T0391761

Preparing for War

The Making of the Geneva Conventions

BOYD VAN DIJK

Great Clarendon Street, Oxford, OX2 6DP,
United Kingdom

Oxford University Press is a department of the University of Oxford.
It furthers the University's objective of excellence in research, scholarship,
and education by publishing worldwide. Oxford is a registered trade mark of
Oxford University Press in the UK and in certain other countries

© Boyd van Dijk 2022

First Edition published in 2022

The moral rights of the author have been asserted

Impression: 3

All rights reserved. No part of this publication may be reproduced, stored in
a retrieval system, or transmitted, in any form or by any means, without the
prior permission in writing of Oxford University Press, or as expressly permitted
by law, by licence or under terms agreed with the appropriate reprographics
rights organization. Enquiries concerning reproduction outside the scope of the
above should be sent to the Rights Department, Oxford University Press, at the
address above

You must not circulate this work in any other form
and you must impose this same condition on any acquirer

Public sector information reproduced under Open Government Licence v3.0
(http://www.nationalarchives.gov.uk/doc/open-government-licence/open-government-licence.htm)

Published in the United States of America by Oxford University Press
198 Madison Avenue, New York, NY 10016, United States of America

British Library Cataloguing in Publication Data

Data available

Library of Congress Control Number: 2021946752

ISBN 978–0–19–886807–1

DOI: 10.1093/oso/9780198868071.001.0001

Printed and bound by
CPI Group (UK) Ltd, Croydon, CR0 4YY

Links to third party websites are provided by Oxford in good faith and
for information only. Oxford disclaims any responsibility for the materials
contained in any third party website referenced in this work.

Contents

Series Editor's Preface	vii
Acknowledgments	ix
Introduction	1
1. The Twisted Road to Geneva	29
1.1 Gathering for the First Time	34
The Government Experts' Conference	36
1.2 Cold War Politics	39
Getting the Soviets on Board	41
1.3 The Diplomatic Conference	44
The Grand Opening	48
2. Making the Civilian Convention	53
2.1 The Rise and Fall of the First Civilian Conventions	57
Developing the Tokyo Draft	59
The Monegasque Rivals	64
2.2 Human Rights in War	67
Civilian Rights in the Shadow of Oradour	71
2.3 Political Prisoners, Statelessness, Torture	75
Faustian Bargains	81
2.4 Protecting Civilians in Wartime	83
Unexpected Soviet Support	87
Death to the Death Penalty	89
Preamble and Protected Persons	91
2.5 Conclusion	95
3. Internationalizing Civil and Colonial Wars	99
3.1 Regulating Civil Wars	101
The Rupture of the First World War	104
The Spanish Civil War	107
3.2 "Studied Vagueness"	110
Troubled Empires	113
3.3 Preparing for a War of Attrition	120
"Manifestly Absurd"	123
3.4 The Fall and Rise of Common Article 3	127
Near-Death	131
Downfall	134
Resurrection	139
3.5 Conclusion	142

vi CONTENTS

4. Fighters in the Shadows — 147

4.1 Partisan Warfare — 150
  The Brussels Conference of 1874 — 156
  "Where there's a Jew there's a partisan, and where there's a partisan there's a Jew" — 159
4.2 The Resistance — 164
  "Traumatized" Architects — 168
4.3 Weaving a Legal Safety Net — 171
  "Creating a Gap Between the Conventions" — 176
4.4 Night and Fog in Geneva — 180
  Black Holes — 186
4.5 Conclusion — 192

5. Indiscriminate Warfare: Bombing, Nuclear Weapons, and Starvation — 197

5.1 Controlling or Banning Indiscriminate Warfare? — 201
  "Weapons of Peace" — 206
  "Peace Zones" — 211
  The Nightmare of Unrestrained Warfare — 217
5.2 Blind Weapons — 220
  "All or Nothing" — 226
  Pictet's Coup de Théâtre — 231
5.3 "A New Auschwitz?" — 235
  The Soviet Game Changer — 240
  The Final Vote — 245
5.4 Conclusion — 249

6. Preparing for the Worst — 253

6.1 Enforcing the Laws of War — 255
  The First World War and Its Aftermath — 258
  Drafting and Enforcing the 1929 Geneva Conventions — 262
6.2 Laying the Foundations of Future Enforcement — 265
  Contemplating a New War Crimes' Regime — 269
6.3 The Stockholm Conference — 273
  The Grave Breaches and Lauterpacht — 277
6.4 Geneva's Endgame — 284
  Subverting Mouton's Proposals — 287
  Protecting Powers, Inquiry, Conciliation, and Dissemination — 290
6.5 Conclusion — 295

Conclusion — 303
  C.1 The Great Humanitarians — 311
  C.2 Geneva's Legacies — 321

Bibliography — 335
Index — 359

Series Editor's Preface

The historiography of the international law regulating organized violence within and between states—known variously as the laws of war and international humanitarian law—has been constitutive of its self-understanding. The pedigree of history as progress towards moderation and humanization, or as the foul charnel house wrought by power and interest, shapes deeply our thinking about the place and role of law in war. Over the past seventy years the 1949 Geneva Conventions have been at the heart of these narratives, both as legal codes to be interpreted and applied, and as totemic documents representing a contested and contestable idea of the lawful conduct of hostilities.

Histories of the Conventions have relied heavily on its official drafting record (*travaux préparatoires*) but this amounts only to what representatives of states choose to say publicly—and is heavily edited in any event. The animating concerns of key drafting states, and the political and diplomatic contexts of their positions, have been reconstructed episodically, usually in relation to one state and one notable provision of the treaties. Moreover, in the hands of lawyers seeking to make an argument about what the treaty drafters "intended"—tools of the trade of legal advocacy in disputes over the meaning of law—pasts become usable in a highly instrumental sense.

In this book, Dr Boyd van Dijk presents an account of the making of the Geneva Conventions like no other. Drawing upon the internal archives of not only the International Committee of the Red Cross, but leading drafting states including the United States, France, the United Kingdom, the Soviet Union, Canada, Australia, and New Zealand—as well as contextual historical sources—Van Dijk reconstructs the competing and converging agendas of these parties through chapters which follow the negotiation of the Conventions on celebrated issues such as the protection of civilians under occupation, internal armed conflicts, partisan and resistance fighters, enforcement, and indiscriminate air bombing and blockades.

He show decisively, and soberingly, that while some states, such as Gaullist France, were concerned to vindicate the sacrifices of their resistance movements through greater protections for civilians under occupation, they also joined the United Kingdom and the United States in seeking to protect prerogatives to suppress anti-colonial rebellion, to starve enemy populations through blockades, and to engage in carpet bombing and use of nuclear weapons should they have to go to war against the Soviet Union and its satellite states.

Van Dijk conveys these debates with a sense of their dramatic moral and political stakes for all involved. The picture of the drafting of the Conventions which emerges is of a legal project for the humanization of war, but equally, a preoccupation with preserving freedom to fight the *next* war in a manner that ensured the advantage of the key drafting parties. Finalized in the immediate aftermath of the Berlin airlift, the Conventions were written, Van Dijk shows, with a sense that conflict with the Soviet Union might be imminent. And for the United Kingdom, France and the Dutch, wars to retain their colonial possessions were looming or already well under way. Like so much of our new historiographies of international law, empire and its maintenance, as well as power politics, entangle the emergence of so-called "humanity law." Delegates and drafters, and the states they represent, are shown to be neither mere peons of interest nor quixotic moralists; the moral judgment of former resistance fighters taken prisoner by Nazi occupation forces and the (less present) testimony of survivors of concentration and extermination camps cast an indelible shadow over debates about the rights of occupiers and the protection of civilians. But equally present were imperatives to retain the possibility "to bomb civilian centers of populations if it suits them," as one UK Foreign Office official explained in a backgrounder to the British Cabinet (Van Dijk, Chapter 5).

It perhaps ought to be no surprise that the making of the Conventions, examined here in a uniquely vivid and comprehensive detail, was an all-too-human affair.

Nehal Bhuta, Edinburgh, January 2021

Acknowledgments

For most of my life, I have never thought about international law. Although I am rooted in the world's city of peace and justice, The Hague's reputation never really resonated with me, nor with the rest of my family. We saw the city less as the cradle of international law than as the place where my grandparents' dining table would bring us together. While they breathed the same air, my working-class grandparents probably never met an international lawyer in their lifetime and always remained isolated from the city's legalist biotope.

My first close encounter with international law happened on the other side of the Atlantic—in New York. Funding my studies at Columbia University, the Huygens Scholarship Program provided me with the opportunity to broaden my intellectual interests as a graduate student. In the wake of 9/11, I was a direct witness to a heavily politicized debate regarding the Geneva Conventions amid the so-called "War on Terror." The idea of writing about the Conventions and their past emerged from a seminar on the laws of war taught by Tanisha Fazal. Her inspiring teaching and intellectual encouragement helped me, at these early stages of my incipient academic career, to find the courage to apply for PhD programs. I owe thanks to her for the example and intellectual stimulus she gave me throughout these formative years. Another debt I owe to Samuel Moyn, whose human rights class inspired my intellectual move to critically historicizing the laws of war, and who has given me steady support ever since those years.

Like so many other historians of Nazi occupation—which was the central theme of my previous book—I felt drawn to the idea of bringing historical insights and context to these post-9/11 discussions with regard to the laws of war. At Columbia, I had the privilege of meeting brilliant students and attending classes from professors whose interest in historicizing global politics strengthened my intellectual appetites. Many thanks to the people on and around the university's campus who have helped spur my interest in history and law—and some of whom have become life-long friends. I also want to thank Diederik van Hoogstraten and Arie Elshout for taking me on board as their associate researcher and teaching the skills of writing. In doing so, they helped me reconnect with my old love of journalism and introduced me to the curiosities of American politics—for better or worse.

X ACKNOWLEDGMENTS

While pursuing my PhD at the European University Institute (EUI), I have received enormous support from many people whose names deserve special mention. The Department of History and Civilization, and Anna Coda Nunziante in particular, generously assisted me as I traveled the world to visit numerous archives, an immense privilege painfully missed in the current pandemic. I am also grateful for the inspirational lessons I was taught by several professors, including Jennifer Welsh and Nehal Bhuta. Their powerful minds and critical thinking have challenged and inspired me in ways they do not even realize. I am also grateful for Nehal's support in inviting me to Edinburgh and laying the framework for the book's publication—including a powerful preface.

I owe a debt of thanks to Martine, Pierre, Loren, and Thomas Casanova, who kindly hosted me in Montpellier while I was taking French classes. As a big-hearted family, they always encouraged me to broaden my horizons. No less thanks to all those generous hosts with whom I have stayed in Paris (Dorit Broxius), Carouge (Cédric Cotter), Cambridge (Emma Stone Mackinnon), Florence (Rutger Birnie), London (Eline van Ommen), Geneva (Zineb Bencheqroun), and across American suburbia. The same applies to my high school and college friends who always provided me with a shelter when I returned to Amsterdam.

On a different level, I am indebted to Dieter Reinisch and Olga Gnydiuk for their wonderful support in joining the hunt for new archival prey. Special thanks goes to the librarians, archivists, and many others who have provided me with access to a forgotten past. This work would not have been possible without the support of the Schweizerischen Bundesarchiv, Tsentral'nyi derzhavnyi arhiv vyschykh organiv vlady ta upravlinnia Ukrainy, the National Archives of Ireland, the Library and Archives Canada (Maria Horne), the National Archives, British Library, National Archives of Australia, Archives New Zealand, Israel State Archives, het Archief van het Nederlandse Rode Kruis (Ton Tielen), het Nationaal Archief, la Bibliothèque du Comité international de la Croix Rouge, les Archives du Comité international de la Croix Rouge (Fabrizio Bensi, Daniel Palmieri, and Jean-Luc Blondel), les Archives diplomatiques Courneuve, les Archives diplomatiques Bruxelles, Columbia University Archives, the Library of Congress, the American Jewish Archives, the New York Public Library, and the National Archives at College Park, Maryland. I am also grateful to Eli Lauterpacht, who allowed me to examine his father's personal papers. His death is a great loss for the entire academic community.

Dirk Moses is probably the most cosmopolitan supervisor alive. We have discussed the laws of war over drinks and food in various places across the globe. He supervised my dissertation on which this book is based and has supported my work since the moment we met on Fiesolean soil. I am grateful for his guidance and critical thinking. Federico Romero, my second reader, has offered advice throughout the entire course of the PhD and gave useful suggestions on how to move its analysis forward. Two powerful minds, Paul Betts and Samuel Moyn, examined the dissertation as committee members and their observations have been very useful for developing the manuscript. They have all helped me discover what it might mean to write a history of making war more humane.

In London, at King's College, I was generously welcomed by Guglielmo Verdirame, who threw me an intellectual life belt. The year after, Walter Ladwig, Joe Maiolo, and Alan James kindly offered me the opportunity to teach at the War Studies Department, whose students have been an enormous pleasure to work with. At Queen Mary, Mira Siegelberg provided intellectual direction and helped me refine my arguments as she lectured a course on human rights history, for which I taught two undergraduate seminars.

In Amsterdam, at the European Studies Department, Michael Wintle and Matthijs Lok provided a stimulating environment with friendly colleagues and motivated students. I am grateful for their role in preventing me from falling deeper into the black hole of academic precarity, which remains a continuing threat to early career scholars, particularly in today's situation of crisis. While in Amsterdam I was lucky to get to know Artemy Kalinovsky, one of the most generous colleagues I have ever met, who constantly gave me useful advice on a whole range of questions. I am thankful to the organizers of the Amsterdam-Utrecht Seminar Global Intellectual History (Annelien de Dijn, René Koekoek, Camille Creyghton, Matthijs Lok, Lucia Admiraal, and Lisa Kattenberg) for the engaging conversations we have had over the past years about law, political thought, and global history.

Thanks to Enno Maessen, Milou van Hout, and Josip Kesic for helping me reach the finish line, and to my generous colleagues in the department, especially Ewa Stanczyk, Hanna Muehlenhoff, Claske Vos, and Sudha Rajagopalan, for being supportive and friendly conspirators. Pola Cebulak always offered advice on the best restaurants in town and took me to festive nights at Iranian bars.

I would like to thank all the organizers and commentators of the fascinating conferences that I have attended over these years. In Florence, I had stimulating conversations with Helen Kinsella, Adam Roberts, Daniel Segesser, and many others. Kirsten Sellars, Peter Holquist, and John Fabian Witt provided terrific feedback on early drafts. In Geneva and Mainz, as part of the Global

xii ACKNOWLEDGMENTS

Humanitarianism Research Academy, I discussed my work with a cohort of extraordinary researchers. A special thanks goes out to the ICRC, Johannes Paulmann, Andrew Thompson, and Fabian Klose for making this all possible. I am also grateful to Gareth Curless and Martin Thomas for allowing me to join their fabulous network and events across the world in a joint effort to historicize insurgency. I have greatly benefited from their ideas, suggestions, and encouraging words—especially those in the early mornings.

In New York, I benefited from intriguing conversations with talented lawyers and historians, including Nicholas Mulder, Karin Loevy, and Brian Drohan. I had the privilege of addressing a cohort of UN diplomats about the history of the Conventions, thanks to Robert Mardini, Chris Harland, and Kosuke Onishi. In Geneva, I had the opportunity of meeting with another group of incisive IHL writers and advocates, from Cédric Cotter, Ellen Policinski, Jean-Marie Henckaerts, Émilie Max, Marco Sassòli to Giovanni Mantilla. In Cambridge, I greatly enjoyed talking about history and law with Joshua Smeltzer, Daniel Allemann, Emma Stone Mackinnon, Ed Cavanagh, Franziska Exeler, Thomas Clausen, Milinda Banerjee, and Lily Chang. In London, I discussed international law over drinks and coffee with Andrei Mamolea, Ioannis Kalpouzos, Sandesh Sivakumaran, George Giannakopoulos, and Jamie Martin. And back in Amsterdam, I profited from conversations with Aden Knaap, Karin van Leeuwen, Katharine Fortin, and Paul van Trigt.

I am also grateful to Jordan Burke, Merel Alstein, Jack McNichol, Lakshmi Amritha, Kristy Barker, Helen Durham, Wim Blockmans, Christ Klep, Tatjana Das, Emmanuel Blanchard, Ned Richardson-Little, Simon Ferdinand, Roel Frakking, Nicola Owtram, Pierre Grosser, Ingo Venzke, Kevin Jon Heller, Miguel Bandeira Jerónimo, Immi Tallgren, Meredith Terretta, Ruud van Dijk, Sundhya Pahuja, Raluca Grosescu, Ángel Alcalde, Sarah Dunstan, Jo Wood, Thomas Vanhauwaert, Glenda Sluga, Mark Lewis, Eva-Maria Muschik, Jan Stöckmann, Gabriela Frei, Chris Goscha, Scott Stephenson, Jo Wachelder, and many, many others for their contributions. The usual disclaimers apply.

Special mention to Karin Hazelhoff Roelfzema, for offering me the opportunity to write a truly international history; Kiran Patel and Anne Orford, for empowering my scholarship; Alison Duxbury and Bruce Oswald, for making the impossible distance between Melbourne and home more bearable; Yayah Siegers-Samaniri and Gert Oostindie, for hosting me as part of a writing retreat in Leiden; Eliav Lieblich, for enabling me to engage with his brilliant students; Ada González-Torres, for giving me an unforgettable tour around the city of Tel Aviv; Pieter Vanhove and Femke Essink, for cheering me on at times when I needed it the most; Jacob Ramsay Smith and Joseph McQuade, for co-organizing an enlightening workshop at Queen Mary; and Marine Guillaume, for sharing her Parisian coffees.

Finally, I would like to thank my dearest friends and family for their reassuring support, dedication, and unfailing love. The greatest gift of this period was to get to know Anne, the most loving, intelligent, beautiful, and extraordinary woman I have ever met in my life. She has brought so much love and joy into my life, and I am grateful for the support I have received from her caring family—Janine, Francis, Hilde, Barry, and their four-legged friends. I am also relieved to know that, despite illness and hardship, both of my parents—Ineke and Wim—will bear witness to the book coming to fruition. Unfortunately, we did not come unharmed out of this difficult time: the passing of our dearest (grand-)mother has hurt us all, and I miss the greatest advocate of my work and life. With my grandmother's death, The Hague is no longer the place where we meet as a family at her dining table; today, it is the object of my research and the pursuit of historicizing international law.

During this endeavor, I also began to realize that the trajectory of international law was much more intimately connected with that of my own family than I had ever imagined. Indeed, it turned out that a letter from the father of my mother's cousin had passed through the same building where the Conventions were negotiated in 1949. As I write in Chapter 2, these negotiations took place at the city's Palais du Conseil General. Previously, the building had served as the headquarters of the ICRC's POW Agency, with its millions of fiches chronicling the lives of POWs across the globe, including the one of the father of my mother's cousin. As a torpedoed sailor who had spent more than forty hours in the water before being taken by the Japanese to a prisoner-of-war camp close to Nagasaki (after the capitulation he passed through the radioactive city as he made his way home), he used his right under the Geneva Convention to send several letters to his beloved family in The Netherlands.

For me, this unique document forms the living testimony of how the history of international law is always rooted in the personal.

Antwerp, March 2020.

———

Elements of this research have appeared as the following articles and chapters:

Mulder, Nicholas, and Van Dijk, Boyd "Why Did Starvation Not Become the Paradigmatic War Crime in International Law?" in *Contingency* in *International Law: On the Possibility of Different Legal Histories*, ed. Ingo Venzke and Kevin Jon Heller (Oxford: Oxford University Press, 2021): 371–388.

Van Dijk, Boyd, "Human Rights in War: On the Entangled Foundations of the 1949 Geneva Conventions," *American Journal of International Law*, Vol. 112, No. 4 (2018): 553–582.

Van Dijk, Boyd, "Internationalizing Colonial War: On the Unintended Consequences of the Interventions of the International Committee of the Red Cross in South-East Asia, 1945–1949," *Past & Present*, Vol. 250, No. 1 (2020): 243–283.

Van Dijk, Boyd, "'The Great Humanitarian': The Soviet Union, the International Committee of the Red Cross, and the Geneva Conventions of 1949," *Law and History Review*, Vol. 37, No. 1 (2019): 209–235.

Figure I.1 The plenary of the diplomatic conference in Geneva (1949). UK delegation leader Robert Craigie (with moustache) is situated in the upper left corner; Albert Lamarle and Georges Cahen-Salvador on the right, not too far from the Nationalist Chinese delegation; and Frede Castberg (bow-tie) in the upper right corner. The delegations of India and the United States are located on the left.
Source/Rights: ICRC Audiovisual Archives, V-P-CER-N-00000B-18H

Introduction

On the morning of 21 April 1949, at the diplomatic conference of Geneva's opening ceremony, the Swiss president of the meeting Max Petitpierre welcomed state representatives from across the world to the city before a crowd of excited spectators. They gathered at Geneva's historic Bâtiment Électoral—also known as the Palais du Conseil Général—to further the idea of humanizing warfare. Their mission was to revise the existing Geneva Conventions in response to the horrific experiences of the Second World War. The representatives all took part in a carefully choreographed ceremony. Bedecked with classical sculptures and Red Cross relics, the venue had the aura of a house of worship. In a powerful address, Petitpierre asked the delegates to heed the heavy moral responsibility that was resting on their shoulders. Indeed, they had been summoned, he believed, by the "millions of civilians who [had] perished in the horrors of the concentration camps" to purge armed conflict of inhumanity.[1]

The representatives answered his call. They unanimously agreed that civilians deserved protection under the Conventions, and updated the existing treaty for prisoners of war (POWs). In addition to this, they established protections for civilians against the threat of indiscriminate bombing, shielded resistance fighters against torture, and extended these principles to civil wars for the first time. Their efforts were to tilt the Conventions in a progressive direction and hence give war a "more humane face."[2] This undertaking, which was professionally managed by the International Committee of the Red Cross (ICRC), was truly universal, with the participation of representatives from Asia, Eastern Europe, the Middle East, and Latin America.[3] The

---

[1] Final Record of the diplomatic conference of Geneva of 1949, Vol. II, Section A, p. 10, Library of Congress (LOC), Washington, DC.

[2] See Theodor Meron, "The Humanization of Humanitarian Law," *The American Journal of International Law*, Vol. 94, No. 2 (2000): 239–278; and Stephen Neff, *War and the Law of Nations: A General History* (Cambridge: Cambridge University Press, 2006), 342.

[3] This notion of "universality" was broadly shared among contemporary Swiss, German, and Francophone reporters writing for different European newspapers. See *La République*, 9 December 1949. The same notion is also apparent in more contemporary publications. See Dominique-Debora Junod, *The Imperiled Red Cross and the Palestine-Eretz-Yisrael Conflict 1945-1952: The Influence of Institutional Concerns on a Humanitarian Operation* (New York: Kegan Paul International, 1996), 270;

Preparing for War. Boyd van Dijk, Oxford University Press. © Boyd van Dijk 2022.
DOI: 10.1093/oso/9780198868071.003.0001

2   PREPARING FOR WAR

ultimate result was the adoption of four new Conventions, thereby satisfying the world's deep-rooted desire for catharsis in the wake of the war's appalling brutality.

That is the received master narrative of the making of the 1949 Geneva Conventions.[4] According to this story, the delegates were primarily motivated by the shock of atrocity and inspired by humanitarian principles, which led them to establish the most important rules for armed conflict ever formulated. These Conventions were the product of liberal humanitarianism, dating back to Henri Dunant's pioneering efforts following the Battle of Solferino in 1859.[5] Building upon this legacy, the world's legal experts gathered in Geneva (Dunant's birthplace) to shake the dust off his original blueprint for humane warfare. Their deliberations were shaped by a skilled cohort of liberal international jurists dedicated to rectifying the Conventions' shortcomings, which the Second World War had so vividly exposed.

This foundation myth of the Conventions has its origins in the aftermath of the diplomatic conference itself, when former protagonists published their own accounts.[6] The British delegate Joyce Gutteridge stressed the importance of the experience of the war in bringing about the support necessary for revising

---

and Mary Ellen O'Connell, "Historical Development and Legal Basis," in *The Handbook of International Humanitarian Law*, ed. Dieter Fleck (Oxford: Oxford University Press, 2013), 16–17.

[4] For important ingredients of this master-narrative, see Jean-Marie Henckaerts, "History and Sources," in *The Oxford Guide to International Humanitarian Law*, eds Ben Saul and Dapo Akande (Oxford: Oxford University Press, 2020), 1–27, 3–6; Gary Solis, *The Law of Armed Conflict: International Humanitarian Law in War* (New York: Cambridge University Press, 2010), 81–84; Meron, "The Humanization of Humanitarian Law," 243–247; Gerald Draper, "The Legal Classification of Belligerent Individuals," in *Reflections on Law and Armed Conflicts: The Selected Works on the Laws of War by the Late Professor G.I.A.D. Draper*, eds Michael Meyer and Hilaire McCoubrey (The Hague: Kluwer, 1998), 196–205, 199–200; Frits Kalshoven, "The History of International Humanitarian Law Treaty-Making," in *Routledge Handbook of the Law of Armed Conflict*, eds Rain Liivoja and Tim McCormack (New York: Routledge, 2016), 94–112; Michael Schmitt, "Military Necessity and Humanity in International Humanitarian Law: Preserving the Delicate Balance," *Virginia Journal of International Law*, Vol. 50, No. 4 (2010): 795–839, 807–808. Some parts of the recent historiography also have had the tendency to frame the Conventions' history through the lens of the Nazi occupation, the Holocaust, and/or the Second World War in the Pacific. Examples include Gerald Steinacher, *Humanitarians at War: The Red Cross in the Shadow of the Holocaust* (Oxford: Oxford University Press, 2017); and Sarah Kovner, *Prisoners of the Empire: Inside Japanese POW Camps* (Cambridge, MA: Harvard University Press, 2020). For a broader discussion of this problematic master-narrative, see Amanda Alexander, "A Short History of International Humanitarian Law," *European Journal of International Law*, Vol. 26, No. 1 (2015), 109–138, 112–113; and Rotem Giladi, "Rites of Affirmation: Progress and Immanence in International Humanitarian Law Historiography," Unpublished Paper.

[5] This image was coined by Swiss publicists even before the diplomatic conference had started. See Georges Perrin, "Dans l'esprit d'Henri Dunant, Avant une Grande Conférence Diplomatique," *La Nouvelle Revue de Lausanne*, 17 March 1949.

[6] For other examples, see: Draft Article "De Diplomatieke Conference te Genève, 21 April–12 Augusts 1949, Een keuze uit de belangrijkste artikelen," no. 1, Collectie Mouton, National Archives of the Netherlands (NA), The Hague; and Frede Castberg, "Franc Tireur Warfare," *Netherlands International Law Review* [1959]: 81–92.

existing international law,[7] while the French drafter Georges Cahen-Salvador wrote about the Conventions' liberal origins.[8] The influential Francophone drafter Paul de la Pradelle encapsulated these views by framing the history of the Conventions in terms of a dichotomy of realism versus idealism, of military necessity versus humanity, with liberal humanitarian values often trumping considerations of power.[9] Glossing over the major divisions at Geneva, many of these Western accounts of the drafting process stressed the role of bipartisanship at this early stage of the Cold War. Influenced by reports of the conference in the Western press,[10] they constructed a powerful memory regime that smoothed over the contested process of formulating the Conventions and accentuated their origins in humanitarianism and the shared experience of struggle against the Axis powers. In this way, this regime bridged the divisions of the incipient Cold War.

The most widely accepted account of the history of the Conventions was presented by the leading ICRC drafter Jean Pictet.[11] In prominent journals and newspapers published after 1949,[12] he emphasized the Conventions' liberal origins and the ICRC's central drafting role.[13] Even though he acknowledged

[7] Gutteridge was one of the few to note the important interwar legacies and the fact that the Conventions had a "different ancestry." However, she did not explain why those interwar proposals failed to be accepted before the start of the Second World War. Joyce Gutteridge, "The Geneva Conventions of 1949," *British Yearbook of International Law*, Vol. 26, No. 294 (1949): 294–326.

[8] Georges Cahen-Salvador, "Les Nouvelles Conventions de Genève Pour la Protection des Victimes de la Guerre Seront Signées Aujourd'Hui," *Le Figaro*, 8 December 1949.

[9] Paul de la Pradelle, *La Conférence Diplomatique et les Nouvelles Conventions de Genève du 12 Août 1949* (Paris: Les Editions Internationales, 1951), 7–8. Resonating with this powerful image of the Conventions' making, one Finnish drafter spoke of a process that reconciled "military views" with the needs "of humanity." Erik Castrén, *The Present Law of War and Neutrality* (Helsinki: Finnish Academy of Science and Letters, 1954), 178.

[10] Some examples are: *Le Courrier Australien* (Sydney, NSW), 7 October 1949; *The Times*, 13 August 1949; *Journal de Genève*, 5 December 1949; *The New York Times*, 9 December 1949; *The Calgary Herald*, 24 April 1950; and the *Baltimore Sun*, 29 March 1950. One ICRC press officer, René Bovey, played a substantial role in shaping early Swiss collective memory concerning the Conventions' adoption. See his publications in *Tribune de Lausanne*, 14 August 1949, and *Journal de Genève*, 13–14 August 1949.

[11] For similar accounts from another former ICRC drafter, see Frédéric Siordet, "Les Conventions de Genève et la guerre civile," *Revue Internationale de la Croix-Rouge*, Vol. 32, No. 375 (1950): 187–212 and Frédéric Siordet, *Inter Arma Caritas: The World of the ICRC during the Second World War* (Geneva: ICRC, 1947).

[12] One prominent example: Jean Pictet, "The New Geneva Conventions for the Protection of War Victims," *American Journal of International Law*, Vol. 45, No. 3 (1951): 462–475.

[13] For examples of this dominant trend in the historiography, see Steinacher, *Humanitarians at War*, 211–236; Schmitt, "Military Necessity and Humanity," 806; David Crowe, *War Crimes, Genocide, and Justice* (New York: Palgrave Macmillan, 2014), 311–318; Caroline Moorehead, *Dunant's Dream: War, Switzerland, and the History of the Red Cross* (New York: Carroll & Graf Publishers, 1999); Howard Levie, "History of the Law of War on Land," *International Review of the Red Cross*, No. 838 (2000): 339–350; and Junod, *The Imperiled Red Cross*, 271. Unsurprisingly, most Swiss observers echoed Pictet's analysis stressing the importance of the Conventions' adoption for ICRC and Swiss neutrality interests. See Tages Anzeiger, Zürich, 18 March 1950; Gazette de Lausanne, 18/19 March 1950; La Nouvelle Revue de Lausanne, 18 March 1950; Feuille d'Avis de Neuchatel, 7 December 1949; Nouvelliste Valaisan, 16 December 1949; Neue Zürcher Zeitung, 10 December 1949; and Basler Nachrichten, 10/11 December 1949.

4   PREPARING FOR WAR

some of their shortcomings, Pictet portrayed the Conventions' history primarily as an inclusive process, one belonging to a transcendent space of morality. On this account, the agreements pushed the arc of global justice slowly in the direction of offering protection to ever more victims of war. This teleological (if not self-serving) image of the Conventions' making, which remains popular today, has several analytical blindspots. For one thing, the narrative that it puts forward could be easily exploited to obscure Great Power politics, and it falls short of explaining why some of the more radical legal proposals circulating prior to 1949 were rejected, as will be shown below.

Pictet's most influential contribution to later understandings of the Conventions' history undoubtedly stems from his leading role in editing the influential ICRC Commentary, which was published between 1952 and 1959.[14] He first introduced the idea of producing such a legal guideline in 1949, in the immediate aftermath of the diplomatic conference.[15] Its aim was to inform contemporaries of the law's more "appropriate" interpretation. Given that it came to be seen as the authoritative account of the Conventions' making, the ICRC's Commentary has had a lasting influence on both academic and popular understandings of this history. Surprisingly few observers have grasped that this document represents just one account, written by just one former drafter, with its own particular aims.[16] Consequently, the Commentary—with its stress on the Conventions' inclusiveness and depoliticized narrative of their contested making—has come to define the dominant view within the broader literature.

———

This book tells a different story. It shows how the final text of the 1949 Conventions, far from being an unabashedly liberal blueprint, was the outcome of a series of political struggles among the drafters, many of whom were not liberal and whose ideas changed radically over time. Nor were they merely a product of idealism or even the shock felt in the wake of Hitler's atrocities. Constructing the Conventions meant outlawing some forms of inhumanity while tolerating others. It concerned a great deal more than simply recognizing

---

[14] For the recently updated ICRC Commentaries on the Third Convention (as well as the First and Second Conventions), see https://ihl-databases.icrc.org/ihl/full/GCIII-commentary (retrieved 10 November 2020).

[15] The idea for a Commentary came originally from Pictet's predecessor (Paul des Gouttes), who had written a commentary on the Sick and Wounded Convention of 1929. Pictet re-addressed his idea after the diplomatic conference had finished. Minutes of Plenary Meeting ICRC, 20 October 1949, no. A PV A PI.19, Les Archives du Comité International de la Croix-Rouge (ACICR), Geneva.

[16] Many of the contributors to the Commentary were former ICRC drafters: Frédéric Siordet, Claude Pilloud, Jean-Pierre Schoenholzer, Jean Pictet, and René-Jean Wilhelm.

INTRODUCTION 5

the shortcomings of international law as revealed by the experience of the Second World War. In making the Conventions, drafters sought to contest European imperial rule, empower the ICRC, challenge state sovereignty, fight Cold War rivalries, ensure rights during wartime, reinvent the concept of war crimes, and prepare for (civil) wars to come.

This book argues that a better way to understand the politics and ideas of the Conventions' drafters is to see them less as passive characters responding to past events than as active protagonists trying to shape the future of warfare. In many different ways, they tried to define the contours of future battlefields by deciding who deserved protection, what counted as a legitimate target, whose lives mattered, whose did not, when these principles applied, and who had the right to enforce them. Outlawing illegal conduct did as much to outline the silhouette of humanized war as to establish the legality of waging war itself.[17] Indeed, given the violent character of decolonization in Asia and the long-term ambitions attributed to the US and the Soviet Union,[18] virtually every drafter accepted the reality of war as a given, if not as a defining feature of their time.[19] Although they did not seek war as such,[20] they prepared for it by means of weaving a new legal safety net in the event that their worst fear should materialize—*si vis pacem, para bellum.*[21]

Looking beyond retrospective narratives reveals a different story of the Conventions' birth and the drafters' role in bringing that about. In this way it becomes possible to see how truly extraordinary some of their work was— even when it fell short of expectations—and the role that ideas played in

[17] Here I draw upon the ideas of Mary Dudziak, "Making Law, Making War, Making America," in *The Cambridge History of American Law, Vol. III*, eds Michael Grossberg and Christopher Tomlins (Cambridge: Cambridge University Press, 2008), 680–717.

[18] Melvyn Leffler, "National Security and US Foreign Policy," in *The Origins of the Cold War: An International History*, eds Melvyn Leffler and David Painter (New York: Routledge, 2002), 15–52, 37

[19] For a broader discussion of the tension between humanizing warfare and perpetuating war, see Samuel Moyn, *Humane: How the United States Abandoned Peace and Reinvented War* (New York: Farrar, Straus and Giroux, 2021); and Pablo Kalmanovitz, *The Laws of War in International Thought* (Oxford: Oxford University Press, 2020), 143–148. For a discussion of the crime of aggression, see Kirsten Sellars, *"Crimes against Peace" and International Law* (Cambridge: Cambridge University Press, 2013); Carrie McDougall, *The Crime of Aggression under the Rome Statute of the International Criminal Court* (Cambridge: Cambridge University Press, 2013); and Richard Tuck, *Rights of War and Peace: Political Thought and the International Order from Grotius to Kant* (Oxford: Oxford University Press, 1999).

[20] It is important to recognize that Petitpierre and many other drafters insisted that they were not seeking war as such: Final Record of the Diplomatic Conference of Geneva of 1949, Vol. II, Section A, p. 10, LOC. Still, ICRC legal experts admitted privately that their efforts to humanize warfare could be seen as anticipating war without trying to perpetuate it: Conference Diplomatique. Rapport Spécial Etabli par Pilloud, 16 September 1949, no. CR-254-1, Les Archives du Comité International de la Croix-Rouge (ACICR), Geneva.

[21] See Marguerite Frick-Cramer, "Contribution à l'élaboration d'une Convention sur les prisonniers, militaires ou civils, tombés au pouvoir de l'ennemi ou d'une autorité non reconnue par eux," *Revue Internationale de la Croix-Rouge et Bulletin Internationale des Société de la Croix-Rouge* [1947]: 228–247.

reimagining warfare internationally. Indeed, had the drafters been primarily driven by the pursuit of power or military necessity, then their ideas would not have mattered at all. Yet this book shows that not to be the case.[22] Instead, it provides deeper insights into how those actors embedded their past experiences into a broader framework that was shaped by ideas, political interests, perceptions, and expectations about what was to come. For example, when demanding rights in interstate wars in response to Vichy and Nazi occupation, French drafters felt forced to bring this progressive project into line with their brutal counterinsurgency campaign in Indochina and other anti-colonial insurgencies they were expecting to face in the (near) future. Similarly, the Soviet Union proposed to regulate civil wars while remaining silent about its suppression of anti-communist insurgencies in Eastern Europe.[23] And the Americans, for their part, disliked discussion of aerial bombardment on account of their fear that restrictions in that theater of war might undermine their capacity to further their interests in the Cold War.

According to these war-making states, victims of colonial torture, anti-communist political prisoners, or those subjected to terrorizing bombing raids were not necessarily "victims of war" to be protected by these Conventions. Drafting was as much about exclusion as inclusion, undertaken for both liberal and illiberal purposes, and all on a remarkably uneven playing field. The Conventions' architects were both pragmatic and visionary in their efforts to restrain inhuman conduct of warfare and, in this way, lay the foundations of a new international legal order. At the same time, it remains critically important to remember that these actors often represented belligerent states that were armed to the teeth.[24] Anglo-American drafters regularly pushed for the most regressive solutions and opposed further restrictions on regulating occupation. This should come as no surprise. After all, these two liberal powers fought the most wars in the twentieth century—more even than Germany.[25] In trying to maintain a free hand in ongoing and future military operations and condoning the use of enormously destructive weapons against their enemies, Anglo-American drafters had to

---

[22] This point, combined with the occasional lack of leverage of dominant state powers over smaller states, problematizes certain legal realist accounts of the Conventions' making. See Wilhelm Grewe, *The Epochs of International Law* (Berlin: De Gruyter, 2001), 663.

[23] For an impressive history of the Soviets at Nuremberg, see Francine Hirsch, *Soviet Judgment at Nuremberg: A New History of the International Military Tribunal after World War II* (Oxford: Oxford University Press, 2020).

[24] On nineteenth-century debates regarding this issue: Kalmanovitz, *The Laws of War in International Thought*, 148–152.

[25] Hew Strachan, "Essay and Reflection: On Total War and Modern War," *The International History Review*, Vol. 22, No. 2 (2000): 341–370, 342.

ask themselves time and again whether they could credibly claim to be upholding the principle of "civilization" in wartime.

All of the actors participating in the drafting process had to engage with public expectations with regard to the effort to humanize warfare.[26] At the very least, they had to look responsive when victims of occupation demanded that so-called Nazi-style counterinsurgency policies, such as the taking of hostages, be outlawed. Further, they could not afford to ignore the precedents set at Nuremberg and other criminal tribunals, which had proclaimed higher standards for the conduct of warfare.[27] This proved especially challenging in debates regarding the Conventions' application to colonial wars, civilians, partisan warfare, and air bombing. Complaining about the Conventions being used "demagogic[ally]" to further Anglo-American interests,[28] the Soviets tried to widen the scope of the agreements to encompass civilian populations. In this way, they hoped to curtail US air power and spread propaganda in the context of the Cold War. In so doing, the Soviets turned the diplomatic conference into a forum for Cold War and anti-colonial politicking, in which Western adversaries could be criticized on an international stage. The latter were made especially vulnerable by their ongoing counterinsurgency campaigns in Asia and Southeastern Europe, which the Soviet Union—their former ally in the Second World War—characterized as being reminiscent of fascist practices.

"Behind the seemingly calm discussion of the Conventions," wrote a Soviet delegate later, "a fierce fight [had been] lingering between [the] delegations."[29] Discussing questions such as regulating civil wars made it possible for some drafting nations to criticize their Cold War rivals and secure their own political

---

[26] On the question of normative pressure in global politics and international lawmaking: Maartje Abbenhuis, *The Hague Conferences and International Politics, 1898–1915* (London: Bloomsbury, 2018), 3; Ayşe Zarakol, "What Made the Modern World Hang Together: Socialisation or Stigmatisation?," *International Theory*, Vol. 6, No. 2 (2014): 311–332; and Giovanni Mantilla, *Lawmaking under Pressure: International Humanitarian Law and Internal Armed Conflict* (Ithaca, NY: Cornell University Press, 2020).

[27] Yuma Totani and David Cohen, *The Tokyo War Crimes Tribunal: Law, History, and Jurisprudence* (Cambridge: Cambridge University Press, 2018); Kevin Jon Heller and Gerry Simpson, *The Hidden Histories of War Crimes Trials* (Oxford: Oxford University Press, 2014); Kevin Jon Heller, *The Nuremberg Military Tribunals and the Origins of International Criminal Law* (Oxford: Oxford University Press, 2011); and Donald Bloxham, *Genocide on Trial: War Crimes Trials and the Formation of Holocaust History and Memory* (Oxford: Oxford University Press, 2001).

[28] Report Soviet-Ukrainian Delegation, no. F. 2, Op. 12cc, Spr. 969, Ark. 60–76, Tsentral'nyi derzhavnyi arhiv vyschykh organiv vlady ta upravlinnia Ukrainy (TSDAVO), Kiev, Ukraine. This point resonates with "an older cynicism toward the term humanity, shaped by Marx's suspicion of the bourgeois concept of humanity as simply class-based special interests dressed up in universalist language." Paul Betts, "Universalism and Its Discontents: Humanity as a Twentieth-Century Concept," in *Humanity: A History of European Concepts in Practice from the Sixteenth Century to the Present*, eds Fabian Klose and Mirjam Thulin (Göttingen: Vandenhoeck & Ruprecht, 2016), 51–70, 64.

[29] Report Soviet-Ukrainian Delegation, no. F. 2, Op. 12cc, Spr. 969, Ark. 60–76, TSDAVO.

8 PREPARING FOR WAR

interests. Drafters had to reckon with mass statelessness, the fall of European empires, and the rise of new hegemonic powers, which transformed international legal conversations profoundly.[30] As one leading ICRC drafter noted, these different factors each played an "enormous role" in how the Conventions were shaped, why they protected some and not others, and why some issues were addressed while others were not.[31]

By placing the history of the Conventions back in the context of decolonization, the Cold War, and global politics, this book shows how the ideas and politics driven by these processes had a profound impact on how the drafters reconfigured international law's genetic code. It also points out why accounts of the emergence of the Conventions that focus exclusively on the experience of the Second World War, or a longer historical development of the idea of humane warfare dating back to Dunant's pioneering advocacy in the 1860s—if not much earlier[32]—fail to explain why some proposals were codified whereas others were scrapped, why the law remained silent on certain key issues, or why states that had been occupied by the Axis powers had not necessarily been brought together by this experience. These accounts cannot resolve the historical puzzle of why, for example, the French accepted an extrajudicial security clause despite the fascist occupation, the British condoned the use of indiscriminate bombing despite the Blitz, several postcolonial states received the idea of regulating wars within empires and states skeptically, or some European victims of occupation refused to ban the death penalty.

At every stage of this drafting process, questions concerning the kind of international law that would exist in future (proxy) wars and the forms of violence it would tolerate were on the line. The stakes were impossibly high: the "fate of millions of human beings depended on what would happen in Geneva," wrote a Swiss reporter.[33] In drafting new rules for warfare, a range of further issues was in question: the sovereignty of states; the ICRC's credibility; the concept of human dignity; the character of international order; and the forms of power and control that that system wished to exert over people's lives in armed conflict. In the process of debating these questions, drafters expressed contrasting ideas about the very meaning of humanity under conditions of armed

---

[30] For an excellent history of statelessness, see Mira Siegelberg, *Statelessness: A Modern History* (Cambridge, MA: Harvard University Press, 2020).
[31] Conference Diplomatique. Rapport Spécial Etabli par Pilloud, 16 September 1949, no. CR-254-1, ACICR.
[32] For an example, see Alexander Gillespie, *A History of the Laws of War* (Portland, OR: Hart, 2011).
[33] *Journal de Genève*, 18 March 1949.

conflict and how this principle would be best served considering the fundamentally inhumane character of war.

Despite these divisions, establishing new rules for warfare created space for a surprising degree of cooperation during the early Cold War. It gave rise to unique opportunities not just for articulating Cold War rivalries, but for fostering East–West collaboration too. Indeed, it is crucial not to overstate the Cold War's impact on the making of the Conventions. Most tellingly, the ICRC found a strategic partner in the Soviet Union, which eventually was keen to endorse its proposals for humanizing warfare. What is more, behind the scenes the French often cooperated with their main Cold War adversary. For their part, the Americans sometimes voted in favor of Soviet suggestions, and vice versa. So, while recognizing the impact of Cold War dynamics, this book also appreciates the extent to which ideas of deterrence and East–West relations can explain the drafters' actions on principal issues.

Some scholars have spoken of the actors involved in the drafting process without making real distinctions between them, ignoring the extraordinary divisions within their ranks. In the British case, for example, there was a broad debate with regard to partisan warfare and civilian protection not only between the different government bodies concerned (that is, between the Cabinet in London and its delegation in Geneva) or different groups within the North Atlantic Treaty Organization (NATO), including victims of Nazi occupation and states now occupying Germany; crucially, there was also discussion and disagreement among the UK's delegates in Geneva. On the one hand, Foreign Office delegates focused on protecting Britain's prestige and the interests of UK nationals who might be detained in occupied territory; on the other, War Office counterparts (supported by the Security Services) tried to exclude different types of irregulars and civilians so as to secure their respective security interests. By analyzing the impact of such divisions among the major drafting parties participating in the negotiations, this book problematizes the often monolithic and essentialist understanding of the drafters' intentions that still prevails in the current literature.

Over the course of this alternative history of the drafting of the Conventions, we meet individuals who defy expectations. We encounter survivors of Nazi persecution who battled against new rules for enforcing the Conventions. We learn about Western drafters who recognized similarities between Soviet proposals and their own and sought to bridge Cold War divisions. We face British drafters who offended their US allies and pressured smaller NATO partners to endorse their proposals. We listen to women who publicly criticized their male counterparts for failing to outlaw nuclear holocaust. We read

10 PREPARING FOR WAR

about postcolonial delegates who took the moral high ground and enjoyed the *Schadenfreude* of witnessing their former imperial rulers struggle in Geneva. And we get to know ICRC legal experts who used the principles of human rights against those in power to demand a more humane version of occupation.

The ICRC played a transformative role, especially in the early stages of these negotiations, by helping to lay the foundations of the drafting process. It created many of the most important proposals for the Conventions, which soon came to seem like obvious responses to the war's atrocities. As a major drafting party, the ICRC inevitably had its own agenda. Indeed, countering parts of the existing scholarship,[34] this book also shows that the organization faced major political dilemmas and rejected utopian schemes for humanized war. "For [this] work to be successful," Pictet admitted, "the secret [was] to keep it realistic [...] nothing is more dangerous than 'unbridled humanitarianism.'"[35]

By unpacking the different considerations behind the ICRC's approach to the Conventions' remaking, this analysis calls into question those accounts that portray the organization as exclusively "idealist," in opposition to "realist" states. This binary schema conceals more than it reveals. *Preparing for War* also explores the political strategies that the ICRC used to keep the Great Powers on board and prevent itself from being sidelined. The latter was no small concern, for the organization was fiercely criticized for its lack of support for several groups of victims during the war—especially Soviet POWs and Jewish civilians. For example, the ICRC opposed plans to categorize the states' own nationals who suffered under persecution (such as German Jews) as "victims of war," as that had the potential to trigger stringent opposition from the Great Powers. To maintain their support, it removed this suggestion made by Holocaust survivors from its list of drafting priorities and frustrated attempts to put it back on. This indicates that the ICRC was not afraid to prioritize its own interests over those of vulnerable minorities.

That last point raises questions about what might have turned out differently. Which radical courses of action were not taken in Geneva in 1949? Each chapter emphasizes the processual character of drafting the Conventions, raising the possibility of alternative paths and unforeseen consequences. These

---

[34] This book challenges those parts of the literature's still state-centered focus either marginalizing, or simply praising the organization's role in establishing rules for warfare. Steinacher's important account of the Conventions' revision following the Holocaust, based for the most part on US and external ICRC sources, largely credits the ICRC's role. However, it pays little attention to its mixed motives, the Conventions' actual drafting, and the impact of decolonization (I found no reference to Common Article 3). See Gerald Steinacher, *Humanitarians at War: The Red Cross in the Shadow of the Holocaust* (Oxford: Oxford University Press, 2017) and Crowe, *War Crimes, Genocide, and Justice.*

[35] Jean Pictet, "The Formation of International Humanitarian Law," *International Review of the Red Cross* [1985]: 3–24, 20–21.

divergent trajectories are either missing or downplayed in existing accounts, which tend to take the final outcome—namely, four treaties with common articles applying to specific armed conflicts—largely for granted. Challenging this view, the book demonstrates the contingency of the negotiations, which might have collapsed at several junctures. In so doing, it shows that the final draft was not the only outcome possible, but one among many different options. Indeed, plans for the Conventions took myriad forms and might have disappeared altogether had specific actors not stood up to defend or advance them.

There were many roads not taken as the drafters imagined alternative visions for humanized war. They considered creating a single Convention for all victims of war, for instance, and initially agreed upon the need to extend this treaty to a whole range of different armed conflicts, potentially including so-called lower-intensity conflicts, which would have radically expanded international law's scope. The Civilian Convention might have featured the cardinal principle of distinction in aerial warfare, specifically outlawed "mental torture," incorporated the category of "refugees" under Article 4, or at least made specific reference to "stateless persons"—one of the most important civilian victim categories of the modern age. The grave breaches system could have been given more teeth and the POW Convention extended to include guerrillas and spies in particular. And Pictet could have insisted that carpet bombing should be strictly banned under these treaties. There were often good reasons for the drafters reaching different conclusions. That said, there was nothing inevitable about the demise of some proposals and the adoption of others.

This book provides the reader with insights into why the drafters finally adopted the four Conventions in the way that they did. At the diplomatic conference of 1949, the UK delegation seriously considered walking out over the issues of partisans, bombing, and the death penalty. The French had their doubts about the Civilian Convention, particularly with regard to its extrajudicial security clause, which has been mentioned above. Initially, the Soviets did not even take part in these negotiations; they would later also fiercely criticize the final version of the Civilian Convention. The Cold War battles fought at Geneva slowed the drafting process enormously, almost bringing disagreements to breaking point on several occasions and prompting concerns as to whether the conference would ever adopt anything significantly binding.

The ICRC, in turn, considered the possibility of dropping the plan for a separate Civilian Convention at various moments so as to assure the participation of all the Great Powers. Essentially, Pictet's drafting team feared that the treaty might never be accepted, especially by the reluctant Anglo-American delegations and their Stalinist opponents. Indeed, both London and Washington

12 PREPARING FOR WAR

seriously thought about not ratifying, or even signing, the Civilian Convention because of its stricter rules for occupation, particularly with regard to enforcing the death penalty. This treaty might never have been adopted had the French and other victims of Axis occupation continued to push for an ever more ambitious Civilian Convention. Until the very end, the major drafting parties expressed doubt as to whether they could ever agree to anything binding that would restrain the conduct of warfare in meaningful ways.

The drafting process remained contingent in nature and took place at numerous levels—from Geneva's tearooms to the global, with critical implications for how these treaties emerged and developed over time. The drafters' views were directly informed by debates about human rights and nuclear weapons at the United Nations (UN). Experts who had formerly been involved in preparing the Allied war crimes tribunals played a prominent role in providing legal advice and shaping the Conventions' principles. The French, for example, wished to put these treaties into dialogue with other international conventions to prevent interstate resistance fighters from falling outside their scope. The Americans, for their part, tried to protect their interests as a war-making power, while the British tried to prevent human rights from overlapping with the laws of war, thereby protecting their colonial and Cold War interests. While stressing their entangled nature, this book demonstrates how the making of the Conventions became part of a much broader global debate as to how exactly the boundaries of international law in and around armed conflict should be demarcated.

Some drafters wanted to construct a new international legal order, others to restrain the powers of occupiers out of fear of an impending invasion. Still others sought to use the treaties as an instrument to fight Communism with greater legitimacy than they otherwise might. In reimagining the central concept of "victims of war," the Conventions cannot be traced back to a common perspective or universal core. Instead, they were hybrid constructs, shaped by different drafters with contrasting political aims. Nevertheless, drafters shared concerns about the state's paradoxical role in humanizing warfare—that is, as both its strongest guarantor and the greatest threat to it. This power to both protect *and* destroy civilian lives, they realized, meant that the right to decide which of the state's two faces would stand out in wartime was the central puzzle to be solved at Geneva.

None of this came easily, however. Pictet, an inexperienced but exceptionally talented drafter, could do little on behalf of civilians, as an ICRC expert short of voting rights at the final diplomatic conference and only taking a direct part in its discussions about the peripheral First and Second Conventions.[36]

---

[36] See Final Record of the Diplomatic Conference of Geneva of 1949, Vol. II, Section A, p. 46, LOC, 2A.

Opposition from the Great Powers meant that the ICRC had to wait for decades before its interwar proposals for civilian protection were ultimately adopted. And UK drafters complained repeatedly about their continental European allies forcing them to accept ever more restrictions with regard to occupation. By retrieving the neglected history of the politics and ideas of the Conventions' making, this book shows the great difficulties that drafters faced in contemplating and defining what a truly humane war might look like.

Together, a concert of different individuals reimagined the very foundations of international law in wartime. There was no prototypical drafter, as is sometimes assumed. Contrary to popular belief, advocates of humanizing warfare were neither fringe utopians nor outright pacifists—to the contrary, the process involved a distinct group of predominantly European and North American men with clashing views and personal experiences of war: former leaders of wartime resistance movements, victims of Nazi persecution, former prisoners of war, doctors, veterans, colonial officials, military officers, ambassadors, academics, and countless others. They acted on behalf of state and non-state interests and assumed a variety of roles as experts, chairs, provocateurs, negotiators, mediators, demagogues, lobbyists, propagandists, reformers, or spokespeople.

The construction of the Conventions, in other words, was not the work of one person alone. The underlying ideas and ideologies motivating this mixed group of actors varied significantly, ranging from socialism to conservatism, from nationalism to Jewish internationalism. Nonetheless, they all agreed on the premise that wars should have limits. Despite being united in a common cause, they never formed a unified and consistent movement. Some drafters were outspokenly anti-imperialist, struggling against efforts to perpetuate European colonial rule. Others became deeply involved in maintaining empire by associating themselves with proposals that sought to defend colonial sovereignty.

Western actors often encouraged the impression that drafting was a scholarly endeavor in which expertise prevailed over practical concerns and activity. In reality, however, drafters had to get their hands dirty, whether by lobbying governments, drinking vodka with Soviet adversaries, tearing up countless drafts, listening to unbearably long speeches, or working at night to finish detailed reports for their respective capitals. Their work was a truly human affair: it gave rise not only to confusion, miscalculations, amateurism, personal rivalries, and error, but also to moments of ingenuity, courage, brilliance, and even heroism. During this drawn-out process, drafters had to grapple with radical changes in how the international legal order was being reimagined in the

14   PREPARING FOR WAR

first half of the twentieth century. In this book, the analysis puts their agency front and center, emphasizing how they had to constantly redefine their ideas, their beliefs, and the boundaries of their roles in this unique effort to revise the Geneva Conventions.

———

As a research topic, the making of the Conventions is anything but new. In many cases, scholars analyzing this process have cast the ICRC as the central protagonist of a depoliticized origin story. In this narrative, Pictet is presented as the "principal artisan" of these rules.[37] This search for a mythologized (male) founder has led to an historiographical amnesia with respect to the contributions made by other drafters, who were sometimes far more important than ICRC men such as Pictet.[38] In the main, scholars have forgotten the names of Cramer, the first female drafter of the Conventions; Morosov, a Soviet legal expert who played a major role in shaping socialist understandings of the Conventions; Cahen-Salvador, an influential French delegate who worked the concept of rights into the drafts; and Oung, a Burmese general who fought against proposals to regulate civil war, as well as many others who played important roles in the drafting process.[39]

After several decades,[40] the received imagery of the Conventions' genesis began to change as the humanitarian reputation of the ICRC—which had in

[37] Catherine Rey-Schyrr, *De Yalta à Dien Bien Phu. Histoire du Comité international de la Croix-Rouge 1945–1955* (Geneva: Georg-CICR, 2007), 244. The UK military jurist Gerald Draper also traced the Conventions' origins back to a mythified idea of Genevan humanitarianism. He even named his published lecture series on humanitarian law after the Red Cross. Gerald Draper, *The Red Cross Conventions* (London: Stevens, 1958), vii–viii, 1–2.

[38] For a critique of such approaches, see Glenda Sluga and Carolyn James, *Women, Diplomacy and International Politics since 1500* (New York: Routledge, 2016).

[39] This tendency to privilege the ICRC's role has been largely cultivated since the early 1950s. The first volume of the organization's history that was written by its own members was Pierre Boissier, *De Solferino à Tsoushima: Histoire du Comité International de la Croix-Rouge* (Paris: Plon, 1963). Boissier briefly acted as the head of the ICRC mission to Algeria, in the early 1960s. He later became the director of the Institut Henry Dunant (IHD), a body founded in 1965 to study Red Cross activities including its history. The Institut, which was dissolved in 1998, would initially play an important role in shaping the ICRC's history through publishing a range of different works. Other former IHD presidents were Dietrich Schindler and Pictet (he acted twice as president).

[40] One important reason for this delay was the lack of access to both state and non-state archives. Before the ICRC archives opened up in the 1990s, most scholars were forced to use only publicly available sources (e.g. the *Revue*, secondary sources, non-ICRC archives, etc.) in order to reconstruct the organization's history, or that of the Geneva Conventions. One example is Dieter Riesenberger, *Für Humanität in Krieg und Frieden: Das Internationale Rote Kreuz, 1863–1977* (Göttingen: Vandenhoeck & Ruprecht, 1992), 214–218. A few other scholars had the opportunity to conduct research in the ICRC archives before 1996. Examples are Véronique Harouel and Dominique-Debora Junod: see Junod, *The Imperiled Red Cross* and Véronique Harouel, *Genève-Paris 1863–1918: Le Droit Humanitaire en Construction* (Geneva: ICRC, 2003). Former ICRC President Boissier said once about its initial refusal to open its archives for outside researchers: "das Internationale Komitee genießt das Vertrauen der Regierungen. Mit diesem Vertrauen als Rückhalt konnte es in den beiden Weltkriegen ein Riesenwerk

INTRODUCTION   15

large part driven the established account—came under critical scrutiny from outside observers.[41] Political scientists have written the first independent studies of the ICRC's institutional history, stressing its political origins over perceptions of its neutrality.[42] Although these contributions have been pioneering, they paid relatively little attention to the Conventions' history, which they left for others to study. Swiss historians, like many Anglo-American scholars, have responded to this turn by providing more hagiographic accounts of the Conventions, particularly with regard to the ICRC's role.[43] Based primarily on the ICRC's Commentary and Swiss archives, this scholarship has taken little account of the role played by other actors and their different political agendas.

One of the most crucial shifts in the scholarship on the Conventions' making took place around the close of the Cold War, with the end of the bipolar world and the revival of liberal internationalism.[44] All of this spurred a growing scholarly trend toward tracing the origins of the international (legal) order and wartime humanitarianism.[45] This shift overlapped with a broader reorientation toward the study of internationalism as well as transnationalism,[46] with

---

vollbringen, das auch heute noch in der Erinnerung aller Menschen fortlebt." Cited from Riesenberger, *Für Humanität in Krieg und Frieden*, 10–11.

[41] Examples are: John Hutchinson, *Champions of Charity: War and the Rise of the Red Cross* (Boulder, CO: Westview Press, 1996); Rainer Baudendistel, *Between Bombs and Good Intentions: The Red Cross and the Italo-Ethiopian War, 1935–1936* (New York: Berghahn Books, 2006); Irène Herrmann, "La Suisse Entre Peur de l'Autre et Devoir Humanitaire," in *La Peur et ses Miroirs*, ed. Michel Viegnes (Paris: Editions Imago, 2009), 109–121; James Crossland, *Britain and the International Committee of the Red Cross, 1939–1945* (New York: Palgrave Macmillan, 2014); and James Crossland, *War, Law and Humanity: The Campaign to Control Warfare, 1853–1914* (London: Bloomsbury, 2019).

[42] David Forsythe, *Humanitarian Politics: The International Committee of the Red Cross* (Baltimore, MD: Johns Hopkins University Press, 1977). For Forsythe's reflections on his role as an outsider, see David Forsythe, *The Humanitarians: The International Committee of the Red Cross* (Cambridge: Cambridge University Press, 2005), x. For recent political science approaches to analyzing the laws of war, see Tanisha Fazal, *Wars of Law: Unintended Consequences of the Regulation of Armed Conflict* (Ithaca, NY: Cornell University Press, 2018).

[43] Examples include Meron, "The Humanization of Humanitarian Law"; Ruti Teitel, *Humanity's Law* (Oxford: Oxford University Press, 2011); François Bugnion, *Le Comité international de la Croix-Rouge et la Protection des Victimes de la Guerre* (Geneva: ICRC, 2000); Rey-Schyrr, *De Yalta à Dien Bien Phu*; and Jacques Moreillon, *Le Comité international de la Croix-Rouge et la Protection des Détenus Politiques* (Lausanne: L'Age d'Homme, 1973).

[44] For a broader overview of recent historiographical trends in the history of the laws of war, see Helen Kinsella and Giovanni Mantilla, "Contestation before Compliance: History, Politics, and Power in International Humanitarian Law," *International Studies Quarterly*, Vol. 64, No. 3 (2020): 649–656.

[45] For the historiography on war, legal diplomacy, and humanitarianism, see Neville Wylie, *Barbed Wire Diplomacy: Britain, Germany, and the Politics of Prisoners of War, 1939–1945* (Oxford: Oxford University Press, 2010); Sibylle Scheipers, *Prisoners in War* (Oxford: Oxford University Press, 2010); Maartje Abbenhuis, Christopher Ernest Barber, and Annalise Higgins, *War, Peace and International Order: The Legacies of the Hague Conferences of 1899 and 1907* (New York: Routledge, 2017); and Heather Jones, *Violence against Prisoners of War in the First World War: Britain, France and Germany, 1914–1920* (Cambridge: Cambridge University Press, 2011).

[46] Mark Mazower, *No Enchanted Palace* (Princeton, NJ: Princeton University Press, 2009); Susan Pedersen, *The Guardians: The League of Nations and the Crisis of Empire* (Oxford: Oxford

16   PREPARING FOR WAR

its focus on processes and principles that transcend the nation-state, such as humanitarianism.[47] In this context, while having previously published on the history of the laws of war,[48] Geoffrey Best's pioneering 1994 study *War and Law since 1945* represents the first attempt at a comprehensive history of the Conventions written by a scholar not involved in drafting them, nor being always directly aligned with the ICRC.[49]

Best's most significant contributions lay in underlining the importance of the Conventions' contested making and in breaking with triumphalist accounts of the ICRC's role.[50] Still, his work suffered from several major shortcomings: first, Best's limited engagement with other archival materials beyond Anglophone sources led him to minimize the important contributions made by Francophone drafters; second, he placed remarkably little emphasis on empire, a crucial aspect of these negotiations;[51] and lastly, some of Best's judgments were informed by an outdated Cold War politics: take, for instance, the way in which he downplayed the substantial Soviet contributions to the Conventions.[52]

Since the turn of the century, scholars working in the discipline of international law have promoted a new turn toward history.[53] As Jennifer Pitts has noted, this "historicizing moment" has given rise to an important dialogue between the fields of international relations,[54] (postcolonial)

University Press, 2015); and Glenda Sluga, *Internationalism in the Age of Nationalism* (Philadelphia, PA: Philadelphia University of Pennsylvania Press, 2015).

[47] For the origins of this shift towards transnationalism, see Akira Iriye, *Global Community: The Role of International Organizations in the Making of the Contemporary World* (Berkeley, CA: University of California Press, 2004). For a recent discussion of new approaches to internationalism, see Glenda Sluga and Patricia Clavin, eds, *Internationalisms: A Twentieth-Century History* (Cambridge: Cambridge University Press, 2016).

[48] Geoffrey Best, *Humanity in Warfare: The Modern History of the International Laws of Armed Conflicts* (London: Weidenfeld and Nicholson, 1980).

[49] The first attempt by a former drafter to write a comprehensive (Francophone) legal history was De la Pradelle's book: De la Pradelle, *La Conférence Diplomatique*.

[50] For the work of ICRC historians, see Bugnion, *Le Comité international de la Croix-Rouge et la Protection des Victimes de la Guerre*; Rey-Schyrr, *De Yalta à Dien Bien Phu*; Jacques Moreillon, *Le Comité international de la Croix-Rouge et la protection des détenus politiques*.

[51] Best once wrote that, despite Britain's atrocious track record in Kenya and various other places, "a British historian may reflect with some pride that his country's record in armed conflicts since it ratified the Conventions (which was however not before 1957) shows care for spirit and letter alike": Geoffrey Best, "Making the Geneva Conventions of 1949: The View from Whitehall," in *Etudes et essais sur le droit international humanitaire et sur les principes de la Croix-Rouge en l'honneur de Jean Pictet*, ed. Christophe Swinarksi (Geneva: ICRC, 1984), 5–15, 15.

[52] Geoffrey Best, *War and Law since 1945* (Oxford: Clarendon Press, 2002), 110–113.

[53] Examples are: Lauren Benton, *Legal Pluralism and Empires, 1500–1850* (New York: New York University Press, 2013); and Martti Koskenniemi, *Gentle Civilizer of Nations: The Rise and Fall of International Law 1870–1960* (Cambridge: Cambridge University Press, 2001).

[54] David Rodin and Henry Shue, *Just and Unjust Warriors: The Moral and Legal Status of Soldiers* (Oxford: Oxford University Press, 2008); Cécile Fabre, *Cosmopolitan War* (Oxford: Oxford University Press, 2012); and Jeff McMahan, *Killing in War* (Oxford: Oxford University Press, 2009).

theory,[55] international law, and history.[56] Various studies have critically engaged with conventional histories of the laws of war by revealing their profoundly hierarchical and exclusive character.[57] This work has not yet produced a comprehensive genealogy of the Conventions' past and originators, for it engages too little with archival materials, among other things.[58] Nevertheless, these critical legal studies are an important inspiration for this book.[59] Drawing on this body of work, this account is not only sensitive to the law's imperial origins; it also sets out to analyze the Conventions' mechanisms of exclusion and hierarchy, which are too often neglected in mainstream scholarship. The book's approach, which is based on extensive archival reading, resonates with a broader trend within postcolonial legal studies, which is concerned to analyze international law's imbrication with European imperial expansion.[60]

[55] Adil Haque, *Law and Morality at War* (Oxford: Oxford University Press, 2017).

[56] Jennifer Pitts, "The Critical History of International Law," *Political Theory*, Vol. 43 (2015): 541–552, 541; and Matthew Craven, "Theorizing the Turn to History in International Law," in *The Oxford Handbook of the Theory of International Law*, eds Anne Orford and Florian Hoffmann (Oxford: Oxford University Press, 2016), 21–37; and Anne Orford, "International Law and the Limits of History," in *The Law of International Lawyers: Reading Martti Koskenniemi*, eds Wouter Werner, Marieke de Hoon, and Alexis Galán (Cambridge: Cambridge University Press, 2015).

[57] For the excellent scholarship on critical approaches to the laws of war, see Karma Nabulsi, *Traditions of War: Occupation, Resistance and the Law* (Oxford: Oxford University Press, 1999); Frédéric Mégret, "From 'Savages' to 'Unlawful Combatants': A Postcolonial Look at International Humanitarian Law's 'Other'," in *International Law and Its Others*, ed. Anne Orford (Cambridge: Cambridge University Press, 2009), 265–317; Helen Kinsella, *The Image before the Weapon: A Critical History of the Distinction Between Combatant and Civilian* (Ithaca, NY: Cornell University Press, 2011); Giovanni Mantilla, *Lawmaking under Pressure*; Chris af Jochnick and Roger Normand, "The Legitimation of Violence: A Critical History of the Laws of War," *Harvard International Law Journal* (1994): 49–95; Eyal Benvenisti and Doreen Lustig, "Monopolizing War: Codifying the Laws of War to Reassert Governmental Authority, 1856–1874," *European Journal of International Law* [2020]: 127–169; Olivier Barsalou, "Preparing for War: The USA and the Making of the 1949 Geneva Conventions on the Laws of War," *Journal of Conflict & Security Law*, Vol. 23, No. 1 (2018): 49–73; and William Hitchcock, "Human Rights and the Laws of War: The Geneva Conventions of 1949," in *The Human Rights Revolution: An International History*, eds Akira Iriye, Petra Goedde, and William Hitchcock (New York: Oxford University Press, 2012).

[58] One example is Michael Barnett's central *Empire of Humanity*, which only briefly discusses the 1949 Conventions. He saw them not so much as a "breakthrough," but rather as a limited product of fear of another war full of brutality. Michael Barnett, *Empire of Humanity: A History of Humanitarianism* (Ithaca, NY: Cornell University Press, 2013), 102–103.

[59] Other important sources of inspiration are: Stefan-Ludwig Hoffmann, "Human Rights and History," *Past & Present*, Vol. 232, No. 1 (2016): 279–310; Amanda Alexander, "International Humanitarian Law, Postcolonialism and the 1977 Geneva Protocol I," *Melbourne Journal of International Law*, Vol. 15 (2016): 15–50; and Samuel Moyn, *The Last Utopia: Human Rights in History* (Cambridge, MA: Harvard University Press, 2010).

[60] Antony Anghie, *Imperialism, Sovereignty and the Making of International Law* (Cambridge: Cambridge University Press, 2004); Sundhya Pahuja, *Decolonizing International Law: Development, Economic Growth and the Politics of Universality* (Cambridge: Cambridge University Press, 2011); Anne Orford, "A Jurisprudence of the Limit," in *International Law and Its Others*, ed. Anne Orford (Cambridge: Cambridge University Press, 2009), 1–34; Adom Getachew, *Worldmaking after Empire: The Rise and Fall of Self-Determination* (Princeton, NJ: Princeton University Press, 2019); Arnulf Becker Lorca, *Mestizo International Law: A Global Intellectual History, 1842-1933* (Cambridge: Cambridge University Press, 2015); Juan Scarfi, *The Hidden History of International Law in the Americas: Empire and Legal Networks* (Oxford: Oxford University Press, 2017); and Umut Özsu,

18 PREPARING FOR WAR

Focusing on transnational and international dynamics,[61] recent historians have opened up humanitarian concepts' multi-dimensional character. They have stressed that human rights can have a conservative trademark;[62] the "malleability" and the "slipperiness" of humanitarian concepts over monolithic notions of humanity;[63] and the mixed origins of international criminal law.[64] Although this body of work encompasses a number of different approaches, each of these works begins from an understanding of how concepts are contested, evolve over time, and are used by different actors for often divergent political objectives. This book has taken this up as a key premise for its analysis of the Conventions' making.

The 9/11 attacks and their aftermath triggered a heavily politicized debate surrounding the Bush Administration's decision to question the extent to which the Geneva Conventions were relevant for the so-called War on Terror.[65] In this context, a "new" history of the laws of war has emerged,[66] to which this book further contributes. Some observers have stressed the importance of contingency, the role of shifting legal boundaries, and how an older tendency to separate law and morality from the politics of warfare was no longer tenable.[67] Such critical interventions have opened up a new space for historicizing the laws of war from

---

Formalizing Displacement: International Law and Population Transfers (Oxford: Oxford University Press, 2015).

[61] David Armitage, "The International Turn in Intellectual History," in *Rethinking Modern European Intellectual History*, eds Darrin McMahon and Samuel Moyn (New York: Oxford University Press, 2014), 232–252; Judith Surkis, Gary Wilder, James W. Cook, Durba Ghosh, Julia Adeney Thomas, and Nathan Perl-Rosenthal, "AHR Forum: Historiographic 'Turns' in Critical Perspective," *American Historical Review*, Vol. 117, No. 3 (2012): 698–813; Patricia Clavin, "Time, Manner, Place: Writing Modern European History in Global, Transnational and International Contexts," *European History Quarterly* [2010]: 624–640; and Akira Iriye and Pierre-Yves Saunier, *The Palgrave Dictionary of Transnational History* (Basingstoke: Palgrave Macmillan, 2009).

[62] See Marco Duranti, *The Conservative Human Rights Revolution: European Identity, Transnational Politics, and the Origins of the European Convention* (Oxford: Oxford University Press, 2017).

[63] Paul Betts, "Universalism and Its Discontents," 62; and Johannes Paulmann, "Conjunctures in the History of International Humanitarian Aid during the Twentieth Century," *Humanity* (2013): 215–238.

[64] Mark Lewis, *The Birth of the New Justice: The Internationalization of Crime and Punishment* (Oxford: Oxford University Press, 2014); and Daniel Segesser, *Recht statt Rache oder Rache durch Recht? Die Ahndung von Kriegsverbrechen in der internationalen wissenschaftlichen Debatte, 1872–1945* (Paderborn: Ferdinand Schöningh, 2010).

[65] David P. Forsythe, *The Politics of Prisoner Abuse: The United States and Enemy Prisoners after 9/11* (Cambridge: Cambridge University Press, 2011).

[66] Examples are: Angela Bennett, *The Geneva Convention: The Hidden Origins of the Red Cross* (Gloucestershire: Sutton Publishing, 2005); John Fabian Witt, *Lincoln's Code: The Laws of War in American History* (New York: Free Press, 2012); Sibylle Scheipers, *Unlawful Combatants: A Genealogy of the Irregular Fighter* (Oxford: Oxford University Press, 2015); James Morrow, *Order within Anarchy: The Laws of War as an International Institution* (Cambridge: Cambridge University Press, 2014); James Whitman, *The Verdict of Battle: The Law of Victory and the Making of Modern War* (Cambridge, MA: Harvard University Press, 2012); and Isabel Hull, *A Scrap of Paper: Breaking and Making International Law during the Great War* (Ithaca, NY: Cornell University Press, 2014).

[67] See David Kennedy, "Reassessing International Humanitarianism: The Dark Sides," in *International Law and Its Others*, ed. Anne Orford (Cambridge: Cambridge University Press, 2009), 131–155.

different perspectives, in terms of both their origins and practice. This book builds upon this scholarship, drawing inspiration from its comparative approaches to exploring legal history.[68] It also makes use of different analytical tools so as to examine clashing views among the Great Powers with regard to the laws of war.

Historicizing the Conventions' changing character confronts readers with Geneva's paradoxes and contradictions. This is not a story of triumph—reconstructing the making of the Conventions means placing them in history. The book shows how key concepts at stake in the agreements, from "non-international armed conflict" to the idea of civilian protection, emerged and accrued meaning. This book also sheds light on the entangled relations among notions of humanity, rights, and warfare, and specifically the role of lawmaking in propelling the emergence of a new international legal order. This approach foregrounds the ways in which both states and international organizations used the Conventions to further their own agendas and interests as new wars loomed on the horizon.[69] Recognition of this extraordinary history allows readers to better grasp the past and politics of the laws of war.

———

The book analyzes the genealogy of the Geneva Conventions through the lens of the five major drafting parties—the ICRC, the United States, the United Kingdom, France, and, to a lesser extent, the Soviet Union. Their proposals reshaped the fabric of the laws of war. The analysis attends to the ICRC's role as an influential non-state actor in conjunction with that of the Swiss Federal Government, whose officials lobbied for a number of ICRC proposals and eventually organized the diplomatic conference in Geneva.[70] Clearly, this Eurocentric selection of actors does not aim at presenting a truly global history, in that it does not show how the world at large engaged with the spectacle of Geneva.[71] At the same time, the book's choice of focus is not meant to deny the ideas and roles played by non-Europeans in these deliberations. Instead,

---

[68] One particularly important source of inspiration was Hull's groundbreaking study of the laws of war during the First World War: Hull, *A Scrap of Paper*.

[69] Guy Fiti Sinclair, *To Reform the World: International Organizations and the Making of Modern States* (New York: Oxford University Press, 2017).

[70] For the history of ICRC–Swiss relations during World War II, see Isabelle Vonèche Cardia, *Neutralité Entre le Comité International de la Croix-Rouge (CICR) et le Gouvernement Suisse* (Lausanne: SHSR, 2012).

[71] Pictet later admitted that it was often said after 1949 that the Conventions were "made by Europeans for Europeans": Pictet, "The Formation of International Humanitarian Law." For a discussion of the Eurocentric nature of international law, see Martti Koskennimi, "Histories of International Law: Dealing with Eurocentrism," *Rechtsgeschichte* (2011): 152–177; and Kinsella and Mantilla, "Contestation before Compliance: History, Politics, and Power in International Humanitarian Law."

20   PREPARING FOR WAR

Preparing for War presents a comparative and entangled history of the ideas and politics of the most influential players who sought to humanize warfare.

It has chosen to focus on this cast of protagonists for three different reasons. First, the book concentrates on those parties that had the most significant impact on these deliberations. These drafters were able to make notable contributions on account of a variety of factors. The ICRC was able to capitalize on its legitimacy, the UK and France on the size of their delegations, the Soviet Union on the central role it played during the process of negotiating the Civilian Convention, and the US on the drafting power that it brought to the table, as well as its status as a superpower. The book discusses the roles played by other, usually less influential actors only as they bear upon the positions adopted by the major drafting parties or where they directly influenced international law's evolution. This leaves room for further study of actors from the Global South.

Second, the book moves beyond the existing literature's tendency to focus on the state. To achieve this, it attends closely to the politics and strategies of the ICRC, an influential non-state actor, and brings together the insights of important scholarly case studies of the role of single states.[72]

The third reason that the analysis looks at these major drafting parties rather than others is that each participated prominently in the entire drafting process, rather than joining the discussions in the postwar period alone. With a few exceptions, the British, the French, the Americans, and the ICRC all took part in the relevant drafting debates both before and after the Second World War. This was not the case for most other major state actors, such as Japan, the two Germanies, or most Latin American states. The governments of these states either lacked resources or interest in the matter, were ignored, or else went uninvited due to their allegiances in the recent war, for instance. For this reason the book pays relatively little attention to their views, save for those of the Soviets during the final stage of the negotiations. Consequently, it analyzes the part played by the Soviets in relation to that of the other major drafting parties or where it directly affected the revision of the Conventions in 1949.[73]

As the organizers of the most important drafting meetings, in which they strove to obtain bipartisan support for the developing proposals, the Swedes and Swiss tended to see the concept of "universality" primarily through the lens of the Second World War and the Cold War. Fear of war between the Soviet

---

[72] Two examples of such singular case studies are Olivier Barsalou, "Preparing for War" and Best, "Making the Geneva Conventions of 1949."

[73] This dimension of the book is mainly based on non-Soviet materials.

Union and its Western adversaries was crucial in this regard in shaping their respective invitation policies, what ideas emerged, how they were codified, and what was left out of these texts. Strikingly, the ICRC, like the Swiss Federal Government, did little to ensure the participation of those who fell outside the bipolar spectrum or came from outside broader Europe. In preparing the first major drafting meeting for government experts in 1947, the ICRC initially invited only the signatories of the United Nations Declaration of 1942. In so doing, the organization excluded Japan's former allies, such as Thailand. In addition, the Swiss did not press hesitant Arab states to send more delegates to the diplomatic conference two years later, let alone ask members of African national liberation movements to attend the debates in the capacity of full delegates, or even as observers.[74]

Reflecting their primary focus on (Western) Europe, the Swiss hosts believed that most non-Europeans had far less wartime "experience" of applying the laws of war than the Europeans did.[75] Allegedly, this made them better able to revise the Conventions. Building upon a pre-existing racialized outlook, the Swiss were reluctant to invite certain non-European revolutionary movements to participate in the talks—whether the Maoists in China or those fighting against colonialism, such as the Indonesian Republicans. Indeed, they only extended invitations to recognized states that had previously signed at least one of the existing Geneva Conventions. In essence, the Swiss feared that broadening participation in that way might prompt severe opposition from the European colonial powers. This resulted in a highly Eurocentric drafting process.

The diplomatic conference finally generated four different treaties with numerous provisions covering a panoply of issues, from hospital ships and chaplains, through the right to water and labor rights for POWs, to sexual violence and reprisals in armed conflict.[76] In the space of a single monograph, it is impossible to cover all of these questions or provide a truly comprehensive history of the Conventions. In view of this, the book adopts a comparative and entangled approach and returns to the original documents. In this way, it

---

[74] It is also a marked contrast with the revision of the Geneva Conventions in the 1970s, when certain national liberation movements did participate. See Mantilla, *Lawmaking under Pressure*.

[75] As noted by Cédric Cotter, it is ironic that the Swiss made such remarks despite not having been involved in an armed conflict for more than a century.

[76] For perspectives on gender and the laws of war, see Judith Gardam, "A Feminist Analysis of Certain Aspects of International Humanitarian Law," *Australian Year Book of International Law* [1992]: 265–278; and Helen Kinsella, "Securing the Civilian: Sex and Gender in the Laws of War," in *Power in Global Governance*, eds Michael Barnett and Raymond Duvall (Cambridge: Cambridge University Press, 2004), 249–272; Kinsella, *The Image before the Weapon*; and Catherine O'Rourke, *Women's Rights in Armed Conflict under International Law* (Cambridge: Cambridge University Press, 2020).

22 PREPARING FOR WAR

examines the views of the major drafting parties on five pre-selected issues of paramount importance: the regulation of civil and colonial wars; restrictions on air-nuclear warfare and blockade; the protection of civilians; the matter of partisan warfare; and how the agreements were to be enforced. These issues went to the heart of the Conventions and each defined the scope of their provisions. Indeed, they have been central to most debates concerning the laws of war in modern history.

Writing a fuller history of the Conventions means returning to the archives, exploring what went on behind the scenes, which ideas shaped Geneva's deliberations, and how these were conceptualized and finally codified into four treaties. The book analyzes the genealogy of the Conventions' making by attending to the principal questions that drafters faced in the period from roughly the end of the First World War up to 1949, emphasizing the immediate post-1945 era in particular. Considering this extended periodization shows how several key principles arose not from the Second but rather from the First World War and its immediate aftermath, before being fundamentally revised in the years between 1944 and 1949.[77] This may come as a surprise. To give one example, although today the idea of a separate Civilian Convention is often presented as an innovation first made after the Second World War, it had actually already been introduced in the 1920s.[78] Studying the Conventions' genealogy, then, requires extending the temporal scope of analysis beyond the direct impact of the Second World War. It even calls for rethinking the *longue durée*, highlighting the importance of radical interwar innovations over tracing the Conventions' past back to Dunant's advocacy in the 1860s.

Preparing for War analyzes the major drafting parties' attitudes by attending to their evolving legal views; the ideas and legitimacy of their proposals; their perceptions of resistance, competing projects, and the law's suggested scope; their informal lobbying efforts; and how the outbreak of new wars shaped the ways in which they interacted.[79] The book recognizes that the laws of war have a longer history, which goes back as far as the ancient world, medieval chivalry codes, and Vattelian conceptions of justice. However, when contemporary observers today refer to "humanitarian law" and its detailed set of rules for

---

[77] Here my position aligns with Neville Wylie and Lindsey Cameron, "The Impact of World War I on the Law Governing the Treatment of Prisoners of War and the Making of a Humanitarian Subject," *European Journal of International Law*, Vol. 29, No. 4 (2018): 1327–1331, 1347–1350; and Hull, *A Scrap of Paper*.

[78] One example: Mark Lewis, *The Birth of the New Justice: The Internationalization of Crime and Punishment* (Oxford: Oxford University Press, 2014).

[79] A few tools are borrowed from Lewis's excellent analysis on the history of international criminal law. See ibid.

civilians, hospitals, supervision, criminal repression, and (non-)international armed conflicts, they are invoking a vocabulary and body of law that is distinctively twentieth-century in origin.

The ICRC and Swiss observers first coined the term "humanitarian law" in the 1940s. It entered common usage in English, Spanish (*derecho humanitario*), German (*humanitäre Völkerrecht*), and French (*droit humanitaire*) only after the diplomatic conference. (The vocabulary of "international humanitarian law" was coined even more recently—in the 1960s.[80]) The experience of reconstructing the exact meaning of this well-known term in different historical contexts has proven challenging, if not exhausting. This is not just because the relevant documents run to hundreds of thousands of pages and are scattered across the globe, with some held in archives difficult to access. The research also had to handle the systemic problem of public minutes being heavily edited.[81] As such, these documents portray a very different picture of how the Conventions were made from that provided by confidential reports by the drafters themselves. Many key decisions, these reports indicate, were made informally, or at least not in public rooms in which minutes were taken and journalists often present.

Exploring the process of forging the Conventions as a history from below, through the eyes of the main protagonists, raised a number of methodological challenges. The fact that Pictet himself believed that the "making of humanitarian law [...] should remain anonymous," to mention just one, made it almost impossible to identify the part played by individual ICRC experts.[82] In addressing this, the analysis spent a great deal of time going through numerous ICRC files that promised to contain information on Pictet's drafting team but said remarkably little about its exact deliberations and disagreements. By focusing on the role of the ICRC's partners, their reports, and other newly excavated primary sources, however, the book has presented a different story, revealing the ICRC's multifaceted role in shaping the Conventions and lobbying for support in Western capitals.

Still, these materials—often derived from state archives—raise their own methodological questions, not least because they were produced for specific audiences with distinctive interests, preconceptions, jargon, and expectations.

---

[80] Alexander, "A Short History of International Humanitarian Law."

[81] For a more detailed study of the problem of using the so-called travaux préparatoires, see Nathan Kurz, "'Hide a Fact Rather than State It': The Holocaust, the 1940s Human Rights Surge, and the Cosmopolitan Imperative of International Law," *Journal of Genocide Research*, Vol. 23, No. 1 (2020): 1–21.

[82] Pictet, "The Formation of International Humanitarian Law," 4.

24   PREPARING FOR WAR

In this book, the analysis has tried to remain alive not only to the potential and limits of these sources,[83] but also to the ways in which state drafters tried to bypass written documentation. Indeed, in the case of some especially controversial actions, state drafters sought to avoid leaving a paper trail in the archival record. Some of the internal reports from ICRC delegates proved especially useful as a means of demystifying these lacunae in the drafting process.[84] This book's compilation of multilingual archival materials, including recently declassified documents, is composed of predominantly Western and a few Soviet sources. Collected from both state and non-state archives, including private collections, these sources offer a unique perspective on the context in which the question of humanizing warfare reentered the arena of global politics.

The chapters that follow trace the evolution of ideas about the meaning of humanitarian law in the twentieth century. Chapter 1 begins by sketching the winding road to Geneva from the ruins of the Second World War to the diplomatic conference of 1949. This introductory chapter of the book presents the most important actors who participated in the process of humanizing warfare, the steps they took to realize that vision, and the compromises that they were willing to accept along the way. Chapter 2 covers the history of the first binding international treaty to recognize human rights protections for enemy civilians in armed conflict. The Civilian Convention, as it became known, provides a set of basic norms that proscribe brutal counterinsurgency campaigns of the sort seen during the world wars, for instance. In line with the book's sub-goals of redrawing alternative drafting routes and reconstructing the drafters' politics, the chapter argues that the treaty's history should be understood as a long struggle featuring several surprising turns of events, which are now largely forgotten.

Chapter 3 provides a new genealogy of Common Article 3, which regulates wars within states and empires (what were termed "non-international armed conflicts"). This was the first binding international legal provision in history that challenged states' absolute sovereignty in their domestic and colonial affairs for humanitarian purposes. The book revives the neglected history of how this central provision, which has received both praise and criticism since 1949, unexpectedly came into being. In reconstructing the contingencies through which the article emerged, this chapter complicates some of the subsequent

---

[83] One example is that the book features a relatively high number of British archival materials. This is the result of the fact that British delegations—compared to the French—had relatively strict and detailed instructions. It forced them to regularly report in detail to London, thereby leaving a detailed paper trace of their actions for later historical research.

[84] One prominent example: Conference Diplomatique. Rapport Spécial Etabli par Pilloud, 16 September 1949, no. CR-254-1, ACICR.

perspectives that have grown up around it. While some have branded Common Article 3 a failure, for many it remains the most innovative outcome of the entire drafting process. Moving beyond these dichotomies, this chapter provides an in-depth analysis of how attempts to internationalize so-called internal wars were profoundly shaped by the dynamics of imperialism and the Cold War.

Chapter 4 provides a micro-history of the attitudes embedded in the Civilian and POW Conventions concerning one of the most contested categories in the history of humanitarian law: the "irregular" fighter on the battlefield. This broad debate led to conflict not just among the Cold War powers, but also within the Western bloc. It raised several crucial questions. Who deserved protection under humanitarian law? Were civilians allowed to take up arms, or would this violate the principles of distinction and passivity? And what should happen to them if they were captured? This chapter notes the importance of decolonization and the Cold War for understanding how drafters' attitudes changed over time and why they came to a far more exclusionary outcome than is often admitted. Indeed, this discussion left a doubtful legacy for both future irregulars resisting occupation and those fracturing empires.

Chapter 5 takes a more overarching view by looking at how the protections to be adopted under future Conventions might endure the dual threat of bombing and blockade. Although the story of Nuremberg's silence on air-nuclear warfare is widely known, this chapter adds a new dimension to this history by revealing how Geneva struggled to obtain rules for protecting civilian populations. In the first part of the chapter, the analysis reconstructs attempts to limit aerial bombing (and blockade) before 1949, which eventually disappeared from the drafters' radar. The remainder of the chapter demonstrates how international law's silence on indiscriminate bombing and its conditional acceptance of starvation as a weapon of war was less the result of a strictly drawn legal distinction between "Hague" and "Geneva law" than a concerted campaign of subversion on the part of a cartel of Western drafters. Unlike some other participants, they believed that limits should be put on the ways in which the central concept of "victims of war" was interpreted. This created a major struggle over whether humanitarian law would become relevant in aerial warfare, with crucial consequences for the Conventions' future.

Chapter 6 poses various questions about how the Conventions' enforcement mechanisms developed. How should one respond to violations of these treaties? To what extent should violent reprisals be allowed under humanitarian law so as to force parties to adhere to their principles? What about criminal repression? And what could be expected from Protecting Powers and the ICRC, given that the doctrine of neutrality came under scrutiny in the years following the Second World War? These key questions became a legal battle-ground. The role of the state and the boundaries of its sovereignty in relation to outside inspectors were especially contentious. These questions foreshadowed contemporary problems. Today, many speak the language of Geneva yet continue to struggle with its dilemma of how to ensure compliance on the battle-field—as the conclusion will show.

Figure 1.1 The gathering hall of the diplomatic conference, with the Red Cross family tree, in Geneva (1949).
Source/Rights: Bibliothèque de Genève Iconographie, FBB-P-GE-05-03-15

1

The Twisted Road to Geneva

The story of how the Geneva Conventions were made starts with war. On 24 November 1944, ICRC legal experts convened to discuss revising the Conventions for the first time. They gathered in Geneva, which was then something of an oasis surrounded by a continent of ruins.[1] From the land of the northern lights to the Greek Peloponnesos in the south, Europe had been pillaged, millions of people killed, and cities obliterated from the sky. Even if many parts of the continent had been liberated, the Germans still occupied vast tracts of land stretching from the Baltic, through Poland and Italy, to the North Sea estuary. While occupied Europeans yearned for the war to end, the ICRC was about to begin its most ambitious plan yet to humanize future warfare on a truly international scale.

The ICRC was a distinctively Swiss institution that, like the Conventions, was born on the European battlefield. In 1859, Henry Dunant witnessed the carnage inflicted upon wounded soldiers during the Battle of Solferino. Deeply concerned by what he witnessed, the Swiss businessman began helping soldiers wounded in wartime and eventually established a new humanitarian organization to uphold their humanity. This institution, which would later become the ICRC,[2] was part of a much broader nineteenth-century movement promoting charity and relief at a transnational scale. Its mission was to reduce human suffering in war by offering humanitarian aid and promoting the Conventions. Dunant's evangelical beliefs played a key motivating role in these efforts to humanize war.

In 1944, as at its foundation, the ICRC's highest governing body, the Committee, was composed mainly of Protestant men from upper-middle-class Genevan families. The first woman to be admitted to this body (in 1918) was Marguerite Cramer, a prize-winning historian and prominent legal expert who had been involved in several international legal negotiations. Indeed, she was

---

[1] Minutes of Seances Commission Juridique, 24 November 1944, no. A PV JUR. 1, Vol. I, Les Archives du Comité International de la Croix-Rouge (ACICR), Geneva.
[2] Gerald Steinacher, *Humanitarians at War: The Red Cross in the Shadow of the Holocaust* (Oxford: Oxford University Press, 2017), 9–10.

Preparing for War. Boyd van Dijk, Oxford University Press. © Boyd van Dijk 2022.
DOI: 10.1093/oso/9780198868071.003.0002

30 PREPARING FOR WAR

the first woman to contribute toward drafting the Conventions (in 1929).[3] Like her male peers, she came from a middle-class family and shared many of their liberal-conservative beliefs. While embracing Swiss neutralism, these delegates often took a cautious approach to contentious issues relating to warfare. In this way, they hoped to make the ICRC more appealing to states and thus multiply their opportunities to humanize warfare.[4]

On 15 February 1945, as Dresden was being burned to ashes by Allied incendiary bombs, the ICRC circulated an official memorandum. In this document, which announced the start of the process of revising the existing Conventions from 1929,[5] the organization demanded better protection for, and access to, prisoners of war and civilians. It also referred to the need to protect populations against the "effects of war"—an allusion to the threat of indiscriminate bombing in the wake of the inferno along the Elbe. Internally, however, ICRC experts remained divided on how to obtain these protections and how the future treaties should be designed.[6]

Whereas Cramer advocated a single Convention in which both military and civilian prisoners would be protected by general principles, so as to maximize legal flexibility in case of unforeseen situations in the future,[7] other ICRC legal experts imagined a separate treaty for civilians, which would include detailed provisions to protect them against ill-treatment.[8] Although initially it preferred two separate treaties, the ICRC kept all of its options open as the process of revising the existing Conventions got underway.[9]

Crucially, the Soviet and British governments responded critically to the ICRC's first suggestions.[10] These plans were initially unacceptable to the Foreign Office, which sought to keep the matter of revising the rules of warfare solidly in the hands of the Allied Great Powers. On top of this, both the

---

[3] For a more detailed biography of Cramer's legal thought, see Boyd van Dijk, "Marguerite Frick-Cramer: A Life Spent Shaping the Geneva Conventions," in *Portraits of Women in International Law: New Names and Forgotten Faces?*, ed. Immi Tallgren (Cambridge: Cambridge University Press, forthcoming).

[4] David Forsythe, *The Humanitarians: The International Committee of the Red Cross* (Cambridge: Cambridge University Press, 2005), 203.

[5] Mémorandum adressé par le Comité International de la Croix Rouge aux Gouvernements des États Parties à la Convention de Genève et aux Sociétés Nationales de la Croix-Rouge, 15 February 1945, ACICR.

[6] Minutes of Seances Commission Juridique, 18 January 1945, no. A PV JUR. 1, Vol. I, ACICR.

[7] The US and France both spoke out in favor of a single Convention at the 1947 conference. General Report Satow of Conference of Government Expert at Geneva, 1947, no. 3795, FO369 (Foreign Office), The National Archives (TNA), Kew.

[8] Minutes of Seances Commission Juridique, 24 November 1944, 17 April 1945, no. A PV JUR. 1, Vol. I, ACICR.

[9] Ibid., 17 April 1945.

[10] Odd Arne Westad, *The Cold War: A World History* (New York: Basic Books, 2017).

Home Office and War Office argued that a Civilian Convention would undermine Britain's vital security interests.[11] Moreover, the Soviets, who were openly hostile toward the ICRC, did not even respond to its memorandum. Moscow fiercely disliked the ICRC on account of the fact that it had failed to criticize Hitler's crimes against Soviet POWs during the war.[12] Given the resistance on the part of these two major Allied powers, the ICRC's plans for the future Conventions were at serious risk of falling apart at an early stage.

What saved the proposals was less the ICRC's persistence than the support it received from De Gaulle's France, Nationalist China, and especially the United States. With the decline of Europe's colonial powers and the rise of ideas of world leadership, Washington had assumed power on the global stage by building the greatest war machine in history.[13] It wished to use this immense power to forge a new international legal order, which would align with its own interests and legal visions. These rested on the foundational assumption that, as a so-called "superior civilization," the United States felt a responsibility to spread its proclaimed ideals of justice, capitalism, interstate non-aggression, and humanized warfare around the world.[14] Meanwhile, US military planners were developing a web of overseas bases, which reached from the Mediterranean to the Pacific. In planning to assume global leadership, the US sought to ensure American military predominance in the event of any type of armed conflict in the future.[15]

Preparing for future wars, US military officials began conducting their own in-house review of the Conventions at the end of the Second World War.[16] Although it acknowledged the importance of the existing treaties in having protected countless US POWs, this study also revealed several gaps that needed to be addressed in light of America's new global role. One of the experts involved in many of these preliminary debates within the US government

---

[11] Geoffrey Best, "Making the Geneva Conventions of 1949: The View from Whitehall," in *Etudes et essais sur le droit international humanitaire et sur les principes de la Croix-Rouge en l'honneur de Jean Pictet*, ed. Christophe Swinarksi (Geneva: ICRC, 1984), 5–15, 7–8.

[12] Giovanni Mantilla, "The Origins and Evolution of the 1949 Geneva Conventions and the 1977 Additional Protocols," in *Do the Geneva Conventions Matter?*, ed. Matthew Evangelista and Nina Tannenwald (Oxford: Oxford University Press, 2017), 35–68, 38–39.

[13] Stephen Wertheim, *Tomorrow, the World: The Birth of US Global Supremacy in World War II* (Cambridge, MA: Harvard University Press, 2020); and Mark Mazower, *No Enchanted Palace: The End of Empire and the Ideological Origins of the United Nations* (Princeton, NJ: Princeton University Press, 2009), 23.

[14] Melvyn Leffler, "The Emergence of an American Grand Strategy, 1945–1952," in *The Cambridge History of the Cold War, Vol I*, ed. Melvyn Leffler and Odd Arne Westad (Cambridge: Cambridge University Press, 2010), 67–89, 67–68.

[15] Melvyn Leffler, "National Security and US Foreign Policy , in *The Origins of the Cold War: An International History*, ed. Melvyn Leffler and David Painter (New York: Routledge, 2002), 15–52, 18.

[16] Mantilla, "The Origins and Evolution of the 1949 Geneva Conventions," 38–39.

32 PREPARING FOR WAR

was Joseph Dillon, a former law professor at West Point. He had worked as provost marshal during the war, in which role he had responsibility for hundreds of thousands of Axis prisoners of war taken in Africa and Europe. As such, he had specialized knowledge of the 1929 POW Convention. This expertise proved useful when he became a leading member of the government's new Interdepartmental Prisoners of War Committee (POWC).[17]

The Truman Administration established the POWC in early 1946 on the advice of the Under Secretary of State Dean Acheson, and devoted extensive resources to it. This new body comprised various representatives from the Navy, Justice, State, Air Force (including Dillon), War, and Interior departments, as well as the American Red Cross.[18] Their main task was to review the 1929 Conventions and develop solutions to any deficits ahead of upcoming drafting meetings. As its name suggests, the POWC was primarily concerned with prisoners of war as opposed to civilians, whom the ICRC sought to protect. Indeed, its initial proposals, of a very detailed character, focused on improving protections for regular US soldiers and clarifying the rules for captor states. This emphasis clearly resonated with Whitehall's opposition to creating a Civilian Convention.

Anglo-American skepticism toward regulating civilian protection was fundamentally at odds with the legal vision promoted by Charles de Gaulle's Provisional Government of France. French officials were keenly interested in protecting civilians and irregulars in future interstate wars. Unlike their Anglo-American wartime allies, the French believed that partisans should be given POW rights; that civilian populations deserved protection against aerial bombing (British and US bombers had destroyed countless French towns and neighborhoods during the German occupation); and that occupying states' powers should be severely curtailed.[19] Unlike its prewar predecessor, which had all but rejected protecting civilians and irregulars (see Chapter 3), this new Gaullist government demanded their protection. What is more, it sought to radically expand the 1929 Conventions by absorbing ever more categories of persons, from stateless people to partisans.

---

[17] Dillon was one of the first state officials after the war to suggest a major revision of the Conventions to the ICRC. Note ICRC on Talks with the Foreign Office, October 1945, no. CR-240-7, ACICR. The XPW Bulletin, February 1950.

[18] Olivier Barsalou, "Preparing for War: The USA and the Making of the 1949 Geneva Conventions on the Laws of War," *Journal of Conflict & Security Law* (2018): 49–73, 54–55. Minutes Prisoners of War Committee, 28 June 1946, Provost Marshal General, no. 672, National Archives and Records Administration (NARA), College Park, MD.

[19] Note Gouvernement Provisoire de la Republique, 9 July 1945, no. 160, Unions Internationales 1944–1960, Les Archives Diplomatiques (LAD), Paris.

The experience of total defeat and brutal counterinsurgency as an occupied country during the Second World War had prompted a radical shift in French legal attitudes. This reversal was facilitated by Henry Frenay's Ministry for Prisoners, Deportees, and Refugees. A former POW and politically conservative leader of the French resistance, Frenay received substantial funding from De Gaulle's government to not just repatriate French subjects but also prepare a revision of the laws of war. This underlines the significance of the Conventions for De Gaulle's larger political aims of restoring France's grandeur on the international stage.[20]

Most strikingly, as a military man, Frenay believed the 1929 POW Convention had been a "wonder" during the war, for it had saved the lives of countless French POWs in German captivity. In a private meeting, he urged his Swiss counterparts to waste no time in convening a diplomatic conference to develop better rules for protecting victims of war.[21] Concerned to hasten this process, Frenay also played a role in convincing De Gaulle's government to establish a special Inter-Ministerial Commission to prepare new proposals.[22] This preliminary body would include members from Frenay's own department, the armed forces, civilian ministries, federations representing former forced laborers and deportees, the National Council of the Resistance, and the French Red Cross. The latter was often represented by Georges Cahen-Salvador, a legal specialist in POW affairs who, after having survived the Holocaust, returned to work for the Conseil d'État.

Whereas Nationalist China was keen to participate in this drafting process, which presented an opportunity to demonstrate its credentials as aspiring Great Power,[23] the British government kept delaying its response to the ICRC's invitation.[24] It continued its attempts to remove civilian protection from the ICRC's drafting agenda. British resistance broke down only in the face of several different factors, above all its main ally, the US, deciding to endorse the

---

[20] Pieter Lagrou, *The Legacy of Nazi Occupation: Patriotic Memory and National Recovery in Western Europe, 1945–1965* (Cambridge: Cambridge University Press, 2003), 113–114, 125; and Olivier Wieviorka, *The French Resistance* (Cambridge, MA: Harvard University Press, 2016), 68–69.

[21] Letter Swiss government legation in Paris, 22 June 1945, no. A.21.31.Paris; II.A.2.3/45; dodis-8245, Swiss Federal Archives (SFA), Bern. Georges Bidault had made similar remarks when meeting with Swiss diplomat (and ICRC partner) Carl Burckhardt in early June 1945. Letter Swiss government legation in Paris, 8 June 1945, II.A.2.3/45; dodis-8244, SFA.

[22] Letter Ministre des Prisonniers de Guerre, Déportés et Réfugiés, 7 August 1945, no. 160, Unions Internationales 1944–1960, LAD.

[23] Note Haller on Responses Great Powers to ICRC Circular, 17 May 1946, no. E2001E#1000/1571#3306 - BD 257, SFA. Letter Chinese Ministry on Government Experts' Conference, 22 July 1946, no. CR-240-7, ACICR.

[24] Even in mid-June 1946, the ICRC was still waiting for a definitive response from the UK government about its attitude toward drafting rules for civilians. Minutes of Seances Commission Juridique, 12 June 1946, no. A PV JUR. 1, Vol. I, ACICR.

34   PREPARING FOR WAR

ICRC's wish to address civilians.[25] Furthermore, UK officials saw Britain as a "civilized" country playing a leading role in shaping international legal norms, and believed that the Conventions remained "the only measure we have of civilized behavior."[26] As these pressures came together, they ultimately felt forced to give in. Having secured the participation of all the Allied Great Powers except for the Soviet Union, the ICRC felt reassured in continuing the revision process by inviting the global Red Cross movement to Geneva in the summer of 1946.

1.1 Gathering for the First Time

After having called on national Red Cross Societies to share their wartime experiences, the ICRC welcomed a record number of delegations from the Middle East, Europe (including the communist Yugoslavs), Latin America, and Asia (except for Japan) to Geneva's town hall.[27] With historic symbolism, the 1946 Red Cross Conference was opened in the Alabama room, where the first Convention had been signed less than a century before. Although this was the most diverse conference of the entire drafting process, the meeting still featured several notable absentees. Not least among these was the German Red Cross, which was still under investigation by Allied denazification officials for its complicity in Hitler's crimes.[28]

Most importantly, the Red Cross Conference endorsed most of the ICRC's proposed revisions to the Conventions. Delegates agreed with the organization's overarching objective of guaranteeing the human person's dignity in wartime. Indeed, this moral imperative served to unify their collective response to Axis atrocities. In addition, they accepted a stunning number of unprecedentedly strict limitations upon occupying powers' rights and even applied these principles to internal wars. Although they were still far from being finalized, these remarkable proposals helped to strengthen the ICRC's resolve in redesigning the 1929 Conventions. Spurred on by Red Cross support, it drew up even more far-reaching proposals for the upcoming government experts' conference, in April 1947.

---

[25] The US Secretary of State had accepted the ICRC invitation on 5 February 1946. Report Government Experts' Conference, 1947 Provost Marshal General, no. 673 PART I, NARA.

[26] Letter Foreign Office to UK Embassy Washington, 19 March 1946, no. 3592, FO369, TNA.

[27] Barsalou, "Preparing for War," 56. The Japanese Red Cross did consider going to Geneva, but lacked the necessary funds; the ICRC was also unwilling to provide these. Minutes of Seances Commission Juridique, 12 June 1946, no. A PV JUR. 1, Vol. I, ACICR.

[28] Minutes of Seances Commission Juridique, 15 May 1946, no. A PV JUR. 1, ACICR.

In preparing for this critical meeting, the ICRC Legal Division faced the "gigantesque" task of developing new drafts for the future Conventions.[29] Eventually, a pragmatically cautious lawyer named Claude Pilloud was appointed to lead this body. Pilloud had practical experience with interpreting the 1929 Convention as a former ICRC inspector of POW camps in occupied France.[30] The task of devising new rules was given to a specialized team of ICRC legal experts under the supervision of Jean Pictet, an ambitious jurist from Geneva who was then thirty-one years of age. Born into a dynasty of bankers also known as Geneva's Rockefeller family, Pictet grew up in a privileged milieu before training in law at the University of Geneva. He joined the ICRC as a promising lawyer in 1937 and was assigned the task of preparing new drafts for the future Conventions. These plans collapsed, however: the diplomatic conference was canceled when war broke out in Europe. This delayed Pictet in his efforts to realize his dream of protecting civilians through humanitarian law.

With the start of the Second World War, Pictet began working as a member of the ICRC Secretariat carrying out the Committee's decisions. As part of this role, he would become the right hand of president Max Huber and one of the Committee's legal counselors, for whom he gave advice on a range of issues.[31] In 1942, with the mass killings of Jews across Hitler's empire, he began preparing the (in-)famous ICRC draft protest against the Holocaust. As is well known today, the Committee never published it.[32] By the end of the war, Pictet had taken charge of the Conventions' preparatory work and began curating draft texts prepared by his subordinates. He also became involved in legal diplomacy, touring Western Europe and North America to sell the ICRC proposals. From 1945 onward, he tried to convince skeptical government officials to support efforts to revise the Conventions in ways that would safeguard the rights of individuals in wartime.

As Pictet was touring the northern hemisphere, the Allied Powers and Jewish organizations were increasingly criticizing the ICRC for its unwillingness to publicly condemn the Holocaust and stand up against Hitler's regime—and to revise the law accordingly. It also faced competition from the United Nations (UN) and neutral Sweden, which sought greater influence in

---

[29] Minutes of Seances Commission Juridique, 30 November 1944, no. A PV JUR. 1, ACICR.

[30] Journal de Genève, 17/18 November 1984.

[31] *Report of the ICRC on its activities during the Second World War, Vol I* (1948), 54–56.

[32] For more details about this debate, see Jean-Claude Favez, *The Red Cross and the Holocaust* (Cambridge: Cambridge University Press, 1999); Vonèche Cardia, *Neutralité Entre le Comité International de la Croix-Rouge et le Gouvernement Suisse* (Lausanne: SHSR, 2012), 21–26; and Steinacher, *Humanitarians at War.*

36 PREPARING FOR WAR

the global humanitarian arena.[33] Despite these setbacks, the ICRC was determined to stake its claim to a place in the challenging postwar environment. To that end, it restarted Pictet's prewar revision process. In strategically pursuing this endeavor, the ICRC hoped to both demonstrate its potential value for Allied states and reshape the international legal order such that wars would become less destructive.

Out of all the major drafting parties, the French remained the strongest supporters of the ICRC's agenda. Although De Gaulle suddenly resigned and tensions arose among communist and anti-communist officials, the Inter-Ministerial Commission continued to push for more robust protection for civilians and irregulars in interstate war. The presence of former partisans and victims of Nazi persecution in the Commission only emboldened it in its attempts to radically alter existing legal structures. After months of deliberation, its members had completely redrafted the original texts of the 1929 Conventions. What is more, they were ready to present a new Civilian Convention. These transformative proposals, which were introduced at the 1947 government experts' conference in Geneva, reset the entire drafting process and reestablished France as a leading player in international legal affairs.

The Government Experts' Conference

While the Nationalists were bogged down in the Chinese Civil War, US diplomats became increasingly anxious about the impact that recent changes in the international system would have on the drafting process. In addition to the Maoist victories, the British were also retreating from India and the eastern Mediterranean, triggering concerns about the specter of communist expansionism.[34] The British requested American assistance, not least in taking over their responsibility over the eastern Mediterranean. This was the lead-up to the so-called Truman Doctrine. Announced in March 1947, this shift in US foreign policy prompted the president's decision to provide aid to allies in Greece and Turkey. The Truman Doctrine became known as a strategy of "containment," which was aimed primarily at preventing communist powers from exploiting (potential) sources of unrest.[35]

---

[33] Steinacher, *Humanitarians at War*, 2.

[34] David Reynolds, "The European Dimension of the Cold War," in *The Origins of the Cold War: An International History*, ed. Melvyn Leffler and David Painter (New York: Routledge, 2002), 125–138, 133.

[35] Leffler, "National Security and US Foreign Policy," 32–33.

In response to these rising Cold War tensions, the POWC became even more interested in protecting US military interests. As part of its preparatory work for the 1947 conference, US preliminary drafters suggested clarifying the rules for captor states and military imprisonment. These proposals were meant to secure US global interests by revising the Conventions' principles accordingly. While trying to protect America's vital security interests, the POWC still tolerated broadening the POW Convention to allow access for civilian internees. This flexibility shown by the US government was influenced by the pressure exerted by Albert Clattenburg, the chief of the US delegation in 1947 and a former wartime expert on civilian internee affairs. Buoyed by European allies' support for the idea,[36] he even suggested a separate Civilian Convention. Given his wartime visits to internment camps for German aliens in the US, for instance, Clattenburg knew what was at stake for civilians and pushed his skeptical government to alter its legal attitude accordingly, as we saw earlier.[37]

The government experts' conference is often treated as merely a stepping stone toward the final diplomatic conference in 1949. In reality, it was a key moment that profoundly shaped future drafting initiatives by the major protagonists. Strikingly, the group of drafters at the government experts' conference remained extremely privileged, for it included the representatives of only a small group of Allied states. In 1947, the ICRC had invited only those governments that had signed the 1942 Declaration of the United Nations, that possessed extensive experience with POW affairs, and whose subjects had recently been imprisoned by Axis states. This meant excluding numerous states, encompassing neutral powers (even Switzerland itself), former Axis nations (Finland, for example), Allied states without extensive experience in matters of wartime captivity (Latin American Allies except Brazil), and those that European colonial powers did not recognize (such as the Indonesian Republic).[38]

Some former enemies of the Axis powers were not invited to participate in this exclusive drafting festival; others refused to come to Geneva. Whereas the Soviet and Yugoslav governments effectively boycotted the ICRC, the Maoists who had fought against the Japanese invader received no invitation. Nationalist China was the only Asian government represented at the 1947 conference.[39]

---

[36] Minutes Prisoners of War Committee, 12 July 1946, 29 August 1946, Provost Marshal General, no. 672, NARA.

[37] Steinacher, *Humanitarians at War*, 191.

[38] Note Pictet for Michel on Invitation Policy for Government Experts's Conference, 21 February 1947, no. CR-240-9, ACICR.

[39] Mark Lewis, *The Birth of the New Justice: The Internationalization of Crime and Punishment* (Oxford: Oxford University Press, 2014), 233.

38 PREPARING FOR WAR

The ICRC's exclusive invitation policy allowed Western European states to dominate its proceedings and neglect Japanese and German experiences of Allied bombing. What is more, it prevented the conference from being directly affected by Cold War politicking, for the major socialist states failed to show up.[40]

The government experts' conference was opened by Max Huber, the ICRC's former president. Its main purpose, he declared, was to find protections for "la personne humaine, son intégrité physique et sa dignité personnelle."[41] The proceedings saw a number of serious clashes between the continental European and Anglo-American delegations. Whereas the European victims of Hitler's empire supported greater protection for civilians and irregulars in occupied territory, the US and Britain sought to protect their security interests as present occupiers in Central Europe, the Middle East, and East Asia. The head of the British delegation, Harold Satow, who had played a prominent role during the war as a member of Whitehall's POW Department, complained that his continental allies suffered from an "ex-occupied" complex. This went especially for the French, including Frenay's left hand and fellow resistance fighter Claude Bourdet. Satow believed that these victims of Hitler's empire had an overly emotional outlook full of blind spots. Unable to think like occupiers, they produced texts, he argued, that would hamper their future ability to put down (anti-colonial) rebellions.[42]

To the surprise of ICRC and French officials, a concerted effort among the continental European delegations led the government experts' conference to accept a remarkable range of prohibitions on arbitrary measures, from hostage taking to collective penalties. The plenary meeting ended with the president talking warmly about the need for peace and the protection of "les droits de l'homme," prompting thunderous applause.[43] Moreover, the ICRC was astonished to hear that the US delegation no longer opposed a separate Civilian Convention. The Americans now argued that this treaty could help to prevent a "repetition of the outrages perpetrated" against US citizens during the Pacific War.[44] The US drafters' ongoing flexibility helped lay the groundwork

---

[40] The exception being the belated Polish delegation. Ibid., 233.

[41] Speech President Government Experts' Conference, 1947, No. CEG_1947_ASSPLEN, La Bibliothèque du Comité international de la Croix Rouge, Geneva (ICRC Library).

[42] Report Conference of Government Expert at Geneva, Home Office delegate, 1947, no. 3795, FO369, TNA; Report Conference of Government Expert at Geneva, General Report Satow, 1947, no. 3795, FO369, TNA; and Mantilla, "The Origins and Evolution of the 1949 Geneva Conventions," 41.

[43] Cable Lamarle on Civilian Convention and Government Expert Conference, 17 April 1947, no. 160, Unions Internationales 1944–1960, LAD.

[44] Report Government Experts' Conference, Provost Marshal General, no. 673 - PART I, NARA. By contrast, the UK delegation believed that there was "no prospect" that the British government would

THE TWISTED ROAD TO GENEVA   39

for the French–ICRC success in obtaining widespread agreement for an ambitious Civilian Convention's draft. Still, the conference remained sympathetic to the idea of fusing this treaty with the existing agreements, thus creating a giant Convention for a variety of purposes. In the ensuing months, drafters continued experimenting with different models for redesigning the existing Conventions.

1.2 Cold War Politics

In the wake of this "coup de théâtre,"[45] most continental European delegations argued that the diplomatic conference should be held "as soon as possible," no later than April 1948. They also discussed the option of meeting outside Switzerland, in Stockholm, where the next Red Cross Conference was planned to be held (the US initially preferred the Swedish capital to Geneva).[46] Pictet, by contrast, argued that the suggested timeline was far too short: his drafting team already lacked the time necessary to prepare detailed proposals and he feared that they might become overburdened.[47] Central European states also opposed the proposal to meet before April 1948, given their worries about the lack of Soviet participation so far.[48]

This lack of Soviet engagement also raised concerns among some of the major drafting parties. Western and Swiss diplomats, who sought to improve diplomatic relations with Stalin's regime, expressed acute anxiety over the issue.[49] Like the ICRC, they feared that without Soviet participation the entire

---

become a signatory of this treaty "for several years" at least. Report Conference of Government Expert at Geneva, Home Office delegate, 1947, no. 3795, FO369, TNA.

[45] Note for Petitpierre on Government Experts' Conference, 30 April 1947, no. E2001E#1000/1571#3306 - BD 257, SFA.

[46] The seventeenth Red Cross Conference in Stockholm had been originally planned for 1942, but had to be postponed as a result of the outbreak of the war in Europe. Introduction Report Conference of Government Experts at Geneva, May 1947, no. 3795, FO369, TNA; and Minutes Prisoners of War Committee, 9 July 1947, Provost Marshal General, no. 672, NARA.

[47] This nuances Barsalou's suggestion that the ICRC wished to "speed up" the drafting process. Barsalou, "Preparing for War," 53.

[48] The Polish and Czechoslovak delegations finally opposed the strict timeline. Previously, the Czechoslovak delegation had agreed with the French to accelerate the drafting process. By the end of the conference, however, the Czechoslovaks had completely reversed their original position. Minutes Plenary Meeting, 26 June 1947, No. A PV A PI.18, ACICR; Report of Proceedings Government Experts' Conference, May 1947, no. 3795, FO369, TNA; and Report Government Experts' Conference, 1947, Provost Marshal General, no. 673 - PART I, NARA.

[49] Boyd van Dijk, "'The Great Humanitarian': The Soviet Union, the International Committee of the Red Cross, and the Geneva Conventions of 1949," *Law and History Review*, Vol. 37, No. 1 (2019): 209–235, 213–214.

40 PREPARING FOR WAR

drafting process might fail catastrophically. With the onset of the Cold War, these concerns became even more pressing.

The Marshall Plan was first announced in June 1947. Although it was officially meant to revive the destroyed European economy, it also changed the entire political landscape.[50] In effect, it accentuated the division of Europe, turning the western German rump state into the future engine of its economic recovery. Unsurprisingly, the Soviet Union saw the plan as a US plot to establish economic and political hegemony over the entire continent. To prevent this, Moscow pressed its Eastern European clients to refuse Marshall aid and demanded that Western communist parties should start undermining the US initiative from within.[51] In the meantime, the Soviets began replacing popular-front governments in Eastern Europe with Stalinist allies, a gradual process of Sovietization that finally culminated in the Prague coup.[52]

The toppling of the Czechoslovak government in February 1948 convinced Western European governments to sign a mutual defense agreement, the Brussels Pact. What is more, they asked Washington to back up this agreement with its massive military power, as part of a broader Atlantic security alliance. At this stage, the Truman Administration was still reluctant to become militarily entangled in Europe if the Republican-dominated Congress continued to oppose it.[53] Indeed, although neither Washington nor Moscow wanted war, and nor did the Marshall Plan immediately trigger the Cold War, fears of military conflict grew exponentially in this period.

Tensions became especially heightened when Stalin decided to close off Berlin in June 1948. By blocking Berlin, he hoped to force the Western powers to reverse their widely disputed decisions regarding Germany's future. This turned out to be a mistake on Stalin's part, for his actions only made the Western powers more convinced that he meant to expand Soviet power across the Eurasian continent. At this stage, Washington increasingly began to approach European politics in terms of deterring Soviet expansionism by building new partnerships. Accordingly, Western powers began holding exploratory talks about another Western alliance, which ultimately led to the establishment of the North Atlantic Treaty Organization (NATO).[54]

---

[50] Westad, *The Cold War: A World History*.
[51] William Hitchcock, "The Marshall Plan and the Creation of the West," in *The Cambridge History of the Cold War, Vol I*, ed. Melvyn Leffler and Odd Arne Westad (Cambridge: Cambridge University Press, 2010), 154–174, 167.
[52] Reynolds, "The European Dimension of the Cold War," 134.
[53] Hitchcock, "The Marshall Plan and the Creation of the West," 168–169.
[54] Westad, *The Cold War: A World History*.

During this period, Washington tried to keep Eurasia outside the Soviet orbit. It built up a new system of alliances, bolstered the capitalist world economy, and sought to preserve its monopoly over atomic weapons.[55] Although war with the Soviet Union remained implausible to most observers, these initiatives made it ever more likely. If war was to break out, US officials argued, they wanted to have the necessary military capacity and legal tools in place so that they could destroy the Soviet enemy. They considered atomic weapons crucial to that enterprise, and would instruct their future negotiators accordingly.[56]

Getting the Soviets on Board

As fears of war grew, the French saw the urgency of persuading the Soviets to take part in this drafting process aimed at limiting its effects. Accordingly, Paris sought to obtain Moscow's participation. Not only were the French anxious about future wars without reciprocity, as had occurred in the German–Soviet War (1941–1945), but the assumption that France and the Soviet Union had undergone "similar wartime experiences" led them to expect that the two states might act as potential drafting allies.[57] The future of the Conventions, they realized, depended upon successfully involving the Soviets.

At this stage, French diplomats began to discuss a range of possible ways in which Soviet participation could be secured with members from the Standing Commission, who were preparing the next Red Cross Conference in Stockholm. Most of these French initiatives led to nothing, however. French diplomats therefore repurposed an older plan to organize a second government experts' conference, this time outside Geneva. Given that the Soviets were not enthusiastic about meeting in Paris, a gathering in Prague was suggested instead. French officials hoped that this would spark Moscow's interest, for the Soviets considered the Czech capital to be in their sphere of influence. At this point, there was a real chance that future drafting meetings would be held outside Switzerland. In any event, the plan to meet in Prague fell apart even before the Prague coup had officially begun: the Czech government "mysteriously" rejected it in January 1948.[58] Contrary to the hopes of French officials, the

---

[55] David Painter and Melvyn Leffler, "The International System and the Origins of the Cold War," in *The Origins of the Cold War: An International History*, ed. Melvyn Leffler and David Painter (New York: Routledge, 2002), 1–14, 3–4

[56] Leffler, "National Security and US Foreign Policy," 33–34.

[57] Van Dijk, "'The Great Humanitarian'," 216–217.

[58] Van Dijk, "'The Great Humanitarian'," 213–223.

42   PREPARING FOR WAR

next drafting meeting would be held in neither Paris nor Prague, but rather Stockholm.

The British government finally started its own internal drafting process while preparing for the next stages of the drafting process. It established two separate Interdepartmental Committees, both of which were composed of members from different military and civil agencies, from the Colonial Office to the Foreign Office. One Committee was to study mainly the Civilian Convention and was placed under the control of the Home Office (the "Home Office Committee"). The other focused largely on the POW and Red Cross Conventions and was led by the War Office (the "War Office Committee"). Crucially, Whitehall stubbornly refused to send an official government delegation to Stockholm, even despite US pressure. Believing that revisions to the Conventions should be handled by states alone, the British government only sent observers.[59] This mistake proved decisive in that it made it possible for the ICRC to push through its revolutionary plans at the meeting in Stockholm.

With the British marginalized, the ICRC had a unique opportunity to gain support for its far-reaching plans at the Red Cross Conference in August 1948. Pictet's visionary legal order took form at this meeting, with Red Cross delegations (including government officials) accepting most of his revolutionary plans. In a radical move, they rejected a whole range of Nazi-style counterinsurgency policies. Indeed, in the preamble to the Civilian Convention the delegations proclaimed the need "to respect the principles of human rights [...] at any time and in all places."[60] Moreover, they endorsed an entirely new treaty for both international and non-international armed conflicts: it was to protect civilians against deportations, torture, and reprisals.[61]

At the same time as the 1948 Red Cross Conference, Swiss government officials organized a special meeting in Stockholm for representatives from the major drafting parties, including several others, to discuss the timing and organization of the final diplomatic conference.[62] Whereas the British observers wanted to postpone this meeting to allow time for more preparatory work,

---

[59] Despite contrary advice from several UK officials, Whitehall saw no reason why it should send an official government delegation to the Stockholm Conference. Accordingly, it sent only observers to Stockholm. Introduction Report, Government Experts' Conference, May 1947, no. 3795, FO369, TNA; Best, "Making the Geneva Conventions of 1949," 12–13; Steinacher, *Humanitarians at War*, 199. The ICRC also asked the UK government to send a full government delegation to Stockholm. Letter Ruegger to Bevin on Stockholm Conference, 24 July 1948, no. 3969, FO369, TNA.

[60] *Revised and New Draft Conventions for the Protection of War Victims* (Geneva: ICRC, 1948), 113.

[61] Lewis, *The Birth of the New Justice*, 253.

[62] Minutes of Meeting at Stockholm Conference, 28 August 1948, no. E2200.40/1000/1565/BD12, SFA.

many other delegations demanded that the conference be held quickly so as to forestall further delays. To strike a compromise, the Swiss suggested two different meetings. The first, which would be held in Geneva and last for about six weeks, aimed to reach an agreement on the Stockholm texts. States would then adjourn for several months to scrutinize the revised texts, before gathering again in that same city for the second meeting, the signature ceremony.[63] By allocating more time, the Swiss persuaded the most important states to accept this plan and received the green light to start preparing the final diplomatic conference(s) in Geneva.[64]

Despite these successes, the Swiss were as yet unsure about the Soviet response to their revision plans. Indeed, it remained unclear whether a Soviet delegation would ever show up in Geneva. The fact that the Soviets sent a letter furiously rejecting an invitation to the 1948 Red Cross Conference gave them little hope. In the letter, the Soviets complained about the invitation extended to "fascist" Spain and the ICRC's unwillingness to denounce Hitler's crimes during the war.[65] Although it rejected these allegations, the ICRC feared that the Soviets might never appear in Geneva and that, in consequence, the conference would be dominated by the Western powers. This, ICRC officials feared, would damage its reputation for impartiality and universality. Still, the Soviets did send two unofficial representatives to observe the debates in Stockholm. These two men also met with Western delegates, including Albert Lamarle, director of the Foreign Ministry's division of international organizations. An experienced French negotiator, Lamarle urged them to take part in the final diplomatic conference.[66]

In early 1949, the French made several last-minute attempts to convince Acheson, the new US Secretary of State, to start a joint campaign to persuade the Soviet Union to participate. The French did everything they could to convince the Americans to help them, from offering to sacrifice the ICRC to threatening not to join the conference themselves.[67] Acheson was unimpressed, however.[68] At this point, most Western observers anticipated that the Soviets would not come to Geneva and had fairly low expectations of the diplomatic

---

[63] Report UK observer at Stockholm Conference, 3 September 1948, no. 328, WO163 (War Office), TNA; and Correspondence on Head of UK Delegation, December 1948, no. 3970, FO369, TNA.

[64] The first Swiss preparations for the diplomatic conference began in late October 1948. Final Report Stenography Service, 29 September 1949, no. E2001E#1967/113#16123/BD 874, SFA; and Preliminary Report of Secretariat, December 1948, no. E2001E#1967/113#16123/BD 874, SFA.

[65] It is telling that despite these objections the Soviets apparently did not object to Spain's participation with regard to the diplomatic conference one year later.

[66] Van Dijk, '"The Great Humanitarian," 213–223.

[67] Correspondence on Russian participation, January–March 1949, no. 4144, FO369, TNA.

[68] See Letter Secretary of State, 26 January 1949, no. 4144, FO369, TNA.

44 PREPARING FOR WAR

conference.[69] As such, they were extremely surprised when, at the very last moment in mid-April 1949, several Soviet satellites unexpectedly announced their intention to participate. Given recent signs that the Soviet Union wanted to start negotiating with the Western powers about lifting the Berlin blockade, Moscow must have seen opportunities for reaching another agreement with them, this time concerning the revision of the Conventions. This remarkable turn of events not only embarrassed those Soviet allies that had previously rejected invitations from Bern, but also prompted Swiss claims that the Soviet arrival in Geneva represented a major victory for their own diplomatic service.[70]

1.3 The Diplomatic Conference

For five months in 1949, international legal attention centered on Geneva. Organized by Swiss federal officials, the diplomatic conference was held in the Palais du Conseil Général. At the time, this building hosted the ICRC's POW Agency and its millions of fiches chronicling the lives of POWs across the globe. These unique documents had to be temporarily stored in nearby military barracks to allow the Swiss hosts to use this building. The Palais was situated along the Rue du General-Dufour in the heart of Geneva, next to the statue of Guillaume Henri Dufour, one of the ICRC's founding members. A local architect redesigned the entire building for the conference; it was also furnished with numerous classical sculptures and chairs from the Genevan canton.[71] Hundreds of beds were reserved in the city's finest hotels to accommodate the world's experts in the laws of war.

The US delegation was accommodated at the Hotel des Bergues, where they enjoyed an exquisite view of the lake of Geneva.[72] The other Great Powers— France, Nationalist China, Great Britain, and the Soviet Union—were hosted nearby. The Swiss also invited members of the Commonwealth (South Africa, however, did not come), Latin American states, Eastern European satellites (although Poland only sent observers), newly independent India, and the State of Israel (despite Arab opposition). The Yugoslavs who had recently broken off

---

[69] Israeli authorities shared the Western assumption that the Soviet Union and its Eastern European allies would probably not show up in Geneva. See Letter M. Kahany to Ministry of Foreign Affairs, 22 December 1948, no. 1838/2 – צה (00071706.81.D5.A0.67), Israel State Archives, Jerusalem (ISA).

[70] See Basler Nachrichten, 19 April 1949.

[71] Final Report Stenography Service, 29 September 1949, no. E2001E#1967/113#16123/BD 874, SFA; and Report Commissaire on Activities from 23 November 1948 to 21 April 1949, no. E2001E#1967/113#16123/BD 874, SFA.

[72] Report US Delegation Diplomatic Conference, 1949, no. 673, Provost Marshal General, NARA.

relations with the Soviet Union participated as observers, along with the ICRC as experts. In total, sixty-four nations were represented, either as official delegates or observers. Not only the Allies but also some of their former Axis enemies, including the wartime Italian fascist Giacinto Auriti, traveled to Geneva for the final stage of the drafting process.[73]

The two Germanies and Japan were notably absent. None of these formerly Axis powers—and previous skeptics of the laws of war—had signed any peace treaty with the Allies and some doubted whether they would ever feel "bound by [these] Conventions."[74] Under pressure from the Chinese, the diplomatic conference decided that Japan could participate only as observers: the Japanese delegation was to remain under the "guidance" of General Douglas MacArthur's American legal advisors.[75] Tokyo itself, however, had no serious interest in humanizing warfare, having renounced war itself in its own constitution.[76]

To Germany, though, the door remained entirely closed. The last nail in the coffin of German participation came when the influential US military governor of Germany, Lucius Clay, argued that they should never talk about war again.[77] Despite these exclusions, the Swiss claimed that the conference

---

[73] This group of former Axis enemies included Finland, Thailand, and Italy, among others. The only known wartime fascist delegate at the diplomatic conference was the head of the Italian delegation (which featured anti-fascist victims such as Aldo Spallicci too): Giacinto Auriti, the former Italian ambassador to Japan promoting Benito Mussolini's interests in Asia. While making the fascist salute, Auriti played a prominent role at a propaganda meeting in Tokyo in 1937, when Italy officially joined the Anti-Comintern Pact. On at least one occasion, at the diplomatic conference, the Soviet delegation made an allusion to Italy's fascist past when exchanging with Auriti. Final Record of the Diplomatic Conference of Geneva of 1949, Vol. II, Section A, p. 10, Library of Congress (LOC), Washington, DC; and Final Record of the Diplomatic Conference of Geneva of 1949, Vol. II, Section B, pp. 492–495, Library of Congress (LOC), Washington, DC.

[74] UK Note on Participation of Various Countries, 12 March 1949, no. 4146, FO369, TNA. Nationalist Chinese representatives also asked critical questions about why Japan was allowed to send observers whereas the two Germanies were not. Minutes of Meeting Heads of Delegation, 20 April 1949, no. 4150, FO369, TNA.

[75] The two indigenous Japanese advisers of MacArthur's delegation were Koichiro Asakai (a career diplomat who later became Japan's ambassador in the United States) and Ayusawa Iwao (who had studied in the US and represented Japan at the International Labour Organization before the war). Cable US delegation to State Department, 2 May 1949, no. 5, RG43-40, NARA; and Letter President Japanese Red Cross to Odier, 9 April 1949, no. CR-221-3, ACICR. As it had renounced war, Tokyo itself was not expressing extensive interest in the matter of humanizing warfare either, making only very basic suggestions for improvement. Memo Clattenburg to State Department on Japanese Government's Views, 15 September 1948, no. 5536, RG43-22, NARA. While observing the negotiations, Ayusawa Iwao felt alienated and asked: "why engage in war at all?" Cited from Sarah Kovner, *Prisoners of the Empire: Inside Japanese POW Camps* (Cambridge, MA: Harvard University Press, 2020).

[76] For a more detailed discussion of Japan's attitude toward the laws of war, especially during the Second World War, see Kovner, *Prisoners of the Empire*.

[77] See Telegram from Military Governor to Foreign Office, 25 March 1949, no. 4146, FO369, TNA; and Telegram Washington to Foreign Office, 29 March 1949, no. 4147, FO369, TNA. According to Donald Bloxham, the real seat of power in post-war German affairs rested with Lucius Clay. Donald Bloxham, *Genocide on Trial: War Crimes Trials and the Formation of Holocaust History and Memory* (Oxford: Oxford University Press, 2001), 26.

46   PREPARING FOR WAR

embodied an idea of "universality." Like the ICRC, they saw the concept of "universality" through the lens of the Second World War and especially the European Cold War, in that they sought to obtain bipartisan support for the future Conventions. Fear of a military confrontation between the Soviet Union and the West played a crucial motivating role in this endeavor.

Strikingly, both the Swiss and ICRC placed far less emphasis on securing the participation of states beyond Europe that fell outside the bipolar spectrum. The Swiss expressed reluctance to invite revolutionary movements (such as the Maoists in China),[78] those fighting against colonialism (including the Viet Minh), or subaltern actors on the verge of obtaining European recognition (Indonesia, for instance). In essence, the fact that the Swiss invited only recognized states that had previously signed at least one of the existing Conventions attests to their persistently Eurocentric outlook. Bern feared that extending invitations to states with disputed statehood statuses (Israel excluded) or anti-colonial actors might prompt trenchant opposition from its European colonial partners. The result was a highly Eurocentric drafting process.

The major drafting parties' delegations differed not just in size, outlook, experience, and background, but in leadership too. Leland Harrison, the former US ambassador in Switzerland who had worked previously with the ICRC on the Conventions, presided over the US delegation and regularly communicated with Acheson himself.[79] Other influential US delegates were Raymund Yingling, the delegation's main legal expert and deputy head, as well as Clattenburg, who had participated throughout this process. Although both men were experts in the laws of war, they did not have major reputations in the discipline of international law. Instead, they had practical experience in legally administrating occupied territories (Yingling) and POW camps (Dillon). Their main objective was to uphold US global interests, more so than in previous meetings.[80] To that end, in trying to formulate practical rules for warfare, they were concerned to defend the United States' monopoly on atomic weapons and upholding many of the rights of occupiers.

Robert Craigie, an experienced diplomat who had served previously in Tokyo until being interned at the start of the Pacific War, chaired the British delegation.[81] He had wide-ranging experience in participating in international conferences.[82] The role of British deputy was split between two different delegates,

---

[78] Note for Swiss Delegation on Invitation Policies, 12 April 1949, no. J2.118#1968/77_bd.13, SFA.

[79] Barsalou, "Preparing for War," 56.

[80] Minutes Meeting on Draft Civilian Convention, 19 April 1949, no. 40, RG43 - 5, NARA.

[81] The former leader of the 1947 delegation, Satow, had to step back for medical reasons, retired, and therefore did not participate in the diplomatic conference as UK delegate.

[82] Letter Foreign Office to Treasury, 13 December 1948, no. 3970, FO369, TNA.

Henry Strutt, from the Home Office, and William Gardner, a War Office hard-liner who had gained practical experience with the POW Convention during the war. Throughout the drafting process, Gardner staunchly defended the rights of detaining powers as an apologist for empire. Whitehall instructed the British delegation to act aggressively. Accordingly, Craigie's team submitted a record number of amendments, which would all but overthrow the Stockholm proposals. These destructive instructions were not only "so far removed from the general opinion" of the conference that the British delegation came close to the brink of disaster,[83] but also delayed the proceedings for several months, as will be shown in the following chapters.[84]

The French were some of the fiercest critics of Britain's proposals. Although officially the French delegation was led by Robert Betolaud (who was one of Frenay's successors), he rarely attended meetings in Geneva. Cahen-Salvador and Lamarle were the real French leaders at the conference: they tried to obtain international recognition for partisans and civilians in interstate wartime. Just as the memories of the fascist occupation shaped French legal attitudes, so too the Cold War and decolonization led French representatives to exclude from the Conventions prisoners taken in colonial wars and communist spies (see Chapter 4).

The "valuable" Swiss government delegation was led by Plinio Bolla, the judge of the confederation's supreme court. He was advised by a female legal expert, Denise Robert, who would later become a prominent international lawyer in Geneva. Working closely together, the ICRC's delegation included five legal experts (including Pictet), all of whom had the right to speak as official experts—but could not vote. As the conference came to a close, the British delegation even contested that one discursive privilege. In trying to silence the ICRC delegation in this way, they hoped to prevent the Genevans from influencing the final votes.[85]

The Soviet delegation, unlike those of other major drafting parties, was led by a military man, named Nikolay Vasilyevich Slavin. As a Red Army liaison with the Western Allies during the war, he had helped repatriate US POWs from liberated German camps. Seen as loyal, Slavin was also present at Dumbarton Oaks in 1944, at which proposals for the UN were being

---

[83] Conference Diplomatique. Rapport Spécial Etabli par Pilloud, 16 September 1949, no. CR-254-1, ACICR; and Report Dutch Delegation Third Commission, 1949, no. 3045, Code-Archief Buitenlandse Zaken, National Archives of the Netherlands (NA), The Hague.

[84] Best, "Making the Geneva Conventions of 1949," 11.

[85] Pilloud said the Swiss delegation was of "valuable support" to the ICRC and helped to reconcile the different viewpoints among the delegates. He also believed Bolla was "brilliant." Conference Diplomatique. Rapport Spécial Etabli par Pilloud, 16 September 1949, no. CR-254-1, ACICR.

48 PREPARING FOR WAR

formulated. Accompanying him in Geneva was Platon Morosov, the leading Soviet legal expert who had recently participated in drafting the Genocide Convention. One of the Soviet objectives in 1949 was to publicly embarrass the Western powers by supporting proposals to strengthen international legal standards in wartime.[86] With some exceptions, Eastern European delegates— including the Czechoslovak representative, Arnöst Tauber—largely followed this propagandistic Soviet line.[87]

India's small delegation included several former servants of the British empire, such as the representative of the Indian Ministry of Defence, Benegal Mukunda Rao. He was joined by Parmeshwar Narayan Haksar, a former student at the London School of Economics and Jawaharlal Nehru's protégé at the Indian Foreign Service. Haksar had begun his career as a legal advisor, but later became more directly involved in Indian politics as principal secretary to Prime Minister Indira Gandhi. Nationalist China was represented by the lawyer Wu Nan-ju. As the serving Chinese ambassador to Switzerland, he had previously attended meetings of the UN Commission on Human Rights in Geneva, working alongside Peng Chun Chang. During the war, Wu Nan-ju had worked at the Foreign Ministry in the mainland city of Chongqing, where he was subjected to bombardment from Japanese airplanes.

The Grand Opening

The first session of the diplomatic conference convened on 21 April 1949 under the presidency of Petitpierre, the well-respected Swiss foreign minister.[88] He was accompanied by five different vice-presidents, including Slavin, Craigie, and Harrison.[89] The drafting work was divided among six major committees, each of which consisted of several special commissions and working parties analyzing specific legal problems. Whereas the major drafting parties from Europe and North America were large enough to participate in many of these

---

[86] Mantilla, "The Origins and Evolution of the 1949 Geneva Conventions," 42.

[87] While not directly affiliated with either camp, the Israelis also noticed that Eastern European delegates "did nothing without prior consultation with the Soviet representatives." Letter Israeli representative in Geneva to E. Gordon, 4 July 1949, no. 1987/6- חצ (00071706.81.D4.ED.29), ISA.

[88] The head of the British delegation adored Petitpierre, calling him "calm, self-possessed, impartial and authoritative" and an "effective and experienced chairman." Interim Report UK delegation, 4 May 1949, no. 4149, FO369, TNA; and Final Report Craigie, 1949, no. 6036, ADM116 (Admiralty), TNA.

[89] The fifth vice-president came officially from outside of Europe: Pedro de Alba. He was the Mexican ambassador in Switzerland.

specialized commissions, smaller delegations such as China's (the Dutch delegation was twice as large) had to be far more selective.[90] Despite this major imbalance in favor of large Western and Eastern bloc delegations, the leader of the Indian representation, Dhiren Mitra, took up the position of chairman of Committee I, which was tasked with drafting the Wounded and Sick and the Maritime Warfare Conventions. He was the first non-white person ever selected for the prestigious post of chairperson of a major drafting committee at a diplomatic conference on the laws of war at large.

Unlike many laws of war conferences in past days, here delegates voted by majority (one state, one vote procedure) and both French and English were the official working languages of the diplomatic conference. Given that many delegates were not fluent in both languages, women played instrumental roles as interpreters, stenographers, editors, and translators. On busy days, different interpreters worked at more than seven different meetings simultaneously to allow the drafters to communicate with one another.[91] Minutes of the plenary were often typed out at night so that they were ready when the delegates returned to the Palais the following morning.[92] Administrators created a sophisticated system for documenting amendments so as to smooth the massive drafting process.[93] Messengers would drive around Geneva to deliver conference documents to hotels where delegates were staying. This enormous logistical operation, which involved an army of drafting servants from across Switzerland and beyond, consumed thousands of work-hours, tons of carbon paper sheets, and millions of stencils.[94]

Unlike their assistants, many drafters were far from being fully prepared when they assembled in April 1949. ICRC legal experts complained about the representatives' lack of proper instructions and detailed knowledge of the laws of war.[95] Like the delegations' expertise, the personal backgrounds of drafters also varied significantly. France, for instance, sent a former resistance fighter named Andrée Jacob to Geneva. Having gone into hiding during

[90] See Report of Irish Delegation at Geneva Diplomatic Conference 1949, 25 November 1949, no. Series DFA-5-341-137-2, National Archives of Ireland (NAI), Dublin.

[91] Final Report Stenography Service, 29 September 1949, no. E2001E#1967/113#16123/BD 874, SFA; and Note by O'Davoren on Interpreters Service, no date, no. E2001E#1967/113#16123/BD 874, SFA.

[92] Report by Service of Redacteurs, 7 September 1949, no. E2001E#1967/113#16123/BD 874, SFA.

[93] Conference Diplomatique. Rapport Spécial Etabli par Pilloud, 16 September 1949, no. CR-254-1, ACICR.

[94] Final Report Stenography Service, 29 September 1949, no. E2001E#1967/113#16123/BD 874, SFA; and Final Report Roneographie, 26 August 1949, no. E2001E#1967/113#16123/BD 874, SFA.

[95] Conference Diplomatique. Rapport Spécial Etabli par Pilloud, 16 September 1949, no. CR-254-1, ACICR.

50 PREPARING FOR WAR

the war on account of her Jewish origins, she became Bourdet and Frenay's comrade-in-arms as part of *Combat*—where women could play a significant role.[96] As an antifascist underground fighter, she forged paperwork for Jews in hiding and helped organize the resistance movement. After the Liberation of France, she joined Frenay's Ministry, where she became directly involved in the Inter-Ministerial Commission.[97] In actively shaping French legal positioning, Jacob could continue to advocate for the rights of deportees on the international stage.[98]

Although men dominated the diplomatic conference, women such as Jacob actively shaped its outcome. They broke several gender barriers, especially in light of the fact that the Hague Peace Conferences of 1899 and 1907 had officially invited no women as legal drafters.[99] One prominent female delegate in 1949 was Joyce Gutteridge, the first woman to act as legal advisor for the Foreign Office; male colleagues often asked for her advice on questions concerning international law in a joint effort to defend the empire's interests.[100] As a communist propagandist, the Romanian delegate Elisabeta Luca was on the opposite side of the political spectrum to Gutteridge. Luca, an antifascist veteran of the Spanish Civil War, left a lasting impression on the conference. During one of the meetings, she gave an extraordinary speech that exposed the unwillingness of Gutteridge's delegation to end indiscriminate bombing (see Chapter 5).

All of these women and men had suffered during the Second World War. Luca's family had been wiped out during the Holocaust. Gutteridge witnessed the terrible destruction caused by the Blitz. German executioners had summarily shot Bourdet's comrades. Slavin had fought in the bloodlands of Eastern Europe. Dillon had personally seen the railroad cars filled with bodies following the liberation of Dachau.[101] Rao had spent time as a POW, having been captured in Italy. Tauber had survived the horrors of Auschwitz. And many more delegates besides had emerged from the war damaged by years of persecution, fighting, bombing, isolation, starvation, torture, and other forms of ill-treatment.

---

[96] Wieviorka, *The French Resistance*, 156–157.

[97] Here I draw upon the pioneering work of Marie-Jo Bonnet.

[98] Pilloud called her work, and that of Lamarle, of "great help" to the ICRC's work. Conference Diplomatique. Rapport Spécial Etabli par Pilloud, 16 September 1949, no. CR-254-1, ACICR.

[99] Tuba Inal, *Looting and Rape in Wartime: Law and Change in International Relations* (Philadelphia: University of Pennsylvania Press, 2013), 15.

[100] Gardner said she was "invaluable and indefatigable in advising us, at any and all times, on legal issues." Report War Office, October 1949, no. 14038, WO32, TNA.

[101] Final Record of the Diplomatic Conference of Geneva of 1949, Vol. II, Section A, p. 10, Library of Congress (LOC), Washington, DC. 2B, 306.

As a result of these deeply personal experiences, the delegates were keenly aware not just of the inhumanity of total warfare or the need to make it less destructive, but also that the fate of "millions of human beings" depended upon their decisions in Geneva.[102] Protecting civilians was among their most pressing concerns. It is also at the core of the next chapter, in which the story of the making of the Conventions is continued.

---

[102] Journal de Genève, 18 March 1949.

Figure 2.1 The worlds of human rights and the laws of war meeting in Switzerland—Eleanor Roosevelt (left) and Max Petitpierre, in 1947.
Source: Ullstein

2

Making the Civilian Convention

Who counts as a civilian? Who does not? And what does this imply for their treatment? The Civilian Convention's architects discussed these questions throughout the 1940s, even as the specter of endless total war was circling above their heads. In essence, they sought to create the very first treaty in history that specifically protects civilians in wartime. This process triggered a long and nearly fatal effort for a new Civilian Convention whose adoption in August 1949 was hailed as a "miracle" by ICRC president Paul Ruegger.[1] These words reflected not just euphoria but also his relief following an almost desperate campaign to safeguard civilians in armed conflict. Several decades later, it is often forgotten how difficult the Civilian Convention's making was and how it could have collapsed at various points in time.

To explain this "miracle," scholars have pointed to a long-term humanitarian development,[2] the impact of the two world wars,[3] or the Holocaust in explaining the treaty's genesis.[4] This chapter argues that the Civilian Convention's genealogy cannot be captured in such terms, and that it was more contingent than has been claimed in the literature.[5] For a long time, drafters seriously

---

[1] Minutes of Seances Commission Juridique, 11 November 1949, no. A PV JUR. 1, Vol. I, Les Archives du Comité International de la Croix-Rouge (ACICR), Geneva. For the general body of (legal) literature regarding the Civilian Convention's origins, see the ICRC's website https://casebook.icrc.org/ (retrieved 12 January 2017); Leslie Green, *The Contemporary Law of Armed Conflict* (New York: Juris Publishing, 2008); Yoram Dinstein, *The Conduct of Hostilities under the Law of International Armed Conflict* (Cambridge: Cambridge University Press, 2004), 113–114; Gerald Draper, *The Red Cross Conventions* (London: Stevens, 1958), 26–48; and Paul de La Pradelle, *La Conférence Diplomatique et les Nouvelles Conventions de Genève du 12 Août 1949* (Paris: Les Editions Internationales, 1951), 62–93.

[2] For the teleological–humanitarian narrative, see Waldemar Solf, "Protection of Civilians Against the Effects of Hostilities under Customary International Law and under Protocol I," *American University International Law Review*, Vol. 1, No. 1 (1986): 117–135.

[3] For the argument stressing the impact of the First World War, see Amanda Alexander, "The Genesis of the Civilian," *Leiden Journal of International Law*, Vol. 20, No. 2 (2007): 359–376. Karma Nabulsi, as one of the first historians of the laws of war, has argued that the most critical precedent for the Geneva Conventions of 1949 was the "1942 London Declaration of War Crimes [...], which proclaimed hostage-taking and other customary occupying army practices a war crime." Karma Nabulsi, *Traditions of War: Occupation, Resistance and the Law* (Oxford: Oxford University Press, 1999), 12–13.

[4] For examples of the Holocaust argument, see Leslie Green, "Grave Breaches or Crimes Against Humanity," *Journal of Legal Studies*, Vol. 8 (1997): 19, 21 and Alexander Gillespie, *A History of the Laws of War, Vol. 2* (Portland, OR: Hart, 2011), 183.

[5] In Geoffrey Best's accounts, one can find a number of important points relevant to the Civilian Convention's origins, but these are for the most part anecdotal and not entirely comprehensive in scope: Geoffrey Best, *War and Law since 1945* (Oxford: Clarendon Press, 2002), 115–116; and

---

Preparing for War. Boyd van Dijk, Oxford University Press. © Boyd van Dijk 2022.
DOI: 10.1093/oso/9780198868071.003.0003

54   PREPARING FOR WAR

considered placing civilians and combatants under the same treaty umbrella, for instance. There existed no master plan. Drafters stayed often silent on the extermination of European Jewry, too.[6] What is more, the Conventions' most influential drafters foresaw a remarkably tight connection between human rights and humanitarian law, a relationship that is much closer than generally admitted in the literature. Scholars have argued that these two fields remained distinct until the 1950s, or until 1968, when the Teheran Resolution called for the application of human rights in wartime.[7]

Crucially, the leading drafters of the Civilian Convention saw an important connection between these two fields of international law. For instance, ICRC drafter Pilloud saw "des points communs évidents" between the drafts he had co-designed for the Conventions and the Universal Declaration of Human Rights (UDHR).[8] Cahen-Salvador, as the head of the Third Committee at the diplomatic conference negotiating the Civilian Convention's final text, believed the treaty safeguarded "human rights" in wartime.[9] Like other influential drafters, Pictet claimed that the non-binding UDHR had remained largely theoretical, whereas its binding equivalent of "Geneva Law [was leading] the way."[10]

Geoffrey Best, *Humanity in Warfare: The Modern History of the International Laws of Armed Conflicts* (London: Weidenfeld and Nicholson, 1980), 322. For Best's views on the connections between human rights and the Conventions, see Best, *War and Law since 1945*, 144–145.

[6] See also Marco Duranti, "The Holocaust, the Legacy of 1789 and the Birth of International Human Rights Law: Revisiting the Foundation Myth," *Journal of Genocide Research*, Vol. 14, No. 2 (2012): 159–186. For a counter viewpoint on the UN debates regarding the Holocaust, see Nathan Kurz, "'Hide a Fact Rather than State It': The Holocaust, the 1940s Human Rights Surge, and the Cosmopolitan Imperative of International Law," *Journal of Genocide Research*, Vol. 23, No. 1 (2020): 1–21.

[7] For a detailed discussion of this debate, see Boyd van Dijk, "Human Rights in War: On the Entangled Foundations of the 1949 Geneva Conventions," *American Journal of International Law*, Vol. 112, No. 4 (2018): 553–582, 553–558. For insightful histories of human rights and humanitarian law, see Amanda Alexander, "A Short History of International Humanitarian Law," *European Journal of International Law*, Vol. 26, No. 1 (2015): 109–138; Katharine Fortin, "Complementarity between the ICRC and the United Nations and International Humanitarian Law and International Human Rights Law, 1948–1968," *International Review of the Red Cross*, Vol. 94, No. 888 (2012): 1433–1454; William Hitchcock, "Human Rights and the Laws of War: The Geneva Conventions of 1949," in *The Human Rights Revolution: An International History*, ed. Akira Iriye, Petra Goedde, and William Hitchcock (New York: Oxford University Press, 2012), 96–98; Kimberly Lowe, "Humanitarianism and National Sovereignty: Red Cross Intervention on behalf of Political Prisoners in Soviet Russia, 1921–3," *Journal of Contemporary History*, Vol. 49, No. 4 (2014): 652–674. For a longer history of rights and the regulation of warfare, see Pablo Kalmanovitz, *The Laws of War in International Thought* (Oxford: Oxford University Press, 2020), 139–1942; and Michael Barnett, *Humanitarianism and Human Rights: A World of Differences?* (Cambridge: Cambridge University Press, 2020).

[8] Claude Pilloud, "La Déclaration Universelle des Droits de l'Homme et les Conventions Internationales Protégeant les Victimes de la Guerre," *Revue internationale de la Croix-Rouge et Bulletin international des Sociétés de la Croix-Rouge*, Vol. 31, No. 364 (1949): 252–258.

[9] *Le Figaro*, 8 December 1949. See also Final Record of the Diplomatic Conference of Geneva of 1949, Vol. II, Section A, p. 10, Library of Congress (LOC), Washington, DC. 2A, 694–696.

[10] Cited from: Agenor Krafft, "The Present Position of the Red Cross Geneva Conventions," *Transactions of the Grotius Society*, Vol. 37 (1951): 146. For similar views from other Francophone

This chapter shows the transformative impact of "human rights thinking" on the making of the Civilian Convention. Borrowing from the work of intellectual historians and the legal philosopher David Luban, it conceptualizes "human rights thinking" both as a metonym for different projects promoting human dignity and limiting state sovereignty and as a conceptual generator for viewing individuals as holders of universalistic rights in armed conflict. In the sense used here, "human rights thinking" is not necessarily the inherent opposite of "humanitarianism." Appropriating human rights thinking and blending it with humanitarian frameworks as a means to challenge a pre-existing exclusive legal regime that privileged wartime occupiers' rights, the Convention's leading architects played a critical role in contesting a whole range of so-called Nazi-style counterinsurgency policies. In their eyes, measures like hostage taking and collective penalties were no longer appropriate tools to enforce the laws of war and to safeguard the political order of Europe.[11]

These policies, they argued, were not just inhumane or lacking in military necessity, but also—and this represents a decisive conceptual shift—a violation of the fundamental rights and dignity of individuals in wartime. An important cause for this shift was a much larger legal–moral alteration in focus from soldiers' rights to protecting civilians in war. The death ratio had flipped during the war at the cost of civilians and the Allies had used human rights notions as a means to condemn brutal Nazi counterinsurgency measures against them.[12] Once the Allies, and their drafters later in Geneva, had agreed to publicly condemn Nazi atrocities such as hostage killings on the basis of universalistic principles,[13] they were forced to reckon with other measures of counterinsurgency as well—potentially including their own. While never fully realized, this agency-driven logic of "cascad[ing] effects" led to new calls for

---

contemporaries, see Marguerite Frick-Cramer, "Contribution à l'élaboration d'une Convention sur les prisonniers, militaires ou civils, tombés au pouvoir de l'ennemi ou d'une autorité non reconnue par eux," *Revue Internationale de la Croix-Rouge et Bulletin Internationale des Société de la Croix-Rouge* [1947]: 228–247; Claude Du Pasquier, *Promenade philosophique autour des Conventions de Genève de 1949* (Lausanne: 1950); and Henri Coursier, "Les Éléments Essentiels du Respect de la Personne Humaine Dans la Convention de Genève du 12 Août 1949, Relative à la Protection des Personnes Civiles en Temps de Guerre," *Revue internationale de la Croix-Rouge et Bulletin international des Sociétés de la Croix-Rouge*, Vol. 32, No. 377 (1950): 354–369.

[11] For more detailed insights about my theorization of rights and warfare, see Van Dijk, "Human Rights in War," 554–556 and David Luban, "Human Rights Thinking and the Laws of War," in *Theoretical Boundaries of Armed Conflict and Human Rights*, ed. Jens Ohlin (2016), 46–47.

[12] Van Dijk, "Human Rights in War."

[13] See Punishment for War Crimes, The Inter-Allied Declaration Signed at St. James's Palace, London, 13 January 1942; Joint Declaration by Members of the United Nations, 10 December 1942.

56 PREPARING FOR WAR

more universalization and less tolerance for brutality in wars, including those involving anti-colonial resistance and irregulars (see Chapters 3 and 4).[14]

Still, nuancing those accounts which stress complementarity between these postwar international legal frameworks,[15] this chapter also shows how the leading drafters initially adopted human rights thinking but ultimately rejected incorporating its discourse and principles within the Convention's text. In effect, they concealed how indebted they were on an intellectual level to conceptions of human rights as a body of legal thought. For example, the ICRC embraced a determinately selective rights agenda in order to safeguard states' sovereignty by producing a new Civilian Convention with a limited outlook. It saw one of the war's primary victims (i.e. the political prisoner) as not necessarily a "protected person" to be covered under this treaty.

The chapter is divided into three sections, each of which deals with a different time period during which the discussion with regard to the Civilian Convention's future took place. As a starting point for this analysis, the first section shows how a punitive pre-1914 legacy was fundamentally challenged around the First World War, as the ICRC was starting to consider "enemy civilians" in need of their own Convention. Next, it will demonstrate why these interwar proposals were first rejected by France and then later neglected by the ICRC itself. The final section shows how these two actors fundamentally changed their attitude after the horrors of the Second World War and in the wake of the early Cold War and decolonization.

Despite initial opposition by several Allied Great Powers, after 1945 the French Inter-Ministerial Commission and ICRC legal experts began discussing new plans to ensure *certain* types of civilians' rights in wartime, thereby laying the basis for the revolutionary Stockholm proposals featuring a prominent reference to human rights. Building up this crucial legacy, this section also demonstrates how a remarkable bipartisan Cold War coalition of ICRC experts, Western European delegates, and Soviet officials triggered a major legal breakthrough in 1949.[16] Still, it is important to realize that this remarkable result was not so much the outcome of design, as scholarship has suggested previously, but rather that of evolving ideas and a long struggle, of a twisted road with several surprising turns of events.

---

[14] Van Dijk, "Human Rights in War."

[15] One example: Ruti Teitel, *Humanity's Law* (Oxford: Oxford University Press, 2011).

[16] The chapter takes a specific approach by focusing on the concept of the civilian and that of their protection against the most endemic forms of arbitrary treatment (reprisals, collective penalties, torture, and so on). This analysis does not extensively discuss issues such as sexual violence, sieging, humanitarian relief, civilian property, blockade, or air-nuclear warfare. The two latter topics will be discussed in Chapter 5.

2.1 The Rise and Fall of the First Civilian Conventions

The foundational concept of the civilian is often said to have been a permanent feature of the law of nations since its very existence. In reality, however, nineteenth-century lawyers hardly ever referred to the term, instead preferring alternative typologies such as "private citizens" and "noncombatants." This concept was built upon two specific assumptions: one, passivity in the face of an occupier's rule; two, non-participation in the fighting, even though individual noncombatants could be working for a regular army as a cook, for instance. Only if recruited as a member of the regular armed forces would their status change legally, making them liable to being made a prisoner of war if captured by the enemy.[17]

In his famous code, the American jurist Francis Lieber tried to give noncombatants a set of basic rights, which were later codified in the Hague Regulations of 1907 with personal liberty added to them.[18] Still, none of these privileges were absolute or universal in scope. For instance, Lieber argued that indigenous populations deemed insufficiently "civilized" were to be excluded.[19] Instead of applying to humanity at large, the laws of war in this period of violence remained highly selective, excluding countless victims of color. More broadly, international law left a punitive legacy for European noncombatants in occupied territory before the First World War broke out.[20]

Despite continuing critique of these methods, international law in this period never strictly outlawed the use of hostage taking, collective penalties, or reprisals, and made noncombatants' protection conditional. Military necessity would often trump its principles.[21] The practice of internment remained lawful despite widespread condemnation of the deaths of thousands of (white) women and children during the recent Boer War.[22] Instead of reassuring them of protection in wartime, international law sought to prevent noncombatants from getting involved in war in the first place so as to limit its effects and

---

[17] Alexander, "The Genesis of the Civilian," 360.

[18] Doris Appel Graber, *The Development of the Law of Belligerent Occupation* (New York: Columbia University Press, 1949), 194–195.

[19] See Helen Kinsella, *The Image before the Weapon: A Critical History of the Distinction Between Combatant and Civilian* (Ithaca, NY: Cornell University Press, 2011).

[20] Frédéric Mégret, "From 'Savages' to 'Unlawful Combatants': A Postcolonial Look at International Humanitarian Law's 'Other'," in *International Law and its Others*, ed. Anne Orford (Cambridge: Cambridge University Press, 2009), 265–317 and Eyal Benvenisti and Doreen Lustig, "Monopolizing War: Codifying the Laws of War to Reassert Governmental Authority, 1856-1874," *European Journal of International Law* [2020]: 127–169.

[21] Best, *Humanity in Warfare*, 96; and Alexander, "The Genesis of the Civilian," 361.

[22] Philippe Papelier, *Le Droit de la Guerre et la Population Civile* (Paris: L'Institut d'Etudes Politiques de Paris, 1955), 10.

58   PREPARING FOR WAR

protect regular soldiers—the overarching aim of this was to keep the political status quo intact.[23]

During the First World War, entire societies were being mobilized, and legal distinctions came under severe pressure as a result.[24] Both sides targeted prisoners of war (POWs) and exposed "civilians"—a term which owes its invention to the First World War—to brutality.[25] From starvation blockade to internment, they committed acts that would soon be described as "atrocities."[26] During this period, Allied propagandists reproduced horrific stories in a bid to make their own cause look more justified.[27] These evolving legal sensibilities around warfare were also captured in the 1919 Allied Commission's report, which drew a line in the sand against brutal counterinsurgency policies, from hostage killing to torture. It would take more than three decades, however, for these practices to be strictly banned under humanitarian law.[28]

Already at the start of the war, the ICRC had established the International Prisoners-of-War Agency. This ICRC body would become the cradle of humanitarian law by developing new international legal principles for regulating warfare. Whereas Cramer began working as co-director of the Agency's department working on behalf of Allied POWs, Frédéric Ferrière was asked to lead its special civilian section.[29] The latter was a Genevan medical expert who had learned about the need to better protect noncombatants in wartime when he served as Red Cross delegate during the Franco-Prussian and Balkan Wars.[30] Both ICRC experts knew what was at stake for civilians after visiting civilian internees and POWs during the war and helping to develop new international legal standards.[31]

---

[23] Benvenisti and Doreen Lustig, "Monopolizing War."

[24] See also Mahon Murphy, *Colonial Captivity during the First World War: Internment and the Fall of the German Empire, 1914–1919* (Cambridge: Cambridge University Press, 2017).

[25] Alexander, "The Genesis of the Civilian."

[26] The internment of civilians generated serious debate among international lawyers, who generally agreed that civilian internment had to be seen as unlawful. Matthew Stibbe, "The Internment of Civilians by Belligerent States during the First World War and the Response of the International Committee of the Red Cross," *Journal of Contemporary History*, Vol. 41, No. 1 (2006): 5–19. For the vast historiography of civilian internment during the First World War, see Rüdiger Overmans, *In der Hand des Feindes. Kriegsgefangenschaft von der Antike bis zum Zweiten Weltkrieg* (Cologne: Böhlau, 1999); Panikos Panayi, *The Enemy in our Midst: Germans in Britain during the First World War* (New York: Berg, 1991); and Annette Becker, *Oubliés de la Grande Guerre: Humanitaire et Culture de Guerre, 1914–1918: Populations Occupées, Déportés Civils, Prisonniers de Guerre* (Paris: Éd Noêsis, 1998).

[27] Alexander, "The Genesis of the Civilian," 368–369; John Horne and Alan Kramer, *German Atrocities, 1914: A History of Denial* (New Haven, CT: Yale University Press, 2001).

[28] "Commission on the Responsibility of the Authors of the War and on Enforcement of Penalties," *American Journal of International Law* [1920]: 112–115.

[29] Stibbe, "The Internment of Civilians by Belligerent States," 10.

[30] James Crossland, *War, Law and Humanity: The Campaign to Control Warfare, 1853–1914* (London: Bloomsbury, 2019), 101.

[31] One example of this was Cramer's role in shaping the Bern Agreements (1918). During the war, belligerents frequently gathered in neutral countries such as Switzerland to discuss the protection

MAKING THE CIVILIAN CONVENTION   59

In June 1918, as the war was still raging across the globe, the ICRC's highest governing body instructed Cramer and Alfred Gautier, one of her legal mentors, to start drafting a new code for the protection of prisoners of war. They drew upon the wartime agreements[32] to produce a broader POW Convention for, especially, male internees and proposed a gendered definition of POWs, according to which women and children could not be interned.[33] Complementing this preparatory work, Ferrière prepared his own report by detailing the war's destructive impact on civilians and questioning a whole range of brutal counterinsurgency policies, from reprisals, deportations, and hostage killing to the use of forced laborers as "slaves."

Developing the Tokyo Draft

Many of these ideas were discussed at the Red Cross Conference in Geneva, in 1921. The French boycotted this meeting because in their view their German counterparts had been reluctant to condemn their home state's wartime violations of international law, and this proved to be a historically important development. The remaining delegates discussed the ICRC ideas in some detail, endorsing a broad prisoner code which would cover POWs and male civilian internees, just as Cramer had suggested.[34] What is more, they agreed with her suggestion to ban reprisals against POWs, which represents another turning point in the history of humanitarian law.[35] Even more remarkable, the conference widened the Convention's scope by including deportees and banning the use of hostage taking. These plans resonated with a wider shift after the war toward recognizing the importance of the individual, their international legal personality, and elementary human rights thinking, with the embryonic notions of rights concepts and potential for "cascading effects" within the strict legal boundaries of state sovereignty.[36]

---

of civilian internees and the repatriation of wounded POWs. As part of this effort, Cramer was able to persuade warring parties to sign the Bern Agreements, which magnified the potential number of POW repatriates. Crucially, this and other wartime agreements gave rise to new international legal standards, convincing the ICRC to take further steps toward humanizing warfare in subsequent days. Neville Wylie, "The 1929 Prisoner of War Convention and the Building of the Inter-war Prisoner of War Regime," in *Prisoners in War*, ed. Sibylle Scheipers (Oxford: Oxford University Press, 2010), 91–108, 94.

[32] Ibid.

[33] ICRC Report, 1921, No. CI_1921_022_FRE_016_HD, La Bibliothèque du Comité international de la Croix Rouge, Geneva (ICRC Library).

[34] Best first noted the ICRC's critical role in addressing the issue of civilian protection after 1919: Best, *Humanity in Warfare*, 232–233.

[35] Frits Kalshoven, *Belligerent Reprisals* (Leiden: Sijthoff, 1971), 71–72.

[36] This idea is based upon earlier work of mine: Van Dijk, "Human Rights in War," 560.

60 PREPARING FOR WAR

By connecting rights with nationality, the 1921 Red Cross Conference permanently shaped humanitarian law's genetic code by linking the individual war victim's rights with the nationality of that person.[37] This implied that only nationals of enemy belligerents would be covered under this new treaty, excluding several groups of civilians. Indeed, it is striking how civilians lacking nationality (e.g. stateless persons), those imprisoned for political reasons (such as conscientious objectors), and the state's own nationals (for instance, Ottoman Armenians) were banned from having the right to have international rights in wartime. This key question relating to the Convention's scope would continue to spark controversy.[38]

In 1921, the conference largely endorsed the ICRC's elementary human rights agenda, instructing its legal experts to establish a special committee to prepare a new draft for a future meeting of plenipotentiaries.[39] This new Special Committee, led by Ferrière himself and composed of five male legal experts (Cramer was not included[40]), would gather regularly between October 1922 and March 1923 to discuss the future prisoners' code. Drawing inspiration from a previous text,[41] Ferrière's Committee decided to break with Cramer's idea of combining civilian and military questions under a broad prisoner code. Instead, thanks to Ferrière's persistence and Cramer's absence, it suggested a separate Civilian Convention.[42] The former expected that this plan would receive support from states in light of their acceptance during the war of similar principles included in bilateral agreements.[43]

For the 1923 Red Cross Conference, the ICRC presented a draft Civilian Convention with only a limited outlook.[44] In the wake of their disappointing intervention in Russia, the Genevans decided to reverse some of the 1921 conference's far-reaching plans to restrain the state's wartime powers to stage counterinsurgency campaigns. They preferred a much less ambitious Civilian

---

[37] For a broader history of nationality and its hierarchies, see Karen Knop, *Diversity and Self-Determination in International Law* (Cambridge: Cambridge University Press, 2004); Mira Siegelberg, *Statelessness: A Modern History* (Cambridge, MA: Harvard University Press, 2020); and Emmanuelle Saada, *Empire's Children: Race, Filiation, and Citizenship in the French Colonies* (Chicago: University of Chicago Press, 2012).

[38] Van Dijk, "Human Rights in War."

[39] Kalshoven, *Belligerent Reprisals*, 71–72.

[40] For a more detailed discussion of Cramer's gradual marginalization after 1921, Boyd van Dijk, "Marguerite Frick-Cramer: A Life Spent Shaping the Geneva Conventions," in *Portraits of Women in International Law: New Names and Forgotten Faces?*, ed. Immi Tallgren (Cambridge: Cambridge University Press, forthcoming).

[41] The International Law Association had already previously distinguished between civilian and military detainment: Kalshoven, *Belligerent Reprisals*, 74.

[42] Letter Lescaze to Werner, 2 June 1923, no. CR-119-1, ACICR.

[43] Letter Ferrière to Lescaze, 8 May 1923, no. CR-119-1, ACICR.

[44] Lowe, "Humanitarianism and National Sovereignty," 652–654.

MAKING THE CIVILIAN CONVENTION   61

Convention, so as to protect the state's sovereignty and its enforcement powers in interstate wartime. In doing so, the ICRC hoped to convince the (liberal) Great Powers of the importance of its proposals. These hopes were crushed, however, as the ICRC faced resistance from those same Great Powers at the next Red Cross meeting, in 1923.[45]

At this meeting—and after the French had occupied the Ruhr area in Western Germany—the French, who had been previously absent, voiced concern about creating a binding treaty for civilians in occupied territory. Despite their formative experience of enemy occupation during the war, their delegation resisted those plans to protect enemy civilians and restrict the state's brutal counterinsurgency measures in wartime. At various moments, the French argued that matters such as hostage taking fell exclusively within the domain of either the state's own sovereignty, or the laws regulating the conduct of hostilities, not early humanitarian law. Like the British after 1945, the French even argued that the law's revision should be decided upon by states alone, not Red Cross Societies.

Having won the war and become an occupying power in Germany—among other places—the French were keen on protecting their sovereignty by blocking any effort to restrain their weapons of counterinsurgency in any substantially meaningful way. Despite Ferrière's persistence, they eventually downgraded the ICRC's originally long list of detailed restrictions and limited the organization's drafting mandate to that of merely a general advisory body, which dealt a serious blow to Ferrière's elementary human rights agenda of developing a separate Convention.[46] Despite the widespread recognition of the need to protect civilians after 1919, the Red Cross delegates showed little sense of urgency four years later when basically giving up Ferrière's project.

After the unsuccessful Red Cross Conference of 1923, and despite his continuing optimism,[47] Ferrière's elementary human rights calls no longer resonated within the broader Red Cross movement. This declining interest in civilian protection can be accounted for by three factors: the continuing opposition from, especially, France, as well as several National Red Cross Societies;[48] Cramer's early departure; and Ferrière's death in 1924.[49] The remaining ICRC

---

[45] Frédéric Ferrière, "Projet d'une Convention Internationale Réglant la Situation des Civils Tombés à la Guerre au Pouvoir de l'Ennemi," *Revue Internationale de la Croix-Rouge et Bulletin international des Sociétés de la Croix-Rouge*, Vol. 5, No. 54 (1923): 560–585.

[46] Minutes of 1923 Red Cross Conference, Commission IV, 29–30 August 1923, ICRC Library.

[47] Letter Ferrière to Lescaze, 6 November 1923, no. CR-119-1, ACICR.

[48] Few National Red Cross Societies responded to an ICRC circular asking for information about the question of civilian protection: Minutes of Meeting Commission Diplomatique, 12 February 1925, no. CR-119-1, ACICR.

[49] See Letter Lescaze to Ferriere, 3 November 1923, and Letter Girardet to Lescaze, 23 November 1923, no. CR-119-1, ACICR.

62   PREPARING FOR WAR

experts certainly lacked their knowledge and level of enthusiasm for protecting civilians in war, and they remained divided over how they should try to achieve this objective.[50] Some believed, perhaps naively, that a proposal such as banning civilian internment might be a major first step toward greater noncombatant protection. When the UK-oriented International Law Association (ILA) adopted this idea in 1924,[51] the ICRC became more and more skeptical about the whole project.

In consultation with the Swiss government, the Genevans decided to put on hold their plans to develop a new treaty for civilians. They were particularly worried about France's continuing opposition. This decision to postpone was further connected to the ICRC's estimation that much greater support existed for the POW Convention, whose drafting process had progressed much further since 1921. Considering codification of this issue as less complicated, the organization ultimately moved away from further developing the Civilian Convention.[52] Protecting the rights of soldiers was considered more politically expedient: the Swiss government also pressured the ICRC not to raise the matter before the POW Convention had been adopted by the Great Powers, expressing concern that it might otherwise amplify the existing Italian and French concerns regarding the POW Convention's drafting process.[53] By the mid-1920s, the ICRC had effectively sidelined Ferrière's plan as a result of pressure from Paris, Bern, and Mussolini's Rome, and because of discord within the organization itself.

After years of silence, the ICRC readdressed the question of civilians only at the diplomatic conference of 1929, discussing the POW Convention and inviting Cramer as the first known woman legal drafter of humanitarian law in history. For this meeting, it had suggested in its proposals not just to renew its elementary rights thinking by prohibiting reprisals against POWs, but also to allow civilian internees to fall under the prisoners' code, just as Cramer had originally suggested. Crucially, this proposal was eventually rejected after opposition from several Great Powers including Great Britain. Instead, the 1929

[50] See Minutes Meeting Commission des Civils, 28 November 1923, no. CR-119-1, ACICR.

[51] For a history of the ILA's efforts on behalf of POWs during this period, see Neville Wylie, *Barbed Wire Diplomacy: Britain, Germany, and the Politics of Prisoners of War, 1939–1945* (Oxford: Oxford University Press, 2010), 46–48; and James Crossland, *Britain and the International Committee of the Red Cross, 1939–1945* (New York: Palgrave Macmillan, 2014), 32–36.

[52] Minutes of Meeting, 30 July 1925, no. CR-119-2, ACICR. A Swiss observer noted after 1945 that Ferriere's plea had reached only "half ears" because his listeners had a "complacent attention to more manageable loads": Reflections of J. du Plessis, no. J2.118#1968/77_BD 11, Swiss Federal Archives (SFA), Bern.

[53] Minutes of Meeting ICRC and Swiss Federal officials, 12 February 1926, no. CR-119-2, ACICR. See also Vonèche Cardia, *Neutralité Entre le Comité International de la Croix-Rouge et le Gouvernement Suisse* (Lausanne: SHSR, 2012), 239–246.

conference accepted a resolution giving the Swiss and ICRC officials a proper mandate to prepare a new diplomatic conference for civilians in wartime.[54] This led to renewed interest on the part of the ICRC for Ferrière's original plan to protect civilians against ill-treatment.[55]

Shortly thereafter, the ICRC established another Special Committee that would be charged with preparing a draft of a Civilian Convention. For a brief period of time, its members discussed a number of drafts which had been prepared by Paul Des Gouttes, a former member of Ferrière's Committee and the ICRC's most important legal expert until Pictet, who took over during the Second World War; the law professor Georges Werner, who had participated in drafting the Declaration of the Rights of the Child; and Suzanne Ferrière (Frédéric's niece).[56] As the first woman after Cramer to enter the ICRC's highest governing body, Ferrière continued Cramer's struggle, and that of her own uncle, to protect civilians in wartime. Apart from advocating on behalf of children's rights, she also created one of the first major drafts for a Civilian Convention that would lie at the basis of the ICRC's future plans.

While extensively discussed,[57] Ferrière's text initially failed to trigger a breakthrough. For unclear reasons, the Committee suddenly stopped its drafting work in 1931, to the regret of Cramer herself.[58] It is difficult to explain this sudden shift in interest, but it seems to have been caused by three important factors: one, a lack of conviction that states would ever accept such a treaty for civilians; two, the ICRC's larger indifference toward this matter; and three, its competing obsessions with the threat of air-gas bombardment for civilian populations at large (see Chapter 5) and its own interests. Despite the rising number of political prisoners across several empires, the ICRC presented a proper draft convention only at the first Red Cross Conference outside of Europe and North America, in 1934.

In Tokyo, with Japan still occupying Manchuria and having failed to ratify the 1929 POW Convention, the Japanese Red Cross organized a new international conference. It sought to boost the empire's prestige following its scandalous withdrawal from the League of Nations one year earlier.[59] The ICRC's

---

[54] Documentation Diplomatic Conference, 1929, no. CR-119-2, ACICR.

[55] Letter Federal Council to ICRC on Civilian Protection, 21 February 1930, no. CR-119-2, ACICR.

[56] Werner Projet Civilian Convention, 1931, no. CR-119-3, ACICR.

[57] For the discussions of this committee in 1931, see Minutes of Meetings Commission Civils, 1931, no. CR-119-2, ACICR.

[58] Letter Frick Cramer on Civilian Convention, 25 October 1933, no. CR-119-3, ACICR.

[59] For more details, see Michiko Suzuki, "History of Disaster, Recovery, and Humanitarianism: The Japanese Red Cross Society in the Modern World, 1877–1945," Ph.D. Dissertation, SOAS, 2019.

64   PREPARING FOR WAR

Special Committee, which met just before the delegates would gather in Tokyo, started re-discussing its old plans for a Civilian Convention, which led to controversy among its members. Whereas the president Huber and Des Gouttes preferred a limited treaty for enemy aliens in belligerent territory, by noting that the 1907 Hague Regulations already provided some protection for those in occupied territory, Ferrière and others demanded a more ambitious scope. Rather than a limited treaty, they sought to draft a Convention applicable to belligerent *and* occupied territory, with stricter limitations against arbitrary treatment.[60]

The Special Committee's final suggestion, based upon drafts by Ferrière, Des Gouttes, and the ILA, made a few critical adjustments—by banning hostage killings, for instance—but its text still featured many loopholes.[61] This draft, which was adopted by the Red Cross Conference in 1934, largely focused its attention upon the protection of enemy aliens in belligerent territory. Echoing the ICRC's elementary human rights thinking, the text applied to armed conflict even if a belligerent was not party to the treaty, and it banned the use of reprisals. But it did not fully articulate the language of rights, and incorporated several limitations that sought to protect state sovereignty. From the state's own nationals to stateless persons, the Tokyo Draft excluded a whole range of civilians.

The Monegasque Rivals

Unlike its Japanese rival, the Monaco Draft was the only explicit human rights text for regulating warfare during the entire interwar period. Even before the Red Cross Conference gathered in Japan's capital, a small group of jurists and military doctors from the Francophone world had met in the principality of Monaco. One prominent expert attending this meeting was Albert De la Pradelle, an influential French international lawyer, who had also participated in the drafting of the Declaration of the International Rights of Man, in 1929. The draft treaty he co-designed five years later was a truly exceptional human rights text.[62]

---

[60] See Minutes of Meeting CV, 12 April 1934, no. CR-119-2, ACICR; and Minutes Meeting on Werner and Des Gouttes Project, 9 March 1934, no. CR-119-3, ACICR.

[61] This text had been originally drafted by the British jurist Hugh Bellot. See Daniel Segesser, *Recht statt Rache oder Rache durch Recht? Die Ahndung von Kriegsverbrechen in der internationale wissenschaftlichen Debatte, 1872–1945* (Paderborn: Ferdinand Schöningh, 2010).

[62] Van Dijk, "Human Rights in War," 563.

The Monaco Draft had several chapters and, in some respects, was more comprehensive than the 1949 Geneva Conventions would ever be. It spoke the language of rights and assured individuals of the freedom to worship, including rules on the protection of religious buildings. The Monaco Draft also recognized the individual's moral dignity in wartime and applied to occupied territory. In terms of regulating air warfare, it reiterated the concept of distinction and placed restraints on the targeting of cities. Despite these remarkable provisions, the rights of individuals were left vulnerable as legal architects made several concessions to state sovereignty and military necessity in order to maximize the Monaco Draft's appeal to the Great Powers in particular.[63]

While trying to meet their concerns, the Monaco Draft triggered no enthusiasm among the major drafting parties. Whereas the ICRC feared this text would undermine its own Tokyo Draft and the 1929 POW Convention, the Great Powers (especially France) opposed it as they were preparing for another interstate war. As the international system was breaking down, and the ICRC had other drafting priorities than the Monaco Draft, the text gradually disappeared from the international legal radar in ensuing years. The lack of political space for imaginative lawmaking was equally relevant for the ICRC's own project. At this stage the organization would only suggest creating a minor draft convention regarding safety localities and hospital towns, which finally collapsed at the start of the Second World War.

Likewise, the Tokyo Draft has never been signed or ratified by a single state. While positively received by the United States,[64] the plan to hold a diplomatic conference in 1937, the year when Pictet joined the ICRC, was opposed by the two other major liberal powers.[65] For Britain and France, this new Tokyo Draft was in many ways insufficient; they argued that its diplomatic success was also highly unlikely due to the ongoing international tensions resulting from the Spanish Civil War and the Sino-Japanese War.[66] In early 1937, when the French government had officially rejected the Swiss–ICRC plan and when skepticism toward the laws of war as a discipline had grown immensely as a result of their flagrant violation in both Ethiopia and Spain, Bern decided to temporarily postpone its plan for a diplomatic conference.[67] Attempts to revive this drafting process following the 1938 Red Cross Conference in London

---

[63] For more details, see ibid., 564.

[64] Note Responses Governments on Plan Diplomatic Conference, 9 October 1936, no. CR-119-3, ACICR.

[65] Report French Delegation Tokyo Conference, 1934 no. 1140, Unions Internationales 1944–1960, Les Archives Diplomatiques (LAD), Paris. See also Best, *Humanity in Warfare*, 233.

[66] Letter Swiss Political Department to Huber, 10 December 1936, no. CR-119-3, ACICR.

[67] Letters Motta to ICRC, 19 February 1937 and 12 March 1937, no. CR-119-4, ACICR.

66   PREPARING FOR WAR

also led to nothing, causing the early death of the Tokyo Draft as an immediate source of protection for civilians in wartime. European Jews were left without any serious international legal protection in Hitler's empire—a crucial element often missing in today's debates regarding the ICRC's failed response to the Holocaust.

How might we explain these interwar failures—in the 1920s, 1931, and the late 1930s—to draft and ratify a Civilian Convention? Two answers to this question have been offered. The first is that the outbreak of war in Europe led to the Tokyo Draft's demise and that of its Monegasque rival, while the second claims that "states" (without mentioning any specific name) lacked concern and therefore bear main responsibility for these failures. Neither explanation is entirely satisfactory, however. By the late 1930s, with the collapse of the international order, the Sisyphean plan to create a Civilian Convention could lead to nothing but failure.

The ICRC's first proposals had been opposed by the French already in the early 1920s, and, contrary to the ICRC's own later statements, it and the Swiss bear some responsibility too. Although they were one of the few interwar advocates of civilian protection, the Genevans did surprisingly little to trigger attention for their plans to protect civilians; they also caused unnecessary delays. The post-1919 window of opportunity was eventually lost. Crucially, the ICRC decided at key moments to give priority to its other drafting plans: the protection of enemy civilians in wartime was never a primary drafting concern and always stood in the shadow of other ICRC projects serving the interests of soldiers and states. Even though human rights thinking had conceptual effects on ICRC plans, it continued to remain at the margins of the organization's legal reasoning in the period before 1939.[68]

The Tokyo Draft did not die all at once, however. It was still being discussed by ICRC legal experts and Jewish organizations during the war as a potential legal weapon against the Holocaust.[69] Still, in publicly condemning Nazi atrocities as violations of "human rights," the Allies transformed this concept into an universalistic battle-cry, while leaving the Tokyo Draft to wither.[70] In doing so, they tried to reaffirm liberal democracy and its principles in their struggle with authoritarian states such as Hitler's empire, which explicitly rejected the validity of individual rights. Washington saw human rights as part of its larger attempt to forge a new international legal order, which was backed by

[68] Van Dijk, "Human Rights in War," 566.
[69] Jean-Claude Favez, *The Red Cross and the Holocaust* (Cambridge: Cambridge University Press, 1999), 85–88.
[70] Van Dijk, "Human Rights in War," 566.

the British mainly because they needed US support to win the war against their Axis adversaries.

Most strikingly, throughout the war, the Allies hardly invoked the Tokyo Draft; nor did they demand its revision after the war had come to an end.[71] It is telling that Allied postwar planning during the war largely neglected the revision of the Hague and Geneva Conventions, in part due to their troubling relationship with these rules. The Soviets, for instance, brutally occupied parts of Eastern Europe; US soldiers in the Pacific violated the 1929 Convention's principles by scalping dead Japanese soldiers;[72] and the Anglo-American governments did not apply the Conventions to the zones they held occupied in Germany and Japan after the end of hostilities. For these reasons, it is not surprising that none of these Allied powers responded very enthusiastically when the ICRC restarted its prewar drafting process to revise the Conventions after 1944.

2.2 Human Rights in War

From 1944 onwards, the ICRC Legal Division began setting out its plans for the future of civilian protection. While unsure whether to support a separate Civilian Convention or not,[73] it expressed a much greater interest in civilian protection than at any previous time in its history. Unlike prior to the Second World War, the ICRC now endorsed both the discourse and the thinking of human rights as an instrument to criticize Nazi-style counterinsurgency measures, developing surprisingly radical plans to significantly widen the Tokyo Draft's scope and its basic provisions regulating civilian protection in occupied territory.[74] Breaking with interwar elementary rights thinking, Pictet's drafting team demanded a complete prohibition against hostage taking, for instance.[75]

Already during the war, the ICRC had condemned this method of warfare on the basis of rights' principles, illustrating the broader wartime shift to

---

[71] Dominique-Debora Junod, *The Imperiled Red Cross and the Palestine-Eretz-Yisrael Conflict 1945–1952: The Influence of Institutional Concerns on a Humanitarian Operation* (New York: Kegan Paul International, 1996), 51–54; and Arieh Ben Tov, *Facing the Holocaust in Budapest. The International Committee of the Red Cross and the Jews in Hungary, 1943–1945* (Geneva: Henry Dunant Institute, 1988).

[72] Article 4, Sick & Wounded Convention, 1929.

[73] Minutes of Seances Commission Juridique, 24 November 1944, no. A PV JUR. 1, Vol. I, ACICR.

[74] Mark Mazower, "Strange Triumph of Human Rights, 1933–1950," *Historical Journal* vol. 47, no. 2 (2004): 379–98; and Eric Weitz, "From the Vienna to the Paris System: International Politics and the Entangled Histories of Human Rights, Forced Deportations, and Civilizing Missions," *American Historical Review*, Vol. 113, No. 5 (2004): 1313–43.

[75] Report ICRC, 1946, no. CSN_1946_DOCCIR_ENG_03, La Bibliothèque du Comité international de la Croix Rouge, Geneva (ICRC Library); and Van Dijk, "Human Rights in War."

68   PREPARING FOR WAR

human rights thinking. For Pictet, the wartime atrocities and the revolutionary historical changes indicated by decolonization, the rise of new hegemonic powers, and mass statelessness required a new interpretation of humanitarian law. In essence, he sought to reinvent the discipline itself. The engraving of human rights as promoted by the Allied powers (the Monaco Draft's human rights agenda played no role) onto the existing Conventions equipped Pictet's team with the necessary instruments to respond to the Axis atrocities.[76] While leaving open the question of whether to have a separate, amalgamated, or reduced Civilian Convention, it demanded that any future treaty should be based upon the principle of rights in war.[77]

Breaking with interwar understandings of belligerent occupation, the 1946 Red Cross Conference supported the ICRC's open-ended human rights agenda. Maurice Bourquin's Belgian delegation presented a major revision of the Tokyo Draft that would impact virtually every future draft. While based in Geneva, he provide valuable advice to Pictet's drafting team.[78] Similar to Bourquin, Red Cross delegates also condemned Nazi-like counterinsurgency policies and demanded robust protections for civilians in interstate wartime. Together with a former political prisoner from Yugoslavia, the Norwegian human rights advocate Frede Castberg (who had also been taken captive by the Nazis during the war) argued that such protections ought to be based upon the UN's agenda of human rights. Fully adopting human rights thinking, he believed it was essential to fundamentally revise the Tokyo Draft, as it featured several elements sanctioning discriminatory policies and political imprisonment. Castberg, who authored a history of the Nazi occupation of Norway,[79] also called for the banning of all forms of arbitrary treatment, especially torture and collective penalties.[80]

Discussing these proposals, the Second Commission approved of stricter limitations upon the occupier's arbitrary powers. It even adopted a proposal to cover political prisoners, which was ultimately rejected by the plenary. This opposition was most likely due to fears about undermining the sovereignty of major states—most Red Cross Societies usually had close ties with their respective host states.[81] By excluding the question of political prisoners, the 1946

---

[76] ICRC Appeal, 24 July 1943, ICRC Library; and Van Dijk, "Human Rights in War," 566–567.

[77] The Legal Division considered a whole range of different alternatives, from amalgamating the POW and Civilian Conventions to creating a "Charter," or "Civil réduit," with a set of basic rights for every detainee against inhumane treatment.

[78] Belgian Proposal Civilian Convention, no. CSN_1946_DOCSN_02, ICRC Library.

[79] Frede Castberg, *Norge under okkupasjonen: Rettslige utredninger 1940–1943* (Oslo: Cappelen, 1945).

[80] See also Minutes of Meetings Commission II, 1946, no. CSN_1946_COMM2_PV_02, ICRC Library.

[81] Minutes of Plenary Meeting, 3 August 1946, ICRC Library.

Red Cross Conference endorsed a human rights agenda that was more limited than others had hoped for. This outcome led to frustration on the part of Gerhart Riegner, a World Jewish Congress observer, who called it "absolutely unsatisfactory."[82]

Representing a transnational Jewish organization defending the rights of the diaspora, Riegner had been actively involved during the war in combating the Holocaust.[83] Most famously, while based in Geneva, in August 1942 he had dispatched an alarming telegram warning the Allies about the Final Solution. No one listened to him, however. Four years later, he again felt disappointed, this time about the 1946 Red Cross Conference's outcome. Its proposals, he argued, dealt insufficiently with the questions of statelessness and human rights protections: he felt that the law's structure and scope were left too vague as well.

Despite these restrictions, Pictet's team, which received advice from both Cramer and Ferrière as former interwar advocates of civilian protection, felt very much strengthened by the outcome of the 1946 Red Cross Conference. In the following months they began creating a revolutionized Tokyo Draft including human rights concepts (e.g. non-renunciation clauses) as a response to the wartime destruction of states. This open-ended human rights agenda did not focus on human dignity alone, or exclusively on humanitarianism, but balanced these out with evolving conceptions of justice, duties, and sovereignty.[84] In his unique brochure, entitled "La défense de la personne humaine dans le droit future," Pictet adopted human rights thinking to a remarkable extent. Indeed, he admitted that his team's core objective was to obtain "le respect de la personne humaine et [...] les droits essentiels de l'homme et sa dignité."[85]

Again, this exceptional statement by the ICRC's most prominent drafter shows the impact of human rights thinking on the ICRC's quickly changing drafting position after 1944. Nevertheless, it is essential to recognize that the organization embraced a distinct understanding of human rights as a drafting concept. In his brochure, Pictet admitted that his team would focus on "enemy civilians" alone.[86] This decision to endorse a Tokyo Draft with a measured outlook caused controversy among Jewish observers and within ICRC echelons.

---

[82] The WJC believed that "the general rules for the protection of human rights should become the basic rules concerning the protection of civilian population also during war-time." Report Riegner on Red Cross Conference Plans, 18 July 1946, Series D106, no. 10, American Jewish Archives (AJC), Cincinnati, OH.

[83] See also James Loeffler, *Rooted Cosmopolitans Jews and Human Rights in the Twentieth Century* (New Haven, CT: Yale University Press, 2016).

[84] Van Dijk, "Human Rights in War," 568.

[85] Jean Pictet, *La Défense de la Personne Humaine dans le Droit Future* (Baden: 1947) 20.

[86] Ibid., 15.

70 PREPARING FOR WAR

As a response to the Nazi terror against German Jews and Communists, some ICRC drafters believed that political prisoners and the state's own nationals needed to be included as well. Like the Red Cross delegates, they claimed that the future Civilian Convention should be more ambitious in scope. As he had done before 1939, Huber again put a brake on widening the law's scope for civilians, arguing that covering the state's own nationals would be ineffective since "reciprocity was [not] granted."[87] While publicly admitting the crucial significance of human rights for regulating warfare,[88] he preferred to leave such matters to the UN.[89] Equally cautious, Pilloud endorsed this positioning.[90]

As they played a key role in these debates, the ICRC finally accepted Huber and Pilloud's advice, endorsing a measured Civilian Convention for "enemy civilians" alone.[91] By adopting this limited version of human rights in war—thus protecting the states' sovereignty in critical ways, as well as opposing Raphael Lemkin's rivaling concept of genocide—the ICRC made a legally strategic decision.[92] In doing so, the organization hoped to gain widespread support from the Great Powers for its own proposals for the future Civilian Convention. It meant, however, breaking a potential drafting link with the UN's projects regarding human rights and outlawing genocide. Despite this legal division of labor, the ICRC still expanded its original plans' scope by covering the previously neglected category of stateless persons, and it prohibited many of the occupier's most arbitrary counterinsurgency measures now deemed inhumane, the most prominent of which was the prohibition of hostage taking.[93] In essence, this drafting outcome demonstrates that the ICRC's turn to human rights was always selective and never legally intersectional, ultimately considering the goal of achieving state support more important than realizing the utopia of humanizing warfare.

---

[87] Report Riegner Spiritual Conference Geneva, March 1947, Series D106, no. 10, AJC.

[88] Speech Huber at Plenary Meeting Government Experts Conference, 14 April 1947, no. CEG_1947_ASSPLEN, ICRC Library.

[89] This resonated with a broader ICRC policy to separate its activities from those of the UN, as had been done in Palestine. See Junod, *The Imperiled Red Cross*, 262–263.

[90] Although agreeing with his colleagues, Pictet initially tried to expand the category's definition to include "Jews and other minorities." Still, his proposal led to no major alteration, as far as textual drafts are concerned. Minutes of Seances Commission Juridique, 6 December 1946, no. A PV JUR. 1, Vol. I, ACICR.

[91] Minutes of Seances Commission Juridique, 6 December 1946, no. A PV JUR. 1, Vol. I, ACICR.

[92] For a deeper history of the concept of genocide and its problems, see Dirk Moses, *The Problems of Genocide: Permanent Security and the Language of Transgression* (Cambridge: Cambridge University Press, 2021).

[93] Initially, the ICRC proved reluctant to strictly ban the use of deportations and collective penalties. ICRC Report on Civilian Convention, 1947, no. CEG_1947_DOC_PROTCIV_ENG, ICRC Library.

Civilian Rights in the Shadow of Oradour

One of the ICRC's strongest supporters in promoting the Civilian Convention was liberated France. Unlike the Third Republic, which had effectively destroyed the Tokyo Draft, De Gaulle's Provisional Government not only resurrected this document but also tried to radically expand it.[94] This critical shift in French legal attitudes with respect to the Civilian Convention can be explained by a few factors, especially the experience of brutal counterinsurgency as an occupied country and the influence of human rights thinking among its most prominent drafters. Indeed, the Inter-Ministerial Commission's proceedings were initially dominated by former deportees, hostages, and political prisoners, all of whom wished to see more robust human rights protections for civilians in occupied territory. The future treaty, they suggested, was to be based upon a number of legal documents, including a French Nuremberg indictment, the Tokyo Draft, and a special human rights report. The latter had been authored by none other than René Cassin, Cahen-Salvador's superior at the Conseil d'État and the French representative at the UN Human Rights Commission.[95]

Using it as a model, the French Inter-Ministerial Commission discussed the Tokyo Draft article by article and made several important suggestions to radically alter its provisions. Among other proposals, it significantly widened the text's originally limited scope by widening it to take in virtually every civilian in occupied territory. Also, it strengthened its protections against the occupier's arbitrary counterinsurgency measures. The French adopted a mixed approach to this issue of guaranteed treatment: on the one hand, they wished to ban deportations and collective punishment, as a response to the massacre at Oradour-sur-Glane in 1944; on the other, military officials opposed plans to completely prohibit the use of reprisals, as they considered reprisals a potentially important means to put pressure on structural violators such as Nazi Germany.[96] By doing so, they initially left a loophole as part of a broader human rights agenda demanding intangible rights for a whole group of civilians in wartime.[97]

---

[94] The initial French plan was to create a wider POW Convention featuring protections for civilians. This plan was finally dropped in late 1946. See Minutes Meeting Interdepartmental, 23 July 1946, no. 160 - BIS, Unions Internationales 1944–1960, LAD.

[95] This point adds an element to existing studies about Cassin's wider influence on post-1945 human rights initiatives. Jay Winter and Antoine Prost, *René Cassin and Human Rights: From the Great War to the Universal Declaration* (Cambridge: Cambridge University Press, 2013).

[96] This sanctioning of the use of reprisals prompted Cahen's later support for the legalization of it at the Stockholm conference—see Chapter 3.

[97] See Minutes Meeting Interdepartmental, 14 November 1946, no. 160 - BIS, Unions Internationales 1944–1960, LAD.; Minutes Meeting Interdepartmental, 10 January 1947, no. 160, Unions

72 PREPARING FOR WAR

Inspired by Cassin's advocacy on behalf of human rights in order to reconstruct liberal values after Vichy's destruction, the Inter-Ministerial Commission stressed the importance of human rights concepts and discourse.[98] Jacob, who was born into a Jewish family, even suggested a preamble for the future Convention with the aim of securing the individual's human dignity without distinction on the basis of race or nationality—a position in line with Riegner's legal vision, as discussed before. Undoubtedly, Jacob wished to protect stateless persons who had been killed en masse during the Nazi occupation.[99] This plan was initially dropped, for mainly diplomatic reasons, following Lamarle's suggestion.[100] Signaling a greater overlap between human rights and humanitarian law, the French Inter-Ministerial Commission's final draft wished to protect "la personne humaine" by measures such as anti-torture and anti-discrimination clauses. This heavily modified Tokyo Draft based on human rights thinking would have a major impact on the discussions taking place at the upcoming government experts' conference, and directly shaped Pictet's thinking about the future drafting of the Conventions.

Contrary to these Francophone drafters, the American and British governments initially expressed little support for a Civilian Convention. In March 1946, while admitting that the present law's inadequacy had made it "easier for the Germans to murder millions of civilians at Auschwitz,"[101] the Foreign Office told the ICRC that it wished to postpone the matter until a later date, a position largely in line with that of the UK government in the period prior to the Holocaust.[102] Britain's resistance to a Civilian Convention caused serious concern on the part of ICRC legal specialists, who were said to fear that it might lead to continuing the "drama" of neglecting the fate of civilians which had existed "since 1907."[103]

Internationales 1944–1960, LAD; Minutes Meeting Interdepartmental, 17 February 1947, no. 160 - BIS, Unions Internationales 1944–1960, LAD.

[98] Ibid.

[99] See Minutes Meeting Interdepartmental, 4 December 1946, no. 160 - BIS, Unions Internationales 1944–1960, LAD; and Minutes Meeting Interdepartmental, 10 January 1947, no. 160 - BIS, Unions Internationales 1944–1960, LAD.

[100] Minutes Meeting Interdepartmental, 17 February 1947, no. 160 - BIS, Unions Internationales 1944–1960, LAD.

[101] Memo Foreign Office on Civilian Convention, 17 June 1946, no. 3592, FO369 (Foreign Office), The National Archives (TNA), Kew.

[102] This was also a reflection of a broader trend in Allied postwar planning, which generally marginalized the role of the ICRC in favor of that of the UN Relief and Rehabilitation Administration (UNRRA) as well as other humanitarian organizations. Crossland, *Britain and the International Committee of the Red Cross*, 203–206.

[103] Minutes Plenary Session ICRC, 20 June 1946, no. A PV A PI.18, ACICR.

As in the case of their British allies, US officials wished to prevent any serious restrictions for their armed forces in case of a future military occupation. While human rights notions were still circulating within the Interdepartmental Prisoners of War Committee (POWC), its members still primarily focused on protecting US soldiers against ill-treatment. Equally important, they were also concerned about minimizing the burden for US occupation authorities in Germany and Japan,[104] thus skeptically receiving the idea of a separate treaty for civilians and/or occupied territory.[105] Still, the POWC left some room for widening the POW Convention's scope for civilian internees in particular. Clattenburg's intervention in this debate was important, as the previous chapter showed—although he wished to exclude those individuals with a dual nationality, such as Japanese–Americans, since this matter was "our business and [should] not come within the [Convention]." [106]

The major drafting parties, except for the Soviets, came to Geneva in April 1947 to discuss plans for civilian protection in the Third Committee. During this crucial meeting, which was attended by Ferrière, Castberg, Jacob, Lamarle, Clattenburg, Brigadier Page (a former British prisoner of war), and various others,[107] the delegates clashed on a number of issues relating to civilian protection. Whereas Anglo-American representatives tried to secure the occupier's interests, the victims of Nazi occupation demanded rights for civilians in occupied territory.[108] The poorly prepared, if not very restrictive, British delegation regularly came into confrontation with its Western European allies about the law's future scope. The main topics of this debate concerned the law's scope and that of its provisions regulating civilians' treatment in relation to brutal counterinsurgency measures.

---

[104] The Anglo-American occupiers expressed little interest in applying the POW Convention's standards to German prisoners of war or to different categories of civilians in occupied Germany. They felt it was impossible to comply with these standards due to the food shortages in postwar Germany and their own respective occupation policies. Civilians, they argued, should be taken care of by the UNRRA, for instance: Crossland, *Britain and the International Committee of the Red Cross*, 190–193.

[105] Minutes Prisoners of War Committee, 28 June 1946, Provost Marshal General, no. 672, National Archives and Records Administration (NARA), College Park, MD; and Minutes Prisoners of War Committee, 2 August 1946, Provost Marshal General, no. 672, NARA.

[106] Minutes Prisoners of War Committee, 29 August 1946, Provost Marshal General, no. 672, NARA; and Minutes Prisoners of War Committee, 12 July 1946, Provost Marshal General, no. 672, NARA.

[107] In his conference speech, Huber affirmed that the Red Cross wished to obtain a "minimum degree of respect and protection to [the] victims [of war]" and that it had a "profound interest" in the work of the United Nations with respect to protecting human rights at an international level. Speech Huber at Plenary Meeting Government Experts Conference, 14 April 1947, no. CEG_1947_ASSPLEN, ICRC Library.

[108] While having suffered the second largest number of civilian victims during the Second World War, the Nationalist Chinese delegation stayed surprisingly silent in the debate regarding civilian protection.

74 PREPARING FOR WAR

With regard to the law's scope, it remained uncertain what form it would take (reduced, amalgamated, or a separate Civilian Convention) and who should fall under it. The influential Third Committee's vice-president, Bourquin, wished to create an amalgamated treaty and prevent civilians from falling outside of its scope.[109] French delegate Bourdet, a former political prisoner in the Nazi concentration camps, demanded to ban political imprisonment, echoing Castberg's earlier suggestion.[110] This idea led to bipartisan opposition from the ICRC and its Anglo-American partners.[111] Whereas the former wished to keep the Great Powers on board, the latter feared that Bourdet's proposal might fatally undermine their future ability to suppress future insurgencies. As a consequence of these divisions, the Third Committee failed to resolve the question of how to arrange the Civilian Convention's precise scope, which once again shows the contested nature of its drafting process.[112]

The Third Committee experienced similar trouble when attempting to define the occupier's rights and its limitations over its subjects. Britain's Commonwealth and American allies sought to protect these by creating dangerous loopholes in the draft, for example by demanding the permissibility of certain "evacuations" on the basis of race, as they had done during the war when forcibly relocating individuals of Japanese ancestry. The insidiousness of, especially, British opposition to robust civilian protection became immediately obvious to Francophone delegations. Realizing what was at stake, French and ICRC delegates fiercely opposed such ideas.[113] In their eyes, exceptions like the ones demanded by Anglo-American drafters would leave the door open for extremely arbitrary treatment. Instead, based upon their own instructions, they suggested prohibiting all kinds of measures that would violate the civilian's rights in wartime.

Due to these continental efforts, the 1947 Government Experts' Conference accepted a whole range of strict prohibitions against arbitrary measures, from hostage taking to collective penalties—to Lamarle's great surprise.[114] The voting majority of the Europeans, combined with the ICRC's decision to avoid making the interwar mistake of prioritizing issues other than the Civilian

---

[109] Minutes of Meeting Commission III, 1947, no. CEG_1947_COMM#_PV_01, ICRC Library.

[110] Minutes of Meeting Commission III, 1947, no. CEG_1947_COMM#_PV_01, ICRC Library.

[111] Report of American Delegation to Government Experts' Conference, 1947, no. 674, Provost Marshal General, NARA.

[112] Minutes of Meeting Commission III, 1947, no. CEG_1947_COMM#_PV_01, ICRC Library; Minutes of Meeting Commission III, 1947, no. CEG_1947_COMM#_PV_02, ICRC Library; and Report Conference of Government Experts at Geneva, Introduction, 1947, no. 3795, FO369, TNA.

[113] Minutes of Meeting Commission III, 1947, no. CEG_1947_COMM#_PV_02, ICRC Library.

[114] Cable Lamarle on Civilian Convention and Government Expert Conference, 17 April 1947, no. 160, Unions Internationales 1944–1960, LAD.

Convention, played an important part in this crucial success. Despite their opposition, US delegates had received flexible instructions allowing them to pragmatically adopt Francophone proposals trying to secure civilians' rights under occupation. Apart from recognizing the normative shift since 1945 to adopt stricter rules for occupation, US flexibility was also influenced—at least to some extent—by recent memories of Japanese atrocities against US citizens in the Pacific.[115] These factors in combination with entangling human rights agendas allowed for the emergence of a new draft for a Civilian Convention, even though many delegates expressed sympathy for a similar plan to amalgamate the four treaties into one giant Convention. The existing draft nonetheless contained several loopholes and its Francophone supporters feared for its future if Britain's opposition were to continue.[116]

2.3 Political Prisoners, Statelessness, Torture

Crucially, however, the British government realized after the Government Experts' Conference that it had to radically change its drafting strategy. Following pressure from its delegation, the ICRC, and French allies,[117] Whitehall realized that it could no longer refuse to discuss civilian protection. Rather than blocking the debate, it started thinking about how to use it for its own purposes while attenuating its effects on Britain's interests in the context of growing East–West tensions and the violent insurgency in Palestine. This special task was given to the Home Office Committee, with two separate working parties: one led by the Home Office focusing on enemy aliens in belligerent territory, and the other led by the War Office studying occupied territory.

As they found "much to criticize" in the 1947 proposals, the two British working parties began to prepare a far stricter draft for the Civilian Convention than was suggested by the ICRC and most other drafting parties. Seeking to obtain greater protections for its colonial, military, and intelligence officials while minimizing their legal burden amid the early Cold War, this text featured fewer detailed requirements and opposed a number of bans against

---

[115] Minutes of Meeting Commission III, 1947, no. CEG_1947_COMM#_PV_01, ICRC Library; and Report of American Delegation to Government Experts' Conference, 1947, no. 674, Provost Marshal General, NARA.

[116] Report French Delegation Government Expert Conference, 30 April 1947, no. 160, Unions Internationales 1944–1960, LAD.

[117] See Minutes Meeting Plenary, 20 June 1946, no. A PV A PI.18, ACICR; and Report Pilloud Meeting in London with Gardner, 28 October 1947, no. CR-238-4, ACICR.

76 PREPARING FOR WAR

arbitrary counterinsurgency policies, such as the use of collective penalties.[118] Underlying this view was British officials' belief that French demands for detailed provisions would make their task as future occupier impracticable. On the other hand—and this marks an even more important shift in the Civilian Convention's drafting history—the initial British draft pragmatically accepted a select number of restrictions as suggested by the 1947 Government Experts' Conference. For instance, it accepted the suggested prohibition of hostage taking, which was in line with the UK wartime manual,[119] and of physically violent interrogations. Still, it rendered some of these restrictions weak by leaving alarming loopholes in them—by excluding forms of "mental torture," for instance.

Desiring to reduce the burden for its administrators in occupied Germany and in preparation for a potential war with the Soviets, the text also excluded various categories of civilians, such as stateless persons and nationals of a non-party belligerent—the Soviet Union still had not signed the 1929 POW Convention. While accepting a Civilian Convention, the UK government never really believed in the project as such. Instead, it desired a treaty with a minimal scope and plenty of assurances for its security and colonial officials in armed conflict.[120] In essence, British officials initially had no appetite for giving up their legal tools in wartime in exchange for settling the grievances of their continental European allies.

Like its British counterpart, the POWC pragmatically accepted large parts of the proposals from 1947. The Pentagon adopted the suggested ban against hostage taking, for instance.[121] The POWC further agreed to ban counterinsurgency measures varying from torture to collective penalties—following the Justice Department's approval—and even reprisals, which the French had initially sanctioned.[122] Unlike the British, the POWC initially approved limiting the use of "moral torture," illustrating the remaining influence of human rights thinking on its members. Still, some US officials expressed fear that this

---

[118] Draft Civilian Convention Home Office Interdepartmental Committee, 1948, no. 2184, HO213, TNA.

[119] Elizabeth Stubbins Bates, "The British Army's Training in International Humanitarian Law," *Journal of Conflict & Security Law*, Vol. 25, No. 2 (2020): 291–315, 6.

[120] Draft Civilian Convention Home Office Interdepartmental Committee, 1948, no. 2184, HO213, TNA.

[121] Minutes Prisoners of War Committee, 24 May 1948, Provost Marshal General, no. 673, NARA.

[122] Minutes Prisoners of War Committee, 18 June 1948, Provost Marshal General, no. 673, NARA. The US Army had initially opposed banning collective penalties as it feared that it might make "completely ineffectual the powers of an occupying authority": Minutes Prisoners of War Committee, 10 October 1947, Provost Marshal General, no. 673, NARA.

MAKING THE CIVILIAN CONVENTION   77

restriction might severely hamper their intelligence capabilities in a future war with the Soviet Union.[123]

What is more, the POWC even restricted the use of the death penalty by accepting a provision (the "law-of-the-occupied" clause) that might allow a state to issue a new law which prohibited capital punishment right before the outbreak of war—a proposal which it would later deeply regret (see below). This rights-related proposal, which sought to maintain the status quo of criminal law in the occupied territory, might seriously constrain the deterring effect of the occupier's actions against insurgent enemies. When in June 1948 Pictet visited Washington to discuss his team's new draft proposals for the Stockholm Conference, the POWC informed him that it had accepted the bulk of them. This remarkable shift produced great relief among leading ICRC officials, including Pictet, who had expected fiercer opposition from Washington and hoped this would lower UK opposition even further.[124]

Since April 1947, Pictet's drafting team had begun developing its first major drafts for the 1948 Stockholm Conference. Although the archival record is patchy,[125] the ICRC officials more directly involved in this effort appear to have been a select group of experts including Pictet, Pilloud, Huber, Ferrière, Jean Meylan (a young lawyer with wartime experience in civilian internee affairs),[126] René-Jean Wilhelm, and Jean Duchosal, who had organized the 1947 conference. They would also regularly receive advice from outsiders, including German lawyers whose nation was officially excluded from this Allied-dominated drafting stage.

Acting as supervisor, Pictet indicated a substantial interest in the work of the UN Human Rights Commission (UNCHR) led by Eleanor Roosevelt, the US chairperson.[127] He was familiar with the UNCHR's work as he read its reports that were being sent by the ICRC's representative in New York; he also

---

[123] Yingling himself said he believed that "moral coercion" (unlike moral torture) would not be deemed to include the banned measures, and that he believed the Intercross draft was therefore acceptable: Minutes Prisoners of War Committee, 24 May 1948, Provost Marshal General, no. 673, NARA.

[124] Minutes Prisoners of War Committee, 25 June 1948, Provost Marshal General, no. 673, NARA.

[125] It is unclear who drafted the first texts for the Civilian Convention as part of the ICRC's drafts for the Stockholm Conference. The roles and contributions of individuals delegates is often unclear. It is also unknown whether Pictet acted merely as supervisor, editor, or co-drafter, or in a combination of these three roles, or how he did so.

[126] From June 1942 onwards, the Swiss jurist Jean Meylan started working at the ICRC as member of the secretariat for POWs and civilian internee affairs. In October 1945, he moved to the Legal Division to become part of the group studying the law's revision. Curiously, he left the ICRC at the end of August 1947. It is unclear what led to his departure. This information has been generously shared by Daniel Palmieri.

[127] In this note, Pictet admitted having a "vif interet" in the Commission's work: Note Pictet for Michel on UN Commission of Human Rights, 17 March 1947, no. CR-240-10, ACICR.

78 PREPARING FOR WAR

observed its gatherings in Geneva in December 1947.[128] The effects of this continuing human rights thinking, combined with the ICRC's endorsement of the 1947 French text, can be illustrated by its first drafts for the future Conventions. These proposals guaranteed humane treatment "in all circumstances" and intangible rights for wartime detainees.[129] Unlike previously, Pictet's drafting team now banned collective penalties based upon human rights principles. It remained uncertain, however, as to whether it should specifically mention stateless persons (even though they were to fall under this treaty) and fully ban the death penalty, for example.[130]

Pushing the ICRC to devote more attention to protecting mothers and children in war, the International Union for Child Welfare (IUCW) proposed to ban the death penalty for children,[131] for example. This presented Pictet's drafters with an apparent dilemma, especially in light of their human rights agenda. They expressed reluctance to accept the IUCW's idea, fearing that it would interfere with existing capital punishment laws of states and that resistance movements might use the ban to circumvent the POW Convention's tough requirements for irregulars. At this stage the ICRC was still concerned to maintain the deterrence offered by the death penalty, which sought to force irregulars to abide by the Conventions.[132]

At a broader level, the ICRC legal experts remained divided whether they should cover (the states' own) political prisoners, especially those without "all the rights of a citizen." This clearly referred to the fate of German Jews who had lost their civil rights as a result of the 1935 Nuremberg Laws. Despite opposition, the experts finally decided to exclude these persons from the future draft.[133] In a public speech, Huber said that the ICRC believed, as a result of its recent wartime experience, that it could only act successfully when "reciprocity was granted," which was not the case with "nationals of persecuting

---

[128] Similar to Pilloud and Duchosal, Pictet had attended some of the meetings of the Commission as an observer: Letter on ICRC Observers to UN Secretariat CDH in Geneva, 21 November 1947, no. CR-243-11, ACICR.

[129] The Legal Division continued to advocate an older plan of trying to ensure protection for those persons whose status was questioned as a result of the destruction of their indigenous state, e.g., citizens from occupied Western Poland: Draft Civilian Convention, 1948, no. CI_1948_B3_01_ENG_03, ICRC Library.

[130] For Article 59, the ICRC included a provision requiring that when a "protected person" commits an offense with intent to harm the occupant, "[b]ut which does not constitute either an attempt on the life or limb of members of the occupying forces or administration, or a grave collective danger, or serious harm to the property of the occupant or of the installations used by him, the only penalty depriving him of liberty to which he is liable shall be interment": Draft Civilian Convention, 1948, no. CI_1948_B3_01_ENG_03, ICRC Library.

[131] Letter UIPE, January 1948, No. CR-238-4, ACICR.

[132] ICRC Note on Remarks UIPE, January 1948, No. CR-221-4, ACICR.

[133] Minutes of ICRC Assembly, 18/25 August 1947, no. CR-238-4, ACICR.

states."[134] For this reason, combined with fears of possible Anglo-American (and Soviet) opposition, the ICRC preferred to work on the basis of reciprocity by respecting interstate sovereignty.[135] By doing so, it outsourced the pressing question of the wartime protection of the state's own nationals to Roosevelt's Commission, despite its own struggles with codifying this crucial issue.

In other words, while "saluting" the UNCHR's efforts to promote human rights,[136] the ICRC wished to have its own Convention, suggesting a distinct treaty for enemy civilians alone. While having a broader human rights vision than Huber, Pictet continued to adhere to that view by demanding that matters "foreign" to this treaty should be ignored completely.[137] When the ICRC began to prepare a public document concerning its relation to the UN's efforts with regard to promoting human rights, Pictet was also warned by colleagues to separate those two matters. In particular, it was feared that connecting human rights and humanitarian law might also give the UN a pretext to take over the ICRC's leading role in the revision process of the Conventions.[138] This parochial mindset helps to explain the later disappearance of "human rights" from the collective memory of most experts of humanitarian law. It is remarkable how the human rights revolution, as a language, a rallying cry, and a conceptual framework, was initially appropriated by the ICRC in the mid-1940s, but finally lost its appeal as a result of various political considerations.[139]

Apart from concerns about the ICRC's international role, the organization also faced reluctance from several Great Powers at this stage, who were considering even the options of either a reduced treaty version or no Civilian Convention at all. In January 1948, following consultations with various governments, ICRC officials warned Pictet that they would probably not support his far-reaching proposals for civilian protection. Pictet himself was said to realize that the UK government in particular posed a major threat to his plans. Pilloud feared, moreover, that a rejection might potentially undermine the already existing 1929 Conventions.[140]

Acting far less cautiously than Pilloud, Pictet, feeling that now was the time to gain progress "dans le domain du droit humanitaire," opposed all the

---

[134] Report Riegner Spiritual Conference Geneva, March 1947, Series D106, no. 10, AJC.

[135] Minutes of Meeting Bureau, 25/27 August 1947, no. CR-238-4, ACICR.

[136] ICRC Note on Human Rights, no. CR-243-11, ACICR.

[137] Minutes Meeting ICRC Delegation Stockholm Conference, 12 August 1948, no. CRI-25 VIII-Dossier 8, ACICR.

[138] Note Dunand for Pictet, 8 December 1947, no. CR-243-11, ACICR.

[139] Van Dijk, "Human Rights in War," 572–573.

[140] Minutes of Meeting Legal Division, 16 January 1948, no. A PV JUR.1, ACICR.

80 PREPARING FOR WAR

alternative plans, such as a reduced Convention which left open the option of creating fallback options in case of severe Anglo-American (and Soviet) opposition. Supported by Huber, Pictet's critical intervention led to a rejection of public discussion of fallback options, thereby effectively defeating Cramer's plan for a giant single treaty and saving Pictet's original idea of a separate and robust Civilian Convention. It appears that the ICRC also drafted a secret resolution for a reduced version in case of the original draft's rejection by Anglo-American drafters. To be sure, ICRC officials took this nightmare scenario very seriously. Realizing that the stakes were high, Pictet's strategy was to persuade the Red Cross Conference to endorse his far-reaching proposals in order to maximize pressure on their host states, especially the Anglo-American powers.[141]

As we have seen previously, the ICRC received critical feedback on its proposals not just from states, but also from the World Jewish Congress (WJC). Apart from recalling the death of millions of Jewish victims during the Nazi occupation—one of the few references to the Holocaust and public criticisms of the ICRC's silence in the face of it[142]—Riegner's organization also advocated a more robust Civilian Convention. The WJC preferred a text based more strictly on human rights as such that would apply to emergencies (see Chapter 3), prohibit racial segregation, and include formerly ignored categories of civilians as well, from political prisoners to persons with a so-called controversial nationality. The latter referenced persons such as the German Jews, whose status had been put into question during the 1930s as a result of Nazi race laws. Moreover, the WJC suggested an extraordinary mechanism adapted from the ICRC's monitoring provision for the POW Convention. This new instrument, it hoped, would allow civilians with a disputed legal status to fall under the Civilian Convention, with the aim of creating an overarching safety net for as many civilians as possible.[143]

---

[141] Minutes of Meeting Legal Division, 16 January 1948, no. A PV JUR.1, ACICR. Pictet also opposed proposals to discuss with partners the ICRC's possible fallback options in case of the Civilian Convention's rejection. He feared that this would give certain reluctant states, possibly the UK and USA, a pretext to reject the entire treaty. Minutes Meeting ICRC Delegation Stockholm Conference, 3 August 1948. The fallback plan was finally dropped about a week later. Minutes Meeting ICRC Delegation Stockholm Conference, 12 August 1948, no. CRI-25 VIII -Dossier 8 Stockholm 1948, ACICR.

[142] Noam Penkower, "The World Jewish Congress Confronts the International Red Cross during the Holocaust," *Jewish Social Studies*, Vol. 41, No. 3/4 (1979): 229–256, 248–249.

[143] The WJC also suggested to ban deportations of protected persons, to forbid forced labor, to allow protected persons to leave the territory in which the conflict occurs, to ban discriminatory food and medical supplying, and to prevent starvation more generally. See Memorandum WJC on Geneva Conventions, August 1948, no. 17, Series B69, AJC.

Faustian Bargains

After these internal discussions had been concluded, the WJC and the major drafting parties met in August 1948 in Stockholm. For a limited period of time, the third sub-committee of the Legal Commission discussed Pictet's far-reaching proposals for a Civilian Convention. In the end they adopted a remarkable number of prohibitions against arbitrary treatment, including the US delegation's suggestion—later deeply regretted—of including the "law-of-the-occupied" clause.[144] Emboldened by this remarkable shift, French delegate Cahen-Salvador spoke of a "moral revolution" and, influenced by Jacob's former plan for a preamble, drafted together with Castberg a similar instrument for the Civilian Convention. This preamble featured a call to protect human rights "at any time and in all places."[145] It included, furthermore, individual protections against violence to life, hostage taking, torture, and summary executions, thereby embracing a limited, if not selective, human rights agenda by keeping the death penalty in place, for instance.[146] The preamble's acceptance nonetheless generated euphoria within the French delegation, demanding as it did the protection of human rights in times of foreign occupation.

Regardless of its skepticism with respect to "human rights" as a central drafting discourse for the Convention and those plans covering the state's own nationals, Pictet's strategy to obtain a robust Civilian Convention had surprisingly paid off. The Stockholm Conference largely accepted his draft, which represented the first major text in history protecting civilians in various territories, with overwhelming support. The Stockholm draft, as it became known, featured a set of human rights-inspired protections against arbitrary treatment, especially those with regard to hostage taking and collective penalties, causing exhilaration among Hitler's victims. Of course, the draft included several loopholes, such as sanctioning deportations within occupied territory, but these remained relatively modest compared to the Tokyo Draft's major gaps.

---

[144] Following a request from the Geneva-based International Union for Child Welfare, the third sub-committee further agreed to ban capital punishment for "persons under eighteen years of age," in order to protect the "child partisan" of the Second World War, or the "child soldier" as such (a term coined only much later). See also David Rosen, *Child Soldiers in the Western Imagination: From Patriots to Victims* (New Brunswick, NY: Rutgers University Press, 2015).

[145] Summary Minutes of Meetings Sub-Committees, August 1948, no. CI_1948_COMJUR_SC, ICRC Library. Clattenburg believed that the preamble was "innocuous in effect and impracticable to oppose in debate." Report of U.S. delegation to the Stockholm Red Cross Conference, Third Subcommission, 1948, Provost Marshal General, no. 672, NARA.

[146] The preamble itself did not ban the death penalty as such, only its extrajudicial use. It is striking that Castberg seemed to defend this position even after the negotiations had come to an end. See Frede Castberg, "Franc Tireur Warfare," *Netherlands International Law Review* [1959]: 81–92, 92.

82 PREPARING FOR WAR

Despite these breakthroughs, the third sub-committee experienced several clashes between the Western European delegations and a minority of Commonwealth and American delegations defending the position of occupiers, which meant protecting the safety of security and intelligence officials. Among other things, they disagreed over the question whether the state's own nationals and irregulars could fall under the Civilian Convention. The human rights activists Castberg and Riegner wished to broaden the treaty's scope for even armed civilians excluded from the POW Convention and for civilian internees in internal conflicts. This plan, touching directly upon states' sovereignty, precipitated major opposition from a surprising coalition of US and ICRC delegates, whose members claimed that the requirement of protecting civilians against their own government belonged to Roosevelt's Commission, not the Civilian Convention.[147] In a similar fashion, Pilloud, like his US partners, cautiously opposed a Danish proposal prohibiting the transfer of the occupier's own nationals into occupied territory, claiming that this overly infringed upon the states' sovereignty.[148]

Pilloud's delegation felt it had to balance, on the one hand, meeting the demands of especially the US delegation seeking to protect its Cold War interests, and on the other hand, supporting the Western European victims of Nazi empire in providing human rights to civilians for interstate occupations. As in the case of other major drafting issues, if it supported far-reaching proposals by Castberg to significantly curtail states' sovereignty, negotiations might break down. However, if it entirely followed the approach taken by its restrictive American partners, the Civilian Convention might remain very limited in scope and be weak too. Pictet's drafters therefore continued to advocate only a selective human rights agenda, opposing many forms of arbitrary counter-insurgency measures while limiting their focus to a select group of enemy civilians.

This Faustian bargain to keep state sovereignty partly intact in exchange for more robust protections for enemy civilians paid off. The fact that the British government had effectively boycotted this meeting also allowed Western European victims to push for ever more rights for civilians in armed conflict.[149] One of Castberg's Danish allies, also a former political prisoner, critiqued

---

[147] Summary Minutes of Meetings Sub-Committees, August 1948, no. CI_1948_COMJUR_SC, ICRC Library; and Report Clattenburg for State Department, September 1948, no. 22, RG 43, 5536, NARA.

[148] Summary Minutes of Meetings Sub-Committees, August 1948, no. CI_1948_COMJUR_SC, ICRC Library.

[149] Van Dijk, "Human Rights in War," 573–574.

the ICRC's decision to completely ignore the fate of political prisoners, a criticism that was shared by Riegner's WJC.[150] Despite opposition from a Commonwealth skeptic, the Legal Commission finally accepted a Danish proposal which sought to protect political prisoners even in times of intrastate war.

This radical proposal, however, was finally replaced by a much weaker alternative resolution, which merely "expressed the hope" that the final diplomatic conference would try to protect political prisoners, without seeking to place them under the Geneva Conventions. Suddenly working side by side, the French and Canadians expressed palpable relief at this turn of events.[151] Ultimately, the Stockholm Conference represented a major success for both France and Pictet. The latter also successfully defeated plans for a reduced Convention within the ICRC.[152] Still, in the following months this highly promising outcome would be seriously put to the test by the UK government in particular.

2.4 Protecting Civilians in Wartime

There existed no ambiguity in Whitehall's response to the outcome of the Red Cross Conference. Influenced by its fear of war in the wake of the Berlin blockade, the War Office sought to protect its overstretched armed forces by demanding a lower logistical–financial burden for humanized war. In light of this it suggested the exclusion of several civilians, from the states' own nationals to stateless persons, arguing that the latter could not be specifically covered. Whitehall adopted these suggestions, anticipating that it would have to accept greater legal responsibility in the context of the ongoing (and possibly future) refugee crises in Europe, with countless displaced persons remaining across the continent. While not against the idea of legally protecting stateless persons, British officials wished to have no specific reference, fearing it might directly affect their strict immigration policies and the burden for their occupying forces.

The War Office further opposed any "obligations on independent government in respect of their own populations." It believed this matter should be dealt with by the UN, even though here too the British were blocking efforts to apply human rights to either Northern Ireland or Britain's colonial territories. British officials preferred to prevent international law from being

---

[150] Cable WJC on Stockholm Conference, 29 August 1948, no. 17, Series B69, AJC.
[151] See Report Canadian Delegation Stockholm Conference, 1948, no. Series 619 - B - 40, RG 25 - Vol. 5020, Library and Archives Canada (LAC), Ottawa, ON.
[152] Minutes Meeting ICRC Delegation Stockholm Conference, 12 August 1948.

84 PREPARING FOR WAR

directly applied to those areas, for instance by opposing the draft's "impracticable" ban on racial discrimination.[153] Nor did the War Office appreciate the former French–Norwegian efforts at Stockholm to draw a connection between human rights and the Civilian Convention, so as to weave a "safety net." Striving to separate these issues from each other, one War Office-official argued that "it will need all our skills [...] to prevent overlap with the "Human Rights" proposals."[154] This official, like the rest of the War Office as well as MI-5, opposed the draft's preamble as it was believed to cast a "blanket" over the two Conventions to safeguard the "principles of human rights in peace as well as in war."[155]

The perceived risk of an armed clash with the Soviets amid the Berlin blockade led to increasing anxiety about Britain's legal tools in humanized war. Considering themselves occupiers first in the case of a confrontation with the Soviet Union, British intelligence and security officials felt most concerned about the existing draft's implications for their ability to suppress (communist) insurgencies. In relation to this point, MI5 felt that the preamble's scope, by including "mental torture," was "far too wide [and] totally unacceptable." For interrogations, it argued, it was essential to use techniques that may be considered "mental torture," which it felt the preamble was prohibiting.[156] The War Office, in a similar fashion, objected to some (though not all) parts of the draft banning forms of arbitrary treatment, such as torture. For instance, to defend its occupying forces against potential communist resistance movements, it wished to maintain the right to take hostages among civilian populations, even though this suggestion was finally opposed by other British officials.[157]

Moreover, the War Office, in connection with the Foreign Office, argued that the Civilian Convention should allow for the death penalty and even derogations—a dangerous principle which might be easily stretched by an "unscrupulous Power," as Nazi Germany had done during the war. In their advice to the Cabinet, these bodies clarified that special circumstances may arise in which it would be impossible to carry out the treaty's requirements, even though they knew that this might cause virulent opposition at the diplomatic conference. During a special meeting in March 1949, Attlee's Cabinet generally agreed

---

[153] Report War Office Interdepartmental Committee on Civilian Convention, 1948, no. 330, WO163, TNA.

[154] Letter Roseway to Kirkpatrick on Draft Texts, 1 November 1948, no. 3970, FO369, TNA.

[155] Note Alexander to Speake on Human Rights, 7 March 1949, no. 4144, FO369, TNA.

[156] Letter Hill to Speake on Stockholm Drafts, 9 November 1948, no. 2185, HO213, TNA.

[157] Revised Briefing for UK delegation, 11 February 1949, no. 4145, FO369, TNA.

with this proposal, but also recognized that it might be "difficult to hold this position since it would be said that, by permitting derogations, [states] were opening the door to breaches of the Convention."[158] While expecting a stable voting majority in Geneva and considering the law's revision primarily a Great Powers affair,[159] the British delegation would soon discover that this prediction was wrong and that it needed to canvass support from the numerous smaller delegations. At the diplomatic conference, it proved nearly impossible to defend those proposals in the face of persistent opposition from French, Soviet, and ICRC drafters.

Though much less aggressive than its British partners, the US POWC also came out as a critic of the Stockholm draft. While not seeking war with the Soviet Union, US military officials did keep the option open and prepared their instructions accordingly. As a consequence of this, they tried to keep US military power largely unrestrained under humanitarian law. With respect to the Civilian Convention, the POWC regretted its previous suggestion to restrict the death penalty.[160] Its main concern, however, lay with minimizing the burden for its armed forces in the context of the occupations it might have to administer in the future, mainly in light of the ongoing East–West tensions. The Americans too sought a reduced burden for their armed forces and likewise questioned the inclusion of various civilians under the existing draft. Furthermore, it wished to place unlawful combatants mostly outside of the Civilian Convention (see Chapter 3). With respect to the preamble, the POWC initially accepted a reference to "human rights," but later removed it as part of its larger objective to prevent certain persons—especially communist spies—from being covered by this treaty.[161]

Regardless of these restrictions, the US POWC discussed only briefly some of the issues highlighted by the British. Crucially, however, it instructed Harrison's delegation to accept the bulk of the Stockholm draft. The instructions noted that mounting stiff opposition to this text might be embarrassing for the State Department as it might also cause a major split within the Western bloc and undermine US prestige.[162] The Americans understood much better

---

[158] Minutes Meeting Cabinet, 28 March 1949, no. 46, CAB130 (Cabinet Office), TNA.

[159] See Report on Voting Strengths, 7 April 1949, no. 4148, FO369, TNA.

[160] The US POW Committee questioned the age barrier for the death penalty and revised the "law-of-the-occupied" clause by suggesting a vague reference to "applicable law at the outbreak of hostilities."

[161] US Draft for the Civilian Convention, 31 March 1949, Provost Marshal General, no. 673, NARA.

[162] Minutes Meeting at Pentagon on US Draft Convention, 14 April 1949, no. 5, RG43 - 40, NARA; and US Draft for the Civilian Convention, 31 March 1949, Provost Marshal General, no. 673, NARA.

86 PREPARING FOR WAR

than the British that it was better to attenuate the Stockholm draft rather than to directly challenge it. The Canadian delegation, too, was instructed to take a strict approach by excluding political prisoners and questioning the preamble's reference to human rights.[163]

Thus, while the major Commonwealth nations wished to have a minimal preamble, or no preamble at all, the French government considered it "an integral part" of its plans with respect to the Civilian Convention. Compared with the strict British ones, the loose French instructions demanded the Stockholm draft's acceptance and considered its preamble an essential means for creating a "backup" for partisans and civilians. Providing them with critical protections against inhumane treatment, this Convention, it said, drew its strength from the UDHR. Indeed, the French—unlike, for instance, the British—saw a direct link between human rights and humanitarian law. On the other hand, they wished to reach a common understanding on these issues with the other Great Powers, especially the Soviet Union. With respect to the latter, the French were even willing to go as far as to offer the option of reconsidering the Civilian Convention "as a whole," as long as the new text would be based upon principles derived from the UDHR and Genocide Convention.[164] The unique French willingness to accept major compromises in exchange for Soviet participation contrasts starkly with the Anglo-American lack of interest in it.

As we saw previously, Pictet's role as a leading drafting actor was gradually decreasing during this final stage of the drafting process, which was dominated by the Great Powers. Apart from advocating the Stockholm draft, the ICRC suggested broadening the treaty's scope by reinserting so-called forgotten categories of civilians. In this regard it thought specifically of neutrals, allied nationals, and especially stateless persons whose status remained largely un-regulated—at least until the signing of the Refugee Convention in 1951.[165] While recognizing the importance of human rights thinking, the ICRC's draft no longer featured a textual reference to "human rights," ignoring the Stockholm resolution on political prisoners as well. The text's main objective was to create a reciprocity-based Civilian Convention, with sufficiently limited scope to obtain support from the Great Powers by protecting the core of their sovereign power.

---

[163] Instructions Canadian Delegation for Civilian Convention, 28 February 1949, 112 - 20, RG19 - Vol 480, LAC.

[164] Instructions French Foreign Ministry, 14 April 1949, no. 161, Unions, LAD.

[165] Remarks and Proposals submitted by the ICRC, 1949, 68–69, ICRC Library.

Unexpected Soviet Support

The plenipotentiaries of the major drafting parties gathered in April 1949 to establish the first Civilian Convention in history. Whereas Bourquin had been the ICRC's preferred candidate for chairing this debate, Cahen-Salvador was finally chosen as the Third Committee's president following French pressure.[166] Having survived the Holocaust, the French–Jewish drafter was determined that the conference would not fail as the Tokyo drafters had done before them, and would protect civilians in war against ill-treatment. The last part of this chapter will focus upon the Third Committee's discussions relating to the Civilian Convention's scope, that is, the preamble and protected persons, as well as the discussion as to the treaty's future protections against different counterinsurgency measures. Since the Committee referred the question of the treaty's scope to a special Drafting Committee, the focus will first be laid on those debates concerning treatment, which led to immediate delays in the drafting process, which had been supposed to end within six weeks.

During the first reading, however, the Committee experienced serious delays as a result of fierce opposition from, especially, Craigie's delegation. More extraordinary, and to the great surprise of the ICRC, the Soviets supported most parts of the Stockholm draft and often collaborated with the Western powers, even at times with their greatest Cold War adversaries. In principle, the Soviets endorsed limitations upon hostage taking—following Stalin's wartime condemnation of this measure—reprisals, collective penalties, and racial discrimination, bringing their views surprisingly closely in line with those of the French and ICRC.[167] At a later stage, Pilloud would admit privately that he "hardly dared to think what would have become of the Civilian Convention without the presence of [the Soviet] delegation."[168]

Contrary to Anglo-American expectations, Soviet military planning at this stage did not yet envision any major invasion of Western Europe in the case of a confrontation with NATO powers.[169] Instead, Stalin wished to build a powerful line of defense in Germany, set up a buffer zone of friendly states

---

[166] Bourquin became the chairperson of the Second and Joint Committees. Conference Diplomatique. Rapport Spécial Etabli par Pilloud, 16 September 1949, no. CR-254-1, ACICR.

[167] Boyd van Dijk, "'The Great Humanitarian': The Soviet Union, the International Committee of the Red Cross, and the Geneva Conventions of 1949," *Law and History Review*, Vol. 37, No. 1 (2019): 209–235.

[168] Conference Diplomatique. Rapport Spécial Etabli par Pilloud, 16 September 1949, no. CR-254-1, ACICR.

[169] Vladimir Pechatnov, "The Soviet Union and the World, 1944–1953," in *The Cambridge History of the Cold War, Vol I*, ed. Melvyn Leffler and Odd Arne Westad (Cambridge: Cambridge University Press, 2010), 90–111, 103.

88   PREPARING FOR WAR

in Eastern Europe, and extend the Soviet Union's borders.[170] Soviet military planning was still "unequivocally defensive."[171] In this period, Soviet operational plans mentioned only defensive actions in Soviet(-aligned) territory to be occupied by NATO forces. Accordingly, Soviet officials imagined the next war to be more like the last one, demanding protection against potential Western occupiers.[172]

This meant that the Anglo-American powers faced much greater opposition in 1949 than they had expected. Whereas most of the delegations believed that the diplomatic conference would be merely technical in nature, making only small alterations to the existing Stockholm draft, the British wished to completely revise it.[173] For this reason, the Canadians felt that there was not "much chance of [the] Civilian Convention being [accepted]."[174] Most strikingly, the leaders of both the American and British delegations began seriously considering the option of not signing the Civilian Convention at this stage. They also proposed to adjourn the conference for half a year.[175] Remarkably, the surprisingly united opposition of former victims of Axis empires rejected both suggestions, giving the conference more time to prevent the Civilian Convention from collapsing.[176]

In this crucial period, the Third Committee would accept a whole range of prohibitions against arbitrary counterinsurgency measures, from reprisals against persons to collective penalties. Contrasting with the interwar difficulties in codifying this matter, the suggested ban on hostage taking did not spark any major debate, leading to its adoption at the very first reading and triggering hopeful coverage in the international press.[177] The Americans had already given up on this point; the British finally did too after they recognized that putting up a fight would meet overwhelming resistance.[178]

---

[170] Ibid., 92.

[171] Vojtech Mastny, "Imagining War in Europe: Soviet Strategic Planning," in *War Plans and Alliances in the Cold War: Threat Perceptions in the East and West*, ed. Vojtech Mastny, Sven Holtsmark, and Andreas Wenger (New York: Routledge, 2006), 15–45, 16.

[172] Ibid., 16–17.

[173] Report of New Zealand Delegation to Diplomatic Conference of Geneva 1949, AAYS 8638 W2054 ADW2054/1220/3/3 (R18524114), Archives New Zealand (ANZ), Wellington.

[174] Interim Report High Commissioner, 19 May 1949, no. 619 - B - 40 - PART 5, RG25 - Vol. 3398, LAC.

[175] Interim Report High Commissioner, 19 May 1949, no. 619 - B - 40 - PART 5, RG25 - Vol. 3398, LAC; Notes on Meeting UK Delegation, 5 May 1949, no. 4151, FO369, TNA; and Report US Delegation Diplomatic Conference, 1949, no. 673, Provost Marshal General, NARA.

[176] Cable on Length of Conference, 9 June 1949, no. 619 - B - 40 - PART 5, RG25 - Vol. 3398, LAC.

[177] Minutes Meeting UK delegation, 11 May 1949, no. 4152, FO369, TNA; and Final Record of the Diplomatic Conference of Geneva of 1949, Vol. II, Section A, p. 664, Library of Congress (LOC), Washington, DC.

[178] Minutes Meeting UK delegation, 3 May 1949, no. 4150, FO369, TNA.

Another prominent issue related to arbitrary treatment that caused a great deal more controversy was that of banning deportations. Many observers saw this as one of the diplomatic conference's most important topics of discussion. Working together, the American and British delegations, in line with their instructions to obtain certain derogations, demanded exceptions, in the case of "imperative military reasons," to Stockholm's rule of prohibiting deportations. By contrast, the ICRC opposed these Anglo-American suggestions, considering them symptomatic of a larger tendency on their part to reduce the law's "mandatory nature" in favor of military necessity.[179] The Soviets opposed it too, but suggested in turn deletion of the words "against their will," with the aim of sanctioning the forced return of anti-Soviet displaced persons as had been agreed at Yalta in 1945.[180] Rejecting all these proposals, the conference finally suggested to ban forcible deportations from and into occupied territory, as had been first suggested by the Danes at Stockholm.[181]

Death to the Death Penalty

Whereas this breakthrough was achieved relatively easily, the discussion with regard to arbitrary counterinsurgency measures centering around the right to life, and the extent to which that right applied in wartime, proved most controversial. The question of the death penalty, mentioned in Article 59 of the Stockholm draft, first came up for debate in the relevant Drafting Committee. Here, the discussion centered on three key issues: the list of offenses to be punished by the death penalty; the definitions of these terms; and the "law-of-the-occupied" clause, which prohibited the death penalty if the laws of the occupied country had done so before the outbreak of hostilities.

While having completely reversed its view on this point, the American delegation, like the British one, feared that the respective clause would make it virtually impossible for occupiers like it to effectively control insurgent occupied territories in case of a future conflict with the Soviet Union, for instance. In various reports, US officials wrote with concerned that many states had recently prohibited the death penalty, making it increasingly difficult to uphold

---

[179] Conference Diplomatique. Rapport Spécial Etabli par Pilloud, 16 September 1949, no. CR-254-1, ACICR.

[180] Report of Canadian Delegation to Geneva Conference, 1949, no. 112–20, RG 19 - Vol. 480, LAC.

[181] Final Record of the Diplomatic Conference of Geneva of 1949, Vol. II, Section A, pp. 759–761, LOC; and Conference Diplomatique. Rapport Spécial Etabli par Pilloud, 16 September 1949, no. CR-254-1, ACICR.

90   PREPARING FOR WAR

the principle if that provision were to be accepted. Equally, they feared that oc-cupied states would quickly enact legislation banning the death penalty before being invaded, destroying the deterrent of the death penalty as such.

The Anglo-American proposal to maintain the death penalty for so-called saboteurs and spies failed to gain support from the Drafting Committee, with the French surprisingly playing no official role in this particular body. Influenced by Stalin's abolishment of the death penalty, the Soviets, with sup-port from the Scandinavians, rejected their plan. When the Committee ac-cepted a Dutch compromise proposal for a permissive list of offenses for the death penalty, the Soviet delegation "hotly disputed" it.[182] Even the restrictive Foreign Office in London felt it was too permissive.[183] While admitting the Dutch–NATO proposal's usefulness from a strictly military perspective, it felt that the list's terms were extremely vulnerable to "a very subjective interpreta-tion." Pushing back against the War Office's wishes, the Foreign Office feared it might undermine the protection of UK nationals in a future occupied area, which shows the significant divisions within the British government over the treaty's future. To bring Craigie's embattled delegation some relief, British dip-lomats suggested removing some of the list's elastic phrases and taking a less strictly military view on the issue.[184]

When this text was introduced at the Civilian Committee, the Soviets, the French, and Pilloud felt it to be a "bitter disappointment."[185] While upsetting the British, Lamarle's delegation came up with a counterproposal to omit cer-tain offenses from the text and re-insert the deleted "law-of-the-occupied" clause.[186] The French, inspired by rights notions and their painful memories of the Nazi occupation, were widely supported. The British were very frustrated—"if a vote had been taken it would most certainly have [...] been carried." To prevent an early defeat, the British, Americans, and Canadians successfully re-ferred the original text back to the respective Drafting Committee. Lobbying hard, the British defeated a fairly popular restrictive Soviet proposal as a result of a French abstention to appease its NATO allies. The British had been able to prevent an early defeat.[187]

In mid-July 1949, the Drafting Committee presented, under Anglo-American pressure, a revised draft without the "law-of-the-occupied" clause.

---

[182] Minutes Meeting UK delegation, 29 June 1949, no. 4158, FO369, TNA.
[183] See Cable Craigie to Foreign Office, 29 June 1949, no. 4155, FO369, TNA.
[184] Note Foreign Office on Death Penalty, 1 July 1949, no. 4155, FO369, TNA.
[185] Minutes of 41e séance de IIIème Commision, 7 July 1949, ICRC Library. For English translation, see Final Record of the Diplomatic Conference of Geneva of 1949, Vol. II, Section A, p. 766, LOC.
[186] Notes of the 56th Meeting UK delegation, 8 July 1949, no. 4157, FO369, TNA.
[187] Ibid.

The French and the ICRC again reacted with intense disappointment. In a secret report, Pilloud later wrote that he felt the British and American delegates basically wanted a provision that would make persons who committed the "slightest fault" lose their basic human rights virtually immediately, and found that many of their proposals were essentially endorsing the very same things for which the Nazis were being punished after the war by the Allied war crimes tribunals.[188] Most strikingly, an informal bipartisan coalition of Eastern and Western European delegations finally succeeded in pushing through an earlier French text containing the "law-of-the-occupied" clause, a shocking result for both Craigie and Harrison. Surprised and dismayed, the US leader called it the "first important point we have lost."[189] The often careful Craigie now even threatened not to sign the Civilian Convention if the plenary were to approve this outcome, placing enormous pressure on NATO allies to give in to his demands.

In London, a decision was taken to instruct Craigie's delegation to continue fighting this draft in exchange for some minimal compromises.[190] Working hand in hand, Harrison and Craigie tried to convince their allies from Western Europe to drop their version of the "law-of-the-occupied" clause. Craigie adduced "all possible arguments," including threats not to sign the Civilian Convention, but they were not moved. In his view, the French had an overly "deep recollection of bitterness and resistance engendered by use of death penalty" and were therefore determined to "restrict this authorization in every way possible."[191] The French, acting together with the Soviets and the Swiss (most likely influenced by the ICRC), succeeded in persuading the final plenary meeting to vote for their text. The British and Americans were shocked, and threatened again to make a reservation or even to not sign the Convention.

Preamble and Protected Persons

The next section will address those debates with respect to the treaty's precise scope, that is, the definition of protected persons and the preamble. With regard to the latter setting out the Civilian Convention's foundational principles

---

[188] Conference Diplomatique. Rapport Spécial Etabli par Pilloud, 16 September 1949, no. CR-254-1, ACICR.
[189] Cable Harrison for State Department, 4 August 1949, no. 5, RG 43 - 40, NARA.
[190] Letter Roseway to Gardner, 25 July 1949, no. 4158, FO369, TNA.
[191] Cable Craigie for Foreign Office, 5 August 1949, no. 4160, FO369, TNA.

92 PREPARING FOR WAR

and objectives,[192] the Commonwealth delegations desired either no preamble or a very limited one lacking substantive elements.[193] The Americans, together with the Nationalist Chinese, sought a short declaratory preamble with a reference to "human rights."[194] Calling the preamble an "integral part" of the Convention, the French continued to use human rights as a rallying cry. The Soviets also demanded a reference to human rights ("of the greatest importance"),[195] but went one step further: their suggested preamble even recognized the right to life, a move calculated to shame the Anglo-American delegations' opposition to banning the death penalty. While expressing sympathy, Pilloud—unlike the Swiss—felt proposals featuring "human rights" should leave this part out. Trying to separate its own work from that of the UN, the ICRC preferred a substantive preamble with a limited scope, leaving out certain civilian categories.[196]

The First and Third Committees both established a Working Party of representatives to discuss the preamble's revision. As had happened in Roosevelt's UNCHR, there was heated debate among the two working parties as the Vatican delegation suggested a reference to the "Divine Origins of Man."[197] Supporting this essentially anti-communist proposal, the UK and US delegations, under pressure from Catholic organizations at home, turned the discussion into a Cold War battleground. The Soviets, supported by India and Mexico, fiercely opposed the Vatican's idea. The entire debate had revealed major divisions between the delegations, which led to increasing support for dropping the preamble entirely. In the following days, after the debates about a compromise proposal, there occurred "dans les couloirs" discussion whether it was better to remove the preamble to prevent these difficult negotiations from affecting other, far more important drafting debates too. Considering the

---

[192] The analysis done here will be limited to the preamble debates which have taken place in the First and Third Committee.

[193] Final Record of the Diplomatic Conference of Geneva of 1949, Vol. II, Section A, pp. 694–697, LOC.

[194] The latter was later dropped. Final Record of the Diplomatic Conference of Geneva of 1949, Vol. II, Section A, pp. 690–694, LOC. It is likely that this decision was taken following discussions with the British. The Americans seemed not to have fully realized the potential problem of recognizing human rights while trying to deny access to the Convention for certain persons, such as spies. This point further nuances those parts of the literature heralding US contributions to developing human rights after 1945. Elizabeth Borgwardt, *A New Deal for the World: America's Vision for Human Rights* (London: Harvard University Press, 2007).

[195] As seen in internal Soviet reports, this notion of rights reflected a particular socialist humanism, which was regarded as being distinct from bourgeois understandings. Paul Betts, "Universalism and its Discontents: Humanity as a Twentieth-Century Concept," in *Humanity: A History of European Concepts in Practice from the Sixteenth Century to the Present*, ed. Fabian Klose and Mirjam Thulin (Göttingen: Vandenhoeck & Ruprecht, 2016), 51–70, 64.

[196] Final Record of the Diplomatic Conference of Geneva of 1949, Vol. II, Section A, pp. 690–694, LOC.

[197] Report of Irish Delegation at Geneva Diplomatic Conference 1949, 25 November 1949, no. Series DFA-5-341-137-2, National Archives of Ireland (NAI), Dublin.

preamble a vital element of the future Convention, the French reacted to these new developments with alarm.[198]

The Soviets were also hardening their position, rejecting the ICRC's compromise with a reference to God and willing to support only "their" Ukrainian amendment lacking any mention of humanitarian law's so-called divine origins. If defeated, the Soviets claimed that they would oppose the preamble itself. As the Ukrainian amendment was rejected,[199] and because the First Committee had informally supported deleting the preamble, the Soviets angrily joined the camp of skeptics opposing the instrument as such.[200] US–French mediation efforts toward a declaratory preamble led to nothing.[201] The Canadians succeeded in obtaining support from a bipartisan coalition to delete the preamble: disappointing Lamarle, the Soviets also blocked his delegation's attempt to re-open the debate at a later stage.[202] The Coordination Committee's decision to ask the First Committee to reconsider its preliminary acceptance of a preamble led to the instrument's death in its infancy.[203] While the French were disappointed, the Soviets saw it is an important success in their larger struggle against Anglo-American drafting strategies.[204] This decision to remove the preamble created lasting ambiguity about the exact relationship between humanitarian law and human rights—a love that dared not speak its name until the Teheran Resolution of 1968.[205]

Nonetheless—and this point is often forgotten in the present literature—Cahen's co-edited preamble may have died as an instrument but its human rights principles lived on, as they were inserted into Common Article 3 by his delegation. Due to this article, the Civilian Convention as a whole did not apply to civil and colonial wars (see Chapter 3), leaving open the question of the extent to which it could protect political prisoners in situations short of recognized armed conflict. In May 1949 the Danish–Jewish delegate Georg Cohn, who had escaped Denmark during the war as part of the famous

---

[198] Cable Lamarle Preamble Civilian Convention, 22 June 1949, no. 161, Unions Internationales 1944–1960, LAD.

[199] Minutes Meeting UK Delegation, 2 July 1949, no. 4157, FO369, TNA; Interim Report UK Delegation until June 10th 1949, no. 20770, ADM1, TNA; and Interim Report Canadian Delegation, 19 July 1949, no. 619 - B - 40 - PART 5, RG25 - Vol. 3398, LAC.

[200] Cable US Delegation Preamble, 2 July 1949, no. 5, RG 43 - 50, NARA.

[201] Cable French Delegation Preamble, 9 July 1949, no. 161, Unions Internationales 1944–1960, LAD; and Final Record of the Diplomatic Conference of Geneva of 1949, Vol. II, Section A, pp. 780–781, LOC.

[202] Cable French Delegation Preamble, 9 July 1949, no. 161, Unions Internationales 1944–1960, LAD; and Final Record of the Diplomatic Conference of Geneva of 1949, Vol. II, Section A, pp. 780–781, LOC.

[203] Final Record of the Diplomatic Conference of Geneva of 1949, Vol. II, Section B, p. 145, LOC.

[204] Report Soviet-Ukrainian Delegation, no. F. 2, Op. 12cc, Spr. 969, Ark. 60–76, Report Soviet-Ukrainian Delegation, no. F. 2, Op. 12cc, Spr. 969, Ark. 60-76, Tsentral'nyi derzhavnyi arhiv vyschykh organiv vlady ta upravlinnia Ukrainy (TSDAVO), Kiev, Ukraine.

[205] Van Dijk, "Human Rights in War."

94   PREPARING FOR WAR

rescue mission of Danish Jews by local resistance fighters, had already asked Petitpierre whether it was permissible to reintroduce the Stockholm resolution on political prisoners for which his country had fought previously.[206] The Swiss president, acting in line with the ICRC's view on this issue, responded negatively to his request, arguing that political prisoners did not fall under the foundational category of "victims of war."[207] In reality, the Swiss president feared the reaction of the Great Powers if this issue were to be raised at any stage during these diplomatic negotiations.

While critical, the individual political prisoner was not the only drafting sacrifice made for the Civilian Convention's birth. After finishing its work, the relevant Drafting Committee presented a formula for the Convention's scope, as defined by its third article, to define who fell under the category of "protected person." Following Anglo-American pressure to prevent a larger legal burden amid refugee crises in Europe and beyond, it had significantly reduced the article's discursive scope by removing the reference to stateless persons, for instance. The loss of this important reference led to fierce criticism from the Austrian jurist Hans Popper, who invoked the recent persecutions of stateless Jews. His proposal reinserting this specific reference to stateless persons back into the draft was rejected.[208]

What is more, the ICRC's original intention behind creating the foundational category of "protected person" was to develop a solution that would maintain the sex-based legal distinction between civilians and combatants. As its drafters noted, however, this approach proved "extremely difficult."[209] Some drafters identified the protected person by means of reproductive capacity and age, while others prioritized nationality as the Civilian Convention's foundational distinction, or wished to completely abolish this difference.[210] In internal debates about who should count as a protected person, ICRC legal specialists invoked a universalist discourse. Nonetheless, they eventually produced a much more narrow definition, as we saw earlier.

In limiting the treaty's scope to enemy civilians in belligerent and occupied territory, ICRC drafters had decided not to fully replicate sex difference. Their aim was to maximize state support and strategically limit the scope of

---

[206] Letter Von Mayden to Petitpierre on Cohn's request regarding pol prisoners, no date, no. J2.118#1968/77_bd.2, SFA.

[207] Letter to Cohn, 19 May 1949, no. J2.118#1968/77_bd.2, SFA.

[208] Final Record of the Diplomatic Conference of Geneva of 1949, Vol. II, Section A, pp. 793–796, LOC.

[209] ICRC Documents for Meeting Division Juridique, 18 August 1947, No. CR-240-10, ACICR.

[210] For example, the International Union of Child Welfare claimed that particular measures in the Conventions should be to the benefit of all children and women, whatever their nationality. Anna Crowe, "'All the Regard Due to Their Sex': Women in the Geneva Conventions of 1949," *Research Working Paper Series Human Rights Program Harvard University* [2016], 10.

humanitarian law, thereby removing political prisoners, including numerous men and women, from the legal radar.[211] This is not to suggest that sex difference did not shape the Convention at all. Distinctions based on sex were profoundly influential and deliberately woven into the treaty's architecture by ascribing a homogenous sex character to different women. This sex difference appeared in several places in the Civilian Convention: in provisions that understood women predominantly as mothers; in rules relating to pregnancy and childbirth; and in the treaty's ambiguous attitude toward sexual violence in wartime.[212]

2.5 Conclusion

In August 1949, drafters accepted the Civilian Convention with overwhelming support. The adoption garnered major plaudits for Ferrière, who was heralded as the "pioneer of the Civilian Convention."[213] This outcome was widely recognized as a revolutionary moment in the history of the laws of war.[214] Unlike previous international treaties, the Civilian Convention placed severe restrictions on brutal counterinsurgency measures in war.[215] This major shift in international legal history was the product of claims that individuals other than soldiers possessed rights as victims of war, in combination with the drafters' continuing use of human rights thinking.[216]

Pushed by cascading effects, drafters of the Civilian Convention pivoted the existing laws of war from concentrating on the protection of soldiers to securing the rights of enemy civilians and adopted a record number of rights for warfare, from the principle of non-discrimination to the right to have rights in wartime. In doing so, they created the first binding international law in history protecting enemy civilians' rights in belligerent and occupied territory. By contrast, the UDHR remained a non-binding list of moral values, the UN Charter said very little about human rights, and the European Convention on Human Rights (ECHR) was signed only a year after the Civilian Convention's

---

[211] Van Dijk, "Human Rights in War," 569–570.

[212] See Kinsella, *The Image before the Weapon*.

[213] The contributions of his niece Suzanne and Cramer were left unmentioned. Final Record of the Diplomatic Conference of Geneva of 1949, Vol. II, Section B, pp. 519–520, LOC.

[214] Hersch Lauterpacht, "The Problem of the Revision of the Law of War," *British Yearbook of International Law* [1952]: 360–382, 360.

[215] On the legality of reprisals and collective penalties: Lauterpacht, "The Problem of the Revision of the Law of War," 361. On the legality of summary executions: Kevin Jon Heller, *The Nuremberg Military Tribunals and the Origins of International Criminal Law* (Oxford: Oxford University Press, 2011), 207–12.

[216] Van Dijk, "Human Rights in War."

96   PREPARING FOR WAR

adoption.[217] Despite these major accomplishments, the Convention was far from perfect and certainly not all-inclusive. To the contrary, the ICRC excluded many civilians from its drafts, with political prisoners among its most prominent drafting victims.[218] The final text also featured a great number of hierarchies. Although the drafters did not ignore sexual violence, they failed to recognize rape as a pressing moral concern, instead prioritizing matters such as the destruction of private property.[219]

The Convention's norms may have been widely adopted since 1949, but they also embodied the pathogen of rights destruction, as they featured several exclusive impulses and could be arranged and understood in seemingly contradictory ways.[220] Among other seeming contradictions, drafters banned racial segregation while leaving Jim Crow and colonial laws unaddressed, and they rejected deportations while expelling millions of Germans from their homes during the Convention's drafting process. For various reasons, drafters were unable or unwilling to see the potentially destructive effects of these new hierarchies and exclusions enshrined in the treaty's text.[221]

For the Anglo-American delegations, the outcome of the Civilian Convention's making was far from pleasing. In August 1949 each considered making reservations or even not signing the Civilian Convention, as a result of its banning of the death penalty, for example.[222] While having achieved a number of drafting triumphs, including obtaining a limited duration clause to prevent the treaty from placing major restraints on prolonged military occupations such as the ones in postwar Germany and Japan,[223] the British and

---

[217] Van Dijk, "Human Rights in War," 579, 582.

[218] "Since 1945 the ICRC has paid increasing attention to one of the most fundamental human rights issues—political prisoners." David Armstrong, "The International Committee of the Red Cross and Political Prisoners," *International Organization*, Vol. 39, No. 4 (1985): 615–642, 615, 626; and Jacques Moreillon, "The ICRC and the Future," *Revue Internationale de la Croix-Rouge* [1983]: 231–245. When reflecting on the diplomatic conference, Pictet admitted in 1999 that political prisoners had been excluded from the final draft of the Geneva Conventions. However, he put the blame on states, rather than the ICRC. Jean Pictet, "De la Seconde Guerre Mondiale à la Conference Diplomatique de 1949," *Revue internationale de la Croix-Rouge*, Vol. 81, No. 834 (1999): 205–208, 207.

[219] Tuba Inal, *Looting and Rape in Wartime: Law and Change in International Relations* (Philadelphia, PA: University of Pennsylvania Press, 2013).

[220] See Shane Darcy, *Judges, Law and War: The Judicial Development of International Humanitarian Law* (Cambridge: Cambridge University Press, 2014), 118–126.

[221] See conclusion; and Van Dijk, "Human Rights in War," 581–582.

[222] Report of Canadian Delegation to Geneva Conference, no. 112–20, RG 19 - Vol. 480, LAC; and Minutes Plenary Meeting, 11 November 1949, no. A PV JUR.1, ACICR.

[223] Other "victories," from the perspective of occupiers, were the lack of a strict ban on reprisals against property, scorched earth policies, blockade, and so on. The US-sponsored plan to have a limited duration clause to limit the occupier's obligations and prevent it from becoming relevant for ongoing US-led occupations would later cause serious troubles in the context of long-lasting and transformative occupations, such as the one in Palestine. See Nehal Bhuta, "The Antinomies of Transformative Occupation," *The European Journal of International Law*, Vol. 16, No. 4 (2005):

Americans felt the treaty dealt with occupiers far too harshly. This created serious concern on their part about legal room for maneuver in case of a future military confrontation with the Soviet Union. As the stakes were high, their decision whether or not to sign the Convention would also be dependent upon humanitarian law's broader attitude toward intrastate war—the very topic that will be further explored in Chapter 3.

721–740; Adam Roberts, "Transformative Military Occupation: Applying the Laws of War and Human Rights," *American Journal of International Law*, Vol. 100, No. 3 (2006): 580–622; and Darcy, *Judges, Law and War*, 96–114.

Figure 3.1 The Government Experts' Conference in Geneva (1947). From left to right: 3. Frede Castberg, 4. Albert Lamarle, 8. Maurice Bourquin, 9. Jean Pictet, 10. Jean Duchosal, and 11. Max Huber.

Source/Rights: ICRC Audiovisual Archives, V-P-HIST-E-06937H

3

Internationalizing Civil and Colonial Wars

For most observers, the adoption of Common Article 3 (CA3) marked a break-through in the history of international law. In extending humanitarian law's scope to non-international armed conflict, it has been said to have broken the bastion of sovereignty in wartime.[1] Gary Solis, author of a standard work on the laws of war, has called the article "the most significant innovation of the [...] Conventions."[2] For her part, the ICRC historian Catherine Rey-Schyrr has called it a "succès le plus marquant,"[3] and Geoffrey Best has referred to it as "the most significant and arguably the most useful article of all."[4] Others, how-ever, such as legal scholar Lindsay Moir, have argued that the article's history "is widely perceived as having been disappointing, to say the least."[5] While hailing it as "a radical breakthrough," German historian Fabian Klose has joined Moir in skepticism concerning CA3's historical track record after 1949.[6]

In other words, the current literature on CA3, which draws heavily on the historically selective ICRC Commentary,[7] has created a puzzling contrast by portraying its history as a major breakthrough, a disappointment—or even both. This chapter moves beyond this dichotomy by using a genealogical ap-proach to explore the contingent and imperial origins of CA3. Since the devil is in the detail, the chapter's guiding principle is to carefully reconstruct the circumstances and mixed motives behind the eventual, unexpected birth of

---

[1] The reference to this ICRC website is: https://www.icrc.org/eng/war-and-law/treaties-custom ary-law/geneva-conventions/overview-geneva-conventions.html (retrieved 26 March 2017). The ICRC's statements seem to have been inspired by some of its previous publications on this matter, in-cluding the Commentary, which herald CA3's creation as a "grand victory." See Frédéric Siordet, "Les Conventions de Genève et la guerre civile," *Revue Internationale de la Croix-Rouge*, Vol. 32, No. 375 (1950): 187–212, 212.

[2] Gary Solis, *The Law of Armed Conflict: International Humanitarian Law in War* (New York: Cambridge University Press, 2010), 96–97.

[3] Catherine Rey-Schyrr, *De Yalta à Dien Bien Phu. Histoire du Comité international de la Croix-Rouge 1945–1955* (Geneva: Georg-CICR, 2007), 239, 264.

[4] Geoffrey Best, *War and Law since 1945* (Oxford: Clarendon Press, 2002), 168.

[5] Lindsay Moir, *The Law of Internal Armed Conflict* (Cambridge: Cambridge University Press, 2002), 67. Basing his views partly on Moir's work, the British intellectual historian David Armitage echoes many of Moir's skepticisms with regard to CA3. See David Armitage, *Civil Wars: A History in Ideas* (New Haven, CT: Yale University Press, 2017), 202–203.

[6] Fabian Klose, "The Colonial Testing Ground: The International Committee of the Red Cross and the Violent End of Empire," *Humanity*, Vol. 2, No. 1 (2011): 107–126, 109.

[7] See Jean Pictet, *The Geneva Conventions of 12 August 1949: Commentary* (Geneva: ICRC, 1958).

Preparing for War. Boyd van Dijk, Oxford University Press. © Boyd van Dijk 2022.
DOI: 10.1093/oso/9780198868071.003.0004

100 PREPARING FOR WAR

the article in 1949. By using such an approach, it demonstrates how the ICRC in particular tried to widen international law's existing scope to civil war and colonial wars outside Europe. It promoted the legal internationalization of internal wars, with critical consequences not just for the organization's own future, but also for the character of international law in subsequent decades.[8]

This chapter stresses the importance of contingency, neglected in the relevant historiography, for explaining how the negotiations developed over time, why they nearly collapsed at various points in time, what alternative plans were rejected, and why Common Article 3 was finally accepted in August 1949.[9] It shows that there was nothing inevitable about this outcome. By unpacking its historical context, the chapter also challenges those parts of the literature that encapsulate a monolithic, context-free, and singular understanding of CA3's history.[10] This reveals the critical importance of imperial and Cold War dimensions for understanding the article's genealogy, and why the Great Powers were eventually willing to accept this provision despite its binding restrictions on their sovereignty while at its most fragile.

The chapter is divided into four sections, each of which deals with the debate concerning the future scope of humanitarian law. As a starting point for this study on Common Article 3 and its genealogy, the opening section evaluates the first major attempts by anti-Bolshevik activists and Red Cross officials to try to internationalize internal conflicts in the wake of the First World War. It further explores the initial experiments of the ICRC concerning a number of plans to apply international legal principles to both civil and colonial wars prior to and just after the Second World War. The second part continues the discussion above and is largely based on minutes of drafting meetings and internal reports from the four major drafting parties participating in the initial post-1945

---

[8] For more details, see Boyd van Dijk, "Internationalizing Colonial War: On the Unintended Consequences of the Interventions of the International Committee of the Red Cross in South-East Asia, 1945–1949," *Past & Present*, Vol. 250, No. 1 (2020): 1–42.

[9] One example: Sandesh Sivakumaran, *The Law of Non-International Armed Conflict* (Oxford: Oxford University Press, 2014), 40–42.

[10] Sivakumaran's brilliant legal account of Common Article 3 does not explain sufficiently, however, how and why the article was accepted. Neither does it point out what motivated states or the ICRC to support or reject different drafts. See Sivakumaran, *The Law of Non-International Armed Conflict*, 156–162; and Rey-Schyrr, *De Yalta à Dien Bien Phu*, 264–267. The best account we have so far is an impressive study of Giovanni Mantilla. Analyzing the drafting process of CA3, Mantilla's excellent political science work is the first account that has extensively used archival materials from several drafting parties. The study has a few limitations, however. For example, it does not highlight the informal deals made between the British, French, and Americans during the most critical stage of this drafting process, and it cannot sufficiently account for the last stage of the drafting process in which pressure-making was less important due to the secret ballot vote (see below). Giovanni Mantilla, *Lawmaking under Pressure: International Humanitarian Law and Internal Armed Conflict* (Ithaca, NY: Cornell University Press, 2020). See also Kathryn Greenman, "Common Article 3 at 70: Reappraising Revolution and Civil War in International Law," *Melbourne Journal of International Law*, Vol. 21 (2020): 1–27.

drafting phase. At these preliminary gatherings, the parties, and particularly the Norwegian human rights advocate Castberg, discussed plans to apply certain human rights principles to internal wars and to extend the scope of the future Conventions. This laid the foundations for the first drafts which were to be discussed at the last two major conferences.

The third section reveals the colonial anxiety expressed by, especially, the French and British about those proposals in light of the ongoing wars of decolonization in Indochina and Palestine, and how these parties tried to exclude so-called small-scale colonial conflicts from humanitarian law's future scope. The last part provides an in-depth account of the final drafting phase by looking at the interrelated ways in which the drafts were finally challenged and made legally imprecise by imperial drafters, thereby protecting their sovereign powers. It makes clear how the dynamics of decolonization, informal deal-making among the Great Powers, and the Cold War left a lasting imprint on the outcome of these deliberations. CA3 emerges from this chapter, then, not so much as a major breakthrough, or an utter failure, or even a foreseen outcome of an original design. Rather, defying common stereotypes, this chapter argues that the final product was the unexpected outcome of ICRC lobbying, of contingency, of unforeseen Soviet support, and of a deceptive attempt by French imperialists to break a major diplomatic deadlock. Indeed, it shows that CA3, as the outcome of tiresome negotiation, was unexpected and was accepted only after all the other alternatives had been either ignored or rejected as impracticable.

3.1 Regulating Civil Wars

Civil wars have been some of the most deadly conflicts in history. The "long" nineteenth century in particular witnessed a great number of them, from the "Taiping Rebellion" to the American Civil War.[11] Before 1949, however, there existed only a handful of international legal provisions regulating such internal wars.[12] They varied from signing ad hoc agreements between the parties involved, to the recognition of belligerency, or of insurgency, through means of international law.[13] Only when an insurgent party complied with some very

---

[11] Armitage, *Civil Wars*, 161–195.

[12] Anthony Cullen, *The Concept of Non-International Armed Conflict in International Humanitarian Law* (Cambridge: Cambridge University Press, 2010), 25.

[13] Lauterpacht: "The difference between the status of belligerency and that of insurgency […] may best be expressed in the form of the proposition that belligerency is a relation giving rise to definite

102 PREPARING FOR WAR

strict criteria[14] and was recognized either formally or tentatively as a belligerent power could it become a subject of international law, including the laws of war.[15] This largely political decision to recognize a situation of belligerency or insurgency led to all parties, including the insurgent one, being expected to adhere to the laws of war.[16] The question whether to recognize that type of situation of fratricide was typically to be answered by the *de jure* government, not by any outside observer.[17]

However, the conditions under which a decision like this could be taken were never clearly defined. Recognition of belligerency, in addition, occurred only if the scale of the conflict was considered large enough and if the interests of (neutral) states were directly at stake, such as the protection of foreign nationals. A civil or colonial conflict, in other words, first had to resemble a conventional interstate war and be brought in line with Eurocentric standards of "civilization" before it could obtain coverage from international law. Given its high threshold of application, the doctrine of belligerency—or even that of insurgency—which often determined the success or failure of a struggle for independence was almost never applied and primarily served the interests of empires, which sought to protect their sovereignty against internationalization at almost all times.[18]

Typically, state officials would describe acts of rebellion or insurrection as "mutiny" or "troubles" and reject international humanitarian access,[19] such as ICRC inspections, and international recognition of such groups as lawful

---

rights and obligations, while insurgency is not." Hersch Lauterpacht, *Recognition in International Law* (Cambridge: Cambridge University Press, 2013, first published in 1947), 270.

[14] Lauterpacht: "These conditions are as follows: first, there must exist within the State an armed conflict of a general (as distinguished from a purely local) character; secondly, the insurgents must occupy and administer a substantial portion of national territory; thirdly, they must conduct the hostilities in accordance with the rules of war and through organized armed forces acting under a responsible authority; fourthly, there must exist circumstances which make it necessary for outside States to define their attitude by means of recognition of belligerency. Recognition of belligerency is in essence a declaration ascertaining the existence of these conditions of fact. To grant recognition of belligerency when these conditions are absent is to commit an international wrong as against the lawful government. The same applies to the premature recognition of belligerency." Lauterpacht, *Recognition in International Law*, 176.

[15] For a legal account of the law of belligerency and recognition, see P.K. Menon, *The Law of Recognition in International Law: Basic Principles* (Lewiston, NY: Edwin Mellen Press, 1994).

[16] Cullen, *The Concept of Non-International Armed Conflict*, 14; and James Rosenau, *International Aspects of Civil Strife* (Princeton, NJ: Princeton University Press, 1964).

[17] See Adam Roberts and Richard Guelff, *Documents on the Laws of War* (Oxford: Oxford University Press, 2000), 481.

[18] The few exceptions of recognition of belligerency were, among others, the struggle for Greek independence in the 1820s and the US Civil War.

[19] In certain cases, states did allow for the intervention by (often government-controlled) National Red Cross Societies. Giovanni Mantilla, "Under (Social) Pressure: The Historical Regulation of Internal Armed Conflicts through International Law," Ph.D. Dissertation, University of Minnesota, 2013, 71–72.

belligerents.[20] They sought to depoliticize (anti-colonial) resistance by disqualifying rebels as "criminals" and prosecuting them by means of harsh penal laws.[21] Indeed, numerous such exclusive emergency and martial laws were enacted by states and empires throughout the modern period. Exemplary in this regard are the strict emergency laws of the French and British Mandates and the brutal colonial legal regime in the Dutch East Indies, for instance.[22]

Contrary to previous scholarship, the Red Cross movement, including the ICRC, never took this strict international legal regime for granted and was hardly a newcomer when it came to regulating civil wars. Indeed, it sought ways to safeguard European victims of intrastate war, with Dunant himself advocating on their behalf during the Paris Commune of 1871.[23] Since the moment it was conceived in the 1860s, the movement has regularly intervened in internal wars, mostly within Europe. To be sure, most of these interventions remained small-scale in nature and centered on providing relief rather than regulating warfare—and failed to protect victims sufficiently. In the main, they were conducted by National Red Cross Societies, not the ICRC, as the latter remained usually reluctant to challenge state sovereignty head on. It would intervene only if it had been invited to do so by its local partners, such as the *de jure* government or the National Red Cross Society, which were often inextricably linked.[24]

Far from surprisingly, attempts at the Red Cross Conference in 1912 to change this status quo were opposed by some of the more powerful states. Inspired by its recent efforts to assist victims of insurrections related to US imperial interventionism in the Western Hemisphere, the American Red Cross pushed for explicit permission for the Red Cross to provide relief to all sides, and for a foreign Red Cross Society to be permitted to offer its services.[25]

---

[20] Stathis Kalyvas, "Civil War," in *The Oxford Handbook of Comparative Politics*, eds Charles Boix and Susan Stokes (Oxford: Oxford University Press, 2007), 416–434, 416.

[21] Cullen, *The Concept of Non-International Armed Conflict*, 11–15, 18. For the historiography on crime and punishment in the colonial world, see Mark Condos, "Licence to Kill: The Murderous Outrages Act and the Rule of Law in Colonial India, 1867–1925," *Modern Asian Studies*, Vol. 50, No. 2 (2016): 479–517; and Kim Wagner, "'Calculated to Strike Terror': The Amritsar Massacre and the Spectacle of Colonial Violence," *Past & Present*, Vol. 233, No. 1 (2016): 185–225. See also Joseph McQuade, *A Genealogy of Terrorism: Colonial Law and the Origins of an Idea* (Cambridge: Cambridge University Press, 2020).

[22] See Seosamh Ó Longaigh, *Emergency Law in Independent Ireland, 1922–1948* (Bodmin: Four Courts, 2006); Daniel Neep, *Occupying Syria under the French Mandate: Insurgency, Space and State Formation* (New York: Cambridge University Press, 2012); and Petra Groen, "Colonial Warfare and Military Ethics in the Netherlands East Indies," in *Colonial Counterinsurgency and Mass Violence: The Dutch Empire in Indonesia*, eds Bart Luttikhuis and Dirk Moses (New York: Routledge, 2014), 25–44.

[23] Mantilla, "Under (Social) Pressure," 69–82; and James Crossland, *War, Law and Humanity: The Campaign to Control Warfare, 1853–1914* (London: Bloomsbury, 2019).

[24] Mantilla, "Under (Social) Pressure," 70–74, 85.

[25] The report's co-editor, who was affiliated with the State Department, said during the conference not to represent the US government's views: Report American delegation, 1912, no. 73, American Red

104   PREPARING FOR WAR

The most powerful opposition to this idea came from a Czarist Russian Red Cross representative, who fiercely resisted the US proposal.[26] The ICRC, fearful of losing support and of directly interfering in states' domestic affairs, sided with the skeptics, including the French Third Republic.[27]

The Rupture of the First World War

Though rejected, the 1912 US proposal did not die in its infancy. After the rupture of the First World War and its aftermath, it was ironically the Czarist Red Cross, changing its pre-1914 legal attitude for reasons of anti-communist politicking, that introduced the idea of providing the Red Cross with a legal mandate to intervene in situations of civil war.[28] This volte face had been triggered by the ideas of Georges Lodygensky, a Russian anti-communist exile living in Geneva.[29] He wrote two articles, published in the ICRC's own journal, denouncing the Bolsheviks' atrocities and advancing plans to prevent a recurrence, with the aim of reestablishing imperial Czarist authority over the empire. With the wartime rise of Bolshevism, he claimed, a new era had begun whereby "new victims" and "new suffering" demanded new rules.[30] The ICRC endorsed his counterrevolutionary project.[31]

Revealing early humanitarian law's anti-communist origins, an aspect that has been largely neglected in the current scholarship,[32] Lodygensky's proposals demanding protection "des droits élémentaires" in internal wars offered a set of

---

Cross, National Archives and Records Administration (NARA), College Park, MD. See Gwendolyn Shealy, *A Critical History of the American Red Cross, 1882–1945* (New York: The Edwin Mellen Press, 2003).

[26] Rosemary Abi-Saab, *Droit Humanitaire et Conflits Internes: Origines et Évolution de la Réglementation Internationale* (Geneva: Institut Henry-Dunant, 1986), 32–34.

[27] Mantilla, "Under (Social) Pressure," 95–96.

[28] For broader historical context, see Tehila Sasson, "From Empire to Humanity: The Russian Famine and the Imperial Origins of International Humanitarianism," *Journal of British History* Vol. 55, No. 3 (2016): 519–537; and Bruno Cabanes, *The Great War and the Origins of Humanitarianism, 1918–1924* (Cambridge: Cambridge University Press, 2014).

[29] Georges Lodygensky, "La Croix-Rouge et la Guerre Civile," *Revue Internationale de la Croix-Rouge* [1919]: 1159–1180; Georges Lodygensky, "La Croix-Rouge et la Guerre Civile (2me article)," *Revue Internationale de la Croix-Rouge* [1920]: 654–670; and Georges Lodygensky, *Face au Communisme, 1905–1950: Quand Genève Était le Centre du Mouvement Anticommuniste International* (Geneva: Slatkine, 2009).

[30] Lodygensky, "La Croix-Rouge et la Guerre Civile," 1159–1180.

[31] Mantilla, *Lawmaking under Pressure*, 54.

[32] Rosemary Abi-Saab mentions Lodygensky's name, but does not further reflect upon his anti-Bolshevik background. See Abi-Saab, *Droit Humanitaire et Conflits Internes*, 35–37. For the ICRC's pro-communist views in the interwar period, see Daniel Palmieri, "Une Neutralité sous Influence? Le CICR, Franco et les Victimes," *Revue Suisse d'Histoire*, Vol. 59, No. 3 (2009): 279–297.

procedures for the Red Cross in order to intervene in Bolshevik Russia, forming a crucial basis for future drafts regulating civil war. He suggested giving POW rights to political prisoners and recognizing the right of intervention for the Red Cross, whether a foreign Red Cross Society or, in a unique situation, the ICRC. He also proposed banning the taking of hostages as a response to the ongoing Bolshevik persecutions of White Russian civilians.[33]

Under the influence of Lodygensky, the ICRC eventually endorsed proposals granting the Red Cross as a whole a proto-legal mandate to intervene in large-scale civil wars.[34] The ICRC further built upon other international initiatives by extending its services to revolutions as well, marking its entry into a new international legal domain by broadening its appeal among (counter-) revolutionaries.[35] This shift was linked directly to the changing international context of the post-war period, with the crumbling of several multinational empires and the emergence of new possibilities for restructuring the existing global order, as well as to the increasingly competitive humanitarian environment emerging after 1919.[36] At this stage, the ICRC witnessed the rise of several humanitarian competitors, above all the League of Red Cross Societies and the League of Nations, and it sought to become involved in the Russian Civil War, where that humanitarian competition was being fought.

The break-up of the German and Austro-Hungarian empires had led to civil strife in Silesia and a communist coup d'état in Hungary, where the ICRC first experimented with prison visits;[37] the independence of Ireland and Finland had caused brutal civil wars; and disappointment with the "Wilsonian moment" prompted several uprisings across the globe.[38] The aspirations of non-European peoples hoping for independence from colonial rule were crushed at the Paris Peace Conference in 1919. At this gathering, the Allied Powers

---

[33] Report Russian Red Cross for Red Cross Conference, 1921, La Bibliothèque du Comité international de la Croix Rouge, Geneva (ICRC Library).

[34] Mantilla, "Under (Social) Pressure," 99. The ICRC acted initially quite reluctantly, which nuances those claims that the ICRC had played a "pioneering role" in this period. Pablo La Porte, "Humanitarian Assistance during the Rif War (Morocco, 1921–6): The International Committee of the Red Cross and 'an Unfortunate Affair,'" *Historical Research*, Vol. 89, No. 243 (2016): 114–135, 119.

[35] Van Dijk, "Internationalizing Colonial War"; and Rainer Baudendistel, *Between Bombs and Good Intentions: The Red Cross and the Italo-Ethiopian War, 1935–1936* (New York: Berghahn Books, 2006), 27–30.

[36] Robert Gerwarth, *Vanquished: Why the First World War Failed to End* (London: Allen Lane, 2016).

[37] See André Durand, *De Sarajevo à Hiroshima* (Geneva: Institut Henry-Dunant, 2009), 164–165; Catherine Rey-Schyrr, *De Yalta à Dien Bien Phu. Histoire du Comité international de la Croix-Rouge 1945-1955* (Geneva: Georg-CICR, 2007), 241–242; and Mantilla, "Under (Social) Pressure," 97.

[38] For the "Wilsonian moment," see Erez Manela, *The Wilsonian Moment: Self-Determination and the International Origins of Anticolonial Nationalism* (Oxford: Oxford University Press, 2007); and Norman Graebner and Edward Bennett, *The Versailles Treaty and Its Legacy: The Failure of the Wilsonian Vision* (Cambridge: Cambridge University Press, 2014).

106 PREPARING FOR WAR

decided to keep hold of their imperial powers by setting up a Mandate system for those territories formerly belonging to the German and Ottoman empires.[39] Disappointment about this and other decisions to maintain imperial rule in a quasi-universal global order provoked a range of insurgencies, leading to increasing concern on the part of the mainly European delegates gathering at the 1921 Red Cross Conference about the humanitarian consequences of these new developments.

Much of the Czarist Russian proposal was finally adopted as part of a special resolution. This non-binding Resolution XIV, notably declaring that all victims of civil wars and revolutions had the right to be helped, not only implicitly condemned the Bolshevik atrocities but also recommended a set of new procedures for Red Cross interventions in civil wars. In particular, it suggested a theoretical model for intervention by different types of Red Cross societies; and it endorsed the direct application of certain humanitarian "principles," even if one side was not formally recognized as a belligerent.[40] Still, Resolution XIV, often hailed as the precursor to CA3, suffered from a number of serious shortcomings: it was of course non-binding, was far from comprehensive, failed to contest the exclusive doctrine of belligerency, and did very little to challenge colonial sovereignty outside Europe.

Despite such loopholes in the statute, in the following years civil war did become increasingly internationalized as the ICRC provided relief to thousands of victims of internal conflicts. Still, its actions focused largely upon Europe, mostly ignoring violence taking place outside of it,[41] and it later faced major problems in gaining access to victims of state terror, for instance in fascist Italy.[42] Following its largely failed mission in Russia in the early 1920s, the ICRC had decided to shift its attention to matters other than regulating civil wars, such as the protection of civilian populations during air bombing (see Chapter 5). The Genevans and their partners broke this status quo only when they began to re-consider in the early 1930s the definition of war itself, in the wake of the Kellogg–Briand Pact of 1928.

To understand why, it is important to realize the international legal implications for the laws of war of this treaty's prohibition on aggression, and look to

---

[39] Megan Donaldson, "The League of Nations, Ethiopia, and the Making of States," *Humanity* [2020]: 6–31.

[40] Résolutions et Voeux de la Xme Conférence Internationale de la Croix-Rouge, 1921, no. 43, American Red Cross Records, National Archives and Records Administration (NARA), College Park, MD.

[41] La Porte, "Humanitarian Assistance during the Rif War."

[42] La Porte's important account of the ICRC's actions during the Rif War has revealed how the 1921 model of working through National Red Cross Societies largely failed. See ibid., 126.

its effects on the practice of justifying wars after the Pact's acceptance. In 1931, during the Japanese invasion into Manchuria, the Red Cross already witnessed how these hostilities were not deemed "war" by Japanese authorities. The latter claimed these acts were so-called self-defense, and later staged "incidents" without filing a diplomatic notice beforehand, which made it virtually impossible for the ICRC to gain access to these disputed war zones.[43] Furthermore, because of the Kellogg–Briand Pact's outlawing of such aggressions, Japan's invasions were difficult to conceptualize from an international legal standpoint, at least from the perspective of advocates of regulating warfare.[44] This led to their invention of the term of "armed conflict," which would constitute the core of future drafts involving wars between or within states in the post-Pact era.

The Red Cross movement formed its response to these problems at its fifteenth conference in, again ironically, Tokyo. As we saw in Chapter 2, at this gathering in 1934, which was organized by the Japanese Red Cross partly in order to improve its government's discredited international image,[45] members agreed upon another resolution, expressing their wish to have humanitarian law applied to undeclared wars as well—described in this case as "armed conflicts not accompanied by a declaration of war," a carefully phrased reference to Japan's legally covert invasion of Manchuria.[46] To be sure, such concept of "armed conflict" had been discussed previously, but it was used much more frequently after 1928, when states became less inclined to declare war formally and preferred to stage hybrid so-called wars of self-defense. This process of recasting war as "armed conflict" had its origins in the interwar period rather than in the years after 1945 with the Nuremberg Trials' condemnation of aggression and CA3's emergence, as is sometimes assumed.

The Spanish Civil War

With the 1934 Monaco Draft staying silent on civil war, the second major interwar testing ground in Europe (after the Russian Civil War) during which the

---

[43] Baudendistel, *Between Bombs and Good Intentions*, 19. Other examples referred to in later ICRC reports were the Chaco War between Bolivia and Paraguay, the conflict between Italy and Abyssinia, and the civil war in Spain. Report on the Interpretation, Revision and Extension of the Geneva Convention of July 27, 1929, Page 1, 1938, no. 79, ARC, NARA.

[44] See Sidney Brown, "Application, en Cas d'Hostilités non Accompagnées d'une Déclaration de Guerre, des Conventions de Genève et de la Convention Relative au Traitement des Prisonniers de Guerre," *Revue Internationale de la Croix-Rouge*, Vol. 16, No. 186 (1934): 457–476.

[45] The Japanese Red Cross had more than two million adult members. Durand, *De Sarajevo à Hiroshima*, 239–242.

[46] Resolution XXXVIII of Tokyo Conference, 1934, no. 46, ARC, NARA.

108 PREPARING FOR WAR

ICRC attempted to widen the law's scope was the Spanish Civil War. This brutal conflict lacked a recognition of belligerency as a result of the major liberal powers' decision to formally endorse a policy of non-intervention, regardless of communist and fascist interventions.[47] Although the 1929 Conventions thus did not necessarily have to come into operation due to this non-recognition of belligerency, the ICRC pushed both sides to create ad hoc agreements and to openly declare their will to abide by the principles of those rules of warfare.[48] Despite their promises to comply with international law, the Republicans and Franco's armed forces both committed major atrocities during the war.[49] Even though often unsuccessful, the ICRC's attempts to gain respect for the Conventions in times of civil war led to renewed interest among its legal experts in the problem of how to legally regulate such conflicts, and about how to apply certain humanitarian principles to such situations.[50]

In October 1937, following the widely criticized Italian invasion of Ethiopia, the ICRC invited a number of experts connected to Red Cross Societies to Geneva in order to discuss the revision of humanitarian law. At this meeting, several issues related to its future scope were addressed. With respect to civil war, the report states that participants discussed in detail the existing treaties' application to "new" types of violent conflicts, including "cases of civil war, [and] conflicts between a mother country and a colony." Illustrating the continuing reluctance of the Red Cross, the idea of directly applying the treaty's provisions to internal conflicts was still not supported because "the principal contingency which it was desirable to provide for, namely civil war, has not been legally covered by it." Although not in favor of extending the Convention's scope, the delegates did feel sympathetic toward the proposition "that the Convention's [...] humanitarian principles must be respected under all circumstances, even when it is not juridically applicable [i.e. in large-scale civil war: BvD]."[51] By avoiding the sensitive question of belligerency, the delegates suggested that the application of the treaty's "moral" principles, not its legal provisions, could be extended to internal conflicts as well—a "splitting idea" that would continue to resonate in Red Cross circles.[52]

---

[47] The ICRC's operations were further hampered by the presence of two opposing Red Cross Societies—one based in Madrid, the other in Burgos.

[48] Most third powers adhered to a policy of non-intervention in the context of the Spanish Civil War. Mantilla, "Under (Social) Pressure," 114–115.

[49] Cullen, *The Concept of Non-International Armed Conflict*, 22.

[50] See Palmieri, "Une Neutralité sous Influence?"

[51] Report on the Interpretation, Revision and Extension of the Geneva Convention of July 27, 1929, Page 7–8, 1938, no. 79, ARC, NARA.

[52] Report on the Interpretation, Revision and Extension of the Geneva Convention of July 27, 1929, Page 7–8, 1938, no. 79, ARC, NARA.

In June 1938, in the wake of the breakdown of the international system, these proposals and the ICRC's own report on the issue of civil war were finally discussed at the Red Cross Conference in London.[53] Co-edited by Des Gouttes, the head of its Legal Division and Pictet's predecessor, the report suggested— without trying to undermine the doctrine of belligerency—specific procedures for how the Red Cross could intervene in times of internal war.[54] Its other suggestion was to create a more detailed list of applicable humanitarian principles. Derived from other texts of early humanitarian law, these principles referred, among other things, to the protection of political prisoners, of interned non-combatants, and the banning of reprisals. This resolution, as it was called, was intended to provide the ICRC and its partners with a "moral basis," not a legal one, for offering their services to the victims of internal wars.[55]

Another resolution discussed at the meeting in London was introduced by the Republican Spanish delegation as a response to the dire situation of those held in Nationalist hands. Most importantly, it proposed a more specific set of rules for regulating civil war. What is hardly surprising, though, is that these proposals were immediately resisted by the other Spanish delegation representing Franco's government, which had been invited by the ICRC.[56] Reflecting the destructive state of the international system at the time, one delegate wondered whether this moment was opportune to establish new rules when "feeling was still running so high." Concerned about the Third Republic's political instability, the French delegate agreed to postpone the discussion. When the Italian and Nazi German delegations also asked for adjournment of the debate, a major stalemate ensued.[57]

In response, the French delegation, while trying not to appear "indifferent to the exigencies of humanity,"[58] suggested a compromise solution by drafting a minimal set of very general principles acceptable to all delegations, and this was approved with just a few amendments. The revised text requested

---

[53] Durand, *De Sarajevo à Hiroshima*, 325–326; and Abi-Saab, *Droit Humanitaire et Conflits Internes*, 40–42.

[54] The original author was the Genevan judge Walter Yung. Max Huber and Paul des Gouttes later co-edited the text.

[55] Report IInd Commission, Summary of the Discussions of the Legal Commission, Page 31, 1938, no. 47, ARC, NARA.

[56] Report IInd Commission, Summary of the Discussions of the Legal Commission, 1938, no. 47, ARC, NARA.

[57] To appease states concerned about protecting their sovereignty and the doctrine of belligerency, he reassured them that "civil and international warfare were entirely different and the same rules could not apply to both." Report IInd Commission, Summary of the Discussions of the Legal Commission, 1938, no. 47, ARC, NARA.

[58] Report French Delegation London Conference, 1938, no. 1141, Unions Internationales 1907–1944, Les Archives Diplomatiques (LAD), Paris.

110 PREPARING FOR WAR

respect for the Conventions' humanitarian principles in times of large-scale civil war and demanded humane treatment for political prisoners. This resolution was approved by the delegates, but it lacked ambition and binding legal provisions for regulating internal wars. More specifically, it exerted few duties on states, failed to specify any of its general principles, or define civil war as such.[59]

Even though the 1938 London resolution featured some proto-legal precedents, such as allowing the ICRC to get involved in large-scale civil wars, it did not fundamentally challenge the sovereignty of (colonial) states with respect to their internal affairs. As a rule, these continued to keep strict control over their penal law policies regulating anti-colonial rebellion and insurgency. Yet this resolution, as well as that of other interwar texts regarding civil war, conveyed an important, now-forgotten dimension about the nature of interwar ICRC legal imaginations of regulating civil war. In many ways these represented significant legal steps in developing the idea of internationalizing conflicts within and outside empires, within and outside Europe, and thus potentially globally. Indeed, these interwar efforts seeking to reimagine state sovereignty within Europe created the foundations for the ICRC's interventions in Indonesia, Indochina, and Palestine immediately after the Second World War, which challenged colonial sovereignty in myriad ways.[60] These often forgotten interventions—and, though less so, those during the wars of decolonization after 1949[61]—were the real testing grounds for the ICRC with regard to internationalizing internal wars on a more global scale.

3.2 "Studied Vagueness"

The Second World War set into motion another wave of decolonization. Whereas Great Britain lost control over India, France was forced to grant independence to Syria and faced rebellion in Algeria. While the European metropole was celebrating Germany's unconditional surrender on 8 May 1945, the French gendarmerie shot anti-colonial activists protesting in the Algerian

[59] Report IInd Commission, Summary of the Discussions of the Legal Commission, 1938, no. 47, ARC, NARA.
[60] Junod, too, has argued that the "British did not forget the link that could be established between the ICRC's practices [on behalf of Palestinian Jews: BvD] and the evolution of international law." Dominique-Debora Junod, *The Imperiled Red Cross and the Palestine-Eretz-Yisrael Conflict 1945–1952: The Influence of Institutional Concerns on a Humanitarian Operation* (New York: Kegan Paul International, 1996), 55, 58.
[61] Klose, "The Colonial Testing Ground."

city of Sétif that same day.[62] With the start of revolutions in Indochina and Indonesia, both the French and Dutch empires experienced major crises, leading to renewed calls for ICRC intervention as a response to the wars of decolonization in South-East Asia and the Middle East.

In this decolonizing world, ICRC delegations started to claim their own place while transforming the international legal system. Among other things, they began contesting ideas of colonial sovereignty and constructed a new global stage for anti-colonial actors. For instance, Indonesian Republicans used the Conventions and the ICRC as a platform to strengthen their own international position. While reflecting on these developments, ICRC legal experts meanwhile started thinking about internationalizing internal war further by developing the Conventions in new, if not unexpected, directions.[63]

The ICRC legal experts first discussed "civil war" in mid-1946, when one of them raised the matter during an internal meeting.[64] Whereas some demanded the law's direct application to internal war, the ever-cautious Huber preferred a more discreet approach, being aware of the imperial powers' distaste toward the idea of giving up their sovereignty and empowering partisans (see Chapter 4). As a leading ICRC legal expert, Huber convinced his fellow drafters to raise the matter of internal war at future conferences only at "its margins."[65] In July 1946, one ICRC official tried again—with Pictet's support—to discuss the issue in more detail, but it again led to nothing. The ICRC finally decided to instruct its delegation to act carefully by suggesting the application of international law to civil war by mere analogy, testifying to its initially cautious attitude in an effort to keep the imperial powers on board.[66]

In mid-1946, several Red Cross representatives came to Geneva to try and change that attitude. One of their important points of discussion was the question of regulating "civil war," which was raised by Pictet on different occasions.[67] Contrary to a popular notion that the ICRC was primarily responsible for inserting the internal war clause, the strongest advocate at this stage for that idea was Castberg, the Norwegian human rights advocate.[68] Seeking to apply human rights in interstate and intrastate wars, he advocated powerfully for the

---

[62] David Painter and Melvyn Leffler, "The International System and the Origins of the Cold War," in *The Origins of the Cold War: An International History*, eds Melvyn Leffler and David Painter (New York: Routledge, 2002), 1–14, 9–10.

[63] For more details, see Van Dijk, "Internationalizing Colonial War."

[64] Note prepared by Meylan on the ICRC's role in Civil War, 29 April 1946, no. A PV JUR. 1, Vol. I, Les Archives du Comité International de la Croix-Rouge (ACICR), Geneva.

[65] Minutes of Seances Commission Juridique, 1 May 1946, no. A PV JUR. 1, Vol. I, ACICR.

[66] Minutes of Seances Commission Juridique, 24 July 1946, no. A PV JUR. 1, Vol. I, ACICR.

[67] Procès-Verbaux de la Commission I, no. CSN_1946_COMM1_PV_01, ICRC Library.

[68] Ibid.

112 PREPARING FOR WAR

internationalization of civil wars and opposed efforts to insert restrictive reciprocity clauses.[69] His enduring support for rights in wartime, his opposition to discrimination and torture, and his sense of the importance of humanizing civil wars charted the path toward the future of CA3.

Due to Castberg's efforts and Pictet's decision to break with his predecessor's approach, the 1946 Red Cross Experts Conference agreed to the internationalization of internal war, even though it undermined its force by means of accepting a reciprocity clause for at least one Convention. This implied that if one of the fighting parties expressly refused to abide by it, this treaty would no longer apply. This clause was intended to put pressure on insurgents in particular to comply with humanitarian law, but Castberg feared that it weakened the treaty's strength by making it vulnerable to manipulation. Still, signaling a major break with the prewar consensus to apply merely "moral" principles to internal wars, the Red Cross delegates agreed, thanks to Castberg's constant pressure, to directly apply international law to "civil war." Nonetheless, the precise scope of this category remained extremely vague.

The major drafting parties knew of course that the result of the 1946 Red Cross Conference was to provide preliminary answers only. Most tellingly, British and American government officials entirely ignored its plan for regulating internal wars. The ICRC, by contrast, took it far more seriously, and its interest and confidence in the matter of internal wars grew exponentially afterwards. Around this period, it also began sending new ICRC delegations to internal wars breaking out around the Mediterranean, in the Middle East, and across Asia. These small but pioneering missions across the globe strengthened the ICRC's resolve in further broadening humanitarian law's scope to internal wars.

In its reports for the 1947 Government Experts' Conference, ICRC legal experts, influenced by their efforts to secure the organization's future in response to Swedish and UN competition as well as Allied criticisms of its wartime record, advanced a proposal that would allow it to offer its services in times of internal war. They also made allusions to dropping reciprocity as a strict legal condition, thereby removing an important conceptual blockage for a future legal revolution, as we will see later.[70] This concept of reciprocity became a point of legal contestation for ICRC legal experts, even though they did not develop the 1946 Red Cross Conference's proposals much further and accepted a reciprocity clause regardless of Castberg's opposition.[71]

---

[69] Norwegian Memorandum, no. CSN_1946_DOCSN_01, ICRC Library.
[70] Van Dijk, "Internationalizing Colonial War."
[71] ICRC Preliminary Documents, no. CEG_1947_DOCPG_ENG_04, ICRC Library.

Unlike the ICRC, the French Inter-Ministerial Commission hardly reflected upon the outcome of the 1946 Red Cross Conference or the question of internal war. Initially, following the outbreak of the war in Indochina, the French even rejected the application of the 1929 Conventions to this conflict; in their view, no situation of belligerency existed and humanitarian law, including ICRC inspections, therefore did not apply. Due to anxieties about French nationals held hostage by Viet Minh forces, the French government changed its attitude somewhat, however, eventually requesting that the ICRC undertake its first mission in Indochina.[72]

When this issue of colonial war first came up for debate in the Inter-Ministerial Commission, in early 1947, the representative of the Ministry of Overseas Territories insisted on the need to protect "white non-combatant populations" against indigenous "massacres"—a reference to a racialized fear of subaltern violence against French colonial settlers.[73] But his warning remained unheard. Devoting most of its attention to partisans and civilians, as we saw earlier, the Inter-Ministerial Commission ignored the matter of internal war almost entirely, thereby poorly preparing French delegations for their future task.

Troubled Empires

By the time the Government Experts Conference gathered in April 1947, the international political landscape had changed considerably. The escalation of the wars in Palestine, Indochina, Indonesia, and Greece around mid-1947 had a direct impact on the way that the major drafting parties responded to the Red Cross plans to extend the Conventions to such types of internal wars. While having inadequately prepared their delegations for this matter, the three major Western Allied powers—France, Great Britain, and the US—were rather surprised when it was raised by Castberg in particular, who played a critical role during this debate. Calling it "new and unexpected," the alarmed British delegate Gardner tried immediately to suspend the debate about internal war in order to discuss the matter internally.[74]

---

[72] Van Dijk, "Internationalizing Colonial War."

[73] Compte-rendu de la Séance Commission Interministérielle, 10 January 1947, no. 160-BIS, Unions Internationales 1944–1960, LAD.

[74] Report Conference of Government Experts at Geneva, Introduction, 1947, no. 3795, FO369 (Foreign Office), The National Archives (TNA), Kew.

114 PREPARING FOR WAR

The question of regulating colonial war led to a whole range of problems, both legally as well as politically, for the imperial powers. Because they could no longer defend their imperial legal visions with antiquated language of "civilization," and because they had accepted ICRC interventions in Palestine, Indochina, and Indonesia, they had to resort to other legal methods to defeat the Red Cross proposals.[75] While regretting the ICRC's endorsement of a reciprocity clause, Castberg continued to push for extending the Conventions' scope to internal wars. Strikingly, the fairly moderate US delegation disliked some of his ideas but was said to be willing to accept a civil war clause for "humanitarian reasons,"[76] despite resistance from Greek royalist allies trying to keep their hands free during the Greek Civil War.

Unlike their US allies, the imperial delegations from France and Britain expressed far greater concern about the Red Cross proposals—while realizing it was impossible to reject them outright, as they had allowed ICRC officials entry into Indochina and Palestine.[77] Lamarle, a former protagonist in French–ICRC negotiations over Indochina and now the head of the French delegation, was said to be concerned, as he feared that a "growing tendency" to widen humanitarian law's scope to even "expeditions colonials" would have important implications for his government's efforts to destroy the Democratic Republic of Vietnam (DRV).[78] He was particularly concerned about the problem of the DRV's possible recognition, whose status as a potential belligerent had been resisted by French authorities thus far.[79] The 1947 conference put existing tensions—between colonial and indigenous claims of sovereignty; and between those for and against recognizing belligerency—under renewed pressure.

---

[75] For a broader history of colonialism, ideas of federalism, and global politics, see Michael Collins, "Decolonization and the 'Federal Moment,'" *Diplomacy and Statecraft* Vol. 24, No. 1 (2013): 21–40; Jennifer Foray, "A Unified Empire of Equal Parts: The Dutch Commonwealth Schemes of the 1920s–40s," *Journal of Imperial and Commonwealth History* Vol. 41, No. 2 (2013): 259–284; Spencer Mawby, *Ordering Independence: The End of Empire in the Anglophone Caribbean, 1947–69* (Basingstoke: Palgrave Macmillan, 2012); James Parker, *Brother's Keeper: The United States, Race, and Empire in the British Caribbean, 1937–1962* (Oxford: Oxford University Press, 2008). Frederick Cooper, *Citizenship Between Empire and Nation: Remaking France and French Africa, 1945–1960* (Princeton, NJ: Princeton University Press, 2014); Gary Wilder, *Freedom Time: Negritude, Decolonization, and the Future of the World* (Durham, NC: Duke University Press, 2015).

[76] Report of American Delegation to Government Experts' Conference, 1947, no. 674, Provost Marshal General, NARA.

[77] Procès-Verbaux de la Commission III, Vol. IV, p. 195, no. 37514, ICRC Library.

[78] Van Dijk, "Internationalizing Colonial War." Lamarle was one of the French officials involved in negotiating a deal with the ICRC for its access into Indochina. It is striking that the Malagasy Uprising was apparently never mentioned.

[79] Note Lamarle on Civilian Convention, 22 April 1947, no. 160, Unions Internationales 1944–1960, LAD.

In the end, the conference adopted a formula developed by Castberg, including a reference to civil war in "colonial" territories, which had been inserted by the Norwegian himself.[80] The US delegation wrote in its final report that

> there was unanimity of opinion as to such extension, and it was agreed to insert the following clause as a general remark: (...) the general humanitarian principles of the present Convention shall remain applicable in case of armed conflict within the frontiers of a State, unless one of the opposing parties expressly announces its intention to repudiate its obligations.[81]

Embarrassed by their Norwegian ally, Washington and its Western European partners did not recommend the application of the treaty's legal provisions, but agreed upon the inclusion of some "general principles," without specifying any of them, in a future draft. Indeed, they left vague the conditions constituting "civil war" and suggested a reciprocity clause, making the text very susceptible to strategic use by imperial powers especially. The British delegation accepted the text only as a "basis" for the debates to come, not as a potential draft.[82] Voicing even greater concern than his Anglophone colleagues, Lamarle inserted a reservation to the text, as he feared that its provisions might legally empower Vietnamese insurgents on the global stage.[83] Still, the Frenchman recognized, as did most of his imperial partners, that this text was far from finalized, and could still be subverted at future meetings.

In preparation for these, Gardner's delegation suggested to their colleagues in London that they look further into the matter of internal war. As the issue was a principle relevant to all the Conventions, both Interdepartmental Committees discussed it extensively. The War Office Committee, chaired by Gardner himself, deliberated on the question of civil war for the first time in October 1947, right after the British government had decided to withdraw from Palestine. Influenced by restrictive legal advice from Gutteridge of the Foreign Office, its members jointly agreed that the POW and Red Cross Conventions would come into operation only when the lawful government had recognized a situation of belligerency.[84]

---

[80] Minutes Bureau, 1947, pp. 10–11, no. CEG_1947_BURCONF_PV, ICRC Library.

[81] Report of American Delegation to Government Experts' Conference, Committee Reports Section 1, 1947, no. 674, Provost Marshal General, NARA.

[82] Van Dijk, "Internationalizing Colonial War."

[83] Minutes Plenary, 1947, p. 32, no. CEG_1947_ASSPLEN, ICRC Library.

[84] Minutes of Meeting War Office Committee, 15 October 1947, no. 326, WO163 (War Office), TNA.

116 PREPARING FOR WAR

The War Office Committee did not however oppose the civil war clause it-self. One reason for this was the perceived need to safeguard the protection of British soldiers held in the "enemy hands" of insurgents.[85] By contrast, showing the wider divisions within the British government, the Home Office Committee took a far more radical approach in opposing the civil war clause. While agreeing that the 1947 proposals for the POW and Red Cross Conventions may be accepted—"in the hope that by so doing, discussion of the precise inten-tions of its proposers may be avoided"—the Home Office Committee did not apply this view to the Civilian Convention. Protecting civilians from their own government should be dealt with by Roosevelt's UNCHR, it argued, partly be-cause it "now expressly avoids the imposition of obligations during a period of emergency." Indeed, UK officials were simultaneously trying to exclude colo-nial conflicts from the UNCHR's drafting radar. For British civil officials, the 1947 proposal for civilian protection directly violated the "fundamental right of the lawful government" to treat insurgents as "traitors," and should therefore be resisted.[86]

In April 1948, during a joint meeting with members from both Committees, British officials gathered again to discuss their division of opinion, seeking agreement on the civil war clause for future debates. In the first place, they agreed that the 1947 text needed stricter limitations to remain in line with ex-isting international law, as they understood it. For instance, they insisted that future Conventions should not impose any obligation on the British govern-ment unless it had recognized a situation of belligerency—which it had denied in the case of the Spanish Civil War, even. Neither the ICRC nor insurgents, British officials claimed, should be able to challenge this authorization: all at-tempts to make the Civilian Convention applicable in times of internal war should be similarly "resisted."[87]

Most critically, the formulae ultimately agreed upon, UK officials argued, should *not* specify what conditions constitute civil war, or who shall decide when those conditions obtain. Like their French allies, the British tried to leave undefined when a civil war clause could be applied, making a future draft ex-tremely vulnerable to strategic use. At all times, British officials stated, the delegation was to leave "open" the questions of what constituted a civil war, and how to decide upon this. As Gardner would later put it, they recognized that there existed an "advantage in a studied vagueness which would allow a

---

[85] Memorandum Gardner for War Office Committee, no. 326, WO163, TNA.
[86] Report Home Office Committee Civilian Convention, 1948, no. 2184, HO213 (Home Office), TNA.
[87] Minutes Meeting Civil War, 5 April 1948, no. 328, WO163, TNA.

lawful government some discretion in deciding whether to agree to apply the Convention."[88]

While the British Interdepartmental Committees were on a collision course, Pictet's drafting team was busy producing the first and eventually far more ambitious drafts of the new Conventions. Its legal specialists took radical steps by including a set of far-reaching articles, some of which would become part of every Convention, that is, the Common Articles. The second article covered the treaty's application and mentioned in its fourth paragraph three specific types of internal conflicts to which its provisions would apply: "civil war, colonial conflicts, and wars of religion," with the latter apparently referring to the antisemitic violence in Nazi Germany in the years before the war's outbreak.[89] In applying the treaty to "colonial conflicts," the ICRC was hoping to give itself a legal mandate to intervene in such wars in the future and to reshape decolonization in new ways.[90]

This list of relevant intrastate violence was placed within one new legal category that has become world famous: "armed conflicts which are not of an international character." As we saw earlier, this concept had its roots in the prewar period, when elements of it had referred, on the one hand, to undeclared interstate wars and, on the other, to the demand of Pictet's predecessor to apply the Conventions' "moral" principles to internal wars.[91] The ICRC legal experts also removed the reciprocity provision, since it might "render this stipulation valueless"—said one of their reports—"as one Party could always allege that its adversary disregarded some specific clause of the Convention." In August 1947, following the ICRC's tragic decision to leave Indochina because of a perceived lack of reciprocity, it had demanded the provision's removal and this was approved of by the leading Assembly.[92]

This may sound like a tiny alteration, but it represents a major shift in the ICRC's legal attitude toward internal wars, now opposing reciprocity as a means to put pressure on fighting parties to comply with humanitarian law. This change of legal attitude, striking at the sovereign's discretionary powers in internal wartime, was most likely triggered by the ICRC's recent challenges

---

[88] Minutes Meeting Interdepartmental Committee, 21 April 1948, no. 328, WO163, TNA.

[89] Draft Revised or New Conventions for the Protection of War Victims, May 1948, LOC. The wording of "civil war" referred to the Spanish and Chinese civil wars and that of "colonial conflicts" to the ICRC's engagements in Indochina, for instance. The reference to "wars of religion" is unclear. British officials later claimed that it might refer to the Holocaust. Letter Foreign Office to Home Office, 17 November 1948, no. 2185, HO213, TNA.

[90] Van Dijk, "Internationalizing Colonial War."

[91] The ICRC appeal of 12 March 1948 similarly discussed the application of the "principles" of the Geneva Conventions. Junod, *The Imperiled Red Cross*, 117–119.

[92] Minutes Meeting Assembly, August 1947, no. CR-238-4, ACICR.

118 PREPARING FOR WAR

in acquiring reciprocal legal support in Southeast Asia, and from the fighting parties in Palestine, for the Conventions' application.[93] Nevertheless, in order to keep the imperial powers on board, the ICRC gave its consent to the demand that the draft should in no way affect the post-war treatment, nor the legal status, of the insurgent party involved.[94]

When the ICRC's drafts with respect to Common Article 2 reached the other major drafting parties, they were almost immediately criticized.[95] The further escalation of colonial and civil wars in Asia, heightening East–West tensions, and the growing American involvement in the Greek Civil War around 1948 led to increasing anxiety among these drafting parties, and their respective preparatory committees, about the plan to extend the Conventions to internal war. The American Interdepartmental Prisoners of War Committee (POWC) disapproved of the ICRC drafts because of their "too broad" provisions.[96] It instructed its delegation to accept merely a civil war clause with a high threshold, combined with a reciprocity clause, "since insurrectionaries cannot be regarded as bound by international conventions."[97]

While expressing far less concern about the matter than its British and French counterparts, the US POWC accepted the idea of a civil war clause, but tried to restore the less binding language agreed upon in April 1947. For this reason, the US delegation was instructed to restrict the debate to merely "traditional humanitarian work" and "strongly oppose any move to discuss political questions," such as extending the treaties to emergencies.[98] US authorities wished to prevent at all times the possibility of the racial violence in the South being scrutinized by means of the Conventions.[99]

---

[93] Van Dijk, "Internationalizing Colonial War"; and Junod, *The Imperiled Red Cross*, 112–113, 116–120.

[94] Draft Revised or New Conventions for the Protection of War Victims, p. 6, May 1948, LOC. The ICRC kept insisting afterwards that giving consent to this demand was essential for the final acceptance of Common Article 3—"without it Article 3 would probably never have been adopted." Commentary published under the general editorship of Jean S. Pictet on the Second Geneva Convention, p. 38, 1960, LOC.

[95] It is relevant to note that the ICRC hardly reflected upon the air bombing dimensions of its proposals for civil and colonial war. It might have been that it was simply reluctant to do so out of fear that it might create even more opposition from its British, French, and American partners, but this remains speculation. It might also be that that the ICRC simply overlooked the entire question.

[96] Minutes Prisoners of War Committee, 17 May 1948, Provost Marshal General, no. 673, NARA.

[97] Report of US delegation to the Stockholm Red Cross Conference, Plenary Sessions of the Legal Commission—Appendix I, 1948, Provost Marshal General, no. 672, NARA.

[98] Position Paper for the Upcoming Stockholm Conference, p. 1, August 1948, no. 22, RG 43, 5536, NARA.

[99] See also Duncan Bell, *Empire, Race and Global Justice* (Cambridge: Cambridge University Press, 2019).

By contrast, Riegner's World Jewish Congress (WJC) promoted a text significantly broadening the scope of the ICRC drafts to even cases of "emergency."[100] This proposal not only challenged the ICRC's mostly pro-government attitude, as well as its trinity of large-scale civil, religious, and colonial conflicts, but also illustrates its legally unsatisfying answer to regulating so-called low intensity conflicts and political prisoners (see Chapter 2). In a later speech, Riegner would explain that numerous other cases of violence failed to develop into conflicts, "because," he said, "of the failure of one party to resist," and that these cases therefore failed to be covered by the existing proposals.[101] Alluding to the pogrom of Kristallnacht in 1938, he stated that "the armed forces of the country literally annihilated thousands of Jews, burning their houses, shops, and synagogues."[102] He introduced an amendment to the article's fourth paragraph which would extend its scope to "cases of emergency, due to violence or disturbances caused by national, racial or religious [though not political: BvD] groups."[103]

These criteria referred directly to the Jewish minorities which had suffered under Nazi or any other anti-Semitic rule, but the major drafting parties feared that they could easily be applied to other groups as well. The amendment could hypothetically be interpreted as giving protection to African-Americans suffering under racially motivated lynching attacks, or to the Viet Minh fighting against French imperial restoration. In its memorandum to the Stockholm conference the WJC tried to specify under which conditions a case of emergency was legally pertinent, by listing cases such as "organized disturbances, rioting, and other acts of physical aggression and violence directed against civilian groups for political and similar ends."[104]

---

[100] Report Legal Commission, Verbatim reports of meetings, p. 2, 1948, no. 22, ARC, NARA. For a broader history of the WJC, see Mark Lewis, "The World Jewish Congress and the Institute for International Affairs at Nuremberg: Ideas, Strategies, and Political Goals, 1942–1946," *Yad Vashem Studies*, Vol. 36, No. 1 (2008): 181–210; Michael Marrus, "The Three Jewish Émigrés at Nuremberg: Jacob Robinson, Hersch Lauterpacht, and Raphael Lemkin," in *Against the Grain: Jewish Intellectuals in Hard Times*, eds Ezra Mendelsohn, Stefani Hoffman, and Richard I. Cohen (New York and Oxford: Berghahn Books, 2014), 240–254.

[101] Report Legal Commission, Verbatim reports of meetings, p. 2, 1948, no. 22, ARC, NARA. With respect to this issue, the WJC had also referred in its memorandum to the article's second paragraph, which stated that the treaty was applicable to cases of occupation, irrespective of whether or not armed resistance had taken place.

[102] Report Legal Commission, Verbatim reports of meetings, p. 2, 1948, no. 22, ARC, NARA. In its pre-circulated memorandum, the WJC more specifically addressed elements from the anti-Jewish persecution in Nazi Germany during the 1930s. Memorandum of the WJC on the Draft Convention for the Protection of Civilian Persons in Time of War submitted to the XVIIth International Red Cross Conference, pp. 4–5, Series B69, no. 17, American Jewish Archives (AJC), Cincinnati, OH.

[103] Report Legal Commission, Verbatim reports of meetings, p. 2, 1948, no. 22, ARC, NARA.

[104] Memorandum of the WJC on the Draft Convention for the Protection of Civilian Persons in Time of War submitted to the XVIIth International Red Cross Conference, pp. 4–5, Series B69, no. 17, AJC.

120 PREPARING FOR WAR

The basic criterion ought to be, the WJC argued, that if state violence caused a "public emergency" it would make "humanitarian intervention," and thus the application of the Conventions, justifiable and even necessary. Riegner was aware, however, that the Conventions were "not to protect the people against their own Government."[105] Nonetheless, he thought it was important for the ICRC to make a strong statement by condemning all actions leading toward the violations of "the principles of such a [Human Rights] Charter."[106] In so doing, he directly challenged the doctrine of belligerency and tried to widen the second article's scope to even non-violent conflicts, for example political persecution, state terror, and racial discrimination. The Stockholm delegations of the major drafting parties, including the ICRC, however, wished to completely exclude precisely these cases from the future Conventions.

3.3 Preparing for a War of Attrition

The British, French, American, ICRC, and WJC delegations traveled to Sweden's capital for the Red Cross conference in August 1948.[107] The Legal Commission was split into a number of sub-commissions, including one to discuss the Sick and Wounded Convention and its future application. Its first meeting took place on 21 August 1948, with the Greek royalist law professor Michael Pesmazoglou presiding. Less than a week later, this sub-commission began to discuss the problem of the treaty's application, causing a great deal of confusion and chaos among the delegates.[108]

According to some delegates, the main cause of this confusion concerned the fact that Pesmazoglou first raised the treaty's application by trying to make the recognition of belligerency dependent upon a majority decision of the UN Security Council's permanent members, a privileged group dominated by states with an anti-communist outlook.[109] Frustrated by its Greek ally's restrictive approach, the US delegation opposed his proposal, introducing another

---

[105] This, Riegner and the ICRC thought, was to be done by the to-be-signed UN Charter of Human Rights, or perhaps the Genocide Convention, for which he had also advocated.

[106] Memorandum of the WJC on the Draft Convention for the Protection of Civilian Persons in Time of War submitted to the XVIIth International Red Cross Conference, pp. 4–5, Series B69, no. 17, AJC.

[107] Abi-Saab, *Droit Humanitaire et Conflits Internes*, 47–49.

[108] Report of US delegation to the Stockholm Red Cross Conference, Plenary Sessions of the Legal Commission—Appendix D, 1948, Provost Marshal General, no. 672, NARA.

[109] Report Clattenburg for State Department, September 1948, no. 22, RG 43, 5536, NARA; and Report Legal Commission, Summary of the debates of the Sub-Commissions, August 1948, no. 22, ARC, NARA.

text with a reciprocity clause.[110] ICRC representative Pictet, acting in line with his instructions, opposed both amendments. Lacking wide support, both the Greek and American proposals failed to pass the vote—one was withdrawn beforehand, the other was rejected.[111]

The fact that the other sub-commission studying the POW Convention finally did adopt a reciprocity clause exemplifies the confusing nature of this ill-coordinated drafting debate—according to US delegate Clattenburg, it was the "most confused discussion experienced during the entire Conference."[112] The WJC proposal first came up for debate and it fell largely on deaf ears. Calling it a "sensitive issue," Pilloud said to abstain.[113] According to a disappointed WJC delegate, he "dismissed [this proposal] whilst the United Nations was [still] discussing the human rights declaration."[114] As a former observer at the UNCHR's meetings in Geneva, Pilloud was very much aware of the problem of the imperial powers trying to suspend that declaration in time of emergency.

However, Pilloud admitted privately that it would be difficult for the Great Powers to ever accept the far-reaching infringements on their sovereignty suggested by Riegner's WJC.[115] Similarly, the Legal Commission almost unanimously thought that the WJC's suggestion undermined the state's sovereign right too severely, and it preferred a more "general clause," as Pilloud liked to put it.[116] The amendment was rejected overwhelmingly, to the relief of the imperial powers.[117]

Around this stage of the debate the US delegation reintroduced the reciprocity clause, to the ICRC's disappointment.[118] William Mott, a legal officer representing the US Navy, stressed that "it would be impossible in the case of a colonial conflict, where one party consisted of bandits, to require them to observe the Convention. That party would not be bound as would be the

---

[110] The US delegation later started to regret inserting a reciprocity clause into the draft for the Sick and Wounded Convention. Report Legal Commission, Summary of the debates of the Sub-Commissions, August 1948, no. 22, ARC, NARA.

[111] To keep states on board, Pictet advanced a third amendment asking for the replacement of the word "provisions" with "humanitarian principles," and this suggestion was received favorably. Report Legal Commission, Summary of the debates of the Sub-Commissions, August 1948, no. 22, ARC, NARA. This fact of lacking specific provisions was also noted in the Commentary of 1960. Jean Pictet, *The Geneva Conventions of 12 August 1949: Commentary* (Geneva: ICRC, 1960).

[112] Report of US delegation to the Stockholm Red Cross Conference, Plenary Sessions of the Legal Commission, Appendix I, 1948, Provost Marshal General, no. 672, NARA.

[113] Minutes CJ, pp. 36–57, no. CI_1948_COMJUR_01, ICRC Library.

[114] Cable WJC Delegation, August 1948, Series B69, no. 17, AJC.

[115] Letter Pilloud to Strahler, 15 June 1948, no. CR-243-11, ACICR.

[116] Minutes CJ, pp. 36–57, no. CI_1948_COMJUR_01, ICRC Library.

[117] Report Legal Commission, Verbatim Reports of Meetings, 1948, no. 22, ARC, NARA; Report British Observer at Stockholm Conference, 3 September 1948, no. 328, WO163, TNA; and Report of US delegation to the Stockholm Red Cross Conference, 1948, Provost Marshal General, no. 672, NARA.

[118] Minutes CJ, pp. 36–57, no. CI_1948_COMJUR_01, ICRC Library.

122 PREPARING FOR WAR

contracting party."[119] Seeking the support of the imperial powers, Washington tried to portray anti-colonial activists as terrorists with no legitimate political demands. Supporting Mott's derogatory statements, the Greek royalist Pesmazoglou stated that the Conventions could not be directly applied to internal wars, as it might lead to a situation in which insurgents could profit from aid being given to them by a protecting power. This might, of course, be a "foreign power with a political interest in supporting them"—a clear reference to the threat of communist involvement in the Greek Civil War.[120]

Dominating the debate, many Western bloc delegations (except some of the Nordic ones) shared an understanding about these issues. The Dutch delegation very much disliked the "far-reaching" ICRC proposals.[121] Most importantly, the French delegation suggested omitting "any attempt," Clattenburg wrote, "to specify the kind of armed conflict which are not international in character."[122] It thus requested the complete removal of every specific reference to colonial conflicts.

The French proposal was presented by Cahen-Salvador himself. He feared that Common Article 2 might be directly applied to his country's escalating counterinsurgency campaign in Indochina against the Viet Minh insurgents. To prevent this, he tried to leave vague the conditions under which the internal war clause would become legally pertinent.[123] Seeking to protect French colonial interests, Cahen-Salvador's amendment was finally accepted by an overwhelming majority, as many delegates either preferred to leave ambiguous the precise scope of the clause, or erroneously believed it sought to widen the law's application.[124] To the ICRC's disappointment, the Stockholm conference also agreed upon a reciprocity clause to the article's fourth paragraph in the POW and Civilian Conventions.

The ICRC had to walk a thin line between, on the one hand, supporting the demands from the Great Powers seeking to protect their major strategic interests and, on the other hand, advocating for its own mission to enhance the

[119] Report Legal Commission, Verbatim Reports of Meetings, 1948, no. 22, ARC, NARA.

[120] Report of US delegation to the Stockholm Red Cross Conference, Plenary Sessions of the Legal Commission, Appendix I, 1948, Provost Marshal General, no. 672, NARA.

[121] Rapport van Nederlandse Delegatie XVII Internationale Rode Kruis Conference te Stockholm, Algemene Artikelen, 1948, Code-Archief Ministerie van Buitenlandse Zaken, no. 3049, National Archives of the Netherlands (NA), The Hague.

[122] Report of US delegation to the Stockholm Red Cross Conference, Plenary Sessions of the Legal Commission, Appendix I, 1948, Provost Marshal General, no. 672, NARA.

[123] The ICRC's remarks from the 1950s simply denied the relevance of imperial concerns by incorrectly stating that the "Stockholm Conference [...] rejected this reference, but did so only because too rigid a definition might allow belligerents to escape their obligations." Analysis for the use of National Red Cross Societies, p. 6, Vol. 2, 1950, LOC.

[124] Report Legal Commission, Verbatim Reports of Meetings, 1948, no. 22, ARC, NARA.

protections for victims of large-scale internal wars. If it supported far-reaching proposals such as the one introduced by the WJC covering "low intensity" conflicts, a stalemate would probably result, or worse. However, if it entirely followed the line laid down by those major states, there was a real chance that Common Article 2 would be nothing more than an impracticable compromise text. It finally pushed the plenary to accept a draft that would internationalize only large-scale internal wars.

"Manifestly Absurd"

Despite these compromises, British civilian agencies still responded anxiously to the 1948 Stockholm drafts, stating that "none of the Conventions should apply to [...] racial riots [or] armed disturbances in the Colonies."[125] The Foreign Office called the draft's relevant section on internal war "totally objectionable."[126] The Security Services stated that "it would be manifestly absurd for the Convention to be [applied to the] Communists in Malaya." They feared that "similar troubles might in the future flare up in other parts of the Colonial Empire [as well]."[127] This places into further doubt the assumption that no legal architect had ever "foreseen" the future outbreak of wars of decolonization—to the contrary.[128]

The Home Office, as in the case of the Foreign Office,[129] the Colonial Office, and the Security Services, focused its attention chiefly on the Civilian Convention, "intensely disliking its mention of civil war."[130] Based upon Gutteridge's restrictive legal advice, it alleged that this element would directly undermine Britain's sovereignty and its stress upon nationals holding "unqualified allegiance." Moreover, it expressed concern that, under influence of the heightening East–West tensions as a result of the Berlin blockade, this might lead to "misrepresentation by subversive interests [i.e. by Communists] in colonial territories."[131] For these reasons, the Home Office Committee—taking a

---

[125] Report Frank Newsam on Civil War, 28 January 1949, no. 2173, HO213, TNA.

[126] Revised Briefing for UK delegation, 11 February 1949, no. 4145, FO369, TNA.

[127] Letter Hill to Speake, 10 November 1948, no. 2185, HO213, TNA.

[128] The head of the ICRC's Commentaries update project Jean-Marie Henckaerts has argued that "it has been in this area [of Common Article 3] that we see the biggest development in the past 60 years; something the drafters of the Conventions couldn't have foreseen at the time." Link: http://blogs.icrc. org/law-and-policy/2017/02/01/behind-the-scenes-updated-commentary-on-the-first-geneva-conv entions/ (retrieved 1 March 2017).

[129] Note Foreign Office Civil War, 25 January 1949, no. 4143, FO369, TNA.

[130] Letter Strutt to Craigie on Civil War, 16 December 1948, no. 3970, FO369, TNA.

[131] Note Foreign Office Civil War, 25 January 1949, no. 4143, FO369, TNA.

124 PREPARING FOR WAR

radically restrictive view on this matter—insisted upon deleting all references to civil war in the future Civilian Convention.

The War Office Committee agreed in principle, but embraced a set of less restrictive diplomatic "methods to [...] secure the exclusion of enemy agents and Franc tireurs" (see Chapter 4).[132] In response, it suggested applying both the POW and Civilian Conventions to a "de facto civil war," such as a major internal war in which belligerent rights had been granted to "law-abiding" insurgents. The War Office, concerned about the protection of its troops, objected to the Home Office Committee's plan to allow punishment of insurgents as "criminals," fearing that this "would almost certainly" lead to brutal counter-reprisals.[133]

In relation to this, signaling a shift in diplomatic attitudes toward regulating internal wars, Gardner admitted that increasing public pressure to apply the Conventions to such armed conflicts as a result of "recent years [of] conflicts in Spain, China, Indonesia, and Palestine [was] almost impossible [...] to resist." By accepting an internal war clause, he argued, the British government would still be able to determine international law's application, thereby securing almost absolute sovereignty in its domestic affairs. To secure its diplomatic–military interests, the War Office Committee thus pragmatically agreed to a weak civil war clause, with the additional reservation that its application could be determined by the state alone, not by insurgents or the ICRC.[134]

Gathering in March 1949, the Labour Cabinet had to finally decide whether it would side with its civilian or military Interdepartmental Committee.[135] Diverging from its usual approach, it decided to adopt the former's views for this question, opposing humanitarian law's direct application to internal conflicts. Why? The Cabinet's decision was influenced by, on the one hand, severe opposition from its two legal ministers who insisted on accepting the Home Office Committee's radical proposals,[136] and, on the other, its growing fears about inciting upheaval across the empire through international legal means. Consequently, it rejected Gardner's less aggressive approach, fearing that it might "jeopardize [its] security," and instructed its delegation to take a most

---

[132] Letter Strutt to Craigie on Civil War, 16 December 1948, no. 3970, FO369, TNA.

[133] Briefing War Office for Cabinet, 26 March 1949, no. 14041, WO32, TNA.

[134] Ibid.

[135] The meeting was attended by Prime Minister Clement Attlee, the Lord Chancellor, the Secretary of State for War, the Home Secretary, the Attorney-General, the Under-Secretary of State at the Foreign Office, Gardner, and Craigie, head of the future UK delegation.

[136] Beckett, from the Foreign Office: "Now, I am afraid there is some truth in this, and it is to be noticed how largely the decisions of Ministers on this matter have been influenced by the legal Ministers, namely the Lord Chancellor and the Attorney-General." Comments Beckett on Letter Craigie, 10 May 1949, no. 4149, FO369, TNA.

restrictive approach.[137] Amplifying its decision, Attorney General Hartley Shawcross, who also served as the British lead prosecutor at the Nuremberg trials, insisted "that <u>none</u> of the Conventions should apply to civil war."[138] If it had to yield on this point, he stressed, then it had to resist "to the bitter end."[139] These strict instructions, the UK delegation leader Craigie realized,[140] left him no choice other than to "settle down to a war of attrition," potentially leading to a götterdämmerung of his delegation's prestige.[141]

The French Inter-Ministerial Commission, too, was hardening its views with regard to internal war around this period, though not to the extent of its aggressive British counterpart. In April 1949, with the escalating Indochina War, the French Foreign Ministry suddenly sounded major alarm, arguing that the Stockholm draft's relevant section was "extremely dangerous." Indeed, it expressed concern that it might empower Vietnamese "brigands" and open the door for communist interventionism in the war. To prevent this, it demanded that insurgents in times of internal war would have to comply with strict conditions, while leaving conspicuously vague the matter of when these applied.[142] Indeed, French diplomats told the British during informal talks precisely what their real, far more destructive strategy entailed.

With regard to internal war, Lamarle's delegation was said to be unwilling to take the lead in this matter. The fear was that doing so might undermine its simultaneous efforts to secure certain human rights provisions for civilians and partisans in occupied territory during interstate wars, an important element that has been overlooked in the existing literature.[143] If the British were to suggest excising the internal war clause, Lamarle added, his delegation would first support it "generally" and then propose a compromise. This text would have to feature "sufficiently widely drawn exceptions [...] to make it largely inapplicable," it was agreed. In the case of this text's defeat, Lamarle's delegation "would gladly accept complete deletion," noted a relieved British official.[144] This imperial plot not only felt awkward for the French victims of Nazi empire, as they opposed the British on many other drafting issues (see Chapters 2 and

---

[137] Minutes Meeting Cabinet, 28 March 1949, no. 46, CAB130, TNA.

[138] The Foreign Office was very pleased with the outcome of the Cabinet meeting. See Report on Cabinet Meeting and Civil War, 31 March 1949, no. 4147, FO369, TNA.

[139] Opinion of Attorney-General on Civil War, April 1949, no. 4148, FO369, TNA.

[140] The leader of the UK delegation, Craigie, was a retired diplomat who had served as the British representative to the UN War Crimes Commission. He was also the ambassador to Japan, until the Second World War broke out in the Pacific.

[141] Report British Delegation, no. 6036, ADM116, TNA.

[142] Report Meeting with French Delegation, 18 April 1949, no. 4150, FO369, TNA.

[143] Mantilla, "Under (Social) Pressure"; and Best, *War and Law since 1945*.

[144] Report Meeting with French Delegation, 18 April 1949, no. 4150, FO369, TNA.

126   PREPARING FOR WAR

4), but it also strengthened, if not emboldened, the British delegation's will to fight on in order to win the expected war of attrition.

Initially, Craigie's efforts to gain similar assurances from his American colleagues appeared fruitful. In February 1949 he had spoken informally with Harrison, the head of the US delegation and an equally experienced diplomat, and his State Department deputy Yingling, who gave him the impression that they shared Whitehall's doubts about the internal war clause. In his reports to London, Craigie wrote that he expected them to oppose plans to directly apply the POW and Civilian Conventions to internal conflicts.[145] He was wrongly informed, however, as the Cabinet's decision to firmly oppose the internal war clause led to significant American opposition.

Unlike the British government, the US POWC had no objection to a civil war clause as such. It only demanded from its own representatives that they take note of one of its main concerns with respect to this issue: the potential extension to cases of "insurrection not stabilized into civil war." In such cases, the POWC instructed, the *de jure* government should have the right to maintain its authority and put down, for instance, a Communist-inspired rebellion "without the hampering restrictions of the Convention."[146] In this context, the Committee remained under the influence of the early Cold War. In other cases of large-scale internal wars, however, the POWC—using the large-scale war of the anti-communist Indonesian Republic as its model[147] — could see room for accepting a substitute paragraph if it met several conditions: most prominently, it had to include a robust reciprocity clause.[148] Continuing its former approach, Pictet's drafting team agreed in principle to the imperial powers' exclusion of "lower intensity" conflicts. In its preparatory report, it claimed that the internal war clause must be applied only if "hostilities not of an international character [...] have taken on such dimensions that their conduct can no longer be regulated by municipal legislation."[149] However, as previously, it did not insist on a more expansive clause: it merely continued pressing for the deletion of reciprocity clauses. Supporting these proposals, Swiss diplomats hoped that their own delegation would endorse them, in order to counter

[145] Minutes of Meeting US and UK delegations, 28 February 1949, no. 4144, FO369, TNA.
[146] United States Draft for the Revision of the Convention for the Protection of Civilians Persons in Time of War of the Committee on Prisoners of War, March 1949, Provost Marshal General, no. 673 - Part 2, NARA.
[147] It is important to realize that the UK and US governments had recognized de facto the insurgent Republican government.
[148] United States Draft for the Revision of the Convention for the Protection of Civilians Persons in Time of War of the Committee on Prisoners of War, p. 2, March 1949, Provost Marshal General, no. 673 - Part 2, NARA.
[149] Remarks and Proposals submitted by the ICRC, 1949, 36–38, ICRC Library.

radical British opposition.[150] Acknowledging its lack of recent experiences with civil war, the Swiss delegation eventually decided to act as a "mediator," thus not making any specific recommendations out of fear of annoying the Great Powers.[151]

3.4 The Fall and Rise of Common Article 3

To the surprise of almost everyone, in April 1949, the Soviet Union decided not just to end its boycott of the ICRC, traveling to Switzerland to participate in the drafting of humanitarian law, but also to endorse its proposals for regulating civil and colonial wars.[152] The Soviet delegation, noted various delegates, initially accepted the Stockholm draft, but later aimed at as far-reaching a clause as possible: "their unstated reason," believed a Canadian delegate, "being that such a clause could create enormous legal troubles for a government trying to put down a Communist-inspired rebellion."[153] During the gathering of the Joint Committee, in which the discussion regarding the relevant common article took place, the communist Hungarian delegate said that the conference's essential aim was to extend humanitarian law's scope "as much as possible." In his view, the Stockholm draft had done undue damage to it by including a reciprocity clause, and this part had to be radically revised.[154]

The Soviet-aligned delegations entered Geneva prepared to endorse the internal war clause as part of the Conventions provided that they would be able to keep the door closed for outside inspectors. Based on Leninist and Stalinist doctrines and the perceived lack of protection for communist insurgents in Greece and elsewhere,[155] Slavin's delegation turned the final stage of the drafting process into a sort of a postcolonial forum in which Western imperial powers could be harshly criticized. As they had done before at the UN, the Soviets tried to incorporate principles of national self-determination and decolonization into the Conventions' genetic code.[156] By using this anti-colonial

---

[150] Note Micheli for Petitpierre, 5 April 1949, no. J2.118#1968/77_bd.13, Swiss Federal Archives (SFA), Bern.

[151] Minutes Meeting Swiss delegation, 5 April 1949, no. J2.118#1968/77_bd.13, SFA.

[152] Jiří Toman, "L'Union Soviètique et le Droit des Conflits Armés," Ph.D. Dissertation, University of Geneva, 1997, 78–79.

[153] Report of Canadian Delegation to Geneva Conference, 1949, no. RG 19, Vol. 480-112-20, Library and Archives Canada (LAC), Ottawa, ON.

[154] Final Record of the Diplomatic Conference of Geneva of 1949, Vol. II, Section B, p. 11, Library of Congress (LOC), Washington, DC.

[155] Toman, "L'Union Soviètique et le Droit des Conflits Armés," 80.

[156] Eric Weitz, *A World Divided: The Global Struggle for Human Rights in the Age of Nation-States* (Princeton, NJ: Princeton University Press, 2019), 297.

128 PREPARING FOR WAR

argument strategically, they obtained a powerful weapon to isolate the Western imperial powers on the global stage.[157] With liberal reporters similarly pushing for the law's extension, Western representatives had no choice but to engage with those Soviet proposals.[158]

The delegations at Geneva repeatedly changed their strategies and views on the internal war clause, but as a whole they advanced roughly four different propositions: (1) that the Stockholm draft should be maintained with a few revisions, such as removing its reciprocity clauses—"the Stockholmers option"; (2) that the Conventions should be applicable to most internal armed conflicts—the official Soviet position; (3) that they should not be applicable at all—the "nuclear option"; or (4) that they should be applicable only in large-scale internal armed conflicts with specially designated characteristics. Many delegations representing liberal empires were advised by their own preparatory committees to support either the third option, that is, the rejection of the article's fourth paragraph; or, especially in harsh diplomatic circumstances, to limit its scope to a bare minimum (option 4).

Fearing uprisings in Quebec,[159] the Canadians agreed to endorse either option 4 or, preferably, the deletion of the article's entire fourth paragraph.[160] Among these skeptical delegations, the Dutch, the New Zealanders, and especially the British remained the most critical of the internal war clause, preferring the nuclear option.[161] In many ways, they had no idea what they were getting into at the diplomatic conference, and expected crucial voting majorities to be obtained relatively easily.[162] The US delegation's draft may have also opposed the Stockholm text's solution, calling it "not satisfactory," but it left significant room to accept an alternative proposal along the lines of option 4.[163]

---

[157] Mantilla, *Lawmaking under Pressure*, 59.

[158] For more details about the impact of normative pressure, see Mantilla, *Lawmaking under Pressure*; Giovanni Mantilla, "Forum Isolation: Social Opprobrium and the Origins of the International Law of Internal Conflict," *International Organization*, Vol. 72, No. 2 (2018): 317–349; and Giovanni Mantilla, "Social Pressure and the Making of Wartime Legal Protection for Civilians," *European Journal of International Relations*, Vol. 26, No. 2 (2019): 444–468.

[159] Report of Canadian Delegation to Geneva Conference, 1949, 10, no. 112-20 RG 19 – Vol. 480, LAC.

[160] Commentary on the Draft Convention for the Protection of Civilians Persons in Time of War of the Interdepartmental Committee on the Revision of the Geneva Conventions, February 1949, RG 19, Vol. 480-112-20, LAC.

[161] Two examples are: British Memorandum on the Proposed New Conventions for the Protection of War Victims, 24th January 1949, A472, W32574, Part 1, National Archives of Australia (NAA), Canberra, ACT; Letter J.J. van Houten to M.W. Mouton, 11 April 1949, no. 272, Archief Rode Kruis Nederland (ARKN), The Hague.

[162] Report on Voting Strengths, 7 April 1949, no. 4148, FO369, TNA.

[163] United States Draft for the Revision of the Convention for the Protection of Civilians Persons in Time of War of the Committee on Prisoners of War, March 1949, Provost Marshal General, no. 673 - Part 2, NARA.

Generally speaking, the US delegation was supported by its loyal Australian allies.

The opening phase of the negotiating process took place in the Joint Committee, where the liberal imperial powers and the so-called Stockholmers, a group of strange bedfellows from both Communist and Western bloc delegations supporting the Stockholm drafts, were divided into different factions. Whereas Pilloud continued to press for deleting the reciprocity clauses, the French delegation feared that the ICRC and other delegates had lost sight of the "rights of States," according to its deputy head Lamarle: "it was impossible to carry the protection of individuals to the point of sacrificing the rights of States."[164]

Lamarle's statement was a painful reminder for Jewish observers of the apparent force of Nazi legalism. It also put pressure on the position of Cahen-Salvador's colleague as a member of a delegation seeking to uphold "civilization" in the post-Nazi period. For this reason, Lamarle apologized the next day, suggesting that by "rights of the State" he had not wished to imply rights in the way that fascist regimes had done in recent times. This slip of the tongue demonstrates the awkward position from which Lamarle and other liberal imperial delegates interpreted this drafting process. They tried to neatly distinguish between the actions of their former Nazi occupier and their own in Indochina. For the French especially, this attempt to apply rights conceptions to European occupation while trying to legally sideline the wars of decolonization proved extremely difficult at times.

After the British opposed the internal war clause, the French proposed, with support from an Italian delegate who feared another civil war after the anti-fascist victory in 1945, a new amendment making it impossible for small-scale "disorder, anarchy or brigandage" to be covered by the Conventions. Only if the armed forces were well organized, belonged to a responsible authority capable of respecting humanitarian law, and held control over a "given territory" could these cases of internal war be protected by it.[165] Despite criticism from Castberg and other "Stockholmers," who argued that states' rights should not prevail over humanitarian considerations, the French proposal enjoyed "a considerable measure of support in the conference," as one delegate reported.[166]

The regressive Burmese delegation, whose government was trying to suppress an insurgency at home, tried to remove the Stockholm draft from the

---

[164] Final Record of the Diplomatic Conference of Geneva of 1949, Vol. II, Section B, pp. 12–13, LOC.
[165] Final Record of the Diplomatic Conference of Geneva of 1949, Vol. II, Section B, p. 10, LOC.
[166] Cable from Australian Delegation to Department of External Affairs, May 6 1949, A472, W32574 - Part 2, NAA.

130 PREPARING FOR WAR

negotiating table. Likewise, the Nationalist Chinese delegate Wu Nan-ju held that that text was "too sweeping" and expressed support for restrictions as proposed by Lamarle and Harrison. The American leader had suggested an alternative, with some Commonwealth support, that would allow the law's application to "certain armed conflicts within the territory of a State party."[167] The treaty, in his view, should be applicable merely to large-scale internal wars in which rebels had gained belligerent rights by having met a specific list of requirements.

This list of conditions (insurgents had to be well organized, exercise de facto authority over persons within a demarcated territory, and so on) would become an important basis for future discussions regarding Common Article 2. The proposed alternative, however, was far from perfect: it did not clearly identify the relevant armed conflict, for instance. Among others, Castberg warned about these dangers and added that if the French proposal was accepted it could lead to a situation in which one party could declare without proof that its opponent was not in a position to ensure order, and then prosecute it by means of harsh penal laws, as the French had done previously.[168]

Whereas the French and American proposals received some criticism,[169] the British plan to basically delete the entire intern war clause was rejected almost unanimously. "There is no doubt," wrote Craigie to the Foreign Office, "[that] we shall be alone in adopting a purely negative attitude on this subject."[170] In this early stage of the discussion, the British leader repeatedly expressed concern about the loss of Britain's prestige, the critical press reports in Britain and Switzerland,[171] and its strained relations with, especially, Harrison's delegation.[172]

Despite all his delegation's lobbying "dans les coulisses,"[173] he realized the impossibility of keeping internal war out, of winning the war of attrition, and asked the Foreign Office to request new instructions.[174]

These revised guidelines, Craigie argued, should be much more flexible and centered around "some formula which, while not dotting i's, would [...] leave the last word to the sovereign powers."[175] In essence, this meant that, while

---

[167] Final Record of the Diplomatic Conference of Geneva of 1949, Vol. II, Section B, pp. 10–16, LOC.
[168] Final Record of the Diplomatic Conference of Geneva of 1949, Vol. II, Section B, pp. 10–16, LOC.
[169] Final Record of the Diplomatic Conference of Geneva of 1949, Vol. II, Section B, pp. 10–15, LOC.
[170] Letter Craigie to Foreign Office, 9 May 1949, no. 4149, FO369, TNA. For criticisms towards the British delegation's actions, see Cable US delegation to State Department, 2 May 1949, no. 5, RG43 - 40, NARA; and Cable Lamarle Civil War, 28 April 1949, no. 161, Unions Internationales 1944–1960, LAD.
[171] Mantilla, Lawmaking under Pressure, 85.
[172] See Minutes of Meeting with Mayhew, 19 May 1949, no. 4151, FO369, TNA.
[173] Letter Craigie to Foreign Office, 9 May 1949, no. 4149, FO369, TNA.
[174] Interim Report UK Delegation, 4 May 1949, no. 4149, FO369, TNA.
[175] Letter Craigie to Foreign Office, 9 May 1949, no. 4149, FO369, TNA.

continuing to principally oppose the internal war clause, Craigie desired to reintroduce Gardner's old plan to create an alternative draft based upon the dictum of so-called studied vagueness, which would leave Britain's colonial sovereignty largely intact. While endorsing his suggestion, the Foreign Office expressed doubts as to whether Whitehall would change its mind on this question.[176]

Near-Death

The skeptics were initially proven right. The hawkish Shawcross, in particular, firmly opposed any proposal that would potentially hinder British colonial officials from punishing insurgents as traitors: "it must be remembered that these Conventions," he told the Foreign Office, "affect the Colonial powers more seriously than any others [...] [and] it is charming to find the USSR [...] advocating the application of the Convention to civil war [as] they have taken pretty good care [...] that civil war could never occur [there again]," he added cynically.[177] Struggling to find support at home, Craigie was forced to delay the conference's proceedings in Geneva until Attlee's Cabinet had decided what it would do next.

The French, too, were starting to rethink their original views on internal war, but in a completely different way—to the disappointment of Harrison's delegation. Hardening their attitude, the French change in tactics seemed to have been caused by a shift from above, namely, Paris, demanding a stricter course on this issue. Responding to the first debates in Geneva, the Ministry of Interior and Ministry of Overseas Territories, which seem not to have been directly involved in the drafting of the Foreign Ministry's instructions, gathered for a special session in early May 1949 to discuss new guidelines for the matter of internal war. Dissatisfied with the Foreign Ministry's previous proposals, they came up with three new instructions: question the conference's competence in internal war affairs; accept the law's application to international wars only; and, in the case of heavy resistance, propose a compromise with a non-binding declaration for specifically internal conflicts (i.e. not signing any binding provision on internal war).[178] Bringing the French and British positions together,

---

[176] See Letter Caccia to Craigie, 12 May 1949, no. 4149, FO369, TNA; Comment Kemball on Letter Alexander, 10 May 1949, no. 4152, FO369, TNA; and Minutes Meeting UK delegation, 13 May 1949, no. 4152, FO369, TNA.

[177] Record of Meeting with Attorney-General, 16 May 1949, no. 4150, FO360, TNA.

[178] Instructions French Foreign Ministry, 9 May 1949, no. 161, Unions Internationales 1944–1960, LAD.

132   PREPARING FOR WAR

these new instructions from Paris failed to convince many of the other delegations at the conference.[179]

In Geneva, meanwhile, the other initial proposals had failed to receive enough support, causing the first major stalemate on internal war. The head of the Swiss delegation, Plinio Bolla, in line with his instructions to act as a mediator, had already proposed organizing a sub-committee that would be charged with designing a compromise formula acceptable to all delegations. The Special Committee, as it became known, was composed of several Western bloc states: the Soviet Union; France; and Britain; Burma, representing the postcolonial Asian delegations; and Uruguay, representing the Latin American ones. They were chaired by Bolla himself. Their first major decision was to agree, by 10 votes to 1, to extend the Conventions to cases of internal armed conflict, making Craigie's original instructions obsolete.[180]

Because the Special Committee had decided to abandon the widely criticized Stockholm text in order to find a new shared agreement,[181] its members decided to establish another sub-committee tasked with creating that compromise text. This First Working Party, as it became known, would include members from the US, France, Australia, and Castberg's Norway.[182] The draft they produced resembled the previous American proposal and featured a belligerency clause combined with a list of alternative requirements (organized military force, determinate territory, etc.).

Additionally, it included the French demand that the legal status of the insurgent party would be unaffected by the treaty's application, and it limited the protecting powers' provisions of the Conventions, unless both parties agreed upon its applicability. More critically, the First Working Party decided on the division of Common Article 2 into two separate clauses: one (Common Article 2) featuring its original three paragraphs and the other (Common Article 2A, in the future: Common Article 3) its fourth paragraph regarding the treaty's application. In the First Working Party's draft, this novel Article 2A would be similar in all but one Convention, the Civilian one, for which it made only the treaty's humanitarian principles pertinent.

On 16 May 1949, the First Working Party's draft was discussed within the Special Committee. Craigie's delegation, while internally expressing support

[179] Cable Lamarle on Civil War, 13 May 1949, no. 161, Unions Internationales 1944–1960, LAD. The American were critical of these new French instructions and suspected that the British were behind them. Cable US delegation to State Department, 15 May 1949, no. 5, RG43 - 40, NARA.

[180] Final Record of the Diplomatic Conference of Geneva of 1949, Vol. II, Section B, p. 43–45, LOC. The British rejected it. The French government's new instructions had not yet arrived in Geneva.

[181] Final Record of the Diplomatic Conference of Geneva of 1949, Vol. II, Section B, p. 45, LOC.

[182] The Working Parties apparently did not take minutes of their proceedings.

for it, continued to try to delay its discussion while awaiting new instructions from London.[183] Using the argument of trying to protect NATO's coherence, the British leader wished to have the Cabinet's approval to canvass for this particular formula, as he told Christopher Mayhew, the Under-Secretary of State serving Ernest Bevin, during a special meeting in Geneva.[184] Lamarle too expressed sympathy for it, but was not fully convinced.[185] Soon after, he returned to Paris. Here, the Ministry of Interior and Ministry of Defense were said to fiercely oppose the First Working Party draft, fearing that it would have "grave consequences" for the escalating Indochina War.[186] The outcome of this meeting was that the French delegation's attitude would harden even further, to the satisfaction of Craigie's delegation.[187]

While openly opposing Lamarle's views, ICRC delegate Pilloud and other former "Stockholmers" found the First Working Party's draft too rigid, asserting that it could never have been applied in any recent civil war.[188] In an indication of the near collapse of the negotiations, he even admitted in private that he would be willing to give up the clause in order to prevent "infection" affecting other crucial drafting debates, such as the Civilian Convention's making.[189] On 25 May 1949, gathering for a joint meeting, the ICRC and Swiss delegation both underlined this panic and discussed a range of fallback options in case of continuing Anglo-French resistance. ICRC President Ruegger even suggested a separate, non-binding declaration for civil war as a last resort, which signals his organization's declining support for the matter.[190]

As Lamarle's attempts in Geneva to revise the First Working Party draft failed to achieve tangible results,[191] the French Foreign Ministry decided in early June 1949 to draft another set of instructions, this time to prevent the negotiations from collapsing. In its final proposal, it was said to be willing to apply the

---

[183] Interim Report UK Delegation, 27 May 1949 no. 4151, FO369, TNA. Craigie: "The policy of the Delegation in this matter is to employ delaying tactics pending reconsideration of the attitude of HM government." Letter Sinclair to Beckett, 18 May 1949, no. 4151, FO360, TNA.

[184] Minutes Meeting with Mayhew, 19 May 1949, no. 4151, FO369, TNA.

[185] Final Record of the Diplomatic Conference of Geneva of 1949, Vol. II, Section B, p. 47, LOC. Cable Lamarle Civil War, 13 May 1949, no. 161, Unions Internationales 1944–1960, LAD.

[186] Instructions French Foreign Ministry, 23 May 1949, no. 161, Unions Internationales 1944–1960, LAD.

[187] Minutes of Meeting UK Delegation, 24 May 1949, no. 4162, FO369.

[188] It is important to recognize that the ICRC's understanding of "civil war" as a legal category was hybrid. For instance, it called the Zionist insurgency in the Mandate of Palestine a "civil war" between the "British and Jews." Final Record of the Diplomatic Conference of Geneva of 1949, Vol. II, Section B, pp. 46–48, LOC.

[189] Cable Lamarle on Civil War, 16 May 1949, no. 161, Unions Internationales 1944–1960, LAD.

[190] Plenary Meeting, 25 May 1949, no. A PV A PI.19, ACICR.

[191] Cable Lamarle on Civil War, 25 May 1949, no. 161, Unions Internationales 1944–1960, LAD.

134 PREPARING FOR WAR

Civilian Convention's preamble and its basic human rights principles, which had been originally drafted by Cahen-Salvador, to internal conflicts without making any reference to belligerency or outside supervision. In doing so, the metropole wished to protect its colonial sovereignty. This plan also seemed to have been influenced by, on the one hand, opposition from its civilian, colonial, and military officials against attempts to directly apply the Conventions to Indochina, which might undermine their ongoing counterinsurgency operations, and, on the other, certain French officials wishing to discursively apply human rights principles in wartime, while seeking to prevent further damage to France's international standing. If this final compromise proposal were rejected, however, the French delegation was instructed to make a reservation to this part of the future Conventions.[192]

Soon after—in mid-June 1949, after having returned from Paris—Lamarle, "embarrassed by [their] position in Indochina,"[193] made his return to Geneva's negotiating table by introducing a proposal that would reset the entire drafting process.[194] This proposal said that "parties" had to endeavor to bring into force all or part of the Conventions' provisions and stipulated that the general human rights principles of the Civilian Convention's preamble should be applied to internal conflicts.[195] In practice, this meant that the French, seeking to protect their colonial interests, still maintained a powerful stand against outside supervision and the inclusion of any legal provision making the treaty directly applicable to such conflicts. Instead, they proposed to apply the preamble's very general principles and prevent any encroachments on the colonial state's sovereignty, to the satisfaction of Craigie's delegation.[196]

Downfall

"This result," one New Zealand delegate wrote in his later report, "eliminates all danger that the new Conventions will be used to encourage rebellion or

---

[192] Instructions French Foreign Ministry on Civil War Clause, 4 June 1949, no. 161, Unions Internationales 1944–1960, LAD.

[193] Report of New Zealand Delegation to Diplomatic Conference of Geneva 1949, AAYS 8638 W2054 ADW2054/1 220/3/3 (R18524114), ANZ.

[194] Best called the French proposal a "magical resolution." Best, War and Law since 1945, 173. A similar sentiment can be found in Rey-Schyrr's important account of the article's creation, which is largely based on Pictet's Commentary. She credits the French for achieving the breakthrough within the negotiations without taking sufficient note of the strategic–imperial motivations behind their proposal. Rey-Schyrr, De Yalta à Dien Bien Phu, 265–266.

[195] Final Record of the Diplomatic Conference of Geneva of 1949, Vol. II, Section B, p. 78, LOC.

[196] Letter UK Delegation to Kemball, 10 June 1949, no. 4152, FO369, TNA.

insurrection."[197] Many of the other skeptical delegations therefore reviewed it positively.[198] Ignoring his Cabinet's new but still strict instructions,[199] Craigie immediately expressed public support for the French proposal: it posed little threat to his government's interests and was in line with his broader agenda of unifying the Western bloc delegations.[200] Whitehall quickly endorsed this line.[201] The Italians eventually accepted the proposal as well.[202] They were joined by two military men: the Burmese Tun Hla Oung, who had previously served the British empire, and the Uruguayan Hector Blanco, representing the opinion of civil war-affected Latin America.[203]

The American delegation, in contrast, showed much less enthusiasm for the French proposal. Yingling, misjudging the diplomatic opportunity, rejected it altogether because he thought it removed all obligations to apply the Convention to internal conflicts and perhaps feared that it would lead to public criticism, if not Soviet resistance.[204] Craigie's attempts to convince him and his chief Harrison to accept the French proposal, by referring to their shared NATO interests, succeeded only partially. The two American delegates, seemingly unsure about the drawn link to their military alliance, preferred to continue to support the First Working Party draft, although they promised not to actively oppose the French proposal.[205] Indeed, they were careful not to alienate their French allies, relying on their support to secure major US interests in relation to the atomic bomb and security clause (see the following chapters).

Considering it the best alternative to the rigid US-supported First Working Party's draft and wishing to prevent a major fiasco, the Swiss–ICRC bloc decided—unlike Castberg—to side with the French, thus prompting hesitant delegations to act similarly.[206] The other critical vote would come from the Soviets, who had rejected the First Working Party's Draft. This time, however,

---

[197] Report of New Zealand Delegation to Diplomatic Conference of Geneva 1949, AAYS 8638 W2054 ADW 2054/1 220/3/3 (R18524114), ANZ.

[198] It is unclear whether this was done first by the French, or later, by the delegates together, although it seems that the former explanation is more plausible than the latter.

[199] Minutes Meeting Cabinet on Civil War, 23 May 1949, no. 46, CAB130, TNA.

[200] Telegram Craigie to Foreign Office, 16 June 1949, no. 4152, FO369, TNA; and Minutes Meeting UK Delegation, 17 June 1949, no. 4155, FO369, TNA.

[201] See Letter Strutt to Kemball, 21 June 1949, no. 4152, FO369, TNA; Letter War Office on French Proposal, 20 June 1949, no. 4153, FO369, TNA; Telegram London to UK delegation, 22 June 1949, no. 4154, FO369, TNA; and Telegram Craigie to Foreign Office, 23 June 1949, no. 4154, FO369, TNA.

[202] Cable Lamarle on Civil War, 23 June 1949, no. 161, Unions Internationales 1944–1960, LAD.

[203] Final Record of the Diplomatic Conference of Geneva of 1949, Vol. II, Section B, p. 78, LOC.

[204] Final Record of the Diplomatic Conference of Geneva of 1949, Vol. II, Section B, p. 79, LOC.

[205] Minutes of Meeting UK delegation, 21 June 1949, no. 4156, FO369, TNA. The French did publicly oppose the First Working Party draft, however. Final Record of the Diplomatic Conference of Geneva of 1949, Vol. II, Section B, pp. 93–95, LOC.

[206] For the Swiss position, see Final Record of the Diplomatic Conference of Geneva of 1949, Vol. II, Section B, pp. 97–99, LOC.

136   PREPARING FOR WAR

they sympathized with the French proposal, asking them to help update the text. Their suggestion led to the creation of the Second Working Party, composed of members from Great Britain, the Soviet Union, France (which was rewarded with the position of chairperson), and a few other delegations. Having isolated itself, the US declined to take part and, to Lamarle's disappointment, did not play an official role in this critical part of the negotiations.[207]

This Second Working Party, as it was called, worked on the French suggestion by turning Common Article 2A into a list of minimum human rights principles for armed conflicts of a non-international character. It included a reference to the old French demand for non-recognition of the status of insurgents, and an anti-discrimination clause, to the Colonial Office's frustration.[208] It also allowed the ICRC to offer its services in internal wars:[209] for fear of undermining its neutrality, the Swiss delegation opposed attempts to make this mandatory.[210]

The Second Working Party's draft featured several major loopholes. It lacked prohibitions on executions, reprisals, and collective penalties. Probably under pressure from Craigie's delegation,[211] the Italians decided to pull back their original proposal to add collective penalties to the draft.[212] Only the Soviet delegation addressed this issue in its alternative draft—which was, in the end, rejected by an overwhelming majority (see below).[213] Internal British reports

---

[207] Final Record of the Diplomatic Conference of Geneva of 1949, Vol. II, Section B, p. 79, LOC; and Cable Lamarle on Civil War, 18 June 1949, no. 161, Unions Internationales 1944–1960, LAD.

[208] Letter Colonial Office, 22 June 1949, no. 4152, FO369, TNA.

[209] Final Record of the Diplomatic Conference of Geneva of 1949, Vol. II, p. 83, LOC.

[210] Final Record of the Diplomatic Conference of Geneva of 1949, Vol. II, pp. 93–95, LOC. The French delegation was not vehemently opposed to this proposal, although it wished to safeguard its sovereignty. See Cable Lamarle on Civil War, 23 June 1949, no. 161, Unions Internationales 1944–1960, LAD.

[211] The Colonial Office, in particular, strongly opposed banning collective penalties. Letter Trafford Smith Colonial Office on Collective Punishment and Civil War, 25 June 1949, no. 4155, FO369, TNA. It is worth quoting from one of his letters to reveal the Colonial Office's strong opposition to this proposal: "the inclusion of this rather general expression would be extremely embarrassing from the Colonial Office point of view for the following reasons. On the one hand, a number of Colonies (notably in Africa) have on their Statute Book collective punishment ordinances which provide that this form of punishment may be used to deal with offenses such as cattle stealing and the like. It would be a very serious thing to deprive the Administrations concerned of their ability to use these provisions [. . .] There are, however, the more difficult cases of the present disturbances in Malaya, and [. . .] the use of punitive bombing in the Aden Protectorate. What is happening in Malaya is certainly an "armed conflict," and it seems equally clear that what might be described as "collective punishment" has been used—e.g. the burning of villages, and so on—and may well be used again. For obvious reasons, we could not agree to limit the authorities in Malaya by the proposed ban on collective punishment. Equally in the case of the Aden Protectorate, the system of punitive bombing is used by which, after due warning, the last sanction imposed by the Administration to secure the handing over of murderess, etc., is to destroy villages from the air. I believe there have also been cases in which punitive bombing has been used to suppress insurrections by local sheiks."

[212] Final Record of the Diplomatic Conference of Geneva of 1949, Vol. II, p. 95, LOC.

[213] The ICRC's Commentary of 1960 also noted the lack of provisions or principles against reprisals. But its authors argued that the principle of humane treatment in CA3 was incompatible with reprisals. Jean Pictet, *The Geneva Conventions of 12 August 1949: Commentary* (Geneva: ICRC, 1960).

seem to indicate that imperial powers may have thought it was too valuable a method to have it forbidden in times of internal war. In their counterinsurgency campaigns, they frequently made use of this method for repression. Consequently, Common Article 2A did not strictly ban the use of reprisals and collective penalties, and this also helps to explain why these practices never disappeared entirely in the decades after 1949.

The Special Committee also admitted in its final report that it had removed a section prohibiting the practice of deportations from the Second Working Party's draft, allegedly because it was "irrelevant in the case of civil war."[214] Deportations of protected persons from occupied territories, however, would be officially forbidden by the Civilian Convention.[215] Neither did the draft specifically address the problems of air bombing, ethnic cleansing, or extermination.[216] The Committee's decision to delete from the text the ban on deportations was probably connected to the fact that imperial powers always invoked measures of population resettlement to suppress insurgencies (see British Malaya in the late 1940s).[217] Prohibiting deportations would thus significantly hamper the imperial powers' strategy to defeat their internal enemies. As such, this issue was made largely taboo.

At the very end of the debate in the Special Committee, in early July 1949, the Soviet delegation introduced another amendment, the most far-reaching one presented up to that point by any state during the entire conference. In communist-controlled media, such as *Pravda*, editors had attacked "Anglo-American" proposals which sought to limit humanitarian law's application to interstate wars and were based upon "aggressive goals [toward] national liberation movements of colonized nations,"[218] but the Soviets had no alternative text to support except for the rejected Stockholm text.[219] Challenging the Western

---

[214] It is telling that a ban on forced movement of civilians in times of internal armed conflict was included only in the later Additional Protocols. Sivakumaran, *The Law of Non-International Armed Conflict*, 51.

[215] Article 49 did allow for the evacuation of a given area if the security of the population or "imperative military reasons" so demand.

[216] Final Record of the Diplomatic Conference of Geneva of 1949, Vol. II, p. 83, LOC.

[217] Russell Crandall, *America's Dirty Wars: Irregular Warfare from 1776 to the War on Terror* (Cambridge: Cambridge University Press, 2014), 170.

[218] In an official report for higher officials, including Secretary of the Central Committee of the Ukrainian Communist Party Nikita Khrushchev, Soviet-Ukrainian delegates said the colonial powers' efforts to question the law's relevance for colonial wars should be considered as part of a larger, concerted attempt by the Anglo-American delegations to undermine the Geneva Conventions. At informal meetings, however, the delegates seemed far more sensitive to inner divisions within the Western bloc, such as the differences existing between the French, British, and American delegations. Report Soviet-Ukrainian Delegation, no. F. 2, Op. 12cc, Spr. 969, Ark. 60–76, Tsentral'nyi derzhavnyi arhiv vyschykh organiv vlady ta upravlinnia Ukrainy (TSDAVO), Kiev, Ukraine.

[219] On the *Pravda* article of 13 May 1949, see Cable U.S. Embassy Moscow to Secretary of State on Pravda Article of 13th May 1949, no. 677, Provost Marshal General, NARA.

138 PREPARING FOR WAR

powers' "covert" drafting tactics, the guiding principle of their new proposal was that almost all the Conventions' provisions would have to be applied to internal conflicts so to provide a "minimum level of humaneness."[220]

The Soviet draft, in line with recent statements at the UN by the leading Soviet legal expert Andrei Vyshinsky in support of the right to self-determination,[221] included a number of rights and prohibitions on reprisals and the killing of civilians, but it failed to present a comprehensive proposal to uphold the Conventions in times of internal conflict. For example, seeking to protect their sovereignty against outside interference, the Soviets excised the paragraphs concerning protecting powers and the legal status of parties involved, which was seen as a potential support for Communist rebels; they also left out the conditions under which the article would apply.[222]

The entire paragraph making special mention of the ICRC's intervention was also removed.[223] Denying the existence of "truly neutral countries" and considering the ICRC an Anglo-American puppet, the Soviets held that providing such international observers access to their camps would inevitably lead to "spying activities" from abroad.[224] While trying to obtain Soviet support for his own proposal, Lamarle rejected the Soviet amendment as kindly as possible. Most other delegates did so as well. As a result, the Soviet proposal was rejected by an overwhelming majority of 9 votes to 1; Slavin's delegation had suffered an embarrassing defeat.[225]

On 8 July 1949, revealing the occasionally dilettante nature of these negotiations, the Special Committee crucified, in a tumultuous vote, the amended draft of the Second Working Party. The French and British were utterly shocked. What had caused this dramatic turn of events? First, the American, Soviet, Norwegian, and Australian delegations maintained their opposition to this text. Second, the Burmese delegate, a former supporter of the French text, had received new instructions to oppose the adoption of *any* text on civil war, as the Anglo-French coalition had originally wanted.[226] Lastly, the Swiss

---

[220] Report Soviet-Ukrainian Delegation, no. F. 2, Op. 12cc, Spr. 969, Ark. 60–76, TSDAVO.

[221] Bill Bowring, "The Soviets and the Right to Self-Determination of the Colonized: Contradictions of Soviet Diplomacy and Foreign Policy in the Era of Decolonization," in *The Battle for International Law: South–North Perspectives on the Decolonization Era*, eds Jochen von Bernstorff and Philipp Dann (Oxford: Oxford University Press, 2019), 404–425, 414.

[222] Final Record of the Diplomatic Conference of Geneva of 1949, Vol. II, Section B, pp. 97–98, LOC.

[223] Ibid.

[224] Report Soviet-Ukrainian Delegation, no. F. 2, Op. 12cc, Spr. 969, Ark. 60–76, TSDAVO.

[225] Final Record of the Diplomatic Conference of Geneva of 1949, Vol. II, Section B, p. 100, LOC.

[226] Cable Lamarle on Civil War, 9 July 1949, no. 161, Unions Internationales 1944–1960, LAD. It is unclear whether this new instruction came straight from Rangoon, or from another Asian capital, since the Burmese delegate was said to represent the so-called Asian vote. Still, the instruction fell in line with the Burmese government's recently adopted policy to reject an ICRC offer to intervene in Burma. For the initial rejection letter, see Letter Burmese Embassy in New Delhi, 23 June 1949, no.

chairman's replacement, the Uruguayan Blanco, had made a crucial mistake.[227] Because he, who supported the French text, thought that he could not cast a vote as a chairperson, the draft was rejected, creating enormous disappointment among the defeated French. Three days later the Special Committee likewise rejected the US-supported First Working Party's draft—this time by a vote of 7 to 4—and the fourth paragraph of Article 2 of the Stockholm draft, by a unanimous vote.[228] The Committee then had to report to the Joint Committee that it had failed to agree upon any draft: it believed at this point that an internal war clause seemed a distant dream.

Resurrection

In the Joint Committee, however, following a sequence of events behind the scenes, the amended Second Working Party draft suddenly rose from the dead. On 19 July 1949 the Committee voted in favor of the text, by 22 votes for, 4 against, and 12 abstentions (mostly the Eastern Bloc). What had caused this sudden breakthrough? Left with no feasible alternatives and highly invested in the matter, the French delegation had started a desperate diplomatic offensive to reopen the debate in the Joint Committee's upcoming session and to regain support for its rejected proposal.[229] Its first successes were to persuade Blanco to make a public statement explaining why he had abstained from supporting, thereby hoping to secure precious Latin American votes, and to gain support from the Great Powers for its renewed offensive.[230]

Like its French counterpart, the British delegation preferred to have no civil war clause at all, but it knew that this approach was risky as it was unlikely to receive immediate support from other delegations seeking different solutions.[231] More critically, Craigie recognized the importance of upholding interallied solidarity and of the fact that the French would only agree to the Anglo-American security clause, and other issues crucial for this coalition, if their own text for

---

BG-017-07-002, ACICR. For the ICRC's engagements in India, Burma, and Pakistan, see Rey-Schyrr, *De Yalta à Dien Bien Phu.*

[227] Minutes of Meeting UK Delegation, 9 July 1949, no. 4157, FO369. Professor de La Pradelle had apparently returned to France for exams. Cable Lamarle on Civil War, 9 July 1949, no. 161, Unions Internationales 1944–1960, LAD.

[228] Final Record of the Diplomatic Conference of Geneva of 1949, Vol. II, Section B, p. 102, LOC.

[229] Minutes of Meeting UK Delegation, 12 July 1949, no. 4158, FO369, TNA.

[230] Minutes of Meeting UK Delegation, 11 July 1949, no. 4158, FO369, TNA.

[231] Minutes of Meeting UK Delegation, 9 July 1949, no. 4157, FO369, TNA.

140 PREPARING FOR WAR

civil war got through.[232] Hence, he decided to seek support for the French text. If rejected, however, then he would vote for no text at all, which remained his favored option.[233] For similar reasons, the Americans, recognizing the improbability of achieving success with their own draft, decided in the end no longer to speak publicly in favor of this First Working Party draft—to Lamarle's satisfaction.[234] He even succeeded in initially convincing the Eastern European delegations to rally for his proposal after it had become clear to them that their own proposal would stand little chance—although in the end they probably abstained.[235]

The final stage of the drafting process took place in the focus of world attention when it was presented to the plenary meetings, at which critical journalists and other observers were present in larger numbers. The Second Working Party's draft on Common Article 2A was renamed by the Drafting Committee into Common Article 3. The plenary meeting was split once again into three groups with different opinions, and it was far from obvious that it would accept the French proposal, which many delegations remained skeptical of. One group, led by the Soviets, said that Common Article 3 did not go far enough; others, such as the Burmese Oung, were not convinced at all; and a large group of delegates were on the fence. During these two dramatic plenary debates, the Burmese military delegate demanded in a long speech the deletion of both Common Articles 2 and 3 from the drafts: "It is because," he said, "of the conflicts arising in certain parts of the world, including mine—conflicts caused by foreign ideologies [i.e. communism: BvD], that I am submitting my amendment."[236]

Although far from publicly, Oung's statements were supported by his former imperial ruler and several Western bloc states, including Canada.[237] Craigie admitted privately that this "was really far more acceptable [...] but that we could not break faith with the French, who had said that they would not now go back on the decision to have a reference to Civil War." His delegation therefore decided to support the Burmese amendment as long as it would not break faith with its French allies.[238]

---

[232] Correspondence on Security and Article 3, 12 July 1949, no. 4156, FO369, TNA.

[233] Letter Craigie to Foreign Office, 19 July 1949, no. 4158, FO369, TNA.

[234] Cable Lamarle on Civil War, 20 July 1949, no. 161, Unions Internationales 1944–1960, LAD.

[235] Lamarle had expected Soviet support but was surprised to see how they had suddenly abstained. Cable Lamarle on Civil War, 20 July 1949, no. 161, Unions Internationales 1944–1960, LAD.

[236] Final Record of the Diplomatic Conference of Geneva of 1949, Vol. II, Section B, p. 327, LOC.

[237] One example: Rapport van de Nederlandse Delegatie bij de Diplomatieke Conferentie, Gemeenschappelijke artikelen van de vier Verdragen, Page 9, no. 3045, Code Archief Buitenlandse Zaken, National Archives of the Netherlands (NA), The Hague.

[238] Minutes of Meeting UK Delegation, 21 July 1949, no. 4160, FO369, TNA.

The deputy head of the Soviet delegation, Morosov, disagreed with this group's reasoning, noting the "unspeakable cruelty and destruction" caused by recent colonial wars, turning the plenary into another East–West confrontation. In his view, the Second Working Party's draft was "intended to restrict the application of the Convention as far as possible [...] The obvious outcome of such a measure is that a large number of important provisions concerning the protection of war victims will not be put into operation."[239] Previously rejected by the Special Committee, his own amendment was once again turned down, this time by 20 votes to 11, with 7 abstentions.[240]

Concerned that he had placed "some of [his imperial] friends in an embarrassing situation," the former British colonial servant Oung asked the chairman to vote on the article by secret ballot—a proposal fiercely resisted by Morosov, who particularly liked to embarrass Craigie's delegation. This Burmese proposal was implicitly supported by the influential American and British delegations,[241] which led to its acceptance.[242] Thanks to an important intervention by president Petitpierre, the more than forty delegations were forced to decide whether to support the French-supported text of Common Article 3 and say "Yes," or to oppose it and thus adhere to Oung's motion by voting "No."[243] In the end, following critical interventions by ICRC and Swiss delegates, who preferred the French motion over the Burmese one,[244] they—including, apparently, the Soviets—went for the former option by adopting Common Article 3 by 34 votes to 12 with 1 abstention. It is not unlikely that the British were among those who voted against this text.[245] Morosov finally congratulated Lamarle on his "success,"

---

[239] Final Record of the Diplomatic Conference of Geneva of 1949, Vol. II, Section B, p. 326, LOC.

[240] Final Record of the Diplomatic Conference of Geneva of 1949, Vol. II, Section B, p. 338, LOC. Internally, the ICRC admitted that it could give its approval to this Soviet amendment. Note Siordet on Civil War Vote, 29 July 1949, no. CR-221-4, ACICR.

[241] Quite tellingly, Lamarle wrote with satisfaction about how the American delegation operated during these plenary meetings. Cable Lamarle Civil War, 29 July 1949, no. 161, Unions Internationales 1944–1960, LAD.

[242] Final Record of the Diplomatic Conference of Geneva of 1949, Vol. II, Section B, p. 339, LOC.

[243] Lamarle said during the plenary meeting that "a few delegations, including my own" thought that there would first be a secret ballot on the proposal of the Burmese. He had already filled in his own voting paper. It is quite likely that he voted in favor of the Burmese proposal before then voting for his own text. But Petitpierre told him that the Burmese proposal was not an amendment; it was a motion to vote "No" on the whole of the article, to reject it outright. He then suggested taking one vote only, which was accepted. Fresh voting papers were spread before the final but secret ballot took place. Final Record of the Diplomatic Conference of Geneva of 1949, Vol. II, Section B, p. 339, LOC.

[244] Lamarle noted that the ICRC was critical in helping to persuade "the most hesitant." It is remarkable how little credit the ICRC historiography gives to this important intervention by the Swiss and ICRC to convince certain hesitant states to vote for the French text. Cable Lamarle Civil War, 29 July 1949, no. 161, Unions Internationales 1944–1960, LAD.

[245] For more details about the exact voting record, see Van Dijk, "The Great Humanitarian," 230–231.

142 PREPARING FOR WAR

one that the surprised ICRC delegation had no longer expected after a truly epic debate.[246]

3.5 Conclusion

The death and resurrection of Common Article 3 demonstrates the contingent nature of the effort to internationalize internal wars through humanitarian law. Originally a human rights text,[247] the article was the very first legal provision of its kind—following the Lieber Code of the US Civil War[248]—to specifically apply certain legal principles to internal armed conflicts for humanitarian purposes. Despite the fact that a considerable number of powerful states, including Great Britain, considered making a reservation to CA3, the regimes of Argentina and Salazar's Portugal were eventually the only ones to do so;[249] Oung's delegation of Burma was one of the few to abstain from voting for the Civilian Convention due to this provision.[250] In enshrining the internationalization of large-scale internal wars in the Conventions, the diplomatic conference won a highly symbolic victory and transformed international law in wartime. In fact, it created a legal revolution whose impact grew as time progressed. Its advocates helped to trigger a shift away from exclusive understandings of belligerency and toward connecting the European dimensions of warfare with those of the colonies.[251]

As anti-colonial actors used the Conventions to strengthen their international claims, they directed the ICRC's attention to internationalizing wars within empires and states, leading to renewed calls for broadening

---

[246] Note Siordet on Civil War Vote, 29 July 1949, no. CR-221-4, ACICR.

[247] It is often forgotten in the literature that the original version of CA3, i.e. the Civilian Convention's preamble, had a distinct history featuring a reference to human rights. Most accounts only recognize an overlap between CA3 and human rights law for the period from the 1960s onward. See Sivakumaran, *The Law of Non-international Armed Conflict*, 42–46; Mantilla, "Under (Social) Pressure," 194. One of the few scholars who has drawn attention to this connection between both fields of international law are Rosemary Abi-Saab and Theodor Meron. See Abi-Saab, *Droit Humanitaire et Conflits Internes*, 59–60; and Theodor Meron, "The Humanization of Humanitarian Law," *The American Journal of International Law*, Vol. 94, No. 2 (2000): 239–278, 246.

[248] Armitage, *Civil Wars*, 185–186; and John Fabian Witt, *Lincoln's Code: The Laws of War in American History* (New York: Free Press, 2012).

[249] The Argentineans apparently made a reservation only when signing the Conventions, but not at ratification. The Argentina reservation stressing that CA3 would be the only article applicable to internal conflicts is now considered legally irrelevant. The far more strict Portuguese reservation was not repeated at ratification, either. Report on Articles Common to All Four Conventions, p. 4, A1838, 1481/1A - Part 7, NAA.

[250] The state only ratified the Geneva Conventions in 1992. Final Record of the Diplomatic Conference of Geneva of 1949, Vol. II, Section B, p. 525, LOC.

[251] Van Dijk, "Internationalizing Colonial War."

humanitarian law's scope. As a consequence, Western imperial delegations came under severe pressure from several delegations to endorse this view. Their resistance to it triggered criticisms from not just the liberal ICRC but also communist drafters seeking to publicly shame their Cold War adversaries. The Soviets realized, however, that they could accept virtually any text as long as it did not infringe upon their sovereign discretion to reject ICRC inspectors (see Chapter 6). Indeed, Moscow had no desire to accept any legal restraint on its ongoing efforts to subjugate Eastern Europe. Like other imperial powers, it expected to be able to control CA3's application should new insurgencies break out in the future.[252]

Although stopping short of calling this outcome "a happy result" because it destroyed the idea of absolute state sovereignty, another UK-aligned delegate also felt relief when CA3 was finally accepted since it lacked, in his view, "any guarantee of real protection to the victims of a civil war."[253] This view reflects the fact that British and French imperialists had succeeded in creating a watered-down text that minimized the weight of its restrictions. This chapter has revealed that almost every kind of violence taking place within states had been considered in the 1940s, but that these two major drafting parties deliberately left CA3's scope vague,[254] thereby excluding emergencies and many other types of internal wars, as well as their victims, from humanitarian law's scope.[255]

This refutes the historiographical stereotype that "the" drafters had not foreseen the juridical gray area of violence considered short of internal armed conflict, such as "disturbances," which were supposedly "new" or "hardly comprehended" around the 1940s for those involved in this process. According to this erroneous logic, such types of allegedly "small wars" became only a matter of international legal concern following the waves of decolonization after 1949, which led to the Second Additional Protocol protecting victims of "all" conflicts occurring within the state's body politic.[256] In reality, Western imperial

[252] For more details, see Boyd van Dijk, "'The Great Humanitarian': The Soviet Union, the International Committee of the Red Cross, and the Geneva Conventions of 1949," *Law and History Review*, Vol. 37, No. 1 (2019): 209–235.

[253] Report of New Zealand Delegation to Diplomatic Conference of Geneva 1949, AAYS 8638 W2054 ADW2054/1 220/3/3 (R18524114), ANZ.

[254] It is no coincidence that the British delegate Gutteridge later wrote that Common Article 3 would apply merely to large-scale conflicts such as "civil war": Joyce Gutteridge, "The Geneva Conventions of 1949," *British Yearbook of International Law*, Vol. 26 (1949): 294–326, 300.

[255] Sivakumaran was one of the few who noted some of these problems earlier—although he does not dwell on why they had occurred in the first place: Sivakumaran, *The Law of Non-International Armed Conflict*, 162.

[256] Richard Baxter, "Humanitarian Law or Humanitarian Politics? The 1974 Diplomatic Conference on Humanitarian Law," *Harvard International Law Journal*, Vol. 16 (1975): 1–26, 4. This view has recently been re-endorsed by Jean-Marie Henckaerts, the head of the ICRC's project to update Pictet's old

144 PREPARING FOR WAR

powers voiced serious concerns already in the 1940s—if not long before—about the impact of anti-colonial violence because they feared more was to come in the future, therefore trying to undermine CA3's proposed framework.

To the ICRC, despite the concessions to imperial powers, this did not detract from the fact that it had broken the taboo about applying international norms to internal wars, and helped to amplify previously marginalized voices in international law. The imperial career of CA3 proves this point. The provision developed into an important asset for anti-colonial activists, such as the Algerian National Liberation Front (FLN). They used the French-designed CA3 most effectively by isolating the French colonizer on the international stage.[257] CA3 is now the area of humanitarian law that is most relevant to today's armed conflicts, with the so-called War on Terror the most prominent example. In 2006, in the *Hamdan v Rumsfeld* case, the US Supreme Court used the article to put an end to the torture of suspected Al Qaeda-operatives (see Conclusion). Elaborating on these points for other irregulars, the next chapter will focus more closely on the debates with regard to the rebirth of the POW Convention in the 1940s.

Commentary. See: http://blog.journals.cambridge.org/2017/02/01/behind-the-scenes-updated-commentary-first-geneva-convention/ (retrieved 9 February 2017).

[257] Matthew Connelly, *A Diplomatic Revolution: Algeria's Fight for Independence and the Origins of the Post-Cold War Era* (Oxford: Oxford University Press, 2002).

Figure 4.1 Soviet leader Nikolay Vasilyevich Slavin (second from right) at the diplomatic conference in Geneva (1949). It was the very first time that the Soviet Union participated in the drafting of a Geneva Convention.
Source/Rights: Ullstein

4

Fighters in the Shadows

Who deserves protection under the POW Convention? Could this treaty include resistance fighters, or would that undermine the distinction between combatants and civilians? In 1960, when his co-edited Commentary for the 1949 POW Convention had come out, Pictet claimed that he and other drafters had "solved [these] most difficult questions […] of 'partisans.'"[1] Since then, many scholars have similarly argued that drafters had significantly expanded humanitarian law's scope to partisans such as those excluded from the Second World War. Emily Crawford, for instance, has argued that "the inclusion of resistance fighters in the Conventions was considered a substantial broadening of the category of combatant and brought persons traditionally considered […] bandits within the ambit of Geneva protection."[2] Crawford's view resonates with that of other scholars stressing the POW Convention's wider scope since 1949.[3]

Strikingly, however, when the Additional Protocols were signed in the 1970s, the International Committee of the Red Cross (ICRC)—trying to explain its

---

[1] Jean Pictet, *The Geneva Conventions of 12 August 1949: Commentary* (Geneva; ICRC, 1960). Unlike Pictet, the Foreign Office-delegate Joyce Gutteridge, and the UK government in general, interpreted Article 4 far more strictly, arguing that "particularly civilians, who, as individuals […] have taken up arms to defend their lives […] were not entitled to the protection of the Prisoners of War Convention." Joyce Gutteridge, "The Geneva Conventions of 1949," *British Yearbook of International Law*, Vol. 26 (1949): 294–326, 313–314.

[2] Emily Crawford, *The Treatment of Combatants and Insurgents under the Law of Armed Conflict* (Oxford: Oxford University Press, 2010), 52–54.

[3] Examples are: Reema Shah and Sam Kleiner, "Running Out of Options: Expiring Detention Authority and the Viability of Prosecutions in the Military Commissions under Hamdan II," *Yale Law Review*, Vol. 32, No. 2 (2014): 465–504, 484; Daphné Richemond-Barak, "Nonstate Actors in Armed Conflicts: Issues of Distinction and Reciprocity," in *New Battlefields Old Laws: Critical Debates on Asymmetric Warfare*, ed. William Banks (New York: Columbia University Press, 2011), 106–132, 114–115; Anicée van Engeland, *Civilian or Combatant: A Challenge for the 21st Century* (Oxford: Oxford University Press, 2011), 40; Roland Otto, *Targeted Killings and International Law: With Special Regard to Human Rights and International Humanitarian Law* (Heidelberg: Springer, 2012), 227; and William Hitchcock, "Human Rights and the Laws of War: The Geneva Conventions of 1949," in *The Human Rights Revolution: An International History*, ed. Akira Iriye, Petra Goedde, and William Hitchcock (New York: Oxford University Press, 2012), 93–112, 98–99. The recently published Oxford Commentary of the Geneva Conventions claims that "The record of the Diplomatic Conference indicates that states supporting the inclusion of such groups envisioned that partisans and guerrillas would be included in this description [of irregulars] in particular." In reality, many of these "supporting states," like France and the Netherlands, excluded anti-colonial guerrillas and other irregulars from these treaties. Andrew Clapham, Paola Gaeta and Marco Sassòli, ed., *The 1949 Geneva Conventions: A Commentary* (Oxford: Oxford University Press, 2015), 896. Using Pictet's Commentary as a source, Carl Schmitt

---

Preparing for War. Boyd van Dijk, Oxford University Press. © Boyd van Dijk 2022.
DOI: 10.1093/oso/9780198868071.003.0005

148 PREPARING FOR WAR

recent success in widening humanitarian law's scope to include anti-colonial guerrillas—claimed that drafters in 1949 had failed to properly deal with partisan warfare, as they could not have foreseen the explosive rise of this activity.[4] These two contrasting views—inclusivity versus exclusivity—now dominate the historiography on this matter. This chapter aims to dig deeper and demonstrate that neither of these two narratives adequately accounts for the restrictive stance of both the POW and the Civilian Convention toward partisan warfare.[5]

The chapter's guiding principle is to critically examine why, how, and under what circumstances the main drafting parties dealt with the right of resistance in times of occupation.[6] It shows how the Anglo-American drafters in particular sought to exclude irregulars, from anti-colonial guerrillas to communist spies, and to legalize their extrajudicial policies to deal with these direct threats to their counterinsurgency designs. On this issue, their views were colored by anxieties caused by rising East–West tensions, decolonization, and the fears of communist "fifth columns." Triggering a massive struggle with the French, the ICRC, and the Soviets, this contentious debate with regard to partisan warfare led eventually to a far more ambiguous outcome than is often presented in the literature so far.

---

argued that "Die Genfer Konventionen erweitern den Kreis der den regularen Kampfern gelichgestllten Personen vor allem dadurch, daß sie die Mitglieder einer 'organisierten Widerstandsbewegung' den Mitfliedern von Milizen und Freikorps gleichstellen und ihnen auf diese Weise die Rechte und Vorrechte der regularen Kombattanten verliehen": Carl Schmitt, *Theorie des Partisanen: Zwischenbemerkung zum Begriff des Politischen* (Berlin: Duncker & Humbolt, 1963), 31. Scheipers has rightly argued that Schmitt was "correct in as far as the codified law recognizes militias and spontaneous risings en masse [...] but other forms of irregulars remained excluded from the law": Sibylle Scheipers, *Unlawful Combatants: A Genealogy of the Irregular Fighter* (Oxford: Oxford University Press, 2015), footnote 4, 183–186.

[4] "What the drafters in 1949 could not have foreseen, was the truly enormous tidal wave of guerrilla activity which in the thirty years following 1945 affected countries which had not yet achieved independence. It was not clear at that time that ultimately guerrilla warfare would be the method of warfare 'par excellence' for liberation movements and that the tide of self-determination would propel these movements forward, without giving thought to the conditions agreed upon in The Hague in another time and for other circumstances": Jean Pictet, *Commentary on the First Additional Protocols to the Geneva Conventions* (Leiden: Martinus Nijhoff Publishers, 1987), 384.

[5] Partisan warfare is framed here as an irregular form of military activity often disconnected from the regular armed forces while targeting an enemy occupier. When discussing the question of partisan warfare, I refer specifically to those debates dealing with codifying international law's scope for irregulars, including guerrillas, partisans, spies, enemy agents, and those suspected of these acts.

[6] In this context, the literature often refers to the question of unlawful combatants. Other typologies used in contemporary English vocabulary for this category of fighters are "unprivileged belligerents," "marauders," "enemy combatants," "irregular combatants," and "illegal combatants." In French there exist similar terms, such as "combattant illegal," "combattant ennemi," and "combattant ennemi illégal," the latter of which clearly resonates with the Bush Administration's wording of "unlawful enemy combatants." See Gary Solis, *The Law of Armed Conflict: International Humanitarian Law in War* (New York: Cambridge University Press, 2010), 224–228.

FIGHTERS IN THE SHADOWS   149

A remarkable aspect of this drafting process is that powerful postwar calls to lower the rather high POW Convention threshold for partisans largely failed.[7] The Convention, admitted US drafter Yingling, would not have "covered many persons acting as 'partisans'" during the Second World War.[8] The Soviets, too, argued that it failed to protect most resistance fighters.[9] Other drafters agreed that the relevant article's reference to "resistance movements" was meant not so much as a robust protection, as some have implied, but rather as an instrument to end a political deadlock. It helped to end the stalemate caused by, on the one hand, continental European pressure to obtain the right of resistance in occupied territory in order to appease political constituents at home, and, on the other hand, the restrictive Anglo-American delegations trying to protect their security interests as potential enemies of future partisans.[10]

In fact, by mid-1948, the ICRC had already given up on its plans to lower the POW Convention threshold for partisans. Pictet's drafting team shifted its attention to providing every captured person with a basic set of human rights protections under the Civilian Convention, with the aim of eradicating the endemic practices of torture and summary executions. The ICRC and others hoped this would allow partisans excluded from the POW Convention to "fall back" on the Civilian Convention, a now largely forgotten but critical chapter in the history of humanitarian law.[11] By contrast, the Anglo-American delegations continuously opposed these plans for an overarching safety net. Rather than bridging these two treaties, they sought "exemptions, [to] decrease

---

[7] Few scholars have registered this problem, except for Scheipers and Yoram Dinstein, an influential Israeli academic and legal practitioner. However, neither of the two pay close attention to the complex drafting history of this particular element. See Yoram Dinstein, *The Conduct of Hostilities under the Law of International Armed Conflict* (Cambridge: Cambridge University Press, 2004), 34 and Scheipers, *Unlawful Combatants*, 2–3. For Solis' critique of Dinstein's views on this issue, see Solis, *The Law of Armed Conflict*, 197–198.

[8] Raymund Yingling and Robert Ginnane, "The Geneva Conventions of 1949," *American Journal of International Law*, Vol. 46, No. 3 (1952): 393–427, 402.

[9] Report Soviet-Ukrainian Delegation, no. F. 2, Op. 12cc, Spr. 969, Ark. 60–76, Tsentral'nyi derzhavnyi arhiv vyschykh organiv vlady ta upravlinnia Ukrainy (TSDAVO), Kiev, Ukraine. Castberg, too, admitted euphemistically that the "solution offered by the Conventions [...] was by no means in accord with the hopes of many members of the Conference." Frede Castberg, "Franc Tireur Warfare," *Netherlands International Law Review* [1959]: 81–92, 83–84.

[10] Report Soviet-Ukrainian Delegation, no. F. 2, Op. 12cc, Spr. 969, Ark. 60–76, TSDAVO.

[11] Some, including Castberg himself, have pointed at this issue before, but have been unable to historically explain how and why this outcome came about. Examples are Castberg, "Franc Tireur Warfare," 83; Knut Dörmann, "The Legal Situation of 'Unlawful/Unprivileged Combatants'," *International Review of the Red Cross*, Vol. 85, No. 849 (2003): 45–74; and Gerald Draper, "The Geneva Conventions of 1949," *Recueil des Cours* [1965]: 113. Others, however, have defined the category of "protected person" as a group of "noncombatants": Solis, *The Law of Armed Conflict*, 234. The major exception to this rule of "neglect" is Hitchcock's excellent article exploring the connections between human rights and the 1949 Geneva Conventions. Based on Anglophone sources, the ICRC Commentaries, and the conferences' minutes, he has shown how human rights played a significant part during these debates in granting rights to both civilians and combatants: Hitchcock, "Human Rights and the Laws of War," 97–98, 106.

[…] protection."[12] They wished to create a gap in order to internationally codify their extrajudicial policies and prevent suspected communist agents from falling under the umbrella of humanitarian law.

Taking an interconnected approach, this chapter is divided into four sections, each of which deals with a specific time period in which the debate concerning irregulars was conceived differently. As a starting point for this study on the POW Convention's scope, its related provisions, and their history, the first section provides a longer history focusing on the invention of the concept of defense before occupation by also considering the law's punitive origins in dealing with partisan warfare. It also demonstrates how this problematic legacy even survived after the First World War's controversies surrounding the *francs-tireurs*. The second section of this chapter takes a closer look at the start of the post-1945 revision process of the POW Convention and how it sought to broaden the concept of defense by turning it into the right of resistance in occupied territory. It does so by means of analyzing the relevant discussions among the major drafting parties roughly up to mid-1947.

This section will show how these first attempts to enhance the protection afforded to partisans mostly failed, thanks to virulent British opposition. The following section continues this debate by looking at the main drafting parties' shift to the Civilian Convention and their evolving ideas in the period around the 1948 Stockholm Conference. This was the moment at which a transformative legal bridge was drawn between the two Conventions, while human rights arose most prominently in the drafting stage. The final section of this chapter gives a detailed account of the last phase of this revision process by analyzing how those Stockholm drafts were finally re-negotiated, and how Anglo-American drafters tried to tear down that same bridge. This section reveals how the outcome of major clashes at the diplomatic conference left a problematic legacy for irregulars fighting in armed conflicts.

4.1 Partisan Warfare

Those advocates longing for greater protection for irregulars did not deal so much with interwar legacies, such as those faced while creating CA3 and the Civilian Convention, but rather with one dating back to a period long before the First World War. The then existing law made an implicit distinction

---

[12] Report Soviet-Ukrainian Delegation, no. F. 2, Op. 12cc, Spr. 969, Ark. 60–76, TSDAVO.

between so-called lawful and unlawful combatants, neither of which was ever explicitly mentioned in the codified laws of war. These notions were legally arranged around two particular elements: belligerent rights and the privilege of POW treatment. While the former right implies that a lawful belligerent is sanctioned by a sovereign and holds the right to kill in times of combat, the latter privilege is closely connected to this status and indicates, by means of the laws of war, whether they can be allowed a degree of positive treatment.[13] To receive this type of protection, the belligerent was to comply with those laws of war; otherwise they would be left in what extrajudicial thinkers like to call a "state of exception": the person belonged to the law, but actually fell outside of it. They were considered a criminal and treated accordingly, for example by summary execution.[14]

The question of how to legally protect and label these different categories without bringing those "criminals" into the scope of the law has been part of continuing debate in the long history of the laws of war. In this section, the chapter will first briefly discuss influential opinions as expressed especially by Vattel and Lieber—widely considered to be two of the most important legal thinkers on this matter—by focusing on their restrictive attitudes toward irregulars, their POW rights, and the highly punitive powers which publicists such as these gave to occupiers to deal with civilian resistance. It will then investigate how this punitive regime was codified from the late nineteenth century onwards, and why it failed to be made less restrictive after the experiences of the First World War.

At the heart of these debates taking place in the modern period was the seminal work on the question of irregulars, *The Law of Nations* (1758), written by the leading Swiss publicist Emer de Vattel.[15] Herein de Vattel laid down the most basic rules meant specifically for warfare that would define future thinking on the treatment of POWs, and on who should fall under this category. Writing at a time when state formation was gaining further traction, Vattel claimed that the "sovereign [was] the real author of war";[16] all other "private wars," he stated, "[that were] carried on between private individual[s]

---

[13] See Carl Schmitt, *Politische Theologie: Vier Kapitel zur Lehre von der Souveränität* (Munich: Duncker & Humblot, 1934).

[14] See Giorgio Agamben, *State of Exception* (Chicago, IL: The University of Chicago Press, 2005); and Giorgio Agamben, *Homo Sacer: Sovereign Power and Bare Life* (Stanford, CA: Stanford University Press, 1998).

[15] For a deeper discussion of Vattel and Lieber's work, see Pablo Kalmanovitz, *The Laws of War in International Thought* (Oxford: Oxford University Press, 2020), 103–111, 128–152.

[16] Emer de Vattel, *The Law of Nations, Or, Principles of the Law of Nature, Applied to the Conduct and Affairs of Nations and Sovereigns, with Three Early Essays on the Origin and Nature of Natural Law and on Luxury* (Indianapolis: Liberty Fund, 2008), § 472.

152 PREPARING FOR WAR

belong to the law of nature properly so called."[17] 'The troops alone carry on the war', he further argued, "while the rest of the nation remain[s] in peace."[18]

Vattel's central assumption in demanding for fighters a state connection was that when civilians would take up arms, this would lead to a "more bloody" war, one that could be terminated only by the "utter extinction of one of the parties"—that is, unrestrained war.[19] Two other critical assumptions were that most of these irregulars fought intermittently, better known today as "farmer-by-day-guerrilla-by-night."[20] They were not regularly organized and did not consistently wear a distinctive sign, as they would take this off following the end of their armed operations. Second, according to this line of thinking, they allegedly treated their captured enemy with greater cruelty than regular soldiers.[21]

In most cases, Vattel, as many of his followers would later say, left little room for violent resistance under occupation, except in some special cases. This comparatively strict conception of the right of resistance, rooted in the eighteenth century, was closely connected to theories of statehood and European "civilized" warfare, particularly its notion of partisan warfare, developed in the wake of the Thirty Years' War. This approach to warfare, which involved small disruptive units behind enemy lines rather than armed civilians unconnected to a regular army, expanded and changed quite substantially in nature around the time of the Revolutionary and Napoleonic Wars.[22] It was during this epoch that the conduct of war as such changed remarkably, as the professional cabinet wars of the previous centuries were replaced by the image of massive people's armies. With the onset of this form of so-called people's wars, a corresponding new type of fighter appeared on the battlefield, purportedly inspired by nationalist or "partisan-like" motives.[23]

These discussions—triggered by reflections on the wars following the French Revolution, with the rise of "new" military formations, from Spanish

---

[17] Ibid., § 469.

[18] Ibid., § 226.

[19] Ibid.

[20] Schmitt, *Theorie des Partisanen*, 11.

[21] For a critical assessment of this discourse on irregular warfare, see Scheipers, *Unlawful Combatants*, 10–14.

[22] Walter Laqueur, "The Origins of Guerrilla Doctrine," *Journal of Contemporary History*, Vol. 10, No. 3 (1975): 341–382, 342.

[23] The rise of this form of "partisan warfare," or, in the words of Clausewitz, "the people in arms" (or *Parteigänger*), partly as a result of the radical changes in Europe's political landscape and its mass mobilization of entire societies and industries for the conduct of warfare, led to what some call the democratization of warfare—which implied not just the greater presence of civilians on the battlefield, but also a greater stress on state-organized discipline and more strictly distinguishing them from regular soldiers. Scheipers, *Unlawful Combatants*, 43–44, 53–54.

guerrillas, to the French *levée en masse*, to the Prussian volunteer corps—heralded a new phase in legal thinking about irregulars' protection. These publicists stayed very close to Vattel's understanding of the matter at stake, although they increasingly divided fighters into two different categories separated by their contrasting images of "discipline" and "state authorization." This situation started to evolve from the late 1840s onwards, when new (civil) wars broke out in which so-called patriotic fighters began to play an ever increasing role. They not only challenged the strict barriers drawn by publicists previously, but also led to a renewed consensus, mainly due to the work of Lieber.[24]

Building upon Vattel's work, in 1862, during the second year of the US Civil War, Lieber published an important brochure on the matter of guerrillas. The work was commissioned by Henry Halleck, then the general-in-chief of the Unionist Army.[25] In this brochure Lieber identified a number of different legal categories of persons resembling irregulars, from the partisan to the "Rising en masse."[26] The spy, unless he had rejoined his army; the rebel; and the conspirator were, in Lieber's view, particularly dangerous and deserved little to no protection. The conspirator, for Lieber, was somebody who had failed to act in a chivalric manner; he had conducted secret agreements leading to a resumption of arms, or had murdered from "secret places"; it was precisely this disdain for secrecy on the part of Lieber that helps to explain the future law's distaste for such methods. Lieber saw little room for protecting those who operated intermittently, in secrecy, or who held no affiliation with the belligerent party's main army; he believed that they should be excluded from the POW framework.[27]

Like many other publicists, Lieber made two "exceptions" to this rule. One exception was for the *levée en masse*, a loose category of irregulars increasingly popularized since the Revolutionary Wars, which he regarded as being in need of some form of privileged protection, mainly as a result of its members' "patriotic" credentials. But this protection was conditioned: the *levée* had to be organized in "respectable numbers, and [has to have] risen in the yet uninvaded or unconquered portions of the hostile country."[28] The other "exception" was the autonomously operating partisan; this very specific category of fighters had been lawfully constituted by means of its papers and it

---

[24] Henry Halleck, *International Law; or, Rules Regulating the Intercourse of States in Peace and War* (San Francisco: H.H. Bancroft & Company, 1861), 383–387, 406.

[25] Francis Lieber, *Guerrilla Parties: Considered with Reference to the Laws and Usages of War* (New York, 1862), 37.

[26] Ibid., 41.

[27] Lieber, *Guerrilla Parties*, 41–43, 49.

[28] Ibid., 47.

154 PREPARING FOR WAR

had operated in liaison with its main army, as opposed to autonomously operating guerrillas, who did not wear a fixed, distinctive sign. The latter, more heterogeneous category was that of the "intermittent guerrilla," the irregular who operated much more autonomously.[29] Partisans by contrast, Lieber argued, functioned under a central command and were paid or commissioned by that regular army; therefore, he argued, this type of irregular fighter should be given POW status.

Lieber was less sure, however, about how far this scope could be extended. Ought it to include guerrillas or the "free-corps," defining this latter category as persons "not belonging" to a regular army but consisting of autonomously operating and "high-minded patriots" authorized, though not individually sanctioned, by their government to take up arms? For Lieber, whose own views on this issue were colored by the historical precedent of the Prussian free-corps fighting during the Napoleonic Wars, the difficulty with this specific fighter category was that its "patriotic" members often lacked discipline.[30]

The final category he identified was indeed that of the guerrilla himself, the legal status of whom was quite different in many respects. He regarded guerrillas as "self-constituted," that is irregularly organized, "by the call of a single individual," and not belonging to any belligerent party.[31] If guerrilla parties were "self-constituted sets of armed men" who "form no integrant part of the organized army," then, according to Lieber, they would no longer would be protected by the law.[32] However, if such a guerrilla party been aided or had aligned itself with the main army of a belligerent party, then it would be "difficult," he admitted, "for the captor of guerrilla-men to decide at once whether they are regular partisans [and, if they are not, to sentence them to a punishment of execution: BvD]." For then the party's members would deserve some form of protection as long as they complied, under a form of reciprocity clause, with the laws of war.[33]

In 1863, Lieber codified many of these elastic and ambiguously defined principles favoring the regular army's interests when drafting his famous

---

[29] Schmitt: that is essentially a person who "vermeidet, die Waffen zu tragen, der aus dem Hinterhalt kämpft, der sowohl die Uniform des Feindes als auch feste oder lose Abzeichen und jede Art von Zivilkleidung als Tarnung benutzt." Schmitt, *Theorie des Partisanen*, 41–42.

[30] Lieber, *Guerrilla Parties*, 44.

[31] Lieber, *Guerrilla Parties*, 39. In the case of the Peninsular War, this situation had been significantly complicated by the fact that the Spanish provisional government had not been recognized by Napoleon, raising the issue of a party to the conflict lacking any belligerent-status for itself, even though it had been aligned with a recognized belligerent, i.e. the "Free-French problem."

[32] Lieber, *Guerrilla Parties*, 50–51.

[33] Lieber, *Guerrilla Parties*, 52.

instructions, *General Order No. 100*.[34] These instructions, promulgated by President Abraham Lincoln as part of his broader Emancipation plans, were used to help the Unionist forces to engage lawfully in their fight with the Confederacy.[35] They featured 157 articles covering a wide range of topics, including the protection of POWs and spying.[36] As Lieber had argued previously in his brochure, they denied POW protection to so-called "bandits," or to those who had committed hostilities without being part of a regular army; they were "not public enemies [echoing Vattel's requirement: BvD], and, therefore, if captured, are not entitled to the privileges of prisoners of war, but shall be treated summarily [i.e. executed: BvD] as [...] pirates," he wrote.[37] But he extended protection to members of the "rising en masse," as long as their part of the country had not yet been occupied, thereby recognizing the concept of armed defense for mostly unoccupied civilians.

Many of these jurists, including Lieber,[38] agreed that few of these protections had any major significance in times of war against so-called "barbarians."[39] This racial hierarchy was based on a three-fold rationale. First, European jurists held the view that non-Europeans were racially inferior; they considered them as lacking the necessary capabilities to apply the body of "civilized" rules of warfare adequately. Second, these groups had not signed any treaty on the laws of war; thus there existed no situation of reciprocity, the critical basis upon which most of these nineteenth-century rules for war were codified.[40] Third, many of those jurists feared that non-European fighters were incapable of showing sufficient restraint in warfare.[41] For that matter, they were concerned about the much older imperial practice of recruiting such forces as auxiliaries for the colonial battlefields.[42]

---

[34] Francis Lieber, *Instructions for the Government of Armies of the United States in the Field, General Orders No. 100* (1863).

[35] See John Fabian Witt, *Lincoln's Code: The Laws of War in American History* (New York: Free Press, 2012).

[36] See Lieber, *Instructions*, Article 49.

[37] Lieber, *Instructions*, Article 82. For his conception of the "public war," see Rotem Giladi, "Francis Lieber on Public War," *Göttingen Journal of International Law*, No. 4 (2012): 447–477.

[38] See Frédéric Mégret, "From 'Savages' to 'Unlawful Combatants': A Postcolonial Look at International Humanitarian Law's 'Other'," in *International Law and Its Others*, ed., Anne Orford (Cambridge: Cambridge University Press, 2009), 265–317.

[39] For the discussion of whether this non-application of the laws of war to the colonies led to more savage and less restrained wars in these areas, rather than in Europe and North America, see Scheipers, *Unlawful Combatants*, 177–179 and Isabel Hull, *Absolute Destruction: Military Culture and the Practices of War in Imperial Germany* (Ithaca, NY: Cornell University Press, 2005), 1–5.

[40] "The perversity of this whole situation of course is that the non-participation of 'non-civilized nations' in humanitarian treaties was not their choice," writes Mégret aptly: Mégret, "From 'Savages' to 'Unlawful Combatants'." See Scheipers, *Unlawful Combatants*, 13–21.

[41] Mégret, "From 'Savages' to 'Unlawful Combatants'."

[42] But certain imperial powers made an exception to this rule as their colonial armies were in a desperate need of indigenous troops to control their vast empires. Because of this, they tolerated the

156 PREPARING FOR WAR

The Brussels Conference of 1874

Many of these principles were finally codified in the wake of the Franco-Prussian War of 1870–1871, with its numerous summary executions of the *francs-tireurs*. The Prussian occupiers claimed that these irregulars had to have been individually sanctioned by the French state and to have been carrying proof of this direct government authorization in order to gain the status of prisoner of war.[43] The French government, on the other hand, disagreed with this point of view, stressing that its Ministry of War's decision to commission the *Garde Nationale Mobile*, and the *francs-tireurs*, by means of a "collective" and "indirect" authorization had been sufficient to make them eligible for such rights, and that they ought not to have been summarily executed, as the Prussians had done.[44]

The young Russian jurist Fyodor Martens, also a prominent legal advisor at the Czarist Foreign Ministry,[45] had been influenced by Lieber's work.[46] He contested some of the restrictive views as presented by German jurists, for instance noting that "the public opinion of the neutral States of Europe [had] found [their] conduct [in the Franco-Prussian War] [...] too cruel."[47] Consequently, Martens proposed, in a letter to the Russian Foreign Ministry, that it should take up the initiative of bringing together European experts to reshape the laws of war and "civilize" future warfare.[48] This symbolized the start of history's first international attempt to codify rules on partisans by creating the first comprehensive code for the conduct of European land warfare.[49]

In 1874, a group of predominantly military experts gathered at the invitation of the Czar in the city of Brussels. They discussed two critical questions with respect to irregulars, and to the question of occupation, which does not form the core of this chapter's focus: what constituted a lawful combatant liable to POW rights? And under what conditions was he truly "authorized" to take up arms?

---

recruitment of certain non-Europeans by making a race-based distinction between "barbarian soldiers" with or without a so-called responsible command, that is, an "officer of a civilized nation." See Scheipers, *Unlawful Combatants*, 43–44.

[43] Scheipers noted that many of these *francs-tireurs* were still treated as POWs when captured by the Germans: Scheipers, *Unlawful Combatants*, 91–92.

[44] Ibid., 88–91.

[45] For more information about Martens, see James Crossland, *War, Law and Humanity: The Campaign to Control Warfare, 1853–1914* (London: Bloomsbury, 2019), 124–125.

[46] Peter Holquist, "By Right of War: Imperial Russia and the Development of the Law of War," unpublished paper, 10–11.

[47] James Spaight, *War Rights on Land* (London, 1911), 45.

[48] Holquist, "By Right of War," 7–8.

[49] Crossland, *War, Law and Humanity*, 126–127.

In other words, they discussed not only the experiences of the Franco-Prussian War, but also continued past efforts to codify the laws of war initiated by the Geneva Conference in 1864 and that of the Saint-Petersburg Declaration of 1868, with its prohibition of certain weaponry. Another other important impetus to these Czarist efforts was the broader calls at the time for further codification of interstate affairs such as weaponry, trade, and warfare.

The draft Martens finally produced, which was loosely based upon the Lieber Code and influenced by his recent tour around the battlefields of the Franco-Prussian War,[50] would set out the future drafting process and ultimately formed the basis upon which the founding articles of the Hague Regulations would be established as well.[51] Unlike the Lieber Code, however, it featured a standardized set of four specific and objective criteria defined in an *ex negativo* fashion for those to be considered part of the regular army and for those yet forming part of it, such as militias and "volunteers."[52] These different military formations had to comply with the following set of conditions: being headed by a responsible person; wearing some distinctive badge habitually (this feature was only assumed implicitly); being recognizable at a distance; carrying arms openly; and, finally, conforming to the laws of war.[53]

Like the Lieber Code, the Russian draft sanctioned the use of the still very privileged *levée en masse* (privileged because its members had to comply at this point with just one condition: respect the laws and customs of war) and it further stated that "armed bands not complying with the above-mentioned conditions shall not possess the rights of belligerents; they shall not be considered as regular enemies, and in case of capture shall be proceeded against judicially." As such, every armed person was still obliged to meet the conditions of regular organization and that of the so-called belligerent nexus: he had to be in some way connected to the main army of the belligerent party.

The conference's special committee in charge of covering these matters was split into roughly two camps: one representing the interests of the two large occupying land armies; the other focused on the naval powers of Great Britain,[54] the Netherlands, and some of the other European powers with

---

[50] Ibid., 126–127.

[51] Holquist, "By Right of War," 10–13, 19.

[52] See also Scheipers, *Unlawful Combatants*, 103–104.

[53] In addition, in the case of capture, their non-combatant members were to enjoy the same rights as prisoners of war, unless they were doctors, ambulance personnel, or clergymen, all of whom could enjoy the rights of neutrality—a further precision of Lieber's somewhat ambiguous remarks on these questions.

[54] The British said to refuse to send a delegate to the conference "unless it was assured that naval matters would not be considered": Morton Royse, *Aerial Bombardment: and the International Regulation of Warfare* (New York: 1928), 7.

158 PREPARING FOR WAR

smaller land armies.[55] As a recently defeated power, the French, who had a very sizable land army, were somewhat aloof during the conference, viewing it as a Russian attempt to limit their abilities to take revenge on Germany.[56] Wilhelmine Germany and Russia, by contrast—representing the greatest land armies in Europe—resisted many of these proposals attempting to restrain the occupier's powers.[57]

In particular, the Germans and their officers—whose own views were shaped, according to Isabell Hull, by their traumatic experiences of the continuing French resistance in occupied territory in the 1870s—tried vigorously to exclude armed civilians from any form of international legal protection, effectively pushing them into a state of exception, and saw many of those proposals as condemnation of their conduct during the Franco-Prussian War.[58] The Russian delegation acknowledged the concept of national defense, but it resisted efforts to sanction the practice of civilian resistance in European occupied territory. Both delegations tried to ensure that they would maintain freedom of action in future wars.[59]

The other camp, represented by the European powers with smaller land armies, was most concerned about the legal–military implications of those ideas. They feared that such considerations would severely restrict their possibility of conscripting a large number of armed civilians into their regular armies at short notice in the face of a large-scale invasion, and that it would lead to an overly privileged occupying power. In the event of war, they desired to have the right to enroll by means of a *levée*, as it was called, "all the available strength of the nation," according to a Belgian delegate, without extending these privileges to their colonial subjects. The British delegation remained, however, cautious: it did not wish to participate in any discussion on "points extending to general principles of international law not already universally recognized and accepted."[60] The French delegation argued that a man acting in self-defense should not be punished; no agreement, however, could be reached on this point.[61] The conference did relatively little to further restrict the occupier's

---

[55] Spaight, *War Rights on Land*, 48.

[56] Holquist, "By Right of War," 29. James Lorimer, *The Institutes of the Law of Nations; A Treatise of the Jural Relations of Separate Communities* (London: Blackwood and Sons, 1883), 338.

[57] Holquist, "By Right of War," 10.

[58] See Isabel Hull, *A Scrap of Paper: Breaking and Making International Law during the Great War* (Ithaca, NY: Cornell University Press, 2014) and Holquist, "By Rights of War," 30.

[59] Crossland, *War, Law and Humanity*, 129.

[60] Lorimer, *The Institutes of the Law of Nations*, 340.

[61] This was caused partly by the conference's own rules of procedure, which stipulated that unanimous agreement for every point of discussion had to be reached. In the 1940s, there existed the majority rule.

authority and discretionary powers, thus underlining many of Lieber's foundational principles.[62]

However, as the Brussels Conference reached its ending, it was becoming obvious that the deadlock on the issue of protecting irregulars could not be broken: the delegates finally agreed to sign a non-binding declaration, to Martens' disappointment. The outcome of this meeting would stir major criticism in the years afterward;[63] to cite British legal scholar James Spaight, it had been "mutually destructive," as it had failed to sign a binding treaty and had produced a text with two opposing stances. On the one hand, it had granted the concept of national defense before occupation to appease the smaller powers' delegations; on the other hand, it had made these privileges conditional upon strict criteria, to meet the Russian–German coalition's demands.[64] Nor did the jurists of the Institute of International Law, originally founded by "The Men of 1873,"[65] alter this outcome to any significant degree.

"Where there's a Jew there's a partisan, and where there's a partisan there's a Jew"

The second major codifying attempt to find a suitable answer to the question of how to legally deal with partisan warfare came with the two Hague Peace Conferences of 1899 and 1907, again following an invitation from the Russian Czar.[66] Their proclaimed objectives were to reduce armaments and the tensions among the Great Powers.[67] In 1899, in the second commission on the codification of land warfare chaired by Martens himself, delegates decided to organize a separate sub-commission, with the task of revising the Brussels draft. This group agreed without too much debate to take over most of its provisions

---

[62] Scheipers, *Unlawful Combatants*, 101–102; and Crossland, *War, Law and Humanity*, 126–127.

[63] On criticisms of the Brussels Conference's outcomes: Lorimer, *The Institutes of the Law of Nations*, 75–76; and Jules Guelle, *Droit International: La Guerre Continental et Les Personnes* (Paris, 1881), 41–55. See also Regina Buß, *Der Kombattantenstatus. Die kriegsrechtliche Entstehung eines Rechtsbegriffs und seine Ausgestaltung in Verträgen des 19. und 20. Jahrhunderts* (Bochum: Universitätsverlag Brockmeyer, 1992).

[64] Spaight, *War Rights on Land*, 54–55.

[65] Martti Koskenniemi, *Gentle Civilizer of Nations: The Rise and Fall of International Law 1870-1960* (Cambridge: Cambridge University Press, 2001), 4.

[66] For more details, see Maartje Abbenhuis, "Civilization at War, 1899-1906," in *The Hague Conferences and International Politics, 1898-1915*, ed. Maartje Abbenhuis (London: Bloomsbury Academic, 2019), 97–120.

[67] Crossland, *War, Law and Humanity*, 173.

160 PREPARING FOR WAR

on spies, but they were much more divided when it came to defining POW rights.[68]

As in 1874, the Hague delegates split into similar camps and again failed to arrive at a solution.[69] Martens put a great deal of energy into this matter, partly out of a fear that this would turn into another fiasco of a conference suggested by the Czar. While being bound by his Russian delegation's view that the Convention's scope should not be widened so as to include the right to resistance in occupied territory,[70] he declared that cases not included in the future code would still leave populations and belligerents "under the protection and empire of the principles of international law." Clearly, then, the alternative text he proposed, later known as the "Martens Clause," was bound to be vague and, in the view of critics, it was evasive as well.

In this, the Hague drafters failed to bring about a satisfying legal answer to the question of regulating partisan warfare. This was in spite of the Second Hague Convention's annex and its first three articles on the definition for POW rights, which created the distinction between the army as such and privileged irregulars such as members of a volunteer corps, fulfilling the Brussels criteria. But it remained virtually impossible for civilians to claim the right to resistance in occupied territory.[71] Even Martens himself later acknowledged many of these problems.[72] His conception of humanitarianism "was a blend of idealism," noted the legal scholar Antonio Cassese, "and a keen desire to advocate the official position of Russia." The Russian's proposition was not so much designed to provide a form of humanitarian protection to irregulars, as some other scholars have suggested, but rather functioned as a way to meet the Czar's interests and avoid bringing the first Hague Peace Conference to a fatal ending.[73]

---

[68] Report on the Proceedings of the Hague Peace Conferences, p. 489–490, Library of Congress (LOC), Washington, DC.

[69] Ibid., 417.

[70] Antonio Cassese, "The Martens Clause: Half a Loaf or Simply Pie in the Sky?" *European Journal of International Law*, Vol. 11, No. 1 (2000): 187–216, 195–196.

[71] Article 1 of the Second Hague Convention's annex: "The laws, rights, and duties of war apply not only to armies, but also to militia and volunteer corps, fulfilling the following conditions: To be commanded by a person responsible for his subordinates; To have a fixed distinctive emblem recognizable at a distance; To carry arms openly; and To conduct their operations in accordance with the laws and customs of war. In countries where militia or volunteer corps constitute the army, or form part of it, they are included under the denomination 'army." Article 2: "The population of a territory which has not been occupied who, on the enemy's approach, spontaneously take up arms to resist the invading troops without having time to organize themselves in accordance with Article 1, shall be regarded a belligerent, if they respect the laws and customs of war." Article 3: "The armed forces of the belligerent parties may consist of combatants and non-combatants. In case of capture by the enemy both have a right to be treated as prisoners of war." See Cassese, "The Martens Clause," 197.

[72] Ibid., 198.

[73] Cassese, "The Martens Clause," 199, 201–202, 208.

By 1907, following the experiences of the South African and Russo–Japanese Wars,[74] the question was still far from resolved: some delegates at the Second Hague Peace Conference even expressed a degree of satisfaction with the way in which the current treaties were organized.[75] In consecutive years, many of these principles were included in the instructions and field manuals of major European armies. Resistance in already occupied territories remained unlawful. The Janus-faced character of those codified laws of war has never been entirely reconciled, many jurists admit: if these sometimes pointed in the direction of rigidity, by excluding a great number of irregulars, they could as easily point in the direction of elasticity, by giving commanders in the field the power to act arbitrarily against them.

During the First World War, the ICRC established the International Prisoners-of-War Agency and closely followed the inter-belligerent conferences, at which states promised to bring an end to the suffering of enemy POWs.[76] These wartime agreements inspired the ICRC's decision in June 1918 to develop a new POW code. It asked two legal experts, including Cramer, to start preparing a new code for the protection of POWs as a response to wartime atrocities. They built upon the wartime agreements in designing a collection of principles on which the future prisoners' code could be centered.

To realize this legal vision, Cramer suggested a gendered definition of POWs that would keep women out of war and allow only mobilizable adult men to be interned. Another defining feature of Cramer's vision for the prisoners' code was her stress on the relevance of promoting elementary human rights thinking.[77] Strikingly, she claimed a whole collection of rights for military prisoners, from the right to correspondence, labor rights, and immunity from reprisals, to the right to life.[78] At a later stage, she even suggested extending

[74] Sakuyé Takahashi, *International Law Applied to the Russo-Japanese War with the Decisions of the Japanese Prize Courts* (London: Stevens, 1908), 89–93.

[75] Report on the Proceedings of the Hague Peace Conferences. The Conference of 1907, Vol. 3, 98, LOC. It is critical to bear in mind that this discussion was essentially about the definition of whom to grant POW status to, less so about defining the concept of lawful belligerency, as some have argued. Scheipers, *Unlawful Combatants*, 100–102.

[76] Heather Jones, *Violence against Prisoners of War in the First World War: Britain, France and Germany, 1914–1920* (Cambridge: Cambridge University Press, 2011); and Neville Wylie and Lindsey Cameron, "The Impact of World War I on the Law Governing the Treatment of Prisoners of War and the Making of a Humanitarian Subject," *European Journal of International Law*, Vol. 29, No. 4 (2018): 1327–1350.

[77] For a definition for the concept of elementary human rights thinking, see Boyd van Dijk, "Human Rights in War: On the Entangled Foundations of the 1949 Geneva Conventions," *The American Journal of International Law*, Vol. 112, No. 4 (2018): 553–582.

[78] Marguerite Frick-Cramer, "A propos des projets de conventions internationales réglant le sort des prisonniers," *Revue Internationale de la Croix-Rouge et Bulletin Internationale des Société de la Croix-Rouge* (1925): 73–84, 82.

162 PREPARING FOR WAR

the law's scope to "francs tireurs civils" as long as they participated "openly" in armed conflict.[79] The fiery controversies around the summary executions of Belgian and French *francs-tireurs* during the First World War,[80] and those triggered by ensuing civil war in Central Europe, had led to increasingly powerful calls for recognizing the legality of resistance in occupied territory.

In July 1929, the major drafting parties except for the Soviet Union gathered in Geneva to decide upon the future of Cramer's co-drafted prisoners' code. The Soviets had developed their own socialist version of a POW code, but the ICRC expressed little interest in it.[81] Even more strikingly, the delegates in 1929 expressed great reluctance to discuss more fundamental matters head on.[82] Acutely aware of the deadlocked debates of Brussels and The Hague and of the broader skepticism of the victorious Allied powers—including France—regarding this issue, and cognizant of the wider consensus in favor of keeping civilians strictly out of armed conflict, drafters were loath to open the Pandora's Box of questions related to partisan warfare.[83] For these reasons, the original Martens Clause and the 1899 Second Hague Convention's first three articles remained virtually unchanged in the decades after. While denying the right to resistance in occupied territory, the non-socialist architects of the 1929 POW Convention simply included a reference to them in the treaty's primary article.[84]

The destructive consequences of this lack of protection for irregulars under humanitarian law, as well as the broad discretionary powers for occupiers, were felt most bitterly by the resistance fighters of the Second World War. In this period Hitler issued an order that captured resistance fighters would be executed and his forces used brutal collective penalties to terrorize enemy civilians.[85] Considering military surrender unacceptable and disliking the 1929 POW Convention's supervisory elements,[86] Stalin had decided not to adhere to

---

[79] Ibid., 81.

[80] See John Horne and Alan Kramer, *German Atrocities, 1914: A History of Denial* (New Haven, CT: Yale University Press, 2001); Hull, *A Scrap of Paper*; and Michael Geyer, "Insurrectionary Warfare: The German Debate about a Levée en Masse in October 1918," *The Journal of Modern History*, Vol. 73, No. 3 (2001): 459–527.

[81] Jiří Toman, "L'Union Soviètique et le Droit des Conflits Armés," Ph.D. Dissertation, University of Geneva, 1997, 385–387.

[82] See Neville Wylie, *Barbed Wire Diplomacy: Britain, Germany, and the Politics of Prisoners of War, 1939–1945* (Oxford: Oxford University Press, 2010), 38–63.

[83] Scheipers has argued that the lack of post-1919 attention to irregular warfare was caused by the fact that the First World War was "one of the few conflicts in which irregular fighters did not play a significant role, at least in the European theaters of war." Scheipers, *Unlawful Combatants*, note 87.

[84] Convention relative to the Treatment of Prisoners of War, Article 1, 27 July 1929.

[85] Olivier Wieviorka, *The French Resistance* (Cambridge, MA: Harvard University Press, 2016), 131.

[86] It is telling that Soviet jurists considered the role of Protecting Powers unacceptable, disliking the 1929 Convention's allegedly bourgeois character and framing the ICRC as a "reactionary" organization.

that treaty, which provided the Nazis with a legal excuse to exclude millions of starving Soviet POWs.[87] They also tried to use some of the law's elastic wordings punitively to justify their genocidal policies—"where there's a Jew there's a partisan, and where there's a partisan there's a Jew."[88] After Hitler's downfall, the Allied judges of the Nuremberg Military Tribunals (NMTs), especially in the cases of the Ministries, High Command, and Einsatzgruppen, rejected many of these justifications outright.[89]

However, in the case of the infamous *Hostage* tribunal, the US judges noted that the partisans of the Balkans and Greece had not met all the Hague Regulations' criteria, and subsequently ruled that their executions by the Germans had not necessarily been unlawful.[90] For the Free French and other European resistance movements, it were precisely these problems "plaguing the war crimes tribunals after World War II" that reminded them of the importance of their wartime claims to broaden the law's scope for partisans.[91] Already during the war, the Free French had disputed the Hague Regulations' strict criteria for belligerency and Berlin's destructive orders to execute captured partisans as so-called *francs-tireurs*.[92]

In August 1944, with the landings at Normandy and the Allied recognition of the French Forces of the Interior (FFI) as being aligned with De Gaulle's belligerent army, the ICRC circulated its own memorandum urging all the parties to grant POW rights to organized partisans.[93] In this document the Genevans invoked the "principles of humanity" and human rights thinking to prohibit the killing of partisans not covered by the law's provisions. They also disputed the importance of belligerent status for granting POW status if partisans

---

The Soviets tried to restrict themselves to the Hague Regulations of 1907, which had no binding supervisory elements. Toman, "L'Union Soviètique et le Droit des Conflits Armés," 389–395.

[87] Toman, "L'Union Soviètique et le Droit des Conflits Armés," 387–389.

[88] Cited from: Scheipers, *Unlawful Combatants*, 125–132.

[89] For the vast historiography on partisan warfare, Nazi occupation, and the Holocaust, see Mark Mazower, *Hitler's Empire: Nazi Rule in Occupied Europe* (London: Allen Lane, 2008); Omer Bartov, *The Eastern Front, 1941–45: German Troops and the Barbarisation of Warfare* (Basingstoke: Palgrave, 2001); Christopher Browning, *Ordinary Men: Reserve Battalion 101 and the Final Solution in Poland* (London: Penguin, 2001); and Ben Shepherd, *Terror in the Balkans: German Armies and Partisan Warfare* (Cambridge, MA: Harvard University Press, 2012).

[90] See Kevin Jon Heller, *The Nuremberg Military Tribunals and the Origins of International Criminal Law* (Oxford: Oxford University Press, 2012).

[91] The quote referring to the war crimes trials comes from the American jurist Richard Baxter. Detlev Vagts, Theodor Meron, Stephen Schwebel, and Charles Keever, *Humanizing the Laws of War: Selected Writings of Richard Baxter* (Oxford: Oxford University Press, 2014), 117–118.

[92] *Report of the ICRC on its activities during the Second World War, Vol I* (1948), 520–521.

[93] For the actual note and its drafting debates, see ICRC appeal on partisans, 17 August 1944, no. G-1154-G.92, Les Archives du Comité International de la Croix-Rouge (ACICR), Geneva. See also Letter Max Huber to Minister for External Affairs, 24 August 1944, no. series A989, 1944/925/1/155, National Archives of Australia (NAA), Canberra, ACT.

164   PREPARING FOR WAR

complied with the Regulations' criteria. Whereas the Germans made no official declaration, the American and British responded remarkably evasively to this ICRC memorandum.[94]

In a special memo, the British War Office admitted that this proposal "clearly" was in the interests of the Allied powers. In securing the law's backing for partisans fighting against the Germans, it would empower the struggle against Hitler's occupation. At the same time, the War Office feared possible resistance in a future occupied Germany threatening the safety of Allied occupation forces. To prevent this, it advised the UK government not to take "any positive line of action" on this issue.[95] This meant that the major Allied powers not only fell short of fully recognizing the right of resistance in occupied territory, but also sealed the fate of partisans by failing to dispute their summary executions head on.

4.2 The Resistance

The rise of the new Gaullist state built upon a mythical ideal of collective resistance, combined with the early recognition of its belligerent status by the ICRC,[96] transformed French legal attitudes toward its postwar project to revise humanitarian law, especially in relation to partisan warfare. The French Inter-Ministerial Commission, which owed its existence to a former resistance fighter (Frenay) who had tried to widen the POW Convention's scope, agreed upon the need to broaden this treaty for resistance fighters and to guarantee them basic human rights against torture. Its members disagreed, however, about *how* to cover irregulars under this Convention.[97] As a result of growing tensions between former resistance fighters demanding a broader scope and a more cautious group of officials from the Ministry of Overseas Territories, the Ministry of War, and the Foreign Ministry, the Inter-Ministerial Commission witnessed a major split on the issue, establishing a sub-committee to solve this critical question.[98]

---

[94] *Report of the ICRC on its activities during the Second World War, Vol I* (1948), 517–518.

[95] For the British War Office's reaction to this memo, see Memo War Office for Imperial Prisoners of War Committee Sub Committee, 11 September 1944, no. series A989, 1944/925/1/155, NAA.

[96] *Report of the ICRC on its activities during the Second World War, Vol I* (1948), 520.

[97] Note Ministère des Prisonniers, Déportés et Réfugiés Révision de la Convention de Genève, 9 July 1945, no. 160, Unions Internationales 1944–1960, Les Archives Diplomatiques (LAD), Paris.

[98] Report Commission Chargée de la Révision et de l'Adaptation des Conventions de Genève aux Circonstances Actuelles, 23 July 1946, no. 160-BIS, Unions Internationales 1944–1960, LAD.

The formula it suggested, which questioned the concept of recognized belligerent status on behalf of the Free French—although not for the Viet Minh—widened the law's scope for "les combattants de l'intérieur organises," a concept that would continue to influence French legal visions on this matter. This seemingly innocent limitation would imply, however, that irregulars operating on their own would not necessarily fall under the POW Convention's umbrella.[99] Due to criticisms about this restriction, another drafting committee was set up, suggesting a compromise text by widening the original proposal's scope through covering "all persons, not belonging to the armed forces, who had been captured during war operations."[100] This new proposal, which potentially covered so-called "fifth columns,"[101] led to renewed opposition from Lamarle. In trying to protect the Republic's hard-won sovereignty, and being aware of Anglo-American sensitivities on this matter, the French diplomat also sought to prevent outside observers from intervening on behalf of such irregulars.[102]

By contrast, the former resistance figure Georges Duhamel demanded basic human rights for every detainee, by giving them protections against torture.[103] Duhamel had gained De Gaulle's favor during the war and also knew about the Conventions, as a former military surgeon. The Ministry of War, seeking to protect its security interests in occupied Germany and Indochina, wanted to keep several criteria for irregulars in place, however—by asking them to wear a fixed insignia, for instance.[104] While expressing sympathy for the proposals from former resistance fighters, Lamarle feared that these would most likely engender opposition from Anglo-American allies.[105] As a diplomat, he was familiar with their concerns regarding this matter. Due to these divisions, the French initially failed to solve the enigma of how to protect partisans without sacrificing their core strategic interests.[106]

[99] Note Ministry of Foreign Affairs Direction Générale des Affaires Administratives, 26 July 1946, no. 160, Unions Internationales 1944–1960, LAD.

[100] The Comité de Rédaction was composed of Jacob; Dominique Perrin, of the Unions Direction; and Claude Chayet, of the Legal Division of the French Foreign Ministry: Textes Proposé à la Commission par le Comité de Rédaction, 1946, no. 160-BIS, Unions Internationales 1944–1960, LAD.

[101] See also Compte-rendu de la Séance Commission Interministérielle, 8 January 1947, no. 160-BIS, Unions Internationales 1944–1960, LAD.

[102] Compte-rendu de la Séance Commission Interministérielle, 14 November 1946, no. 160-BIS, Unions Internationales 1944–1960, LAD.

[103] Compte-rendu de la Séance Commission Interministérielle, 8 January 1947, no. 160-BIS, Unions Internationales 1944–1960, LAD.

[104] Vandaele's comments triggered a fierce response from Pierre Hemery, who had been formerly held at the slave labor camp of KL Dora-Mittelbau. In his view, none of the "maquisards" had ever worn any fixed insignia and removed them once their operations were over. Compte-rendu de la Séance Commission Interministérielle, 8 January 1947, no. 160-BIS, Unions Internationales 1944–1960, LAD.

[105] Compte-rendu de la Séance Commission Interministérielle, 8 January 1947 and 22 February 1947, no. 160-BIS, Unions Internationales 1944–1960, LAD.

[106] Compte-rendu de la Séance Commission Interministérielle, 22 February 1947, no. 160-BIS, Unions Internationales 1944–1960, LAD. See also Projet de Convention Relative au Traitement des

166 PREPARING FOR WAR

In late 1946, Pictet's drafting team had produced an important internal memorandum concerning the protection of resistance fighters that would transform the ICRC's views on this matter for years to come. This document was based upon the organization's wartime experiences in occupied France and Italy.[107] It said that the 1929 POW Convention had to be revised in light of the recent war's "nombreuses difficultés" with respect to partisan warfare. Pictet's drafting team preferred a specific definition with detailed provisions over a general provision like the Martens Clause ("too vague").[108] Echoing their human rights agenda, they argued that the future treaty should guarantee intangible rights[109] for non-recognized regular armed forces (e.g. the Free French) and collectively organized resistance movements (the FFI).[110]

In this context, Pictet limited those rights to only those irregulars who had a connection with at least one recognized belligerent party and had complied with the Regulations' strict criteria for POW status.[111] For instance, referring to the prototype of De Gaulle's Free French, he wished to cover organized resistance movements whose government had formerly existed (i.e. the Third Republic), and had been recognized as such by at least one of the war's major belligerents. This meant, however, that he potentially excluded a whole range of resistance movements, such as Frenay's own *Combat*, which officially lacked

Prisonniers de Guerre, no. CEG_1947_DOC_FRAN, La Bibliothèque du Comité international de la Croix Rouge, Geneva (ICRC Library).

[107] Draft Pictet Notice Concernant l'Article Premier de la Convention Relative au Traitement des Prisonniers de Guerre, 1946, no. CR-240-5, ACICR.

[108] Draft Pictet Notice Concernant l'Article Premier de la Convention Relative au Traitement des Prisonniers de Guerre, 1946, no. CR-240-5, ACICR.

[109] This formed a response to the ICRC's recent wartime experiences of witnessing how many detained fighters whose government or authority had been destroyed (i.e. Polish POWs), or who went into exile (i.e. Dutch soldiers re-interned by the Germans), or who had not been recognized (i.e. Free French fighters), or whose collaborating counterparts had agreed to certain "special agreements" (i.e. Vichy/ Quisling's collaborating government), had been excluded from the law's protection. Pictet wanted to prevent this from happening again by making the rights of a prisoner of war intangible and irrespective of the belligerent party's exact status.

[110] In this context, he referred to three particular historical prototypes: the Gaullists, representing the Committee of National Liberation (CFLN), whose members had refused the German terms of the Armistice (unlike Pétain's followers), the Italian "Badoglistes," representing the 1943-established authority led by General Pietro Badoglio, and the "partisans," of the *Forces Françaises de l'Intérieure* (FFI), established in February 1944. Pictet also raised the problem of "surrendered enemy personne" (SEP), a *debellatio* type of category invented by the Allies after the unconditional surrender of German and Japanese soldiers. The ICRC had difficulty reaching them as they were not considered official prisoners of war, falling under the Third Geneva Convention. For the history of ICRC–Allied discussion on the issue of SEP, see James Crossland, *Britain and the International Committee of the Red Cross, 1939–1945* (New York: Palgrave Macmillan, 2014), 190–195.

[111] The ICRC report on partisan warfare during the Second World War testifies to its Eurocentrism. See Statut et Traitement des Partisans, no. G-1153-G.92, ACICR.

that belligerent connection and/or a sufficiently organized apparatus meeting the law's strict requirements.[112]

Focusing his attention exclusively on Western Europe, Pictet had scant interest in those resistance movements opposing colonial rule. At this stage, the question of the Viet Minh's belligerent status in relation to partisan warfare appeared not to have been on his mind. For Pictet, it was more important to cover those organized resistance movements which resembled "groupements nationaux qui, combattant en unités plus ou moins compactes, continuaient la lutte en territoire occupé (par exemple les FFI)."[113] Continuing the law's nineteenth-century focus on patriotism, he thus initially limited the POW Convention's protection to "patriotic" movements, rather than other forms of political resistance such as anti-colonialism.

Although he questioned some of the existing law's requirements, by criticizing the demand for irregulars to carry their arms openly, Pictet initially remained reluctant to entirely remove these.[114] As we saw before, he remained a pragmatist at heart. Other ICRC officials responded critically, however, to parts of the partisan memorandum, preferring to lower the law's threshold for intermittent resistance fighters even further. The objective of these critics was to allow irregulars such as Frenay's *Combat* to work secretly rather than to force them to carry their arms openly, or to wear a distinctive sign at all times, which would have made them extremely vulnerable.[115] Ultimately, the ICRC, influenced by cautious officials such as Huber and because of fears of undermining the cardinal principle of distinction, left the question of partisans open for debate at the 1947 Government Experts' Conference.

Whereas the ICRC and French drafters extensively discussed the question of irregulars before April 1947, British and American preparations focused on completely different topics, such as strengthening the existing regulations for military imprisonment so as to better protect their armed forces in response to the killing of Allied POWs by Axis captors. The fact that both major Allied powers had extensive wartime experience of dealing with questions of partisan warfare (e.g. Hitler's infamous *Kommandobefehl*, plus the Ex Parte Quirin trials of 1942) did surprisingly little to change this outlook.[116] The US POWC

---

[112] Wieviorka, *The French Resistance*, 1; and Rod Kedward, *In Search of the Maquis: Rural Resistance in Southern France, 1942–1944* (Oxford: Oxford University Press, 1993).

[113] Draft Pictet Notice Concernant l'Article Premier de la Convention Relative au Traitement des Prisonniers de Guerre, 1946, no. CR-240-5, ACICR.

[114] Preliminary Documents Submitted by the ICRC, Vol. II, no. CEG_1947_DOCPG_ENG_01, ICRC Library.

[115] Note Colombo for Pilloud, 23 December 1946, no. CR-240-5, ACICR.

[116] See Louis Fisher, *Nazi Saboteurs on Trial: A Military Tribunal and American Law* (Lawrence, KA: University Press of Kansas, 2003).

168 PREPARING FOR WAR

continued to focus its attention on issues other than expanding the law's scope for irregulars throughout these immediate postwar years. While discussing the POWC's early restrictive drafts for the POW Convention, the US internment expert Clattenburg even claimed that they "would have been very helpful to the FFI in France."[117]

"Traumatized" Architects

When the Americans and British arrived in Geneva in April 1947, they acted as enemies of future irregulars, seeking to limit the Convention's access for resistance fighters. They also expected continental European allies to follow this line. Henry Phillimore, a former British prosecutor at Nuremberg,[118] played a crucial role during these 1947 negotiations: he constantly opposed efforts by Lamarle's delegation to widen the law's scope for irregulars.[119] During these proceedings, former resistance figures such as Pierre Bellan and Bourdet—who had been questioned by the Gestapo—demanded greater protection for irregulars under humanitarian law against torture. Yet at the POW Committee's very first meeting, their delegation asked for improved protection in the case of (non-recognized) resistance movements.[120]

These far-reaching proposals, which were supported by most other formerly occupied nations whose governments depended upon their links with wartime resistance movements for their legitimacy in the post-Nazi era, took Phillimore's poorly prepared delegation by complete surprise, forcing it to reserve its opinion on this issue.[121] Having expected a far more restrictive attitude from his fellow occupier in Germany and overlooking the substantial differences within the French state concerning partisan warfare, Phillimore felt that its delegation lacked a sense of reality by seeing "all questions through the

---

[117] Minutes Prisoners of War Committee, 28 June 1946 and 28 February 1947, Provost Marshal General, no. 672, National Archives and Records Administration (NARA), College Park, MD.

[118] An Eton graduate, Henry Phillimore had served during the war as a legal officer at the Prisoner of War Department to interpret the existing laws of war. When the war was coming to an end, he began preparing cases against Nazi war criminals; finally he joined the British prosecuting team at Nuremberg.

[119] British views also reflected a broader distrust among members of British POW departments towards the ICRC, which had its origins in their recent wartime experiences. See Crossland, *Britain and the International Committee of the Red Cross*, 206–207. Moreover, this restrictive British attitude stands in marked contrast to the British position in 1874, when it sought to protect its interests as a small land power.

[120] Minutes Meetings Commission II, Vol. III, 1947, no. CEG_1947_COMM2_PV_01, ICRC Library.

[121] Report Conference of Government Experts at Geneva, 1947, no. 3795, FO369 (Foreign Office), The National Archives (TNA), Kew; and Minutes Meetings Commission II, Vol. III, 1947, no. CEG_1947_COMM2_PV_01, ICRC Library.

eyes of defeat [rather than those] of a detaining power, an occupying power, or a victorious power."[122] Still, he expressed sympathy since "many, if not all, of [the French] had [...] been in German occupation camps and they, their relatives and friends had had bitter [wartime] experiences."[123]

By invoking their personal experiences as former victims of Hitler's empire at the negotiating table, these continental European delegates gained unique moral authority over their Anglo-American (and ICRC) counterparts. Indeed, Phillimore realized he could not entirely ignore their arguments and felt constrained in his ability to publicly pressure his European allies to take Western security interests more seriously.[124] Likewise, the ICRC appreciated the French positioning, but remained reluctant to publicly speak in favor of their far-reaching proposals widening the law's scope for partisans. Pilloud, for instance, called it a "delicate topic," claiming that it was "impossible" to include every irregular.[125]

While initially the French and British both saw room for compromise,[126] the POW Committee, discussing the issue of partisans in greatest detail, experienced a major deadlock. Frustrated, the British, like the Americans, complained that their Western European allies were still unable to think in terms other than "those of their experiences under occupation."[127] In particular, they disliked the fact that none of them seemed to be "conscious of the problems which they [would be] confront[ed with] if the circumstances were reversed"—that is, a future scenario in which major Western powers occupied enemy lands.[128] As these gaps were not to be bridged any time soon, Phillimore suggested a special sub-committee, but its members again failed to agree upon a compromise formula acceptable to both sides.[129]

Viewing him as a legal expert,[130] the ICRC asked the former Nuremberg prosecutor to draft a separate text that could be used as a template for

---

[122] Report Conference of Government Experts at Geneva, 1947, no. 3795, FO369, TNA.

[123] Report Conference of Government Experts at Geneva, no. 3795, FO369, TNA.

[124] Giovanni Mantilla, *Lawmaking under Pressure: International Humanitarian Law and Internal Armed Conflict* (Ithaca, NY: Cornell University Press, 2020), 41.

[125] Minutes Meetings Commission II, 1947, no. CEG_1947_COMM2_PV_01, ICRC Library, Geneva.

[126] See Report Conference of Government Experts at Geneva, 1947, no. 3795, FO369, TNA; Minutes meetings Commission II, 1947, no. CEG_1947_COMM2_PV_01, ICRC Library; and Cable Lamarle to Foreign Ministry on POW Convention and Partisans, 15 April 1947, no. 160, Unions Internationales 1944–1960, LAD.

[127] Report Conference of Government Experts at Geneva, 1947, no. 3795, FO369, TNA.

[128] Report of American Delegation to Government Experts Conference, 1947, no. 674, Provost Marshal General, NARA.

[129] Minutes Meetings Commission II, 1947, no. CEG_1947_COMM2_PV_01, ICRC Library.

[130] Letter Phillimore to Max Huber, 5 November 1945, no. CR-240-7, ACICR; and Letter Huber to Phillimore, 5 October 1945, no. CR-240-7, ACICR.

170 PREPARING FOR WAR

further discussion. The ICRC misjudged the situation completely, however. Unsurprisingly, Phillimore created a text which fell in line with British interests by demanding strict conditions for resistance fighters to fall under the future POW Convention. Among other things, they had to have effective control over a certain territory, carry their arms openly, and wear a distinctive sign, and could potentially be prosecuted for their acts in wartime. This restrictive proposal immediately triggered heavy opposition from the French and many other delegations: Bourdet, as former second-in-command of *Combat*, argued that such types of proposal would make partisan warfare "more terrorist."[131]

In principle, as shown in previous chapters, the Americans preferred a far less restrictive approach than that advocated by Phillimore. The British regressiveness had much to do with the insurgency they were fighting in Palestine. Informally, Phillimore admitted that partisan warfare would become more relevant in the future and deserved humanitarian law's attention, but at this time he felt it was necessary to prioritize the "very serious threat to [British] armed forces" in Palestine.[132] This factor, combined with the (belated) arrival of the Stalinist Polish delegation which sought to obstruct Phillimore's delegation on this issue,[133] made it obvious to everyone "that no agreement could be reached."[134] The result was that the POW Committee failed to agree upon the military Convention's scope since many realized that another opportunity for discussion would arise at future drafting meetings.

The outcome of the 1947 Government Experts' Conference caused frustration on the part of all participating major drafting parties. Whereas the British and Americans blamed its failure on the allegedly traumatized victims of Hitler's empire, the French saw their stubbornness as a major cause. Equally disappointed, Pictet's drafting team was becoming increasingly skeptical about achieving greater protection for irregulars through the POW Convention. In June 1948, president Ruegger, together with Pictet, admitted during a US POWC meeting which they attended in Washington that if it would accept the ICRC's new drafts for the Conventions then "he was willing to rest the subject." While he "had evidently hoped that more protection might be accepted

---

[131] Cable Lamarle to Foreign Ministry on Partisans POW Convention, 16 April 1947, no. 160, Unions Internationales 1944–1960, LAD. See also Minutes Meetings Commission III, 1947, no. CEG_1947_COMM3_PV_03, ICRC Library.

[132] Cable Lamarle to Foreign Ministry on Partisans POW Convention, 16 April 1947, no. 160, Unions Internationales 1944–1960, LAD.

[133] Minutes Meetings Bureau, 1947, no. CEG_1947_BURCONF_PV, ICRC Library. See Report of American Delegation to Government Experts Conference, 1947, no. 674, Provost Marshal General, NARA.

[134] Report of American Delegation to Government Experts Conference, 1947, no. 674, Provost Marshal General, NARA.

for partisans," he appreciated that widening this treaty scope would "probably" lead to only more violations.[135]

4.3 Weaving a Legal Safety Net

By mid-1948, when fears of war were on the rise, Pictet's drafters had thus largely given up on their original plan to widen the POW Convention's scope. In their new draft, they copied the Hague Regulations' criteria and Phillimore's demand for effective control of a territory by resistance movements. Of course, they had made a few critical suggestions for this treaty, extending its scope even to colonial wars and thereby potentially including the Viet Minh. They also sought to prevent the exclusion of prisoners whose status was contested, but these two proposals did little to challenge the still restrictive outlook of the foundational article of the Convention for most irregulars. The most important change in the ICRC's attitude with respect to this matter had taken place in another domain, however. As we saw in Chapter 2, it had begun advocating, under the influence of human rights thinking, a regime of minimum protection for every enemy civilian under the Civilian Convention.

What is most fascinating is that the ICRC had decided in early 1948, when it presented its new drafts to the other major drafting parties, to make it possible for irregulars excluded from the restrictive POW Convention to fall under the Civilian one. Pictet's drafting team admitted in its proposals that "should [...] [persons applying for POW rights: BvD] be refused, for any reason, the application of these international Conventions [i.e. the POW Convention: BvD], they shall be protected by the present Convention [the Civilian Convention], in so far as they have a right thereto under the present Article [Article 3]."[136] By covering an impressive range of irregulars, the ICRC tried to guarantee all of them the rights of appeal, humane treatment, a fair trial, and access to outside inspectors. This major shift, largely overlooked in the literature,[137] blurred the distinction between fighters and non-combatants more than ever before.

Whereas Pictet tried to prevent irregulars from being excluded from these Conventions, the British War Office Committee, which was tasked with revising the POW Convention, tried to achieve the very opposite. In mid-1947,

---

[135] Minutes Prisoners of War Committee, 25 June 1948, no. 673, Provost Marshal General, NARA. No minutes of this meeting have been found in the ACICR.

[136] Draft Revised or New Conventions for the Protection of War Victims, 1948, LOC.

[137] A major exception to this rule is Dörmann, "The Legal Situation of 'Unlawful/Unprivileged Combatants'."

172 PREPARING FOR WAR

Gardner—who acted as its chairperson, defending a hardline position—drafted an influential memorandum in which he expressed major concern about plans to allow many irregulars to fall under humanitarian law.[138] He particularly disliked those concepts which might possibly cover ' "terrorist' elements in Palestine." Defending the empire's interests, Gardner's principal aim was to demand that irregulars come out into the open and meet a so-called "objective test [...] which an Occupying Power can itself regard as fair."[139] This meant that irregulars either had to come out of the shadows to fight against a regular occupier in an open battle, leading to their inevitable destruction, or work secretly and, if captured, suffer maltreatment by that same army.

When the War Office Committee discussed this memorandum in September 1947, British security officials agreed that it was imperative to prevent their commanders in the field from being "handicapped" and that "terrorists campaigning against law and order" in colonial territories be covered. Arthur Dove, the War Office's Deputy Director of Military Operations, agreed that it was important to give "the maximum protection to any of our own people dropped within enemy lines." Once hostilities ceased, however, he argued that "those responsible for acts of subversive terrorism" should be excluded. Having previously served in Palestine, Dove's thinking with respect to this issue was also colored by anxieties concerning the protection of "our forces in Palestine at present." Likewise, one legal advisor from MI-5 wished not to "handicap [us] in dealing with such a situation as existed in Palestine."[140]

Although less restrictive than Gardner's original proposal, the War Office Committee maintained a regressive and extrajudicial attitude with respect to treating irregulars, particularly those challenging British rule. Its report said clearly that those operating in "colonial, mandated or trustee territory in which a rebellion is in progress" could never fall under humanitarian law (see Chapter 3).[141] It is crucially important to recognize that partisans operating elsewhere were asked to meet conditions they could never meet in practice, or that would lead to their inevitable defeat.[142] Essentially, the War Office was trying to internationally legalize its extrajudicial counterinsurgency policies previously used in colonial wartime.

---

[138] Minutes of War Office Committee 17 September 1948, no. 326, WO163 (War Office), TNA.

[139] Memorandum on Partisans by the Chairman for Consideration of Second Meeting of Committee, 18 August 1947, no. 326, WO163, TNA.

[140] Minutes of Meeting War Office Committee, 17 September 1947, no. 326, WO163, TNA.

[141] Report of the Sub-Committee on the Definition of Partisans, 13 February 1948, no. 327, WO163, TNA.

[142] The General Staff had also given its approval of the report.

Discussing the Civilian Convention, the Home Office Committee added that "enemy agents and suspected enemy agents whilst entitled to be treated humanely, should not have the right to benefit by certain particular provisions [e.g. Protecting Power connections: BvD] of the proposed [Civilian] Convention."[143] The problem, however, was that it left unclear what "humane treatment" precisely meant. The ICRC would not be allowed to visit prisons where those persons would be questioned, for instance. Detaining officials were also granted highly discretionary powers when interrogating those suspected of hostile activities. These recommendations sanctioning the use of extrajudicial interrogation measures emerged from deeply rooted anxieties among British security officials, whose views were dominant at this stage, and increasingly in relation to the threat of communist "fifth columns," as we will see later.

In September 1947, the US POWC restarted its reexamination of the POW Convention. Unlike the British, it still adopted a remarkably moderate approach to the issue of treating irregulars. Although it shared British concerns about the threat of communist spies, the POW Committee's debates revealed far less anxiety about this matter at this stage of the drafting process—which it would soon profoundly regret.[144] With human rights thinking remaining present in State Department circles, it endorsed Clattenburg's proposal for a general clause with minimum human rights protections for all kinds of detainees. On the other hand, it knew that the existing draft was still rigid enough to safeguard most of its security interests. In June 1948, when Pictet had come to Washington, US officials—including Yingling—admitted frankly that they were "perfectly aware" that their plans for the POW Convention left most partisans isolated.[145]

When the major drafting parties met in Stockholm in August 1948, there was hardly any time available to discuss "difficult passages" such as those relating to partisans.[146] Discussing the POW Convention, the Juridical Committee's second sub-committee first removed Phillimore's original

[143] Report Home Office Committee on the Civilian Convention, 1947, no. 2184, HO213 (Home Office), TNA.

[144] With respect to irregulars' protection, it was more interested in issues varying from the protection of civilian air crews, considering Japan's "Enemy Airmen's Act" from August 1942; medical personnel; chaplains; the merchant marine; and so on.

[145] Based on his meeting with US officials, Pictet wrote in a memo for Pilloud: "Les experts se sont ralliés au texte de l'article 3 relatif aux partisans qu'ils jugent la meilleure formule, tout en étant parfaitement conscients que cet article n'aurait pas couvert la plupart des cas de résistance de la dernière guerre." Note Pictet for Pilloud on US Views, 9 July 1948, no. CR - 238-5, ACICR.

[146] Report UK Observer Stockholm Conference, 1948, no. 328, WO163, TNA; and Memo F. Palmer on Stockholm Conference to External Affairs, 30 August 1948, no. 619 - B - 40 - PART 3, RG25 - Vol 3398, Library and Archives Canada (LAC), Ottawa, ON.

174   PREPARING FOR WAR

demand for partisans to have effective control over a territory.[147] British observers disapproved of Clattenburg's human rights clause: during informal talks,
Gardner told his mostly indifferent US colleague about his opposition to this
"completely impossible provision." Demonstrating his major anxiety about this
clause, Gardner feared it would give protection to "spies, war criminals, unau-
thorized underground movements and the like." When the US proposal was
finally accepted by the conference, he noted how "French [...] representatives
[...] received it with open smiles,"[148] with former resistance fighters Jacob and
Bellan being visibly present there.

Studying the Civilian Convention, the Stockholm Conference's third sub-
committee focused on the ICRC's proposal to create a bridge between the two
treaties. Unfortunately the specifics of this debate are unavailable, due to a lack
of detailed minutes. One report from the Dutch delegation suggests that the
Canadians rejected this proposal whereas the ICRC continued to support it,
though cautiously.[149] In the end, the third sub-committee accepted a confusing
section which said that "the nationals of the country where the conflict takes
place and who are not covered by other international conventions, are likewise
protected by the present Convention."[150]

This section, which applied to internal conflicts as well, left unclear how it
should be interpreted in times of interstate occupation. Neither did it specifically address the status of resistance fighters as such. Cohn's delegation thus
suggested adding an extra line stating clearly that "the protection of members of
the underground movement has been provided for in the [POW Convention].
In case of doubt, members of the underground movement shall benefit at least
by the same protection as that ensured to civilian populations."[151] This Danish
proposal seems to have failed to reach codification, only being mentioned in
the minutes as a possibility for future debate.

In the end, the 1948 Stockholm Conference made a few remarkable steps
toward protecting irregulars. Most prominently, it recognized, for the first

---

[147] It also rejected Cohn's far-reaching proposal to ask for partisans the same requirements as the
levée, a proposal that would be accepted only in the 1970s with the Additional Protocols. See Protocol
Additional to the Geneva Conventions of 12 August 1949, and relating to the Protection of Victims of
International Armed Conflicts (Protocol I), Article 44. Geneva, 8 June 1977.

[148] Report UK Observer Stockholm Conference, 1948, no. 328, WO163, TNA.

[149] Rapport van de Nederlandse Delegatie Stockholm Conferentie, 1948, no. 71, Ministerie van
Sociale Zaken, National Archives of the Netherlands (NA), The Hague.

[150] Convention for the Protection of Civilians Persons in Time of War, 1948, 114, no. CI_1948_
PROJET_ENG_04, ICRC Library.

[151] Summary Debates Sub-Commissions of the Legal Commission, no. 22, American Red
Cross, NARA.

time in history, human rights in wartime and the right of resistance in both occupied and colonial territory under the POW Convention, which challenged international law's racialized foundations. The treaty's fourth article made it far more difficult for detaining powers to eliminate "doubtful categories" of prisoners. The practice of summary executions was now increasingly stigmatized under humanitarian law.[152] On the other hand, the conference maintained strict conditions for irregulars, which spelled a failure to fully protect them through the POW Convention. Compared to the original 1929 Convention, this new text required them to comply with three additional conditions, leaving continental Europeans very disappointed.[153] The question of how to create a possible safety net between the two treaties for excluded irregulars was not sufficiently answered either, fomenting further controversy in the following year.

Despite these shortcomings, the Stockholm Conference's outcome represented a legal breakthrough for the protection of irregulars. This can be accounted for by considering two important factors. First is the absence of British opposition due to its decision not to send any government delegates with full voting rights to Stockholm. "There is no doubt," admitted the New Zealand delegate afterward, "that the UK and those countries which have supported its views have lost heavily as a result of their silence at Stockholm [...] Occupying powers [...] were shorn of the right to punish adequately the hostile acts of the local inhabitants."[154] Second, as a result of the flexible instructions from the State Department, the US delegation acted "très souple," according to the surprised French delegation, which had expected much fiercer opposition.[155] Indeed, US delegates almost never pressed for any solution: if they met severe opposition, they would drop their proposal or make a reservation. The lack of pressure from these two usually restrictive major drafting parties created the conditions which enabled the French and ICRC to successfully push through proposals to safeguard basic rights for irregulars in armed conflict.

---

[152] Revision of the POW Convention, no. CI_1948_PROJET_ENG_03, ICRC Library.

[153] The Danish delegation, therefore, made a reservation to this part of the draft. Summary Debates Sub-Commissions of the Legal Commission, no. 22, American Red Cross, NARA.

[154] Report of New Zealand Delegation to Diplomatic Conference of Geneva 1949, AAYS 8638 W2054 ADW2054/1220/3/3 (R18524114), Archives New Zealand (ANZ), Wellington.

[155] Instructions US Government for Basil O'Connor, Chairman of the US Delegation, August 1948, no. 22, RG43 - 5536, NARA; and Report Bellan Conventions Internationales—Protection des Prisonniers de Guerre, October 1948, no. 159 - TER, Unions Internationales 1944–1960, LAD.

176 PREPARING FOR WAR

"Creating a Gap Between the Conventions"

The British government reacted to these Stockholm drafts with great skepticism. In late 1948, while preparing for the final diplomatic conference, Gardner drafted another restrictive memorandum, in which he objected to Clattenburg's accepted clause and to covering "[illegitimate] hostile acts on the part of private enemy individuals." For him, it was essential that if one person committed a hostile act against the occupier, then this person ceased to be a non-combatant protected under the Civilian Convention. In such a case, he argued, that person should meet an "objective test" which allows for access to the POW Convention's rights.[156] A later briefing for Attlee's Cabinet confirmed that the occupier could ultimately determine whether this person had met that test's requirements—"the ones of proof would be on the partisan."[157]

Influenced by anxieties surrounding the threat of communist spies and as a result of the ongoing insurgency in British Malaya, the final UK memorandum, which excluded even suspects of hostile operations, created controversy within Whitehall itself. The Home Office and MI-5 wished to entirely exclude enemy agents, and anti-colonial guerrillas in particular. As we saw earlier, the Foreign Office continued to express concern about the fate of its subjects held captive by a future enemy and the possible repercussions for Britain's prestige. Not seeing the need to "trouble the PM [Attlee] on this point," the two sides finally agreed to solve the matter between themselves.[158] Their final proposal was to officially give every detainee the right to be humanely treated, although they deliberately failed to clearly define this point in their suggestions, leaving future prisoners and their rights in limbo.

This lack of definitional clarity was the result of the continuing internal split among the British drafters concerning what humane treatment precisely entailed, a debate which has powerful echoes in later extrajudicial regimes such as that of the "War on Terror." UK intelligence officials deliberately drew an important distinction between "physical violence and cruelty" and "mental violence and cruelty," without clarifying these different terms. In private conversations, they argued that "mental torture must be used [...] for an effective interrogation."[159] Furthermore, MI-5 tried to make it impossible for outside inspectors such as the ICRC to monitor the situation of these suspects held in

---

[156] Draft Memorandum to the Swiss edited by Gardner, 14 January 1949, no. 4142, FO369, TNA.

[157] Memorandum by the Secretary of State for Foreign Affairs and the Secretary of State for War, 10 March 1949, no. 33, CAB129 (Cabinet Office), TNA.

[158] Letter B. A. Hill to Speake on Civilian Convention, 10 November 1948, no. 2185, HO213, TNA.

[159] Letter B. A. Hill to Speake on Civilian Convention, 9 November 1948, no. 2185, HO213, TNA.

extrajudicial detention. In principle, this meant that the Secretary of State were to be given the "unfettered and final decision [...] as to who is to be suspected of being an enemy agent [that was] not challengeable in the Courts or by the Protecting Power."[160]

These proposals were finally discussed at a critical meeting of the British Cabinet, which was attended by Prime Minister Attlee, Foreign Secretary Ernest Bevin, and Home Secretary James Ede, who had recently opposed the abolition of the death penalty in Britain.[161] In the end they decided to endorse the memorandum's suggestions, while stressing that detainees "are always to be humanely treated."[162] On the other hand, the Cabinet attenuated this proposal by cutting the potential link between the two treaties. Also, British officials continued to question the Stockholm draft's strict prohibitions against *every* form of torture.[163] Hence, they tried to exclude from the texts suspects of hostile acts, illustrated by a revealing comment from Gardner during an internal meeting of his delegation at the start of the diplomatic conference, in April 1949:

[Our] object [...] [is] to combat the view that everybody should be protected by one Convention or another. We were deliberately creating a gap between the Conventions to cover people who did not conform to the recognized laws of war [...] and we ought to have it firmly in mind that we wanted the genuine suspect to be in the gap, and not in the Conventions. Each delegate should have it clearly in mind that we deliberately wanted to exclude from all Conventions not merely spies, francs-tireurs and saboteurs, but also the persons who were suspected of these operations.[164]

This revealing remark demonstrates the British delegation's extrajudicial inclination, which was caused by its continuing anxieties with regard to the interests of its security officials in Europe and Asia. These anxieties were fueled by rumors in Whitehall about the threat of communist "fifth columns" in the wake of East–West tensions.

Although the increasingly dominant Pentagon realized it was impossible to fully revise the Stockholm drafts,[165] it shared many of those British concerns

---

[160] Letter B. A. Hill to Speake on Civilian Convention, 10 November 1948, no. 2185, HO213, TNA.
[161] The minutes of the Cabinet meeting focus on outcome, rather than the process. This makes it difficult to determine the precise nature of its debates.
[162] Letter H. A. Strutt to Craigie on Civilian Convention, 16 December 1948, no. 3970, FO369, TNA.
[163] See Revised Draft Brief for UK Delegation, 11 February 1949, no. 4145, FO369, TNA.
[164] Notes of Third Meeting of the UK Delegation, 22 April 1949, no. 4149, FO369, TNA.
[165] Still, the Pentagon regretted the attitude of their Stockholm delegation, which accepted a whole range of "relatively idealistic provisions" that limited their powers in wartime. Craigie's Report on

178 PREPARING FOR WAR

relating to the threat of communist agents. Shaping US legal attitudes, the Berlin blockade triggered greater fears of war with the Soviet Union and the threat of domestic subversion.[166] The growing hysteria in Washington surrounding the alleged threat of Soviet spies had a direct impact upon its preparations for the upcoming diplomatic conference, in 1949. For this reason the US POWC hardened its attitude, opposing Clattenburg's original plan for a human rights clause.[167] It also suggested, following recommendations from the Attorney General's Department of Justice, cutting the link between the two treaties by means of a special security clause for the Civilian Convention.

This potentially destructive extrajudicial clause would place captured enemy agents temporarily beyond the scope of humanitarian law. By trying to block prisoners from circulating valuable intelligence through external inspectors, US officials hoped to protect their security interests as they were preparing for war.[168] Much had happened in the years since US officials had accepted the Civilian Convention and shaped its protection for noncombatants and against inhumane treatment. They realized that protecting their armed forces against severe restrictions might be useful in a future war with the Soviets and other potential enemies, instructing the delegation to create a wedge between the Conventions and ditch Clattenburg's human rights clause.

While the French government still considered the issue of partisans a major priority, it would no longer push so hard on it if this were to directly undermine obtaining a common understanding with the other Great Powers. After the Prague Coup and Berlin blockade, Paris realized that its new military alliance with London and Washington was essential for its security in the case of a potential invasion by the Soviet Union or a revived Germany.[169] When meeting in Paris, the British convinced Lamarle, as a moderate French diplomat, to take their mutual defense interests as founding NATO members more seriously, for instance with regard to spies. Although he had addressed this matter

---

the Diplomatic Conference, November 1949, no. 6036, ADM116 (Admiralty), TNA; and Minutes of Meeting at the Pentagon on the Civilian Convention, 14 April 1949, no. 5, RG 43, 40, NARA.

[166] Odd Arne Westad, *The Cold War: A World History* (New York: Basic Books, 2017); and Melvyn Leffler, "National Security and US Foreign Policy," in *The Origins of the Cold War: An International History*, ed. Melvyn Leffler and David Painter (New York: Routledge, 2002), 15–52, 37.

[167] See Text of US Draft for Diplomatic Conference, March 1949, no. 22, American Red Cross, NARA.

[168] Boyd van Dijk, "Human Rights in War: On the Entangled Foundations of the 1949 Geneva Conventions," *American Journal of International Law* (2018): 553–582, 574. See Minutes Prisoners of War Committee, 31 March 1949, no. 673, Provost Marshal General, NARA.

[169] Odd Arne Westad, *The Cold War: A World History* (New York: Basic Books, 2017); and Melvyn Leffler, "The Emergence of an American Grand Strategy, 1945–1952," in *The Cambridge History of the Cold War, Vol I*, ed. Melvyn Leffler and Odd Arne Westad (Cambridge: Cambridge University Press, 2010), 67–89, 80.

internally, he admitted that his government had not fully "appreciated the dangers of allowing suspected spies coming under the Conventions."[170] This statement was in accord with his government's broader agenda of seeking a better understanding with major NATO allies on issues of common military interest.

With respect to partisans, the French Foreign Ministry endorsed a double solution by, on the one hand, limiting the POW Convention's scope for collective resistance in occupied territory, and, on the other hand, assuring basic rights for individuals under the Civilian Convention. As part of this scheme, the French delegation was instructed to bring the two treaties "into harmony" with each other by means of the preamble featuring human rights, which remained an instrumental element for its overall drafting agenda. Indeed, the French delegation consistently aimed at banning torture and improving the "procédure judiciaire" in times of interstate war. Unlike the British, they saw overlap rather than a contrast between the Geneva Conventions, the Genocide Convention, and the Universal Declaration of Human Rights (UDHR).[171] The French envisaged a direct link between human rights and humanitarian law as long as the Indochina War was excluded. The fact that Bourdet, who had recently criticized French escalation of the war, was no longer part of its delegation appears to have prevented major internal dissent on this issue.

While working more closely with NATO allies, the French still wished to obtain contractual reciprocity with the Soviets and even saw them as potential drafting allies, deflecting expected Anglo-American opposition. While Craigie would later complain that they were often "unduly apprehensive of any opposition to the Soviets,"[172] the Soviets expressed suspicion about such accommodation among Western delegations.[173] The Soviets and the ICRC were arguably the strangest partners at this stage of the drafting process.[174] At the diplomatic conference, although ideological opposites, the two parties often worked together and supported each other's proposals, endorsing the Stockholm drafts from 1948. The ICRC largely accepted these texts, although it made a few

---

[170] Record of Conversations held in Paris between French delegation and the British, 18 April 1949, no. 4150, FO369, TNA.

[171] Instructions French Foreign Minister for French Delegation, 14 April 1949, no. 161, Unions Internationales 1944–1960, LAD.

[172] Craigie's Report on the Diplomatic Conference, November 1949, no. 6036, ADM116 (Admiralty), TNA.

[173] Boyd van Dijk, "'The Great Humanitarian': The Soviet Union, the International Committee of the Red Cross, and the Geneva Conventions of 1949," *Law and History Review* (2019): 209–235; and Report Soviet-Ukrainian Delegation, no. F. 2, Op. 12cc, Spr. 969, Ark. 60-76, TSDAVO.

[174] Unfortunately, the ACICR provides very few insights into the ICRC's actions during this particular stage of the drafting process.

180 PREPARING FOR WAR

important clarifications, for instance by removing Clattenburg's clause in favor of the Civilian Convention's preamble.[175]

Taking part for the first time in a global effort to create new rules for POW protection, the Soviets took a far more aggressive approach by actively opposing their Cold War adversaries' proposals. They believed these Anglo-American powers were using the Convention as a means "to prepare [for] a new war." In their view, the Anglo-American delegations were exploiting humanitarian law as a means to spy on them, to "demoralize" Soviet soldiers by suggesting that being a prisoner of war "is very convenient," and to reinforce a so-called "war psychosis."[176] In essence, the Soviets, based upon their wartime policies and ideological preconceptions,[177] wished to widen the POW Convention's scope to take in as many anti-imperial irregulars as possible, with the exception of suspected "war criminals"—which prompted concern among Anglo-American delegates about the treatment of their bomber pilots in case of Soviet capture.[178]

In line with this position, the Soviets constantly demanded that the law's strict conditions for partisans be softened. This proposal was in line with Soviet understandings of "just war" theory and their wartime experiences under Nazi rule. Moscow claimed that the summary executions of Soviet partisans by the German occupiers had been unlawful. By contrast, Anglo-American delegates wished to keep the POW Convention's scope highly restricted and to create a security clause that would deny irregulars broader legal access.[179] The Soviets saw such restrictive proposals as Anglo-American attempts to "create all possible loopholes" in the Conventions, if not to repeat Hitler's atrocities.[180]

4.4 Night and Fog in Geneva

The final stage of the drafting process triggered an epic struggle over the protection of partisans in future armed conflicts. Yet during the POW Committee's very first discussions, major disputes erupted around the sixth paragraph of

---

[175] See Draft Convention relative to the Treatment of Prisoners of War, 1949, no. CD_1949_DOCTRAV_ENG_03, ICRC Library; and Draft Convention for the Protection of Civilian Persons in Time of War, 1949, no. CD_1949_DOCTRAV_ENG_04, ICRC Library.

[176] Report Soviet-Ukrainian Delegation, no. F. 2, Op. 12cc, Spr. 969, Ark. 60-76, TSDAVO.

[177] For more details on this issue, see Toman, "L'Union Soviètique et le Droit des Conflits Armés," 517–518.

[178] Report Soviet-Ukrainian Delegation, no. F. 2, Op. 12cc, Spr. 969, Ark. 60-76, TSDAVO.

[179] Van Dijk, '"The Great Humanitarian,'" 225.

[180] Ibid., 226–227.

the Stockholm draft's article on organized resistance movements. As in 1947, this question created a deep split between the Anglo-American and the continental European delegations, including the Soviets, who were willing to go "to almost any length," complained Craigie.[181] During this stage of the debate, his delegation received very little support for its alternative proposals. Lamarle called them "too elastic" and "too imprecise." The Soviets found them a "retrograde step."[182]

This deep antagonism between parties from opposite sides of the Iron Curtain surprised most delegates. The New Zealand delegation wrote later that

> it was not appreciated [...] that so many governments would send delegations to Geneva with unqualified instructions to support the Stockholm text. It was not realized that opposition to many of the provisions of that text would come as a complete and unpleasant surprise to many of the countries which are favorably disposed towards us.[183]

Considering his own proposals completely "rational," the self-righteous Craigie expressed disappointment with the lack of support he received from European allies, whose legal attitude he characterized as the "reverse of realistic."[184] He believed it must have been rather paradoxical for observers to witness how the Western Europeans were supporting their potential occupier "to outvote the Anglo-Saxon countries," even though officially there existed no Soviet invasion plans until the 1950s.[185]

While remaining confident about his chances of securing Britain's core interests,[186] Craigie was now confronted with a major problem within his own delegation. The unyielding Gardner was in the midst of a personal rivalry with US delegates in the POW Committee. According to Gardner, they staged "a series of violent attacks grossly misrepresenting UK proposals."[187] Other delegates, too, had noticed how these Anglo-American delegates were fighting an

---

[181] Craigie's Report on the Diplomatic Conference, November 1949, no. 6036, ADM116, TNA.

[182] Compte-rendu de la Séance Commission II, 27 April 1949, no. CD_1949_Comm2_CR03, ICRC Library.

[183] The report itself is not signed by any New Zealand official. However, considering its style and expertise, it is likely written by Baxter himself. Report of New Zealand Delegation to Diplomatic Conference of Geneva 1949, AAYS 8638 W2054 ADW2054/1220/3/3 (R18524114), ANZ.

[184] Craigie's Report on the Diplomatic Conference, November 1949, no. 6036, ADM116, TNA.

[185] Report of New Zealand Delegation to Diplomatic Conference of Geneva 1949, AAYS 8638 W2054 ADW2054/1220/3/3 (R18524114), ANZ; and Craigie's Interim Report of Geneva Conference, 4 May 1949, no. 20770, ADM1, TNA.

[186] Craigie's Interim Report of Geneva Conference, 4 May 1949, no. 20770, ADM1, TNA.

[187] Report on the Work of the War Office Members of the UK delegation, 1949, no. 14038, WO32, TNA.

182 PREPARING FOR WAR

embarrassing "oratory duel."[188] During a meeting of this UK delegation, the personally frustrated Gardner warned his fellow delegates that "if the present state of affairs continued [...] the delegation should return home and refuse to sign the Conventions as they stand." This would represent the last stand of the British delegation's fight against the partisan. By contrast, the far more diplomatically attuned Craigie preferred to stay in Geneva to make the drafts "workable" rather than going home, a view which he eventually pushed through.[189] These divisions nonetheless reveal the significant tensions that beset the fragile Anglo-American coalition, endangering its bargaining position and the negotiations as a whole, if not the protection of detainees in the hands of future occupiers.

In the following days, the head of the isolated British delegation would try to persuade Harrison to control his delegates in the POW Committee, an attempt which initially failed to yield any results.[190] Fierce confrontations between the delegations continued, to Harrison's disappointment. While appreciating French moderation, he anxiously reported how their British allies were "losing votes."[191] The Soviets were successfully undermining their proposals in various Committees, thus creating a split within the Western bloc that deeply worried the US delegation.[192] In the following weeks, the two major NATO powers informally pressured their Western European allies to take seriously their allegedly "common" security interests as members of the Western defense bloc.

Meanwhile, the POW Committee was facing deadlock over the question of who to allow to access the POW Convention. When the Committee decided to create a Special Committee with a Working Party, the chairing of this body spurred yet more tension among Harrison and Craigie's associates. The American delegate's suggestion to nominate Gutteridge led to fierce criticism from the latter. She felt this was done with "nefarious intent [...] to railroad the Stockholm draft [...] through the Committee, knowing that [I] could not object without a risk of seeming partiality and [our] delegation could not criticize [it] without appearing to censure [me]." Gardner, the most hardline British delegate of all, agreed with her.[193]

---

[188] Conference Diplomatique. Rapport Spécial Etabli par Pilloud, 16 September 1949, no. CR-254-1, ACICR.

[189] Minutes of Meeting UK Delegation, 4 May 1949, no. 4150, FO369, TNA.

[190] Minutes of Meeting UK Delegation, 4 May 1949, no. 4150, FO369, TNA.

[191] Cable US delegation for State Department on Diplomatic Conference, 9 May 1949, no. 5, RG 43 - 40, NARA.

[192] See Cable US delegation for State Department on Diplomatic Conference, 2 May 1949, no. 5, RG 43 - 40, NARA.

[193] Minutes of Meeting UK Delegation, 14 May 1949, no. 4152, FO369, TNA.

When these two British delegates suggested dropping some of their demands, Craigie responded that he was "not happy" about this sudden move by his colleagues. Thereafter, he tried to improve the hostile relations between the two most powerful Western delegations through informal talks with Yingling, Harrison, Lamarle, Cahen-Salvador, and the Dutch jurist Willem Mouton, also a former exile in London advising his Anglophone government there (see Chapter 6), who would come to play a critical role as a mediator in this transatlantic struggle.[194] These behind-the-scenes talks concerned three new proposals with respect to partisans and the POW Convention: a Belgian amendment; a British proposal with support from the United States; and Cohn's suggestion to reject belligerent equality altogether.

The Belgian and British proposals, which demanded a fixed emblem and effective control over lower units by partisans, led to criticism from both the ICRC and the Soviets, who felt these plans "might [be] easily given an arbitrary interpretation."[195] The other proposal from Cohn to delete "belligerent equality," a principle which said that the law's obligations apply equally to every belligerent regardless of whether its acts of war had been unlawful or not,[196] would substantially lower the threshold for resistance fighters.

For instance, it would allow individual civilians acting against genocide to lawfully take up arms in occupied territory.[197] It can hardly be called surprising that the Israeli Major Arieh Steinberg,[198] "bearing in mind the terrible suffering undergone by [my] people,"[199] responded positively:

Up to the last war combatants alone were involved in the event of conflict. That was no longer the case during the Second World War, in the course of which a belligerent Power was manifestly bent on exterminating a whole people, massacring women and children in cold bold. What should a people do in such circumstances? Should it not rightly and dutifully seek to defend itself?[200]

---

[194] Minutes of Meeting UK Delegation, 14 May 1949, no. 4152, FO369, TNA.

[195] Final Record of the Diplomatic Conference of Geneva of 1949, Vol. II, Section A, pp. 428–430, LOC.

[196] Minutes of Meeting UK Delegation, 19 May 1949, no. 4152, FO369, TNA; and Van Dijk, "Human Rights in War."

[197] Final Record of the Diplomatic Conference of Geneva of 1949, Vol. II, Section A, pp. 423–427, LOC.

[198] Based on the wartime experience of the Holocaust, the Israelis endorsed a position almost diametrically opposed to the one they would endorse three decades later. During the negotiations of the Additional Protocols in the 1970s they, considering themselves occupiers first, rejected a set of very similar proposals then introduced by the Palestine Liberation Organization (PLO), and other national liberation movements, to improve the position of guerrillas in particular.

[199] Final Record of the Diplomatic Conference of Geneva of 1949, Vol. II, Section A, p. 426, LOC.

[200] Final Record of the Diplomatic Conference of Geneva of 1949, Vol. II, Section A, pp. 426–427, LOC.

184 PREPARING FOR WAR

More surprisingly, Cahen-Salvador's delegation, supposedly influenced by Lemkin's advice and because of its instructions to draw connections with the Genocide Convention,[201] expressed sympathy for Cohn's proposal. Craigie's delegation, however, saw it as an attempt to place Western defense interests at risk, rejecting it outright.[202] In private, Craigie said that Cohn's "narrow and obstinate leadership" had much too powerful an influence over his Scandinavian allies, who often voted with the Soviets.[203] Unsurprisingly, the latter also supported enlarging the law's scope for those irregulars fighting on behalf of a "just cause."[204]

While Cohn's amendment was eventually rejected, the Belgian proposal and the existing Stockholm draft received significant support. When the chairman mistakenly put out a preliminary vote,[205] the Belgian plan gained approval from the British and the French (the latter following British lobbying efforts). The original Stockholm draft received equally marked support, with the Soviets, Indians, and, most surprisingly, Americans approving it.[206] In voting with the Soviets to outvote its own British and French allies, the US delegation created a great deal of surprise among the delegates present at this session.[207] What it reveals, however, is a continuing lack of Anglo-American coordination, and personal rivalries undermining relations among their representatives participating in the POW Committee.

---

[201] In August 1948, at the United Nations, Raphael Lemkin had told French officials that "a national, ethnic or religious group under the threat of systematic destruction by the occupying power would find themselves in a state of self-defense." He argued that this principle of self-defense had to be extended to a national, ethnic, or religious group under "threat of its existence" and to "partisans, in the case of the occupant's plan to systematically to destroy [them]." He found it essential, therefore, to carefully lower the requirements for them. It is quite likely that Lemkin's remarks influenced Lamarle's delegation, and the French Foreign Ministry, to support the Danish proposal and to partly base their instructions upon the Genocide Convention as such. Note to French Foreign Minister, 16 August 1948, no. 159 - TER, Unions Internationales 1944–1960, LAD; and Instructions French Foreign Minister for French Delegation, 14 April 1949, no. 161, Unions Internationales 1944–1960, LAD.

[202] Report on the Work of the War Office Members of the UK delegation, 1949, no. 14038, WO32, TNA; and Minutes of Meeting UK Delegation, 20 May 1949, no. 4152, FO369, TNA.

[203] Craigie's Report on the Diplomatic Conference, November 1949, no. 6036, ADM116, TNA. Pilloud too acknowledged that some of Cohn's interventions were "curieux" and "very often incomprehensible." Conference Diplomatique. Rapport Spécial Etabli par Pilloud, 16 September 1949, no. CR-254-1, ACICR.

[204] Van Dijk, "The Great Humanitarian," 225–226.

[205] Final Record of the Diplomatic Conference of Geneva of 1949, Vol. II, Section A, pp. 443–447, LOC.

[206] The Indian Ministry of Defence had previously supported the restrictive views of the British delegation. However, at the diplomatic conference the Indian delegation, which played a minimal role during these negotiations, took a slightly less pro-British view on the matter. See Note Indian Ministry of Defence, 21 October 1948, no. CR-240-13, ACICR.

[207] See Minutes Meeting UK Delegation, 3 June 1949, no. 4153, FO369, TNA; Report on the Work of the War Office Members of the UK delegation, 1949, no. 14038, WO32, TNA; and Cable US delegation for State Department, 4 June 1949, no. 5, RG 43–40, NARA.

FIGHTERS IN THE SHADOWS   185

By early June 1949, following the article's first reading, the delegates feared that no additional protection for future partisans would eventually be reached. After the mistaken vote, Craigie successfully persuaded Harrison to work together in the near future on defense-related issues such as the treatment of irregulars, an argument that had failed to work in the debate regarding Common Article 3 (see Chapter 3).[208] By invoking their common interests as members of the NATO alliance facing a common Soviet threat, Craigie was able to lift his delegation out of its isolation while putting pressure on Harrison to keep control over his own delegates, openly fighting with UK representatives in the POW Committee. Although they did so only "with obvious reluctance,"[209] these US delegates eventually bent to Harrison's directive. Thus, the Anglo-American bloc solidified as the Soviet position appeared increasingly weak.

By convincing his French, Italian, and US partners to work together as NATO allies on defense-related questions,[210] the diplomatically savvy Craigie eventually lowered support for plans to significantly expand the law's scope for resistance fighters. As time went on, he wrote:

Opinion veered more and more towards our own more realistic approach […] This change in sentiment was due not only to sustained argument in committee but also to discreet and continuous lobbying by members of our delegation outside the conference. As an example it may be mentioned that, in the case of the Atlantic Treaty Powers, the appeal to the ideals of "Western Union" was usually effective when dealing with some important point relating to our common defence.[211]

This view was later partially confirmed by Pilloud who wrote that that the fear of war between East and West played an "enormous role" in reuniting the initially split Western bloc.[212] The deadlock over the question of partisans was finally broken when the Dutch mediator, Mouton, also representing a founding NATO member, introduced a few compromise proposals.[213] One important

[208] Craigie's Report on the Diplomatic Conference, November 1949, no. 6036, ADM116, TNA.
[209] Ibid.
[210] Minutes of Meeting UK delegation, 24 June 1949, no. 4157, FO369, TNA.
[211] Craigie's Report on the Diplomatic Conference, November 1949, no. 6036, ADM116, TNA.
[212] Conference Diplomatique. Rapport Spécial Etabli par Pilloud, 16 September 1949, no. CR-254-1, ACICR.
[213] Mouton's other proposal was to combine elements from the Martens Clause with those of human rights law. This meant that "even in cases where the decision of the courts […] would not allow these persons to benefit [from the POW Convention], they shall nevertheless remain under the safeguard and rule […] of international law as derived from the usages prevailing among civilized nations, of human rights and the requirements of public conscience." Due to its potentially wide scope, Mouton's proposal was rejected: Final Record of the Diplomatic Conference of Geneva of 1949, Vol. II, Section A,

186 PREPARING FOR WAR

idea which he suggested was a plan to replace the disputed paragraph with a simple reference to resistance movements, leaving the status quo intact.[214] While appearing to widen the POW Convention's scope, Mouton's proposal in fact left in place some conditions which made the treaty's scope stricter than for other irregulars, such as the *levée en masse*.

Although grasping the problem, the Committee's members were sufficiently shaken by the degree of hostility during these debates to accept this weak diplomatic compromise proposal.[215] Once the French and British had prevented, in the Joint Committee, the POW Convention from being directly applied to resistance fighters in colonial wars, the plenary voted overwhelmingly in favor of this revised article. In it, the Anglo-American restrictive agenda was largely secured, and the Soviets and French received the reference to resistance movements they had sought to satisfy their leaders and constituents at home. But they failed to provide future resistance fighters with sufficient protection under humanitarian law.

Black Holes

Apart from restricting the POW Convention's scope, Anglo-American delegates also proposed a security clause that would seek to block the door for excluded resistance fighters to access the Civilian Convention. The Third Committee, where this clause was discussed, had witnessed another split between the ICRC

p. 478–482, LOC. Mouton also reintroduced the idea of holding hearings for irregulars whose status had been questioned. He was inspired by the experiences of summarily executed Dutch resistance fighters whose combatant status had been contested by the Germans. This proposal helped to create the important "Article 5 hearings," a vital screening procedure designed to temporarily protect those persons whose status was unclear or contested. This provision helped to break the endemic practice of summary executions. It is striking how little attention the literature has paid to this invention. Exceptions are Dinstein, *The Conduct of Hostilities*, 41; and Solis, *The Law of Armed Conflict*, 228–231. Mouton's proposal to allow non-recognized "organized resistance movements" to fall under the same compromise text was finally dropped. This proposal was again based on the experience of Dutch resistance fighters during the Second World War who had fought for the Dutch government in exile (not recognized by the Germans). Mouton realized his proposal could potentially apply to colonial resistance movements, and, following British counsel, dropped it. Report on the Work of the War Office Members of the UK delegation, 1949, no. 14038, WO32, TNA. Mouton's decision to drop his proposal later made it difficult for anti-colonial and/or secessionist resistance movements to gain the POW Convention's background. They lacked either a belligerent connection or a government whose authority had been diplomatically recognized *before* the outbreak of hostilities. For the relevant Kassem case of 1969, see Solis, *The Law of Armed Conflict*, 240–243.

[214] Final Record of the Diplomatic Conference of Geneva of 1949, Vol. II, Section A, pp. 478–482, LOC.
[215] Article 3 of the POW Convention also features certain protections for other new "irregular categories," such as the merchant marine, civilian air crews, and so on. As these do not cover the question of partisan warfare, I have decided not to discuss them in this chapter.

and the French—seeking to assure human rights for every enemy civilian in interstate war and prevent a repetition of Hitler's "Night and Fog" decree[216]—and the closely collaborating Commonwealth–American delegations, arguing in favor of excluding most irregulars from both Conventions.[217] While different in approach, the proposals for a security clause of this latter group shared the objective of creating a black hole rather than a bridge between the POW and Civilian Conventions, thereby creating fears of a return of the Nazi forced disappearances that had been condemned by the Nuremberg Trials.[218]

While the ICRC and others asked Pilloud and human rights lawyer Castberg to find a compromise solution for this problem, the three major NATO powers decided to join forces to deal informally with this issue.[219] The Soviets were kept in the dark again. Working in consultation with the restrictive Australians, whose draft for a security clause lay at the basis of these discussions, the leaders of the British, American, and French delegations came together regularly to discuss a future security clause for the Civilian Convention.[220] One of their first proposals was to temporarily exclude individual suspects of hostile activities with continuing access to a Protecting Power.[221] This plan raised opposition from the Pentagon,[222] as well as from the British General Staff and the Security Services,[223] who feared that it would

[216] See Cable Lamarle to Foreign Ministry on Diplomatic Conference, 2 May 1949, no. 161, Unions Internationales 1944–1960, LAD; and Instructions French Foreign Minister for French Delegation, 14 April 1949, no. 161, Unions Internationales 1944–1960, LAD.

[217] Cable Lamarle to Foreign Ministry on Diplomatic Conference, 2 May 1949, no. 161, Unions Internationales 1944–1960, LAD.

[218] Minutes of Meeting at Cabinet Office, 30 May 1949, no. 46, CAB130, TNA; Minutes of Meeting at Cabinet Office, 24 June 1949, no. 46, CAB130, TNA; and Brief for Australian Delegation, no. series A1838, 1481/1A PART 1, NAA. For more background into Nuremberg and enforced disappearance, see Brian Finucane, "Enforced Disappearance as a Crime under International Law: A Neglected Origin in the Laws of War," *Yale Journal of International Law* (2010): 171–197, 175–177.

[219] To the disappointment of the ICRC, Castberg was called back to Oslo at the end of June. His role as the leader of the Scandinavian delegations was taken up by Cohn. It is unclear why Castberg had to return home, or whether anyone had pressured Oslo to do so. Castberg had been previously considered for the position of president or vice-president of a Committee, but his English and French were not considered good enough by Swiss officials. The pressure of the French to have Cahen appointed as president of the Third Committee made an end to these talks, according to Pilloud. Note ICRC on Presidents and Vice-Presidents, 11 April 1949, no. CR-221-4, ACICR; and Conference Diplomatique. Rapport Spécial Etabli par Pilloud, 16 September 1949, no. CR-254-1, ACICR.

[220] Report on Debate Committee III by Hodgson, 1949, no. series A1838, 1481/1A PART 8, NAA.

[221] Telegram Craigie to Foreign Office on Security Clause, 2 July 1949, no. 4156, FO369, TNA.

[222] The Army Intelligence Division in particular was against it. The Justice Department, however, had originally thought that the proposed resolution would be acceptable. In view of the Army's arguments, however, it had sided with the Army's position. See Minutes of Meeting at State Department, 7 July 1949, no. 674, Provost Marshall General, NARA; and Cable State Department to Harrison on Security Clause, 8 July 1949, no. 5, RG 43 - 40, NARA.

[223] The British General Staff rejected the proposal, fearing that it "would mean that the knowledge of apprehension of spies [...] must be passed to the Protecting Power with no guarantee that this in turn does not reach the ears of our adversary [...] Also apprehended person would resist interrogation

188 PREPARING FOR WAR

undermine their most vital intelligence interests as part of the larger Cold War struggle.[224]

Whitehall's new instruction to accept a strict security clause once again caused dissension within Craigie's own delegation. The Foreign Office representatives feared not only severe European opposition and damage to Britain's prestige, but also that it would undermine the protection for future British nationals held in enemy hands. By contrast, the War Office representatives and others preferred to secure their most critical security interests in the wake of the ongoing insurgency in Malaya and East–West tensions.[225] While the British delegation in Geneva successfully delayed the discussions there, Gardner and Gutteridge, as the two leading representatives from both camps, were sent to London to attend a special meeting of the Interdepartmental Committee.[226]

For this meeting, Craigie wrote a secret letter in which he analyzed the situation and gave policy recommendations. He, like the Americans, knew that key to the success of this operation to exclude so-called hostile elements was gaining French support, and thereby the crucial votes from smaller delegations sitting on the fence. In his letter, Craigie described how the question of "security" was bound up in a much larger policy debate involving the key issue of internal wars, now the recipient of Paris' strongest interest. "The French," wrote Craigie, "say that they can only afford to be conciliatory on [the security clause] if their proposals on civil war (now in jeopardy) go through. So you will see the matter is not free from complexity!"[227] Concerns of a Soviet occupation, said Craigie, sidelined any proposal that would legitimize "wholesale arrests [...] to which the Germans had recourse in the last war."[228]

Craigie knew that French anxieties surrounding the debate concerning colonial war could be exploited for his own delegation's extrajudicial agenda. As the Special Committee had previously rejected the French-sponsored Second Working Party text (see Chapter 3), the French were becoming very concerned about the Conventions being directly applied to the Indochina War, which it sought to exclude altogether. In response, according to Craigie, the French

knowing full well that within three months he would come under the Protecting Power. Accordingly, no time limit can be accepted": Cable Foreign Office to Craigie, 9 July 1949, no. 4156, FO369, TNA.

[224] Cable State Department to Harrison on Security Clause, July 8 1949, no. 5, RG 43-40, NARA.
[225] Minutes of Meeting UK delegation, 8 July 1949, no. 4157, FO369, TNA.
[226] Minutes of Meeting UK delegation, 8 July 1949, no. 4157, FO369, TNA; and Letter Craigie on Security Clause, 12 July 1949, no. 4156, FO369, TNA.
[227] Letter Craigie on Security Clause, 12 July 1949, no. 4156, FO369, TNA.
[228] Once occupied, "their troubles [would be] on their own heads for having accepted the British text which completely exempted suspected persons," wrote Craigie. Letter Craigie on Security Clause, 12 July 1949, no. 4156, FO369, TNA.

seemed willing to accept a less destructive security clause if the Americans, especially, would support their plans for the Civilian Convention and the exclusion of colonial war. In other words, the crucial debate surrounding the security clause was directly connected to a wider discussion within the Western bloc about colonial war, civilian protection, NATO solidarity, loyalty, and allegiance as such.

While pushing the Interdepartmental Committee in London to make concessions,[229] Craigie played diplomatic chess on different boards by joining the ongoing informal talks with his French and US counterparts in Geneva. French war veterans minister Betolaud had just arrived with new instructions from his democratic socialist Cabinet, demonstrating the matter's importance to the Republic's highest leadership. Seeking to obtain Anglo-American support with respect to discussions regarding colonial war, he accepted a less strict security clause with application to occupied territory. Craigie, however, wished to specifically exclude suspects of hostile acts in "belligerent territory," referring to the threat of communist spies in France.[230] While agreeing with his British colleague, Harrison refused to speak publicly in favor of his plan out of fear of losing French support for his own proposals and losing American prestige. Swiss reporters were meanwhile framing these liberal proposals as "communist methods," noting the paradoxical fact of the illiberal Soviets defending human rights in Geneva.[231]

If Craigie's proposal were defeated, he reported to Washington, the British delegation would support its own draft for the security clause. Harrison was confident that it would go through with French support "even if [the] British cannot go along." He knew, at the same time, that "chances of getting anything without French support [were] practically nil."[232]

When the Interdepartmental Committee in London decided to give in to its delegation's demands—this being combined with support from Acheson's State Department—the new compromise proposal came to look increasingly appealing.[233] This new draft distinguished between the treatment of suspects in occupied and belligerent territory.

In the former case, French pressure made sure that it significantly limited the occupier's powers in case of enemy invasion. On the other hand, in belligerent

---

[229] Letter Craigie on Security Clause, 12 July 1949, no. 4156, FO369, TNA.
[230] Cable Harrison to State Department on Security Clause, 13 July 1949, no. 5, RG 43-40, NARA.
[231] Journal de Genève, 19 July 1949.
[232] Cable Harrison to State Department on Security Clause, 13 July 1949, no. 5, RG 43-40, NARA.
[233] Cable Foreign Office for Craigie on Outcome of Interdepartmental Meeting, no. 4156, FO369, TNA; and Cable US Delegation, 18 July 1949, no. 5, RG 43-40, NARA.

190 PREPARING FOR WAR

territory, where the French government was still in charge, the detaining power
would be able, according to one Commonwealth delegate,

> to subject enemy agents to a grueling and lengthy questioning, accompanied
> perhaps by deprivation of food and sleep. Such treatment, though not inhu-
> mane, may amount to physical or moral coercion. If it does, such questioning
> will be lawful in the case of suspects in the territory of a belligerent, but not in
> the case of suspects in occupied territory.[234]

This plan put the French in a difficult position: on the one hand, it would protect its core security interests with respect to communist spies at home and
appease their major NATO allies.[235] On the other hand, it generated fear that
it would open the door to arbitrary treatment and place its diplomatic prestige
at risk. In the end, the French decided "unwillingly" to accept it, by prioritizing
the interests of the NATO alliance at the expense of marginalized irregulars.[236] The compromise text was approved by a majority of 5 votes (UK, USA,
Canada, France, Switzerland) to 1 (USSR), with 1 abstention (NATO member
Norway).[237]

When this draft was discussed in the Civilian Committee and the plenary,
the American and British delegates pushed their Western European allies to
(publicly) support it. Pilloud later wrote that this pressure was "almost analo-
gous" to that of the Soviets on their satellites.[238] The Soviet-aligned delegates,
who had been excluded from these informal talks, viciously attacked this draft.
Having escaped the Holocaust by going into hiding, the Czechoslovakian
lawyer Pavel Winkler said that it would "reintroduce police methods known
only too well from the time of the National-Socialist occupation." Likewise,

---

[234] Report of New Zealand Delegation to Diplomatic Conference of Geneva 1949, AAYS 8638 W2054
ADW2054/1220/3/3 (R18524114), ANZ.

[235] Conference Diplomatique. Rapport Spécial Etabli par Pilloud, 16 September 1949, no. CR-254-1,
ACICR; and Cable Lamarle to Ministry of Foreign Affairs on Security, 16 July 1949, no. 161, Unions
Internationales 1944–1960, LAD.

[236] Conference Diplomatique. Rapport Spécial Etabli par Pilloud, 16 September 1949, no. CR-254-
1, ACICR.

[237] Pilloud was especially disappointed about the Swiss decision to support this draft. Conference
Diplomatique. Rapport Spécial Etabli par Pilloud, 16 September 1949, no. CR-254-1, ACICR. While
leaving out the role of the Soviets, Hitchcock has argued that "the humanitarian states in the 1949 negotiations—France, Norway, Sweden, Denmark—conceded to the British that spies and saboteurs should
not be granted all the protections [of the] Fourth Convention." It is important to note that within this
"humanitarian bloc," there existed subtle differences between its members. Neither does Hitchcock full
appreciate the informal deals made between the Great Powers: Hitchcock, "Human Rights and the Laws
of War," 101.

[238] Conference Diplomatique. Rapport Spécial Etabli par Pilloud, 16 September 1949, no. CR-254-
1, ACICR.

FIGHTERS IN THE SHADOWS   191

Soviet delegate Morosov felt it echoed the spirit of the anti-communist witch hunts in Washington.[239]

When the Soviets introduced their own proposal on this matter, however, the ICRC expressed little support for it. One crucial reason for this was that the Soviets admitted publicly that this plan had no relevance for their own "suspects of spying," as these were of "domestic concern," outside of the scope of the Conventions.[240] Pictet's colleagues knew enough. While defeated, the Soviets continued to use other subversive measures to undermine, if not embarrass, the Anglo-American delegations in this diplomatic arena. As their Cold War adversaries had done in the debate regarding the internal war clause (see Chapter 3), they suggested a secret ballot to enable Western European delegations skeptical of the security clause to vote against this proposal, which was only narrowly rejected by the conference. The French, for their part, wished to raise the matter at the plenary and tried to subvert the original English draft by means of revising its French translation in a more progressive fashion.[241] When the British and Americans opposed these covert attempts to corrupt their plans, Lamarle admitted that his delegation was "running the risk of an echec," potentially undermining the Western bloc's cohesion and its own strategic interests in other crucial debates. After "lengthy negotiations," the delegates accepted a revised French translation.[242]

This raised immediate opposition from the ICRC and Soviets, who deemed it substantially different from the original English text.[243] In their view, this new translation reopened the debate with regard to the security clause—a proposal which would need a two-thirds majority, according to the conference's rules of procedure. To the ICRC's frustration, the influential Swiss president Petitpierre however ignored these rules (Pilloud: "abuse," "unedifying") following pressure from the major Western powers to put out a vote for this particular text, which was eventually lost by the Soviets. The plenary then approved both texts, accepting the security clause and, Pilloud feared, placing irregulars at great risk.[244]

---

[239] Final Record of the Diplomatic Conference of Geneva of 1949, Vol. II, Section A, pp. 796–798, LOC.

[240] Ibid.

[241] Conference Diplomatique. Rapport Spécial Etabli par Pilloud, 16 September 1949, no. CR-254-1, ACICR; and Report Dutch Delegation Third Commission, 1949, no. 3045, Code-Archief Buitenlandse Zaken, NA.

[242] Cable Lamarle to Foreign Ministry on Security, 8 August 1949, no. 161, Unions Internationales 1944–1960, LAD.

[243] Pilloud: this text was "absolutely different" even for somebody with "only weak knowledge of English." Conference Diplomatique. Rapport Spécial Etabli par Pilloud, 16 September 1949, no. CR-254-1, ACICR.

[244] Pilloud wrote that it was "difficult for the Swiss" who had not experienced war for more than decades to say anything against a "state who had come to lead and win the largest war in history." Conference Diplomatique. Rapport Spécial Etabli par Pilloud, 16 September 1949, no. CR-254-1, ACICR.

192 PREPARING FOR WAR

4.5 Conclusion

The rocky reception given to the idea of recognizing the right of resistance in occupied territory demonstrates its contentious nature as it became part of humanitarian law's imagination. While the ICRC and Western Europeans were disappointed with the final outcome, and some considered even making a reservation to the security clause, in the end only a few states publicly opposed it. The divided Anglo-American coalition had succeeded in preventing the POW Convention from lowering its threshold for most partisans. Although this treaty widened its scope for "regular armed forces" whose authority had not been recognized (a category which has been hardly applied since 1949) to appease Western European resistance communities, as well as recognizing a broader shift toward the right of resistance in occupied territory, the final text provided little protection against inhumane treatment for most individual resistance fighters. This chapter has shown that Article 4 of this treaty made a textual reference, but this did not lead to lowering its legal threshold. On the contrary, it covertly added two extra requirements (military organization, connection with a belligerent party). The reference to "organized resistance movements' was meant as a means to break a diplomatic deadlock, not to open the door for more irregular outsiders.

Nor has the term received much currency since 1949. Most irregulars in future armed conflicts and occupations (e.g. in Cyprus or Palestine) found it hard to gain protection under this treaty. The fact that the 1929 POW Convention did not directly apply to internal wars either "removed one of the most serious complications," as a relieved Commonwealth delegate noted afterwards.[245] The fact that this element recognizing a safety net for partisans has been largely forgotten since 1949 has a great deal to do with past Anglo-American efforts to erase this element from the Conventions' text and from legal memory more generally.

They largely succeeded in deleting textual references recognizing that link and obtained a "totalitarian" security clause (according to their Dutch NATO ally[246]) which would "virtually [...] deprive" irregulars of the treaty's protections. For this reason, the same Commonwealth delegate said it was of "the greatest importance" that those persons should always try to fall under the more protective POW Convention. This extrajudicial security clause, which

---

[245] Report of New Zealand Delegation to Diplomatic Conference of Geneva 1949, AAYS 8638 W2054 ADW2054/1220/3/3 (R18524114), ANZ.

[246] Report Dutch Delegation Third Commission, 1949, no. 3045, Code-Archief Buitenlandse Zaken, NA.

FIGHTERS IN THE SHADOWS   193

allowed "no impartial observer," gave states "virtually unlimited" powers, and removed the detainee "indefinitely" from the Protecting Powers' eyes,[247] caused significant concern on the ICRC side.[248] After 1949 it would be invoked by those state officials who wished to remove irregulars from the law's protection (see Conclusion).

As we saw earlier, the most promising element for irregulars was the ICRC–French plan to create a safety net between the two Conventions. Strikingly, its existence was largely acknowledged by most of the delegates present at the diplomatic conference. Even the same Commonwealth skeptic cited above admitted in his private report: "if [partisans] do not receive the protection afforded by the Prisoners of War Convention, they will automatically receive the protection afforded by the new Civilian Convention."[249] Indeed, many roads were not taken by the delegates in 1949—for instance, they could have explicitly codified the safety net; the ICRC might have specifically prohibited "mental torture"; the French could have rejected the security clause; and the Foreign Office could have insisted on the rights of British subjects with greater force.

Despite these shortcomings, the drafting process with regard to irregulars led to major tensions and concern among French, British, American, Soviet, and other major drafting parties. As we have seen previously, there were some major differences of opinion between the members of their preparatory committees, which also sheds light on the pressurized civil–military relations within these state polities, and among Western bloc allies in particular. Anglo-American drafters often experienced divisions within their own ranks, causing embarrassing clashes in public.[250] In the meantime, the Soviets could easily benefit from these internal fractures by accusing their Cold War adversaries of reintroducing Nazi police methods.[251]

---

[247] Agamben, *State of Exception*, 4. Report of New Zealand Delegation to Diplomatic Conference of Geneva 1949, AAYS 8638 W2054 ADW2054/1220/3/3 (R18524114), ANZ.

[248] Conference Diplomatique. Rapport Spécial Etabli par Pilloud, 16 September 1949, no. CR-254-1, ACICR.

[249] Report of New Zealand Delegation to Diplomatic Conference of Geneva 1949, AAYS 8638 W2054 ADW2054/1220/3/3 (R18524114), ANZ. Mouton, a strong advocate of greater protection for resistance fighters: "That persons who do not fall under Article 3 [of the POW Convention: BvD] are automatically protected by other Conventions is certainly untrue [...] These people, if they do not belong to Article 3 [...] might be shot and that is a decision which we do not want to leave in the hands of one man [for which he tried to create the Article 5 procedure: BvD]." Final Record of the Diplomatic Conference of Geneva of 1949, Vol. II, Section B, p. 271, LOC. His acting minister, Joseph Luns, the NATO secretary-general in the 1970s, would later refute this claim when responding to questions from Dutch MPs. See Handelingen Tweede Kamer, 24 February 1954, The Hague.

[250] Memorandum from DJB/MZ External Affairs to Secretary, April 1st 1949, Series A1838, 1481/1A PART 1, NAA.

[251] Final Record of the Diplomatic Conference of Geneva of 1949, Vol. II, Section A, pp. 796–798, LOC.

194 PREPARING FOR WAR

In summary,[252] this chapter has shown in detail how the debates about partisan warfare in its widest sense had taken off already in the 1940s, far prior to the 1970s when the Protocols were negotiated. It has often been argued, even by the ICRC itself, that the original drafters had either not foreseen or imagined guerrilla warfare, as such—it was "new" to those involved in this process in the 1940s. Others have suggested that the 1949 Conventions merely reflected the European wartime experiences with this issue. According to this logic, only from the 1960s on did it become a matter of international legal concern, with the new wave of wars of national liberation and Palestinian resistance to Israel's occupation. These developments, many argue, finally led to the widening of humanitarian law's scope and "minimum protections" for guerrillas epitomized by the signing of the Additional Protocols in 1977.[253]

---

[252] Keith Suter, *An International Law of Guerrilla Warfare: The Global Politics of Law-Making* (London: Frances Pinter, 1984), 13–14. De La Pradelle, whose own French work on this matter is largely unknown in the Anglophone world, wrote by far the most comprehensive account of the Conventions' revision. In this work, he admitted that Article 4's solution remained "imparfait" and was to form "un précédent utile à exploiter pour obtenir la grande reconnaissance internationale des mouvements de résistance." Paul de la Pradelle, *La Conférence Diplomatique et les Nouvelles Conventions de Genève du 12 Août 1949* (Paris: Les Editions Internationales, 1951), 62. US military jurist Richard Baxter also recognized that "it is reasonable to suppose that guerrillas and members of resistance movements will more frequently than not fail to conform to these standards." Richard Baxter, "So-Called 'Unprivileged Belligerency': Spies, Guerrillas, and Saboteurs," *British Yearbook of International Law* [1951]: 327–328. Best argued too that "the 1949 solution of this problem was, in truth, no solution at all": Geoffrey Best, *War and Law since 1945* (Oxford: Clarendon Press, 2002), 132. See also Erik Castrén, *The Present Law of War and Neutrality* (Helsinki: Finnish Academy of Science and Letters, 1954), 149; Remigiusz Bierzanek, "Le Statut Juridique des Partisans et des Mouvements de Résistance Armée: Évolution Historique et Aspects Actuels," in *Mélanges Offerts à Juraj Andrassy: Essays in International Law in Honour of Juraj Andrassy*, ed. Vladimir Ibler (The Hague: Martinus Nijhoff, 1968), 54–77, 68. While focusing almost exclusively on Article 4 of the POW Convention, Scheipers has stressed the importance of three mostly political–diplomatic factors: "certain political considerations"; the role of the French "switching sides" due to their occupying interests in postwar Germany; and the fact that the Convention's revision "bears the mark of the strategic interests of major states at the time of its codification" (without making clear which strategic interests). The main innovations of this postwar revision process were, in Scheipers' eyes, their increasing protection for civilians and the creation of Common Article 3. She does not address the linkage between the two Conventions, the Civilian Convention's security clause, or any other related provision, such as the "hearing procedure." Sibylle Scheipers, "'Unlawful Combatants': The West's Treatment of Irregular Fighters in the 'War on Terror,'" *Orbis*, Vol. 58, No. 4 (2014): 566–583, 575–576; and Scheipers, *Unlawful Combatants*, 144–145, 231. Nabulsi has not provided a comprehensive historical account of this matter either. Karma Nabulsi, *Traditions of War: Occupation, Resistance and the Law* (Oxford: Oxford University Press, 1999), 13–14.

[253] Examples of this tendency are Robert Delhunty, "Is the Geneva POW Convention 'Quaint'?" *William Mitchell Law Review*, Vol. 33 (2007): 1636; Henri Meyrowitz, "Les Guerres de Libération et les Conventions de Genève," *Politique Étrangère*, Vol. 39, No. 6 (1974): 607–627, 608–610; and Michael Meyer and Hilaire McCoubrey, *Reflections on Law and Armed Conflicts. The Selected Works on the Laws of War by the Late Professor Colonel G.I.A.D. Draper* (The Hague: Kluwer Law International, 1998), 199. US legal scholar Rosa Brooks writes similarly that "inevitably, the Geneva Conventions were "out of date" from the moment they entered into force": Rosa Brooks, "The Politics of the Geneva Conventions: Avoiding Formalist Traps," *Virginia Journal of International Law*, Vol. 46, No. 197 (2005–2006): 197–207, 198. For the discussion on the idea as propagated by the Bush Administration that the Geneva Conventions are "quaint" and "obsolete" by virtue of their alleged lack of application in a "new kind of war," that of fighting a global "War on Terror," see John Yoo, *War by Other Means* (New York: Atlantic Monthly Press, 2006); Renée de Nevers, "The Geneva Conventions and New Wars,"

There are three problems with this historiographical line of thinking. First of all, it tends to ignore the fact that the plans allegedly introduced in the 1970s were hardly new.[254] In fact, many of them had already been coined in the 1940s by different delegations. Second, some of these proposals were condemned to obscurity by Anglo-American drafters, whose rejection of them stemmed from the firm conviction that they would be fighting against guerrillas in future wars with communist forces, separatists, and/or anti-colonial groups. Lastly, an important problem with the argument about the origins of the 1970s debates regarding guerrilla warfare is that it tends to ignore the critical role of agency of different drafters.

For example, the French did not rely exclusively upon their own wartime experiences while re-imagining the POW and Civilian Conventions, as has been often assumed in the literature. While the delegation was composed of former resistance fighters, it also drew on the state's roles as a member of the newly established NATO alliance and as a fighting colonial power in Indochina. The logic often invoked in the literature implying that the Conventions themselves are "backward-looking" and almost by definition "outdated" or "ill-prepared" due to the changing character of war, that their drafters merely reflected upon their past record but failed to foresee their present or future challenges,[255] is thus a very one-sided claim, if not a historically inaccurate one.[256] The implication that French resistance fighters themselves lacked foresight or were unable to comprehend the nature of guerrilla warfare, or its increasing popularity, fails the test of historical scrutiny. As we will see in the next chapter, many of these questions would return as the ICRC began campaigning against the threat of indiscriminate warfare.

Political Science Quarterly, Vol. 121, No. 3 (2006): 369–395; and Anthony Dworkin, "Rethinking the Geneva Conventions," *Global Policy Forum* (2003). For a critical account of the "new wars thesis," see Scheipers, *Unlawful Combatants*, 1–32, 207–211, 228–232; and Edward Newman, "The 'New Wars' Debate: A Historical Perspective Is Needed," *Security Dialogue*, Vol. 35, No. 2 (2004): 173–189.

[254] To be sure, today's often invoked concept of "continuous combat function" was first comprehensively described by the ICRC in its 2009 report. See Nils Melzer, *Interpretive Guidance on the Notion of Direct Participation in Hostilities under International Humanitarian Law* (Geneva: ICRC, 2009).

[255] Schmitt was thus only partially correct when he claimed that "Die Formulierungen der Genfer Konventionen haben europäische Erfahrungen im Auge, nicht aber die Partisanenkriege Mao Tse-tungs und die spätere Entwicklung der modernen Partisanenkrieges." Schmitt, *Theorie des Partisanen*, 29.

[256] One example is Karen Greenberg, *The Torture Debate in America* (Cambridge: Cambridge University Press, 2008), 314.

Figure 5.1 The Stockholm conference (1948). In the front row: the delegations of Burma, Argentina, Afghanistan, and Australia. In the upper right corner: the ICRC delegation, including Jean Pictet, and the French delegation, Albert Lamarle and Andrée Jacob.
Source/Rights: ICRC Audiovisual Archives, V-P-HIST-E-06965

5

Indiscriminate Warfare: Bombing, Nuclear Weapons, and Starvation

On the night of 9/10 March 1945, several weeks after the firebombing of Dresden, two American airmen boarded a B-29 plane.[1] Their mission was to destroy Japan's capital. After a flight of several hours they reached their destination, Tokyo, dropping a shower of napalm on its working-class neighborhoods. This triggered an immense firestorm that incinerated roughly 100,000 Japanese civilians.[2] The Americans repeated the same destructive routine a few days later when they firebombed the city of Kobe, destroying countless homes and hospitals. This series of incendiary raids by American B-29s ultimately killed more Japanese civilians than the two nuclear attacks on Hiroshima and Nagasaki combined.[3]

On their return, the two American airmen (Robert Nelson and Algy Augunas) were intercepted by a Japanese fighter lurking in the dark. After a dogfight, the US plane crashed on Japanese soil. The two American airmen survived but were quickly captured by Japanese forces and sent to a nearby prison. Here they discovered the denial of their prisoner of war status by their Japanese captors under the Enemy Airmen's Act (1942). This Japanese law removed the protection of the laws of war from those Allied fliers who had indiscriminately bombed Japanese cities. When the two Americans were eventually put on trial, they were found guilty of violating the laws of war and sentenced to the death penalty by a Japanese military tribunal. The two men were executed as war criminals.[4]

---

[1] Marilyn Young, "Bombing Civilians: From the Twentieth to the Twenty-First Centuries," in *Bombing Civilians: A Twentieth-Century History*, ed. Yuki Tanaka and Marilyn Young (New York: Free Press, 2010); and Sven Lindqvist, *A History of Bombing* (New York: New Press, 2001).

[2] Sheldon Garon, "On the Transnational Destruction of Cities: What Japan and the United States Learned from the Bombing of Britain and Germany in the Second World War," *Past & Present*, Vol. 247, No. 1 (2020): 235–271, 250–251.

[3] Jeremy Black, *Air Power: A Global History* (Lanham, MD: Rowman & Littlefield, 2016); and Robert Nelson and Christopher Waters, "The Allied Bombing of German Cities during the Second World War from a Canadian Perspective," *Journal of the History of International Law*, Vol. 14, No. 1 (2012): 87–122.

[4] Record of Yokohama Trials, 1 July 1948, United States of America vs. Eitaro Uchiyama, 1 July 1948; and Sarah Kovner, "A War of Words: Allied Captivity and Swiss Neutrality in the Pacific, 1941–1945," *Diplomatic History*, Vol. 41, No. 4 (2017): 719–746.

Preparing for War. Boyd van Dijk, Oxford University Press. © Boyd van Dijk 2022.
DOI: 10.1093/oso/9780198868071.003.0006

198 PREPARING FOR WAR

Infuriated by this decision, after Japan's surrender the American government demanded prosecution of the Japanese officials involved in this process. In 1947, the Americans set up a special war crimes tribunal in the city of Yokohama, still suffering from the severe damage caused by wartime US bombing raids. Unsurprisingly, the respective Japanese officials were found guilty of violating the laws of war by failing to provide the American airmen with a fair trial. The fact that both had taken part in the killing of tens of thousands of Japanese civilians did not matter to the US judge. Whereas the commanding Japanese general was sentenced to hanging, several of his associates were given long-term prison sentences. Washington hoped these trials would send a powerful signal to future captors of US airmen, as tensions with the Soviet Union were escalating at the time.

Most tellingly, the legal architects of the Conventions opted for a similar solution when they tried to solve the problem of regulating indiscriminate bombing in the wake of the Second World War. Like the US judges in 1947, they deliberately sidelined the question of the legality of air-nuclear warfare while prohibiting belligerents from depriving enemy prisoners of the right to a fair trial and executing captured bomber pilots.[5] In this regard, it is crucial to consider why the Civilian Convention, which aims to protect enemy civilians, remains silent on two of the greatest threats to their safety: air and nuclear bombing.[6] Why, after the war's terror bombings, have no rules for air warfare been substantially revised, apart from protecting those instigating them? Why does the Civilian Convention fail to specifically mention the principle of distinction?[7] And why, after the war's mass starvation campaigns, was depriving civilians of food not specifically prohibited by the drafters?

Since 1949 many observers of humanitarian law have neglected these key questions, or even claimed erroneously that the Civilian Convention was supposed to protect "humanity from another […] Dresden firestorm."[8] An

---

[5] Articles 129 and 130, POW Convention, 1949.

[6] Pictet admitted, in 1999, that "states" (the ICRC never wished to publicly identify one or more in particular) had been largely responsible for the exclusion of nuclear warfare from the Civilian Convention. See Jean Pictet, "De la Seconde Guerre mondiale à la Conference diplomatique de 1949," *International Review of the Red Cross*, Vol. 81, No. 834 (1999): 205–208, 207.

[7] Wade Mansell and Karen Openshaw have argued (erroneously) that the "crucial, traditional distinction between combatant and non-combatant was retained and remained central": Wade Mansell and Karen Openshaw, "The History and Status of the Geneva Conventions," in *The Geneva Conventions under Assault*, ed., Sarah Perrigo and Jim Whitmann (London: Pluto Press, 2010), 18–41, 23. Similarly, some scholars have suggested, on the basis of a selective reading of the final drafts, that the 1949 Conventions lay down a principle of civilian protection against air bombing, thereby ignoring Geneva's acceptance of indiscriminate bombing following massive US government pressure. John Tirman, *The Deaths of Others: The Fate of Civilians in America's Wars* (Oxford: Oxford University Press, 2011), 8–9.

[8] This quote comes from an online article written by the Geneva-oriented BBC journalist Imogen Foulkes: Imogen Foulkes, "Geneva Conventions Laws of War 'Need Fixing'," *BBC News* Link: http://www.bbc.co.uk/news/world-europe-35023029 (retrieved 6 May 2017). See also William Boothby, *The*

almost exclusive focus on the drafting outcome over its process has led to a problematic historiographical amnesia, also bypassing a range of unique attempts to regulate air-atomic warfare and blockade in the first half of the twentieth century. Others, however, have argued that humanitarian law's silence on these matters is the result of a then-strict boundary drawn between "Hague Law" and "Geneva Law," one exclusively regulating the war's conduct, the other the protection for "victims of war."[9] "The means of waging war," argues Solis in his seminal work, "[were] issues left to [...] 'Hague Law' [and therefore] one [found] no mention in the Geneva Convention of [...] matters as [...] distinction."[10] Likewise, Swiss legal scholar Dietrich Schindler has suggested that the International Committee of the Red Cross (ICRC) evinced little interest in the question of regulating the war's conduct, considering it "part of the Hague law."[11]

This popular "design" argument, which tends to overlook the importance of those attempts dating back earlier than the 1970s to regulate the conduct of air bombing and blockade, now largely dominates the relevant historiography, with a few small exceptions.[12] While questioned by some,[13] the idea of a widely

---

Law of Targeting (Oxford: Oxford University Press, 2012), 25–26, 168–170; Ingrid Detter, *The Law of War* (Farnham: Ashgate, 2013), 307–320; Theodor Meron, "The Humanization of Humanitarian Law," *The American Journal of International Law*, Vol. 94, No. 2 (2000): 239–278, 245–246; and Shane Darcy, *Judges, Law and War: The Judicial Development of International Humanitarian Law* (Cambridge: Cambridge University Press, 2014), 204.

[9] Some have suggested that the Civilian Convention's rules on civilian protection had a particular relevance for air bombing. See Mark Selden, "A Forgotten Holocaust: US Bombing Strategy, the Destruction of Japanese Cities, and the American Way of War from the Pacific War to Iraq," in *Bombing Civilians: A Twentieth-Century History*, ed. Yuki Tanaka and Marilyn Young (New York: New Press, 2010), 77–96, 88–92.

[10] Solis, *The Law of Armed Conflict*, 82–83. For a similar design argument, see Robert Kolb and Richard Hyde, *An Introduction to the International Law of Armed Conflicts* (Oxford: Hart, 2008).

[11] See Dietrich Schindler, "International Humanitarian Law: Its Remarkable Development and Its Persistent Violation," *Journal of the History of International Law* (2003): 165–188, 170. Following the signing of the Additional Protocols in 1977, former US negotiator George Aldrich wrote that "for the first time since the Hague Conventions of 1907" an attempt had been made to regulate the war's conduct: George Aldrich, "New Life for the Laws of War," *American Journal of International Law*, Vol. 75, No. 4 (1981): 764–783, 777.

[12] One notable exception is Gillespie's important account of the history of the laws of war. In his work, he notes how both the Nuremberg Trials and the Geneva Conventions stayed silent on indiscriminate air bombings. He attributes this silence to the Cold War and decolonization, but does not provide a satisfying answer as to how these factors affected the decision-making process in particular: Alexander Gillespie, *A History of the Laws of War Vol. II* (Portland, OR: Hart, 2011), 36–37. Other examples are: Geoffrey Best, *Humanity in Warfare: The Modern History of the International Laws of Armed Conflicts* (London: Weidenfeld and Nicholson, 1980), 233; and the ICRC legal expert Yves Sandoz, who has noted the crucial role of the US in blocking discussions on air bombing: Yves Sandoz, "Le Demi-siècle des Conventions de Genève," *International Review of the Red Cross*, Vol. 81, No. 834 (1999): 241–264, 242–243.

[13] Yoram Dinstein, *The Conduct of Hostilities under the Law of International Armed Conflict* (Cambridge: Cambridge University Press, 2004), 23; and François Bugnion, "Droit de Genève et Droit de la Haye," *International Review of the Red Cross*, Vol. 83, No. 844 (2001): 901–922, 908.

200 PREPARING FOR WAR

accepted distinction between "Hague Law" and "Geneva Law" was popularized after 1949 by former Anglo-American delegates and by the ICRC itself.[14] In its Commentary for the Civilian Convention, while turning a blind eye to previous attempts to regulate air-atomic warfare, the ICRC claimed that air bombing had always fallen "within the purview of the Hague Conventions."[15]

Taking a limited scope by analyzing only the questions of distinction and the protection of particularly civilian populations against air-atomic bombing and, to a lesser extent, blockade, this chapter challenges the strictly drawn distinction between "Hague" and "Geneva Law" found in the literature. It argues that the ICRC and others discussed both air bombing and blockade already in the interwar period, if not earlier, and has attempted to raise awareness about the issue ever since the start of the Second World War. Both questions played a far more central role in the drafting of the Conventions than is often assumed. This chapter provides new historical evidence and explanations by placing into question the later justifications found in the literature for the fact that Geneva refused to codify air-atomic warfare and blockade in a strict manner.

---

[14] US delegate Raymund Yingling pointed out clearly that he felt that the Conventions "do not constitute restrictions upon the use of modern combat weapons. For example, modern warfare unfortunately and often may involve the killing of civilians in proximity to military objectives, as well as immense destruction of property. Rather, these provisions cover only persons protected by the conventions, e.g. prisoners of war and the inhabitants of occupied territory." Joyce Gutteridge wrote that the drafters had been faced with the "impossibility in the circumstances of modern war" to draw "the rigid line which used to divide members of combatant forces and civilians": Joyce Gutteridge, "The Geneva Conventions of 1949," *British Yearbook of International Law*, Vol. 26 (1949): 294–326, 319; and Raymund Yingling and Robert Ginnane, "The Geneva Conventions of 1949," *The American Journal of International Law*, Vol. 46, No. 3 (1952): 393–427, 427.

[15] Pictet, Jean, *The Geneva Conventions of 12 August 1949: Commentary* (Geneva; ICRC, 1958), 10. The ICRC Commentary: "It is, perhaps, a pity from the humanitarian point of view that the conference adopted this course; for no one questions the necessity for restrictive rules in this sphere. It may nevertheless have been wise not to overload the Convention, as this might have jeopardized its chance of ratification by the Powers. Besides, the limitation of means of waging war is a matter which comes traditionally within the purview of the Hague Conventions, whose object is to codify the laws of war in the strict sense of the term." See Jean Pictet, "Les Principes du Droit International Humanitaire," *International Review of the Red Cross*, Vol. 48, No. 573 (1966): 411–425, 412–413. In the 1980s, when trying to justify the ICRC's previous policies, the new Commentary for the Additional Protocols similarly stated that the diplomatic conference in 1949 had lacked a proper mandate to regulate air-atomic warfare, since this matter "fell under the Hague Law." Claude Pilloud, *Commentary on the Additional Protocols of 8 June 1977 to the Geneva Conventions of 12 August 1949* (Geneva: ICRC, 1987), 583. ICRC Commentary: "The Diplomatic Conference of 1949 did not have a mandate to deal with that particularly delicate area, which at that time fell under the Hague Law laying down the rights and duties of belligerents in the conduct of military operations and restricting the choice of the means to be used for inflicting damage. Although Geneva law had been developed in great detail in 1949, and adapted to the requirements of the time, the Hague law had not evolved to the same extent, while the techniques of warfare had developed enormously during the two World Wars. The written rules which could be invoked for protecting civilians against the dangers of hostilities dated back to 1907, when aerial bombardment did not yet exist. Such was the tragic absurdity of the situation."

The major Western powers, seeking to gain recognition for "extermination with [...] recognized weapons of war,"[16] played a critical part in suppressing attempts by socialist, neutralist, and ICRC officials to place limits upon virtually unrestrained air power and *Hungerblockade*. They later justified these restrictive efforts by considering both matters as belonging exclusively to "Hague Law" rather than "Geneva Law." By replicating this deceptive justification as the reason Geneva had stayed "silent" on the matter of, especially, air-atomic warfare, scholarship has created a form of historical silence, relegating to oblivion the enormous struggle that took place to prevent the diplomatic conference from regulating indiscriminate warfare, with critical consequences for how we understand the Conventions today.

While enriching the literature's limited focus on Tokyo and Nuremberg's virtual silence with respect to air bombing, this chapter adds a new dimension to this debate and counters existing perspectives. Its main claims are split across three different sections, the first of which deals with the interwar attempts to revise the existing rules for air(-gas) bombardment and blockade. The next section shows how, and to what extent, the ICRC was willing to go along with far-reaching attempts to protect civilian groups through international law and disarmament campaigns. Building upon this discussion, the section that follows explains how the Red Cross as a whole used those interwar legacies during the 1940s to reaffirm the collapsed principle of distinction. It demonstrates how a major debate occurred within and outside the ICRC concerning how, and to what extent, it should try to regulate indiscriminate warfare. In 1948, at the Stockholm Conference, the ICRC set its own precedent for protecting civilian populations, igniting controversy among Anglo-American officials. This exemplar was later used by the Soviets to turn the diplomatic conference into a Cold War battleground, threatening the future of the negotiations as a whole.[17]

5.1 Controlling or Banning Indiscriminate Warfare?

The international legal regulation of indiscriminate warfare started long before the Wright brothers first took off in their airplane. Already in the 1860s,

---

[16] Minutes of Meeting UK Delegation, 16 June 1949, no. 4155, FO369 (Foreign Office), The National Archives (TNA), Kew.

[17] This part adds an important element to existing studies on immediate postwar attempts to regulate atomic warfare under international law. See Gro Nystuen, Stuart Casey-Maslen, and Annie Golden Bersagel, *Nuclear Weapons under International Law* (Cambridge: Cambridge University Press, 2014); and Darcy, *Judges, Law and War*, 188–199.

Lieber wrote that, "as civilization [had] advanced during the last centuries," noncombatants should be spared as much as the "exigencies of war" would admit. Likewise, the 1868 St. Petersburg Declaration recognized the importance of protecting noncombatants to the greatest degree allowed by "calamities of war," whereas the first Geneva Convention demanded respect for neutralized military hospitals.[18] At this point there existed widespread agreement that the only legitimate object of war was to weaken the enemy's forces, not noncombatants or medical facilities. This nineteenth-century understanding of distinction was not without critical exceptions, however.

In case of "blockade," for example, the law of nations tolerated the weapon of starvation. When besieging a demarcated area, belligerents were permitted to deny noncombatants and food suppliers from either entering or leaving this locality—Lieber: "[one can] starve the hostile belligerent, armed or *unarmed* [emphasis added, BvD], so that it leads to the subjection of the enemy."[19] Merchants from neutral states would be exempted only if they abstained from trading so-called contraband goods with the enemy.[20] In case of (naval) bombardment, the norm of distinction often superseded that of military necessity. In fortified towns, military considerations tended to prevail over distinction: according to many contemporary publicists, so long as artillery (or naval) fire would remain restricted within a short range of a fortified area, that principle of distinction would remain practical.[21] As we saw previously, this conception of non-combatanthood was a highly discriminatory one, excluding a whole range of persons, especially those indigenous peoples who suffered from colonial starvation policies.[22]

Put differently, the parameters of non-combatant immunity, as it was later called,[23] were never absolute or definitively determined.[24] Rather, the term

---

[18] Neve Gordon and Nicola Perugini, "'Hospital Shields' and the Limits of International Law," *European Journal of International Law*, Vol. 30, No. 2 (2019): 439–463, 444.

[19] Article 17, Lieber, *Instructions for the Government of Armies of the United States in the Field, General Orders No. 100* (1863); and Neve Gordon and Nicola Perugini, *Human Shields: A History of People in the Line of Fire* (Berkeley, CA: University of California Press, 2020).

[20] For detailed discussions of the concept and history of contraband, see Nicholas Mulder, *The Economic Weapon: Interwar Internationalism and the Rise of Sanctions, 1914-1945* (forthcoming), xxii—xxiii and Isabel Hull, *A Scrap of Paper: Breaking and Making International Law during the Great War* (Ithaca, NY: Cornell University Press, 2014), 164.

[21] Morton Royse, *Aerial Bombardment: and the International Regulation of Warfare* (New York: 1928), 150.

[22] Helen Kinsella, *The Image before the Weapon: A Critical History of the Distinction Between Combatant and Civilian* (Ithaca, NY: Cornell University Press, 2011); Alex De Waal, *Mass Starvation: The History and Future of Famine* (Cambridge: Polity, 2018), 67–73; and Mike Davis, *Late Victorian Holocausts: El Nino Famines and the Making of the Third World* (London: Verso, 2002).

[23] Igor Primoratz, *Civilian Immunity in War* (Oxford: Oxford University Press, 2010).

[24] See also Pablo Kalmanovitz, *The Laws of War in International Thought* (Oxford: Oxford University Press, 2020), 111–115.

was conditioned by available technology, ideas of military necessity, blockade, civilizational scope, and the demands of modern capitalism. In 1856, the Congress of Paris tried to codify some of these foundational notions into one text for maritime warfare, partly as a response to the recent boom of inter-continental trade making states ever more dependent upon foreign foodstuffs. The 1856 Declaration of Paris placed a set of basic restraints on blockade in an attempt to prevent future European wars from being haunted by the specter of starvation.[25] Less than two decades later, the Brussels Conference tried to repeat this codifying effort for land warfare, arguing that only fortified towns could be bombarded; urban areas not fortified by troops could not be attacked, nor might hospitals be directly targeted.[26]

Therefore, the restrictive German delegation in 1899 suggested replacing the Brussels test of fortification for that of defense, whether a town was defended or not. While accepting this plan, the First Hague Conference failed to provide a clear set of criteria for the test itself. Neither did it effectively regulate bombardment. Of course, it had accepted certain rules for protecting monumental places, but these were meant to prevent wanton destruction rather than strictly regulating bombardment itself. Gathered at the Czar's behest with the proclaimed ambition of reducing armaments, this meeting not only proved unable to meet this objective but also refused to ban submarine warfare, to the disappointment of outside observers.[27] Ultimately, it accepted only two prohibitionary declarations relating to indiscriminate warfare: on the use of poison gas, passed with near unanimity, and on bombing from balloons.[28]

The question of whether the German proposal related to targeting also applied to air bombing created significant controversy at both Hague conferences. At the first meeting, in 1899, the Czarist Russian delegation had proposed to prohibit bombing from so-called non-dirigible balloons. This weapon, which

---

[25] Nicholas Mulder and Boyd van Dijk, "Why Did Starvation Not Become the Paradigmatic War Crime in International Law?" in *Contingency in International Law: On the Possibility of Different Legal Histories*, ed. Ingo Venzke and Kevin Jon Heller (Oxford: Oxford University Press, 2021), 371–388.

[26] This legal theorem was predicated upon an outdated system of a defensive line composed of fortified towns. This outdated conception eventually gave way to one of defense positions built upon extended lines of forts with non-fortified towns. For a broader discussion of civilian targeting, see Alexander Downes and Kathryn McNabb Cochran, "It's a Crime, But Is It a Blunder?" in *Civilians and Warfare in World History*, ed. Nicola Foote and Nadya Williams (London: Routledge, 2017), 288–312; Michael Horowitz and Dan Reiter, "When Does Aerial Bombing Work? Quantitative Empirical Tests, 1917–1999," *Journal of Conflict Resolution*, vol. 45, no. 2 (2001): 147–173; Alexander Downes, *Targeting Civilians in War* (Ithaca, NY: Cornell University Press, 2008); and Stathis Kalyvas, *The Logic of Violence in Civil War* (Cambridge: Cambridge University Press, 2006).

[27] Andrew Webster, "Reconsidering Disarmament at the Hague Peace Conference of 1899, and After," in *War, Peace and International Order? The Legacies of the Hague Conferences of 1899 and 1907*, ed. Maartje Abbenhuis (London: Routledge, 2017), 69–85, 78.

[28] Ibid., 69.

204 PREPARING FOR WAR

the Russians had tried but failed to develop, was militarily ineffective and thus was hardly ever used in actual combat. It is no surprise that the delegates easily agreed to the Russian proposal.[29] The US delegation, aware of the ongoing experiments with airplanes at home, convinced the other delegates to limit the prohibition on bombing from balloons to a period of only five years.[30] In other words, if military necessity was at issue, there existed virtually no robust international rule to prevent noncombatant populations from being targeted.[31]

Still, it is vitally important to remember that few jurists at the time deemed as acceptable bombardment for so-called "psychological reasons." There existed a widespread taboo on bombing noncombatants accepted as such in order to erode, to undermine, the nation's will to fight—certainly in the context of European interstate wars. Equally important, few attempts were made to codify this norm, out of fear of undermining the army and navy's ability to effectively wage war.[32] More generally, contemporaries were reluctant to draft rules that would significantly hinder states' military operations. For these reasons, the Hague Regulations accepted the bombing of open towns if considered a military necessity and placed naval bombardment outside this test's scope.[33] Indeed, the use of bombardment was thus not unregulated, but rather deregulated: the commander in the field or on the seas was allowed to fire indiscriminately if this was considered a military necessity.[34]

The question of bombardment arose again after the balloon declaration had expired and while the Second Hague Conference was gathering in 1907. In the years leading up to this meeting, the technology for the dirigible balloon had improved dramatically. Leading this effort, the French and Germans both adopted dirigible balloons into their regular armies. Previously in favor of prohibition, the two leading air powers and Russia now demanded international recognition for the legality of air bombing, endorsing its regulation as a result. In their view, this new method of warfare deserved the same type of regulation as any other firing device. Other empires disagreed, however. Whereas the Austro-Hungarians wished to prohibit air bombing to protect their massive

---

[29] Royse, *Aerial Bombardment*, 23–28, 32, 46.

[30] Ibid., 35–36.

[31] Ibid., 154–159.

[32] The Institute of International Law condemned bombardments that were "destined solely to bring about the submission of the country": Royse, *Aerial Bombardment*, 161.

[33] "The reason given for this departure from the land warfare rules was that naval forces could not land forces and take possession of a place in order to carry out the necessary destruction. Bombardment without landing forces might thus be essential": Ibid., 162–164.

[34] Ibid., 165.

land army, the British feared that it threatened their own metropolitan safety and naval supremacy.[35]

The Italian and Russian proposal to regulate air bombings eventually led to the creation of the historic Article 25, placing air bombing under the same category as land bombardment. The French removed the specific reference to air bombing to prevent "undue accentuation." The final version legalizing air bombing brought it under the existing—and permissive—land bombardment regime originally proposed by the Germans, thereby securing the major air powers' key interests.[36] Despite internal support for banning aerial warfare, the Institute concurred with its legalization in 1911, as Italian airplanes dropped their first bombs on colonial Libya. Paradoxically, apart from legalizing this weapon while refusing to readdress disarmament, the Second Hague Conference also extended the prohibition of the original balloon declaration until the next Hague Peace Conference—which never met.[37] This document failed to be ratified due to opposition from the major air powers: applying to wars with signatories only, the balloon declarations never became truly restrictive during the First World War.[38]

As the Second Hague Conference refused to extend the laws of land warfare to the maritime world,[39] Whitehall decided to invite the world's naval powers to London to obtain clearer and written rules for naval warfare. In the end, the participants drafted a declaration which tightened the rules on blockade by developing an elaborate set of contraband provisions that sought to prevent hunger blockade. Whereas the British received guarantees against the targeting of their merchant shipping by German submarines, Berlin obtained the right to import foodstuffs through neutral Holland's ports. However, when the British refused to ratify this agreement, the London Declaration's future looked bleak, as a new generation of British, American, and French naval thinkers were preparing for total warfare on the high seas.[40] They considered an all-out maritime offensive on enemy food supply lines, as well as the bombardment of noncombatant populations, as legitimate means to destroy the enemy in a so-called knockout blow—this same conception would lie at the

---

[35] Royse, *Aerial Bombardment*, 55–56, 59, 65–66, 105.

[36] Similarly, they implicitly admitted that while being spared "as far as possible," hospitals could be targeted if they were being used as human shields: Article 27, Hague Regulations 1907. See Gordon and Perugini, *Human Shields*.

[37] Royse, *Aerial Bombardment*, 113–119.

[38] Hull, *A Scrap of Paper*, 225.

[39] Webster, "Reconsidering Disarmament," 79; Hull, *A Scrap of Paper*, 142–143.

[40] Hull, *A Scrap of Paper*, 142–144; and Mulder and Van Dijk, "Why Did Starvation Not Become the Paradigmatic War Crime in International Law?"

206 PREPARING FOR WAR

origins of strategic bombing thinking that grew in popularity during the First World War.[41]

"Weapons of Peace"

During this catastrophic conflict, during which ideas of indiscriminate warfare welcomed the end of the proclaimed principle of distinction, blockade was regulated by only a non-ratified declaration. The most pertinent rules for air bombing concerned a few articles from the Hague Regulations, arguing that bombardment of open towns remained generally prohibited. However, none of these provisions did much to restrain the actual conduct of air bombing, nor that of blockade. British government officials publicly defended starvation blockade as a legitimate weapon to defeat the Central Powers, and it led to mass civilian death.[42] Starvation among civilians was the main cause of noncombatant death during this global war.[43]

Most French border cities were being systemically bombed already by 1915. When the city of Freiburg was targeted by French airplanes in reprisal, German authorities relocated nearby camps with Allied prisoners of war toward the city center, with the aim of creating human shields for the protection of German civilians.[44] As the air war progressed, increasingly belligerents began to directly target urban areas, calling their bombing operations reprisals or deliberately blurring the concept of undefended towns—and this despite continued criticism of strategic bombing in Allied parliaments.[45] The doctrine of military objective proved practically impossible as a result of the air weapon's lack of accuracy.

During the First World War, Red Cross hospitals were deliberately targeted and zeppelin raids spread terror among civilian populations.[46] In turn, the

---

[41] Mulder, *The Economic Weapon*, xxix–xxx, xxviii; and David Morgan-Owen and Louis Halewood, "Introduction: Strategy, Economics, and the Sea," in *Economic Warfare and the Sea: Grand Strategies for Maritime Powers, 1650–1945*, ed. David Morgan-Owen and Louis Halewood (Liverpool: Liverpool University Press, 2020), 1–22, 6–7; Luís Paulo Bogliolo, "Governing from Above: A History of Aerial Bombing and International Law," Ph.D. Dissertation, University of Melbourne, 2020, 4; and Thomas Hippler, *Governing the Skies: A Global History of Aerial Bombing* (London: Verso, 2017).

[42] Hull, *A Scrap of Paper*, 165 and Mulder, *The Economic Weapon*, viii–ix.

[43] Mulder, *The Economic Weapon*, viii–ix.

[44] Gordon and Perugini, *Human Shields*.

[45] Agnieszka Jachec-Neale, *Concept of Military Objectives in International Law and Targeting Practice* (London: Routledge, 2014), 19; Hull, *A Scrap of Paper*, 302–303. For a broader history, see Amanda Alexander, "The 'Good War': Preparations for a War against Civilians," *Law, Culture and the Humanities*, Vol. 15, No. 1 (2016): 227–252.

[46] Gordon and Perugini, *Human Shields*.

British were committed to the policy of hunger blockade in order to defeat the Central Powers. Despite protests from Scandinavian neutrals and attempts by the United States to mediate between the fighting parties to end both hunger blockade and unrestricted submarine warfare,[47] neither Germany nor the Allied powers wished to revise these policies. By the end of the war, both sides realized not just that the principle of distinction had virtually collapsed but also that indiscriminate warfare had transformed the nature of warfare, if not the international order more broadly.[48]

In the period after the war, during which blockade had played a decisive role in defeating the Central Powers according to Allied leaders,[49] the victorious liberal powers addressed the issue internationally, contributing to the development of economic warfare as the League of Nation's most valuable "weapon of peace."[50] At Versailles, while prohibiting gas weaponry for the defeated states and making disarmament a central part of the League's Covenant, the Allies envisaged blockade as a crucial weapon in the future struggle against aggression. It is striking that advocates of this approach through the League of Nations forthrightly admitted that such a blockade might trigger mass civilian death. Still, they believed it was a price worth paying for bolstering a new international institution that might prevent or stop war.[51]

It is less surprising, however, that Red Cross Societies from Scandinavian neutrals were less convinced by this reframing of blockade as a weapon of peace. Concerned about its impact on the livelihoods of civilians, the Swedish Red Cross delegation proposed in 1921, at the first postwar Red Cross Conference, to restrict aerial warfare and temporarily lift blockade to provide relief to women and children.[52] By contrast, the British argued, in a Lieberian fashion, that such "remitting [of] the stringency of blockade would [only] prolong war."[53] At the same time,[54] the ICRC tried to resurrect the principle of

---

[47] Hull, *A Scrap of Paper*, 170–178.

[48] Mulder, *The Economic Weapon*, 106.

[49] This statement reflects the opinion of Allied leaders at the end of the First World War—not necessarily that of historians today. Hull, *A Scrap of Paper*, 170; Mulder, *The Economic Weapon*, 137.

[50] Mulder, *The Economic Weapon*, 113.

[51] Mulder and Van Dijk, "Why Did Starvation Not Become the Paradigmatic War Crime in International Law?"

[52] Expressing concern about potential League sanctions, interwar German elites often supported Scandinavian campaigns to limit the power of blockade: Mulder and Van Dijk, "Why Did Starvation Not Become the Paradigmatic War Crime in International Law?"

[53] Report UK delegation to Red Cross Conference, 1921, no. 8598/12, ADM1 (Admiralty), TNA.

[54] A Greco-German Mixed Arbitral Tribunal, under the Peace Treaty of Versailles of 1919, made two controversial decisions in the interwar period about claims for damages for the destruction of property and loss of life as a result of German air raids. For a discussion of these verdicts, see Georg Schwarzenberger, *International Law as Applied by International Courts and Tribunals, Volume II, The Law of Armed Conflict* (London: Stevens, 1968), 144–150.

208 PREPARING FOR WAR

distinction by demanding from Allied states and the League the prohibition of indiscriminate warfare—especially the use of gas, even though this weapon killed proportionally few combatants during the war, and had not been used against interstate civilians at that stage.[55]

At the 1921 Red Cross Conference the ICRC tried to prohibit gas and limit air bombing to military objectives alone;[56] the latter was rejected by several state representatives, who considered it ineffective or impracticable. Following the Swedish proposal, the Red Cross Conference's appeal from 1921 to apply the existing rules more strictly never amounted to recognizing their insufficiency, as demonstrated during the First World War.[57] Crucially, this meant that questions regarding blockade and air warfare, whether taking place in "civilized" Europe or in the colonies, were deliberately left in the hands of major states, especially those soon gathering at the disarmament conference in Washington.[58]

From 1921 until early 1922, the world's most powerful states discussed the regulation of the use of indiscriminate weaponry, from gas warfare to military airplanes, as a critical pre-condition for maintaining peace. On blockade, they agreed to recognize submarines as legitimate weapons of war by enforcing cruiser rules while remaining silent about hunger blockade. Most of the fundamental issues with respect to economic warfare were left unresolved.[59] By contrast, the conference was far less accommodating with regard to gas warfare, initiating an effort to prohibit this less destructive weapon that in 1925 led to the signing of the Geneva Protocol, a treaty which banned the first use of gas in interstate wars.[60] By excluding colonial wars,[61] they deliberately left a gap in this treaty that could be exploited by imperial powers to suppress anti-colonial insurgencies by using (tear) gas weaponry.[62]

On air warfare, no agreement was reached, and the matter was then forwarded to a special expert group. This Committee, which gathered in neutral

---

[55] See Bugnion, "Droit de Genève et Droit de la Haye," 910–911.

[56] Minutes of Meetings Red Cross Conference Commission VII, 1921, La Bibliothèque du Comité international de la Croix Rouge, Geneva (ICRC Library).

[57] Ibid.

[58] Resolution Red Cross Conference XII Limitation de la Guerre, 1921, ICRC Library.

[59] Hull, *A Scrap of Paper*, 209, 272.

[60] Andrew Webster, "Making Disarmament Work: The Implementation of the International Disarmament Provisions in the League of Nations Covenant, 1919–1925," *Diplomacy & Statecraft*, Vol. 16, No. 3 (2006): 551–569, 561–562.

[61] See also Güneş Murat Tezcür and Doreen Horschig, "A Conditional Norm: Chemical Warfare from Colonialism to Contemporary Civil Wars," *Third World Quarterly*, Vol. 42, No. 2 (2020): 1–19.

[62] Erik Linstrum, "Domesticating Chemical Weapons: Tear Gas and the Militarization of Policing in the British Imperial World, 1919–1981," *Journal of Modern History*, Vol. 91, No. 3 (2019): 557–585, 566, 570, 573.

The Hague until February 1923 and was chaired by the leading American jurist John Bassett Moore, was composed of representatives from the Netherlands plus the five major Allied powers, one of whom was Albert De la Pradelle.[63] An influential Parisian professor of international law, De la Pradelle helped to create the first drafts, based upon British and American proposals, for the regulation of air warfare.[64] This text, which represents the first comprehensive attempt to regulate bombing from the sky up to that point, would have a significant impact on the development of the laws of war in the coming decades.

The document's drafters agreed that the existing Hague rules for air bombardment from 1907 were completely outdated.[65] That new text, they agreed, should condemn terror bombing, as had been practiced by Germany's zeppelin raids, and be based on a British-sponsored text codifying the wartime doctrine of military objectives.[66] The delegates recognized a number of objects that should be spared or could be lawfully targeted, one of which was munition factories, which left the door open for strategic bombing. Regardless of this, bombing of urban areas outside the army's operations remained prohibited. However, if operating in a town, the area could be bombed as long as this was done "proportionally"—the first time this key principle was explicitly codified in legal history. In theory, the principle suggested that if there existed a reasonable presumption that the target was sufficiently militarily important in proportion to the danger posed to civilians, that particular area could be bombed.[67] In this way, drafters made the cause of civilian protection secondary to the interests of bombing.

Whereas these men hoped to place at least some restraints on the air weapon, interwar advocates of strategic bombing believed that civilian targeting represented a more "humane" alternative to the horrors of trench warfare. Hugh Trenchard, the founder of Britain's Royal Air Force (RAF), believed that air bombing could "induce the enemy government, by pressure from the population, to sue for peace, in exactly in the same way as starvation by blockading the country would force the government to sue for peace."[68] Like many other

---

[63] Nelson and Waters, "The Allied Bombing of German Cities during the Second World War from a Canadian Perspective," 93.

[64] For the proposals of the different delegations, see Texts Proposed by Delegations, 1922–1923, no. 4, Nederlandse Delegatie Commissie tot Herziening van het Oorlogsrecht, National Archives of the Netherlands (NA), The Hague.

[65] See Reports and Texts Proposed by Subcommittees, 1922–1923, no. 4, Nederlandse Delegatie Commissie tot Herziening van het Oorlogsrecht, NA; and General Report of Jurists, 1923, no. 5, Nederlandse Delegatie Commissie tot Herziening van het Oorlogsrecht, NA.

[66] Ben Saul, *Defining Terrorism in International Law* (Oxford: Oxford University Press, 2006), 273.

[67] Dutch Report Hague Conference, 1923, no. 1802, Archief Buitenlandse Zaken A-Dossiers, NA.

[68] Cited from: Hippler, *Governing from the Skies*.

210 PREPARING FOR WAR

bombing advocates, he wondered why it would be less humane to bomb civilians from the sky than to legally starve them on the ground, or to inflict mass combatant death in the trenches.[69]

Trenchard's argument resonated with the global spread of air power not only as a weapon of "peace" but also as a cost-effective means to police giant empires. From the French to the British, almost every major imperial power in the 1920s used bombing and/or chemical weapons against anti-colonial insurrectionists.[70] In addition to this, leading air power advocates such as Giulio Douhet defended the use of air-gas warfare to hasten the surrender of enemies.[71] Laying the foundations for the theory of the "knockout blow," which allegedly could lead to a quick victory by means of air-gas warfare, he argued that such means could improve the assumed potential of blockade in ending wars and preventing protracted trench-warfare conflicts.[72] These interwar notions of indiscriminate warfare either as a weapon of "peace," or as a cost-effective means to police massive empires on the cheap, foreshadowed later incendiary bombing campaigns and re-shaped the development of international law.[73]

Civilians were now increasingly seen as the preferred target and not the object of protection, as suggested by Moore's Committee.[74] The Hague Air Rules, as they became known, were therefore never ratified by states out of fear of sacrificing an allegedly decisive weapon. Still, these rules for air warfare had a transformative impact on the development of international law at different levels. Most obviously, the document featured cardinal principles such as proportionality and inspired later efforts, such as the 1954 Hague Convention, to create safety zones and protect monumental buildings in war.[75] At the same time, it is equally revealing that the ICRC, afraid to get involved in "political

---

[69] Ibid.

[70] Black, *Air Power*, 18, 49–51.

[71] See also Azar Gat, *Fascist and Liberal Visions of War: Fuller, Liddell Hart, Douhet, and Other Modernists* (Oxford: Oxford University Press, 1998).

[72] Black, *Air Power*, 43, 59.

[73] Bogliolo, "Governing from Above," 16.

[74] Hippler, *Governing from the Skies*; Bogliolo, "Governing from Above," 8; Alexander, "The 'Good War'," 229.

[75] This element, referring to the protection of monumental buildings, has inspired many, including the creators of the Monaco Draft (see below). De La Pradelle was also part of this effort. Building upon earlier precedents set by Versailles and a Dutch private initiative, the Hague Air Rules also influenced the drafters of the Roerich Pact from the 1930s and the Convention for the Protection of Historic Buildings, a project led by Belgian international jurist Charles de Visscher. These plans usually did not cover the protection of civilian populations as a whole and are therefore not further discussed here. For more background information, see Wayne Sandholtz, *Prohibiting Plunder: How Norms Change* (Oxford: Oxford University Press, 2009), 116–125; and Ana Filipa Vrdoljak, *International Law, Museums, and the Return of Cultural Objects* (Cambridge: Cambridge University Press, 2008).

issues" such as legally codifying air bombing, placed remarkably little emphasis on these new rules designed by the former Allies.

"Peace Zones"

In the mid-1920s, resonating with the approach of other international legal actors, ICRC legal officials far from ignored the matter of indiscriminate warfare, but decided to leave its codification to the Great Powers.[76] Throughout this period they adopted different approaches to promote improved legal regulation.[77] While remaining on the sidelines of efforts by global women's movements and the neutral US government to allow food transports to pass through a blockade (which was rejected by the League under British and French pressure),[78] the Red Cross continued to pressure states to ratify new international rules against indiscriminate warfare. The ICRC had no direct involvement in Allied efforts to codify new rules for gas warfare but did raise states' awareness of the lack of ratifications of the Protocol, which banned chemical and bacteriological warfare. Paradoxically, while demanding compliance with this newly signed treaty, the ICRC invested a great deal of effort in developing civil defense as a response to its possible violation.

This cautious, if not contradictory, approach exemplifies broader international concerns about the threat of attacks on major cities using gas and high explosives.[79] Indiscriminate warfare as a contested method in wartime triggered intense public debate and anxiety in the interwar period.[80] In 1925, when the Red Cross Conference had come to an end, the ICRC began further deepening its expertise with respect to developing measures of civil defense to protect civilian populations against air-gas warfare.[81] Around this time, the

---

[76] Alexander, "The 'Good War,'" 229. For a broader discussion, see Christiane Wilke, "How International Law Learned to Love the Bomb: Civilians and the Regulation of Aerial Warfare in the 1920s," *Australian Feminist Law Journal*, Vol. 44, No. 1 (2018): 29–47.

[77] Richard Overy, *The Bombing War: Europe 1939-1945* (London: Penguin Books, 2014), 24.

[78] Mulder, *The Economic Weapon*, 155–156, 299–300. On gender and distinction: Judith Gardam, "Gender and Non-Combatant Immunity," *Transnational Law and Contemporary Problems* [1999]: 345–370; Laura Sjoberg, "Gendered Realities of the Immunity Principle: Why Gender Analysis Needs Feminism," *International Studies Quarterly*, Vol. 50, No. 4 (2006): 889–910; and Kinsella, *The Image before the Weapon*.

[79] Report ICRC for 1925 Red Cross Conference, 1925, ICRC Library; and Black, *Air Power*, 44. For a broader Red Cross critique of this approach, see Minutes of Meetings Red Cross Conference Commission V, 1925, ICRC Library.

[80] Max Hastings, *Bomber Command* (New York: Dial Press, 1979), 41–43.

[81] The ICRC also pushed the signatories of the Conventions to ratify the Protocol. For the history of the ICRC's efforts with regard to chemical warfare in the interwar period, see Estelle Pralong, *La Guerre Chimique: de la Grande Guerre à la Guerre d'Abyssinie. Les Faiblesses du Nouvel Ordre International* (Geneva: MA Thesis, 2002). See also Annette Becker, "La Guerre des Gaz, entre Tragédie, Rumeur,

212 PREPARING FOR WAR

ICRC hosted several expert meetings on civilian defense, published on the topic in the *Revue*, established a special information center for it, and called for humanitarian exceptions in the case of blockade by the League of Nations in future "sanction wars."[82]

Still, while codifying the 1929 Conventions, the ICRC proved unwilling to outlaw either the League's weapon of hunger blockade or air bombardment.[83] Often seen as the most prominent legal innovation of the interwar period, these treaties however stayed largely silent on the threat of indiscriminate warfare.[84] While failing to ban reprisals against hospitals in the Sick & Wounded Convention, the main innovation of these treaties was to outlaw the use of prisoners of war as human shields.[85] Pushing for this element, the British admitted internally that they were more keen on protecting their air power through this proposal than on preventing their troops from being used as human shields, as had occurred during the First World War.[86] Despite these limited outcomes, the Red Cross nonetheless kept pushing the Great Powers discussing indiscriminate warfare at the disarmament conference in Geneva to prohibit air bombardment ("the Benes resolution") and other indiscriminate weapons targeting civilian populations.[87]

Opening in 1932, the world disarmament conference took place in Geneva[88] in the wake of Japan's first terror bombing campaign against Shanghai, which immediately captured the public imagination, prompting calls for a complete prohibition.[89] At the meeting, the British proposed restricting aerial bombing

---

Mémoire et Oubli," in *Vrai et Faux dans la Grande Guerre*, ed. Christophe Prochason and Anne Rasmussen (Paris: Découverte, 2004), 257–276; Olivier Lepick, *Les Armes Chimiques* (Paris: Presses Universitaires de France, 1999); Leo van Bergen, "The Poison Gas Debate in the Inter-War Years," *Medicine Conflict and Survival*, Vol. 24, No. 3 (2008): 174–187; and Ludwig Haber, *The Poisonous Cloud: Chemical Warfare in the First World War* (Oxford: Oxford University Press, 1986).

[82] Sidney Brown, "Le Rôle de la Croix-Rouge en cas d'Application de l'Article 16 du Pacte de la Société des Nations, et de Blocus en Temps de Guerre," *Revue Internationale de la Croix-Rouge* (1930): 234–282, 234–235, 249–250.

[83] Mulder and Van Dijk, "Why Did Starvation Not Become the Paradigmatic War Crime in International Law?"

[84] See also Neville Wylie, "The 1929 Prisoner of War Convention and the Building of the Interwar Prisoner of War Regime," in *Prisoners in War: Norms, Military Cultures and Reciprocity in Armed Conflict*, ed. Sibylle Scheipers (Oxford: Oxford University Press), 91–106.

[85] While largely ignoring the weaponization of civilians, Nuremberg prosecutors used this ban from the 1929 Convention to charge German soldiers with violating the laws of war through the employment of Allied prisoners of war as so-called human shields: Gordon and Perugini, *Human Shields*. Article 17 of the 1934 Tokyo Draft argued that the 1929 Convention's ban on human shields was applicable to civilian internees "by analogy."

[86] Report of Sub-Committee of Imperial Defence, 1925, no. 64, CAB16 (Cabinet Office), TNA; Gordon and Perugini, *Human Shields*.

[87] *Report of the ICRC on its activities during the Second World War, Vol I* (1948), 684.

[88] It was held at the same building where the diplomatic conference would take place in 1949.

[89] N. C. Fleming, "Cabinet Government, British Imperial Security, and the World Disarmament Conference, 1932–1934," *War in History*, Vol. 18, No. 1 (2011): 62–84, 69.

while sanctioning the use of colonial air policing: on the one hand, they sought to protect metropolitan Britain from aerial attack; on the other hand, they considered RAF bombing as a crucial weapon for ensuring imperial security.[90] By contrast, the Soviets supported the proposed ban on air bombing and suggested economic non-aggression pacts to stop hunger blockade in interstate wars.[91] These disarmament talks finally collapsed in the early 1930s, with the departure of Hitler's delegation from Geneva, given Britain's concerns about its imperial security, and because of stifling French resistance as a result of a lack of concrete security guarantees against potential German aggression.[92]

In the wake of these major setbacks, international organizations other than the ICRC took up the torch of finding new means to protect civilian populations against the dangers of air bombing.[93] While some believed prohibition was the only effective means to stop this, the ICRC leadership believed it had no choice other than to focus on developing civil defense as a practical though limited means to approach that goal.[94] As ICRC president, Huber publicly acknowledged that regulating air bombardment no longer fell "within [the Red Cross] province," and it rejected German calls for prohibiting hunger blockade.[95] As fears over the potential of air power grew significantly over time, other international organizations began developing so-called "peace zones" as a response to the greater sophistication of bombers in the 1930s.[96]

This spatial answer to the rising threat of strategic bombing, also a response to fears about the social breakdown it might generate, was first developed after

---

[90] Fleming, "Cabinet Government," 65–67, 84. See also David Omissi, *Air Power and Colonial Control: The Royal Air Force 1919–1939* (Manchester: Manchester University Press, 1990); and Priya Satia, *Spies in Arabia: The Great War and the Cultural Foundations of Britain's Covert Empire in the Middle East* (Oxford: Oxford University Press, 2008).

[91] The suggested prohibition on hunger blockade would not count for the Soviet empire itself, however. The Ukrainians would quickly learn this lesson after the conference ended. Mulder, *The Economic Weapon*, 306–307; and Jiří Toman, "L'Union Soviètique et le Droit des Conflits Armés," Ph.D. Dissertation, University of Geneva, 1997, 425.

[92] See Fleming, "Cabinet Government," 63–64; Peter Jackson, "France, the Problems of Security and International Disarmament after the First World War," *Journal of Strategic Studies*, Vol. 29, No. 2 (2006): 247–280, 254; and Saul, *Defining Terrorism in International Law*, 276.

[93] See Carolyn Kitching, *Britain and the Geneva Disarmament Conference* (New York: Palgrave, 2003).

[94] Minutes of Meetings Red Cross Conference Commission III, 1930, ICRC Library; and Red Cross Conference Resolution V Protection des Populations Civiles Contre la Guerre Chimique, 1930, ICRC Library. For the "Dutch origins" of this resolution, see Leo van Bergen and Maartje Abbenhuis, "Man-Monkey, Monkey-Man: Neutrality and the Discussions about the 'Inhumanity' of Poison Gas in the Netherlands and International Committee of the Red Cross," *First World War Studies*, Vol. 3 (2012): 1–23.

[95] Mulder and Van Dijk, "Why Did Starvation Not Become the Paradigmatic War Crime in International Law?"

[96] Black, *Air Power*, 62.

214 PREPARING FOR WAR

1929, when the Lieux de Genève Association (LGA)[97] was established by the military physician Georges Saint-Paul and the Red Cross humanitarian Robert Jacquinot.[98] These two Frenchmen proposed safety zones for medical services and civilian populations to find refuge from air attacks. They were used most successfully during the Sino-Japanese War. In Shanghai, Jacquinot himself established a unique Red Cross-marked safety zone that saved the lives of countless Chinese civilians.[99] Taking up this idea, the International Congress of Military Medicine and Pharmacy (ICMMP) became an ardent advocate of safety zones and took major steps toward codifying this concept internationally.

In 1934, an affiliated group of Francophone military doctors and the international jurist De la Pradelle gathered in Monaco. The latter had previously taken part in the creation of the Hague Air Rules, and this legacy can be easily discovered in the final text agreed upon by the participants.[100] This document featured implicit references to the Hague Air Rules and endorsed hospital and "security towns" as protective methods against air bombing.[101] By contrast, the Monaco Draft, as it came to be called, remained silent about the threat of hunger blockade and aligned itself with the League's blockading power. The text equally formed a response to a post-1919 skepticism toward the laws of war as a discipline, whose utopian energy had to be "reconstructed" after its loss during the First World War, in the eyes of these French wartime veterans.[102]

The drafters behind the Monaco Draft wished to "humanize war" or even "humanize air war,"[103] a term legally theorized by a group predominantly composed of military doctors.[104] The Monaco Draft included several chapters and

---

[97] In 1937, the organization was moved to Geneva and named the International Association for the Protection of Civilian Populations and Historic Buildings in Wartime: Jiri Toman, *The Protection of Cultural Property in the Event of Armed Conflict* (Aldershot: Dartmouth Publishing, 1996), 447.

[98] Henry Dunant had played with the idea of safety zones already in the nineteenth century, but the concept of safety zones really emerged only in the late 1920s as a response to the threat of aerial bombardment: *Der Spiegel*, 1 April 1953. Marcia Ristaino, *The Jacquinot Safe Zone: Wartime Refugees in Shanghai* (Stanford, CA: Stanford University Press, 2008), 55–56.

[99] Ristaino, *The Jacquinot Safe Zone*, 1–2, 57–59, 65; and Mulder, *The Economic Weapon*, 447.

[100] It is no coincidence that De la Pradelle's descendant mentioned his influence on the final draft. He also dedicated his book to the royal family of Monaco, whom he had represented at the conference, and who had supported the interwar initiative. Paul de La Pradelle, *La Conférence Diplomatique et les Nouvelles Conventions de Genève du 12 Août 1949* (Paris: Les Editions Internationales, 1951), 186–187.

[101] Jan Burgers, "The Road to San Francisco: The Revival of the Human Rights Idea in the Twentieth Century," *Human Rights Quarterly*, Vol. 14, No. 4 (1992): 447–477, 452–453.

[102] See Albert de La Pradelle, Jules Voncken, and Fernand Dehousse, *La Reconstruction du Droit de la Guerre* (Paris: 1936).

[103] The concept of humanizing air warfare ("*L'Humanisation de la Guerre Aèrienne*") comes from a later publication. The brochure featured a preface by de La Pradelle. J. Charpentier, *L'Humanisation de la Guerre Aèrienne* (Paris: Éditions Internationales, 1938).

[104] Ironic, because their primary task in war was to treat wounded soldiers in order to bring them back to the front for the war machine. See Meron, "The Humanization of Humanitarian Law." For a recent critique of the "humanization" concept, see Samuel Moyn, "Toward a History of Clean and Endless War," *Just Security* (9 October 2015).

in some respects was more comprehensive than the 1949 Conventions would ever be.[105] There existed provisions for medical services, and the protection of civilian populations was referenced; prisoners of war should be protected too, it stated. And, unlike the existing Conventions, it featured basic rules on the use of air bombardment that were mostly based upon the Hague Air Rules. It demanded, for instance, protection for monumental buildings, in line with earlier plans, and it placed limits on the targeting of military objectives in urban areas, restricting the use of air bombing.

Not surprisingly, these far-reaching proposals prompted virtually no support, let alone enthusiasm, among the leading air powers. Initially, the Belgian government had promised to host a diplomatic conference—an initiative that was warmly greeted by the 1934 Red Cross Conference in, of all places, Tokyo. This initiative soon lost its momentum, though.[106] After lengthy discussion, recognizing the lack of Great Powers' support for this attempt to regulate air bombing at a time of rising international tensions, the European hosts decided not to follow up on it for fear of a diplomatic fiasco.[107] The plan to discuss the Monaco Draft at a diplomatic conference had died at an early stage.[108]

By mid-1935, the ICMMP was left with little choice but to seek support from other international organizations, the most prominent of which was the ICRC. The Genevans were initially reluctant to ally with any of these initiatives from French humanitarians,[109] fearing that such measures might be ineffective against air bombing and that cooperation in such a politically sensitive area might undermine their neutrality, if not lead to encroachments on the Geneva Conventions.[110] The Monaco Draft touched directly upon matters already covered by the new Tokyo Draft or existing treaties and, according to Huber, had gained little support among the Great Powers—especially France, as a leading

---

[105] Boyd van Dijk, "Human Rights in War: On the Entangled Foundations of the 1949 Geneva Conventions," *American Journal of International Law*, Vol. 112, No. 4 (2018): 553–582.

[106] It is worth mentioning that the Red Cross conference did so, considering the significant overlap between the Tokyo Draft and the Monaco Draft. In 1934, at its conference in Tokyo, the Red Cross endorsed the Belgian initiative wholeheartedly, following ICMMP secretary and Belgian military doctor Jules Voncken's particular plea for it. Tokyo Red Cross Conference Resolution XXXVII, 1934, ICRC Library.

[107] Once the news had reached The Hague, the authorities expressed opposition: considering themselves the exclusive guardians of these rules of war, Dutch officials argued that the matter fell exclusively within their competence, thus objecting to their neighbor's initiative—and Brussels immediately pulled back. Thereafter, the Dutch authorities realized they were left with the unsettling burden of having to organize a third peace conference, which few states wanted.

[108] See Minutes Commissie van Advies voor Volkenrechtelijke Vraagstukken on Monaco Draft, 1934–1939, no. 74, Commissie van Advies voor Volkenrechtelijke Vraagstukken, NA.

[109] Ristaino, *The Jacquinot Safe Zone*, 58–59, 153.

[110] Margot Kleinfeld, "The 1934 Monaco Draft: How the Military Medical Services Worked to Strengthen the Laws of War," *International Review of the Armed Forces Medical Services*, Vol. 88, No. 1 (2015): 91–97, 93–94.

216   PREPARING FOR WAR

air power.[111] The combination of the international system's breakdown and the lack of true will among states to tackle the Herculean task of taming indiscriminate warfare led to the demise of the Monaco Draft in the following years.[112]

As a result of these considerations, the ICRC decided in mid-1936—as it was intervening in the Ethiopian–Italian War, where the air-gas weapon was being extensively "tested" on black civilians and against Red Cross hospitals— to reject the regulation of aerial bombing and the creation of security zones for noncombatants.[113] Mainly concerned with possible violations of the Red Cross emblem, the ICRC turned a blind eye to the numerous violations of the principle of distinction by Mussolini's bomber forces.[114] Indeed, the ICRC, acting in line with its racial biases toward Europeans and against black Africans, was unwilling to go any further than investigating violations of the Red Cross emblem and formulating a draft convention for the protection of hospital towns for soldiers.

This inconclusive approach to regulating indiscriminate warfare failed to capture the public imagination. For example, the ICRC circular announcing its plans for a unambitious draft convention triggered little response from either states or Red Cross Societies. In 1937, the organization hosted a meeting with experts to design a first draft, but it evoked minimal interest. One year later, at the Red Cross Conference in London, the ICRC had to report that its draft treaty had received virtually no support, leading to its slow death over the succeeding years. Apart from this codification failure, the American delegation pushed for a non-binding resolution that appealed to the fighting parties in China and Spain to stop targeting civilians, which triggered an Italo-German counter-offensive indicting the Anglo-American weapon of blockade.[115]

Nor did the ICMMP's attempts to widen the Sick and Wounded Convention's scope for wounded civilians lead anywhere. The most ambitious attempt to codify new rules for air warfare took place in a room outside of the Red Cross Conference: in 1938, as tensions in Europe were rising and the British and Nazi leaders both publicly claimed that the "direct and deliberate bombing of non-combatants [was] illegal,"[116] the ICMMP endorsed an International

---

[111] Minutes Meeting Legal Division, 13 May 1936, no. A PV JUR.1, Les Archives du Comité International de la Croix-Rouge (ACICR), Geneva.

[112] Some also raised doubts about the text's feasibility and its practicability. Minutes Meeting Legal Division, 13 May 1936, no. A PV JUR.1, ACICR.

[113] Minutes Meeting Legal Division, 8 June 1936, no. A PV JUR.1, ACICR.

[114] Gordon and Perugini, *Human Shields*; and Rainer Baudendistel, *Between Bombs and Good Intentions: The Red Cross and the Italo-Ethiopian War, 1935–1936* (New York: Berghahn Books, 2006).

[115] Report Commission I London Conference, 1938, no. 47, American Red Cross, National Archives and Records Administration (NARA), College Park, MD.

[116] Cited from: Nelson and Waters, "The Allied Bombing of German Cities during the Second World War from a Canadian Perspective," 97.

Legal Association (ILA) draft on air warfare which had been drafted under De la Pradelle's chairmanship.[117] Still, this text, which prohibited incendiary weapons and endorsed the Monaco Draft's safety zones, was also virtually ignored by those same Great Powers, who were preparing for a terrifying air war against civilian populations. Nationalist China also voiced skepticism about the proposed safety zones, fearing that these might "release the [enemy] from the obligation to respect non-military objectives [outside of them]."[118]

The Nightmare of Unrestrained Warfare

The gradual breakdown of the international system after 1929, combined with the Great Powers' continuing opposition to the principle of distinction,[119] essentially condemned from the start attempts to codify rules for the protection of civilian populations. Nevertheless, the legacies of the Monaco group, ILA, Soviet non-aggression pacts, Scandinavian neutrals, and others shaped the ICRC's actions on behalf of civilian populations during the Second World War. In April 1939, signaling his early interest in this issue, Pictet wrote—in the first article of his long career—that the Hague Regulations were far from adequate to protect civilians in a future European air war, and thus suggested considering alternatives such as safety zones as a means of transforming the ICRC's attitude toward this question.[120] When the war in Europe broke out his organization made several last-minute appeals to the major belligerents—which major neutral powers like the United States initially supported as well—to spare civilian populations and mark prisoner of war camps with special emblems.[121]

Although these appeals made implicit references to the Monaco Draft as well as the Hague Air Rules, even suggesting safety zones for civilians,[122] the ICRC continued to prioritize its neutrality interests over those of civilians.

---

[117] It also helped to establish a new journal and study center ("Comité de Luxembourg") to improve expertise on protecting civilian populations in a future armed conflict. The official name for the study center was the "Comité International d'Information et d'Action pour la Protection de la Population Civile en temps de Guerre." It was co-founded in July 1938 by Voncken and De la Pradelle who took up the role of secretary-general. See *La Protection de la Population Civile en Temps de Guerre* (1938), ICRC Library. De La Pradelle was acting president of the ILA.

[118] Report Commission II London Conference, 1938, no. 47, American Red Cross, NARA.

[119] Alexander, "The 'Good War,'" 250.

[120] Jean Pictet, "La Protection Juridique de la Population Civile en Temps de Guerre," *Revue internationale de la Croix-Rouge et Bulletin international des Sociétés de la Croix-Rouge*, Vol. 21, No. 244 (1939): 268–289.

[121] See Hastings, *Bomber Command*, 55–56; and de La Pradelle, *La Conférence Diplomatique*, 187–189.

[122] The ICRC made various appeals to the belligerents in 1939, 1940, 1943, and 1944.

218 PREPARING FOR WAR

Tellingly, it refused to declare so-called open cities as a humanitarian response to the lack of civilian protection against air bombing, since this "[fell] outside [of] its proper sphere of action."[123] The ICRC remained also silent on the Anglo-American campaign of unrestricted air warfare. By contrast, it acted far more assertively in the domain of bending blockade, by staging a successful relief campaign in 1942 for the starving Greek civilian population. This unique ICRC operation was never repeated, though: the major United Nations powers wished to maintain pressure on Hitler's empire by blocking its access to valuable food markets.[124]

Mass starvation remained the norm as long as belligerents sought to deprive enemy civilians of foodstuffs so as to secure their government's surrender. The most extreme version of this destructive thinking was the Nazi Hunger plan to deliberately starve Slav and Jewish civilians in occupied Eastern Europe. Although the Nazis were unique in these genocidal designs to annihilate entire civilian groups by means of starvation, they were certainly not the only major power which tried to prevent enemies from obtaining mass calories.[125] The United States, for instance, unleashed a brutal campaign of starvation on Japan's home and occupied islands in order to trigger the specter of mass famine. By laying minefields and through unrestricted submarine warfare, Washington hoped to quicken Japan's surrender.[126] As the blockade and air war by the UN progressed, the civilian/combatant distinction came under increasing pressure, and eventually broke down entirely, to the despair of the few critics in the Anglophone world.[127]

Attacking enemy civilians and combatants with fire bombs or hunger blockade came to be seen as permissible. Thousands of Allied prisoners of war (POWs) paid the ultimate price for it, being killed by "friendly" bombs or torpedoes.[128] Throughout the war, British claims of "precision bombing" had no basis in actual practice either.[129] The RAF bombed German cities indiscriminately and the Germans used Allied POWs as human shields to protect civilians against such aerial bombardments: Pictet's greatest fear, of unrestrained

---

[123] *Report of the ICRC on its activities during the Second World War, Vol I* (1948), 704.

[124] Mulder and Van Dijk, "Why Did Starvation Not Become the Paradigmatic War Crime in International Law?"

[125] Lizzie Collingham, *The Taste of War: World War Two and the Battle for Food* (London: Allen Lane, 2011), 5.

[126] Mulder and Van Dijk, "Why Did Starvation Not Become the Paradigmatic War Crime in International Law?"

[127] Black, *Air Power*, 134; and Hastings, *Bomber Command*, 171.

[128] *Report of the ICRC on its activities during the Second World War, Vol I* (1948), 319–320; and Sarah Kovner, *Prisoners of the Empire: Inside Japanese POW Camps* (Cambridge, MA: Harvard University Press, 2020).

[129] Black, *Air Power*, 122–123; and Hastings, *Bomber Command*, 170.

warfare, had become a painful reality.[130] In March 1944,[131] as the Allied campaign of area bombing was reaching its destructive zenith, the ICRC tried to persuade the major belligerents to protect civilian populations against indiscriminate bombing.

The ICRC's proposal to recover Jacquinot's preexisting model by establishing mass safety zones for civilians was rejected by the Americans and Japanese and ignored by the British, who failed to respond. Whitehall showed more interest in preventing captured RAF "terror fliers" from being lynched by the Germans than in ending its own policy of "morale bombing."[132] The Americans, too, considered safety zones as a dangerous limitation upon their air power and feared they might be used by the Axis powers as a form of human shielding. By contrast, the Japanese argued that the ICRC should act far more aggressively by forcing the major Allies to abide by the 1907 Hague Regulations, as they had originally promised.[133] The only positive response to the ICRC's proposal came from Hitler's government, which viewed it as a subversive weapon to disrupt the attritional Allied bombing campaign through humanitarian law.[134]

To sum up, throughout the interwar period, ICRC attempts to protect civilian populations faced a wall of resistance from the Great Powers and reveal several important points for the Conventions' later development. They show how the ICRC adapted continuously while demanding that attention be paid to the dangers of air warfare, gas weaponry, and blockade. Far from overlooking issues other than strict "Geneva Law," the ICRC adopted different approaches,

---

[130] For the ICRC's efforts during the war on behalf of civilian populations, see ICRC Dossiers Protection des Populations Civiles, no. CR-225-2, CR-225-3, CR-225-4, CR-225-5, ACICR; and *Report of the ICRC on its activities during the Second World War, Vol I* (1948), 210, 312. See also Kovner, "A War of Words," 745.

[131] During the war, the LGA made attempts to form an international body to supervise over the protection of historical buildings. This project was eventually abandoned to prevent the creation of another international body competing with existing ones, including the ICRC. The idea was later entrusted to an organization that emerged from the Allied war alliance—the United Nations Educational, Scientific and Cultural Organization. UNESCO, as it was called, helped to prepare the 1954 Hague Convention on the protection of monumental buildings against air warfare, whose origins date back to the interwar Hague Air Rules and the Monaco Draft: Toman, *The Protection of Cultural Property in the Event of Armed Conflict*, 447. For a history of UNESCO, see Paul Betts, "Humanity's New Heritage: Unesco and the Rewriting of World History," *Past & Present*, Vol. 228, No. 1 (2015): 249–285. On the concept of an international air force see Roger Beaumont, *Right Backed by Might: The International Air Force Concept* (Westport, CO: Praeger, 2001).

[132] Saul, *Defining Terrorism in International Law*, 280–281.

[133] *Report of the ICRC on its activities during the Second World War, Vol I* (1948), 699–700. For the Japanese government's invocation of the 1907 Hague Regulations to condemn US indiscriminate bombing, see Yuki Tanaka, "The Atomic Bombing, The Tokyo War Crimes Tribunal and the Shimoda Case: Lessons for Anti-Nuclear Legal Movements," in *Beyond Victor's Justice? The Tokyo War Crimes Trial Revisited*, ed. Yuki Tanaka, Timothy McCormack, and Gerry Simpson (Leiden: Brill, 2011), 291–310, 305.

[134] During the war, local initiatives were started to establish safety zones or open cities in particular areas, towns, or major cities. See de La Pradelle, *La Conférence Diplomatique*, 187–189.

220 PREPARING FOR WAR

from filing appeals to limited codification, and tried to widen the law's scope to the protection of civilian populations. Still, the ICRC's cautious approach was not enough to revive the principle of distinction and was far less ambitious than that of other actors interested in indiscriminate warfare, such as the LGA or the Soviet Union.

While the proposals from these interwar pioneers were often rejected, many of the principles underlying them were re-adapted by the ICRC in the 1940s—a continuity with the ICRC's policies in other domains, as we saw in previous chapters. Leading ICRC officials felt forced to balance their neutrality, their close ties with the Western imperial powers, and the broader international consensus in support of hunger blockade as the League's enforcement weapon of last resort. Remarkable as it may seem today, the guardian of humanitarian law was willing to tolerate starvation as a legitimate means of warfare to safeguard the international order as a whole. This meant that the ICRC did not wish to get directly involved in the drafting of new rules against such means of indiscriminate warfare, leaving this issue to the League's major powers. While not ignoring the question of unrestrained warfare, the ICRC eventually centered its efforts on pressuring states to comply with those new rules, protecting prisoners of war, and bending blockade in interstate wars. However, and this is the last point, these ICRC efforts to protect victims of war evolved over time, from focusing on codification to stimulating civil defense, mainly as a consequence of the rapidly changing international environment and the technological improvement of war-making from the 1930s onwards.

5.2 Blind Weapons

While the Allies were bombing German cities, in late 1944 Pictet's drafting team restarted its prewar process of drafting the Geneva Conventions. Unlike before the war, Huber addressed the need to codify new rules for the protection of civilian populations, recommending that the opening ICRC circular include a reference to this vital matter. For this reason, the final version of this document re-addressed the prewar draft regarding safety localities and, representing a major break with that period, demanded new rules for civilian protection at large, possibly including enemy civilians under siege.[135] In the wake of the German rocket campaign, this new step into the field of codifying air

---

[135] Minutes of Meeting Legal Division, 18 January 1945, no. A PV JUR.1, ACICR.

war marked a break with the ICRC's prewar reluctance to regulate this matter through humanitarian law.[136]

In the following months, the ICRC adopted a two-tier strategy to prepare for the upcoming meeting of the Red Cross experts in 1946. First, it recognized the practical disappearance of the principle of distinction, the lesson that starving civilians often did not trigger government surrender, and the need to renew attention to the obligations of those targeting enemy territory.[137] The ICRC's most prominent response to those threats was its official appeal to states after the nuclear attacks on Japanese cities, in which it recommended the 1925 Geneva Protocol's extension to atomic warfare.[138] In 1945, building upon the interwar anxieties around air-gas warfare, there existed a wide consensus that the Protocol had succeeded in its mission, despite the terrible fate of Jewish civilians. As a consequence of this perceived "success," the ICRC hoped to extend the Protocol's ban to atomic weapons, triggering a wider debate within the Red Cross movement about "humanizing air war."[139]

Alongside publicly pressuring states, the ICRC's second approach after 1945 was to demand new codified rules for the protection of civilian populations, from safeguarding civilian hospitals to prohibiting bombing reprisals against medical facilities.[140] It also drafted plans to empower the role of humanitarians fighting against hunger blockade, stressing the duties of occupiers and contesting the blockaders' wide discretionary powers.[141] The ICRC asked its partners from Red Cross Societies whether it was "opportune and even possible to restrict aerial bombardment, and to limit the destruction caused by the ever increasing improvement of armaments." This cautious approach reflected the ICRC's persistent concerns about protecting its neutrality, the pressure of domestic Swiss audiences,[142] and maintaining support from the

---

[136] Charles Maier, "Targeting the City: Debates and Silences about the Aerial Bombing of World War II," *International Review of the Red Cross*, Vol. 87, No. 859 (2005): 429–444, 436.

[137] Mulder and Van Dijk, "Why Did Starvation Not Become the Paradigmatic War Crime in International Law?" and ICRC Report for the Red Cross Experts, 1946, no. CSN_1946_DOCCIR_ENG_04, ICRC Library.

[138] ICRC Appeal on Atomic Weapons, 5 September 1945, ICRC Library.

[139] Echoing this, a Stalinist Polish resolution accepted by the Red Cross Board of Governors in mid-1946 demanded that the Red Cross suggested the extension of the Protocol's ban to atomic warfare.

[140] Preliminary Conference of National Red Cross Societies for the Study of the Conventions and of Various Problems relative to the Red Cross, 1946, no. CSN_1946_DOCCIR_ENG_01, ICRC Library.

[141] Mulder and Van Dijk, "Why Did Starvation Not Become the Paradigmatic War Crime in International Law?"

[142] In postwar Switzerland, following the bombings of German and Japanese cities, the idea of "safety zones" made a strong comeback. There were powerful calls to establish wide safety zones to protect civilian populations. For this history, see Dominique-Debora Junod, *The Imperiled Red Cross and the Palestine-Eretz-Yisrael Conflict 1945–1952: The Influence of Institutional Concerns on a Humanitarian Operation* (New York: Kegan Paul International, 1996), 157–158.

222 PREPARING FOR WAR

reluctant Anglo-American powers. Throughout the 1940s, the ICRC believed it was highly dependent upon retaining the support of these two leading Allied powers while codifying rules for warfare on behalf of civilian populations.

As the war came to an end, Anglo-American officials presented blockade and air-nuclear warfare as war-winning strategies that had brought down the Axis powers.[143] In their taxonomies of indiscriminate warfare, they argued that precision bombing and blockading enemy societies were acceptable methods of warfare, allegedly causing only "incidental" civilian death, whereas deliberate extermination, human shields, and mass pillage by the Nazi occupiers were not and needed to be outlawed.[144] The United States envisaged blockade, nuclear weapons, chemical weaponry, and air bombing as four weapons crucial for the preservation of a favorable postwar military balance that would ensure its national security. Whereas the Americans and British had aircraft carriers and major strategic bomber forces, the Soviet Union did not have such capabilities to directly strike the enemy from afar.[145] It is precisely due to this lack of retaliatory capability that the Anglo-American alliance tried to legitimize blockade and air-nuclear power through the fabric of international law, to prepare for a future military confrontation with the Soviet Union.[146]

Allied indiscriminate warfare was eventually integrated into the international legal institutions established by the Allies after 1945. The presence of Allied blockade in the UN Charter as an enforcement weapon illustrates its presumed legality.[147] From the Genocide Convention's failure to specifically address starvation to Nuremberg's silence on the threat of air bombing,[148] postwar international law largely sidelined the principle of distinction. Prosecutors at the Nuremberg and Tokyo trials condemned only the use of human shields and executions of Allied "terror fliers" as war crimes, not indiscriminate bombing itself.[149] Strikingly, one of the leading Allied figures behind this method of

---

[143] Inspired by Black, *Air Power*, 43.

[144] Hastings, *Bomber Command*, 182. See also A. Grayling, *Among the Dead Cities: The History and Moral Legacy of the WWII Bombing of Civilians in Germany and Japan* (New York: Walker Books, 2009); and Pierre-Etienne Bourneuf, *Bombarder l'Allemagne: L'offensive alliée sur les villes pendant la Deuxième Guerre mondiale* (Paris: Presses Universitaires de France, 2014).

[145] David Holloway, *The Soviet Union and the Arms Race* (New Haven, CT: Yale University Press, 1984), 231.

[146] Mulder, *The Economic Weapon*, 157.

[147] Ibid., 511.

[148] Nelson and Waters, "The Allied Bombing of German Cities during the Second World War from a Canadian Perspective," 109–110.

[149] Gordon and Perugini, *Human Shields*; Mulder and Van Dijk, "Why Did Starvation Not Become the Paradigmatic War Crime in International Law?"; and Saul, *Defining Terrorism in International Law*, 281. See also Radhabinod Pal, *International Military Tribunal for the Far East: Dissentient Judgment of Justice Pal* (Tokyo: Kokusho-Kankokai, 1999).

warfare later admitted that "if [the war] had been lost [we] would have been prosecuted [by the victorious Axis powers] as war criminals."[150]

In August 1946, at the Red Cross Conference in Geneva, Pictet's drafting team was therefore confronted with a difficult dilemma. When (South-)Eastern European delegates introduced proposals to effectively ban atomic warfare and to contest hunger blockade, a discussion ensued as to whether these could be part of the future Conventions, and to what extent the ICRC would be willing to challenge its major Western donors, that is, the United States and Great Britain. Under the influence of Anglo-American officials, the Red Cross Conference agreed not to immediately place on its drafting agenda the question of air bombing, although it accepted some basic rules on the protection of civilian hospitals and for those civilians who gave help to wounded bomber pilots, on the condition these would not be hidden from the occupier.[151] Still, the issue of air bombing resurfaced for debate in the Third Committee on Red Cross Affairs, where a Stalinist Polish delegate re-submitted his country's original resolution on atomic warfare. This revised text banning the use of atomic energy for military purposes was accepted by the plenary as a means to put pressure on the ongoing UN disarmament talks. So, while considering the use of atomic weapons illegal, the Red Cross experts remained silent on *how* to get rid of these means: as before the war, they were hesitant to codify limitations upon the use of air weapons, leaving this to the Great Powers gathering at the United Nations.[152]

The major Allies had founded in 1946 a special UN Atomic Energy Commission to establish international control over nuclear energy.[153] President Truman's initial plan with this initiative was to promote international security by collaborating with the Soviet Union in a bid to reduce nuclear armaments. His representative to the UNAEC, Bernard Baruch, called for a supranational authority with powerful enforcement mechanisms to inspect nuclear facilities.[154] At the same time, leading US policymakers and military

[150] Quoted from Nelson and Waters, "The Allied Bombing of German Cities during the Second World War from a Canadian Perspective," 107.

[151] Interestingly, the original idea of requiring civilians to hand over captured wounded enemy soldiers to the occupier had come from the United States. As we will see later, the British reserved their attitude towards this provision. See Minutes Prisoners of War Committee, 14 August 1946, no. 672, Provost Marshal General, NARA; Minutes of Meetings Commission I, 1946, no. CSN_1946_PV_01, CSN_1946_COMM1_PV_03, ICRC Library; Report ICRC for 1947 Conference, no. CEG_1947_DOC_CGREV_ENG, ICRC Library; and Memorandum by the Secretary of State for Foreign Affairs and the Secretary of State for War, 10 March 1949, no. 33, CAB129 (Cabinet Office), TNA.

[152] Minutes of Meeting Plenary, 1946, no. CSN_1946_PLENCOMM2_PV, ICRC Library.

[153] Robert Brown, *Nuclear Authority: The IAEA and the Absolute Weapon* (Washington, DC: Georgetown University Press, 2015), 41.

[154] Lorenz Luthi, *Cold Wars: Asia, the Middle East, Europe* (Cambridge: Cambridge University Press, 2020), 336–337.

224   PREPARING FOR WAR

officials believed that the bomb remained essential to ensuring American national security and for reshaping the international system in line with their core interests.[155] The Soviets, on the other hand, did not approve of the Baruch Plan because of its proposed loss of sovereignty and their growing distrust of the Americans, which was quickly rising at the time, producing a stalemate at the UNAEC.[156]

These stalemated UN debates, together with the diffuse outcome of the 1946 Red Cross Conference, prompted a critical debate within Pictet's drafting team about whether to limit air-nuclear warfare and blockade through humanitarian law. There existed widespread agreement that the interwar period had proven that limiting air warfare through international legal means was "doomed to fail," according to one ICRC official. In his view, the organization should focus on protecting prisoners of war and hospitals, and broadening safety zones; others, however, pushed for eradicating hunger blockade. Their long-term goal was to move humanitarian law away from belligerent rights to civilian protection and to gain recognition for the ICRC as a potential blockade-bender. This would force future blockading states to allow the free passage of relief supplies for starving civilians in wartime.[157]

Both Huber and Pictet initially agreed with these plans. While recognizing that the best means to stop "blind" or indiscriminate warfare was through a prohibition, for strategic reasons the ICRC decided to resist attempts to strictly regulate air-nuclear warfare and to depoliticize relief by staying silent on the root causes of mass famine.[158] Instead, it wished to codify the ICRC's wartime campaign in Greece as a model to stop hunger blockade while readdressing its pre-war designs for civil defense by applying them to different parts of the civilian population.[159] These revised but still cautious ambitions, it was believed, would have a much higher chance of actual codifying success, despite the Anglo-American wartime opposition to safety zones.

In August 1945, when the French Inter-Ministerial Commission had started its internal drafting process, there occurred a similar discussion among French drafters on how to deal with the threat of air warfare and blockade for civilian populations. Following the mass pillage by the Nazi occupiers and the

---

[155] Barton Bernstein, "The Quest for Security: American Foreign Policy and International Control of Atomic Energy, 1942–1946," *The Journal of American History*, Vol. 60, No. 4 (1974): 1003–1044, 1036; and David Rosenberg, "The Origins of Overkill: Nuclear Weapons and American Strategy, 1945–1960," *International Security*, Vol. 7, No. 4 (1983): 3–71, 11–12.

[156] Brown, *Nuclear Authority*, 43–44; and Luthi, *Cold Wars*, 336–337.

[157] Mulder and Van Dijk, "Why Did Starvation Not Become the Paradigmatic War Crime in International Law?"

[158] Ibid.

[159] Minutes of Meeting Legal Division, 6 December 1946, no. A PV JUR.1, ACICR.

destructive Allied bombings of French urban areas,[160] triggering furious protests from De Gaulle's Free French,[161] Paris expressed support for creating limited safety zones and for better protecting civilians "against the effects of war"—a typology that had wider implications than air warfare alone, potentially including hunger blockade. Considering these issues of a "political" nature, the French formed a special sub-committee under closer military supervision to discuss them.[162] Within this drafting body, French military officials expressed sympathy for plans to create safety zones and localities to protect soldiers and civilian populations against air warfare, but criticized their impracticability.

Moreover, the French Air Force feared, as did the Army, that such zones would impair Western air power, potentially endangering French security and putting the (German, Soviet, or Vietnamese) enemy at a strategic advantage. Although the actual implementation of De Gaulle's initiative to turn France into an atomic military power did not start until the end of the Indochina War, Paris still recognized the vital importance of (nuclear) air power for policing its empire on the cheap and ensuring national security in the long term.[163] French military officials also feared the enemy might use safety zones as a human shield to cover its armed forces against air attack, as the Germans had done during the liberation of France.[164]

In addition to this, the diplomat Lamarle—once again—noted that such ambitious proposals to create mass safety zones for civilians might generate powerful opposition from Anglo-American allies, thereby placing already endangered French plans for civilian protection and the future of the entire negotiations at great risk.[165] Understanding that Anglo-American air power would play a crucial role in preparing for a future war with the Soviet Union, the French diplomat recommended a more measured approach aimed at preventing major resistance.[166] Accordingly, the French Inter-Ministerial

---

[160] See Claudia Baldoli and Andrew Knapp, *Forgotten Blitzes: France and Italy under Allied Air Attack, 1940–1945* (London: Continuum, 2012) and Matthew Evangelista, "Myron Taylor and the Bombing of Rome: The Limits of Law and Diplomacy," *Diplomacy & Statecraft* (2020): 278–305.

[161] Overy, *The Bombing War*.

[162] Note Ministry of Foreign Affairs on Interdepartmental Committee, 26 July 1946, no. 160, Unions Internationales 1907–1944, Les Archives Diplomatiques (LAD), Paris.

[163] Charles Cogan, "From the Fall of France to the Force de Frappe: The Remaking of French Military Power, 1940–1962," in *The Fog of Peace and War Planning: Military and Strategic Planning under Uncertainty*, ed. Talbot Imlay and Monica Duffy Toft (New York: Routledge, 2006), 224–248, 224–228. Black, *Air Power*, 178.

[164] Compte-rendu de la Séance Commission Interministérielle, 31 January 1947, no. 160 - BIS, Unions Internationales 1907–1944, LAD.

[165] Compte-rendu de la Séance Commission Interministérielle, 22 February 1947, no. 160 - BIS, Unions Internationales 1907–1944, LAD.

[166] Black, *Air Power*, 151.

226 PREPARING FOR WAR

Commission suggested that military safety localities be recommended, with the possibility of safety zones for civilians raised only if their major Western allies did not react with irritation at the upcoming meeting.[167]

"All or Nothing"

When the Government Experts gathered in April 1947, British and American delegates indeed voiced fierce opposition to the issue. At the time, US military planners were already preparing for an air-nuclear offensive by developing lists of civilian targets in the Soviet Union.[168] Although the American Red Cross had wished to formulate new rules for the protection of civilian populations against this threat, the US POWC merely showed interest in ensuring that POWs would never be used as human shields against their own air power.[169] While admitting that it was "impossible" to prevent hospitals from being targeted, US government officials left the entire question of regulating air-atomic warfare for UN bodies to take up. They believed that "in atomic warfare the objective must necessarily be all or nothing so far as very widespread areas of destruction are concerned."[170] Creating a precedent for later US actions, Clattenburg argued in Geneva that the ICRC's plans for extended safety zones for civilian populations simply fell outside of the conference's competence, and his delegation wished to keep the weapon of blockade intact by emphasizing the duties of occupying states.[171] Just as Clattenburg criticized the binding character of the ICRC's proposals against hunger blockade, his British allies accepted the relevant text only as a "basis" for future debate, not as a potential draft.[172] Despite the Blitz, the UK delegation also rejected the formulation of rules for safety zones as part of these Conventions.

Both major air-naval powers argued that most limitations on air warfare and blockade were unacceptable—except for those helping to protect their pilots and prisoners of war—and that nuclear weapons lay outside the Red Cross's competence. While the French tried to persuade their two allies to accept at

---

[167] Compte-rendu de la Séance Commission Interministérielle, 18 March 1947, no. 160 - BIS, Unions Internationales 1907–1944, LAD.

[168] Cited from: Holloway, *The Soviet Union and the Arms Race*, 227–228.

[169] Minutes Prisoners of War Committee, 1 July 1946, Provost Marshal General, no. 672, NARA; and Minutes Prisoners of War Committee, 21 October 1947, Provost Marshal General, no. 673 - Part I, NARA.

[170] Minutes Prisoners of War Committee, 16 August 1946, Provost Marshal General, no. 672, NARA.

[171] Minutes of Meetings Commission III, 1947, no. CEG_1947_COMM3_PV_03, ICRC Library.

[172] Mulder and Van Dijk, "Why Did Starvation Not Become the Paradigmatic War Crime in International Law?"

least smaller sanitary localities and the right of free passage of relief for occupied nations, the Americans went no further than vaguely leaving the question of safety zones for commanders in the field to decide upon.

Acknowledging their failure, the delegates asked the ICRC to further study these questions.[173] Following this disappointment, the conference delegates began to hear rumors circulating about a Stalinist Polish resolution condemning the use of means of mass destruction, a typical reference to the threat of atomic warfare. Alarmed, the US delegation immediately attempted to silence the rumors by killing the resolution before it was even introduced. In private, US government officials expressed serious concern that the Stalinist attempt to condemn atomic weapons would be used as an excuse by the Soviets, in any future war, for not applying the Conventions, and that it would place a legal taboo on their nuclear monopoly.

While it had made slow progress during the war, the Soviet atomic bombing project had been relaunched after the attack on Hiroshima. After this horrific event Stalin realized the weapon's true strategic importance, immediately ordering a crash program to develop a Soviet bomb.[174] He also demanded the development of Soviet missiles, a strategic bomber force, and air defenses to create a powerful Soviet deterrent against overwhelming American firepower.[175] Accordingly, the Soviet-aligned delegates in Geneva tried to contest America's nuclear monopoly and re-addressed interwar Soviet plans to abolish interstate hunger blockade.[176] The Polish resolution, under US pressure, was eventually forwarded to the plenary session for discussion, providing Clattenburg's team with time to prepare a counter-offensive.[177]

At the respective plenary meeting, the Allied Brazilian contingent—most likely in coordination with Clattenburg's delegation—introduced a counter-resolution calling for peace without referring to the sensitive question of weapons regulation. Whereas the French supported it, the tiny Eastern European contingent fiercely opposed the Brazilian proposal, triggering the first major East–West confrontation over atomic warfare at a postwar drafting meeting. To prevent further escalation, a British compromise text leaving out all sensitive issues was accepted by the plenary, to overwhelming applause. The Poles had accepted it after talks with Lamarle, acting as mediator, and

---

[173] Report of American Delegation to Government Experts' Conference, 1947, no. 674, Provost Marshal General, NARA.

[174] Holloway, *The Soviet Union and the Arms Race*, 90, 114–116.

[175] Ibid., 245–246.

[176] Ibid., 157.

[177] Report of American Delegation to Government Experts' Conference, 1947, no. 674, Provost Marshal General, NARA.

228 PREPARING FOR WAR

calls from the ICRC, which feared that failing to agree upon a peace resolution would create an embarrassing precedent amid rising East–West tensions.[178]

The outcome of the 1947 Government Expert Conference nonetheless proved disappointing from the perspective of civilian populations at large. Among other things, the Allied experts failed to abolish the weapon of starvation, removed—under British pressure—the demand for civilians who assisted wounded bomber pilots to hand them over to the occupier, and rejected mandatory safety zones.[179] The conference did endorse the criminalization of hospital targeting and prohibited reprisals against such facilities.[180] While frustrated about those stricter rules for occupiers (see Chapter 2), the US delegation expressed relief about the lack of substantial rules for limiting air warfare, particularly its nuclear equivalent.[181] Washington's preferred course of keeping the regulation of weapons within UN bodies that it controlled, and preventing the law's drafting from placing restraints on their massive air power to counter a Soviet threat, had largely succeeded. Despite these concessions, the ICRC became increasingly interested in formulating new rules for the protection of civilian populations and prisoners of war, and against the weapon of hunger blockade.

As it had done previously, Pictet's drafting team continued to make use of a multifaceted approach to regulate air warfare and blockade as part of its larger effort to design a set of more radical proposals for the 1948 Stockholm Conference. The ICRC had to walk a fine line between recognizing (socialist) Red Cross demands on behalf of civilian populations and maintaining good working relations with its major liberal allies to secure the Civilian Convention's success—and prevent its downfall in the postwar era. While doing so, it made several compromises by accepting the US POWC's suggestion to prohibit the immediate punishment of wounded bomber pilots and those civilians taking care of them.[182] As we saw before, the relationship with the US hegemon was

---

[178] Cable Lamarle on Polish Resolution, 26 April 1947, no. 160, Unions Internationales 1907–1944, LAD.

[179] The British opposed this proposal recommended by the United States to place an obligation on the civilians to hand over wounded soldiers to the occupying power, in light of the "assistance given to your [RAF] airmen by the peoples of the occupied countries." Report Conference of Government Expert at Geneva, 1947, no. RC_report-1947, ICRC Library; and Report Proceedings Commission I, 1947, no. 3795, FO369, TNA.

[180] Report Conference of Government Expert at Geneva, 1947, no. RC_report-1947, ICRC Library.

[181] Report of American Delegation to Government Experts' Conference, 1947, no. 674, Provost Marshal General, NARA.

[182] Draft Convention for the Sick & Wounded, 1948, no. CI_1948_PROJET_ENG_01, ICRC Library; Draft Convention for Prisoners of War, 1948, no. CI_1948_B3_01_ENG_02, ICRC Library. For the US POWC's suggestions in this direction, see Minutes Prisoners of War Committee, 14 August 1946, Provost Marshal General, no. 672, NARA.

considered critically important for making Pictet's drafting plan a success: this was a crucial reason why the Genevan himself and other leading ICRC officials paid Washington a special visit in June 1948, around the start of the Berlin blockade.

To avoid Anglo-American opposition, the ICRC continued to reject the idea of directly regulating air warfare through revision of humanitarian law while endorsing mandatory safety zones and so-called neutralized zones, with which it began experimenting in Palestine, to protect civilian populations.[183] At the same time, it adopted a remarkably ambitious approach by requiring a blockading state to authorize food supplies in both occupied and belligerent territory, which struck at the root of the weapon of starvation,[184] and by embracing earlier proposals to put pressure on states to ban so-called "blind weapons," the ICRC's equivalent of the humanization-of-war-terminology from the Monaco Draft for indiscriminate warfare.[185] In February 1948, while preparing for the Stockholm Conference, Pictet himself had also suggested adapting an originally socialist resolution banning atomic weapons.[186]

To Pictet's mind—revealing his continuing concern about nuclear warfare—this prohibition did not go far enough and should include all "armes aveugles,"[187] a term he understood as referring to indiscriminate weapons such as rockets, atomic bombs, gas warfare, and "tapis de bombes."[188] Unlike Pictet, the far more cautious and pragmatic Pilloud believed such a proposal would seriously upset Anglo-American allies, threatening the future of the entire revision process, while putting the Soviet bloc "on the advantage"—and thereby revealing his anti-Soviet credentials. He recommended instead a limited resolution endorsing the 1925 Protocol's extension to atomic weapons. While his fears were downplayed, the ICRC accepted Pictet's potentially far-reaching resolution.

It is difficult to assess what exactly motivated the ICRC to make this bold decision and at that time, in light of its continuing concerns about

---

[183] For the history of the ICRC and safety zones in Palestine, see Junod, *The Imperiled Red Cross*, 155–163.

[184] Draft Civilian Convention, 1948, no. CI_1948_B3_01_ENG_03, ICRC Library.

[185] Meetings of Meetings The League of Red Cross Societies, ICRC, and the Swedish Red Cross, mid-January 1948, no. CRI - 25 IV—Dossier 4, ACICR.

[186] The only scholar who has previously noted this "awkward" situation for the ICRC is Junod, who wrote an important dissertation (based mainly on ICRC sources) on the ICRC in Palestine: Junod, *The Imperiled Red Cross*, 238–239.

[187] Pictet would continue to use this term after 1949, for instance in his groundbreaking essay from 1966 providing a more systematic theory for IHL. See Jean Pictet, "Les Principes du Droit International Humanitaire," 522.

[188] Minutes of Meeting Bureau Stockholm Conference, 17 February 1948, no. CRI - 25 IV—Dossier 4, ACICR.

230 PREPARING FOR WAR

safeguarding the drafting process in the wake of Washington's growing skepticism. It is likely that the ICRC felt pressured to take action on behalf of civilian populations due to domestic Swiss opposition and its neglect by other international bodies, from the UN International Law Commission (ILC) and especially the UNAEC, where neither Moscow nor Washington was genuinely willing to compromise.[189] Moreover—and this is a crucial point to add— some leading ICRC drafters, such as Wilhelm and Pictet, saw the Stockholm Conference as a crucial opportunity to put serious pressure on major states to accept greater limitations on indiscriminate warfare while sharing their disappointment about the Nuremberg decision to stay silent on the recent war's terror bombings, taken as a result of Anglo-American opposition to its discussion.

While recognizing this opposition, other ICRC officials were said to believe there existed a sizable force in Washington—possibly a reference to the American Red Cross—favoring a prohibition on atomic weapons. As such, they were willing to take a risk. It is not unlikely that they had heard about such views on their trip to Washington, when, for instance, they met members of the American Red Cross who held that position (see below). In August 1948 there was surprisingly little debate about the ICRC's plans to create mandatory safety zones and neutralized zones.[190]

With the Air Force expressing no major opposition to those plans, the US delegation had received remarkably flexible instructions from the State Department accepting both suggestions while demanding an end to human shielding.[191] By contrast, the Canadian delegation, fearing the potential effect of the proposals for Western air power, argued against mandatory safety zones, demanding they be made "wholly permissive" at the final diplomatic conference and rejecting the binding nature of the ICRC proposals against blockade.[192] The US delegation quickly realized it might have made a serious mistake on the question of safety zones, and advised the State Department to reconsider its views on this issue.[193]

---

[189] Bernstein, "The Quest for Security," 1044.

[190] The ICRC also finally succeeded in preventing a specific mention of its own name, or that of Switzerland, as had been requested by Swiss activists. Junod, *The Imperiled Red Cross*, 251–252.

[191] Report of US delegation to the Stockholm Red Cross Conference, 1948, Provost Marshal General, no. 672, NARA; Minutes of Meeting Commission Juridique, no. CI_1948_COMJUR_SC, ICRC Library; Minutes Prisoners of War Committee, 18 June 1948 and 3 August 1948, Provost Marshal General, no. 673, NARA; and Text US Draft POW Convention, 1948, no. 669, Provost Marshal General, NARA.

[192] See also Report Australian Observer Stockholm Conference, September 1948, no. Series: A472; Control: W32574 PART 1, National Archives of Australia (NAA), Canberra, ACT.

[193] Report of US delegation to the Stockholm Red Cross Conference, 1948, Provost Marshal General, no. 672, NARA.

Pictet's Coup de Théâtre

Once Pictet's resolution became known, the US delegation split immediately, and became divided into two camps. As head of the group, president of the American Red Cross, and the influential leader of the League of Red Cross Societies,[194] Basil O'Connor broke with his instructions and said to refrain from voting against this resolution, shocking his government colleagues including Clattenburg. To his mind, accepting the resolution would lead to "unnecessary publicity" and undermine his country's interests as part of the " 'Cold War' now going on"—a reference to the Berlin crisis.[195] In his view, neither Washington nor the American Red Cross could afford to be seen as an advocate for using atomic weapons while fears of war were growing as the Soviets kept Berlin under siege.

Accordingly, the American lawyer recommended accepting Pictet's resolution. As a government representative in favor of unrestricted air power, Clattenburg abhorred O'Connor's dissent and tried to force him to reconsider his view, but the president was unwilling to do so. Instead, he said he would abstain from voting and directed his government colleagues to act similarly.[196] However, when Pictet's resolution was brought to the vote, O'Connor shifted his approach somewhat, saying he could not abstain from voting for it, and instructing his colleague of the League to do similarly. While the delegation's head raised his hand in support of Pictet's resolution, his government colleagues abstained, leading to an embarrassing defeat.[197] The French and Canadian government delegates also abstained.[198] However, by not actively lobbying against the resolution, these Western powers enabled the Commission Juridique to accept Pictet's resolution with overwhelming support.

Surprised, Clattenburg's government colleagues tried to prevent further embarrassment by seeking to unify their delegation's opposing views. The presence of journalists at the plenary meeting where Pictet's resolution would be re-discussed caused even greater alarm about a potential international outcry.

---

[194] It is important to highlight that the League of Red Cross Societies had previously made statements in the direction of banning nuclear weapons entirely.

[195] Instructions State Department for US Delegation Stockholm Conference, August 1948, no. Series 1, RG 43–48-B, NARA.

[196] Memo Clattenburg on Resolution Humanization of War, 10 September 1948, no. Series 22, RG 43 - 5536, NARA.

[197] Memo Clattenburg on Resolution Humanization of War, 10 September 1948, no. Series 22, RG 43 - 5536, NARA; and Report of US delegation to the Stockholm Red Cross Conference, 1948, Provost Marshal General, no. 672, NARA.

[198] Report Canadian Delegation Stockholm Conference, 1948 no. Series 619 - B - 40, RG 25 - Vol. 5020, Library and Archives Canada (LAC), Ottawa, ON.

232 PREPARING FOR WAR

Delegates feared that reporters, detecting a painful split within their delegation, would use it as a means to embarrass them before the eyes of the world as
American pilots, viewed until Hitler's downfall as "terror fliers," were hailed as
Berlin's guardian angels during the Soviet blockade.[199] Acting in liaison with
the State Department, US government delegates discussed the option of putting forward a counter-resolution, as had been done in April 1947, to take the
sting out of Pictet's far-reaching proposal. Due to a lack of time, this plan was
dropped. A new plan was discussed with allies, including French government
officials who also opposed a blockade-related resolution, to make a special an-
nouncement at the plenary session about the option of states abstaining.

This special statement recognized that any state delegation abstaining held
that the issue of regulating the conduct of war fell outside the competence of
the Red Cross Conference. The text, which argued that such matters ought to
be exclusively in UN hands, was eventually read out before Pictet's resolution
was put to a vote at the respective plenary session. Privately, Clattenburg stated
that this was an effort to deceive journalists into thinking that nobody opposed
the goal of limiting air-atomic warfare at a time of increasing arms buildup.
His plan worked. Lacking official socialist representation, few journalists apparently registered the Western dissension concerning Pictet's resolution.
Following the acceptance of the text, a satisfied Clattenburg noted in his report
how the trick had succeeded in "distract[ing] public attention from the split
vote in [our] delegation."[200]

In his reports, Clattenburg warned the State Department that it should
better prepare its delegations for such conferences. In particular, he was fright-
ened that the future US delegation might have to face similarly unacceptable
initiatives to discuss limiting air-atomic warfare at the diplomatic conference.
To counter this threat, he advised the State Department to prepare a special
counter-resolution, as had been done in April 1947, which could be used to
neutralize any attempt to place limitations upon US air power and its nuclear
monopoly. This text, he argued, had to be "incisive […] attractive to the Red
Cross['s] mind and […] detract from the possibility of favorable consideration
[…] of less political[ly] desirable resolutions." Regarding the latter, he meant
a text that impaired his government's strategic interests and dominant position
within the relevant UN bodies discussing disarmament.[201] Clattenburg's advice

---

[199] Hippler, *Governing from the Skies*.
[200] Memo Clattenburg on Resolution Humanization of War, 10 September 1948, no. Series 22, RG 43
- 5536, NARA.
[201] Memo Clattenburg on Resolution Humanization of War, 10 September 1948, no. Series 22, RG 43
- 5536, NARA.

must have played a role in the extensive preparations by the State Department for an upcoming clash on this issue at the diplomatic conference.[202]

Interestingly, a French Red Cross delegate proposed a separate resolution that "condemned blockade" as a weapon of war—Lamarle's government delegation refused to endorse this text in an attempt to keep their Anglo-American allies on board. Still, Clattenburg's delegation prevented—surprisingly, with the help of another French Red Cross representative with closer government ties (Cahen-Salvador)—the resolution from being extensively discussed, and also avoided hospitals from being used as human shields by adding the words "as far as possible."[203] The Americans felt most strongly about the ICRC proposals bending blockade that might directly undermine their naval power "from the point of view of [our] naked survival."[204]

The British government's mistake of not sending a full delegation to Stockholm enabled the Genevans to push through their proposals with help from European victims of Allied blockade and Nazi pillage.[205] Still, Cahen-Salvador's co-edited preamble, which codified the principle of distinction for the first time, was called "innocuous in effect" by US government representatives.[206] Neither they nor the British saw any harm, at this stage, in accepting this provision.[207] While generating more concern, Pictet's non-binding resolution never became mandatory as such, nor did the conference outlaw the weapon of starvation. Equally, the British and Americans saw mandatory safety zones as an impracticable solution to deal with the threat of air bombing for metropolitan civilians.

The British, under pressure from the Chiefs of Staff, opposed those zones for both practical and military reasons. In their view, safety zones would undercut British defense plans and impose too large a burden on their armed forces.[208] Based upon lessons drawn from the RAF's bombing campaigns, the

---

[202] For a history of US engagement with the fate of civilians in war, see John John Tirman, *The Deaths of Others: The Fate of Civilians in America's Wars* (Oxford: Oxford University Press, 2011).

[203] Minutes of Commission Juridique, 1948, no. CI_1948_COMJUR_02, ICRC Library; and Report of U.S. delegation to the Stockholm Red Cross Conference, 1948, Provost Marshal General, no. 672, NARA.

[204] Report Clattenburg on Stockholm Conference, 10 September 1948, no. Series 22, RG 43 - 5536, NARA.

[205] For Best's apologetic views with regard to blockade ("blockade is more humane than bombardment"), Geoffrey Best, *War and Law since 1945* (Oxford: Clarendon Press, 2002), 282–283.

[206] It is more likely that Castberg—as a supporter of safety zones—and not Cahen-Salvador inserted the principle of distinction. Memo Clattenburg Stockholm Conference Civilian Convention, 12 October 1948, no. 22, RG 43 - 5536, NARA.

[207] Briefing for UK delegation, February 1949, no. 4145, FO369, TNA; and US Draft for the Civilian Convention, 31 March 1949, Provost Marshal General, no. 673, NARA.

[208] Report War Office Interdepartmental Committee on Civilian Convention, 1948, no. 330, WO163 (War Office), TNA.

234   PREPARING FOR WAR

British believed a future war with the Soviets would be even more destructive and virtually without limit.[209] They also feared that the Stockholm proposals would "greatly weaken the weapon of blockade,"[210] and that the Soviets would exploit these loopholes by freely importing food supplies despite a blockade. Whereas the British delegation would have to "firmly oppose" the right of free passage for food supplies and refuse mandatory zones before accepting a permissive version,[211] the American one was instructed to immediately demand non-mandatory zones and, under pressure from the armed forces, delete any binding restrictions on blockade.[212]

The French, preoccupied with garnering support from all the Great Powers even at the expense of the ICRC itself, no longer evinced much interest in safety zones, seeing them as a potential liability in their quest to gain bipartisan support for the Civilian Convention's provisions for occupation. While ignoring Anglophone criticisms, the ICRC restated its desire for mandatory safety zones as well as a preamble with the principle of distinction included.[213] More importantly, emboldened by his success at Stockholm, Pictet even raised internally the possibility of replacing the old Hague Regulations with the new Conventions with regard to indiscriminate warfare, since the drafts for these treaties overlapped, and because he knew that the Dutch government would express no opposition.[214]

As he had done in most other debates, the senior ICRC drafter Huber, however—fearing such a move would prompt severe Great Power opposition—demanded that those fields be kept legally separate and that atomic weapons be left to the UNAEC, even though the Baruch Plan had already collapsed. By mid-1948, the prospects for international control of nuclear energy looked bleak. Whereas American nuclear warfare planning grew increasingly urgent, Stalin was determined to acquire his own bomb.[215] In turn, keen to end this cycle of indiscriminate warfare, the young ICRC delegate Wilhelm raised the

---

[209] Overy, *The Bombing War.*

[210] Briefing for UK delegation, February 1949, no. 4145, FO369, TNA.

[211] Briefing for UK delegation, February 1949, no. 4145, FO369, TNA.

[212] US Draft for the Civilian Convention, 31 March 1949, Provost Marshal General, no. 673, NARA; and Memo US Delegation for State Department, 2 May 1949, no. Series 5, RG 43 - 40, NARA.

[213] Remarks and Proposals submitted by the ICRC, 1949, ICRC Library. The ICRC later claimed that Dunant had been the first to address the idea of safety zones. The LGA, however, thought that the ICRC had taken over its ideas without properly crediting them. Annoyed, Pictet believed it was impossible to make them understand that those ideas belonged to "all men of good will," not the LGA alone. Minutes of Plenary Meeting ICRC, 16 December 1948, no. A PV A PI.19, ACICR.

[214] Report Meeting Pictet and Pilloud in The Hague, 1 June 1948, no. 304, Archief Rode Kruis Nederland (ARKN), The Hague; and Copy of Memo François, 28 April 1949, no. 5, Collectie Mouton, NA.

[215] Holloway, *The Soviet Union and the Arms Race*, 162–165, 228.

Stockholm resolution as a potential mandate for the organization to intervene in relation to limiting air bombing, but this led to renewed opposition from another senior law professor, Paul Carry. He, like Huber, rejected their younger colleagues' proposal to go beyond their original mandate. Traumatized by the failures of the interwar period, he reminded them of the resolution's lack of support from the Great Powers, especially Britain and the US. The ICRC accepted the professorial advice, leaving Pictet's initiative aside to be dealt with after 1949, with devastating consequences for civilian populations (see Conclusion).[216]

The ICRC's decision not to specifically focus on air-atomic warfare (e.g. by subsuming the criminalization of hospital targeting under the meta-category of grave breaches[217]) was probably taken in coordination with the Swiss Federal Government. Bern had assured the Great Powers that it would not raise legal issues they considered of a "political nature," and would focus on matters related to "victims of war" alone. The Swiss delegation later publicly admitted these assurances were calculated to increase the diplomatic conference's "prospects of success" and prevent an Anglo-American walk out.[218] A later Canadian report also admitted that if the Swiss had addressed arms regulation head on, then its delegation "and [those of] other countries [i.e. the United States: BvD] might [have] very well refused to attend."[219]

5.3 "A New Auschwitz?"

To the surprise of nobody, in 1949 the two major victims of Allied bombing and blockade failed to receive a proper invitation to the diplomatic conference: the Japanese could send only US-supervised observers, while the two Germanys were excluded. In the meantime, American military planners were calculating that a future strategic bombing campaign against the Soviet Union might cause more than two million civilian deaths and reduce Soviet industrial capacity by almost 40 percent.[220] Fearing alienation of their American allies, French and ICRC delegates kept a low profile at this conference while delegates were

---

[216] Minutes of Meeting ICRC Legal Division, 16 March 1949, no. A PV JUR.1, ACICR.

[217] For more details, see Remarks and Proposals submitted by the ICRC, 1949, ICRC Library.

[218] Final Record of the Diplomatic Conference of Geneva of 1949, Vol. II, Section A, p. 504, LOC.

[219] Report of Canadian Delegation to Geneva Conference, 1949, no. 112-20, RG 19 - Vol. 480, LAC. Possibly for fear of alienating the Soviets, the Swiss apparently did not provide for a pre-agreed agenda, leaving space for others to raise issues outside the conference's considered mandate.

[220] Holloway, *The Soviet Union and the Arms Race*, 228–229.

236   PREPARING FOR WAR

discussing the politically sensitive question of air-atomic warfare.[221] Using Pictet's resolution strategically, the Soviets first addressed the matter as part of their larger "peace" offensive to place limitations upon Western air power while trying to embarrass their delegations internationally.

Upholding the Stockholm drafts, the Soviet-aligned delegates put forward proposals to bend blockade (despite their continuing siege of West Berlin), criminalize indiscriminate bombing, limit the massive destruction of property, and create mandatory safety zones. On this issue, the ICRC received public support from the Soviet delegation.[222] Even as the Soviets drew on Pictet's proposals, they made clear that their plans would remain socialist in character. As its proposals to secure the weapon of starvation came under severe pressure, Craigie's delegation was forced to change its strategy from opposing to modifying articles concerning blockade. Its new approach was to revise the relevant provisions in accordance with the Admiralty's most important interests.[223]

To prevent the NATO alliance from suffering an embarrassing defeat, Castberg's delegation from Norway introduced a compromise text that secured most of Britain's concerns with regard to free passage of food while assuaging the fears of European victims of Nazi pillage in relation to supplying occupied territory with sufficient foodstuffs. Ultimately, the Admiralty accepted this Norwegian compromise because it secured most of its interests by creating "very widely drawn" discretionary powers to reject outside food relief.[224] NATO powers agreed on the need to secure a weapon with which it could slowly destroy the enemy in a future armed conflict. For these reasons, a majority of the relevant committee accepted the revised amendment in spite of continuing Soviet resistance.[225]

Demonstrating their anxious legal mindset, the Anglo-American delegations tried to make the relatively innocuous mandatory safety zones permissive again. They were supported in this stance by, once again, the Nationalist Chinese, as well as a few Western Europeans who had had disappointing recent experiences with this measure.[226] Questioning its practicability, they wished

---

[221] ICRC historian Rey-Schyrr has given a short overview of this debate, but does not dwell on it. She simply notes that the ICRC tried to stay out of any political controversy to protect its neutrality. Catherine Rey-Schyrr, *De Yalta à Dien Bien Phu. Histoire du Comité international de la Croix-Rouge 1945–1955* (Geneva: Georg-CICR, 2007), 282.

[222] As his father was sick, de La Pradelle's son introduced the proposal rooted in the Monaco Draft on safety zones at the relevant Committee meeting. Letter Replacement for Monaco Delegation, 11 April 1949, no. 161, Unions Internationales 1944–1960, LAD.

[223] Mulder and Van Dijk, "Why Did Starvation Not Become the Paradigmatic War Crime in International Law?"

[224] Records Meeting Cabinet Office on Blockade, 24 June 1949, No. 21475, ADM1 (Admiralty), TNA.

[225] Mulder and Van Dijk, "Why Did Starvation Not Become the Paradigmatic War Crime in International Law?"

[226] This section refers to the Stockholm drafts with respect to Article 11, 12, and 12A.

to make it an option rather than an obligation for belligerents.[227] As divisions continued, the French, acting once again as mediators, suggested a permissive text that was based upon a similar proposal from another Committee. As well as accepting this compromise, the delegates also agreed to neutralized zones applying even to states' own nationals.[228] Seeing no immediate threat to their air power or sovereignty as such, the Anglo-American delegates willingly accepted both proposals without a mandatory character.

In a surprising move, the Soviets then used Article 29, which guaranteed individual protected persons of human rights protections against torture, as another means to place limitations upon Western air power. By using human rights strategically against the liberal powers, the Soviet communists tried to widen the provision's individualized scope to mass ill-treatment of entire groups through extermination. The major Western powers saw this move as a backdoor attempt to ban strategic bombing and nuclear warfare entirely. The Soviets and their allies, referring to the recent war's extermination of civilians— even to the Holocaust itself—received support from formerly occupied nations and also from the Nationalist Chinese delegation, whose leader had personally witnessed Japan's terror bombing.[229] Complaining about their allies' complacency and "unrealistic" behavior, the self-righteous Anglo-American delegates once again claimed their continental European allies had an "emotional outlook" on the issue, while ignoring their allegedly mutual interests as members of the Western alliance.[230]

Having recognized its potential threat to their core interests as leading NATO bomber nations,[231] Craigie's delegation began to work more closely with its American allies to defeat the Soviet proposal on procedural grounds. Although they had disagreements about what approach to take,[232] their mutual goal was to ensure that whatever was accepted would in no way restrict Western air power from being used against the Soviet Union—or anti-colonial

---

[227] Final Record of the Diplomatic Conference of Geneva of 1949, Vol. II, Section A, pp. 626–629, LOC.

[228] Final Record of the Diplomatic Conference of Geneva of 1949, Vol. II, Section A, pp. 630, 785, LOC.

[229] Minutes of Meeting Third Committee, no. CD_1949_COMM3_CR11, ICRC Library.

[230] Cable US Delegation on Opposition at Diplomatic Conference, 10 May 1949, no. Series 5, RG 43 - 40, NARA; and Craigie's Report on Diplomatic Conference, November 1949, no. 6036, ADM116, TNA.

[231] Interim Report UK Delegation until 16 May 1949, no. 20770, ADM1, TNA; and Minutes of Meeting UK Delegation, 3 June 1949, no. 4153, FO369, TNA.

[232] The British and Americans had several disagreements, for instance, with regard to the question of authorized work for prisoners of war. Whereas Gardner wished to reintroduce the ICRC draft with a specific list of targetable industries in which POWs would not be authorized to work, the US Air Force delegate Dillon remained in favor of maintaining the Stockholm draft. He also said that "today war was a conflict between whole nations, and during hostilities everything assumed a military character." Final Record of the Diplomatic Conference of Geneva of 1949, Vol. II, Section A, pp. 272, 343, LOC.

238 PREPARING FOR WAR

actors, for that matter. To this end, they argued that the Soviet proposal belonged rather to the preamble or to the Joint Committee, or simply called the text an encroachment on the UN Genocide Convention. None of these attempts to wield the procedural weapon succeeded, however. Harrison's delegation, for its part, applied a special drafting technique instead to destroy the Soviet proposal's most threatening element, which hinted indirectly at limiting US air power.

In a shrewd move, the American delegation changed this particular element by applying it only to individual protected persons rather than to the civilian population as a whole, which the original amendment did.[233] This prohibited Nazi-style extermination of civilians while preventing limitations upon Western air power. In the Western-dominated Drafting Committee in which this revised text was later discussed, the US delegation pressured its Western European allies to endorse the drafting adjustment it had proposed. Craigie's delegation was unsure whether this risky approach would pay off in the end, but finally acceded to its major ally's demand.[234] After two long debates the Drafting Committee's majority accepted, by 6 votes to 1 (the Soviets opposed), the revised proposal banning Nazi-style extermination of individual protected persons, not airborne group-annihilation.[235]

Feeling betrayed and outflanked by the American counter-offensive, the Soviets fiercely criticized their Western European partners for dropping support for their original amendment.[236] Following Anglo-American combined lobbying, the conference's plenary accepted the UK-sponsored proposal despite Craigie's continuing concerns about it. Privately, he admitted that if it was to be ever ratified, then it could never apply to "extermination with the *recognized* weapons of war [emphasis added: BvD], as protected persons might well be inadvertently killed in legitimate operations, possibly even in large numbers."[237] The Soviets, for their part, pilloried the fact that the conference's "demagogic" speeches invoking the principles of "humanity" were being given

[233] Boyd van Dijk, "Human Rights in War: On the Entangled Foundations of the 1949 Geneva Conventions," *American Journal of International Law*, Vol. 112, No. 4 (2018): 553–582.

[234] Minutes of Meeting UK Delegation, 17 June 1949, no. 4155, FO369, TNA; and Minutes of Meeting UK Delegation, 21 June 1949, no. 4156, FO369, TNA.

[235] The Soviets recognized immediately the "false character" of this US adjustment and characterized it as an attempt to take away the responsibility from "murderers," e.g. bomber pilots who had indiscriminately targeted enemy cities. See Report Soviet-Ukrainian Delegation, no. F. 2, Op. 12cc, Spr. 969, Ark. 60-76, Tsentral'nyi derzhavnyi arhiv vyschykh organiv vlady ta upravlinnia Ukrainy (TSDAVO), Kiev, Ukraine; and Report of Canadian Delegation to Geneva Conference, 1949, no. 112-20, RG 19 - Vol. 480, LAC.

[236] Report Soviet-Ukrainian Delegation, no. F. 2, Op. 12cc, Spr. 969, Ark. 60–76, TSDAVO; and Final Record of the Diplomatic Conference of Geneva of 1949, Vol. II, Section A, pp. 712–713, LOC.

[237] Minutes of Meeting UK Delegation, 16 June 1949, no. 4155, FO369, TNA.

while American delegates were already preparing for another war in which they might kill civilians on a massive scale—as they indeed would do in Korea just one year later.[238]

While expressed privately, those Anglo-American views about their intention to destroy entire cities eventually became more widely known among the informed public, especially those parts critical of past Allied bombing campaigns. This occurred following reports in the press, both at home and in communist outlets, which spread Cold War propaganda. In the context of East–West rivalries, these publications had significance for British worries about their prestige. Causing concern among UK officials who saw themselves as paragons of justice,[239] these embarrassing reports from Swiss and foreign journalists triggered questions from Labour MPs to Attlee's Cabinet concerning the veracity of the rumor. Projecting an image of Anglophone "civilization," Bevin's Foreign Office denied every allegation, but it admitted privately that "if we give [the MPs] the whole story, [then] there might be numerous supplementaries which would be more difficult to answer." In a separate memo, a Foreign Office official noted that "all the great Powers intend to bomb civilian centers of populations if it suits them."[240] These revealing statements were a reflection of Cold War anxiety as much as a deeper skepticism about the impossibility, if not undesirability, of actually limiting air warfare through international law.

The sequence of Soviet defeats over Article 29A and other provisions raised broader concern about the Soviets' acceptance of the final outcome, if not possible Soviet repercussions that might follow.[241] Not only British, but especially French and Swiss officials tried to prevent a Soviet walkout by acting as mediators. As we saw previously, Craigie's team viewed these Francophone mediation attempts as unnecessarily accommodating of their main Cold War adversary. The Swiss, in particular, came to play a significant role in averting a total collapse of these negotiations when, after their recent defeat over Article 29A, the Soviets presented a resolution that was seen as a threat to the future of the entire drafting process.[242] Indeed, delegates began expressing major

---

[238] The Soviet-Ukrainian report refers specifically to the ICRC's use of the principles of humanity and the protection of war victims. However, it did not distinguish between the ICRC and Anglo-American powers, as it saw the former as an Anglo-American puppet serving capitalist interests. Report Soviet-Ukrainian Delegation, no. F. 2, Op. 12cc, Spr. 969, Ark. 60–76, TSDAVO.

[239] See *The Sunday Observer*, 3 July 1949.

[240] See Correspondence on Parliamentary Questions, 4 and 5 July 1949, no. 4156, FO369, TNA.

[241] See Interim Report UK Delegation until June 10th 1949, no. 20770, ADM1, TNA; and Report UK Delegation of Meeting Committee III, 21 June 1949, no. 4153, FO369, TNA.

[242] Hodgson confirmed this sequence of events: Report Hodgson on Committee III, no. Series: A1838, 1481/1A PART 8, NAA.

240 PREPARING FOR WAR

anxiety about a potential collapse, which they believed could have disastrous consequences for victims of war in future armed conflicts.

The Soviet Game Changer

On 6 July 1949, at the close of the Third Committee's second reading of the Civilian Convention, Soviet leader Slavin—ironically a former wartime liaison for US bombers based in the Soviet Union[243]—presented a game-changing resolution that took most Western delegates by complete surprise[244] and created a "sensation."[245] In his remarkable statement, Slavin tried to make up for the Convention's "chief defect" in failing to protect civilian populations against the "most dangerous consequences of modern warfare." He called the use of atomic weapons incompatible with international law and urged governments to ratify the 1925 Protocol—the United States had not yet done this as it considered chemical weapons of crucial importance for its national security.[246] Having nearly completed its own nuclear weapons program, the Soviet Union nevertheless re-appropriated Pictet's blind weapons resolution and the preamble's reference to distinction as a drafting weapon to directly attack the US delegation and to foment another Cold War battle.[247]

Taken aback, the French chairperson Cahen-Salvador questioned the Soviet resolution's admissibility, arguing that it fell outside of his committee's competence. Feigning unawareness of the Stockholm resolution (despite his prominent role at this conference),[248] Cahen-Salvador thought that the Soviets should have given him prior warning. Likewise, an Australian representative who was a staunch ally of Harrison's delegation tried to rule out the Soviet resolution on procedural grounds, calling it a breach of the "rules of fair play." Although allowed to speak only briefly, Morosov severely criticized

---

[243] See Serhii Plokhy, *Forgotten Bastards of the Eastern Front: American Airmen behind Soviet Lines and the Collapse of the Grand Alliance* (Oxford: Oxford University Press, 2019).

[244] Following Clattenburg's advice, the State Department had prepared early for such a Soviet attempt to ban atomic warfare. See Cables on Soviet Proposal Atomic Energy, May 1949, no. Series 5, RG43 - 40, NARA.

[245] Final Report Craigie, November 1949, no. 4164, FO369, TNA.

[246] The US ratified only after the Vietnam War. See Overy, *The Bombing War*; and Webster, "Making Disarmament Work," 564.

[247] It is telling that the Soviets removed Pictet's original reference to all blind weapons, including rockets and carpet bombing. In other discussions, the Soviets had publicly stated they did not wish to ban all indiscriminate weapons, merely atomic and gas weapons. Final Record of the Diplomatic Conference of Geneva of 1949, Vol. II, Section A, p. 757–762, LOC.

[248] Despite their attendance, Lamarle and Cahen were said not to have known about this Stockholm resolution. Cable Lamarle Soviet Motion, 7 July 1949, no. 161, Unions Internationales 1944–1960, LAD.

Cahen-Salvador's ruling out of his proposal. It was hypocritical, he argued, as the French had recently introduced a similar type of resolution on another matter (see Chapter 6), and in violation of the Stockholm resolution banning weaponry such as nuclear arms.

While Cahen-Salvador reserved the resolution's admissibility for the next meeting, Western delegates were alarmed by this new Soviet resolution. As nuclear weapons were regarded as a central element in Western preparations for war against the Soviet Union,[249] Yingling immediately called Washington, expressing concern about this latest development in Geneva. Acheson's State Department called an emergency meeting in the nation's capital with officials from various civil and military agencies to discuss the Soviet resolution. Swift deliberation yielded the view that the text was "completely unacceptable," a propagandistic attempt to embarrass the US government on the international stage. Playing a key role here, the Joint Chiefs of Staff felt their delegation in Geneva had to oppose "any action that accepted any jurisdiction" on atomic weapons for this diplomatic conference.[250]

Acheson's State Department, too, expressed concern about the Soviet resolution, considering it a direct attempt by the Soviets to circumvent the stalemated UN negotiations on international control over nuclear arms. Considering its much weaker position within Red Cross fora, Washington wanted the discussion on this matter to continue within the UNAEC, over which it held tighter control by means of a stable majority and where the Soviets were being blamed for stalemate. As such, Washington instructed the delegation to oppose any resolution on nuclear weapons for procedural reasons, unless it recognized that regulating methods of war belonged exclusively to the UN's respective bodies.[251]

By contrast, a delegate from the British Foreign Office—whose government had decided in 1947 to develop its own nuclear bomb[252]—feared that this US approach of using the procedural weapon to kill the Soviet resolution might be a dead-end. The plan to argue that the conference's invitation or its rules of procedure made it impossible to discuss this text was considered "useless."[253] After speaking to Swiss officials, the delegate argued that ruling out the text or preventing its discussion would "result in interminable procedural wrangling"

---

[249] Holloway, *The Soviet Union and the Arms Race*, 228.

[250] Minutes of Meeting at the State Department on Soviet Resolution, 7 July 1949, no. 669, Provost Marshal General, NARA.

[251] Ibid.

[252] Black, *Air Power*, 157.

[253] While a "strict chairman" provided some leeway, this UK delegate felt it was not enough to kill the resolution in its entirety. Note Alexander for Craigie, 7 July 1949, no. 4156, FO369, TNA.

242 PREPARING FOR WAR

and further loss of precious Western prestige at a time of East–West tensions. Their other fear was that it might "very well drive the Russians to walk out of the conference." They considered the idea of allowing the resolution to be discussed and then moving for its closure, thereby limiting speeches to one per side, lobbying for support, and finally pressing for a vote.[254]

In the meantime, acting clearly in favor of Anglo-American interests, Cahen-Salvador approached Slavin directly, urging him to drop his resolution altogether.[255] Again unsurprisingly, Slavin objected. In turn, Cahen-Salvador threatened to discuss merely the text's receivability rather than its substance. Once again, Slavin refused. While cooperating on issues of shared NATO interest, the French and British delegations felt forced to come up with an alternative drafting tactic.[256] In addition to canvassing for votes from smaller states, the British gathered their Commonwealth allies for an emergency meeting to discuss a joint strategy to defeat the Soviet resolution.

The participants agreed that discussion of the text's substance should be avoided and that it should be argued that the conference had no competence on this issue. In this regard, the former delegate Gardner reminded them of the successful precedent of having defeated a similar Stalinist resolution on procedural grounds at the conference in 1947.[257] Referring to this precedent, Lamarle's delegation agreed that an attempt should be made to defeat the Soviet resolution on procedural rather than substantive grounds. While fearing repercussions from the Soviets, his delegation agreed to this strategy for mainly diplomatic reasons: to protect the Western bloc's cohesion and shared NATO interests, and to give preference to the UN's lead in this context.[258]

While the French and British were united concerning goal and strategy, Craigie was far less certain about which tactic would defeat the Soviet resolution. He preferred to take a back seat in this debate, hoping to protect his delegation's already damaged reputation which had been weakened by actions in other debates. At the same time, he saw opportunities to malign the Soviets and spread Cold War propaganda by blaming them for the recent impasse at the UNAEC to control nuclear energy. The British leader suggested a counter-resolution that called for peace without addressing weapons, which

---

[254] Correspondence on Strategy to Defeat Soviet Resolution, 7–12 July 1949, no. 4156, FO369, TNA.

[255] Alternatively, the French chairperson suggested that he delay the text's discussion or to forward it to the plenary, as it was germane to all four Conventions. President Petitpierre agreed with the latter idea. Cable Lamarle Soviet Motion, 7 July 1949, no. 161, Unions Internationales 1944–1960, LAD.

[256] This account was confirmed only indirectly by one British source. Cahen's precise informal actions at this stage of the drafting process remain unclear. Correspondence on Strategy to Defeat Soviet Resolution, 7–12 July 1949, no. 4156, FO369, TNA.

[257] Minutes of Meeting UK Delegation, 7 July 1949, no. 4157, FO369, TNA.

[258] Cable Lamarle Soviet Motion, 7 July 1949, no. 161, Unions Internationales 1944–1960, LAD.

was inspired by a previous British text that had defeated the Stalinist resolution from 1947.[259] The text argued that the matter lay outside this conference's competence, while expressing a pious hope that the UN would shortly arrive at a balanced judgment in this regard. Bevin's Foreign Office approved this tactic, but instructed Craigie to coordinate his actions with NATO allies and to prevent being dragged into any major controversy that would further compromise the international position of the British, which had triggered critical questions in the House of Commons.[260]

Expressing even more anxiety than the British, Acheson's State Department asked the Soviet resolution to "be killed" on the basis of procedure and competence.[261] This led to informal conversations between Harrison, Craigie, leading French delegates, and Petitpierre, who implicated Swiss neutrality in shielding NATO air power. They agreed to a letter, drafted by Yingling, which opposed the Soviet resolution on procedural grounds and denied the conference's competence in this regard. Fearing further international outcry, they agreed that discussing the resolution's substance should be avoided at all times.[262] The aim was to suppress the text on procedural grounds and develop a coordinated approach to empower Cahen-Salvador's position as chairperson; he could then rule it out.[263] Behind the scenes, the leading NATO powers would lobby for support to ensure that, in the event of a Soviet challenge, the majority would support his decision to place their resolution out of order.[264]

This risky strategy paid off—at least initially. Prior to the debate, the French, British, and Americans had collected signatures from smaller states and their closest partners for their counter-resolution empowering Cahen's position as chair. The Belgian professor Bourquin initially hesitated to endorse this aggressive strategy, possibly fearing a damage to his academic reputation.[265] The Americans also continued to put pressure on Cahen-Salvador to rule out this resolution.[266] French leaders Betolaud and Lamarle, anticipating a hostile Soviet response, were against Cahen-Salvador taking a partisan position as

---

[259] Secret Memo Craigie for Foreign Office, 8 July 1949, no. 4156, FO369, TNA.

[260] The Foreign Office accepted an alternative resolution similar to Craigie's plan if the Soviets would persist in their efforts. This counter-resolution would have to be agreed upon among the major Western powers, said London. Response Foreign Office on Soviet Resolution, 12 July 1949, no. 4156, FO369, TNA.

[261] Cable State Department to Yingling, 8 July 1949, no. Series 677, Provost Marshal General, NARA.

[262] Report of Canadian Delegation to Geneva Conference, 1949, no. 112-20, RG 19 - Vol. 480, LAC.

[263] Minutes of Meeting UK Delegation, 14 July 1949, no. 4158, FO369, TNA.

[264] Letter Alexander to Foreign Office, 15 July 1949, no. 4157, FO369, TNA.

[265] See Cable Dutch Delegation on Soviet Resolution, 22 July 1949, no. 3044, Collectie Code-Archief Buitenlandse Zaken, NA; and Note Telephone Call, 15 July 1949, no. 2976, Collectie Code-Archief Buitenlandse Zaken, NA.

[266] Report of Canadian Delegation to Geneva Conference, 1949, no. 112-20, RG 19 - Vol. 480, LAC.

244 PREPARING FOR WAR

chairperson, but the Frenchman himself stated that he felt compelled to rule out the resolution on the basis of the conference's rules of procedure. More likely, however, is that pressure from Anglo-American delegates drove Cahen-Salvador's decision to kill the Soviet bill on procedural grounds.[267]

In the Third Committee, at the actual debate, US leader Harrison first raised a point of order to lock discussion on the substance of the Soviet resolution. Cahen-Salvador then declared the text out of order. As expected, the Soviets were furious, but the Frenchman held tight control and quickly silenced them by setting out a vote. The resolution was declared inadmissible by 34 votes to 8, with only the Soviet bloc voting in favor of this text.[268] Even some of their closest non-communist partners, Finland and Israel, feared to speak and/or vote in favor of their resolution—one abstained, the other decided to have another coffee.[269] When a Soviet delegate tried to address the Committee he was silenced by Cahen-Salvador, but, after a vote, was finally given the right to speak. Calling the procedure "unfair," the Soviet delegate announced that his delegation would resubmit its resolution at a future plenary session.[270]

Cahen-Salvador's crude behavior toward the Soviets was subsequently criticized by the delegates and in the local Genevan press as unfair,[271] and Anglo-American tactics were derided as overly aggressive. In a secret report, ICRC delegate Pilloud later wrote that Cahen-Salvador's decision to accept Harrison's point of order and to rule out the resolution was "abusive."[272] Calling

---

[267] It is more likely that this statement was included in the cable to assure the French Foreign Ministry, in Paris. It would have been difficult to explain that Cahen did not necessarily act in accordance with the conference's rules of procedure. Cable Lamarle on Soviet Resolution, 20 July 1949, no. 161, Unions Internationales 1944–1960, LAD.

[268] Among the most notable abstainers were Finland, Burma, and Ethiopia. Among the 11 absentees were the Israelis and a number of Latin American countries. The Israelis had been offered a deal by the Soviets: if they supported their resolution on atomic weapons as well as their position with regard to Article 74 of the POW Convention, the Soviets would vote in favor of the Israeli proposal to recognize the Red Star of David as an official emblem. Letter E. Gordon to M. Fischer, 20 July 1949, no. Arrow – 5/184 (00071706.81.D3.D5.01), Israel State Archives, Jerusalem (ISA).

[269] It is telling that Israeli authorities had internally discussed the risk of antagonizing the Soviets by rejecting their resolution. They feared that the Soviets might retaliate by refusing to support their major offensive to gain recognition for the Red Star of David as part of the Conventions. Letter Division of International Organizations to Maurice Fischer, 10 July 1949, no. 1987/6 - ‏נצ‎ (00071706.81.D4.ED.29), ISA. According to an AP press report, the only non-communist state to support the Soviet resolution during the later plenary debate was Israel. AP Press Report, 9 August 1949, no. Arrow – 7/2016 (00071706.81.D4.FA.3F), ISA.

[270] Final Record of the Diplomatic Conference of Geneva of 1949, Vol. II, Section A, pp. 799–805, LOC.

[271] *Journal de Genève*, 20 July 1949.

[272] Conference Diplomatique. Rapport Spécial Etabli par Pilloud, 16 September 1949, no. CR-254-1, ACICR. It is remarkable how Best has largely adopted the Western propaganda surrounding the Soviet resolution. Basing his views on Anglophone sources, he called the Soviet resolution "in defiance of the agreed rules of procedure and all norms of conference behavior." After that, he presented a pro-Anglophone view on the issue—"this was no hour for softness." Best, *War and Law since 1945*, 112–113.

his appointment regrettable,[273] the ICRC's legal expert felt that the Frenchman was "ignorant" about the rules of procedure and lacked tact in his role as chairperson, a feeling shared by other delegates.[274] Disgusted by Cahen-Salvador's actions, Petitpierre, who had previously been involved in preparing the basis for this "abusive" drafting tactic, was categorically opposed to any "attempt to stifle discussion in plenary as [had been done in the Third Committee]."[275] The aggressive Anglo-American tactics, the delegate concurred, should be revised if the Soviet resolution was to be discussed at the final plenary session.

The Final Vote

In the following days, whereas French and ICRC officials kept an understandably low profile, both Petitpierre and the diplomatically experienced Craigie tried to persuade Soviet and US delegates to prevent further procedural bloodshed.[276] A frustrated Craigie failed to persuade his Soviet counterpart to accept his utterly vague counter-resolution, however.[277] Nor did Petitpierre's mediating efforts have any results. Realizing who they were dealing with, the Soviets wanted to talk only about their own resolution, while the Americans considered the very idea of discussing it "useless," still preferring to use the procedural weapon.[278]

Acheson's State Department finally instructed its delegation to defeat the Soviet resolution on procedural grounds. It represented, in their view, a covert Soviet attempt to undermine the United States' position within the UNAEC, even though Truman himself had recently given up on this effort to control nuclear energy.[279] The resolution was seen as an attempt to push through their previously rejected plan for nuclear disarmament without international control.

---

[273] While having preferred Bourquin as chair, Pilloud believed Cahen had been chosen not for his skills, but only because of "extremely violent pressure" from the French delegation. Conference Diplomatique. Rapport Spécial Etabli par Pilloud, 16 September 1949, no. CR-254-1, ACICR.

[274] In a similar vein, the British heard from their Commonwealth allies that they had "won on votes [...] but lost on points." See Cable Dutch Delegation on Soviet Resolution, 22 July 1949, no. 3044, Collectie Code-Archief Buitenlandse Zaken, NA.

[275] Notes on Discussions Soviet Resolution, 27 July 1949, no. 4158, FO369, TNA.

[276] The British leader suggested a vague counter-resolution that rejected the conference's competence. The US delegation, expressing little enthusiasm for the notion, was willing to accept it only if the Soviets did so as well. If not, then they would either abstain or oppose it and use the same procedural weapon to defeat the Soviet resolution instead.

[277] The Soviet suggestions offered in response to his proposal were rejected by Craigie. Notes on Discussions Soviet Resolution, 27 July 1949, no. 4158, FO369, TNA.

[278] Cable Yingling to State Department on Soviet Resolution, 3 August 1949, no. 677, Provost Marshall General, NARA.

[279] Rosenberg, "The Origins of Overkill," 21–22.

246 PREPARING FOR WAR

Accepting any resolution might cause "an embarrassing precedent," said the State Department under Acheson's guidance. Essentially, it feared that any resolution would counteract the General Assembly's (GA) earlier decision to endorse international control and provide the Soviets with an opening to push through their rejected proposal. In connection to this, the State Department also feared that it would damage its dominant position within the UNAEC (unlike the diplomatic conference), where it held a majority.[280]

For these reasons, Secretary of State Acheson, who had participated in previous US debates with regard to its role at the UNAEC, instructed the US delegation to oppose any substantive resolution. While leaving some space for revision of Craigie's original resolution, his instruction was interpreted as a recommendation to defeat the Soviet resolution on procedural grounds alone. However, if, because of procedure, the only choice would be between the Soviet resolution and Craigie's, then the delegation could vote for the latter text.[281] When informed, the anxious UK delegation sounded the alarm, claiming that Washington had the wrong impression of "the general feeling" in Geneva. In its view, the delegates desired an alternative resolution rather than another procedural fight. Like the French, the British still feared that a procedural fight might be lost, possibly putting the Soviets at an advantage.[282] Bevin's Foreign Office, which played a critical role at this stage of the negotiations, was asked to persuade the State Department to revise its new instructions.[283]

In New York, however—signaling the multilayered nature of these negotiations—the US and Canadian delegations to the UN were pushing their British counterpart to drop Craigie's resolution in Geneva. Echoing the State Department's views, the Canadian delegation argued that resolution "would be extremely embarrassing" and claimed that "any concessions to the Russians would be a mistake." As discussions about atomic energy were about to restart in New York, the Commonwealth–US bloc believed that accepting Craigie's resolution would be "particularly unfortunate." Seeking to forestall any compromise of the authority of the UNAEC, the bloc pressured the British to accept Craigie's resolution.[284] Soon after, the British leader received instructions to drop it and use the procedural weapon instead.[285]

---

[280] Letter British Embassy Washington to Foreign Office, 4 August 1949, no. 4158, FO369, TNA.

[281] Cable Yingling to State Department on Soviet Resolution, 3 August 1949, no. 677, Provost Marshall General, NARA.

[282] Report of Canadian Delegation to Geneva Conference, 1949, no. 112-20, RG 19 - Vol. 480, LAC.

[283] Minutes of Meeting UK Delegation, 6 August 1949, no. 4162, FO369, TNA.

[284] Correspondence on Craigie's Resolution on Atomic Bombs, 8 August 1949, no. 4160, FO369, TNA.

[285] His fear that it might be used by the Soviets as a "moral victory does not seem very important to us," wrote the Foreign Office in a reply. Instructions Foreign Office on Atomic Bomb Resolutions, 6 August 1949, no. 4158, FO369, TNA.

INDISCRIMINATE WARFARE   247

Once the British and French had given in to Acheson's demands,[286] the major Western powers had to prepare a drafting tactic for the plenary meeting to defeat the Soviet resolution on procedural grounds. They soon found out that Petitpierre, unlike Cahen-Salvador, was far less accommodating than in previous times and remained unwilling to act as a puppet.[287] Their new strategy was to secretly canvass votes for a point of order to oppose the conference's competence on nuclear weapons. The British and Americans were relieved to hear that the confrontational Australian representative William Hodgson was eager to take up the burden of publicly defending their position in the face of Soviet opprobrium and critical Swiss reporters.[288] Like the Anglo-Americans, the Soviets prepared their allies for the upcoming battle, demanding that they speak publicly in favor of their resolution.

Initially sidestepping the vote on the four Conventions, president Petitpierre opened the debate on the Soviet resolution's receivability. Following Slavin's introduction of this text, Hodgson took the floor and rejected the plenary's competence, arguing that the issue belonged exclusively to the UN. The Soviet bloc responded fiercely, claiming that the Australian was defending the extermination of civilian populations. The Romanian delegate Luca, a victim of the Holocaust, gave a remarkable speech in which she mentioned her family's tragic fate of extermination, asking the delegates whether anyone could imagine a "new Auschwitz"—one of the few obvious references to Jewish wartime suffering. Luca: "if, in a future war, the parties to the conflict can employ means of extermination such as asphyxiating gases, gas chambers and atomic bombs, what is the use of [this] Convention?"[289] By connecting genocide with US resistance to control of nuclear and gas weaponry, she placed the Western bloc delegates in an extremely uncomfortable position.

The most important intervention was not made by Luca, nor by Hodgson, but by the Swiss delegate Bolla, who was widely seen as a respected legal expert. During the plenary session, to Pilloud's disappointment, he publicly spoke against the Soviet resolution's receivability.[290] The judge Bolla believed that it

---

[286] No cable seems to have been exchanged between Paris and Geneva—at least none that has been preserved in the French archives I have consulted. It is not unlikely that a telephone call took place, or that the French delegation had been given discretion to adopt its own course in coordination with the US delegation. Cable Lamarle on Soviet Resolution, 11 August 1949, no. 161, Unions Internationales 1944–1960, LAD.

[287] Report of Canadian Delegation to Geneva Conference, 1949, no. 112-20, RG 19 - Vol. 480, LAC.

[288] Introduction Report of Australian Delegation, 1949, no. Series A1838, Control: 1481/1A Part 3, NAA.

[289] Final Record of the Diplomatic Conference of Geneva of 1949, Vol. II, Section B, 495–509, LOC.

[290] Conference Diplomatique. Rapport Spécial Etabli par Pilloud, 16 September 1949, no. CR-254-1, ACICR. Basing his view largely on Anglophone sources, Best appears not to recognize the mixed

248 PREPARING FOR WAR

would violate his delegation's promise to the Western Great Powers to refrain from discussing the regulation of these methods of war, therefore opposing the conference's competence on this issue. Whereas Petitpierre saved face by expressing unwillingness to rule out this Soviet resolution, his Swiss delegation effectively did so by openly rejecting its receivability. This "essential" intervention, to quote Lamarle, convinced hesitant delegations to vote against the Soviet resolution, and it saved Petitpierre's reputation as a Swiss statesman.[291] The text was rejected by 35 votes to 9, with 5 abstentions, creating immediate concern in the local Swiss press about whether or not the Soviets would finally sign the Conventions.[292]

While the Soviets saw this as a majority controlled by the "Anglo-American bloc,"[293] the Indians deliberately abstained to flag their more independent course vis-à-vis the most aggressive tactics used by the major Cold War powers.[294] While trying to become part of the family of nations, the neutralist Indians simultaneously sought to distance themselves from this Cold War division, and their former colonial ruler, at the diplomatic conference.[295] Seeking to repair the ruined atmosphere, the Mexican delegation introduced another resolution which called for peace in vague terms. The resolution noted that the Conventions had "been drawn up in atmosphere of complete harmony [to] spare the victims of war all possible suffering." This pious statement deliberately concealed the enormous struggle that had led to the exclusion of air-atomic warfare from the Civilian Convention's scope, complained the Soviet delegation. Similarly, communist newspapers across the world decried the decision, causing anxiety among Western diplomats.[296] The plenary finally removed the Mexican resolution's relevant section, reducing its text to an empty shell with an undefined call for peace amid fears of another catastrophic war.

---

feelings of many delegations about the aggressive tactics used by the Anglo-American powers. Best, *War and Law since 1945*, 113.

[291] Cable Lamarle on Soviet Resolution, 11 August 1949, no. 161, Unions Internationales 1944–1960, LAD. For positive characterizations of Bolla, see Final Report Craigie, November 1949, no. 4164, FO369, TNA; and Report of Canadian Delegation to Geneva Conference, 1949, no. 112-20, RG 19 - Vol. 480, LAC.

[292] *Journal de Genève*, 7 August 1949. According to an AP press report, the only non-communist state to support the Soviet resolution during the plenary debate was Israel. AP Press Report, 9 August 1949, no. Arrow – 7/2016 (00071706.81.D4.FA.3F), ISA.

[293] Report Soviet-Ukrainian Delegation, no. F. 2, Op. 12cc, Spr. 969, Ark. 60–76, TSDAVO.

[294] The Indian delegation believed, under influence from a jurist delegate, that the issue properly belonged to the GA. This was another reason why it did not vote in favor of the Soviet resolution.

[295] Luthi, *Cold Wars*, 288.

[296] See Memo Canadian Embassy Moscow on Soviet Press Reports, 18 August 1949, no. Series 619 - B - 40 - PART 5, RG25 - 3398, NARA.

5.4 Conclusion

Resurrecting the principle of distinction in the context of East–West tensions produced a toxic political cocktail. Throughout this drafting process, the Soviet and Anglo-American blocs clashed frequently over the question of limiting indiscriminate warfare. By abusing the rules of procedure and turning allies into puppets, the Americans finally managed to exclude the matter of air-nuclear warfare from the final drafts, creating a major loophole that enabled the indiscriminate targeting of civilian populations. The final drafts provide few means to stop or limit the effects of these weapons in any respect except for prohibiting human shields, which served US security interests well. By humanizing blockade, drafters also rejected Nazi-style starvation policies such as killing civilians fleeing from a siege,[297] without necessarily challenging the legality of starvation as a weapon of war itself.[298]

The Civilian Convention neither featured a preamble recognizing the principle of distinction, nor guaranteed absolute protection for hospitals against air bombing.[299] On safety zones, American and British officials recognized they provided little protection and posed no real threat to their hegemonic air power.[300] Their main concern was to protect their dominant position within the UN and prevent the placing of limitations upon the "arsenal of democracy" in relation to its broader struggle with Soviet totalitarianism—a Cold War logic that could easily justify the use of mass killing in the service of global justice. Moreover, internal discussions within American and British drafting parties leave little ambiguity about what they understood as being left of the principle of distinction. It has been rightly noted that the Civilian Convention protected civilians against brutality while staying silent on the two greatest threats to their safety, that is, air and atomic warfare. This critique, appearing in several media outlets in Switzerland, forced Petitpierre at the Conventions' signature

---

[297] This challenged parts of the outcome of the High Command Trials, which had acquitted German generals for such actions. Kevin Jon Heller, *The Nuremberg Military Tribunals and the Origins of International Criminal Law* (Oxford: Oxford University Press, 2012).

[298] Mulder and Van Dijk, "Why Did Starvation Not Become the Paradigmatic War Crime in International Law?"

[299] Gordon and Perugini, "'Hospital Shields' and the Limits of International Law," 459.

[300] See Gutteridge, "The Geneva Conventions of 1949," 321; and Report of War Office Delegates Diplomatic Conference, 1949 no. 14038, WO32, TNA. Other delegations largely agreed with this observation. Report of New Zealand Delegation to Diplomatic Conference of Geneva 1949, AAYS 8638 W2054 ADW2054/1 220/3/3 (R18524114), Archives New Zealand (ANZ), Wellington. Yingling also argued that safety and neutralized zones were "purely exhortatory." Yingling and Ginnane, "The Geneva Conventions of 1949." Draper later wrote naively that safety zones might "provide a haven [...] should an armed conflict involving the use of nuclear weapons break out." Gerald Draper, *The Red Cross Conventions* (London: Stevens, 1958), 82.

250 PREPARING FOR WAR

ceremony to publicly defend their legacy of excluding indiscriminate warfare (see Conclusion).[301]

This chapter has also revealed the problematic assumption found in the literature concerning the importance of design over struggle, and of the drafting outcome over its process. It is important to reemphasize that humanitarian law's silence on air-atomic bombing was not by design, as has often been suggested, but was the outcome of a major clash within and between various parties, within the ICRC, and among the Soviet and Western blocs. The widespread notion that the exclusion of air-atomic warfare was related to the idea that "Geneva Law" covered only victims of war does not sustain historical scrutiny. Such a position completely overlooks the numerous attempts made by various drafters to regulate the methods of warfare under the Red Cross umbrella. Neither does it properly explain why, how, and under what circumstances the issue eventually failed to become extensively codified. For instance, the literature does not properly distinguish between the Anglo-American approval of regulating some methods of war, such as pillage and human shields, but not others.

This chapter argues that the Civilian Convention's silence on air-atomic warfare is best understood not as an outcome of a strict distinction drawn between Hague and Geneva Law, but rather as that of a concerted Anglo-American attempt to place air warfare and, to a lesser extent, blockade outside the scope of humanitarian law, with devastating consequences for civilian populations in armed conflict. Seeking to protect their hegemonic air power,[302] British and American officials tried to minimize at all costs the space for discussion on the protection of civilian populations, an attitude that would continue to persist throughout the Cold War.

It is also important to realize that throughout the twentieth century, significant voices with sharply different backgrounds and political views supported regulating indiscriminate warfare under forms of humanitarian law. This chapter has demonstrated how the issue of regulating air-atomic warfare was never ignored. Throughout the immediate postwar years, the ICRC was pressed from various sides to respond to indiscriminate bombings and hunger blockades. During this period, the ICRC's approach to starvation was initially shaped by its wartime experiences. Still, it refused to outlaw a useful tool of anti-communist containment for fear of hostility from its Western

---

[301] Speech Petitpierre at Signature Ceremony, 8 December 1949, no. E2800#1967/59#522, Swiss Federal Archives (SFA), Bern.

[302] It is sometimes argued that CA3 provided rules for colonial air warfare. This view would not have been accepted by most delegates—especially not the British. See Boothby, *Laws of Targeting*, 432–433.

allies.[303] At the same time, the ICRC succeeded at Stockholm in breaking the taboo on hunger blockade and nuclear warfare in surprisingly effective ways. Paradoxically, while trying to prevent an East–West confrontation, Pictet's resolution was later re-appropriated by the Soviets to turn the diplomatic conference into a space for fighting an epic Cold War struggle—soon afterwards they conducted their first nuclear test on the Kazakhstani steppe.

Regardless of these clashes and the failure to regulate indiscriminate warfare, one should not forget the crucial but mixed legacies of this period. As early as 1950, following the first signature ceremony of the new Conventions, ICRC president Ruegger appealed to the signatories of these treaties to take the necessary steps to reach an agreement on banning atomic weapons and "all non-directed missiles," a clear reference to Pictet's resolution from 1948.[304] That appeal, ignoring the Convention's silence on the issue, symbolizes the start of the ICRC's continuing efforts during the Cold War and long after to promote rules against air-atomic warfare to protect civilian populations. It is no coincidence that Pictet and Wilhelm, as former proponents of controlling indiscriminate weapons, would feature in the endeavor to formulate rules for air-atomic warfare culminating in the 1956 New Delhi Draft Rules. During this post-1949 period the ICRC continued to re-adapt older ideas and vocabularies for its own advocacy efforts, from safety zones, military objectives, "blind weapons," and bending blockade to codifying a ban on nuclear warfare, with the hope of resurrecting the collapsed principle of distinction.

---

[303] Mulder and Van Dijk, "Why Did Starvation Not Become the Paradigmatic War Crime in International Law?"

[304] See Bugnion, "Droit de Genève et Droit de la Haye," 912.

Figure 6.1 The UK prosecutor Henry Phillimore at Nuremberg. He later participated in the 1947 Government Experts' Conference and the 1948 meeting in Geneva to create the Grave Breaches proposals.

Source/Rights: Shuttershock, link: https://www.shutterstock.com/editorial/image-editorial/colonel-h-j-phillimore-obe-barristeratlaw-in-action-at-the-nuremberg-trials-box-640-91811154-ajpg-5699505a

6

Preparing for the Worst

How should one respond to violations of the Geneva Conventions? By allowing violent reprisals to occur so as to force belligerents to stop breaking the law? Or would punishing violators be a more humane deterrent? In case of a trial, how can proceedings be organized in line with conceptions of justice and humanity? Could such a court sit during wartime, or only once hostilities had completely ceased? What role might the Conventions play if each party accuses the other of violating these rules? What can be expected from Protecting Powers given that many neutral states gradually died out after 1945? Some have proposed establishing a new international supervisory body in response to this disappearance. But to what extent would this endanger the future of the ICRC, the oldest international humanitarian body in history?

These questions are not just central to international law today; they also profoundly shaped the development of enforcement mechanisms for the Conventions more than seven decades ago. In designing a suite of new enforcement provisions after the Second World War, most drafters realized what was at stake. The war's atrocities had already undermined people's faith in the project of humanizing warfare; were they to be unsuccessful in fighting impunity on the battlefield through the mechanisms of enforcement, then outside observers would lose their last remaining hope in this endeavor. The challenge was complicated by the fact that the task of developing new enforcement mechanisms proved infinitely more complex, if not controversial, than some had imagined. Indeed, it raised highly technical questions that bore directly upon the extremely sensitive issue of state sovereignty.

This chapter explores the problems and dilemmas that drafters faced in their efforts to establish provisions for enforcement, emphasizing how this project accelerated a slow shift in the history of the laws of war. Historically, responsibility for enforcing this body of international law lay primarily with states, which were endowed with an arsenal of punitive powers. Until the mid-twentieth century, international law allowed for collective penalties, reprisals, and other brutal measures to punish or deter potential violators.[1] However, this

---

[1] Eyal Benvenisti and Doreen Lustig, "Monopolizing War: Codifying the Laws of War to Reassert Governmental Authority, 1856–1874," *European Journal of International Law* [2020]: 127–169.

Preparing for War. Boyd van Dijk, Oxford University Press. © Boyd van Dijk 2022.
DOI: 10.1093/oso/9780198868071.003.0007

254 PREPARING FOR WAR

changed as a result of the destructive experiences of two world wars, combined with formative debates about internationalism, humanitarianism, sovereignty, and individual rights. From the early 1920s onwards, drafters began experimenting with more humane and more international ways of enforcing the laws of war. Indeed, they established a set of pioneering instruments to give outside inspectors more leverage over states unwilling to relinquish their sovereign power.

This process ultimately culminated in heated debates in Stockholm and Geneva, in which Anglo-American, Soviet, Western European, and other delegates argued over whether to place significant restraints on state sovereignty in an attempt to realize the utopia of full application. Many of the formerly occupied countries proposed prohibiting reprisals as the "most potent means" of enforcing the Conventions.[2] Through radical ideas like this, they sought to precipitate a broader shift from state to international responsibility for enforcement, and from violent to non-violent enforcement measures. To this end, they proposed disseminating the Conventions around the world, among many other things. As the book has already intimated, these ideas were not simply reactions to what had gone wrong previously: drafters were also keen to confront new challenges posed by the breakup of empires and the Allied Grand Alliance, not least the reinvention of neutrality as a central enforcement concept in the laws of war.

In this chapter, the term "enforcement" has been used broadly to refer to the many ways in which drafters imagined how the Conventions should be applied and what provisions were needed to ensure their observance.[3] Save for the question of dissemination, which connects more directly with enforcement, related issues such as implementation (e.g. publishing revised field manuals) fall outside of the scope of this analysis.[4] This chapter reconstructs the making of those provisions that have shaped the Conventions' strategies of enforcement, from settling disputes to respect, through ICRC visits to Protecting Powers, to investigating and punishing violations. In revisiting these debates, the chapter furthers the book's larger objective by

---

[2] Gerald Draper, "The Implementation of the Modern Law of Armed Conflicts," *Israel Law Review*, Vol. 8, No. 1 (1973): 1–22, 4.

[3] Geoffrey Best, *War and Law since 1945* (Oxford: Clarendon Press, 2002), 142.

[4] For studies related to implementation, see Adam Roberts, "The Laws of War: Problems of Implementation in Contemporary Conflicts," *Duke Journal of Comparative & International Law*, No. 6 (1995): 11–78, 14; and Gentian Zyberi, "Enforcement of International Humanitarian Law," in *Human Rights Institutions, Tribunals and Courts: Legacy and Promise*, ed. Gerd Oberleitner (Singapore: Springer, 2019), 377–400.

establishing why and how drafters tried to prepare for the worst—in this case: unrestrained warfare.

6.1 Enforcing the Laws of War

Before the twentieth century, those who advocated regulating warfare had always been willing to tolerate brutal enforcement measures in order to preserve state power, as Chapters 2 and 3 demonstrated.[5] Among other instruments, they accepted reprisals and summary executions of suspected violators as a deterrent. The assumption behind many of these measures was that the threat of reciprocal brutal action could keep enemies in check and ensure compliance on the battlefield.[6] However, this approach effectively opened the gates to a cycle of violent reprisals, in that it gave both sides license to break the law temporarily as a means of forcing the other party to comply again. Behind a veneer of legality, advocates of enforcement justified the use of brutal measures and accepted serious human suffering as a means of upholding international legal principle.

For European observers, the Franco-Prussian War (1870–1871) laid bare the inhumane consequences of this enforcement regime. During the conflict, the belligerents were accused of misusing the Red Cross emblem and conducting savage reprisals.[7] They expelled enemy aliens from their territory as part of a larger campaign of total warfare. Shocked, lawyers began devising a new set of institutions and concepts to minimize the inhumane effects of such wars. The ICRC made its first visit to a prisoner-of-war (POW) camp as an officially neutral observer during this conflict and states began developing an incipient framework of Protecting Powers to strengthen compliance with the laws of war.[8] This new framework involved a new international legal practice,

---

[5] For a history of (early) modern enforcement mechanisms, see Pablo Kalmanovitz, *The Laws of War in International Thought* (Oxford: Oxford University Press, 2020), 118–122.

[6] Draper, "The Implementation of the Modern Law of Armed Conflicts," 7–9.

[7] Jan Lemnitzer, "International Legal History: From Atrocity Reports to War Crimes Tribunals—The Roots of Modern War Crimes Investigations in Nineteenth-Century Legal Activism and First World War Propaganda," in *War Crimes Trials and Investigations: A Multi-Disciplinary Introduction*, ed. Jonathan Waterlow and Jacques Schuhmacher (Basingstoke: Palgrave, 2019), 111–156, 120.

[8] Jacques Moreillon, *Le Comité international de la Croix-Rouge et la Protection des Détenus Politiques* (Lausanne: L'Age d'Homme, 1973), 42. The task of a prisoner representative was to receive and distribute humanitarian aid. The idea behind this institution was apparently first suggested during the Franco-Prussian War, and became an accepted practice during the First World War. The prisoner representative also played a key role in providing information for ICRC delegates visiting POW camps. For this reason, drafters of the 1949 Conventions provided them with a real status under humanitarian law. Howard Levie, "Prisoners of War and the Protecting Power," *American Journal of International Law*, Vol. 55, No. 2 (1961): 374–397.

256 PREPARING FOR WAR

whereby belligerents and their citizens were represented by a Protecting Power in enemy territory. This established a crucial precedent for the further development of the laws of war and their enforcement in the century to come.[9]

Another important shift prompted by the Franco-Prussian War came in the form of increasing calls for international criminal punishment and inquiry. Many observers of the conflict wished to investigate and punish those who had violated the 1864 Geneva Convention through misuse of the Red Cross emblem.[10] The most prominent advocate of this punitive approach was a lawyer and cofounder of the ICRC named Gustave Moynier, who insisted on punishing violations of the treaty at a truly international level.[11] Signatory states did not receive these suggestions warmly, though. Unwilling to give up their sovereign power, they opposed any proposal for international jurisdiction in this period.[12] Rather than entrust the responsibility for enforcing the Convention to a clique of international investigators and prosecutors, these states retained it for themselves.[13]

The 1906 Geneva Convention is a case in point.[14] This treaty, which broadened the existing Convention's provisions for sick and wounded soldiers, silenced attempts to internationalize repression and supervision. Despite Moynier's active involvement, its architects were reluctant to adopt a paragraph that would concretely further internationalization. Although they expressed a desire that disputes concerning the application of the Convention could be forwarded to the Permanent Court of Arbitration, the drafters still gave primacy to the sovereign.[15] States were merely asked to adjust domestic penal codes in line with the Convention's principles, which proved illusory in

[9] Levie, "Prisoners of War and the Protecting Power"; David Forsythe, "Who Guards the Guardians: Third Parties and the Law of Armed Conflict," *American Journal of International Law*, Vol. 70, No. 1 (1976): 41–61, 42.

[10] Lemnitzer, "International Legal History," 120; and Mark Lewis, *The Birth of the New Justice: The Internationalization of Crime and Punishment* (Oxford: Oxford University Press, 2014), 16.

[11] Daniel Segesser, *Recht statt Rache oder Rache durch Recht? Die Ahndung von Kriegsverbrechen in der internationale wissenschaftlichen Debatte, 1872–1945* (Paderborn: Ferdinand Schöningh, 2010), 90–95. For a critical history of Moynier's implication in European colonial brutality, see Samuel Moyn, *Humane: How the United States Abandoned Peace and Reinvented War* (New York: Farrar, Straus and Giroux, 2021).

[12] Lewis, *The Birth of the New Justice*, 17.

[13] Yves Sandoz, "The History of the Grave Breaches Regime," *Journal of International Criminal Justice*, Vol. 7, No. 4 (2009): 657–682, 658.

[14] The 1899 Hague Conference had almost absorbed the Geneva Convention. The ICRC successfully convinced the conference not to discuss its revision, in part because of Edouard Odier's intervention. Just a few years later, the ICRC decided to gather the long-awaited Second Geneva Conference to revise the old Convention: James Crossland, *War, Law and Humanity: The Campaign to Control Warfare, 1853–1914* (London: Bloomsbury, 2019), 186.

[15] On the Permanent Court of Arbitration: Andrei Mamolea, "Saving Face: The Political Work of the Permanent Court of Arbitration," in *Experiments in International Adjudication: Historical Accounts*, ed. Ignacio de la Rasilla and Jorge Viñuales (Cambridge: Cambridge University Press, 2019), 193–210.

any case, meaning that hardly any state changed its laws accordingly.[16] Still, the 1906 Convention took the first steps toward early conceptions of dissemination in that it obliged states to instruct their soldiers and population about the Convention's principles.[17]

Just as states were reluctant to give up their sovereign power, the ICRC was unwilling to compromise on its doctrine of neutrality. The Genevans perceived Moynier's idea of deterring violations of the Convention through sanctions as a direct threat to their core task of providing humanitarian assistance. The ICRC feared that this punitive strategy would jeopardize its delicate relationship with states, which was seen as necessary if it was to maintain access to wounded soldiers on the battlefield. To prevent this from happening and secure its core principles, it argued that states should prosecute violations of the Convention through their own domestic criminal systems. Accordingly, it saw its task in wartime as one of merely forwarding complaints of violations to states, which proved another illusion of belle époque enforcement.[18]

The 1899 and 1907 Hague Conferences did little to change this reliance on domestic jurisdiction. Still, they did launch several new concepts relating to enforcement: compensation, relief societies for POWs, and, most importantly, inquiry.[19] In 1899, the Russian delegate Martens had introduced the idea of an impartial commission of inquiry that might investigate violations and thus forestall reciprocal action, potentially preventing all-out war.[20] Although far from perfect, this approach would quickly prove its immense potential. With Great Britain and Czarist Russia on the verge of war over the "Dogger Bank incident" in 1904, it helped to ease tensions by demonstrating that Russian warships had only accidentally targeted British fishermen.[21]

---

[16] Lewis, *The Birth of the New Justice* and Yves Sandoz, "The Dynamic but Complex Relationship Between International Penal Law and International Humanitarian Law," in *The Legal Regime of the International Criminal Court: Essays in Honor of Professor Igor Blishchenko*, ed. José Doria, Hans-Peter Gasser, and Cherif Bassiouni (Leiden: Martinus Nijhoff, 2009): 1049–1069, 1052.

[17] Convention for the Amelioration of the Condition of the Wounded and Sick in Armies in the Field, Article 26, 6 July 1906.

[18] Lewis, *The Birth of the New Justice*, 16.

[19] Elizabeth Stubbins Bates, "Towards Effective Military Training in International Humanitarian Law," *International Review of the Red Cross*, Vol. 96, No. 895/896 (2014): 795–816, 799. Article 1 of Hague Convention IV of 1907 did include an obligation to "issue instructions" (orders, not education) to troops in line with the 1906 Convention. Arthur Eyffinger, "Friedrich Martens: A Founding Father of the Hague Tradition," *ENDC Proceedings*, Vol. 15 (2012): 13–43, 30.

[20] John Merrills, *International Dispute Settlement* (Cambridge: Cambridge University Press, 2017); and Larissa van den Herik, "An Inquiry into the Role of Commissions of Inquiry in International Law: Navigating the Tensions between Fact-Finding and Application of International Law," *Chinese Journal of International Law* [2014]: 507–537, 509–510.

[21] Eyffinger, "Friedrich Martens," 30, 36.

258 PREPARING FOR WAR

Although they laid the foundations for several future mechanisms, the drafters of the Hague Conventions failed to design a comprehensive system for enforcement. Among other shortcomings, they made use of neither criminal sanctions nor Protecting Powers to promote compliance.[22] Although this outcome clearly stemmed from states' reluctance to give up sovereign power at a time of growing geopolitical rivalries, there is at least one more factor to be reckoned with.[23] This is that the drafters were equally unwilling to rule out existing enforcement mechanisms such as reprisals. This irresolution enabled states to inflict massive suffering among soldiers and civilians during the First World War without having to fear immediate international legal retribution.[24]

The First World War and Its Aftermath

With the outbreak of the First World War, belligerents rapidly moved to imprison a gigantic number of soldiers and civilians.[25] They were often exposed to extremely poor conditions: confinement, starvation, intimidation, torture, as well as forced labor. Propagandists severely undermined the position of these victims of war, who were often depicted as subhuman creatures. The war's totalizing logic and the brutal reprisals against POWs only worsened their suffering. These dynamics would profoundly shape future approaches to enforcing the laws of war, in four specific ways.[26]

First, with regard to supervision, the war enabled the emergence of the ICRC and Protecting Powers on the global stage, with the former winning the Nobel

---

[22] Lewis, *The Birth of the New Justice*, 17; and Shane Darcy, "Laying the Foundations: Commissions of Inquiry and the Development of International Law," in *Commissions of Inquiry: Problems and Prospects*, ed. Christian Henderson (London: Hart Publishing, 2017), 4. The first commission of inquiry to investigate violations of the laws of war was the International Commission to Inquire into the Causes and Conduct of the Balkan Wars (1913). This Carnegie Endowment-sponsored committee represents a unique precedent, and it was the first experiment with this type of investigation. It also advocated for the deployment of commissions of inquiry during times of war, which had been never done before. See also William McHenry Franklin, *Protection of Foreign Interests: A Study in Diplomatic and Consular Practice* (Washington: 1947), 79.

[23] Roberts, "The Laws of War: Problems of Implementation in Contemporary Conflicts," 21.

[24] Segesser, *Recht statt Rache oder Rache durch Recht?* 319.

[25] Mahon Murphy, *Colonial Captivity during the First World War: Internment and the Fall of the German Empire, 1914–1919* (Cambridge: Cambridge University Press, 2017).

[26] Heather Jones, *Violence against Prisoners of War in the First World War: Britain, France and Germany, 1914–1920* (Cambridge: Cambridge University Press, 2011); and Neville Wylie and Lindsey Cameron, "The Impact of World War I on the Law Governing the Treatment of Prisoners of War and the Making of a Humanitarian Subject," *European Journal of International Law*, Vol. 29, No. 4 (2018): 1327–1331.

Peace Prize in 1917. For belligerents on both sides, these institutions lowered concerns about the safety of their soldiers in enemy captivity.[27] For much of the war, the most powerful Protecting Power working on behalf of Allied POWs held by the Central Powers was the United States.[28] Its representatives would inspect camps containing prisoners across Europe and report on the conditions in which they were being held.[29] In 1917, when the US finally entered the war as an Allied belligerent, Switzerland took over its role as the world's most important Protecting Power.[30] What is more, it offered its diplomatic good offices for negotiation among the belligerents, which produced a set of repatriation agreements allowing sick POWs to recover in the Alps. As the chapter goes on to show, these unique agreements would create important legal precedents for the postwar period.[31]

Second, the war set another crucial precedent created in the domain of enforcement. This concerned the transformation of the ICRC's role in wartime, during which neutral Genevan delegates visited hundreds of camps with military and civilian prisoners to monitor the conditions in which they were being held. Indeed, the ICRC's POW Agency compiled and circulated detailed information about how prisoners were treated in captivity, despite the absence of a Geneva Convention to specifically regulate these matters. The organization also engaged in humanitarian diplomacy in a bid to convince belligerents to repatriate sick POWs to neutral territories such as Switzerland.[32] Still, it proved extremely difficult to operate without a proper Convention and in occupied territories, especially in Eastern Europe—if not far beyond Europe. Despite these shortcomings, the ICRC's work during the war would pave the way for key post-1919 efforts to strengthen the external supervision of humanitarian law.

Third, the war prompted the (re-)emergence of international criminal law through new concepts including "crimes against humanity" and "war crimes."

---

[27] Franklin, *Protection of Foreign Interests*, 95.

[28] Ibid., 88–89.

[29] "This work, carried out on a scale never before attempted, gained world-wide recognition and paved the way which led to the POW Convention signed [in] 1929": Ibid., 99–100.

[30] Strikingly, after becoming an Allied belligerent in 1917, the US government resisted the activities of Protecting Powers. At this stage, it rejected the view that the Swiss could act as a Protecting Power to inspect US camps with Germans POWs: Levie, "Prisoners of War and the Protecting Power."

[31] Especially in the period between 1917 and 1918, many international conferences took place in the territories of Protecting Powers to facilitate such agreements between belligerents to mitigate the suffering of POWs and civilian internees. Some of the most famous outcomes of these meetings are the Bern Agreements of March and April 1918. Cédric Cotter, "(s')Aider Pour Survivre": Action Humanitaire et Neutralité Suisse Pendant la Première Guerre Mondiale, Ph.D. Dissertation, University of Geneva, 2017.

[32] Cotter, "(s')Aider Pour Survivre."

260 PREPARING FOR WAR

Neither of these terms were frequently invoked before the war.[33] In some respects, their new prominence during the war was due to Allied propagandists, who often used them to indict "German lawlessness" and thus incite hatred of a racialized enemy.[34] In 1915 the Allies also coined the concept of "crimes against humanity" in response to the Armenian genocide perpetrated by their Ottoman enemies.[35] In embracing criminal law, liberal Allied jurists helped to criminalize atrocities and develop new institutions to deter future crimes, such as fact-finding bodies and war crimes tribunals.[36]

Fourth, in 1919 the Paris Peace Conference established a new commission of inquiry to investigate breaches of international law by the Central Powers.[37] Even though it tended to avoid the vocabulary of "war crimes," this commission would help to develop a historic list of violations of the laws of war that would play a transformative role in international legal history. The list was intended as a means of structuring evidence of criminality before a future criminal tribunal would start its proceedings.[38] The Allied fact-finders even contemplated the prosecution of thousands of individuals by collecting massive amounts of evidence against them. Ultimately, however, Allied governments lacked the political will to prosecute these war criminals. Instead, they delegated responsibility for this to former perpetrator states. This proved a fatal misjudgment, for the trials in Leipzig and Istanbul sentenced only a handful of war criminals before being closed down entirely.[39]

Despite these failures, the first postwar experiments with fact-finding and war crimes' trials were historically significant, creating several important conceptual legacies. Most critically, they laid down the intellectual groundwork

---

[33] Daniel Segesser, "The Punishment of War Crimes Committed against Prisoners of War, Deportees and Refugees during and after the First World War," *Immigrants & Minorities*, Vol. 26 (2008): 134–156, 135.

[34] Lemnitzer, "International Legal History," 124.

[35] Alan Kramer, "The First Wave of International War Crimes Trials: Istanbul and Leipzig," *European Review*, Vol. 14, No. 4 (2006): 441–455, 442; and Kerstin von Lingen, *"Crimes against Humanity": Zur Ideengeschichte der Zivilisierung von Kriegsgewalt, 1864–1945* (Paderborn: Schoeningh, 2018).

[36] Segesser, "The Punishment of War Crimes Committed against Prisoners of War, Deportees and Refugees during and after the First World War," 137.

[37] Lemnitzer, "International Legal History," 127.

[38] Cherif Bassiouni, "The United Nations Commission of Experts Established Pursuant to Security Council Resolution 780 (1992)," *The American Journal of International Law*, Vol. 88, No. 4 (1994): 784–805, 784–785.

[39] This is not to deny, however, the domestic and international impact of the Istanbul and Leipzig trials. In many ways, they represent a significant legal precedent for the use of domestic courts to try individuals for international crimes. Kramer, "The First Wave of International War Crimes Trials," 445–446; and Daniel Segesser, "Dissolve or Punish? The International Debate amongst Jurists and Publicists on the Consequences of the Armenian Genocide for the Ottoman Empire, 1915–23," *Journal of Genocide Research*, Vol. 10, No. 1 (2008): 95–110.

for the later emergence of enforcement concepts such as individual criminal responsibility. This meant that even heads of state could be individually prosecuted for war crimes, an idea that was endorsed by the Red Cross Conference of 1921.[40] Indeed, at this meeting Red Cross delegates contemplated the future of the Conventions' enforcement mechanisms. In so doing, they not only laid down several principles for settling disputes over the application of the laws of war, such as giving states the right to ask the Permanent International Court of Justice (PICJ) to give a verdict; they also discussed international criminal courts as a potential means of deterring states from violating these treaties.

Nevertheless, for Red Cross delegates such as these, criminal repression was never the most important tool for promoting compliance in humanized war. Instead of embracing the "new justice," to quote one historian,[41] they saw fact-finding and supervision as more effective measures by which to realize the dream of full(er) application. Red Cross delegates wished to elevate the ICRC's role by potentially incorporating its members into a new neutral control body, which would enforce the application of the law by supervising camps during wartime. This mobile "commission of neutrals," as it was called, was to act as the world's most important wartime supervisory body, with access to "all places of internment" and "necessary information."[42] It was claimed it left no camp unsupervised.[43]

This Red Cross proposal imagined an entirely new form of supervision in wartime, making the Protecting Powers look much less relevant. It also embedded Geneva's new and old international organizations in a transnational verification body with the task of investigating alleged violations. In assigning penalties for violations, this new verification structure required the League of Nations to get involved if a transgressing member state did not follow up on its reports. In that extreme scenario, the League's Council would need to place sanctions on this perpetrator state were it to leave violations unpunished. As part of their response to postwar demands for stronger enforcement, then, Red Cross drafters directly implicated the ICRC's neutrality in a broader scheme of international sanctions, with potential far-reaching consequences for the development of international law.[44]

---

[40] Kramer, "The First Wave of International War Crimes Trials," 450–451.

[41] Lewis, *The Birth of the New Justice*, 17.

[42] Report UK Delegation to Red Cross Conference, 1921, no. 8598/12, ADM1 (Admiralty), The National Archives (TNA), Kew.

[43] Levie, "Prisoners of War and the Protecting Power."

[44] Nicholas Mulder, *The Economic Weapon: Interwar Internationalism and the Rise of Sanctions, 1914–1945* (forthcoming).

262 PREPARING FOR WAR

Drafting and Enforcing the 1929 Geneva Conventions

To be sure, this plan to fully internationalize enforcement never got off the ground. When diplomatic drafters gathered in Geneva in 1929, they adopted a much less ambitious system of enforcement. In turning institutions such as the ICRC and Protecting Powers into humanitarian law's most preferred supervisors, they undermined the more internationalized equivalents discussed above. Neither the ICRC nor Protecting Powers were strengthened to the extent that they could challenge states decisively, for example by keeping their prisons closed for outside inspection—regardless of Soviet fears in this regard. This would prove especially problematic during the Second World War in dealing with prisoners belonging to so-called spectral states, such as Polish POWs and Polish–Jewish internees after 1939, for they lacked the diplomatic recognition crucial for those interstate structures to operate, following the destruction of their indigenous Polish state by the totalitarian occupiers.[45]

In relation to spectral phenomena, the 1934 Monaco Draft contained far more ambitious provisions for enforcement than the 1929 Conventions ever did. In an attempt to internationalize enforcement to nearly the fullest possible degree, drafters of this text had adopted various forms of fact-finding, supervision, and criminal repression from the interwar period. Forcing states to cooperate with investigations into wartime violations, they called for an international criminal court to take action if any serious violation was alleged. Similarly, they diminished the role of neutral Protecting Powers in favor of fully internationalizing external supervision. Having sought to place firmer restraints on state sovereignty and empowering international enforcement in this way, these proposals were rejected by virtually every state on the grounds that they subverted their sovereign power too severely.[46]

This litany of disappointments in the interwar period made the work of external supervisors extremely hard during the Second World War. The fact that Japan,[47] Nazi Germany, and the Soviet Union shut out Protecting Powers and the ICRC for much of the war made the situation more difficult still. The scope of their supervisory work was essentially limited to parts of Western Europe, North America,

---

[45] Sandoz, "The Dynamic but Complex Relationship Between International Penal Law and International Humanitarian Law," 1052–1053; Forsythe, "Who Guards the Guardians: Third Parties and the Law of Armed Conflict," 43; Frédéric Siordet, "Les Conventions de Genève de 1949: Le Problème du Contrôle," *Revue internationale de la Croix-Rouge* [1951]: 695–718, 707; and Franklin, *Protection of Foreign Interests*, 150–153.

[46] Paul de La Pradelle, *La Conférence Diplomatique et les Nouvelles Conventions de Genève du 12 Août 1949* (Paris: Les Editions Internationales, 1951), 351.

[47] Franklin, *Protection of Foreign Interests*, 129–130.

PREPARING FOR THE WORST   263

and the Middle East; more than 70 percent of the world's POWs never met any external supervisor.[48] This trend worsened with the dramatic decline in the number of neutral states as the war escalated. Tiny states such as Switzerland had to manage the colossal task of policing camps across the globe. Accordingly, the interwar system of supervision had gradually fallen apart by the end of the war.[49]

Having said this, the collapse of this supervisory framework was not complete. In a great number of cases supervisors could still act meaningfully: they kept countless prisoners alive and informed families at home about their lives in captivity.[50] Despite these achievements, the ICRC never used its access to publicly pressure Nazi Germany to end its genocidal killings of Jewish and Slav prisoners.[51] In some situations, Germany even used the ICRC's presence across the Reich to whitewash certain elements of its destructive policies.[52] Ultimately, the Holocaust was stopped not by international inspectors exposing its gruesomeness, but by Allied victory in the war.

Even before the last Nazi death camp closed, the Allies had begun developing new legal concepts and institutions. In preparation for prosecution of Nazi war criminals once the war was over, the Allies established the United Nations War Crimes Commission (UNWCC) in 1943. Composed of future drafters including Mouton and Craigie, this inquiry body started collecting great amounts of evidence of war crimes in anticipation of future trials.[53] (In the end, however, the preparations for the Nuremberg trials were conducted later by US prosecutors in occupied Germany, led by Robert "Justice" Jackson.[54]) By embracing notions of individual criminal responsibility and rejecting superior orders as a lawful defense in court, the Nuremberg trials left critically important legacies for subsequent enforcement.[55] Indeed, the Allies skyrocketed

[48] See also Hamza Eroglu, La représentation internationale en vue de protéger les intérêts des belligérants (Neuchatel: Imprimerie Richème, 1949), 64; Siordet, Siordet, "Les Conventions de Genève de 1949: Le Problème du Contrôle," 716; and Levie, "Prisoners of War and the Protecting Power."

[49] Switzerland would act as Protecting Power for more than thirty-five states. See Levie, "Prisoners of War and the Protecting Power"; and Best, War and Law since 1945, 148.

[50] Neville Wylie and James Crossland, "The Korean War and the Post-War Prisoners of War Regime, 1945–1956," War in History, Vol. 23, No. 4 (2016): 439–456.

[51] Lewis, The Birth of the New Justice, 238.

[52] For a history of the infamous ICRC visit to KZ Theresienstadt, see Sébastien Farré, "The ICRC and the Detainees in Nazi Concentration Camps (1942–1945)," International Review of the Red Cross, No. 888 (2012): 1381–1408, 1382–1383; and Sébastien Farré and Yan Schubert, "L'illusion de l'objectif. Le délégué du CICR Maurice Rossel et les photographies de Theresienstadt," Le Mouvement Social [2009]: 65–83.

[53] Darcy, "Laying the Foundations," 9–10; Lewis, The Birth of the New Justice, 16; and Sandoz, "The Dynamic but Complex Relationship Between International Penal Law and International Humanitarian Law," 672.

[54] Bassiouni, "The United Nations Commission of Experts," 787.

[55] Paola Gaeta, "Part VII Accountability/Liability for Violations of the Law in Armed Conflict," in The Oxford Handbook of International Law in Armed Conflict, ed. Andrew Clapham and Paola Gaeta

these principles into the international legal hemisphere by organizing tribunals across Europe and Asia often along similar lines to the Nuremberg principles.[56] The Allies were determined not to repeat the mistake of making perpetrator states responsible for their own prosecutions after the First World War. This demonstrates to some degree that they were able to learn at least some lessons from the past.[57]

Of course, this does not mean that the Allies were perfect students of international law. On the contrary, the trials they organized at Nuremberg, Tokyo, and many other places were imperfect experiments in international criminal justice; some leading ICRC officials even had the impression that this represented "victors' justice."[58] In their view, the Allies both failed to give German defendants a fair trial and ignored the criminal behavior among their own armed forces during the war. What is more, in only prosecuting crimes against humanity that were directly connected to interstate aggression, they also prevented post-war criminal justice from being used as a tool by anti-colonial activists to prosecute their own colonial crimes.[59] Radhabinod Pal, a dissenting anti-colonial judge representing India at the Tokyo trials, said that this demonstrated how liberal Allied empires tried to use international law as a smokescreen behind which they sought to reestablish colonial rule in Asia.[60] Although Lemkin was disappointed by some of the trials too, he was more

(Oxford: Oxford University Press, 2014), 737–765, 738–739. See also Kim Priemel and Alexa Stiller, *Reassessing the Nuremberg Military Tribunals: Transitional Justice, Trial Narratives, and Historiography* (New York: Berghahn Books, 2014).

[56] See also Kevin Jon Heller, *The Nuremberg Military Tribunals and the Origins of International Criminal Law* (Oxford: Oxford University Press, 2011); Yuma Totani and David Cohen, *The Tokyo War Crimes Tribunal: Law, History, and Jurisprudence* (Cambridge: Cambridge University Press, 2018); and Kevin Jon Heller and Gerry Simpson, *The Hidden Histories of War Crimes Trials* (Oxford: Oxford University Press, 2014).

[57] Segesser, "The Punishment of War Crimes Committed against Prisoners of War, Deportees and Refugees during and after the First World War," 150.

[58] Gerald Steinacher, *Humanitarians at War: The Red Cross in the Shadow of the Holocaust* (Oxford: Oxford University Press, 2017). For the historiography of the Tokyo trials, see Yuma Totani, *The Tokyo War Crimes Trial: The Pursuit of Justice in the Wake of World War II* (Cambridge, MA: Harvard University Press, 2008); Neil Boister and Robert Cryer, *The Tokyo International Military Tribunal: A Reappraisal* (Oxford: Oxford University Press, 2008); Barak Kushner, *Men to Devils, Devils to Men: Japanese War Crimes and Chinese Justice* (Cambridge, MA: Harvard University Press, 2015); and Kirsten Sellars, *Trials for International Crimes in Asia* (Cambridge: Cambridge University Press, 2016).

[59] Peacetime crimes could be technically prosecuted, but they had to be directly linked to the execution of war crimes or crimes of aggression: Gaeta, "Part VII Accountability/Liability for Violations of the Law in Armed Conflict," 741–743.

[60] Radhabinod Pal, *International Military Tribunal for the Far East: Dissentient Judgment of Justice Pal* (Tokyo: Kokusho-Kankokai, 1999); Milinda Banerjee, "India's 'Subaltern Elites' and the Tokyo Trial," in *Transcultural Justice at the Tokyo Tribunal*, ed. Kerstin von Lingen (Leiden: Brill, 2018), 262–283; and Milinda Banerjee, "Decolonization and Subaltern Sovereignty: India and the Tokyo Trial," in *War Crimes Trials in the Wake of Decolonization and Cold War in Asia, 1945–1956*, ed. Kerstin von Lingen (London: Springer, 2018), 69–91.

concerned about the Allied decision to drop "his" vocabulary of genocide in favor of prewar concepts such as crimes against humanity.[61]

6.2 Laying the Foundations of Future Enforcement

Despite the immense interest in criminal repression, once the war was over virtually no drafter made it central to their initial proposals for the future Conventions. Instead of strengthening the position of criminal prosecutors, they devoted most of their attention to empowering Protecting Powers and ICRC inspectors within the existing framework. During this opening stage of the drafting process, continental European drafters, including the ICRC, argued that the preexisting system of external supervision had proven its value, despite the fact that most prisoners had never seen an inspector during the war. They recommended the system's enlargement,[62] broadening the mandate of external inspectors by giving them access to previously excluded categories of persons, of whom civilians were the most important.

What is most striking, though, is that ICRC drafters were initially very reluctant to get on board with any proposal invoking criminal repression. In fact, many of them were highly critical of the work of Allied prosecutors of German war criminals.[63] Whereas Huber expressed concern about the rights of German defendants, his partner Burckhardt disapproved of the entire project of Allied war crimes tribunals, calling them "Jewish revenge."[64] The resistance toward criminal repression among leading ICRC officials had a direct impact on the initial proposals for enforcement, which said very little about prosecuting violations and focused almost entirely on the rights of POWs accused of war crimes.

---

[61] Philippe Sands, *East West Street: On the Origins of Genocide and Crimes against Humanity* (London: Weidenfeld & Nicolson, 2017). For a critical analysis of Lemkin's conception of genocide, see Dirk Moses, *The Problems of Genocide: Permanent Security and the Language of Transgression* (Cambridge: Cambridge University Press, 2021).

[62] The UK drafter Harold Satow wrote in a later report for the POW Department that "without the help given by Protecting Powers [the POWs'] lot in the [Second World War] would most certainly have been very much harder than it actually was." Report of British POW Department during World War II, 1950, no. Series 619 - B - 40, RG 25 - Vol. 5020, Library and Archives Canada (LAC), Ottawa, ON.

[63] This complicates the view that "the ICRC has always endeavored to find ways to improve implementation of [IHL] and, to this end, to incite the states to fight against impunity for war crimes." Sandoz, "The Dynamic but Complex Relationship Between International Penal Law and International Humanitarian Law," 1067. See also Giovanni Mantilla, "The Origins and Evolution of the 1949 Geneva Conventions and the 1977 Additional Protocols," in *Do the Geneva Conventions Matter?* ed. Matthew Evangelista and Nina Tannenwald (Oxford: Oxford University Press, 2017): 35–68, 48.

[64] Gerald Steinacher, *Humanitarians at War: The Red Cross in the Shadow of the Holocaust* (Oxford: Oxford University Press, 2017), 126.

266 PREPARING FOR WAR

At this stage, ICRC legal experts saw criminal repression primarily through the lens of POW protection. Above all, they were concerned that war crimes' trials would compromise their own position of neutrality, and undermine the protection of POWs, as well as that of the German Red Cross. (Again, at that time the German Red Cross was under Allied investigation for their former allegiances with the Nazi regime.[65]) For these reasons, the ICRC's proposals for the 1946 Red Cross Conference contained virtually nothing about war crimes. They placed far more emphasis on strengthening Protecting Powers, speeding up inquiry procedures, protecting POWs, and demanding diplomatic privileges for ICRC inspectors.

Those who wished to turn the ICRC into a potential arbitrator or global investigator of war crimes were met with nothing but resistance from its own legal experts. As long as ICRC members saw their "chief duty" in wartime as that of remaining neutral humanitarians,[66] advocates of expanding its mandate would receive no support from Geneva. The ICRC also developed more elaborate plans about how to disseminate humanitarian law more globally. The most important development regarding enforcement on the side of the ICRC was the increasing criticism it leveled at the use of reprisals as a lawful means of deterring states from violating the Conventions.[67] Having been so destructive during the war, reprisals came to be seen as a direct attack on the rights of individuals. In a remarkable volte face, this mechanism entirely lost its previous standing as a potentially effective instrument of promoting compliance.[68]

Whereas ICRC legal experts expressed almost no interest in repressing violations through humanitarian law, their colleagues from the US POW Committee took the opposite view, demanding a new regime for bringing war criminals to trial in the wake of the "Nuremberg moment." In line with their initial self-understanding as promoters of ideas of American justice on the international stage, they developed a new provision stating that violations of the Conventions would amount to "war crimes."[69] This far-reaching proposal did

[65] Lewis, The Birth of the New Justice, 238–239.

[66] Report ICRC, 1946, no. CSN_1946_DOCCIR_ENG_01, La Bibliothèque du Comité international de la Croix Rouge, Geneva (ICRC Library).

[67] Agreeing with the ICRC and testifying to the growing norm against reprisals, the World Jewish Congress had also rejected in 1942 the use of violent Allied reprisals to force the Nazis to stop the Holocaust. Instead, it preferred the use of rescue actions and war crimes trials. Lewis, The Birth of the New Justice, 156–157.

[68] Report ICRC, 1946, no. CSN_1946_DOCCIR_ENG_01, ICRC Library; Lewis, The Birth of the New Justice, 234.

[69] Minutes Prisoners of War Committee, 28 June 1946, Provost Marshal General, no. 672, National Archives and Records Administration (NARA), College Park, MD.

not trigger any serious resistance among somewhat inattentive US military officials at this stage, as they were far more concerned with rejecting any reference to superior orders as a legitimate excuse for war crimes in order to safeguard military discipline within their own ranks.[70] Their support for strengthening the position of Protecting Powers and ICRC inspectors also indicates the lessons the US military had learned from recent wartime experiences in Europe, the Middle East, and the Pacific.[71]

The support shown by the world's hegemon for a war crimes chapter in the future Conventions was more widely shared among delegates attending the 1946 Red Cross Conference. While being closely aligned with the ICRC, Bourquin's delegation representing Belgium showed its support for it by reintroducing the Monaco Draft's chapter on sanctions.[72] This growing consensus in favor of criminal repression entirely reset the drafting process with regards to enforcing the Conventions. Combining interwar ideas with post-war criminology, drafters pressured the ICRC to reevaluate its original position with regard to criminal repression. Whereas it had previously resisted or marginalized such calls, now the organization began to slowly realize that the increasing support for more powerful deterrents against war crimes had to be translated into new proposals to base humanitarian law's enforcement provisions on more criminological foundations.[73]

More remarkably still, some of the most creative proposals for enforcement came not from the Western liberal powers, but from socialists. To develop new enforcement mechanisms, the Yugoslav delegation proposed an international tribunal (despite Soviet ambivalence) and a more rapid inquiry procedure in wartime. At the same time, it questioned the ICRC's credibility, emphasizing how the organization had failed to stand up to fascist occupiers during the war. The Yugoslavs cast doubt on the ICRC's neutral position within the proposed framework, demanding that the UN Security Council serve as the guardian of the Conventions instead, condemning any violation of these rules.[74] As part of these efforts, the Yugoslav delegation also promoted dissemination of the Conventions on a global scale. This suggestion received far more support than

---

[70] Minutes Prisoners of War Committee, 16 August 1946 and 29 August 1946, Provost Marshal General, no. 672, NARA.

[71] Minutes Prisoners of War Committee, 12 July 1946, Provost Marshal General, no. 672, NARA. See also Sarah Kovner, "A War of Words: Allied Captivity and Swiss Neutrality in the Pacific, 1941–1945," *Diplomatic History*, Vol. 41, No. 4 (2017): 719–746.

[72] Report ICRC on Documentation Delegations, 1946, no. CSN_1946_DOCSN_02, ICRC Library.

[73] Lewis, *The Birth of the New Justice*, 229–230.

[74] Report ICRC on Documentation Delegations, 1946, no. CSN_1946_DOCSN_02, ICRC Library.

268 PREPARING FOR WAR

the campaign to marginalize the ICRC.[75] For now, the organization's future was guaranteed—as long, that is, as the Western Great Powers did not decide otherwise.

The 1946 Red Cross Conference created a number of important precedents for future drafting debates regarding enforcement. Despite fierce opposition from Yugoslav and Polish delegates, it agreed to accept the ICRC's role within the proposed framework. The ICRC was saved largely by the more dominant liberal delegates from Western Europe, whose experiences with this body during the war were far more positive than those of their Eastern European counterparts.[76] Beyond guaranteeing the ICRC's future, Red Cross delegates also embraced the important concepts of war crimes and fact-finding in formulating new mechanisms for enforcement.[77]

By connecting international criminal law with conceptions of fact-finding, the Red Cross Conference merged two ideas that Bourquin and Pictet had discussed previously. These two key legal actors—the former being one of the latter's intellectual mentors—had already suggested that, where allegations of violations were made, parties should have the right to ask the International Court of Justice (ICJ) to organize a proper inquiry procedure. The outcome of this would then determine whether those claims were factual.[78] This approach, they hoped, would lead to the emergence of a new division of international legal labor: whereas fact-finders would support future prosecutions by establishing the facts on the ground, courts would use these findings in their legal proceedings to punish those judged guilty.[79]

---

[75] The Yugoslav argument was based upon the premise that an informed public opinion had instilled major "fear" among the Germans regarding the use of gas against combatants on the battlefield (ignoring the terrible fate of gassed Jewish civilians). Along these lines they suggested a massive propaganda campaign to disseminate the Conventions on a global scale in order to ensure their future success. Report ICRC on Documentation Delegations, 1946, no. CSN_1946_DOCSN_02, ICRC Library.

[76] The Yugoslav delegation even stated that "the 1929 Convention played no role for us; it was as if she did not exist." See Report Minutes of Commission II, 1946, no. CSN_1946_COMM2_PV_01, ICRC Library. For Gallopin's response to Yugoslav criticisms: Report Minutes of Commission II, 1946, no. CSN_1946_COMM2_PV_03, ICRC Library.

[77] Again, it is not always clear to what extent the Red Cross experts made a distinction between minor and major violations. Occasionally they referred to core principles when raising the question of violations, suggesting a difference between minor and serious breaches. See Report Minutes of Commission II, 1946, no.CSN_1946_COMM2_PV_02, ICRC Library; and Summary Report, 1946, no. CSN_1946_P_CONFRE_ENG_RES, ICRC Library.

[78] There exists little archival proof suggesting any causal link between the UNWCC's work and the inquiry proposals under discussion here. It is striking that the UNWCC as a precedent was hardly specifically discussed during these debates.

[79] Summary Report, 1946, CSN_1946_P_CONFRE_ENG_RES, ICRC Library.

Contemplating a New War Crimes' Regime

In the months following the Red Cross Conference, ICRC legal experts began developing new proposals for the upcoming conference of Allied experts, in April 1947. The proposals they submitted were a mixture of old and new plans: they reformed existing ideas for dissemination and created novel provisions for substitutes in case Protecting Powers could no longer operate. Although ICRC drafters adopted many of the plans suggested by Red Cross partners, one can only take this argument so far. Most importantly, it does not properly account for the fact that the ICRC had to operate strategically in a minefield of global politics.[80] As shown in previous chapters, its legal experts felt forced to maintain a delicate balance between meeting the demands of Red Cross delegates and preventing the Great Powers from walking out. Their task of upholding support for the Conventions proved especially difficult when it came to the debate around war crimes first addressed by the US.[81]

Whereas the younger generation of ICRC legal experts, including Pilloud (a member of the International Association of Penal Law), believed that including the concept of war crimes in their proposals was an "extremely interesting idea," older delegates feared it might endanger the entire project. Given her wartime experiences, Cramer believed that traditional ICRC mechanisms for promoting compliance in wartime had proven to be more effective, regardless of the war's atrocities.[82] This criminological reluctance is revealing in that it indicated a deeper divide among the members of its legal elite: while some went along with the post-Nuremberg turn toward punitive measures, others feared that such efforts would compromise the ICRC's neutrality and its other established principles.[83]

At this stage, the ICRC began slowly contemplating a new war crimes regime. Its eventual decision to adopt the language of war crimes was influenced by several considerations, one of which being that Nuremberg had recently decided to consider violations of the 1929 Conventions as war crimes.

---

[80] Strikingly, though, the practice of good offices apparently was never successfully applied during the Second World War.

[81] Preliminary Documents for Conference, 1947, no. CEG_1947_DOCPG_ENG_01, ICRC Library.

[82] Marguerite Frick-Cramer, "Contribution à l'élaboration d'une Convention sur les prisonniers, militaires ou civils, tombés au pouvoir de l'ennemi ou d'une autorité non reconnue par eux," *Revue Internationale de la Croix-Rouge et Bulletin Internationale des Société de la Croix-Rouge* [1947]: 228–247.

[83] Lewis, *The Birth of the New Justice*, 242. To be sure, Cramer did not object to criminal repression as such, believing it represented the "only effective way to prevent reprisals." However, she continued to emphasize mechanisms of supervision and diplomacy over sanctions. Marguerite Frick-Cramer, "Contribution à l'élaboration d'une Convention sur les prisonniers, militaires ou civils, tombés au pouvoir de l'ennemi ou d'une autorité non reconnue par eux," *Revue Internationale de la Croix-Rouge et Bulletin Internationale des Société de la Croix-Rouge* [1947]: 228–247.

270 PREPARING FOR WAR

Furthermore, the US government's initial support for a war crimes regime gave additional political impetus for pushing in this direction. As a result, the ICRC began to gradually shift its position on war crimes. Whereas previously it had considered the project of war crimes as basically anti-humanitarian, it now cautiously supported it as significant to guaranteeing the law's future. While preferring other enforcement measures, its legal experts gradually came to appreciate the relevance of the concept of war crimes for their larger goal of promoting compliance on the battlefield.[84]

When these new ICRC proposals were introduced at the Government Experts' Conference in 1947, the UK delegation was shocked. Phillimore, its leading delegate, expressed a "complete reservation" regarding the part covering war crimes. The former prosecutor at Nuremberg was particularly anxious about a Dutch proposal, put forward by Mouton, to combine automatic inquiry with universal jurisdiction. In creating a global web of criminal repression, this plan would place severe restraints on Britain's sovereignty, he feared.[85] To avoid being isolated, Phillimore accepted the proposal relating to inquiry, though only in light of his colleagues' "very strong feelings" in support of it. Still, he was anxious that inspectors would be allowed to move freely around the battlefield wherever they pleased and that this would dramatically affect Britain's military operations, possibly making these extremely vulnerable.[86]

The US delegation continued to support the war crimes project, despite resistance on the part of Britain, its main ally.[87] The plan was also supported by France, despite its lack of serious internal debate with regard to the issue.[88] The US delegation remained reluctant, however, to get fully on board with Mouton's far-reaching proposal for a criminal court with universal jurisdiction to enforce the Conventions. The Dutchman also wished to force states to punish and extradite violators, thus undermining their sovereignty in critical ways. Although the US successfully pushed back against many of these proposals,[89]

---

[84] Lewis, *The Birth of the New Justice*, 241–242.

[85] The New Zealanders and South Africans also made a reservation. Report Plenary Government Expert Conference, 1947, no. CEG_1947_ASSPLEN, ICRC Library.

[86] Report Government Experts Conference, 1947. no. 673 - PART I, Provost Marshal General, NARA; and Report UK delegation to Government Experts' Conference, 1947, no. 2967, BT64 (Board of Trade), TNA.

[87] Report Government Experts Conference, 1947. no. 673 - PART I, Provost Marshal General, NARA.

[88] Report Minutes of Commission I, 1947, no. CEG_1947_COMM1_PV_03, ICRC Library. I found only a single (and tiny) reference to repression in French preliminary discussions. See Compte-rendu de la Séance Commission Interministérielle, 12 February 1947, no. 160-BIS, Unions Internationales 1944-1960, Les Archives Diplomatiques (LAD), Paris.

[89] Report Minutes of Commission I, 1947, no. CEG_1947_COMM1_PV_03, ICRC Library; Lewis, *The Birth of the New Justice*, 244–245.

Mouton convinced them to accept at least some basic provisions for criminal repression.[90]

It is worth paying closer attention to this pivotal figure in the making of the Conventions' criminal enforcement measures. After completing his legal studies, Mouton began teaching international law in the colony of the Dutch East Indies. With the outbreak of the Second World War, he came to London to work in exile as the main legal advisor for the Dutch prime minister; in mid-1945, he was also appointed as the new Dutch representative at the United Nations War Crimes Commission (UNWCC). Working in London under regular aerial bombardment, he became part of a transnational network of jurists and diplomats, including Craigie and Lauterpacht. As the war came to an end, Mouton drew upon this wartime experience in writing a doctoral dissertation on war crimes, which he defended at the University of Leiden in 1947. In the meantime, he successfully used his international criminal expertise to convince his Anglo-American allies of the necessity of incorporating the notion of war crimes into the Conventions' framework.[91]

In addition to codifying war crimes, the 1947 Government Experts' Conference had to answer an intricate set of questions concerning the problem of external supervision. What role should drafters attribute to Protecting Powers in humanized war? How were states to organize the system for supervising POW camps if they were to avoid damaging their sovereignty too gravely? What could be expected from Protecting Powers if the concept of humanitarian neutrality was becoming fundamentally suspect after 1945—at least in socialist eyes? Should the ICRC remain the preferred humanitarian actor in wartime? Or should it be replaced by a new international controlling body, especially given the Soviet boycott of the Genevan organization? Would the ICRC not be better served if another, more powerful actor assumed responsibility for enforcing the Conventions?[92]

For the French delegate Cahen-Salvador, the answers to these questions were clear. He suggested internationalizing the system of supervision by means of a new "international organism" to monitor the Conventions' application in line with interwar Francophone ideas. He feared that without this framework the treaties might become a "dead letter."[93] His concern about the existing system's

---

[90] Boyd van Dijk, "The Guardians: An International History of the Dutch and 'Hague Law', 1944–1949," in *Shaping the International Relations of the Netherlands, 1815–2000*, ed. Rimko van der Maar, Ruud van Dijk, Samuel Kruizinga, and Vincent Kuitenbrouwer (London: Routledge, 2019).

[91] Ibid.

[92] Best, *War and Law since 1945*, 153.

[93] See Compte-rendu de la Séance Commission Interministérielle, 6 February 1947, no. 160-BIS, Unions Internationales 1944–1960, LAD.

272 PREPARING FOR WAR

ineffectiveness stemmed directly from France's problematic experiences with it during the German occupation. Instead of allowing Protecting Powers to supervise French POWs and civilian internees, Vichy had signed a separate agreement with Nazi Germany, resulting in numerous problems and controversy.[94] As a former victim of Vichy, Cahen-Salvador put forward a mechanism whereby an international substitute organism would intervene in the event of Protecting Powers being sidelined. He also left the door open for the ICRC to take up this new role.[95]

Whereas Cahen-Salvador saw room for ICRC involvement as a potential global substitute for Protecting Powers, French diplomats such as Lamarle had little faith in Geneva's future in this regard. Given the Soviet boycott of the ICRC, Lamarle knew that this plan might easily fall apart.[96] He imagined that a potential war between the Soviet Union and the Western bloc might leave no room for neutrality or reciprocity; for its part, Geneva would be either destroyed or occupied by the Red Army.[97] As he prepared for this scenario, Lamarle realized that Cahen-Salvador's plan could never really work in practice as long as the Soviets boycotted the ICRC. He began working with US officials in an effort to overcome these problems, appeasing Soviet concerns by sidelining the ICRC and developing proposals for full(er) internationalization.[98]

The 1947 Government Experts' Conference had made room for the emergence of initiatives such as these in adopting the phrase "competent international body." This decision may not have been meant to undermine the ICRC's

---

[94] The June 1940 armistice agreement had stipulated that French soldiers would remain POW until a peace treaty was signed. Until that stage, they would remain under the protection of the 1929 POW Convention. As the peace treaty failed to materialize, Vichy leader Philippe Pétain decided to sign a separate agreement with Nazi Germany whereby ambassador Georges Scapini would supervise and negotiate the conditions for French POWs without direct application of the 1929 Convention. After the war, this decision was widely criticized and Scapini was punished by a French court for his collaboration with the German occupier. Raffael Scheck, "The Prisoner of War Question and the Beginnings of Collaboration: The Franco-German Agreement of 16 November 1940," *Journal of Contemporary History*, Vol. 45, No. 2 (2010): 364–388, 364–367.

[95] Compte-rendu de la Séance Commission Interministérielle, 6 February 1947, no. 160-BIS, Unions Internationales 1944–1960, LAD.

[96] Ibid.

[97] This view was held more widely among the former Allies, such as US government official Clattenburg who made a similar statement: "Clattenburg observed that in a future war it will be more difficult than in the past to attempt to apply rules to minimize human suffering for various reasons, such as […] the greater difficulty in finding genuine neutrals to supervise observance of the rules. He commented that in a future war neutral countries will probably be fewer and that a future war may involve ideology to such an extent that genuine neutrality will be impossible." Minutes Prisoners of War Committee, 9 July 1947, Provost Marshal General, no. 672, NARA.

[98] Cable Lamarle on Soviet Absence, 21 April 1947, no. 160, Unions Internationales 1944-1960, LAD; Minutes Prisoners of War Committee, 7 August 1947, Provost Marshal General, no. 672, NARA; and Boyd van Dijk, "'The Great Humanitarian': The Soviet Union, the International Committee of the Red Cross, and the Geneva Conventions of 1949," *Law and History Review*, Vol. 37, No. 1 (2019): 209–235.

position directly, but it did make it possible for later critics to claim that it had.[99] Indeed, some drafters feared that suggesting the creation of a new body for supervising the law globally had "endanger[ed the ICRC's] activities."[100] These rumors created alarm at the ICRC headquarters, where it was widely agreed that the "competent international body" posed a direct threat to its own privileged position within the proposed Conventions. In response, its officials devised a new strategy to prevent France and other countries from marginalizing the ICRC on the international legal stage.[101]

Once again, this conference had mixed consequences for the debate regarding the Conventions' making, in this case with respect to enforcement. It accepted an extraordinary number of ideas seeking to promote compliance: empowering the law's mechanisms for mediation; ICRC supervision without the approval of a detaining power; substitutes; inquiry; and the concept of war crimes. The introduction of the latter provision was achieved through continued US lobbying, which, in the so-called Nuremberg moment, wished to avoid the "repetition of the outrages perpetrated upon [our citizens] in the last war."[102] Although these plans for enforcement were still far from finalized at this early stage, they pushed the drafting process in several new directions, with vital implications for how its key protagonists operated in the following months.[103]

6.3 The Stockholm Conference

Preparing for the Stockholm Conference in August 1948, Pictet's drafting team faced the difficult task of having to develop a coherent draft text on the basis of a set of "extrêmement vague" proposals.[104] It immediately removed references to "war crimes" and the "competent international body."[105] As its officials

---

[99] Minutes of Commission III, 1947, no. CEG_1947_COMM3_PV_01, ICRC Library.

[100] Report Conference of Government Expert at Geneva, 1947, no. RC_report-1947, ICRC Library; and Minutes of Commission II, 1947, no. CEG_1947_COMM2_PV_05, ICRC Library.

[101] Documentation for Assembly, 25 August 1947, no. no. CR-238-4, Les Archives du Comité International de la Croix-Rouge (ACICR), Geneva; and Best, *War and Law since 1945*, 151.

[102] Report Government Experts' Conference, 1947, Provost Marshal General, no. 673 - Part I, NARA; and Best, *War and Law since 1945*, 156–157.

[103] UK officials said after the 1947 conference that drafters had "mistakenly concluded" that some governments were in favor of replacing the ICRC because of their support for the "international competent body" reference. Regardless of these criticisms, the UK was generally in favor of the ICRC as a supervisory institution "established by tradition and capable within [its] own [limited] humanitarian sphere." Best, *War and Law since 1945*, 152.

[104] Documentation for Assembly, 25 August 1947, no. no. CR-238-4, ACICR.

[105] The ICRC drafts for the Stockholm reference make hardly any mention of war crimes, except for a short reference in the Sick & Wounded Convention's text. This shows, more broadly, that the ICRC at this stage showed little enthusiasm for the concept of war crimes. In essence, it decided not to further

274 PREPARING FOR WAR

noted, this rather opportunistic approach was influenced by the wish to secure the ICRC's future and certain legal considerations, namely trying to avoid overlapping with ongoing negotiations at the UN. As shown in previous chapters, Pictet's drafting team both drew inspiration from these and established several boundaries between them so as to ensure the principle of *lex specialis* and prevent further competition.[106]

Pictet's drafting team also had to decide whether it would continue with the war crimes project that had originally been started by the US government. In February 1948, two ICRC delegates from Paris came to see Pictet to air concerns regarding criminal repression.[107] One of them was Pierre Boissier, who had recently attended various war crimes trials in France. In light of his experience of these cases, he was gravely worried about the rights of war criminals and their alleged lack of judicial guarantees. Given that he expected trials like these to spread across the globe in the coming years, if not decades, he believed that new liberal safeguards were needed to protect POWs from arbitrary treatment.[108] To realize this ambition, he and Pictet had discussed the idea of developing a more liberal war crimes chapter to defend suspects' rights through humanitarian law. These were to be guaranteed, Boissier argued, through fixed punishments and liberal safeguards. This entailed nothing less than fully incorporating criminal repression into the framework of the Conventions.[109]

Listening to Boissier's demands, Pictet recognized that criminal repression deserved far more attention as a drafting concern than he and others had given it thus far. Among other things, he appreciated Boissier's demand for liberal safeguards (such as due process) as a means of preventing future legal proceedings from becoming Stalinist show trials. At least initially, he was less convinced by Boissier's calls for a move beyond domestic jurisdiction and for the ICRC to assume a more central role in the debate regarding criminal repression.[110] Pictet's remarkably confined legal imagination in this domain gradually began to expand, however. His drafting team eventually circulated a new report for the Stockholm Conference, in which they began engaging with contemporary

develop its principles through establishing rules with regard to procedure, courts, and penalties, as the organization would do from late 1948 onwards.

[106] Minutes Prisoners of War Committee, 23 January 1948, Provost Marshal General, no. 673 - Part I, NARA; and Minutes of Reunion of Bureau/CJ, 25–27 August 1947, no. CR-238-4, ACICR.

[107] Minutes Prisoners of War Committee, 23 January 1948, Provost Marshal General, no. 673 - Part I, NARA; and Minutes of Reunion of Bureau/CJ, 25-27 August 1947, no. CR-238-4, ACICR.

[108] Response Pictet on Report Boissier, 7 April 1948, no. CR-238-4, ACICR.

[109] Report Boissier, 23 March 1948, no. CR-238-4, ACICR; and Response Pictet on Report Boissier, 7 April 1948, no. CR-238-4, ACICR.

[110] Ibid.

debates regarding the future of international criminal law more seriously than ever before.[111]

In this report, the ICRC admitted that the future of the Conventions depended upon addressing this matter: "without any [...] sanctions [...] even intensified supervision [e.g Protecting Powers and ICRC inspections: BvD], would be of no avail."[112] Following discussions with Boissier, Allied lawyers, and Red Cross humanitarians, ICRC legal experts now recognized that the pre-war approach of endorsing domestic jurisdiction and protecting state sovereignty was "entirely inadequate."[113] The report suggested several alternatives, from developing a special criminal repression chapter to creating a separate annex and asking states to deal with the matter on their own—the ever-cautious Pilloud called this the "best solution."[114] Ultimately, Pictet's drafting team hoped that its partners would take the first step at Stockholm by adopting proposals for universal jurisdiction and curtailing state sovereignty.[115]

Before the 1948 Stockholm Conference, the US government suddenly changed its attitude completely with regard to criminal repression. In stark contrast to its previous stance, it was now doubtful about its original plan to incorporate war crimes into the future treaties.[116] From early 1948 onwards, as Cold War tensions were on the rise, US military officials in particular began expressing increasing concern with regard to this question. Addressing the notion of war crimes, some suggested, was "inconsistent with the whole idea" of the Conventions.[117] In their view, these treaties had to be based upon national sovereignty. They should be free of notions of universal jurisdiction and, being "humanitarian" in nature, of ideas of punishment too. Whereas the ICRC was looking to limit state sovereignty, US drafters were moving in the opposite direction.[118] They saw ideas of universal jurisdiction as a potential threat to their interests in the emerging Cold War—though both liberal parties, the ICRC and

---

[111] Minutes of Meeting Bureau, 14 April 1948, no. CR-238-5, ACICR.

[112] Report ICRC "Repression of Infringements of the Humanitarian Conventions" for Stockholm Conference, June 1948, no. CI-1948_B3_06_ENG, ICRC Library.

[113] Ibid.

[114] Minutes of Commission Juridique at Stockholm Conference, August 1948, no. 18382, ICRC Library; and Report ICRC "Repression of Infringements of the Humanitarian Conventions" for Stockholm Conference, June 1948, no. CI-1948_B3_06_ENG, ICRC Library.

[115] Ibid.

[116] Minutes Prisoners of War Committee, 5 November 1947, Provost Marshal General, no. 673 - Part I, NARA.

[117] Minutes Prisoners of War Committee, 2 April 1948, Provost Marshal General, no. 673 - Part I, NARA; and Memorandum Young on War Crimes and Penal Issues, 23 January 1948, Provost Marshal General, no. 669, NARA.

[118] Strikingly, after meeting with Pictet in Washington, US officials gained the (wrongful) impression that he "appeared in substantial agreement" with their idea of deleting war crimes. Minutes Prisoners of War Committee, 25 June 1948, Provost Marshal General, no. 673 - Part I, NARA.

276 PREPARING FOR WAR

United States, agreed on the necessity of several legal safeguards for suspects, as will be shown below.

At this stage, the foreign policy objectives of the Truman Administration began to gradually prioritize the struggle against the Soviet Union. In line with this, it sought to bring Germany and Japan safely into the Western alliance by winding down the entire war crimes project.[119] In pursuit of these ends, Washington opposed the war crimes chapter and tried to protect from ill-treatment any future US prisoner of war whom the communist enemy might accuse of war crimes. Hoping to assure US soldiers that they would be visited by external supervisors, US delegates still placed some of their trust in the ICRC despite having mixed feelings about its potential effectiveness in a war with the Soviet Union (see below).[120] Still, they recognized that pressing for liberal safeguards at the meeting in Stockholm might unintentionally lead to a discussion of the war crimes chapter more generally, which they had asked to avoid.[121]

Washington's allies from Britain supported its new campaign against the war crimes chapter, which formed part of a larger shift in Western foreign policy objectives at the start of the Cold War. Echoing US officials, the British government voiced doubts about the ICRC's report, officially on the ground that it undermined the Conventions' "humanitarian" nature. In fact, Whitehall wanted war crimes to go unmentioned in the texts of these treaties.[122] To secure this common objective, Anglo-American officials did their best to keep this matter off the drafting agenda, both at the Stockholm Conference and beyond. In trying to circumvent the issue of war crimes and ignoring their own recent violations of the 1929 Convention concerning this issue,[123] they

---

[119] Donald Bloxham, *Genocide on Trial: War Crimes Trials and the Formation of Holocaust History and Memory* (Oxford: Oxford University Press, 2001), 27.

[120] Clattenburg: "On the whole the ICRC played at Stockholm the part of a conservative and jealous Swiss organization which blandly believes that it can continue unhampered in its humane activities because its activities have always been impartial and humane [...] The fact that those humane activities have on occasion aided enemies of the Soviet regime [i.e. Hitler's Germany] and that the majority of persons connected with the Committee are persons why by profession or birth belong to classes distrusted by communists does not seem to have permeated the consciousness of the Committee." Memo Clattenburg on ICRC role at Stockholm Conference, 15 September 1948, no. Series 22, RG 43 - 5536, NARA; Minutes Prisoners of War Committee, 19 November 1947, Provost Marshal General, no. 673 - PART I, NARA; and Memorandum Young on War Crimes and Penal Issues, 23 January 1948, Provost Marshal General, no. 669, NARA.

[121] Minutes Prisoners of War Committee, 5 November 1947, Provost Marshal General, no. 673 - Part I, NARA.

[122] Minutes Prisoners of War Committee, 18 May 1948, Provost Marshal General, no. 673 - Part I, NARA; and Letter Kuppinger to Gardner, 2 June 1948, no. 1143, HO213 (Home Office), TNA.

[123] In 1946, the US Supreme Court had argued in the Yamashita case that Article 60 of the 1929 Geneva Convention providing accused POWs with access to Protecting Powers applied only to those "persons who are subjected to judicial proceedings for offenses committed while prisoners of war." US military officials feared that this ruling would undermine the protection of future US POWs charged with violations of the Geneva Conventions: J. V. Dillon, "Development of Law Relative to Treatment of Prisoners

PREPARING FOR THE WORST   277

demanded extra protection for POWs accused of war crimes prior to their capture. In this way, while trying to exclude irregulars who were not even accused of war crimes (see Chapter 4), they sought to protect their regular armed forces should they be taken prisoner by the Soviet enemy. This double-edged agenda, advanced by the two major liberal powers, prompted significant debate at the 1948 conference.[124]

The Grave Breaches and Lauterpacht

With the British government delegation absent at the Stockholm Conference, US delegates were virtually alone in their struggle against the war crimes chapter. Despite this, they successfully convinced other delegations to drop both the old definition of war crimes, which had been put forward by US drafters in 1947, and Mouton's plan for an international criminal tribunal.[125] His continuing advocacy in support of universal jurisdiction terribly frustrated his US allies, who expected solidarity among, if not loyalty from, Western European partners.[126] Given that the delegates had little time to discuss the complex question of war crimes in detail, not to mention the convoluted drafting methods used at the meeting, the plan for domestic jurisdiction was pushed through without Mouton and other critics being offered a real opportunity to challenge, let alone revise, it.[127]

The exception was Mouton's success in helping the ICRC to obtain a non-binding resolution demanding that the ICRC be allowed to further investigate the question of war crimes for an upcoming "conference." The French delegate Cahen-Salvador endorsed both internationalized supervision and the ICRC's proposal that a special chapter on criminal repression be created, despite opposition from his Anglo-American allies.[128] The French supported the war crimes

---

of War," 1950, Provost Marshal General, no. 670, NARA. In the same year, US authorities in postwar occupied Germany treated German POWs accused of war crimes as ordinary criminals, not necessarily as POWs protected by the 1929 Convention. The ICRC complained that they were trying avoid treating the German accused as prisoners of war under the Convention: Lewis, *The Birth of the New Justice*, 245.

[124] Minutes of Meeting with ICRC officials in Washington, 24 June 1948, Provost Marshal General, no. 669, NARA.

[125] Rapport van de Nederlandse Delegatie Stockholm Conferentie, 1948, no. 71, Ministerie van Sociale Zaken, National Archives of the Netherlands (NA), The Hague.

[126] Memo Clattenburg on Plenary Sessions of the Legal Commission, 26 November 1948, no. Series 22, RG 43–5536, NARA.

[127] Lewis, *The Birth of the New Justice*, 255.

[128] Minutes of Commission Juridique at Stockholm Conference, August 1948, no. 18382, ICRC Library. While meeting with ICRC officials, Lamarle confirmed that his government was now actively

278 PREPARING FOR WAR

resolution as well.[129] The ICRC interpreted this resolution as a call to develop a new war crimes chapter before the start of the diplomatic conference rather than deferring it to the Red Cross Conference planned for 1952, to the surprise of some Anglo-American officials.[130] This bold move triggered a momentous shift in the debate with regard to criminal repression.[131]

Seen in the round, the Stockholm Conference established dissemination, inquiry, supervision, and conciliation as the most crucial tools for enforcing humanitarian law. To start with conciliation: as a set of methods for settling international disputes, the delegates chose to give Protecting Powers the means to offer their diplomatic good offices if belligerents disagreed over the application of the Conventions. They were unable, however, to resolve the more pressing question as to whether proposed substitutes could still operate in light of the ongoing East–West tensions. In attempting to overcome this problem, the French again suggested a new international control body to strengthen enforcement. Despite having been rejected previously, this proposal now resonated with broader US concerns regarding the ICRC as a potential supervisor due to the continuing Soviet boycott.[132]

Although it appreciated the ICRC's efforts on behalf of US POWs during the Second World War, Washington was doubtful as to whether this organization could continue as the preferred external supervisor in the Conventions.[133] To resolve this, US representatives (both government and American Red Cross officials) tabled proposals that would minimize its weight within this framework, reinserting the language of the "competent international body" that the ICRC had previously deleted.[134] The ICRC's desperate lobbying behind the scenes

working on the question of criminal sanctions, considering it of their "greatest interest." Minutes of Meeting Lamarle and Michel, 20 March 1948, no. CR-238-4, ACICR.

[129] It is striking that some US delegates appear to have mistakenly believed that this resolution was meant for the next Red Cross conference, not for the diplomatic conference in 1949. Memo Clattenburg on Plenary Sessions of the Legal Commission, 26 November 1948, no. Series 22, RG 43–5536, NARA; and Report of US delegation to the Stockholm Red Cross Conference, 1948, Provost Marshal General, no. 672, NARA.

[130] Memo Clattenburg on Plenary Sessions of the Legal Commission, 26 November 1948, no. Series 22, RG 43–5536, NARA.

[131] Minutes of Commission Juridique at Stockholm Conference, August 1948, no. 18382, ICRC Library.

[132] Memo Clattenburg on ICRC role at Stockholm Conference, 15 September 1948, no. Series 22, RG 43–5536, NARA; and Memo Clattenburg on Plenary Sessions of the Legal Commission, 26 November 1948, no. Series 22, RG 43–5536, NARA.

[133] Clattenburg criticized the ICRC's "reluctance to contemplate the fact that a future war [...] will not be one of a character in which [it] can operate successfully." Memo Clattenburg on ICRC role at Stockholm Conference, 15 September 1948, no. Series 22, RG 43–5536, NARA.

[134] Wylie and Crossland, "The Korean War and the Post-war Prisoners of War Regime, 1945–1956," 9. US representatives noticed how the ICRC had removed the reference to the "competent international

helped to prevent these proposals from being accepted by the conference.[135] Given that another French amendment challenging the ICRC's position was defeated, delegates left the interrelated questions of substitutes and Protecting Powers unresolved.[136]

Despite failing to figure out the riddles of supervision, the Stockholm delegates did accept many of the ICRC's proposals for inquiry. They were assured that state sovereignty would be safe under these plans. Rather than forcing delegates to accept an investigative agency on a permanent basis, these proposals merely recommended ad hoc commissions whose findings were not necessarily binding. Thanks to this cautious approach, this set of ideas emerged from Stockholm almost unscathed. Although far from perfect, these proposals had some advantages, one being that states would have the right to request an investigation even if one of the parties would not immediately agree to it.[137]

The ICRC's immediate response to this part of the Stockholm meeting's outcome was still disappointment, given that it produced only weak sovereign-friendly results with respect to criminal repression and, to some extent, inquiry too. In preparing for the diplomatic conference, it made several suggestions for improvement in these areas so as to make the reports produced by future inquiry committees binding on every party. Despite Pictet's initial reservations, it also forced states to punish those considered guilty of violations.[138] Indeed, his drafting team became increasingly focused on repression as a key organizing principle for enforcement, as against traditional ICRC approaches such as conciliation. Given the growing resistance offered by the US hegemon, the ICRC's turn toward criminal repression posed significant risks for its own position and its core principles, not to mention for the drafting process it was leading as chief revisor of the Conventions.

To discuss the question of criminal repression ahead of the diplomatic conference, Pictet's drafting team invited four international legal experts—Mouton, Lauterpacht, Phillimore, and Jean Graven—to Geneva in December 1948. These men (the possibility of inviting female experts was not even considered) were chosen on account of their expertise in international criminal

---

body" in order to prevent any "alteration of the structure of the Committee itself." Memo Clattenburg on ICRC role at Stockholm Conference, 15 September 1948, no. Series 22, RG 43–5536, NARA.

[135] Wylie and Crossland, "The Korean War and the Post-War Prisoners of War Regime, 1945–1956," 9.
[136] Note on Stockholm Conference, 3 September 1948, no. 159 - TER, Unions Internationales 1944–1960, LAD.
[137] Best, *War and Law since 1945*, 157.
[138] Remarks and Proposals submitted by the ICRC, 1949, ICRC Library; and Report Comité d'Experts, December 1948, CR-238-7, ACICR.

280 PREPARING FOR WAR

law and involvement in previous conferences. Like Lauterpacht, Mouton was a
"natural choice," for he remained a constant advocate of universal jurisdiction
and international courts as means of strengthening enforcement.[139] Because
of their belief that neutrals would play virtually no role in future "ideological"
wars and that reprisals were to be "absolutely" prohibited, these experts preferred criminal repression in enforcing these Conventions.[140]

Although he was not the ICRC's first choice, Jean Graven, the Swiss professor
of criminal law and member of the International Association of Penal Law
(IAPL) (before becoming its president in the 1960s), would play a key role in
this formative debate. Like Mouton and Lauterpacht, Graven was enthusiastic
about the idea of universal jurisdiction and endorsed the "revolution[ary]"
precedent of the Nuremberg trials (on which Lauterpacht had worked previously).[141] As a former reporter on the trials for Geneva's most important
newspaper,[142] Graven also wished to make violators of the Conventions individually responsible.[143] The British prosecutor Phillimore was another veteran
of the Nuremberg trials. As previously, in this debate he preferred trials to take
place following the end of hostilities, rather than during the war as the Soviets
had done at Kharkov (1943), for instance,[144] and to assure defendants of liberal safeguards to prevent them from being treated arbitrarily in future court
cases.[145]

In six meetings with these international criminal experts at its headquarters, the ICRC was represented by its most formidable legal experts, including
Pilloud, Pictet, Boissier, and Huber. The latter acted as the group's chairperson.
They set the meetings' agenda and sometimes voiced dissenting opinions. In
addition to developing a set of common articles, their shared objective was to
balance the two imperatives of punishing violators and protecting defendants
against unfair treatment.[146] The ICRC experts sought to turn the Conventions'

[139] Lewis, *The Birth of the New Justice*, 257.

[140] Report Comité d'Experts, December 1948, CR-238-7, ACICR.

[141] The ICRC had originally preferred Paul Logoz, a Swiss judge and ICRC member: Lewis, *The Birth of the New Justice*, 259. For the Graven quote, see Romane Laguel and Damien Scalia, "Jean Graven: Interdisciplinary and International Criminal Lawyer," in *The Dawn of a Discipline*, ed. Frédéric Mégret and Immi Tallgren (Cambridge: Cambridge University Press, 2020), 358–380, 366.

[142] Laguel and Scalia, "Jean Graven," 359, 367.

[143] Lewis, *The Birth of the New Justice*, 259; and Laguel and Scalia, "Jean Graven," 364.

[144] Franziska Exeler, "Nazi Atrocities, International Criminal Law, and War Crimes Trials: The Soviet Union and the Global Moment of Post-World War II Justice," in *The New Histories of International Criminal Law: Retrials*, ed. Immi Tallgren and Thomas Skouteris (Oxford: Oxford University Press, 2019), 189–219; and Tanja Penter, "Local Collaborators on Trial: Soviet War Crimes Trials under Stalin (1943–1953)," *Cahiers du monde russe*, Vol. 49, No. 2/3 (2008): 341–64. See also Valentyna Polunina, "The Khabarovsk Trial: The Soviet Riposte to the Tokyo Tribunal," in *Trials for International Crimes in Asia*, ed. Kirsten Sellars (Cambridge: Cambridge University Press, 2015), 121–145.

[145] Lewis, *The Birth of the New Justice*, 257.

[146] Report Comité d'Experts, December 1948, CR-238-7, ACICR.

penal provisions into a set of global standards for states to use as a model in drafting post-war criminal legislation. These standards would ensure several liberal safeguards for defendants in humanized war.[147]

The key figures in this debate were Lauterpacht, Mouton, Graven, Huber, Phillimore, and Pilloud; they were seen as the most knowledgeable experts of international criminal law in the room, if not the world. Their discussions came to center on five key issues: defining violations, grave breaches, universal jurisdiction, superior orders, and an international criminal court. Beginning with the latter, Graven keenly supported Mouton's proposal to reference an international court of this kind. Despite his skepticism about the Genocide Convention, the Swiss professor reminded his colleagues of its recent inclusion of such a reference in its text.[148] Pilloud, however, feared that such an allusion might clash directly with the ICRC's overarching wish to avoid any "intimate relationship" with the UN's work (for the UN's General Assembly had recently adopted the Genocide Convention). Concerned to avoid upsetting the Great Powers by interfering with the UN's efforts, Pilloud recommended "caution" in codifying Mouton's proposal.

At the same time, Graven worried that if Mouton's proposal was rejected then the only remaining path for criminal repression would be that of national tribunals. Recalling the Leipzig Trials' failure to punish German war criminals after the First World War, he tried to convince his colleagues to opt in favor of the proposal.[149] Others, however, worried that Mouton's idea might reduce prosecutors' effectiveness in the long run. For example, Lauterpacht voiced the concern that an international court would be flooded with "hundreds of cases." To prevent this, he suggested appending a so-called neutral element (e.g. an ICRC delegate) to national courts to ensure their impartiality and effectiveness. Acting pragmatically, the drafters finally emphasized states' joint responsibility to repress violations of the Conventions, rejecting Mouton's proposal of referencing an international court.[150]

Another major point of controversy in the discussions related to Lauterpacht's suggestion that courts should not accept defendants' pleas of superior orders. This plan, which was based upon the 1945 London Charter (for which Lauterpacht had been consulted by Jackson), was opposed by

---

[147] Lewis, *The Birth of the New Justice*, 259.

[148] For his critique of the Genocide Convention, see Laguel and Scalia, "Jean Graven," 375–377.

[149] For a broader discussion of Graven's support for international courts, see ibid., 366–367.

[150] The drafters admitted that an international tribunals would "doubtless" be the best instrument to prosecute violations, but wondered whether it was realistic. Remarks and Proposals submitted by the ICRC, 1949, p. 21, ICRC Library.

282 PREPARING FOR WAR

Phillimore, Lauterpacht's former colleague.[151] Having worked on Britain's prosecuting team at Nuremberg, he cautioned that superior orders were sometimes tolerated as an excuse in different penal systems. Moreover, Boissier argued that Lauterpacht's proposal further undermined the accused's already precarious position in his view. To underline this point, he even claimed that the punishment of German executioners of French partisans had been unfair on various grounds. One can imagine that Lauterpacht must have been taken aback by this apologetic assertion; some of his own family members had been killed by the Nazis.[152]

To strike a compromise, Graven and Huber made several alterations to Lauterpacht's original proposal, accepting certain situations in which mitigating circumstances obtained.[153] Another hotly debated issue was Graven's suggestion that they design a web of universal jurisdiction: he proposed several Nuremberg principles, including individual criminal responsibility. Despite Pilloud's warning that no victor would ever accept universal jurisdiction except for dealing with the vanquished, these proposals received widespread support, creating a legal breakthrough.[154] Among other achievements, Graven attained the promise that states would be forced to punish violators, allow trials to occur (even if they were far from the original site of the violation), facilitate extradition and prosecute even those who could not be extradited. Despite pushback against these proposals, Graven successfully convinced his partners to add several layers of universal jurisdiction on top of the framework of national tribunals that had previously been agreed upon.

Still, the drafters continued to circle around two questions fundamental to humanitarian law's criminological future: what actually constituted a violation of the Conventions? And upon which legal principles should such an understanding of contravention be based? For Lauterpacht, who fused human rights thinking with ideas of criminal repression, a violation extended to any act in wartime causing serious bodily harm or deprivation of liberty. Such misdeeds amount to war crimes, he argued. For Huber, the criterion had to be the degradation of the human personality. In emphasizing this point, he aligned with Lauterpacht's human rights thinking, as well as that of Graven.[155] To

---

[151] Katherine O'Byrne and Philippe Sands, "Trial before the International Military Tribunal at Nuremberg (1945–46)," in *Landmark Cases in Public International Law*, ed. Eirik Bjorge and Cameron Miles (London: Hart Publishing, 2017), 189–220, 201.

[152] Report Comité d'Experts, December 1948, CR-238-7, ACICR.

[153] Remarks and Proposals submitted by the ICRC, 1949, p. 19, ICRC Library, 1949.

[154] Report Comité d'Experts, December 1948, CR-238-7, ACICR.

[155] Laguel and Scalia, "Jean Graven," 363, 374. Here I diverge from the widespread belief that "international criminal law, humanitarian law, and human rights were still separate domains at this point in history": Lewis, *The Birth of the New Justice*, 267.

establish these ideas in law, Huber even suggested that the final act of the future Conventions was to imply covering violations of other treaties relating to the laws of war (e.g. the 1907 Hague Regulations).[156]

This surprisingly daring plan to cover rules regarding air bombing, in particular, was put forward by one of the most cautious ICRC experts. Still, Huber believed that the future repression chapter could not be limited to acts other than aerial bombardment. Unlike Mouton, who drew a different lesson from their shared experience of having been exposed to the threat of enemy bombing, Lauterpacht disagreed with Huber's suggestion on the grounds that strategic bombing could not be considered a war crime. This indicates the limitations of Cantabrigian human rights thinking. However, Ruegger, the ICRC president, believed that Huber's proposal might be "unexpectedly successful" if it were proposed at the future diplomatic conference, noting how a separate proposal at a 1925 arms trafficking meeting had ultimately led to the banning of gas weaponry in wartime. Despite being unwilling to codify Huber's plan, the group did agree to allude to it in the margins of preliminary documents shared among the diplomatic drafters of 1949.[157]

The question remained as to what constituted a violation of the Conventions and whether one should distinguish between so-called major and minor violations—the former being prosecutable, the latter not necessarily so. Some wondered whether they should refer not to violations but instead to war crimes, to underline the Nuremberg judgment. Although Lauterpacht continued to speak the trials' language of war crimes, Pilloud defended the decision to remove these words at the Government Experts' Conference in 1947. Indeed, he opposed any attempt to include this language of war crimes in future texts. To find a compromise between these positions, Graven and Phillimore came up with a new organizing principle for criminal sanctions, coining the famous phrase "grave breaches."

The final remaining question to be agreed upon, then, was that of which acts constituted a grave breach of the Conventions. To what extent does employing POWs in the war effort by the enemy violate the Conventions to a criminal level? Should rape be criminalized specifically (the final text remained silent about this)? At what point does the bombing of cities cross the threshold of legal gravity? While having no qualms about excluding partisans, Phillimore asked whether the "moral torture" inflicted on families as a result of them being uninformed about loved ones in captivity can be seen as a grave breach

---

[156] Report Comité d'Experts, December 1948, CR-238-7, ACICR.
[157] Remarks and Proposals submitted by the ICRC, 1949, pp. 22–23, ICRC Library. 1949.

284 PREPARING FOR WAR

(he thought that it could). Others feared that defining a grave breach would unintentionally suggest tolerance of "minor violations," despite the serious bodily harm these might cause. For this reason, the drafters deliberately silenced all talk about specific examples of "minor" breaches and made sure that the mirroring notion of "grave" breaches was sufficiently broad as to allow judges to interpret it in a potentially humane fashion.

After dozens of hours deliberating these points, the group emerged with four legally revolutionary common articles, which gave rise to a whole new system of criminal repression for the Conventions. This unique framework had its origins in a range of different principles, from universal jurisdiction, through human rights thinking, to contrasting notions of state sovereignty. Whereas the language of war crimes was deliberately left out, the drafters did adopt several Nuremberg principles, such as the refusal to accept arguments pertaining to superior orders. In addition to this, they gave national courts priority over international ones, while forcing states to extradite persons accused of grave breaches. They argued that no defendant could be easily stripped of their rights.[158] Given that the ICRC, as a non-governmental organization, could not introduce these proposals at the diplomatic conference, Mouton convinced his own delegation to present them at the relevant session in Geneva.

6.4 Geneva's Endgame

US delegates at the diplomatic conference in 1949 were shocked by the proposals. It was said that Yingling was not amused by his allies' "sharp practice." He tried to use the late introduction of these texts as an excuse to call the relevant amendment out of order.[159] At some point, the US delegation even threatened to refuse to sign the Conventions if those proposals were adopted by the conference.[160] As Washington had instructed its members to undermine the Stockholm proposals for enforcement in key areas, Yingling was determined to defeat these attempts to codify the Nuremberg principles. Whereas most drafters attending the meeting saw these post-war trials as a formative moment in the history of international law, the influential US delegate held the opposite view. Yingling placed far more emphasis on the dangers that they allegedly

---

[158] Lewis, *The Birth of the New Justice*, 261; and Best, *War and Law since 1945*, 161.

[159] Cable Yingling to State Department on Article 119, no. 5, RG43 - 40, NARA.

[160] Cable Yingling to State Department on Article 119, May 1949, no. 5, RG43 - 40, NARA; and Final Report Craigie, November 1949, no. 4164, FO369 (Foreign Office), TNA.

posed. Above all, his delegation was interested in protecting US sovereign power from outside interference.

Robert Quentin-Baxter, the former assistant of the New Zealand judge at the Tokyo trials, felt that Yingling was trying to undermine the ICRC's proposals by "denying the authority of the Nuremberg and Tokyo judgments."[161] In private conversations, the US delegate apparently told the New Zealander delegate "quite frankly" that he "was, and had always been, opposed to the holding of war trials." Expressing regret about his country's involvement in Nuremberg after his experiences as the State Department's legal advisor for the occupied areas, Yingling insisted that the Conventions "should contain no provision which acknowledged [...] the authority of the Nuremberg judgment." Quentin-Baxter believed it would have been wiser if his US allies had not espoused such views, given the central role that they had played in the Nuremberg trials.[162]

Despite also having been a key player in the Nuremberg trials, the UK government had also instructed its delegation to "resist any reference to [...] war crimes."[163] The War Office called the ICRC proposals "completely unacceptable." Its officials advised the British Cabinet to consider the matter carefully. The Conventions, the War Office argued, must not be extended to cover "every isolated misdeed [such as the] extensive destruction to property [i.e. from air bombing: BvD]."[164] Following this advice, Attlee's Cabinet instructed its delegation to "oppose any reference [...] to war crimes." Still, it would be allowed to accept some of the Nuremberg principles such as individual criminal responsibility, though only if it was pressed. The delegation was not to lose sight of the bigger picture—of protecting Britain's sovereignty, if not the integrity of its municipal laws.[165]

The British delegation was forced to change its strategy, however: not only did the conference accept the ICRC proposals for discussion, but both Britain and the US feared that the Soviets might exploit this opportunity to spread Cold War propaganda.[166] As in earlier drafting debates, their approach was to "to render [these ICRC proposals] as innocuous as possible."[167] Shawcross, the

---

[161] As noted before, the New Zealand report is not signed by any New Zealand official. However, considering its style and expertise, it is most likely written by Quentin-Baxter. Report of New Zealand Delegation to Diplomatic Conference of Geneva 1949, AAYS 8638 W2054 ADW2054/1220/3/3 (R18524114), Archives New Zealand (ANZ), Wellington.

[162] Ibid.

[163] Memorandum by the Secretary of State for Foreign Affairs and the Secretary of State for War, 10 March 1949, no. 33, CAB129 (Cabinet Office), TNA.

[164] Report War Office on Grave Breaches Proposals, 25 March 1949, no. 4147, FO369, TNA.

[165] Minutes of Cabinet Meeting on War Crimes, 28 March 1949, no. 14041, WO32 (War Office), TNA.

[166] Notes on Meeting UK Delegation, 5 May 1949, no. 4151, FO369, TNA. See also Cable on Dutch Proposal, 17 June 1949, no. Series 619 - B - 40, RG 25 - Vol. 3398, LAC.

[167] Final Report Diplomatic Conference, 1949, no. 6036, ADM116 (Admiralty), TNA.

286 PREPARING FOR WAR

former prosecutor at Nuremberg and now Attorney-General of the UK, made several alterations to the proposed texts so as to make them more acceptable to his government.[168] In so doing, he advised the UK delegation in Geneva to look more closely at the "gutted" text of the Genocide Convention for inspiration in revising the ICRC's proposals.[169] In this way, he hoped to prevent them from doing further damage to Britain's sovereign power.

While the Anglo-American delegations were exploring ways of countering the ICRC's efforts to break their sovereign power, the French sat on the fence. While awaiting new instructions from Paris, Lamarle's delegation reserved its view on the grave breaches plan and tried to prevent further tensions with Anglo-American allies. As the chapter goes on to show, at this stage the French were primarily interested in obtaining the conference's support for their proposals with regard to supervision (and other questions discussed in previous chapters).[170] Given the French's initial lack of interest, the grave breaches debate was handled privately among members of the UK, US, and Dutch delegations. In these negotiations behind closed doors, Mouton played a key role in trying to reconcile his Anglo-American counterparts' regressive position with the support shown by the Western European bloc, which demanded more powerful instruments against grave breaches.[171]

Mouton felt that the International Law Commission (ILC) was making "very slow progress and [...] unlikely to produce anything for some years to come."[172] He also expected that the UN would remain deadlocked as a result of East–West tensions. For these reasons, he sought to force states to accept at least some obligations with regard to criminal repression.[173] At Shawcross's suggestion, the new proposals that emerged from these backdoor negotiations drew inspiration from the restrictive model of the Genocide Convention. As such, they aimed to restore the state's sovereign powers in several key ways.

Despite these compromises, Mouton did maintain several elements of the original ICRC proposals. The composite solution referenced contested concepts such as the ban against superior orders, or even an international court.

---

[168] Opinion Attorney-General on War Crimes, 11 April 1949, no. 4147, FO369, TNA.

[169] The term "gutted" comes from Adam Weiss Wendt's fascinating book. Adam Weiss-Wendt, *The Soviet Union and the Gutting of the UN Genocide Convention* (Madison: University of Wisconsin Press, 2017).

[170] Cable Lamarle on Violations of the Conventions, 4 May 1949, no. 161, Unions Internationales 1944–1960, LAD.

[171] Van Dijk, "The Guardians."

[172] Mouton made this claim in part because he wished to challenge the premise behind the Anglo-American argument pointing to the ILC as a better forum for dealing with war crimes than the Conventions' revision process. Best, *War and Law since 1945*, 159.

[173] Minutes of Meeting Craigie and Mouton on the Question of War Crimes, 5 May 1949, no. 4149, FO369, TNA and Van Dijk, "The Guardians."

The latter proposal was dropped, however, following resistance from Yingling, who fiercely opposed any suggestion of universal jurisdiction.[174] Mouton's proposals prompted criticism from UK government officials too. The War Office reacted furiously to his suggestion that acts such as the "unlawful extensive destruction of property" should be criminalized. Acting as its central delegate in Geneva, Gardner was shocked, having been left entirely in the dark by the Foreign Office negotiator. He wished to make a reservation to the Conventions if these proposals were adopted.[175] Like other War Office delegates, he feared that the criminological innovations would seriously damage Britain's bombing capability and "impose great handicaps on [our] military commanders."

Foreign Office delegates were much less alarmed, however. Unlike their War Office colleagues, they believed that Mouton's plans represented a "standard of decent conduct [recognized by all] civilized nations [such as Britain]."[176] Given her idea of Britain as a "civilized" nation trying to abide by international legal standards, and that nations other than Britain would commit grave breaches, Gutteridge felt duty bound to endorse the proposals. She also realized that a majority of the conference might favor large parts of Mouton's suggestions.[177] For these reasons, Foreign Office delegates were willing to take them more seriously than their War Office colleagues. Weeks of lonely resistance to various proposals in favor of strengthening the Conventions had severely damaged the UK delegation's reputation among allies in Geneva. Striking a compromise, the Foreign Office and its delegates hoped, might prevent further damage to its already precarious position.

Subverting Mouton's Proposals

With the UK General Staff wanting to have nothing "included in the Conventions which would restrict [the] freedom to carry out [its] operations, particularly bombing,"[178] Foreign Office negotiators had no choice but to return to the drafting table. Ultimately they were able to convince Mouton to make several alterations to his original proposals by taking the Genocide

---

[174] Cable Yingling to State Department on Dutch Proposal, 16 May 1949, no. 5, RG43 - 40, NARA and Cable Yingling on Dutch Proposal, 21 May 1949, no. 5, RG43 - 40, NARA.

[175] Correspondence on Sanctions, 3–16 June 1949, no. 46, CAB130, TNA; and Minutes Meeting UK Delegation, 3 June 1949, no. 4153, FO369, TNA.

[176] Minutes Meeting UK Delegation, 3 June 1949, no. 4153, FO369, TNA.

[177] For Britain's similar reasoning in relation to the Genocide Convention—"to save its prestige and accommodate public opinion"—see Lewis, *The Birth of the New Justice*, 186.

[178] Correspondence on Sanctions, 3–16 June 1949, no. 46, CAB130, TNA.

288 PREPARING FOR WAR

Convention's more restrictive outlook as a model. The resulting text was introduced to the Special Committee in late June 1949. It scrapped several references to universal jurisdiction, superior orders, and those parts with the potential to restrict the use of air bombing.[179] Moreover, it significantly shortened the list of grave breaches, removing references to acts such as dangerous work (to please the War Office) and transferring persons in fear of persecution (to prevent the UK from being prosecuted for deporting Soviet citizens after 1945, as had been agreed at Yalta).[180]

Craigie reported to London that his delegation had "succeeded [...] in securing omission from [the] list of grave breaches of all those points to which [the] War Office see objection[s] except that relating to destruction of property for which there appears to be wide support." Still, this wording was significantly curtailed by its revision into "unlawful, wanton and extensive destruction of property, not justified by military necessity." This prevented any threat to Britain's air bombing capability. "It is difficult to see," he argued, "how this definition could be held to interfere with bombing."[181] The new text also carefully avoided any reference to "crimes" that the Soviets had wished to see codified.[182]

Moscow's instructions with regard to criminal repression had largely focused on the Stockholm drafts, though with some important reservations. Influenced by the legal advice of Morosov, who had acted as a member of the Soviet delegation at the Tokyo trials, the Soviets aimed to replace the vocabulary of "breaches" with that of "crimes" so as to affirm Soviet legal orthodoxy while also recognizing the seriousness of violating these Conventions.[183] They also asked for a two-year deadline by which states had to incorporate these new criminal provisions into their domestic legislation. This was resisted by most liberal states, in part because the deadline would be extremely difficult to meet—and they knew that it would force them to speed up their slow ratification procedures, as we will see in the next chapter. Both Soviet proposals, therefore, were quickly defeated by a wide margin.

A similar fate awaited another Soviet proposal, which suggested that enemy soldiers considered "war criminals" should not be protected as POWs but rather should be seen as liable to punishment. In many ways, this idea directly threatened the liberal safeguards promoted by the ICRC and Lauterpacht's

---

[179] Van Dijk, "The Guardians."
[180] Final Report Craigie, November 1949, no. 4164, FO369, TNA.
[181] Van Dijk, "The Guardians."
[182] Best, *War and Law since 1945*, 163.
[183] The Western powers opposed many of these Soviet plans for both political and legal reasons. For instance, the notion of war crimes had different meanings on opposite sides of the Iron Curtain. Best, *War and Law since 1945*, 158; and Lewis, *The Birth of the New Justice*, 268–269.

Committee.[184] Moreover, Anglo-American officials voiced concern that it might jeopardize the safety of their own bomber pilots, for the Soviet proposal "might afford a pretext enabling a belligerent [e.g. the Soviet Union] to treat as war criminals members of the armed forces who [...] took part in bombing raids on cities."[185] The proposal was quickly defeated by the Western powers, prompting the Soviets to repeat that the West was too soft on war criminals.[186]

The most inflammatory suggestion put forward by the Soviets was to extend Mouton's list of grave breaches through the addition of a new clause criminalizing the "extermination of civilian populations," an indirect reference to air and atomic bombing. In putting forward this proposal, the Soviet delegation tried to embarrass its Anglo-American adversaries publicly by turning Geneva into a diplomatic battleground of the Cold War. In so doing, the Soviets assumed the "great humanitarian" role, presenting far-reaching proposals that could neither be agreed by their opponents nor even be implemented by their own officials. Following the defeat of this proposal (which would have criminalized various acts, including indiscriminate bombing), the Soviets shifted their strategy. Now, they sought to ban the use of atomic bombs almost entirely (see Chapter 5).[187]

Still, it would be wrong to suggest that the Soviets were working in an entirely different legal atmosphere from their Western counterparts. Crucially, both sides meant to protect their sovereignty from outside interference, and accordingly they preferred to codify national tribunals, domestic jurisdiction, and national penal codes. The Soviets opposed any suggestion that their own political prisoners might be included under the Conventions or that an international criminal court might be established along the lines envisaged by Mouton. The Soviets saw the Nuremberg trials as an exception, not the rule for future international law. This regressive view resonated with their earlier opposition to internationalization during the making of the Genocide Convention and the Soviet Union's broader legal orthodoxy on the issue.[188]

The final text that emerged from the delegates' debate on criminal repression was significantly restricted as compared to Mouton's original proposals. Still, Anglo-American delegates were far from pleased about the result, accepting it only "unwillingly."[189] Despite their disappointment, they had nonetheless

---

[184] Van Dijk, "The Great Humanitarian," 225.
[185] Report of New Zealand Delegation to Diplomatic Conference of Geneva 1949, AAYS 8638 W2054 ADW2054/1220/3/3 (R18524114), ANZ.
[186] Lewis, *The Birth of the New Justice*, 268.
[187] Van Dijk, "The Great Humanitarian," 227–228.
[188] Lewis, *The Birth of the New Justice*, 212.
[189] Minutes Prisoners of War Committee, 27 October 1949, Provost Marshal General, no. 673 - Part I, NARA.

290   PREPARING FOR WAR

succeeded in protecting key areas of their sovereignty through making several informal deals with other delegations. The outcome of the conference also disappointed many liberal observers, both within and outside Switzerland.[190] Neither side was entirely pleased about the final text,[191] which shows that it appeared a bad compromise: it spoke the language of universal jurisdiction without placing serious restraints on state sovereignty.

The fact that the system of grave breaches did not make "much practical difference during the Cold War" only bolsters this skeptical view. Having said that, Pilloud's fears—that the ICRC's original proposals for criminal repression might have to be sacrificed to keep the Great Powers on board or that they would interfere with the ILC's efforts to codify the Nuremberg judgment—proved unfounded. The question remains, however, whether pleasing the powerful has been the best strategy for developing criminal law provisions in light of the ambiguous outcome reached in August 1949.[192]

Protecting Powers, Inquiry, Conciliation, and Dissemination

The final puzzle that drafters had to solve was how to codify an area of enforcement that had taken a notoriously long time to develop—that is, supervision. The French delegation, for whom supervision was "absolument indispensable," tried to empower inspectors, such as they would be able to properly enforce the Conventions.[193] This effort was shaped by several considerations: that of securing the safety of future French POWs; preventing the repetition of the Vichy scenario, in which Protecting Powers had been sidelined; anticipating a continuing Soviet boycott of the ICRC; and the possibility of a new war in which there were no neutral Protecting Powers left.[194] To meet these various challenges, the French demanded a more rigorous system of supervision with stronger substitutes and less sovereign discretion, so as to prevent the reemergence of legal black holes in wartime.

Whereas the French were keen on empowering supervisors in exchange for sacrificing their own sovereign power—except for its colonial implications,

---

[190] Gazette de Lausanne, 13 July 1949. For the informal dealmaking with Greek and Italian delegates, see Letter Alexander to Beckett, 5 July 1949, no. 4156, FO369, TNA.

[191] To give one example, the Canadian delegation had "no enthusiasm for this compromise text and abstained in the final vote." Report of Canadian Delegation to Geneva Conference, 1949, no. 112-20, RG 19 - Vol. 480, LAC.

[192] Lewis, *The Birth of the New Justice*, 267–269.

[193] Instructions French Foreign Minister for French Delegation, 14 April 1949, no. 161, Unions Internationales 1944–1960, LAD.

[194] Levie, "Prisoners of War and the Protecting Power," 35.

PREPARING FOR THE WORST   291

other Great Powers were primarily interested in keeping their sovereignty intact. British delegates disapproved of those proposals that placed binding and significant restrictions on their sovereignty and burdened the Protecting Powers with numerous tasks (the latter concern was shared by Petitpierre himself).[195] They feared that these plans would severely undermine the existing system of (ICRC) supervision, which they felt had done its job during the war in protecting British assets and subjects.[196] In particular, War Office delegates feared that the proposals might enable supervisors to operate close to the frontline, thereby undermining Britain's military operations through revealing confidential information. To prevent this, Gardner again hinted that if curious Protecting Powers could not be kept away from the future battlefield then the UK delegation might make another reservation to the Conventions.[197]

Despite its fierce resistance to empowering supervision, the UK delegation did not voice support for the Soviet proposal, which would have shut out Protecting Powers for reasons of "security," that is, to stop them infringing upon state sovereignty.[198] Although he shared many of the Soviets' concerns, Craigie believed these plans would "prevent a Protecting Power [from] functioning at all."[199] Like his Foreign Office colleague Gutteridge, Craigie feared for his delegation's reputation should other delegations have the impression that it was standing in the way of a broad post-war consensus in favor of empowering supervision. Australian allies called out the dubious intent behind the destructive Soviet proposals. Describing their experiences as a former Protecting Power for Poland during the Soviet occupation, they recalled how an "unscrupulous power" had closed the door on "security" grounds. In light of this the British had no choice but to oppose the Soviet plan, which led to its rejection by the conference.[200]

In the meantime, ICRC delegate Pilloud had noticed how the Soviet delegation was essentially in favor of the Stockholm drafts, save for those parts that

---

[195] Minutes Meeting UK Delegation, 20 April 1949, no. 4151, FO369, TNA.

[196] The UK delegation ultimately recognized the ICRC as a "responsible, independent, impartial and efficacious instrument" for enforcing the Conventions. See Report Craigie on Common Articles, 7 October 1949, no. 6036, ADM116, TNA; and Note Jean Duchosal for Ruegger on Lunch with Gardner, 31 May 1949, no. CR-238-9, ACICR.

[197] Report War Office Delegates, October 1949, no. 13038, WO32, TNA.

[198] Wylie and Crossland, "The Korean War and the Post-War Prisoners of War Regime, 1945–1956," 6, 10.

[199] Interim Report UK Delegation, 22 June 1949, no. 4154, FO369, TNA. Like the Foreign Office, the US State Department drew from the experience of the Second World War that Protecting Powers were "an essential feature" in the observance of the Geneva Conventions: Franklin, *Protection of Foreign Interests*, 228.

[200] Report Joint Committee on Common Articles, no. series A1838, 1481/1A Part 7, National Archives of Australia (NAA), Canberra, ACT.

292 PREPARING FOR WAR

related to Protecting Powers.[201] Soviet opposition boiled down to three key issues: whether Protecting Powers could operate on Soviet territory; who could act as its substitute; and who could decide upon all of this.[202] The Soviet delegation staunchly defended state sovereignty in wartime, aggressively opposing any suggestion that Protecting Powers might be strengthened. This immediately triggered concern among Western delegations. They were said to be worried that the Soviets might table more aggressive motions in other debates that were vital to Western interests (such as that on guerrilla warfare) or even, in the most extreme case, walk out of the conference. Losing Soviet involvement, Pilloud feared, would have potentially catastrophic consequences for the future of the Conventions and that of the ICRC and their Swiss hosts.[203]

These Western concerns came to a head when the French delegate Cahen-Salvador readdressed his delegation's old plan to fully internationalize the system of substitutes by establishing a so-called high international committee. This new body was to be composed of thirty "distinguished" experts.[204] It was said to be modeled on parts of the 1934 Monaco Draft,[205] and on the Board of Governors of the League of Red Cross Societies, in which the Soviets had participated. Paradoxically, this French attempt to convince the Soviets to get on board with external supervision only strengthened their opposition to it. The French offer to replace the ICRC with the proposed high international committee also failed to interest the Soviet delegation. In fact, the latter did not back any of these initiatives, all of which aimed to prop up the system of Protecting Powers.[206]

It is important to remember, though, that the Soviets were hardly the only critics of Cahen-Salvador's plan to create an internationalized substitute. Nor was this the only plan threatening the ICRC's position as a neutral inspector. Red Cross Societies had previously suggested a whole range of plans for internationalizing or diversifying the composition of the ICRC so as to strengthen its overall appeal as a supervisory body in humanized war.[207] In private, the

[201] Conference Diplomatique. Rapport Spécial Etabli par Pilloud, 16 September 1949, no. CR-254-1, ACICR.
[202] Wylie and Crossland, "The Korean War and the Post-War Prisoners of War Regime, 1945–1956," 10.
[203] Wylie and Crossland, "The Korean War and the Post-War Prisoners of War Regime, 1945–1956," 10–11.
[204] Best, *War and Law since 1945*, 154.
[205] Quite insightfully, de La Pradelle later compared the concept to the Schuman Plan placing Franco-German steel and coal production under a higher authority: de La Pradelle, *La Conférence Diplomatique*, 8, 232.
[206] Wylie and Crossland, "The Korean War and the Post-War Prisoners of War Regime, 1945–1956," 7–8; and Instructions French Foreign Minister for French Delegation, 14 April 1949, no. 161, Unions Internationales 1944–1960, LAD.
[207] Wylie and Crossland, "The Korean War and the Post-war Prisoners of War Regime, 1945–1956," 8.

ICRC vehemently opposed these proposals out of fear of losing its leading role in supervising adherence to the Conventions. The Swiss delegation too feared that in diminishing the most important Swiss humanitarian actor on the global stage, these plans might undermine their vital national interests.[208] As a former Protecting Power, the Australians also opposed Cahen-Salvador's proposal, which they called "completely impracticable."[209]

As the world's hegemon, the US had the decisive voice in this debate concerning external supervision. If it backed the French plan, then the ICRC's future might be at stake; if it did not, then its French allies would be humiliated. This poignant dilemma was made easier, however, by the fact that Yingling felt that the proposed system was "impracticable."[210] The plan raised difficult questions about how this new international body was to be composed, where it would be located, and how it was to be financed. Nor was it entirely clear whether it could actually operate in practice. With concerns proliferating, Anglo-American delegates persuaded their French allies to withdraw their draft article in favor of a non-binding resolution, which would allow them to save face. This latter resolution would merely recommend that states discuss the high international committee plan through regular diplomatic channels once the conference was over. The resolution was accepted.[211]

With the eventual collapse of the idea of the international high committee,[212] the only remaining hope for advocates of enhanced supervision was the Stockholm text for substitutes. To their disappointment, the two Cold War superpowers both opposed any serious restrictions on their sovereignty when it came to choosing which substitute to accept. Some delegates tried to push back, reintroducing the old system of tripartite consent and forcing states to accept proposed substitutes. Nevertheless, "everybody [...] recognized that this [was] no more than a pious hope."[213] The Soviets eventually even made a reservation to the final version of this article for substitutes, both out of concern about their sovereignty and because of the fact that the ICRC was considered

---

[208] Minutes Meeting UK Delegation, 2 July 1949, no. 4157, FO369, TNA.

[209] Report Joint Committee on Common Articles, no. series A1838, 1481/1A Part 7, National Archives of Australia (NAA), Canberra, ACT.

[210] Minutes Prisoners of War Committee, 18 July 1950, Provost Marshal General, no. 673 - Part I, NARA.

[211] Report Craigie on Common Articles, 7 October 1949, no. 6036, ADM116, TNA.

[212] After the diplomatic conference, US government officials discussed the French plan to finally establish a new high international supervisory committee. In the end, Washington killed the plan, fearing it would undermine the ICRC's position. It also considered the UN as a potential substitute of last resort in case of communist resistance. Minutes Prisoners of War Committee, 18 July 1950, Provost Marshal General, no. 673 - PART I, NARA; and Memo French Embassy to State Department, 26 April 1950, Provost Marshal General, no. 673 - PART I, NARA.

[213] Report War Office Delegates, October 1949, no. 13038, WO32, TNA.

294 PREPARING FOR WAR

the substitute of last resort.[214] This system of substitutes died at birth; it never became fully operational during the Cold War.[215]

Reflecting upon the broader outcome of the debate regarding supervision, advocates of international inspectors admitted that the final text did not meet their expectations. As one drafter wrote, the Protecting Power—or the substitute that took its place—could not "dictate [nor] supervise; it [could] only observe, recommend and report."[216] It required the state's agreement every step of the way.[217] The Civilian Convention's security clause further undermined the position of Protecting Powers (see Chapter 4), enabling states to place protected persons temporarily beyond the supervisor's radar on the grounds that they might pose severe security concerns in interstate wartime. This deeply concerned ICRC legal experts, who were worried about prisoners' rights and their own position as future inspectors in armed conflict. Given that the success of the Conventions depended on their supervision and that socialist states had rejected Protecting Powers, Pilloud's colleagues realized that the prospects looked bleak.

What, then, could still promote compliance on the battlefield?, the drafters asked. One remaining option for fighting impunity on the battlefield was inquiry. The ICRC had originally proposed that reports made by inquiry commissions should be binding on states, forcing them to comply with the findings. This would have to lead in turn to the punishment of those considered guilty of grave breaches.[218] None of the Great Powers, however, would accept any binding inquiry procedure for humanized war, even though the US government had originally proposed a similar idea in the 1920s.[219] The text that they finally accepted was virtually the same as the existing one in the 1929 Convention, which, as Craigie later admitted, could be easily "circumvented by [...] refusing to agree upon an umpire." The leader of the UK delegation was also said to be relieved that his government could never be forced to consent to any inquiry procedure.[220]

---

[214] When the Vatican suggested becoming the substitute of last resort, the British delegation appreciated the idea but said euphemistically that they were "afraid [that] it would not recommend itself to the USSR and its satellites." Minutes Meeting with Papal Nuncio, 5 May 1949, no. 4151, FO369.

[215] De La Pradelle, *La Conférence Diplomatique*, 346.

[216] Report of New Zealand Delegation to Diplomatic Conference of Geneva 1949, AAYS 8638 W2054 ADW2054/1220/3/3 (R18524114), ANZ.

[217] Draper, "The Implementation of the Modern Law of Armed Conflicts," 13.

[218] Remarks and Proposals submitted by the ICRC, 1949, ICRC Library.

[219] Minutes Meeting UK Delegation, 18 June 1949, no. 4155, FO369, TNA. Representing the War Office, Gardner regarded these proposals for inquiry as "crying for the moon." Letter Gardner to Craigie, 13 January 1949, no. 4142, FO369. See also Wylie and Crossland, "The Korean War and the Post-War Prisoners of War Regime, 1945–1956."

[220] Report Craigie on Common Articles, 7 October 1949, no. 6036, ADM116, TNA; and Final Report Craigie, November 1949, no. 4164, FO369 (Foreign Office), TNA.

Years of negotiations had led to this destructive outcome. Reflecting upon this, the Monegasque drafter De la Pradelle hoped to prevent enforcement from becoming a dead letter and save conciliation procedures from a similar fate. Beyond sharing his expertise, he was able to gather an influential coalition of likeminded drafters who wished to protect the procedures from annihilation by UK drafters. For instance, they defeated a British proposal to prevent states from being forced to meet in neutral territory to settle disputes over the application of the Conventions in wartime.[221] They were much less successful, however, in stopping the Danish delegation from promoting ICJ involvement in this context. Just as Lamarle and Yingling opposed this idea on practical grounds, noting that the ICJ had never met during the war, Gutteridge feared the court would never succeed in actually bringing enemies together in The Hague to resolve disputes over the Conventions.[222]

The most powerful opposition to the Danish proposal, however, came from the Soviet-aligned bloc.[223] As with the formation of the Genocide Convention, the Soviet delegation refused the ICJ's jurisdiction when it came to settling disputes over the law's application. In Geneva, they argued that this same plan was still "impracticable" because some states (Switzerland included) had not even signed up to the UN. In reality, they were determined to stop the Soviet Union being brought before a court dominated by non-communist judges. Immediately after the Soviets warned Western partners that they might not sign the Conventions if the Danish plan was adopted, the French suggested a compromise solution. They put forward a non-binding resolution that alleviated Soviet concerns, averting a walkout and thereby preserving the Conventions' future in the socialist world.[224]

6.5 Conclusion

After years of negotiations, drafters remade the Conventions' enforcement procedures in a remarkably contentious way. This process to promote compliance on the battlefield can be best understood as a struggle between two

---

[221] Report Craigie on Common Articles, 7 October 1949, no. 6036, ADM116, TNA.

[222] Minutes Meeting UK Delegation, 16 June 1949, no. 4155, FO369, TNA.

[223] Again, it is important to stress that that Soviet view was also shared by several Western actors. For example, the War Office was equally against reference to the ICJ in wartime. Final Report Craigie, November 1949, no. 4164, FO369 (Foreign Office), TNA.

[224] Report of Canadian Delegation to Geneva Conference, 1949, no. 112-20, RG 19 - Vol. 480, LAC; and Report Craigie on Common Articles, 7 October 1949, no. 6036, ADM116, TNA. Pradelle was pretty devastated about this outcome: Best, *War and Law since 1945*, 158.

296 PREPARING FOR WAR

powerful blocs and contrasting notions of sovereignty, rights, justice, and global governance. On one side was a diverse group of Soviet and Anglo-American delegates, who were concerned to oppose restraints on their sovereign power. On the other were the continental European powers plus the ICRC, which defended a far more robust system of enforcement. In various debates, they demanded Protecting Powers, substitutes, inquiry, criminal repression, and conciliation. However, both sides did agree on the premise that these principles should not be extended to colonial emergencies.[225] The outcome of the discussions, then, was a set of common articles that rested heavily on the will of the state.

Shifting from the years of post-war idealism to the cautious post-1948 period of Cold War skepticism, drafters adopted a text that emphasized the state's role in enforcing the Conventions. They diminished the impact of proposals aimed to establish binding inquiry and cement the jurisdiction of the ICJ. Furthermore, the work of international investigators of grave breaches was made virtually impossible.[226] Domestic jurisdiction was made the organizing principle for dealing with such violations. Overall, instead of strengthening the Conventions in response to the gross violations perpetrated in the Second World War, drafters weakened enforcement mechanisms in various areas to reconstruct their sovereign power in the wake of imperial breakdown.

The political demands of post-war reconstruction, decolonization, and the Cold War were often seen as more important than the moral imperative to learn lessons from the past. Drafters gave up on the issue of external inspectors out of fear of compromising the secrecy of military operations.[227] They decriminalized strategic bombing to allay Anglo-American concerns about losing their dominant air power, which was deemed critical in the face of Soviet dominance on land. They also allowed states to prosecute their own violators, despite the fiasco of the Leipzig Trials. By rendering "virtually non-existent" the obligation that states should extradite their own suspects,[228] drafters willingly accepted the risk of impunity. In recent times, the Nuremberg and Tokyo trials had shown that no state would ever prosecute their own perpetrators. These

---

[225] The Soviet position on this question remains ambiguous (see Chapter 3). On the ICRC: although the organization wished to make the principle of respect indirectly applicable to large-scale internal armed conflicts, it was unwilling to extend these to colonial emergencies of a "lower threshold" such as so-called low-intensity conflicts.

[226] Best, *War and Law since 1945*, 155–157.

[227] Pradelle agreed that the system of Protecting Powers would have little impact in the future: de La Pradelle, *La Conférence Diplomatique*, 346–347. Draper, "The Implementation of the Modern Law of Armed Conflicts," 13–14.

[228] Draper, "The Implementation of the Modern Law of Armed Conflicts," 22.

war crimes tribunals condemned neither Soviet aggression against Poland nor the atomic bombing of Hiroshima by US airmen.[229]

What can explain this limited and disappointing outcome? First, different historical factors account for why the two Cold War superpowers hardened their attitude toward enforcement midway through 1949.[230] Preparing for war, the US and Soviet Union prioritized their key interests over strengthening enforcement of the Conventions. As such, they bear primary responsibility for those drafting failures with regard to enforcement. Whereas the US wished to appease its military officials' concerns, the Soviets sought to protect their sovereignty in relation to their own carceral archipelago. In mediating between these two demands, these major Cold War enemies effectively pushed in a remarkably similar direction. They favored drafting formula that lacked accuracy and would secure maximum sovereign power in key areas, from inquiry to international courts.[231]

Second, the Anglo-American desire to privilege supervision over prosecution from 1948 onwards, combined with Soviet demands in the opposite direction, created a toxic legal cocktail. Given Soviet and postcolonial states' resistance to Protecting Powers and/or the ICRC, it was clear to most drafters that enhanced supervision was little more than a pipe dream.[232] The Protecting Powers were given countless tasks without having the actual ability to execute them effectively.[233] Inquiry inspectors, it was realized, would not be allowed to enter most states' territories. In giving the sovereign carte blanche, the most powerful states had turned key instruments for enforcing the Conventions into virtually useless tools—and that at the very moment they were needed the most, as violent decolonization and Cold War proxy wars were taking off.[234]

Contrary to what many scholars have argued, this restricted outcome did not come about because drafters had merely focused "on past experience, rather than to try to imagine new situations that may be presented in the future."[235] The historical record is far more subtle than this. Instead of looking just at the past, drafters incorporated the lessons they had learned into their projections about the future, as well as their disagreements over current affairs. The delegations fiercely disputed a wide variety of issues: inquiry, access to the

---

[229] Lewis, *The Birth of the New Justice*, 183.
[230] Ibid., 226.
[231] De La Pradelle, *La Conférence Diplomatique*, 222.
[232] Draper, "The Implementation of the Modern Law of Armed Conflicts," 14; Mantilla, "The Origins and Evolution of the 1949 Geneva Conventions," 47.
[233] Best, *War and Law since 1945*, 149–150.
[234] Roberts, "The Laws of War: Problems of Implementation in Contemporary Conflicts," 30.
[235] Georges Abi-Saab, "Le Renforcement du Système d'Application des Régles du Droit Humanitaire," *Military Law and Law of War Review*, Vol. 12, No. 2 (1973): 223–240, 227.

298 PREPARING FOR WAR

battlefield, talking with POWs without witnesses, and so on. Drawing historical conclusions on the basis of past experiences, they placed these in a larger
perspective that was shaped by considerations regarding national sovereignty,
the Cold War, and decolonization. As we saw in previous chapters, the process
of drafting the law was as much a struggle among claims concerning the past,
present, and future as it was a competition over ideas, power, and influence.

These struggles were particularly intense when it came to the question of enforcement. Indeed, it is far from an exaggeration to say that in no other debate
did power and ideas clash so fiercely. Far from being seen as two sides of the
same coin, sovereignty and humanity were pitted against one another. As this
chapter has revealed, although sovereignty may have been victorious in this
battle, by no means did it win the war conclusively.[236] In fact, drafters recognized that the task of enforcing the Conventions was no longer an exclusively
internal affair of states: sovereignty in wartime had been changed forever.[237] In
addition to this, they prohibited the old principle of law enforcement through
reprisals. In its place, they gave rise to an unprecedented range of counter-prin-
ciples: from the right of complaint for POWs, through global dissemination, to
ICRC supervision.

The ICRC came out of this gargantuan struggle stronger than at any previous time in its international legal history.[238] Preparing for an impending war,
Western liberal powers recognized (unlike in 1929) that alternatives to the
ICRC appeared much less appealing and that without this organization there
would be no officially neutral supervisors left.[239] In trying to win the support
of Great Powers the ICRC made several compromises, proposing various adjustments to the Conventions' drafts so as to accommodate their sovereign
concerns. Alternative plans promoted by the French, which aimed to establish

---

[236] Best, *War and Law since 1945*, 148.

[237] Roberts, "The Laws of War: Problems of Implementation in Contemporary Conflicts," 28. Craigie
went even so far as to claim that "much of the suffering caused unlawfully and unnecessarily during the
last war might have been avoided had [the Grave Breaches] formed a part of international law at that
time." Final Report Diplomatic Conference, 1949, no. 6036, ADM116, TNA.

[238] Mantilla, "The Origins and Evolution of the 1949 Geneva Conventions," 47.

[239] Geoffrey Best, "Making the Geneva Conventions of 1949: The View from Whitehall," in *Etudes
et essais sur le droit international humanitaire et sur les principes de la Croix-Rouge en l'honneur de Jean
Pictet*, ed. Christophe Swinarksi (Geneva: ICRC, 1984): 5–15, 9. Even one of its fiercest critics, the
World Jewish Congress, had noted with "the highest satisfaction" how some states had tried to empower
the ICRC's supervisory role. Memorandum of the WJC on the Draft Convention for the Protection of
Civilian Persons in Time of War submitted to the XVIIth International Red Cross Conference, Series
B69, no. 17, American Jewish Archives (AJC), Cincinnati, OH. Strikingly, in 1929, both Washington
and London had argued that the interests of their soldiers captured by the enemy would be best served
by Protecting Powers, not the ICRC. However, the experiences of the Second World War, the end of
US neutrality—i.e. that of its status as the world's most powerful Protecting Power—and the rise of the
US as a global warmaking power changed this dynamic almost completely. Wylie and Crossland, "The
Korean War and the Post-War Prisoners of War Regime, 1945–1956."

a new international control committee, were all voted down. As a result, the ICRC's name is mentioned more frequently than ever before in these treaties: it truly became *the* preferred international humanitarian actor in wartime.[240] The emergence of the UN in this period did little to change this, for it had boycotted the laws of war in that same year, removing the subject entirely from its own drafting agenda, and being born as a wartime alliance rather than as a neutral arbitrator.

Another small success in the area of enforcement was the diplomatic conference's support for provisions relating to dissemination. The ICRC's ambition to spread the Conventions' principles among armed forces and civilian populations around the world received widespread support from delegations.[241] Even the most skeptical participant, Great Britain, promised to follow up on this initiative.[242] As time went on, this small step in the history of the laws of war would have significant consequences, in that it enabled the rise of the ICRC's later dissemination campaigns in the Global South especially. In various parts of the world, ICRC delegates would experiment with teaching numerous courses on this body of international law, as well as the fundamental principles of the Red Cross. Even more strikingly, in promoting rules for interstate warfare, the ICRC also applied these conceptions to armed conflicts taking place within states and empires. Not only that, but ICRC teachers instructed non-state armed groups engaged in intrastate warfare, which accelerated the rise of these Conventions to the global stage after 1949.[243]

Still, it would be wrong to follow some commentators in inflating the importance of some of these legacies of 1949 for dissemination.[244] Some practitioners now argue that by adding the words "ensure respect" to Common Article 1, at the start of each of the four Conventions, drafters forced states to take joint responsibility for enforcing them.[245] Based upon Pictet's Commentary, this

---

[240] Roberts, "The Laws of War: Problems of Implementation in Contemporary Conflicts," 32; Wylie and Crossland, "The Korean War and the Post-War Prisoners of War Regime, 1945–1956"; and Best, *War and Law since 1945*.

[241] Draper, "The Implementation of the Modern Law of Armed Conflicts," 17.

[242] Final Report Craigie, November 1949, no. 4164, FO369 (Foreign Office), TNA.

[243] See also Jessica Stanton, "Rebel Groups, International Humanitarian Law, and Civil War Outcomes in the Post-Cold War Era," *International Organization*, Vol. 74, No. 3 (2020): 523–559; Tanisha Fazal, *Wars of Law: Unintended Consequences in the Regulation of Armed Conflict* (Ithaca, NY: Cornell University Press, 2018); and Hyeran Jo, *Compliant Rebels: Rebels Groups and International Law in World Politics* (Cambridge: Cambridge University Press, 2015).

[244] Some have already noted that the "drafting history of the Geneva Conventions [...] does not support an(y) intention of the drafters to accord this provision [of Common Article 1] an external compliance meaning": Robin Geiss, "The Obligation to Respect and to Ensure Respect for the Conventions," in *The 1949 Geneva Conventions: A Commentary*, ed. Andrew Clapham, Paola Gaeta, and Marco Sassòli (Oxford: Oxford University Press, 2015), 109–134, 121.

[245] Frits Kalshoven, *Reflections on the Law of War: Collected Essays* (Leiden: Martinus Nijhoff, 2007), 695–698.

300 PREPARING FOR WAR

argument has been used to make states co-responsible for whatever violation allies commit.[246] Despite being well intended, this interpretation has no basis in its recorded history. In fact, in the original article the words "ensure respect" meant something subtly different, namely that states should guarantee that their civilian populations would also respect the Conventions—potentially even in civil wars.[247] Indeed, any attempt to interpret this provision (which was hardly ever discussed at the drafting table) more broadly would have triggered massive resistance from the Great Powers.[248] This raises the larger question of what the legacies of the 1949 Conventions are for enforcement today.

The final chapter will show how over time some of the meanings attributed to humanitarian law developed beyond what its designers initially had in mind when laying its foundations. Some provisions took on entirely different meanings, starting a whole new legal life. Whereas at first Common Article 1 was primarily seen as a minor recommendation that the Conventions be taught widely, it has since become a key legal instrument, used to pressure powerful states to take responsibility in the global campaign to put an end to unrestrained warfare.[249]

[246] Examples include Dieter Fleck, "International Accountability for Violations of the Ius in Bello: The Impact of the ICRC Study on Customary International Humanitarian Law," *Journal of Conflict & Security Law*, Vol. 11, No. 2 (2006): 179–199, 182; Birgit Kessler, "The Duty to 'Ensure Respect' Under Common Article 1 of the Geneva Conventions: Its Implications on International and Non-International Armed Conflicts," *German Yearbook of International Law*, Vol. 44 (2001): 498–516, 498; and Umesh Palwankar, "Measures Available to States for Fulfilling their Obligation to Ensure Respect for International Humanitarian Law," *International Review of the Red Cross*, No. 298 (1994): 227–240.

[247] This view is corroborated by the analyses of Roberts, "The Laws of War: Problems of Implementation in Contemporary Conflicts," 29–30, and Kalshoven, *Reflections on the Law of War*, 677, 691–692.

[248] Frits Kalshoven is right to note that the diplomatic conference spent "conspicuously little time and energy" on draft Article 1. Kalshoven, Kalshoven, *Reflections on the Law of War*, 691.

[249] Roberts, "The Laws of War: Problems of Implementation in Contemporary Conflicts." See also Knut Dörmann, Liesbeth Lijnzaad, Marco Sassòli, Philip Spoerri, and Jean-Marie Henckaerts, *Commentary on the First Geneva Convention* (Cambridge: Cambridge University Press, 2016); and Oona Hathaway, Emily Chertoff, Lara Domínquez, Zachary Manfredi, and Peter Tzeng, "Ensuring Responsibility: Common Article 1 and State Responsibility for Non-State Actors," *Texas Law Review*, Vol. 95 (2017): 539–590.

Figure 7.1 Max Petitpierre (right) and Soviet leader Nikolay Vasilyevich Slavin (left) at a special signature ceremony, in Bern (1949).
Source/Rights: Ullstein

Conclusion

The making of the Geneva Conventions reached its apotheosis in the final signature ceremony. On 8 December 1949, thirty-eight state representatives reassembled in the old conference hall in Geneva for the signing of the new treaties.[1] They sat around an old mahogany table that had been used for the first Convention's signature ceremony in 1864. Several decades later, it once again served as the symbolic altar of humanity, allegorically fulfilling Dunant's promise.[2] According to Swiss journalists, the passing of the four Conventions represented nothing less than "an infinitely precious gain for humanity" and an "historic date in the history of the Red Cross."[3]

Echoing these words, president Petitpierre ended the ceremony by making a celebratory speech in which he declared the adoption of the Conventions a milestone in the history of both international law and Switzerland. States had proclaimed new protections and updated the old treaties to guarantee rights in armed conflict. Like his euphoric ICRC colleagues,[4] Petitpierre believed that this had decisively shaped the future of warfare.[5] Indeed, he argued that in securing "rights and respect for the human person" in wartime, the Conventions shared the "spirit" of the Universal Declaration of Human Rights (UDHR). With this in mind, he not only reminded the attendees of the declaration's upcoming anniversary a few days later, but also stressed their common principles and significance.[6]

---

[1] *Journal de Genève*, 9 December 1949; and Letter M. Kahany to Ministry for Foreign Affairs, 9 December 1949, no. 1987/6- חצ (00071706.81.D4.ED.29), Israel State Archives, Jerusalem (ISA).

[2] Landbote, Winterthur, 10 December 1949.

[3] Nouvelliste Valaisan, 10 and 16 December 1949.

[4] Pilloud also called the Civilian Convention's adoption a "success" but still expressed considerable reservations. Minutes Plenary Meeting, 11 November 1949, no. A PV JUR.1, Les Archives du Comité International de la Croix-Rouge (ACICR), Geneva; and Conference Diplomatique. Rapport Spécial Etabli par Pilloud, 16 September 1949, no. CR-254–1, ACICR.

[5] Minutes of Signature Ceremony, December 1949, no. CD_1949_ACTES_FRE_32, La Bibliothèque du Comité international de la Croix Rouge, Geneva (ICRC Library).

[6] Minutes of Signature Ceremony, December 1949, no. CD_1949_ACTES_FRE_32, ICRC Library. Several newspaper articles also noted the overlap between the Conventions and the 1948 Universal Declaration of Human Rights. Neue Zürcher Zeitung, 10 December 1949.

Preparing for War. Boyd van Dijk, Oxford University Press. © Boyd van Dijk 2022.
DOI: 10.1093/oso/9780198868071.003.0008

304 PREPARING FOR WAR

While celebrating the adoption of the Conventions, Petitpierre further warned the signatories not to become morally complacent at a time of escalating Cold War tensions:

> If we can congratulate ourselves on the fact that our Conference has accomplished the aims which were planned for it, we know, nevertheless, that it has not solved […] any of the great problems which weigh today so heavily on the life of the nations. But we desire to express the earnest wish that the feeling of humanity, which […] inspired the Conventions we have just signed, may develop and may one day give the nations a sense of their common interests, which are greater than anything that divides them. This feeling of humanity […] will then no longer limit itself to lessening the evils of war, but will undertake the task of fighting the very idea of war and of ensuring that peace is finally victorious.[7]

In addition to defending the Conventions against pacifist critics, Petitpierre's remarks also served another purpose: that of fending off attacks from the socialist signatories.

The Swiss magistrate implicitly countered criticisms from socialist delegates who were arguing that the drafters should have banned nuclear warfare by adopting the Soviet resolution on this matter. They considered the Conventions "faulty" on various points.[8] One of those most critical of the socialist delegates in Geneva was the Hungarian representative—and former resistance fighter—Anna Kara. While Western delegates celebrated the acceptance of the Conventions,[9] she bluntly confronted them with the "obvious defects" of the new rules that they had adopted. In particular, she criticized the drafters' unwillingness to avert nuclear holocaust in adopting the Anglo-American security clause, which made "any hope of realizing [the Civilian Convention's] principles illusory."[10]

Despite these misgivings at a time of preparations for war, every socialist state in Eastern Europe—including the Soviet Union—signed the Conventions,

---

[7] Minutes of Signature Ceremony, December 1949, no. CD_1949_ACTES_FRE_32, ICRC Library.

[8] ARC, 10 December 1949, no. 619 - B - 40 - PART 6, RG25 - Vol. 3398, Library and Archives Canada (LAC), Ottawa, ON.

[9] It is important to remember that the US delegation signed three Conventions in August 1949, not the Civilian Convention. In December 1949, the US government representative signed the Civilian Convention with the death penalty reservation. Minutes of Signature Ceremony, December 1949, no. CD_1949_ACTES_FRE_32, ICRC Library.

[10] Minutes of Signature Ceremony, December 1949, no. CD_1949_ACTES_FRE_32, ICRC Library; and Final Record of the Diplomatic Conference of Geneva of 1949, Vol. I, pp. 346–347, Library of Congress (LOC), Washington, DC.

with only a few reservations.[11] Their main concern was to preserve their sovereignty by calling for reservations to those parts of the enforcement system that entailed outside supervision, as will be shown below.[12] The Albanians and Yugoslavs signed the Conventions one after another.[13] Some of the Western signatories, by contrast, faced much greater resistance to their efforts to get the treaties adopted and ratified.[14] US military officials were upset about the Civilian Convention's restrictions and the onerous responsibilities that it placed on future occupiers of enemy lands: they were particularly keen to minimize the administrative burden of future US occupations.

Before the signature ceremony, the US Army had already signaled its alarm about the death penalty article and humanitarian law's burdensome obligations for occupying powers.[15] These concerns were very much shared by the British War Office in London. Its representatives demanded that attention be paid immediately to how the Conventions might potentially limit their ability to suppress future insurgencies, not least as a result of Common Article 3.[16] In trying to secure their interests as future enforcers of liberal Western occupation regimes, Anglo-American military officials called for several reservations to the Conventions. By contrast, civilian agencies and former Anglo-American drafters put forward instrumental arguments in a bid to convince their nations' leadership to adopt these treaties with only measured reservations.[17]

In Washington, US diplomats and former civilian drafters such as Yingling argued that it was imperative for the Truman Administration to sign the Conventions "from the standpoint of prestige and as inducement to others"— that is, the Soviet enemy. Similarly, the former UK drafter Craigie argued that

[11] The Soviet Union was unable to attend this signature ceremony due to travel issues. The Soviet delegates, together with the Belorussians and Ukrainians, signed the Conventions a few days later, in Bern. They made several reservations to the treaties: *Pravda*, 13 December 1949; *St. Galler Tagblatt*, 13 December 1949; *National Zeitung*, 13 December 1949; and *Neue Berner Zeitung*, 14 December 1949.

[12] For the Soviet reservations, see Final Record of the Diplomatic Conference of Geneva of 1949, Vol. I, pp. 355–356, LOC. The Soviet decision to sign the Conventions without freeing thousands of German POWs led to critical reactions from several Swiss-German newspapers. See *Appenzeller Zeitung*, 13 December 1949; and *Anzeiger, Affoltern*, 15 February 1950.

[13] Maoist China made declarations of adherence to the Conventions during several stages of the Korean War. The official moment of accession occurred in 1956—so after hostilities had ended.

[14] It is important to note that ratification and implementation are not the same and should be analyzed separately. The complex question of implementation is not discussed in this book. Giovanni Mantilla, "Conforming Instrumentalists: Why the USA and the United Kingdom Joined the 1949 Geneva Conventions," *European Journal of International Law*, Vol. 28, No. 2 (2017): 483–511.

[15] Minutes Prisoners of War Committee, 27 October 1949, no. 673 - PART I, Provost Marshal General, National Archives and Records Administration (NARA), College Park, MD; and Mantilla, "Conforming Instrumentalists," 497.

[16] Mantilla, "Conforming Instrumentalists," 503.

[17] After drafting for several months, Craigie admitted that the Conventions did provide "very real" benefits to the "victims of a future war." Final Report Craigie, November 1949, no. 4164, FO369 (Foreign Office), The National Archives (TNA), Kew; and Mantilla, "Conforming Instrumentalists," 503.

306   PREPARING FOR WAR

his government should "make as few reservations as possible."[18] He represented the Foreign Office, which supported his reasoning that Britain should avoid further harm to its already damaged prestige. The UK Attorney General Shawcross echoed this view, warning that it was "becoming conspicuous amongst the countries of the world for the rigidity of our attitude"[19] and demanding a quick adoption.[20] What brought civilian officials and former (civilian) drafters together was a shared concern for Britain's reputation amid the global struggle of the emerging Cold War.

Given the sensitivities and deep inter-ministerial divisions surrounding the adoption of the Conventions, the UK Cabinet was asked to make the final judgment. Labour ministers were advised to make a reservation to the death penalty article and coordinate any future actions with their American allies.[21] For their part, US government officials continued to wrestle with the question of whether to adopt the Conventions as they were. Whereas military representatives even preferred to make revisions to the existing texts, their civilian counterparts feared that renewing talks over the outcome of the contentious deliberations at Geneva might open something of a Pandora's Box.[22]

Washington gave its approval for the signing of the Conventions only a few days before the ceremony in Geneva was set to commence. It made a reservation to the death penalty article, which Britain and many other NATO allies, including the Netherlands, replicated—to the shock of Dutch survivors of Nazi persecution.[23] As ever, the French were an outlier among the major NATO member states: like Nehru's India, they signed all four Conventions without making a single reservation.[24] In doing so, Paris implicitly rejected the reservation that its most important NATO allies had made to the death penalty article. At the same time, the French signatories remained deliberately silent about

---

[18] Quoted from: Mantilla, "Conforming Instrumentalists," 497, 503.

[19] Letter Attorney-General to Beckett, 27 November 1949, no. 46, CAB130 (Cabinet Office), TNA.

[20] Mantilla, "Conforming Instrumentalists," 503–505.

[21] Ibid.

[22] Ibid., 498.

[23] In February 1954, when the Dutch reservation for the death penalty was first discussed in the Dutch parliament, the acting minister Joseph Luns faced major criticism from especially the communist Rie Lips-Odinot, a former resistance fighter and prisoner of KZ Ravensbrück. Replying to her criticisms, Luns had to admit embarrassingly that his government believed that it could "not be ruled [out] that the Netherlands might find itself one day in the position of occupying power." The Dutch reservation was revoked in the 1970s. Boyd van Dijk, "The Guardians: An International History of the Dutch and 'Hague Law', 1944–1949" in *Shaping the International Relations of the Netherlands, 1815–2000*, eds Rimko van der Maar, Ruud van Dijk, Samuel Kruizinga, and Vincent Kuitenbrouwer (London: Routledge, 2019).

[24] To be sure, France was far from the only NATO member state which dissented from Anglo-American reservation behavior. For instance, the Belgians and Italians also signed the Conventions without reservations. Minutes of Signature Ceremony, December 1949, no. CD_1949_ACTES_FRE_32, ICRC Library. Nationalist China signed the Conventions on 10 December 1949. India did so on 16 December 1949.

CONCLUSION 307

their government's refusal to apply Common Article 3 to the war it was fighting in Indochina. The Swiss decision not to invite Ho Chi Minh's representatives to the ceremony allowed the French to celebrate the adoption of humanitarian law without being confronted with French atrocities against Vietnamese civilians.

After concluding the ceremony, president Petitpierre rallied all of the delegates to ratify the Conventions quickly. In a highly symbolic move to promote their neutrality politics and the ICRC's activities,[25] the Swiss were the first to ratify.[26] Since then, a record number of states has followed this precedent by signing up to the Conventions, creating a belt of ratifications that now stretches across the world. In disseminating its principles globally, the ICRC has played a critical role in facilitating this legislative breakthrough. Today, the Conventions are among the most ratified treaties in world history; what is often forgotten, however, is that it took years—if not decades—to achieve this remarkable outcome.[27]

One critical factor initially hindering the immediate adoption of the Conventions by the Great Powers was the outbreak of the Korean War, which convinced them (with the exception of France) to postpone ratification for the foreseeable future.[28] Although he was originally in favor of a quick ratification, the US Secretary of State Acheson argued that hostilities and exchanges of prisoners of war (POWs) in Korea needed to be settled first before moving forward legislatively. Likewise, the UK government decided to revise its original plan of swiftly ratifying the Conventions following the outbreak of the war. In fact, the British delayed the ratification process for years, in part because they feared that publicly adhering to the Conventions might impair their ongoing counter-insurgency campaign in Kenya.[29]

Once rumors began circulating about an upcoming Soviet ratification, both Anglo-American powers felt forced to resume the momentum of their ratification procedures. Further delays, they feared, might endanger NATO's preparations for war with the Soviets and add fuel to the fire of anti-Western Soviet propaganda.[30] In trying to prevent this, the new US Secretary of State, John Foster Dulles, commissioned a special report to convince the US Senate

---

[25] It is striking that numerous Swiss and Western European newspapers saw the Conventions' adoption as proof of the importance of Swiss neutrality and the ICRC's activities. Examples include *La Métropole*, 19 August 1949; *Basler Nachrichten*, 10/11 December 1949; and *Le Progrès*, 8 December 1949.

[26] *La Suisse*, Geneva, 18 March 1950; *Gazette de Lausanne*, 18/19 March 1950; *La Nouvelle Revue de Lausanne*, 18 March 1950; and *Tages Anzeiger*, Zurich, 18 March 1950.

[27] Minutes of Signature Ceremony, December 1949, no. CD_1949_ACTES_FRE_32, ICRC Library; and Mantilla, "Conforming Instrumentalists," 487.

[28] The state of France acceded in 1951.

[29] Mantilla, "Conforming Instrumentalists," 499, 506–507.

[30] Ibid., 499.

308　PREPARING FOR WAR

to ratify the Conventions.[31] In this document, he argued that the United States "has always taken pride in its leading role [in establishing] humane standards for the protection of the [...] defenseless in time of war [...] and greatly contributed to the making of the Conventions." While it has no basis in historical fact, this popular image of the United States as a gentle civilizer in the field of modern warfare since Lieber continues to resonate. Indeed, it continues to figure quite prominently in the country's collective memory of its role in the drafting of the Conventions.[32]

Senate Committee hearings were held in 1955, with the State Department stressing that the Conventions were important in advancing US interests. Given that a large number of states—and the Soviet Union in particular—had already ratified the Conventions, its officials contended, US claims to prominence on the world stage were now at risk of being compromised. To avoid this scenario, the State Department argued that ratifying the Conventions was important not just militarily but also politically, in that it would serve to maintain US prestige during an especially tense moment of the Cold War. Whereas the US Senate ratified soon after the hearings were over, UK legislators took until 1957 to pass the Geneva Conventions Act.[33]

This period of the early Cold War saw the emergence of a popular mythology which celebrated the adoption of the Conventions as a "universal moment," in which states worked in concert with the ICRC to prevent the previous war's atrocities (to paraphrase several Swiss and foreign newspaper reports).[34] This uplifting narrative accentuated the importance of Western liberal values in humanizing warfare, as well as the successful precedent set by the Civilian

[31] Stephen Kinzer, *The Brothers: John Foster Dulles, Allen Dulles, and Their Secret World War* (New York: St. Martin's Griffin, 2014).

[32] Cited from Mantilla, "Conforming Instrumentalists," 500. Jane Mayer: "America had done more than any nation on earth to abolish torture and other violations of human rights [...] These international treaties [e.g. the 1949 Geneva Conventions], many of which were hammered out by American lawyers in the wake of the harrowing Nazi atrocities of World War II [...]" Jane Mayer, *The Dark Side: The Inside Story of How the War on Terror Turned into a War on American Ideals* (New York: Doubleday, 2008), 7–12; and Gary Solis, *The Law of Armed Conflict: International Humanitarian Law in War* (New York: Cambridge University Press, 2010), 81. See also Gerald Steinacher, *Humanitarians at War: The Red Cross in the Shadow of the Holocaust* (Oxford: Oxford University Press, 2017), 193, 218–236; Tobias Kelly, "What We Talk about When We Talk about Torture," *Humanity*, Vol. 2, No. 2 (2011): 327–343, 328–329. For a critique of those mythmaking accounts, see Samuel Moyn, "From Antiwar Politics to Antitorture Politics" in *Law and War*, eds Austin Sarat, Lawrence Douglas, and Martha Merrill Umphrey (Stanford, CA: Stanford University Press, 2014), 154–197; Samuel Moyn, "Martti Koskenniemi and the Historiography of International Law in the Age of the War on Terror" in *The Law of International Lawyers: Reading Martti Koskenniemi*, eds Wouter Werner, Marieke de Hoon, and Alexis Galán (Cambridge: Cambridge University Press, 2017), 340–359; and Darius Rejali, *Torture and Democracy* (Princeton, NJ: Princeton University Press, 2007).

[33] Mantilla, "Conforming Instrumentalists," 500, 506, 510–511.

[34] *Journal de Genève*, 5 December 1949.

Convention.[35] It also emphasized the Swiss leadership's role in bridging East–West divisions and bringing states from across the globe together in Geneva.[36] This one-dimensional version of history not only endowed the earlier struggle against fascism with meaning (despite Auriti's prominent role at the signature ceremony) but also depoliticized a highly contentious drafting process, thus helping to secure widespread state support.[37]

While it is certainly true that responses to the Conventions were overwhelmingly positive, especially in Switzerland, this is only part of the narrative that was spun around the inception of humanitarian law.[38] This story credited Swiss diplomacy with getting the Soviets on board, without acknowledging the latter's contributions to the formulation of the rules in question.[39] It promulgated the idea that the Conventions protected partisans, without registering the fact that they broadly marginalized them.[40] It emphasized the diplomatic conference's universality, overlooking its exclusion of the decolonizing world and the two Germanies. It also underlined the importance of the adopted provision for safety zones while ignoring the drafters' acceptance of indiscriminate bombing.[41] These blind spots ultimately produced a myth of the Conventions' birth that could be used to influence Western and specifically Swiss audiences.

Indeed, ICRC and Swiss officials played a central role in cementing a mythologized image of the emergence of the Conventions in the years after 1949. During this period, they published a large number of articles in newspapers and journals (both Swiss and foreign) promoting their uplifting interpretation of the Conventions as a product of liberal and inclusive thinking.[42] As the

[35] It is striking how many (Swiss) journalists stressed the importance of the Civilian Convention's adoption without taking note of Common Article 3's successful breakthrough. Examples include *Neue Zürcher Zeitung*, 10 December 1949; and *Feuille d'Avis de Neuchatel*, 7 December 1949.

[36] The New York Times, 9 December 1949; and Basler Nachrichten, 10/11 December 1949.

[37] This idea is inspired by Francine Hirsch, *Soviet Judgment at Nuremberg: A New History of the International Military Tribunal after World War II* (Oxford: Oxford University Press, 2020), 415.

[38] *La Métropole*, 19 August 1949. US, UK, and New Zealander delegates largely agreed that the diplomatic conference had to be considered a success. Report of New Zealand Delegation to Diplomatic Conference of Geneva 1949, AAYS 8638 W2054 ADW2054/1220/3/3 (R18524114), Archives New Zealand (ANZ), Wellington. See also Paul de la Pradelle, *La Conférence Diplomatique et les Nouvelles Conventions de Genève du 12 Août 1949* (Paris: Les Editions Internationales, 1951), 7; and Minutes of Seances Commission Juridique, 11 November 1949, no. A PV JUR. 1, Vol. I, ACICR. Strikingly, World Jewish Congress activists also positively received the Civilian Convention's adoption, arguing that "its existence during WWII would have meant life for millions of civilians and the rescue of 6.000.000 murdered innocent Jews." *Jewish Advocate*, 29 June 1950.

[39] For example: Neue Zürcher Zeitung, 10 December 1949.

[40] *The Times*, 13 August 1949.

[41] *Le Courrier Australien*, 7 October 1949.

[42] As noted before: *Tribune de Lausanne*, 14 August 1949; and *Journal de Genève*, 13–14 August 1949. See also Cédric Cotter and Ellen Policinski, "A History of Violence: The Development of International Humanitarian Law Reflected in the International Review of the Red Cross," *Journal of International Humanitarian Legal Studies*, Vol. 11, No. 1 (2020): 36–67, 51.

310 PREPARING FOR WAR

most famous ICRC lawyer and a former leading drafter of the Conventions, Pictet wrote numerous pieces for the organization's own journal in which he replicated this popular mythology. Furthermore, he played a prominent role in managing the Commentary project, which sought to safeguard the ICRC's role as the guardian of the Conventions. In shaping collective legal memory, these different initiatives served to shield the myths of humanitarian law's past from outside criticism.[43]

During this period, the most influential critiques of this established narrative came largely from the (European) Left. Norwegian communists criticized their government's rejection of the Soviet resolution outlawing nuclear warfare.[44] Pacifist critics, who argued that humanization of warfare was illusory, triggered a fierce response from Swiss conservatives.[45] And the French socialist Bourdet mocked Anglo-American obstructionism, while criticizing his own government's effort to undermine the colonial war clause. Although he described the final version of the Conventions as "un net progrès," Bourdet rejected Stalinist propaganda questioning Geneva's contributions.[46] For all their ferocity, none of these left-wing criticisms was able to overcome the established narrative cultivated by conservative and liberal ICRC advocates.

The latter were able to push their storyline through in part because the world was less interested in the adoption of the Conventions than the Swiss hosts had originally expected.[47] The relatively scant attention paid to the process of deliberation and ratification by the foreign media allowed the Swiss to control the narrative around the making of the Conventions.[48] At the same time, the Swiss wondered about the reasons for this dearth of external interest in the creation of the most important rules ever formulated for armed conflict. In addition to blaming the proceedings' "theoretical character" and several other factors, they believed that the lack of a stark political controversy (except for the Soviet resolution on nuclear warfare) in particular contributed to the wider world's apparent disinterest—an outcome which they could have foreseen in light of

---

[43] Cotter and Policinski, "A History of Violence," 53.

[44] *Friheten*, 11 August 1949.

[45] *Basler Nachrichten*, 10/11 December 1949.

[46] *Combat*, 8 December 1949.

[47] *Journal de Genève*, 5 December 1949. The dominant cohort of Swiss, French, British, American, and Italian journalists formed almost 90 per cent of the total number of journalists present at the diplomatic conference. More than a third of the total number of journalists were Swiss. There was only a tiny number of reporters from outside Europe—four from the Middle East (Egypt and Iraq), three from Asia (China and India), one from the Caribbean (Haiti), and zero from Africa. See Report of the activities of the Service d'information, 12 August 1949, no. E2001E#1967/113#16123/BD 874, Swiss Federal Archives (SFA), Bern.

[48] The lack of world attention to the diplomatic conference was also noticed by reporters themselves. See Trouw, 21 July 1949.

their efforts to depoliticize Geneva's deliberations.[49] What is more, they realized that outsiders felt unable to celebrate the humanization of warfare with "exuberant adulation," to quote one Swiss reporter. For most observers, the task of creating new rules for warfare was of secondary moral importance to that of overcoming "a hopelessly gloomy world situation"—an obvious reference to the Cold War tensions that further escalated after the ceremony.[50]

C.1 The Great Humanitarians

As every chapter in this book has shown, creating a new international legal order for warfare amid existential fears of cataclysmic conflict posed a real struggle for all of the parties involved. They regularly clashed and changed their minds on the question of how to limit the effects of warfare. Considering their political, ideological, and other differences, it would have been extraordinary if they had done otherwise. French officials, to give one example, suddenly embraced humanitarian law—a volte face from their position before the Second World War. Few had expressed serious interest in issues other than POW protection before 1940; indeed, at crucial moments they had opposed attempts to broaden its scope. Even the Monaco Draft, which was co-drafted by French military doctors, had garnered little support in Paris. As a victorious power, which occupied parts of Germany for a period after the First World War and wished to keep its hands "free" in case of another invasion,[51] the Third Republic was initially skeptical of initiatives aiming to codify humanitarian law in areas other than POW protection.

This attitude changed radically, however, after the Republic's total defeat in mid-1940. The rise of a post-Vichy state built upon a mythical ideal of collective resistance and civilian suffering under fascist occupation played a crucial part in radically changing French attitudes toward humanitarian law after 1944. These altered perceptions were institutionalized by a group of former victims of war, from deportees to resistance fighters, as well as Frenay's own Ministry for Prisoners, Deportees, and Refugees. They now embraced humanitarian

---

[49] Report of the activities of the Service d'information, 12 August 1949, no. E2001E#1967/113#16123/ BD 874, Swiss Federal Archives (SFA), Bern.

[50] *Basler Nachrichten*, 10/11 December 1949. The Australian *Daily Telegraph*, 15 December 1949: "we should all be very thankful that 45 High Contracting Parties can get together and agree about the rules of war. But we would all be much more thankful if they agreed not to have any more war."

[51] For the debates on the French occupation of Germany and the laws of war, see Rotem Giladi, "The Phoenix of Colonial War: Race, the Laws of War and the 'Horror on the Rhine'," *Leiden Journal of International Law*, Vol. 30, No. 4 (2017): 847–875.

law, aiming to gain international recognition for their wartime hardships and interests as a colonial power and a formerly occupied nation. These ranged from recognizing their suffering under the fascist yoke, through safeguarding France's interests in Indochina, to protecting its human resources in the metropolitan areas in case of another invasion by a foreign power, whether a revived Germany or the Soviet Union.

Throughout the 1940s the French tried, under pressure from Frenay's former comrades, to gain acknowledgment for their wartime efforts and those of the Free French Forces by codifying the right of collective resistance. Their main objectives were to restrict the occupier's powers and protect (stateless) civilians, goals that they attempted to achieve through reimagining notions of human rights for interstate occupation. Indeed, at Stockholm, Cahen-Salvador infused human rights law into humanitarian law in order to protect individual rights in armed conflicts.

The French played a truly extraordinary role in creating a fairly robust Civilian Convention. Their unique part in mediating between East and West and among the split Western bloc members was crucial. Nonetheless, the French had to bring these progressive efforts in line with their other obligations as members of the NATO alliance and as a fighting colonial power in Indochina. Among other things, they removed the original reference to colonial wars and prevented Common Article 3 from recognizing the Viet Minh as a belligerent. By limiting the final text's scope and reducing the weight of its legal obligations, they succeeded in protecting their colonial state's authority to decide whether it would apply in the future to colonial Algeria, for instance, instead of leaving this decision to international bodies. They also ratified the security clause despite having fiercely battled against it at Geneva.

Thus, the French, far too often seen as being exclusively motivated by their wartime memories, in reality adopted a far more measured, if not highly ambiguous, legal position during this drafting process. While designing new individual rights protections, they had to reckon with France's colonial and military interests as a Western bloc member. This proved especially challenging in the debate regarding partisans' protection: whereas the French, who feared another occupation, tried to empower resistance fighters, Anglo-American allies saw things in a totally different light. They also expressed frustration about France's lack of reflection as a present (and future) occupier in Germany and Austria.

These destabilizing, if not potentially alarming, Western divisions were solved only due to French concerns about losing their endangered proposal for Common Article 3 and, more importantly, because of severe Anglo-American

CONCLUSION 313

pressure. At the same time, the latter's crushing defeat in the tumultuous debate on the death penalty painfully revealed the limits of Anglo-American drafting power. By strategically positioning itself between these delegations and the Soviet-aligned ones, and thanks to its role as the leading representative of the bipartisan bloc of formerly occupied nations, Lamarle's delegation held a unique position that was highly disproportionate to its diminished military power.

The US position is equally difficult to pin down. Prior to the Second World War, American state officials and international lawyers had shown remarkably little interest in European debates on regulating the conduct of warfare. Their main interests lay in codifying peace,[52] matters related to the Western hemisphere, and gaining protections for exclusively their armed forces through ratifying the 1929 POW Convention.[53] By contrast, US officials expressed far less interest in (inter)war legal attempts to protect civilians; they opposed, for instance, a range of initiatives to end indiscriminate warfare. As has already been indicated, the Interdepartmental Prisoners of War Committee's (POWC) name, as well as its initial proposals with regard to improving protections for US military personnel, demonstrated a primary interest in affairs other than those relating to civilians.

The US government's narrow focus on this drafting process gradually broadened around mid-1947. Following the gathering of the government experts' conference, it realized that their continental European allies were broadly in favor of a robust Civilian Convention. Consequently, US drafters began contemplating options to further develop this treaty in line with their own purposes, initially suggesting even a limit on the death penalty. Adopting some of these plans, the Stockholm conference put stricter limits on the occupier's powers. This result was partly the outcome of a strategic miscalculation on the part of the US delegation, whose officials back home realized the mistakes they had made only after the fact.

Their views hardened even further after August 1948, with rising East–West tensions and as new proposals were prepared for the final diplomatic conference. In this crucial drafting phase, Washington began to understand that the popular but far-reaching Stockholm drafts posed a real threat to its primary interests as a potential occupying power. As fears of war with the Soviet Union

---

[52] Daniel Gorman, *The Emergence of International Society in the 1920s* (New York: Cambridge University Press, 2012), 259–284.
[53] See also Elizabeth Grimm Arsenault, "The Domestic Politics of International Norms: Factors Affecting US Compliance with the Geneva Conventions," Ph.D. Dissertation, Georgetown University, 2010.

314 PREPARING FOR WAR

and of communist spies grew significantly, it began toughening its views on a range of essential questions, from partisan warfare, through enforcement, to civilian protection. While their work is sometimes heralded as promoting humanitarian law in the 1940s, US officials saw the Conventions increasingly through the exclusionary prism of the Cold War. Most strikingly, they began considering these four treaties as a potentially useful instrument with which to fight communism in a future war. War planning against the Soviet Union emerged as a key drafting priority for US officials.[54] Accordingly, the POWC made a number of far-reaching suggestions: among other things, it recommended excluding communist spies, suppressing discussion on nuclear warfare,[55] silencing the war crimes debate, and strengthening the occupier's position.[56] Although far more restrictive in perception, the US drafters—unlike the British—understood that it was diplomatically unwise to *fully* revise the Stockholm drafts.

When introducing its proposals at the diplomatic conference, the US delegation faced a tough start nonetheless. Although it received regular support from Latin American and other smaller delegations, it witnessed how the Western bloc had split and that the Soviets were winning alarmingly many early votes—at least according to US delegates. In the POW Committee, the latter openly clashed with their British counterparts as a result of personal rivalries and a lack of coordination. The disastrous vote on the death penalty proved to US officials the need to increase cooperation among the divided Western powers.

By improving inter-allied coordination, breaking rules of procedure, and suppressing internal dissent, the leaders of the Anglo-American delegations mostly restored the broken Western unity, thereby enabling US successes in later debates concerning the security clause and air-atomic warfare.[57] The

---

[54] Melvyn Leffler, *The Specter of Communism: The United States and the Origins of the Cold War, 1917–1953* (New York: Hill and Wang, 1994), 64–65; and Melvyn Leffler, *A Preponderance of Power: National Security, the Truman Administration, and the Cold War* (Stanford, CA: Stanford University Press, 1992), 266–267.

[55] Leffler, *A Preponderance of Power*, 221–223.

[56] US historian Samuel Moyn has alluded to some of these points before, even though he also suggested that "if the new Geneva Conventions [...] were forged and adopted uncontroversially by colonial powers as well as by the United States [...] it was in part because they were compatible with counterinsurgency viewed as necessary in a new era of restive natives." While not incorrect, the diplomatic controversy was of course much more significant than Moyn suggested. Moreover, some of the restrictive Anglo-American propositions were simply rejected—see the disastrous vote on the death penalty. Samuel Moyn, "From Antiwar Politics to Antitorture Politics," 154–197.

[57] While grossly misrepresenting the (early) history of the laws of war, Carl Schmitt's critique of postwar America in creating a set of new hierarchies that would allow it to act virtually without restraint in its engagement with the future enemy—in this case, alleged communist spies or civilian populations in the Soviet Union—has some analytical value here. Carl Schmitt, *The Nomos of the Earth in the International Law of the Jus Publicum Europaeum* (New York: Telos Press, 2003), 309–322. For a broader critique of Schmitt's work, see Martti Koskenniemi, "International Law as Political Theology: How to

importance of Cold War politics should not be overestimated, however. On some occasions the Americans voted against proposals from their own allies and in favor of those sponsored by their main Cold War adversary. The US delegation's legal attitudes were certainly based on Cold War projections, but this does not mean that its members had uniformly embraced a single set of ideas to counter every Soviet proposal.

Thus, while the US usually operated more flexibly, the British were often seen as obstructive and unyielding, mainly due to their strict instructions from the metropole. Their inflexible agenda can be at least partly explained by Cold War and imperial politics. From the very start, Whitehall, considering itself an occupier first and foremost, had opposed the ICRC's efforts to create a robust Civilian Convention and to widen the law's scope for "terrorists." Initially it preferred to conduct talks outside Red Cross circles, effectively boycotting the Stockholm conference. When they finally fully participated, the British generally tried to minimize the law's scope and weaken its protections for the occupied while strengthening those for their own security officials. Essentially, they saw themselves as (imperial) occupiers, while ignoring the evanescence of legal positions and considering the threat of occupation largely hypothetical, to the surprise of some European continentals.[58]

From 1947 onwards, as tensions in Palestine and over postwar Germany were on the rise, the British began to see the Conventions' revision increasingly through the lens of the occupier. Their overarching aim was bringing humanitarian law in line with their security interests in order to effectively fight communism and anti-colonial guerrillas. The War Office wished to protect its armed forces from being attacked from the rear; the Security Services demanded that "mental torture" be sanctioned; the Air Force wanted its air power to be secured; the Colonial Office tried to prevent international law from interfering with its discriminatory policies; and the Home Office tried to exclude communist spies from the future Conventions. The result of these destructive impulses was the British delegation's isolation even at the very start of the diplomatic negotiations.

In 1949, at the conference in Geneva, the UK delegation's hopes proved misplaced as its members immediately faced an uphill battle. The US delegation

---

Read Nomos der Erde?" *Constellations* (2004): 492–511; and Jason Ralph, "The Laws of War and the State of the American Exception," *Review of International Studies*, Vol. 35, No. 3 (2009): 631–649.

[58] *Combat*, 8 December 1949. For the "evanescence" of legal positions during the First World War, see Isabel Hull, *A Scrap of Paper: Breaking and Making International Law during the Great War* (Ithaca, NY: Cornell University Press, 2014), 208.

316   PREPARING FOR WAR

expressed frustration with regard to their unwillingness to compromise and because of their efforts to defend acts that were widely regarded as being legally impermissible, at least since Nuremberg. Craigie's delegation was forced to give in. In the following weeks, he pressured Whitehall to revise its instructions on central issues and also persuaded Harrison to cooperate more closely on military issues of mutual concern—that is, not Common Article 3. This helped to relieve the pressure from his own delegation and to extract French concessions. Craigie knew that he could achieve success and defeat Soviet opposition only if he convinced the other major Western power to agree on a common position— the debate on the security clause illustrated this point very clearly.

Despite major setbacks, over time the increasing Western bloc cooperation bolstered the Anglophone position. The British were extremely relieved to see that the final texts excluded spies and other irregulars while remaining largely silent on indiscriminate bombing. Although they disliked the restrictions on the death penalty, there existed a dominant perception that the outcome could have been much worse. They agreed that they had lost the death penalty battle but won the drafting war in Geneva. As such, the British ratified the Conventions with only a reservation for the provision on the death penalty, as mentioned before.

It is crucial to repeat that this outcome had been beyond the ICRC's wildest dreams for most of the drafting process: even during the diplomatic conference it had witnessed how British and US representatives were discussing "delaying action on the Civilian Convention until a later time."[59] Throughout the drafting process, the ICRC, as a small non-state actor in need of powerful friends and operating in a state-controlled environment, expressed genuine concern as to whether or not the Great Powers would ever accept a Civilian Convention. After 1945 the ICRC was also severely pressured by various parties, both internally and externally, to change its proposals for the future Conventions.[60]

This meant that Pictet's drafting team had to bear in mind the sensitivities of all the Great Powers while preparing its own drafts for the first drafting conferences. If the ICRC moved too far in regulating colonial war the British and French might walk away; if it legally constrained the use of nuclear weapons Washington and many of its NATO allies would do the same; and if it did not take Soviet concerns seriously they might never take part. While desperately trying to secure its own neutral interests and exclusive Swiss composition, the ICRC adopted a more limited agenda than is often assumed, excluding

---

[59] Report US Delegation Diplomatic Conference, 1949, no. 673, Provost Marshal General, NARA.
[60] See also Steinacher, *Humanitarians at War*, 211–228.

certain "clashing" or "sensitive" topics, such as political prisoners, from its list of drafting priorities. It tried to balance justice with military necessity while ensuring state support as a lesson of the war's lack of full reciprocity, and crafted a vision of humanitarian law that was less restrictive than that promoted by Huber and more modest than that which Pictet had pleaded for.

As much as Swiss and ICRC drafters proclaimed the force of humanity, they could not ignore the political realities around them. They realized it was unlikely that the Great Powers would ever agree to sweeping changes to international law that would directly expose them to rigorous external supervision.[61] Instead, they tried to protect civilians without seriously restraining air-atomic warfare; they sought to be inclusive without incorporating every person; and they were inspired by human rights without actually referencing them.

Moreover, Swiss and ICRC drafters had little time for those who chose to fight for the cause of peace. They defended the humanization of warfare as a righteous cause while hoping that it would ultimately lead to peace itself. In the meantime, they demanded restrictions on the conduct of warfare by frequently adopting concepts previously coined by other drafting actors. Take, for instance, the ICRC's adoption of an originally anti-communist initiative to intervene in cases of civil war, or that of Francophone doctors who had demanded safety zones for parts of the civilian population. At the same time, in codifying the provision of Common Article 3, they broke absolute sovereignty in crucial areas and won a major symbolic victory on the legal stage. In adopting the concept of safety zones, they also helped advance ideas for civilian protection in times of air warfare that continue to be invoked, especially since the 1990s.[62]

Most importantly, by adopting a more Great Power-friendly agenda, the ICRC's central aim was less to have a draft that would meet all of its demands than to have one that would be "universally" accepted. Equally important, the Great Powers did not come to love the ICRC as the drafting process evolved, but increasingly liked the alternatives less.[63] If the organization drew one lesson from the war, it was the importance of obtaining reciprocity between belligerents. Although not afraid to directly challenge the Great Powers, the ICRC and the Swiss government usually tried to accommodate their demands to prevent

---

[61] James Loeffler, *Rooted Cosmopolitans: Jews and Human Rights in the Twentieth Century* (New Haven, CT: Yale University Press, 2018), 124.

[62] Marcia Ristaino, *The Jacquinot Safe Zone: Wartime Refugees in Shanghai* (Stanford, CA: Stanford University Press, 2008), 153.

[63] Geoffrey Best, "Making the Geneva Conventions of 1949: The View from Whitehall," in *Etudes et essais sur le droit international humanitaire et sur les principes de la Croix-Rouge en l'honneur de Jean Pictet*, ed. Christophe Swinarksi (Geneva: ICRC, 1984), 5–15, 9–10; and Steinacher, *Humanitarians at War*, 111.

318 PREPARING FOR WAR

negotiations from collapsing.[64] Ironically, the Genevans found a major strategic partner in their ideological arch enemy, the Soviet Union, not because of their shared ideological views—to the contrary—but rather as a result of their overlapping aims in supporting the Stockholm drafts.

As is well known today, the ICRC's relations with the Soviet Union were historically adverse. The tensions between the two opposing sides in the wake of the wars in Eastern Europe led to a total collapse of Swiss–Soviet connections after 1939. Stalin's paranoia with regard to the organization's bourgeois composition and outlook did not help much, either.[65] Whereas during the Second World War the Soviets had believed the ICRC was a "pro-fascist" organization, afterward they argued that it had reinvented itself as "an important instrument in the hands of the Anglo-American bloc."[66] Still, by endorsing the Stockholm texts, the two former adversaries became strange bedfellows at the diplomatic conference, working toward similar goals with ideologically distinct agendas.

As we saw before, humanitarian law was not of exclusively Western liberal design. In fact, all but one of the chapters in this book have shown how the Soviet delegation and its close partners made a major contribution to the law's final product. Whereas parts of the literature claim that Soviet contributions were either biased or limited,[67] this book has revealed the Soviet delegation's mixed but essential legacy in developing the Civilian Convention, including Common Article 3. The Soviets acted in remarkably close cooperation with Francophone partners and introduced powerful proposals to stop inhumane measures in wartime such as the death penalty.

While often working together with Western partners, the Soviets brought occasionally legally unorthodox proposals to the negotiating table. Take, for example, their suggestion to consider captured soldiers, such as bomber pilots, who were suspected of war crimes as criminals liable to punishment rather than protection as prisoners of war—a proposal rejected by the diplomatic conference, triggering a Soviet reservation. Another distinctive Soviet contribution to the drafting process was its suggestion to give far more extensive protections to irregulars who were fighting for a so-called "just cause." In response

[64] Minutes of Signature Ceremony, December 1949, no. CD_1949_ACTES_FRE_32, ICRC Library.
[65] Boyd van Dijk, "'The Great Humanitarian': The Soviet Union, the International Committee of the Red Cross, and the Geneva Conventions of 1949," *Law and History Review*, Vol. 37, No. 1 (2019): 209–235.
[66] Report Soviet-Ukrainian Delegation, no. F. 2, Op. 12cc, Spr. 969, Ark. 60–76, Tsentral'nyi derzhavnyi arhiv vyschykh organiv vlady ta upravlinnia Ukrainy (TSDAVO), Kiev, Ukraine.
[67] One of the few historians who has noted the Soviet impact on the Geneva Conventions is Paul Betts, "Universalism and its Discontents: Humanity as a Twentieth-Century Concept," in *Humanity: A History of European Concepts in Practice from the Sixteenth Century to the Present*, eds Fabian Klose and Mirjam Thulin (Göttingen: Vandenhoeck & Ruprecht, 2016), 51–70, 65.

CONCLUSION 319

to its country's wartime experiences with fighting guerrilla warfare against an enemy aggressor and based on its unique notion of just war theory, the Soviet delegation, similar to the French, wished to soften the law's strict conditions for irregulars fighting for such a cause. They also proposed to eradicate torture and summary execution. As we saw in Chapter 4, the Anglo-American bloc for its part tried to keep the scope of the Conventions for such irregulars to a dangerous minimum.[68]

The Soviets made the diplomatic conference into a sort of postcolonial forum in which imperial Western double standards could be vilified. The former endorsed the Conventions' application to colonial war by seeking to prevent the Stockholm draft's scope from being restricted. At the same time, the Soviets and their allies staunchly defended state sovereignty by preventing outside observers from entering their prison archipelagos. Accordingly, Slavin's delegation prevented political prisoners from accessing the Civilian Convention, refused to adopt penetrating enforcement mechanisms, and denied the ICRC a mandate to visit Soviet prisons. It is telling that they removed from their own plan for applying the Conventions to wars within empires those elements regarding outside supervision, the conditions under which the provision would apply, and those who would determine its application, thereby preventing humanitarian law's automatic application to anti-Soviet rebellions.[69]

A far more alluring Soviet contribution to humanitarian law's making was their essential, though now largely forgotten, role in facilitating the Civilian Convention's breakthrough. Against the outcome expected by most delegates, the Soviet delegation, working alongside Western European and ICRC experts, powerfully supported efforts to limit occupiers' powers and to empower civilian protection. Slavin's men and women wished to restrict, if not outlaw, the use of hostage taking, torture, indiscriminate bombing, reprisals, and the death penalty, following Stalin's order of 1947.[70] By supporting many of the ICRC's proposals on these matters, the delegation frequently succeeded in defeating many of the Anglo-American proposals of a more restrictive nature. The result ("an undoubtable success"[71]) was a fairly robust Civilian Convention.[72]

---

[68] Van Dijk, "The Great Humanitarian."
[69] Ibid.
[70] Ibid.
[71] Report Soviet-Ukrainian Delegation, no. F. 2, Op. 12cc, Spr. 969, Ark. 60–76, TSDAVO.
[72] Ironically, after the Cold War, CA3 was used to prosecute certain Communist crimes in times of non-international armed conflict. See Tamás Hoffmann, "Individual Criminal Responsibility for Crimes Committed in Non-International Armed Conflicts: The Hungarian Jurisprudence on the 1956 Volley Cases" in *Criminal Law Between War and Peace: Justice and Cooperation in Criminal Matters in International Military Interventions*, eds Stefano Manacordan and Adan Nieto (Cuenca: Ediciones de la Universidad de Castilla-La Mancha, 2009), 735–753.

320   PREPARING FOR WAR

As seen previously, Pilloud admitted privately that he "hardly dared to think what would have become of the treaty without the presence of [the Soviet] delegation."[73]

The Soviet delegation also turned Geneva into a Cold War battleground through its support for potentially wide-ranging legal principles and by "cladding [itself] in a white sheet and posturing as the champion of the 'humanitarians'."[74] In doing so, it assumed the role of a "great humanitarian" by trying to embarrass particularly those "who oppose[d] working drafts on practical and legal grounds," according to concerned Anglo-American drafters.[75] By contrast, the Soviets believed the Anglo-American powers were making use of the Conventions as a weapon "to prepare [for] a new war."[76]

In their view, the major Western powers were exploiting the Conventions as a means to spy on them, to "demoralize" Soviet soldiers by implying that being a POW "is very convenient," and to reinforce a so-called "war psychosis."[77] The leading Soviet newspaper *Pravda* published various articles attacking the Western bloc's alleged "war mongering" by critically reporting on its resistance to Soviet-sponsored proposals to abolish indiscriminate bombing. Aside from their propagandistic nature, these Soviet reports testified to a wider fear of an upcoming war, whereby the Conventions would be used "without a doubt" by the Anglo-American bloc to properly prepare for it.[78]

In the Soviet mind, the Anglo-American delegates were trying to secure "maximum guarantees for their prisoners of war" while "creating all possible loopholes" and using the pro-American ICRC to "broaden [their] intelligence and sabotage activities on [Soviet] territory."[79] What is striking is less the Soviet perception of Western powers than the fear of war shared by its Cold War adversaries.[80] The widespread fear of war played a key role in the "tragic irony," as described by Bourdet, that the diplomatic conference, which sought to regulate war instead of ensuring perpetual peace, was one of the few moments

---

[73] In a similar way, he noted that the Soviets, who continued to be suspicious of such Western accommodation, had been "very useful" from his organization's perspective. Rapport Spécial Etabli par Pilloud, 16 September 1949, no. CR-254-1, AICRC. For the Soviet suspicions, see Report Soviet-Ukrainian Delegation, no. F. 2, Op. 12cc, Spr. 969, Ark. 60–76, TSDAVO. For British frustration about Western European accommodation towards the Soviet delegation, see Craigie's Report on Diplomatic Conference, November 1949, no. 6036, ADM116 (Admiralty), TNA.

[74] Craigie's Report on Diplomatic Conference, November 1949, no. 6036, ADM116, TNA.

[75] Cable US delegation on Diplomatic Conference, 2 May 1949, no. 5, RG 43 – Entry 40, NARA.

[76] Report Soviet-Ukrainian Delegation, no. F. 2, Op. 12cc, Spr. 969, Ark. 60–76, TSDAVO.

[77] Report Soviet-Ukrainian Delegation, no. F. 2, Op. 12cc, Spr. 969, Ark. 60–76, TSDAVO.

[78] Van Dijk, "'The Great Humanitarian.'"

[79] Report Soviet-Ukrainian Delegation, no. F. 2, Op. 12cc, Spr. 969, Ark. 60–76, TSDAVO.

[80] Conference Diplomatique. Rapport Spécial Etabli par Pilloud, 16 September 1949, no. CR-254-1, AICRC.

of the early Cold War in which both sides could agree upon anything legally binding.[81]

The diplomatic conference succeeded not because the Great Powers completely agreed on every particular; rather, each had its own reasons for supporting Geneva's work. The United States wished to better protect its soldiers who fell into enemy captivity; France was primarily concerned with safeguarding civilians and irregulars; the Chinese wanted recognition for their wartime suffering; the Soviets demanded major limitations while objecting to foreign interference; and the British wished to preserve their international reputation. Despite these different agendas, the Great Powers were able to discern enough overlap among their interests to agree on a revision of international law at this tense stage of the Cold War and decolonization.

C.2 Geneva's Legacies

Among Pictet's drafting team, the acceptance of the Geneva Conventions occasioned both euphoria and a sobering sense of reality. Recognizing that the Conventions remained an unfinished project, the group had already begun preparing plans to revise the newly signed treaties in the 1950s. One decade later, following the diplomatic revolution represented by the Third World's rise on the global stage, this led to the official start of a new drafting process.[82] In response to the Conventions' perceived shortcomings, the Irish signatory (and former veteran of the guerrilla struggle against British rule) Seán MacBride famously lobbied the Third World bloc to support the introduction of a special resolution at the Teheran Conference in 1968.[83] In many ways, the supporters of this text continued the drafters' calls for the protection of rights in armed conflict by transforming its principles in ways that would reshape humanitarian law's future.[84]

In terms of Geneva's legacies, it is striking that despite the immense controversy surrounding the adoption of Common Article 3, MacBride and

---

[81] *Combat*, 8 December 1949; and *Neue Zürcher Zeitung*, 10 December 1949.

[82] Most tragically, the revived drafting process could not take place at the old conference hall (the Bâtiment Électoral/Palais) after it burned down in 1964.

[83] For a description of MacBride's special signature ceremony, see *Journal de Genève*, 20 December 1949. See also Roland Burke, *Decolonization and the Evolution of International Human Rights* (Philadelphia, PA: University of Pennsylvania Press, 2010); and Steven Jensen, *The Making of International Human Rights: The 1960s, Decolonization, and the Reconstruction of Global Values* (Cambridge: Cambridge University Press, 2017).

[84] Boyd van Dijk, "Human Rights in War: On the Entangled Foundations of the 1949 Geneva Conventions," *American Journal of International Law*, Vol. 112, No. 4 (2018): 553–582.

322 PREPARING FOR WAR

others carried on pursuing the ICRC's agenda of applying the concept of rights to armed conflict and internationalizing wars within states after 1949.[85] Following the outbreak of new wars of decolonization and proxy wars in Africa and Asia,[86] they continued to discuss the possibility of applying humanitarian law to wars within empires, or even to political prisoners in situations deemed to fall short of "armed conflict."[87] The anti-apartheid activist Nelson Mandela would become the most famous beneficiary of this latter initiative. This shows how drafters' attempts to apply notions of human rights to internal armed conflicts in 1949 had generated a critical shift in attitudes toward sovereignty itself. Gradually it gave rise to a revitalized form of humanitarian legal thinking, which has only grown in importance as new wars have broken out.

Although CA3's final text had been designed by European imperialists, anti-colonial activists exploited its principles and language of internationalization to oppose colonial rule, and increasingly engaged with humanitarian law. In 1957, they welcomed the Red Cross movement into the Third World (i.e. New Delhi) for the first time. Although it was hardly anti-colonial, the ICRC facilitated that agenda, in that it was willing to use its right of initiative to invite Global South actors and to intervene in wars of decolonization, despite their marginalization from CA3's restrictive scope. While imperial powers refused to apply the article for years, anti-colonial actors were able to make use of its platform as a megaphone to voice their claims.[88] In direct response to these struggles, the ICRC would later push to widen CA3's existing scope and thus garner support for its principles in the context of the wars of decolonization in Algeria, Kenya, and elsewhere in the Global South.

Despite these achievements, the ICRC believed CA3's initial defects deserved additional revision in the years after 1949. Postcolonial developmental

---

[85] See also Eleanor Davey, "Decolonizing the Geneva Conventions: National Liberation and the Development of Humanitarian Law," in *Decolonization, Self-Determination, and the Rise of Global Human Rights Politics*, eds Dirk Moses, Marco Duranti, and Roland Burke (Cambridge: Cambridge University Press, 2020), 375–396; and Jessica Whyte, "The 'Dangerous Concept of the Just War': Decolonization, Wars of National Liberation, and the Additional Protocols to the Geneva Conventions," *Humanity* [2018]: 313–41.

[86] Odd Arne Westad, *The Global Cold War: Third World Interventions and the Making of Our Times* (Cambridge: Cambridge University Press, 2005).

[87] For a broader discussion of the Third World and the laws of war after 1949, see Georges Abi-Saab, "The Third World and the International Legal Order," *Revue Egyptienne de Droit International*, Vol. 29 (1973): 27–66; Georges Abi-Saab, "The Newly Independent States and the Rules of International Law: An Outline," *Howard Law Journal*, Vol. 8, No. 2 (1962): 95–121; and Mohammed Bedjaoui, *Law and the Algerian Revolution* (Brussels: International Associations of Democratic Lawyers, 1961).

[88] See Brian Drohan, *Brutality in an Age of Human Rights: Activism and Counterinsurgency at the End of the British Empire* (Ithaca, NY: Cornell University Press, 2018), 4; Giovanni Mantilla, *Lawmaking under Pressure: International Humanitarian Law and Internal Armed Conflict* (Ithaca, NY: Cornell University Press, forthcoming), 96–97; and Fabian Klose, "The Colonial Testing Ground: The International Committee of the Red Cross and the Violent End of Empire," *Humanity* [2011]: 107–126.

states, which had just regained their sovereignty, however felt little sympathy for these plans to update CA3. Nonetheless, they could not dictate or reject all of them, partly due to the normative pressure exerted by Pictet's ICRC. Although they had paradoxically become defenders of parts of Geneva's Eurocentric legacies,[89] states in the Global South also challenged the fact that the Conventions did not recognize wars of national liberation as international armed conflicts.[90] Geneva's decision to consider anti-colonial conflicts as a mirror image (i.e. non-international armed conflicts, NIACs) sometimes led to fierce Third World critique.

In the following years, postcolonial states and Pictet's legal experts began revising the existing Conventions in response to these formative debates. Most importantly, the opening article of the First Additional Protocol proscribed colonialism and classified national liberation movements as international legal subjects.[91] As such, it broke with Geneva's Eurocentric inheritance.[92] By contrast, the ICRC drafters of the Second Additional Protocol sought to further develop Common Article 3, though they eventually had to accept a higher threshold due to widespread state opposition.[93] Disappointed, they and other advocates of humanitarian law gradually shifted away from creating more black letter law for wars within states. In the succeeding decades they focused instead on developing customary law, international criminal justice, and *opinio juris* concepts.[94] Despite its initial defects, Common Article 3 remains highly relevant today: in the 1990s, the International Criminal Tribunal for the former Yugoslavia used it as a crucial means to prosecute war crimes committed during the Balkan Wars.[95] More recently, the US Supreme Court appealed to it in stigmatizing the torture of Al Qaeda detainees during the "War on Terror" (see below).[96]

---

[89] Jochen von Bernstorff, "The Battle for the Recognition of Wars of National Liberation" in *The Battle for International Law: South–North Perspectives on the Decolonization Era*, eds Jochen von Bernstorff and Philipp Dann (Oxford: Oxford University Press, 2019), 52–70, 55.

[90] Von Bernstorff, "The Battle for the Recognition of Wars of National Liberation," 70; and Helen Kinsella, "Superfluous Injury and Unnecessary Suffering: National Liberation and the Laws of War," *Political Power and Social Theory*, Vol. 32 (2017): 205–31.

[91] Amanda Alexander, "International Humanitarian Law, Postcolonialism and the 1977 Geneva Protocol I," *Melbourne Journal of International Law*, Vol. 17, No. 1 (2016): 15–50.

[92] Von Bernstorff, "The Battle for the Recognition of Wars of National Liberation," 69–70.

[93] On the Additional Protocols of 1977, see David Forsythe, "Legal Management of Internal War: The 1977 Protocol on Non-international Armed Conflicts," *American Journal of International Law*, Vol. 72, No. 2 (1978): 272–95; and Mantilla, *Lawmaking under Pressure*, 132.

[94] Giovanni Mantilla, "The Origins and Evolution of the 1949 Geneva Conventions and the 1977 Additional Protocols" in *Do the Geneva Conventions Matter?* eds Matthew Evangelista and Nina Tannenwald (Oxford: Oxford University Press, 2017), 35–68; and Sandesh Sivakumaran, "Making and Shaping the Law of Armed Conflict," *Current Legal Problems*, Vol. 71, No. 1 (2018): 119–160.

[95] Shane Darcy, *Judges, Law and War: The Judicial Development of International Humanitarian Law* (Cambridge: Cambridge University Press, 2014).

[96] See Supreme Court of the United States, *Hamdan v. Rumsfeld*, 29 June 2006.

324 PREPARING FOR WAR

Building upon its success in Geneva, the ICRC worked assiduously to disseminate the Civilian Convention's principles in the decades after 1949. Most strikingly, it often went much further than the treaty strictly allowed for. For example, its advocates strategically used some of the Convention's principles to pressure states into treating political prisoners humanely, regardless of their legal exclusion. Furthermore, they began addressing gender-related questions that had been sidelined in 1949. These efforts led to a record number of ICRC prison visits as part of a wider normative shift that dramatically shaped the future of the law, which increasingly took account of women's dignity and their experiences in wartime.[97] What this uplifting story does not fully convey, however, is that the Civilian Convention did little to protect civilians—including women and children—against indiscriminate warfare in the years after its signing. The Korean War, in which so-called recognized weapons of war were widely used to destroy urban areas, painfully revealed the implications of the treaty's silence with regard to mass civilian death inflicted by bombing.[98]

When intervening on the Korean peninsula in 1950, the United States publicly proclaimed that targeting civilians was unacceptable. As the war escalated, however, it soon decided to disregard this principle, targeting Korean civilians indiscriminately and rejecting the ICRC's proposal to create safety zones in accordance with the Civilian Convention. By the end of the war, most North Korean cities had been obliterated by US bombers.[99] ICRC legal experts responded by trying to fill Geneva's lacunae. Building upon Pictet's resolution against "blind weapons," they sought to reaffirm the principle of distinction, which had collapsed in the civilian netherworld of the Korean War.[100]

Subaltern victims of US bombing insisted on absolute prohibitions against civilian targeting.[101] In the face of the fierce opposition from Anglo-American drafters, however, the ICRC chose to demand only basic restrictions on indiscriminate bombing.[102] These efforts eventually led to the adoption of the

[97] Andrew Thompson, "Humanitarian Principles Put to the Test: Challenges to Humanitarian Action during Decolonization," *International Review of the Red Cross*, Vol. 97, No. 897/898 (2015): 45–76.

[98] Sahr Conway-Lanz, *Collateral Damage: Americans, Noncombatant Immunity and Atrocity after World War II* (Abingdon: Routledge, 2006); and John Tirman, *The Deaths of Others: The Fate of Civilians in America's Wars* (Oxford: Oxford University Press, 2011), 59–122.

[99] Conway-Lanz, *Collateral Damage*, 47–50, 59; Tami Davis Biddle, *Rhetoric and Reality in Air Warfare: The Evolution of British and American Ideas about Strategic Bombing* (Princeton, NJ: Princeton University Press, 2002), 296; and Odd Arne Westad, *The Cold War: A World History* (New York: Basic Books, 2017).

[100] Mantilla, *Lawmaking under Pressure*, 108.

[101] For a pioneering history of air warfare and international law after 1949, see Luís Paulo Bogliolo, "Governing from Above: A History of Aerial Bombing and International Law," Ph.D. Dissertation, University of Melbourne, 2020, 134–198.

[102] Mantilla, *Lawmaking under Pressure*, 60.

(non-binding) New Delhi Rules in 1957. Some of the principles laid down in this agreement were finally re-adapted for the Protocols precisely two decades later. Crucially, when it came to formulating rules for warfare from the skies, these new treaties established insufficient protections from aerial attacks for civilians. This was mainly down to their permissive nature and continuing Anglo-American obstructionism.[103] Moreover, the regulation of nuclear warfare remained a legal taboo after 1949 due to NATO and Russian resistance— even today, it remains Geneva's most controversial silence.[104]

Another important shortcoming of the Civilian Convention was its inability to consider starvation as a grave breach of humanitarian law. Anglo-American drafters had successfully prevented the conference from placing severe restrictions on the use of starvation as a weapon, with the Biafrans becoming its most prominent victim group in the 1960s.[105] In this period the Nigerian government placed a legalized blockade on the breakaway polity, raising the specter of mass famine and thousands of civilian deaths. The ICRC asked whether it could have access to these victims. Despite the organization invoking its right of initiative under CA3, this effort was met with state opposition. Instead of granting the ICRC's request, the Nigerian central government applied the Civilian Convention's permissive blockade article, exploiting its extensive discretionary powers to subvert the ICRC's operations in Biafra.[106]

Humanitarian law did little to alleviate the ICRC's precarious situation in Nigeria—let alone to recognize that black lives mattered. The Civilian Convention privileged the rights of the blockader, requiring its consent to allow ICRC relief flights to be flown into the famine-struck province. This draconian requirement prompted Western liberals and humanitarian competitors to level major criticisms at the ICRC. In their view, it was imperative that the ICRC challenge the belligerents' unwillingness to accept relief flights, and not adhere strictly to "outdated" rules. Most famously, the French doctor Bernard

---

[103] Bogliolo, "Governing from Above."

[104] The Treaty on the Prohibition of Nuclear Weapons was signed on 7 July 2017 in New York, and entered into force in January 2021.

[105] See Thierry Hentsch, *Face au Blocus: Histoire de l'Intervention du Comité International de la Croix-Rouge dans le Conflit du Nigéria, 1967–1970* (Geneva: Droz, 1973); Eleanor Davey, *Idealism beyond Borders: The French Revolutionary Left and the Rise of Humanitarianism, 1954–1988* (Cambridge: Cambridge University Press, 2015); Marie-Luce Desgrandchamps, "'Organising the Unpredictable': The Nigeria–Biafra War and Its Impact on the ICRC," *International Review of the Red Cross*, No. 888 (2012): 1409–1432; Dirk Moses and Lasse Heerten, *Postcolonial Conflict and the Question of Genocide: The Nigeria-Biafra War, 1967–1970* (Abingdon: Routledge, 2018); and Alex De Waal, *Mass Starvation: The History and Future of Famine* (Cambridge: Polity, 2018).

[106] Nicholas Mulder and Boyd van Dijk, "Why Did Starvation Not Become the Paradigmatic War Crime in International Law?" in *Contingency in International Law: On the Possibility of Different Legal Histories*, eds Ingo Venzke and Kevin Jon Heller (Oxford: Oxford University Press, 2021), 371–388.

326 PREPARING FOR WAR

Kouchner argued that saving suffering Biafrans served a higher moral purpose than strictly following the principles of humanitarian law. The ICRC's operations ended abruptly in 1969 when one of its airplanes was shot down, forcing its legal experts to come to terms with Geneva's legacy in enabling starvation.[107]

After Biafra, Pictet's colleagues had to recognize that the ICRC's failed operations there were at least partly attributable to the Conventions' unwillingness to restrict blockading rights. As Third World victims of starvation gathered in Geneva for a discussion of the Protocols in the 1970s, the drafters formulated a historically unique (though conditional) prohibition against starvation. Nonetheless, the Reagan Administration—as well as a number of other important states, including India—opposed ratifying the Protocols. This left a dangerous legal gray zone in place. Since the adoption of the Protocols, states have continued to starve enemy civilians, from the UN sanctions regime against Iraq in the 1990s to the most recent famines in Yemen and Syria. To this day, the question of whether it is permissible to block civilians' access to food supplies as means of pressuring enemy states remains fraught and continues to spark debate among international lawyers.[108]

In addition to criticizing Western blockades, Third World states fervently campaigned on behalf of so-called "freedom fighters."[109] In particular, they contested the POW Convention's strict criteria for determining POW status. These forced anti-colonial irregulars to identify and distinguish themselves, thereby making them easy targets for regular imperial armies. This contestation resonated with a similar argument that French victims of fascist occupation had advanced in 1949, which demanded protection for interstate resistance fighters. Afro-Asian states turned this argument on its head by analogizing that "freedom fighters" were no different from those anti-fascist irregulars, and by trying to widen the POW Convention's scope after Cahen-Salvador's delegation had failed to achieve this in 1949.[110] Indeed, the 1970s saw the re-adaptation of more proposals that had previously been rejected. After the diplomatic

---

[107] Nicholas Mulder and Boyd van Dijk, "Why Did Starvation Not Become the Paradigmatic War Crime in International Law?" in *Contingency in International Law: On the Possibility of Different Legal Histories*, eds Ingo Venzke and Kevin Jon Heller (Oxford: Oxford University Press, 2021), 371–388.

[108] Hull, *A Scrap of Paper*, 166. For recent discussions on starvation, international law, and (non-)international armed conflicts, see Federica d'Alessandra and Matthew Gillett, "The War Crime of Starvation in Non-International Armed Conflict," *Journal of International Criminal Justice*, Vol. 17, No. 4 (2019): 815–847; and Simone Hutter, *Starvation as a Weapon: Domestic Policies of Deliberate Starvation as a Means to an End Under International Law* (Leiden: Brill, 2015).

[109] Didier Fassin, *Humanitarian Reason: A Moral History of the Present* (Berkeley: University of California Press, 2012).

[110] Helen Kinsella and Giovanni Mantilla, "Contestation before Compliance: History, Politics, and Power in International Humanitarian Law," *International Studies Quarterly*, Vol. 64, No. 3 (2020): 649–656.

conference in 1949, the ICRC and Afro-Asian experts sought to ensure that captured anti-colonial irregulars were accorded basic human rights by re-addressing plans which had been opposed. This ultimately led to a widening of API's scope, ensuring that most irregulars (with the exception of mercenaries) fell under rather than between the Geneva Conventions and escaped the black hole of the security clause. As socialist drafters had previously hoped, this empowered "freedom fighters' with a "just cause," thereby subverting Geneva's exclusionary legacies.[111]

As seen previously, Geneva's enforcement mechanisms fell short of the ICRC's expectations. The Great Powers, especially the Soviets, had deliberately weakened its proposals in crucial areas so as to protect their sovereignty from outside interference. To that end, they crippled the system of Protecting Powers, neutered the concept of substitutes, and made the grave breaches unable to deter illicit state behavior.[112] While empowering the ICRC's position, the Great Powers deliberately denied the organization's delegates enough power to exercise their supervisory role fully, making them look toothless in the killing fields of the Cold War.[113] Although Francophone experts attempted to fix some of Geneva's most systemic enforcement problems, these efforts after 1949 proved futile.[114]

In the 1970s the ICRC and other drafting bodies reflected upon these discouraging outcomes. In response, they readdressed a whole range of previously rejected proposals for propping up Geneva's weak enforcement framework. Among other plans, these actors proposed a global fact-finding body, reintroduced the concept of automatic substitutes, and took steps to extend these notions to wars within states for the first time. As they had done in 1949, the Soviets opposed proposals such as these, which contested their sovereignty in vital areas. Many Third World states were similarly concerned to shield their sovereignty from outside interference, having attained it only recently and often under violent conditions. As such, they were reluctant to go along with far-reaching enforcement proposals.[115]

Given this resistance, Geneva's weak enforcement system remained largely in place after 1977. Protecting Powers became obsolete and ad hoc fact-finding

---

[111] Mantilla, "The Origins and Evolution of the 1949 Geneva Conventions and the 1977 Additional Protocols," 58.

[112] Ibid., 61.

[113] Mantilla, "The Origins and Evolution of the 1949 Geneva Conventions and the 1977 Additional Protocols," 53–54. See also Paul Thomas Chamberlin, *The Cold War's Killing Fields: Rethinking the Long Peace* (New York: Harper, 2019).

[114] De La Pradelle, *La Conférence Diplomatique*, 347–349.

[115] Mantilla, "The Origins and Evolution of the 1949 Geneva Conventions and the 1977 Additional Protocols," 53–54, 61.

328 PREPARING FOR WAR

commissions remained dormant—a "sleeping beauty"—for a long time.[116] Geneva's system of enforcement had no serious impact during the Cold War, except for ICRC supervision.[117] Geneva's lonely supervisors were aided in their efforts only from the 1980s onward, when several international bodies came of age. These institutions, which ranged from UN bodies, through criminal courts,[118] to several human rights groups (especially Human Rights Watch and Amnesty International), promoted compliance on the battlefield. That said, the system of enforcement remains the eternal headache of humanitarian law.

This became painfully clear in the wake of 9/11, when the Conventions suddenly became a key point of contention in US political debates regarding the Bush Administration's decision to sanction torture.[119] The government's legal advisors dismissed the Conventions as "quaint" and/or irrelevant in their struggle against Al Qaeda and the Taliban. In so doing, they precipitated the emergence of a new global program of brutal interrogation, which broke with the Conventions' principles on humane treatment. In 2006, in the well-known *Hamdan v Rumsfeld* case, the US Supreme Court used CA3 to put an end to this system of global torture, or at least tried to alleviate its most inhumane aspects. US legal advisors also met internal resistance on the part of state lawyers from the later administration and external opposition from civil rights groups.[120] This reflected a period of correction empowered by Barack Obama's presidency, even if not a single perpetrator was ever held accountable for ordering or executing torture.[121]

During the US occupation of Iraq after 2003, the Bush Administration's former legal advisor John Yoo argued that so-called Iraqi saboteurs could fall under the Civilian Convention, although he also continued to stress that the Conventions could not cover members of the Taliban or Al Qaeda.[122] In an

---

[116] Frits Kalshoven, "The International Humanitarian Fact-Finding Commission: A Sleeping Beauty?" *Humanitäires Völkerrecht* [2002]: 213–216.

[117] David Forsythe, "Who Guards the Guardians: Third Parties and the Law of Armed Conflict," *American Journal of International Law*, Vol. 70, No. 1 (1976): 41–61, 45–46; and Gentian Zyberi, "Enforcement of International Humanitarian Law" in *Human Rights Institutions, Tribunals and Courts: Legacy and Promise*, ed. Gerd Oberleitner (Singapore: Springer, 2019), 377–400.

[118] William Schabas, *The International Criminal Court: A Commentary on the Rome Statute* (Oxford: Oxford University Press, 2010),

[119] Ian Hurd, *How to Do Things with International Law* (Princeton: Princeton University Press, 2017), 103–128. See also Richard Abel, *Law's Wars: The Fate of the Rule of Law in the US "War on Terror"* (Cambridge: Cambridge University Press, 2019).

[120] Jens David Ohlin, *The Assault on International Law* (Oxford: Oxford University Press, 2015).

[121] Charlie Savage, *Power Wars: Inside Obama's Post-9/11 Presidency* (New York: Little, Brown & Company, 2016).

[122] For a more detailed insider's account of these debates within the Bush Administration, see Jack Goldsmith, *The Terror Presidency: Law and Judgment Inside the Bush Administration* (New York: W.W. Norton & Co, 2009).

op-ed for the *Wall Street Journal*, Yoo tried to justify his claims by deliberately using the loopholes in the treaty's security clause to condone the strict handling, if not brutal ill-treatment, of detainees in Iraqi belligerent territory by making these applicable to those held in occupied territory, framed as "Iraqi saboteurs"—an extrajudicial argument that is strikingly reminiscent of the position adopted by Anglo-American drafters in 1949.

The term "saboteur" was mentioned only in the fifth article's sentence covering occupied territory, not in the section regarding belligerent territory to which Yoo was referring.[123] Usually, a "saboteur" had significantly more protections than a "suspect" detained in belligerent territory. However, Yoo put the Iraqi saboteur under the article's far stricter section on belligerent territory, such as would "permit the use of more coercive interrogation approaches to prevent future attacks."[124] By invoking the most permissive feature of the security clause, he tried to justify the US government's extrajudicial policies that were being used in detention facilities in Iraq. In the 1950s, Pictet's experts had warned of precisely this danger: namely, that this security clause might enable extrajudicial detainment "under conditions which are almost impossible to check."[125]

This story shows that the principles established by the Conventions had both inclusive and exclusive impulses and could be invoked by actors from across the political spectrum—even by Yoo himself. The Conventions could be invoked to serve many purposes; appealing to them did not automatically imply an attempt to alleviate the suffering of others. Indeed, the rise of a destructive drone empire under Obama's watch reminds us that the defenders of humanitarian law can also tolerate terrible inhumanity.[126] In a similar vein, the drafters understood and arranged the Conventions in seemingly contradictory ways (only seemingly contradictory because they often saw matters very differently to our contemporary view). Among other apparent contradictions, they rejected deportations while expelling millions of Germans from their homes after 1945 and banned extermination in response to the Holocaust while

---

[123] Convention relative to the Protection of Civilian Persons in Time of War, Article 5, 12 August 1949.

[124] John Yoo, "Terrorists Have No Geneva Rights," *The Wall Street Journal*, 26 May 2004. This manipulation of the security clause was registered by the jurist Jason Callen. He made note of it in an email he sent to Jack Goldsmith, then the head of the Office of Legal Counsel. See Email Jason Callen to Jack Goldsmith on Yoo's Article in The Wall Street Journal, 26 May 2004, from https://www.thetorturedatab ase.org/files/foia_subsite/pdfs/DOJOLC000121.pdf (retrieved 23 February 2016).

[125] Jean Pictet, *The Geneva Conventions of 12 August 1949: Commentary* (Geneva; ICRC, 1958); and Conference Diplomatique. Rapport Spécial Etabli par Pilloud, 16 September 1949, no. CR-254-1, AICRC.

[126] Samuel Moyn, *Humane: How the United States Abandoned Peace and Reinvented War* (New York: Farrar, Straus and Giroux, 2021); Thomas Gregory, "Drones, Targeted Killings, and the Limitations of International Law," *International Political Sociology*, Vol. 9, No. 3 (2015); 197–212.

330 PREPARING FOR WAR

privately discussing the use of nuclear weapons, which would lead to civilian annihilation.[127]

Today, it is possible to look back and see what drafters could not—or did not want to—see. For instance, they banned acts such as pillage but failed to strictly outlaw sexual violence, despite its brutality and frequent occurrence in wartime.[128] Nevertheless, it should come as little surprise that drafters failed to develop a comprehensive legal package more than seventy years ago. The inability to fully eradicate wartime suffering today should humble contemporary observers and soften criticism of what drafters did accomplish in 1949. It should also recall the significant political capital that they invested in humanizing warfare—the risks they took, the persuasion this required, the struggles they fought, and the prices they paid in their attempts to secure widespread support among the Great Powers. All of this underlines how distant that goal remains today, despite shared experiences of mass violence and geopolitical rivalries.

Although the women and men who drafted the Conventions made lasting contributions, they had to grapple with historical circumstances and contingencies that they could not possibly hope to control alone. They were products of their time. As such, they worked hard to find common ground in Stockholm, in their respective capitals, and in Geneva, eventually creating a remarkably extensive and detailed package of new rules for warfare. It represented the greatest, most enduring attempt of the twentieth century in setting an ambitious agenda for humanized war. This campaign of limiting the effects of warfare, which emerged from the ruins of two world wars and in response to new threats of war, presented neither a clear nor a final recipe for palliative care in wartime that would place strict limitations on what is legally permitted and proscribed. The drafting process resembled less an ivory tower, in which blueprints are conceived in splendid isolation, than a political arena, in which actors contemplate and struggle over different proposals and the stakes are often impossibly high.

In the face of postwar rivalries among the Western and Eastern bloc states, Pictet's originally ambitious drafting agenda seemed destined to fail. Nevertheless, he and other drafters succeeded in spawning a new legal

---

[127] Van Dijk, "Human Rights in War," 581–582.

[128] The ICRC noted how "countless women of all ages [had been] the victims of the most abominable outrages during the war [...] in occupied territories, very many cases of rape occurred." But it did not call for the outlawing or criminalization of sexual violence, only the protection of women's "honor." ICRC Report, 1947, No. CEG_1947_DOC_PROTCIV_ENG, ICRC Library; and Tuba Inal, *Looting and Rape in Wartime: Law and Change in International Relations* (Philadelphia, PA: University of Pennsylvania Press, 2013).

vocabulary—humanitarian law; reenergized an older conversation about how humanity might be protected from its worst impulses; and shaped the ideas of legal theorists, moral philosophers, military officers, and other practitioners for decades to come. Although they encouraged others to constantly update these new rules and to engage in fresh types of hermeneutic activism, the main conceptual building blocks of humanitarian law, such as the principle of civilian rights, have remained in place. Indeed, almost every international document and rule relating to warfare since 1949 takes the Geneva Conventions as a cornerstone for regulating warfare. Humanitarian law has now moved to the center of global politics and has often been invoked by those demanding an end to brutal occupations and other inhumane acts in armed conflict. From Palestinian survivors of collective penalties to Ukrainian doctors, Congolese rebels to Sri Lankan activists, ICRC delegates to Latin American families of missing relatives—all of these different groups now speak Geneva's language of rights, justice, and humanity.[129]

At the same time, celebrating the impact of the Conventions should not lead to analytical complacency. The warnings that were already being voiced at the genesis of the Conventions should not be forgotten. Lauterpacht, a former drafter of the grave breaches principles, worried that the law's core idea of humanizing warfare might be too hierarchical, if not selective, in its central aims. Some were concerned that in leaving aerial bombing deregulated while outlawing so-called minor evils (e.g. torture), the Conventions would send the wrong signal: humanized war, they feared, might lower the threshold of war itself. Why should we devote political energy, they asked, to limiting the effects of future wars rather than eradicating their root causes? The importance of this question has not diminished in the contemporary age of endless war.[130]

It is striking that an extraordinary number of questions that shaped debates in Geneva several decades ago continue to resonate today. Whereas in 1949 the system of supervision that drafters developed remained embryonic, now there exist fact-finding bodies, social media activism, global investigative reporters, UN missions, human rights groups, and so forth. Pictet's drafters also

---

[129] Acte d'Engagement Auprès de l'Appel de Genève pour la Protection des Soins de Santé Pendant les Conflits Armés, APCLS, 18 August 2019, Archives Geneva Call, Geneva. See also Jessica Stanton, *Violence and Restraint in Civil War: Civilian Targeting in the Shadow of International Law* (Cambridge: Cambridge University Press, 2017); Olivier Bangerter, "Reasons Why Armed Groups Choose to Respect International Humanitarian Law or Not," *International Review of the Red Cross*, Vol. 93, No. 882 (2011): 353–384; and Hyeran Jo, *Compliant Rebels: Rebel Groups and International Law in World Politics* (New York: Cambridge University Press, 2015).

[130] Moyn, *Humane*; Rosa Brooks, *How Everything Became War and the Military Became Everything: Tales from the Pentagon* (New York: Simon and Schuster, 2019); and Van Dijk, "Human Rights in War," 581–582.

332 PREPARING FOR WAR

contemplated regulating new (aerial) weaponry, but this was never put into practice. In the contemporary world, activists are more concerned about the Conventions than ever before—yet they often feel powerless to halt indiscriminate bombing and blockade.[131] They wonder whether societies really are better off for having agreed to these rules; although many states piously claim to uphold the Conventions, they do little to enforce or adhere to them.

It is certainly true that a global wave of radical nationalism and violence—all in the wake of broader political and technological developments—threatens some of the core principles of humanitarian law, with civilians bearing the brunt of the damage.[132] For example, the ICRC has already expressed growing concern about the threat of escalating cyber attacks, which target civilians indiscriminately.[133] In the wake of global efforts to develop pioneering cyber manuals,[134] it has set new norms for the protection of civilians and their property in weaponized cyberspace. In tackling this problem, Brad Smith, the president of Microsoft, has launched a new initiative named a "digital Geneva Convention."[135] Along with Swiss officials, he has proposed that the private sector and its millions of customers worldwide can be protected by modeling a new cyber accord on the framework of the Civilian Convention. Most strikingly, the central task of this treaty, according to Smith, was that of upholding the principle of distinction in wartime by protecting "civilian infrastructure."[136]

Nothing could have been further from the historical reality, however. As shown in Chapter 5, Western drafters deliberately scrapped the principle of

---

[131] Alexander Downes, *Targeting Civilians in War* (Ithaca, NY: Cornell University Press, 2008).

[132] Benjamin Valentino, Paul Huth, and Sarah Croco, "Covenants without the Sword: International Law and the Protection of Civilians in Times of War," *World Politics*, Vol. 58, No. 3 (2006): 339–77. On the question of crisis and the laws of war, see Ian Clark, Sebastian Kaempf, and Christian Reus-Smit, "Crisis in the Laws of War? Beyond Compliance and Effectiveness," *European Journal of International Relations*, Vol. 24 (2018): 319–343; Christine Chinkin and Mary Kaldor, *International Law and New Wars* (Cambridge: Cambridge University Press, 2017); Ioannis Kalpouzos, "Double Elevation: Autonomous Weapons and the Search for an Irreducible Law of War," *Leiden Journal of International Law*, Vol. 33, No. 2 (2020): 289–312.

[133] See Article "The ICRC at Davos: Tech Partnerships, Augmented Reality, and the Cruelty of War," 22 January 2018, from https://www.icrc.org/en/document/icrc-davos-tech-partnerships-augmented-reality-and-cruelty-war (retrieved 15 October 2020); and Article "President Maurer Calls on International Community to Follow Global 'Compasses' and Actively Tackle Future Digital Challenges," 24 September 2019, from https://www.efd.admin.ch/efd/en/home/dokumentation/nsb-news_list.msg-id-76529.html (retrieved 15 October 2020).

[134] Michael Schmitt, *Tallinn Manual on the International Law Applicable to Cyber Warfare* (Cambridge: Cambridge University Press, 2013).

[135] Smith's proposal for a "Digital Geneva Convention" was echoed by French President Emmanuel Macron as part of the "Paris Call for Trust and Security in Cyberspace," 11 December 2018. See also David Sanger, *The Perfect Weapon: War, Sabotage, and Fear in the Cyber Age* (New York: Broadway Books, 2019).

[136] Brad Smith, "Transcript of Keynote Address at the RSA Conference 2017: The Need for a Digital Geneva Convention," 14 February 2017, from https://blogs.microsoft.com/on-the-issues/2017/02/14/need-digital-geneva-convention/ (retrieved 15 October 2020).

distinction in trying to preserve the comparative military advantages of their NATO alliance. To be sure, in criticizing this image of the past, the book does not mean to disqualify recent initiatives to contain cyber warfare. Rather, it seeks to point to a deeper problem: that while the Conventions have taken on an almost sacral status as the world's moral compass in wartime, some of their long-standing historical mechanisms go unrecognized. As a consequence, when contemporaries look back on the inception of the Conventions, they often espy a story of humanity trumping power and atrocity. What they tend to overlook, however, are the political dilemmas involved in this struggle to impose limitations on humanity's worst impulses, with problematic consequences for how advocates remember this troubling past, if not a direct warning from history, decades later.

Indeed, what unites both critics and supporters of the Conventions is a collective amnesia about how—and why—these rules were made in the first place, what hidden legal potentials remain, and what drafters deliberately left deregulated as they finalized their proposals. Some have defined themselves as Pictet's heirs without taking note of his broader agenda, which contained several blind spots. Others frame the Conventions' drafters as the tragic victims of Great Power politics.[137] This book is different in that it reinserts their politics back into history and engages critically with those who have shaped humanitarian law. Humanizing warfare brought together actors from across the Cold War divide and from different backgrounds in the common pursuit of insisting that even wars have limits. Although they adhered to contrasting ideas of ethics, ideology, politics, and nationality, these commitments were often rooted in their former struggle against the Axis powers. They fiercely disagreed, however, over the character of the limits they established and who had the right to define them for future armed conflicts.

While far from fully realized, that powerful vision of humanity and brutality restrained continues to inspire humanitarians today. Few could have imagined this in 1944, when the ICRC began revising the Conventions and the contours of a new international legal order were starting to come into view through the ruins of war.[138]

---

[137] Inspired by Loeffler, *Rooted Cosmopolitans*, 299.
[138] *La République*, 9 December 1949.

Bibliography

A. Archives

Australia
NAA—National Archives of Australia, Canberra
Series A462
Series A472
Series A989
Series A1838

Canada
LAC—Library and Archives Canada, Ottawa
RG 19
RG 25

France
LAD—Les Archives Diplomatiques Courneuve, Paris
Unions Internationales 1907–1944
Unions Internationales 1944–1960

Ireland
NAI—National Archives of Ireland, Dublin
Series: DFA-5-341-137-2

Israel
ISA—Israel State Archives, Jerusalem
Series 00071706.81.D4.ED.29
Series 00071706.81.D5.A0.67
Series 00071706.81.D3.D5.01
Series 00071706.81.D4.FA.3F

New Zealand
ANZ—Archives New Zealand, Wellington
Series: AAYS 8638 W2054 ADW2054/1 220/3/3

Switzerland
ACICR—Les Archives du Comité international de la Croix Rouge, Geneva
A PV JUR.1
A PV A PI.18
A PV A PI.19
CR - 119 - CR 254
CRI - 25
ICRC Library—La Bibliothèque du Comité international de la Croix Rouge, Geneva
SFA—Schweizerischen Bundesarchiv, Bern
E2001E
E2200

336 BIBLIOGRAPHY

E4390
E2800
J2.118

The Netherlands

NA—National Archives of the Netherlands, The Hague
Collectie Mouton
Ministerie van Sociale Zaken
Code-Archief Buitenlandse Zaken: A-Dossiers
Code-Archief Buitenlandse Zaken
Commissie van Advies voor Volkenrechtelijke Vraagstukken
Nederlandse Delegatie Commissie tot Herziening van het Oorlogsrecht
ARKN—Archief Rode Kruis Nederland, The Hague
Series 170-310

Ukraine

TSDAVO—Tsentral'nyi derzhavnyi arhiv vyschykh organiv vlady ta upravlinnia Ukrainy (TSDAVO), Kiev
Op. 12cc, Spr. 969, Ark. 60-76.

United Kingdom

NA—National Archives, Kew
FO—Foreign Office
ADM—Admiralty
CAB—Cabinet Office
FO—Foreign Office
HO—Home Office
WO—War Office

United States

AJC—American Jewish Archives, Cincinnati
Series B69 - B83
Series D4 - 106
NARA—National Archives and Records Administration, College Park
Provost Marshal General
RG 43
American Red Cross

B. Printed Primary Documents

Newspapers and Magazines

Anzeiger, 15 February 1950
Appenzeller Zeitung, 13 December 1949
Baltimore Sun, 29 March 1950
Basler Nachrichten, 19 April 1949; 10/11 December 1949
Combat, 8 December 1949
Daily Telegraph, 15 December 1949
Feuille d'Avis de Neuchatel, 7 December 1949
Friheten, 11 August 1949
Gazette de Lausanne, 13 July 1949; 18/19 March 1950
Jewish Advocate, 29 June 1950

Journal de Genève, 18 March 1949; 20 July 1949; 7 August 1949; 13–14 August 1949; 5 December 1949; 9 December 1949; 20 December 1949; 17/18 November 1984
La Métropole, 19 August 1949
Landbote, Winterthur, 10 December 1949
La Nouvelle Revue de Lausanne, 17 March 1949; 18 March 1950
La République, 9 December 1949
La Suisse, 18 March 1950
Le Comtois, 8 December 1949
Le Courrier Australien, 7 October 1949
Le Figaro, 8 December 1949
Le Progrès, 8 December 1949
National Zeitung, 13 December 1949
Neue Berner Zeitung, 14 December 1949
Neue Zürcher Zeitung, 10 December 1949
Nouvelliste Valaisan, 10 December 1949; 16 December 1949
Pravda, 13 May 1949; 13 December 1949
St. Galler Tagblatt, 13 December 1949
Tages Anzeiger, 18 March 1950
The Calgary Herald, 24 April 1950
The New York Times, 9 December 1949
The Sunday Observer, 3 July 1949
The Times, 13 August 1949
The Wall Street Journal, 26 May 2004
Tribune de Lausanne, 14 August 1949
Trouw, 21 July 1949

Contemporary Literature

Abi-Saab, Georges, "The Newly Independent States and the Rules of International Law: An Outline," *Howard Law Journal* 8:2 (1962): 95–121.

Abi-Saab, Georges, "Le Renforcement du Système d'Application des Régles du Droit Humanitaire," *Military Law and Law of War Review* 12:2 (1973): 223–240.

Abi-Saab, Georges, "The Third World and the International Legal Order," *Revue Egyptienne de Droit International* 29 (1973): 27–66.

Baxter, Richard, "So-called 'Unprivileged Belligerency': Spies, Guerrillas, and Saboteurs," *British Yearbook of International Law* 28:323 (1951): 327–328.

Baxter, Richard, "Humanitarian Law or Humanitarian Politics? The 1974 Diplomatic Conference on Humanitarian Law," *Harvard International Law Journal* 16 (1975): 1–26.

Bedjaoui, Mohammed, *Law and the Algerian Revolution*, Brussels: International Association of Democratic Lawyers, 1961.

Brown, Sidney, "Le Rôle de la Croix-Rouge en cas d'Application de l'Article 16 du Pacte de la Société des Nations, et de Blocus en Temps de Guerre," *Revue Internationale de la Croix-Rouge* (1930): 234–282.

Brown, Sidney, "Application, en Cas d'Hostilités non Accompagnées d'une Déclaration de Guerre, des Conventions de Genève et de la Convention Relative au Traitement des Prisonniers de Guerre," *Revue Internationale de la Croix-Rouge* 16:186 (1934): 457–476.

Castberg, Frede, "*Norge under okkupasjonen: Rettslige utredninger 1940-1943*," Oslo: Cappelen, 1945.

Castberg, Frede, "Franc Tireur Warfare," *Netherlands International Law Review* (1959): 81–92.

Castrén, Erik, *The Present Law of War and Neutrality*, Helsinki: Finnish Academy of Science and Letters, 1954.

338   BIBLIOGRAPHY

Charpentier, J, *L'Humanisation de la Guerre Aèrienne*, Paris: Éditions Internationales, 1938.

Coursier, Henri, "Les Éléments Essentiels du Respect de la Personne Humaine Dans la Convention de Genève du 12 Août 1949, Relative à la Protection des Personnes Civiles en Temps de Guerre," *Revue internationale de la Croix-Rouge et Bulletin international des Sociétés de la Croix-Rouge* 32:377 (1950): 354–369.

Draper, Gerald, *The Red Cross Conventions*, London: Stevens, 1958.

Draper, Gerald, "The Geneva Conventions of 1949," *Recueil des Cours*, 1965.

Draper, Gerald, "The Relationship Between the Human Rights Regime and the Law of Armed Conflicts," *Israel Yearbook of Human Rights* 191 (1971).

Draper, Gerald, "The Implementation of the Modern Law of Armed Conflicts," *Israel Law Review* 8:1 (1973): 1–22.

Du Pasquier, Claude, *Promenade philosophique autour des Conventions de Genève de 1949*, Lausanne: 1950.

Eroglu, Hamza, *La representation international en vue de protéger les intérêts des belligérants*, Neuchatel: Imprimerie Richème, 1949.

Ferrière, Frédéric, "Projet d'une Convention Internationale Réglant la Situation des Civils Tombés à la Guerre au Pouvoir de l'Ennemi," *Revue Internationale de la Croix-Rouge et Bulletin international des Sociétés de la Croix-Rouge* 5:54 (1923): 560–585.

Frick-Cramer, Renée Marguerite, "A Propos des Projects de Conventions Internationales Réglant le Sort des Prisonniers," *Revue Internationale de la Croix-Rouge et Bulletin international des Sociétés de la Croix-Rouge* 7:74 (1925): 73–84.

Frick-Cramer, Renée Marguerite, "Contribution à l'élaboration d'une Convention sur les prisonniers, militaires ou civils, tombés au pouvoir de l'ennemi ou d'une autorité non reconnue par eux," *Revue Internationale de la Croix-Rouge et Bulletin international des Sociétés de la Croix-Rouge* (1947): 228–247.

Graber, Doris Appel, *The Development of the Law of Belligerent Occupation*, New York: Columbia University, 1949.

Guelle, Jules, *Droit International, La Guerre Continental et Les Personnes*, Paris, 1881.

Gutteridge, Joyce, "The Geneva Conventions of 1949," *British Yearbook of International Law* 26:294 (1949): 294–326.

Halleck, Henry, *International Law; or, Rules Regulating the Intercourse of States in Peace and War*, San Francisco: H.H. Bancroft & Company, 1861.

Krafft, Agenor, "The Present Position of the Red Cross Geneva Conventions," *Transactions of the Grotius Society* 37 (1951).

Lauterpacht, Hersch, "The Problem of the Revision of the Law of War," *British Yearbook of International Law* 29 (1952): 360–382.

Lauterpacht, Hersch, *Recognition in International Law*, Cambridge, UK: Cambridge University Press, 2013, first published in 1947.

Lieber, Francis, *Guerrilla Parties: Considered with Reference to the Laws and Usages of War*, New York: 1862.

Lodygensky, Georges, "La Croix-Rouge et la Guerre Civile," *Revue Internationale de la Croix-Rouge* (1919): 1159–1180.

Lodygensky, Georges, "La Croix-Rouge et la Guerre Civile (2me article)," *Revue Internationale de la Croix-Rouge* (1920): 654–670.

Lodygensky, Georges, *Face au Communisme, 1905-1950: Quand Genève Était le Centre du Mouvement Anticommuniste International*, Geneva: Slatkine, 2009.

Lorimer, James, *The Institutes of the Law of Nations; A Treatise of the Jural Relations of Separate Communities*, London: Blackwood and Sons, 1883.

McHenry Franklin, William, *Protection of Foreign Interests: A Study in Diplomatic and Consular Practice*, Washington, DC: 1947.

BIBLIOGRAPHY   339

Oppenheim, Lassa, *International Law. A Treatise Volume II*, New York: Longmans, Green and Co, 1912.

Pal, Radhabinod, *International Military Tribunal for the Far East: Dissentient Judgment of Justice Pal*, Tokyo: Kokusho-Kankokai, 1999.

Papelier, Philippe, *Le Droit de la Guerre et la Population Civile*, Paris: L'Institut d'Etudes Politiques de Paris, 1955.

Pictet, Jean, "La Protection Juridique de la Population Civile en Temps de Guerre," *Revue internationale de la Croix-Rouge et Bulletin international des Sociétés de la Croix-Rouge* 21:244 (1939): 268–286.

Pictet, Jean, *La Défense de la Personne Humaine dans le Droit Future*, Baden: 1947.

Pictet, Jean, "The New Geneva Conventions for the Protection of War Victims," *American Journal of International Law* 45:3 (1951): 462–475.

Pictet, Jean, ed., *The Geneva Conventions of 12 August 1949: Commentary*, Geneva: ICRC, 1958.

Pictet, Jean, ed., *The Geneva Conventions of 12 August 1949: Commentary*, Geneva: ICRC, 1960.

Pictet, Jean, "Les Principes du Droit International Humanitaire," *International Review of the Red Cross* (1966): 411–425.

Pictet, Jean, "The Formation of International Humanitarian Law," *International Review of the Red Cross* (1985): 3–24.

Pictet, Jean, ed., *Commentary on the First Additional Protocols to the Geneva Conventions*, Leiden: Martinus Nijhoff Publishers, 1987.

Pictet, Jean, "De la Seconde Guerre Mondiale à la Conference Diplomatique de 1949," *Revue internationale de la Croix-Rouge* 81:834 (1999): 205–208.

Pilloud, Claude, "La Déclaration Universelle des Droits de l'Homme et les Conventions Internationales Protégeant les Victimes de la Guerre," *Revue internationale de la Croix-Rouge et Bulletin international des Sociétés de la Croix-Rouge* 31:364 (1949): 252–258.

Pilloud, Claude, *Commentary on the Additional Protocols of 8 June 1977 to the Geneva Conventions of 12 August 1949*, Geneva: ICRC, 1987.

de la Pradelle, Albert, Jules Voncken, and Fernand Dehousse, *La Reconstruction du Droit de la Guerre*, Paris: 1936.

de la Pradelle, Paul, *La Conférence Diplomatique et les Nouvelles Conventions de Genève du 12 Août 1949*, Paris: Les Editions Internationales, 1951.

Royse, Morton, *Aerial Bombardment: And the International Regulation of Warfare*, New York: 1928.

Siordet, Frédéric, *Inter Arma Caritas: The World of the ICRC during the Second World War*, Geneva: ICRC, 1947.

Siordet, Frédéric, "Les Conventions de Genève et la Guerre Civile," *Revue Internationale de la Croix-Rouge* 32: 375 (1950): 187–212.

Siordet, Frédéric, "Les Conventions de Genève de 1949: Le Problème du Contrôle," *Revue international de la Croix-Rouge* (1951): 695–718.

Spaight, James, *War Rights on Land*, London: 1911.

Takahashi, Sakuyé, *International Law Applied to the Russo-Japanese War with the Decisions of the Japanese Prize Courts*, London: Stevens, 1908.

Vattel, Emer de, *The Law of Nations, Or, Principles of the Law of Nature, Applied to the Conduct and Affairs of Nations and Sovereigns, with Three Early Essays on the Origin and Nature of Natural Law and on Luxury*, Indianapolis: 2008.

Yearbook of the International Law Commission 1949. Summary Records and Documents of the First Sessions Including the Report of the Commission to the General Assembly, New York: United Nations, 1956.

340 BIBLIOGRAPHY

Yingling, Raymund, and Robert Ginnane, "The Geneva Conventions of 1949," *The American Journal of International Law* 46:3 (1952): 393–427.

C. Secondary LiteratureAbbenhuis, Maartje, Christopher Ernest Barber, and Annalise Higgins, eds., *War, Peace and International Order: The Legacies of the Hague Conferences of 1899 and 1907*, New York: Routledge, 2017.

Abbenhuis, Maartje, *The Hague Conferences and International Politics, 1898-1915*, London: Bloomsbury, 2018.

Abel, Richard, *Law's Wars: The Fate of the Rule of Law in the US "War on Terror"*, Cambridge, UK: Cambridge University Press, 2019.

Abi-Saab, Rosemary, *Droit Humanitaire et Conflits Internes: Origines et Évolution de la Réglementation Internationale*, Geneva: Institut Henry-Dunant, 1986.

Agamben, Giorgio, *Homo Sacer. Sovereign Power and Bare Life*, Stanford, CA: Stanford University Press, 1998.

Agamben, Giorgio, *State of Exception*, Chicago, IL: The University of Chicago Press, 2005.

Akande, Dapo, and Ben Saul, eds., *The Oxford Guide to International Humanitarian Law*, Oxford: Oxford University Press, 2020.

Aldrich, George, "New Life for the Laws of War," *American Journal of International Law* 75:4 (1981): 764–783.

d'Alessandra, Federica, and Matthew Gillett, "The War Crime of Starvation in Non-International Armed Conflict," *Journal of International Criminal Justice* 17:4 (2019): 815–847.

Alexander, Amanda, "The Genesis of the Civilian," *Leiden Journal of International Law* (2007): 359–376.

Alexander, Amanda, "A Short History of International Humanitarian Law," *European Journal of International Law* 26:1 (2015): 109–138.

Alexander, Amanda, "International Humanitarian Law, Postcolonialism and the 1977 Geneva Protocol I," *Melbourne Journal of International Law* 15 (2016): 15–50.

Alexander, Amanda, "The 'Good War': Preparations for a War against Civilians," *Law, Culture and the Humanities* 15:1 (2016): 227–252.

Alexandrowicz, Charles, David Armitage, and Jennifer Pitts, eds., *The Law of Nations in Global History*, Oxford: Oxford University Press, 2017.

Anghie, Antony, "Finding the Peripheries: Sovereignty and Colonialism in Nineteenth-Century International Law," *Harvard International Law Journal* 40:1 (1999): 1–80.

Anghie, Antony, *Imperialism, Sovereignty and the Making of International Law*, Cambridge: Cambridge University Press, 2004.

Antonopoulos, Constantine, "The Relationship between International Humanitarian Law and Human Rights," *Revue Hellénique de Droit International* 63:2 (2010): 599–634.

Arendt, Hannah, *The Origins of Totalitarianism*, New York: Harcourt Brace & Company, 1979.

Arendt, Hannah, *On Revolution*, Penguin: London, 1990.

Armitage, David, *Civil Wars: A History in Ideas*, New Haven, CT: Yale University Press, 2017.

Armstrong, David, "The International Committee of the Red Cross and Political Prisoners," *International Organization* 39:4 (1985): 615–642.

Bailey, Sydney, *Prohibitions and Restraints in War*, Oxford, UK: Oxford University Press, 1972.

Baldoli, Claudia, and Andrew Knapp, *Forgotten Blitzes: France and Italy under Allied Air Attack, 1940-1945*, London: Continuum, 2012.

Bangerter, Olivier, "Reasons Why Armed Groups Choose to Respect International Humanitarian Law or Not," *International Review of the Red Cross* 93:882 (2011): 353–384.

Banks, William, *New Battlefields Old Laws. Critical Debates on Asymmetric Warfare*, New York: Columbia University Press, 2011.

Barnett, Michael, *Empire of Humanity: A History of Humanitarianism*, Ithaca, NY: Cornell University Press, 2013.

Barnett, Michael, *Humanitarianism and Human Rights: A World of Differences?* Cambridge, UK: Cambridge University Press, 2020.

Baudendistel, Rainer, *Between Bombs and Good Intentions: The Red Cross and the Italo-Ethiopian War, 1935-1936*, New York: Berghahn Books, 2006.

Baughan, Emily, "The Imperial War Relief Fund and the All British Appeal: Commonwealth, Conflict and Conservatism within the British Humanitarian Movement, 1920-1925," *Journal of Imperial and Commonwealth History* 40:5 (2012): 845–861.

Barsalou, Olivier, "Preparing for War: The USA and the Making of the 1949 Geneva Conventions on the Laws of War," *Journal of Conflict & Security Law* 23:1 (2018): 49–73.

Bartov, Omer, *The Eastern Front, 1941-45: German Troops and the Barbarisation of Warfare*, Basingstoke: Palgrave, 2001.

Bassiouni, Cherif, "The United Nations Commission of Experts Established Pursuant to Security Council Resolution 780 (1992)," *The American Journal of International Law* 88:4 (1994): 784–805.

Beaumont, Roger, *Right Backed by Might: The International Air Force Concept*, Westport, CO: Praeger, 2001.

Becker, Annette, *Oubliés de la Grande Guerre: Humanitaire et Culture de Guerre, 1914-1918: Populations Occupées, Déportés Civils, Prisonniers de Guerre*, Paris: Éd Noêsis, 1998.

Becker Lorca, Arnulf, *Mestizo International Law. A Global Intellectual History, 1842-1933*, Cambridge, UK: Cambridge University Press, 2015.

Bell, Duncan, *Empire, Race and Global Justice*, Cambridge, UK: Cambridge University Press, 2019.

Bennett, Angela, *The Geneva Convention. The Hidden Origins of the Red Cross*, Gloucestershire: Sutton Publishing, 2005.

Benton, Lauren, *Legal Pluralism and Empires, 1500-1850*, New York: New York University Press, 2013.

Benvenisti, Eyal, and Doreen Lustig, "Monopolizing War: Codifying the Laws of War to Reassert Governmental Authority, 1856-1874," *European Journal of International Law* (2020): 127–169.

van Bergen, Leo, "The Poison Gas Debate in the Inter-war Years," *Medicine Conflict and Survival* 24:3 (2008): 174–187.

van Bergen, Leo, and Maartje Abbenhuis, "Man-Monkey, Monkey-Man: Neutrality and the Discussions about the "Inhumanity" of Poison Gas in the Netherlands and International Committee of the Red Cross," *First World War Studies* 3 (2012): 1–23.

Berman, Nathaniel, *Passions et Ambivalences: Le Colonialisme, le Nationalisme et le Droit International*, Paris: Pedone, 2007.

Bernstein, Barton, "The Quest for Security: American Foreign Policy and International Control of Atomic Energy, 1942-1946," *The Journal of American History* 60:4 (1974): 1003–1044.

von Bernstorff, Jochen, and Philipp Dann, eds., *The Battle for International Law: South-North Perspectives on the Decolonization Era*, Oxford: Oxford University Press, 2019.

Best, Geoffrey, *Humanity in Warfare: The Modern History of the International Laws of Armed Conflicts*, London: Weidenfeld and Nicholson, 1980.

Best, Geoffrey, *War and Law Since 1945*, Oxford: Clarendon Press, 2002.

Betts, Paul, "Humanity's New Heritage: Unesco and the Rewriting of World History," *Past & Present* (2015): 249–285.

342   BIBLIOGRAPHY

Bhuta, Nehal, "The Antinomies of Transformative Occupation," *The European Journal of International Law* 16:4 (2005): 721–740.

Biddle, Tami Davis, *Rhetoric and Reality in Air Warfare: The Evolution of British and American Ideas about Strategic Bombing*, Princeton, NJ: Princeton University Press, 2002.

Bjorge, Eirik, and Cameron Miles, eds., *Landmark Cases in Public International Law*, London: Hart, 2017.

Black, Jeremy, *Air Power: A Global History*, Lanham, MD: Rowman & Littlefield, 2016.

Bloxham, Donald, *Genocide on Trial: War Crimes Trials and the Formation of Holocaust History and Memory*, Oxford: Oxford University Press, 2001.

Bloxham, Donald, and Dirk Moses, eds., *Oxford Handbook of Genocide Studies*, Oxford: Oxford University Press, 2010.

Bogliolo, Luís Paulo, Governing from Above: A History of Aerial Bombing and International Law, Ph.D. Dissertation, University of Melbourne, 2020.

Boissier, Pierre, *De Solferino à Tsoushima: Histoire du Comité International de la Croix-Rouge*, Paris: Plon, 1963.

Boix, Charles, and Susan Stokes, eds., *The Oxford Handbook of Comparative Politics*, Oxford: Oxford University Press, 2007.

Boothby, William, *The Law of Targeting*, Oxford: Oxford University Press, 2012.

Borgwardt, Elizabeth, *A New Deal for the World: America's Vision for Human Rights*, London: Harvard University Press, 2007.

Bourneuf, Pierre-Etienne, *Bombarder l'Allemagne: L'offensive alliée sur les villes pendant la Deuxième Guerre mondiale*, Paris: Presses Universitaires de France, 2014.

Brooks, Rosa, "The Politics of the Geneva Conventions: Avoiding Formalist Traps," *Virginia Journal of International Law* 46:197 (2005–2006): 197–207.

Brooks, Rosa, *How Everything Became War and the Military Became Everything: Tales from the Pentagon*, New York: Simon and Schuster, 2019.

Brown, Robert, *Nuclear Authority: The IAEA and the Absolute Weapon*, Washington, DC: Georgetown University Press, 2015.

Browning, Christopher, *Ordinary Men: Reserve Battalion 101 and the Final Solution in Poland*, London: Penguin, 2001.

Bugnion, François, *Le Comité international de la Croix-Rouge et la Protection des Victimes de la Guerre*, Geneva: ICRC, 2000.

Bugnion, François, "Droit de Genève et Droit de la Haye," *International Review of the Red Cross* 83:844 (2001): 901–922.

Burgers, Jan, "The Road to San Francisco: The Revival of the Human Rights Idea in the Twentieth Century," *Human Rights Quarterly* 14:4 (1992): 447–477.

Burke, Roland, *Decolonization and the Evolution of International Human Rights*, Philadelphia: University of Pennsylvania Press, 2013.

Buß, Regina, *Der Kombattantenstatus. Die kriegsrechtliche Entstehung eines Rechtsbegriffs und seine Ausgestaltung in Verträgen des 19. und 20. Jahrhunderts*, Bochum: Universitätsverlag Brockmeyer, 1992.

Cabanes, Bruno, *The Great War and the Origins of Humanitarianism, 1918-1924*, Cambridge, UK: Cambridge University Press, 2014.

Cassese, Antonio, "The Martens Clause: Half a Loaf or Simply Pie in the Sky?," *European Journal of International Law* 11:1 (2000): 187–216.

Chamberlin, Paul Thomas, *The Cold War's Killing Fields: Rethinking the Long Peace*, New York: Harper, 2019.

Chatriot, Alain, "Georges Cahen-Salvador, Un Réformateur Social dans la Haute Administration Française (1875-1963)," *Revue d'Histoire de la Protection Sociale* (2014): 103–128.

Chesterman, Simon, ed., *Civilians in War*, London: Lynne Rienner, 2001.

Chinkin, Christine, and Mary Kaldor, "Double Elevation: Autonomous Weapons and the Search for an Irreducible Law of War," *Leiden Journal of International Law* 33:2 (2020): 289–312.

Chotzen, Anna, "Beyond Bounds: Morocco's Rif War and the Limits of International Law," *Humanity* 5:1 (2014): 33–54.

Clapham, Andrew, Paola Gaeta, Marco Sassòli, eds., *The 1949 Geneva Conventions. A Commentary*, Oxford: Oxford University Press, 2015.

Clark, Ian, Sebastian Kaempf, and Christian Reus-Smit, "Crisis in the Laws of War? Beyond Compliance and Effectiveness," *European Journal of International Relations* 24 (2018): 319–343.

Clavin, Patricia, "Time, Manner, Place: Writing Modern European History in Global, Transnational and International Contexts," *European History Quarterly* 40:4 (2010): 624–640.

Collingham, Lizzie, *The Taste of War: World War Two and the Battle for Food*, London: Allen Lane, 2011.

Collins, Michael, "Decolonization and the 'Federal Moment'," *Diplomacy and Statecraft* 24:1 (2013): 21–40.

Condos, Mark, "Licence to Kill: The Murderous Outrages Act and the Rule of Law in Colonial India, 1867–1925," *Modern Asian Studies* 50:2 (2016): 479–517.

Connelly, Matthew, *A Diplomatic Revolution. Algeria's Fight for Independence and the Origins of the Post-Cold War Era*, Oxford: Oxford University Press, 2002.

Conway-Lanz, Sahr, *Collateral Damage: Americans, Noncombatant Immunity and Atrocity after World War II*, Abingdon: Routledge, 2006.

Cooper, Frederick, *Citizenship Between Empire and Nation: Remaking France and French Africa, 1945-1960*, Princeton, NJ: Princeton University Press, 2014.

Cotter, Cédric, and Ellen Policinski, "A History of Violence: The Development of International Humanitarian law Reflected in the International Review of the Red Cross," *Journal of International Humanitarian Legal Studies* 11:1 (2020): 36–67.

Cotter, Cédric, (s')Aider pour survivre. Action Humanitaire et Neutralité Suisse Pendant la Première Guerre Mondiale, Ph.D. Dissertation, University of Geneva, 2017.

Crandall, Russell, *America's Dirty Wars: Irregular Warfare from 1776 to the War on Terror*, Cambridge, UK: Cambridge University Press, 2014.

Crawford, Emily, *The Treatment of Combatants and Insurgents under the Law of Armed Conflict*, Oxford: Oxford University Press, 2010.

Crossland, James, *Britain and the International Committee of the Red Cross, 1939-1945*, New York: Palgrave Macmillan, 2014.

Crossland, James, *War, Law and Humanity: The Campaign to Control Warfare, 1853-1914*, London: Bloomsbury, 2019.

Crowe, Anna, "'All the Regard Due to Their Sex': Women in the Geneva Conventions of 1949," *Research Working Paper Series Human Rights Program Harvard University* (2016).

Crowe, David, *War Crimes, Genocide, and Justice*, New York: Palgrave Macmillan, 2014.

Cryer, Robert, *The Tokyo International Military Tribunal: A Reappraisal*, Oxford: Oxford University Press, 2008.

Cullen, Anthony, *The Concept of Non-International Armed Conflict in International Humanitarian Law*, Cambridge, UK: Cambridge University Press, 2010.

Darcy, Shane, *Judges, Law and War*, Cambridge, UK: Cambridge University Press, 2014.

Davey, Eleanor, *Idealism Beyond Borders: The French Revolutionary Left and the Rise of Humanitarianism, 1954-1988*, Cambridge, UK: Cambridge University Press, 2015.

344 BIBLIOGRAPHY

Davis, Mike, *Late Victorian Holocausts: El Nino Famines and the Making of the Third World*, London: Verso, 2002.

Delhunty, Robert, "Is the Geneva POW Convention 'Quaint'?" *William Mitchell Law Review* 33 (2007).

Desgrandchamps, Marie-Luce, "'Organising the Unpredictable': The Nigeria-Biafra War and its Impact on the ICRC," *International Review of the Red Cross* 94:888 (2012): 1409–1432.

Detter, Ingrid, *The Law of War*, Farnham: Ashgate, 2013, 307–320.

van Dijk, Boyd, "Human Rights in War: On the Entangled Foundations of the 1949 Geneva Conventions," *American Journal of International Law* 112:4 (2018): 553–582.

van Dijk, Boyd, "'The Great Humanitarian': The Soviet Union, the International Committee of the Red Cross, and the Geneva Conventions of 1949," *Law and History Review* 37:1 (2019): 209–235.

van Dijk, Boyd, "Internationalizing Colonial War: On the Unintended Consequences of the Interventions of the International Committee of the Red Cross in South-East Asia, 1945-1949," *Past & Present* 250:1 (2020): 1–42.

Dinstein, Yoram, *The Conduct of Hostilities under the Law of International Armed Conflict*, Cambridge, UK: Cambridge University Press, 2004.

Donaldson, Megan, "The League of Nations, Ethiopia, and the Making of States," *Humanity* (2020): 6–31.

Doria, José, Hans-Peter Gasser, and Cherif Bassiouni, eds., *The Legal Regime of the International Criminal Court: Essays in Honor of Professor Igor Blishchenko*, Leiden: Martinus Nijhoff, 2009.

Dörmann, Knut, "The Legal Situation of 'Unlawful/Unprivileged Combatants'," *International Review of the Red Cross* 85:849 (2003): 45–74.

Dörmann, Knut, Liesbeth Lijnzaad, Marco Sassòli, Philip Spoerri, and Jean-Marie Henckaerts, eds., *Commentary on the First Geneva Convention*, Cambridge, UK: Cambridge University Press, 2016.

Doswald-Beck, Louise, and Silvain Vité, "International Humanitarian Law and Human Rights Law," *International Review of the Red Cross* 293 (1998): 94–119.

Downes, Alexander, *Targeting Civilians in War*, Ithaca, NY: Cornell University Press, 2008.

Drohan, Brian, *Brutality in an Age of Human Rights: Activism and Counterinsurgency at the End of the British Empire*, Ithaca, NY: Cornell University Press, 2018.

Durand, André, *De Sarajevo à Hiroshima*, Geneva: Institut Henry-Dunant, 2009.

Duranti, Marco, "The Holocaust, the Legacy of 1789 and the Birth of International Human Rights Law: Revisiting the Foundation Myth," *Journal of Genocide Research* 14:2 (2012): 159–186.

Duranti, Marco, *The Conservative Human Rights Revolution: European Identity, Transnational Politics, and the Origins of the European Convention*, Oxford: Oxford University Press, 2017.

Dworkin, Anthony, "Rethinking the Geneva Conventions," *Global Policy Forum*, 2003.

Engeland, Anicée van, *Civilian or Combatant. A Challenge for the 21st Century*, Oxford: Oxford University Press, 2011.

Evangelista, Matthew and Nina Tannenwald, eds., *Do the Geneva Conventions Matter?* Oxford: Oxford University Press, 2017.

Evangelista, Matthew, "Myron Taylor and the Bombing of Rome: The Limits of Law and Diplomacy," *Diplomacy & Statecraft* (2020): 278–305.

Eyffinger, Arthur, "Friedrich Martens: A Founding Father of the Hague Tradition," *ENDC Proceedings* 15 (2012): 13–43.

Fabre, Cécile, *Cosmopolitan War*, Oxford: Oxford University Press, 2012.

Farré, Sébastien, and Yan Schubert, "L'illusion de l'objectif. Le délégué du CICR Maurice Rossel et les photographies de Theresienstadt," *Le Mouvement Social* (2009): 65–83.

Farré, Sébastien, "The ICRC and the detainees in Nazi concentration camps (1942-1945)," *International Review of the Red Cross* 94:888 (2012): 1381–1408.

Fassin, Didier, *Humanitarian Reason: A Moral History of the Present*, Berkeley, CA: University of California Press, 2012.

Favez, Jean-Claude, *Une Mission Impossible?: Le CICR, les Déportations et les Camps de Concentration Nazis*, Lausanne: Payot, 1988.

Favez, Jean-Claude, *The Red Cross and the Holocaust*, Cambridge, UK: Cambridge University Press, 1999.

Fazal, Tanisha, "Why States no Longer Declare War," *Security Studies* 21:4 (2012): 557–593.

Fazal, Tanisha, *Wars of Law: Unintended Consequences of the Regulation of Armed Conflict*, Ithaca, NY: Cornell University Press, 2018.

Finnemore, Martha, *National Interests in International Society*, Ithaca, NY: Cornell University Press, 1996.

Finucane, Brian, "Enforced Disappearance as a Crime under International Law: A Neglected Origin in the Laws of War," *Yale Journal of International Law* (2010): 171–197.

Fisher, Louis, *Nazi Saboteurs on Trial: A Military Tribunal and American Law*, Lawrence, KA: University Press of Kansas, 2003.

Fleck, Dieter, "International Accountability for Violations of the Ius in Bello: The Impact of the ICRC Study on Customary International Humanitarian Law," *Journal of Conflict & Security Law* 11:2 (2006): 179–199.

Fleck, Dieter, ed., *The Handbook of International Humanitarian Law*, Oxford: Oxford University Press, 2013.

Fleming, N.C., "Cabinet Government, British Imperial Security, and the World Disarmament Conference, 1932-1934," *War in History* 18:1 (2011): 62–84.

Foote, Nicola, and Nadya Williams, *Civilians and Warfare in World History*, London: Routledge, 2017.

Foray, Jennifer, "A Unified Empire of Equal Parts: The Dutch Commonwealth Schemes of the 1920s-40s," *Journal of Imperial and Commonwealth History* 41:2 (2013): 259–284.

Forsythe, David, "Who Guards the Guardians: Third Parties and the Law of Armed Conflict," *American Journal of International Law* 70:1 (1976): 41–61.

Forsythe, David, *Humanitarian Politics: The International Committee of the Red Cross*, Baltimore, MD: Johns Hopkins University Press, 1977.

Forsythe, David, "Legal Management of Internal War: The 1977 Protocol on Non-international Armed Conflicts," *American Journal of International Law* 72:2 (1978): 272–295.

Forsythe, David, *The Humanitarians: The International Committee of the Red Cross*, Cambridge, UK: Cambridge University Press, 2005.

Forsythe, David, *The Politics of Prisoner Abuse: The United States and Enemy Prisoners after 9/11*, Cambridge, UK: Cambridge University Press, 2011.

Fortin, Katharine, "Complementarity between the ICRC and the United Nations and International Humanitarian Law and International Human Rights Law, 1948-1968," *International Review of the Red Cross* 94:888 (2012): 1433–1454.

Gardam, Judith, "A Feminist Analysis of Certain Aspects of International Humanitarian Law," *Australian Yearbook of International Law* (1992): 265–278.

Gardam, Judith, "Gender and Non-Combatant Immunity," *Transnational Law and Contemporary Problems* (1999): 345–370.

Garon, Sheldon, "On the Transnational Destruction of Cities: What Japan and the United States Learned from the Bombing of Britain and Germany in the Second World War," *Past & Present* 247:1 (2020): 235–271.

346 BIBLIOGRAPHY

Gat, Azar, *Fascist and Liberal Visions of War: Fuller, Liddell Hart, Douhet, and Other Modernists*, Oxford: Oxford University Press, 1998.

Gerwarth, Robert, *Vanquished: Why the First World War Failed to End*, London: Allen Lane, 2016.

Getachew, Adom, *Worldmaking after Empire: The Rise and Fall of Self-Determination*, Princeton, NJ: Princeton University Press, 2019.

Geyer, Michael, "Insurrectionary Warfare: The German Debate about a Levée en Masse in October 1918," *The Journal of Modern History* 73:3 (2001): 459–527.

Giladi, Rotem, "Francis Lieber on Public War," *Göttingen Journal of International Law* 4 (2012): 447–477.

Giladi, Rotem, "Rites of Affirmation: Progress and Immanence in International Humanitarian Law Historiography," Unpublished Paper.

Giladi, Rotem, "The Phoenix of Colonial War: Race, the Laws of War and the 'Horror on the Rhine,'" *Leiden Journal of International Law* 30:4 (2017): 847–875.

Gildea, Robert, *Fighters in the Shadows: A New History of the French Resistance*, Cambridge, MA: Harvard University Press, 2015.

Gillespie, Alexander, *A History of the Laws of War*, Portland, OR: Hart, 2011.

Goldsmith, Jack, *The Terror Presidency: Law and Judgment Inside the Bush Administration*, New York: W.W. Norton & Co, 2009.

Gordon, Neve, and Nicola Perugini, "'Hospital Shields' and the Limits of International Law," *European Journal of International Law* 30:2 (2019): 439–463.

Gordon, Neve, and Nicola Perugini, *Human Shields: A History of People in the Line of Fire*, Berkeley, CA: University of California Press, 2020.

Gorman, Daniel, *The Emergence of International Society in the 1920s*, New York: Cambridge University Press, 2012.

Graebner, Norman, and Edward Bennett, *The Versailles Treaty and its Legacy: The Failure of the Wilsonian Vision*, Cambridge, UK: Cambridge University Press, 2014.

Grayling, Anthony, *Among the Dead Cities: The History and Moral Legacy of the WWII Bombing of Civilians in Germany and Japan*, New York: Walker Books, 2009.

Green, Leslie, "Grave Breaches or Crimes Against Humanity," *Journal of Legal Studies* 8 (1997).

Green, Leslie, *Essays on the Modern Law of War*, Ardsley, NY: Transnational Publishers, 1999.

Green, Leslie, *The Contemporary Law of Armed Conflict*, New York: Juris Publishing, 2008.

Greenberg, Karen, *The Torture Debate in America*, Cambridge, UK: Cambridge University Press, 2008.

Greenman, Kathryn, "Common Article 3 at 70: Reappraising Revolution and Civil War in International Law," *Melbourne Journal of International Law* 21 (2020): 1–27.

Gregory, Thomas, "Drones, Targeted Killings, and the Limitations of International Law," *International Political Sociology* 9:3 (2015): 197–212.

Grewe, Wilhelm, *The Epochs of International Law*, Berlin: De Gruyter, 2001.

Grossberg, Michael, and Christopher Tomlins, *The Cambridge History of American Law, Vol. III*, Cambridge, UK: Cambridge University Press, 2008.

Grimm Arsenault, Elizabeth, The Domestic Politics of International Norms: Factors Affecting US Compliance with the Geneva Conventions, Ph.D. Dissertation, Georgetown University, 2010.

Haber, Ludwig, *The Poisonous Cloud. Chemical Warfare in the First World War*, Oxford: Oxford University Press, 1986.

Hastings, Max, *Bomber Command*, New York: Dial Press, 1979.

Hathaway, Oona, Emily Chertoff, Lara Domínquez, Zachary Manfredi, and Peter Tzeng, "Ensuring Responsibility: Common Article 1 and State Responsibility for Non-State Actors," *Texas Law Review* 95 (2017): 539–590.

Haque, Adil, *Law and Morality at War*, Oxford: Oxford University Press, 2017.

Harouel, Véronique, *Genève-Paris 1863-1918. Le Droit Humanitaire en Construction*, Geneva: ICRC, 2003.

Heller, Kevin Jon, *The Nuremberg Military Tribunals and the Origins of International Criminal Law*, Oxford: Oxford University Press, 2012.

Heller, Kevin Jon, and Gerry Simpson, eds., *The Hidden Histories of War Crimes Trials*, Oxford: Oxford University Press, 2014.

Henderson, Christian, *Commissions of Inquiry: Problems and Prospects*, London: Hart, 2017.

Hentsch, Thierry, *Face au Blocus: Histoire de l'Intervention du Comité International de la Croix-Rouge dans le Conflit du Nigéria, 1967–1970*, Geneva: Droz, 1973.

van den Herik, Larissa, "An Inquiry into the Role of Commissions of Inquiry in International Law: Navigating the Tensions between Fact-Finding and Application of International Law," *Chinese Journal of International Law* (2014): 507–537.

Hippler, Thomas, *Governing the Skies: A Global History of Aerial Bombing*, London: Verso, 2017.

Hirsch, Francine, *Soviet Judgment at Nuremberg: A New History of the International Military Tribunal after World War II*, Oxford: Oxford University Press, 2020.

Hoffmann, Stefan-Ludwig, "Human Rights and History," *Past & Present* 232:1 (2016): 279–310.

Holloway, David, *The Soviet Union and the Arms Race*, New Haven, CT: Yale University Press, 1984.

Holquist, Peter, *By Right of War*, forthcoming.

Holquist, Peter, By Right of War: Imperial Russia and the Development of the Law of War, Unpublished Paper.

Horne, John, and Alan Kramer, *German Atrocities, 1914: A History of Denial*, New Haven, CT: Yale University Press, 2001.

Horne, John, ed., *A Companion to World War I*, Chichester: Wiley-Blackwell, 2012

Horowitz, Michael, and Dan Reiter, "When Does Aerial Bombing Work? Quantitative Empirical Tests, 1917-1999," *Journal of Conflict Resolution* 45:2 (2001): 147–173.

Howard, Michael, George Andreopoulos, and Mark Shulman, eds., *The Laws of War: Constraints on Warfare in the Western World*, New Haven, CT: Yale University Press, 1994.

Hull, Isabel, *Absolute Destruction: Military Culture and the Practices of War in Imperial Germany*, Ithaca, NY: Cornell University Press, 2004.

Hull, Isabel, *A Scrap of Paper: Breaking and Making International Law during the Great War*, Ithaca, NY: Cornell University Press, 2014.

Hurd, Ian, *How to Do Things with International Law*, Princeton, NJ: Princeton University Press, 2017.

Hutchinson, John, *Champions of Charity: War and the Rise of the Red Cross*, Boulder, CO: Westview Press, 1996.

Hutter, Simone, *Starvation as a Weapon: Domestic Policies of Deliberate Starvation as a Means to an End Under International Law*, Leiden: Brill, 2015.

Ibler, Vladimir, ed., *Mélanges Offerts à Juraj Andrassy. Essays in International Law in Honour of Juraj Andrassy*, The Hague: Martinus Nijhoff, 1968.

Imlay, Talbot, and Monica Duffy Toft, eds., *The Fog of Peace and War Planning: Military and Strategic Planning under Uncertainty*, New York: Routledge, 2006.

Inal, Tuba, *Looting and Rape in Wartime: Law and Change in International Relations*, Philadelphia, PA: University of Pennsylvania Press, 2013.

Iriye, Akira, *Global Community: The Role of International Organizations in the Making of the Contemporary World*, Berkeley, CA: University of California Press, 2004.

348 BIBLIOGRAPHY

Iriye, Akira, and Pierre-Yves Saunier, eds., *The Palgrave Dictionary of Transnational History*, Basingstoke: Palgrave Macmillan, 2009.

Iriye, Akira, Petra Goedde, and William Hitchcock, eds., *The Human Rights Revolution. An International History*, New York: Oxford University Press, 2012.

Irvin-Erickson, Douglas, The Life and Works of Raphael Lemkin: A Political History of Genocide in Theory and Law, Ph.D. Dissertation, Rutgers University, 2014.

Jachec-Neale, Agnieszka, *Concept of Military Objectives in International Law and Targeting Practice*, London: Routledge, 2014.

Jackson, Peter, "France, the Problems of Security and International Disarmament after the First World War," *Journal of Strategic Studies* 29:2 (2006): 247–280.

Jensen, Steven, *The Making of International Human Rights. The 1960s, Decolonization and the Reconstruction of Global Values*, Cambridge, UK: Cambridge University Press, 2016.

Jo, Hyeran, *Compliant Rebels: Rebels Groups and International law in World Politics*, Cambridge, UK: Cambridge University Press, 2015.

Joas, Hans, *The Sacredness of the Person. A New Genealogy of Human Rights*, Washington, DC: Georgetown University Press, 2013.

Jones, Heather, *Violence Against Prisoners of War in the First World War: Britain, France and Germany, 1914-1920*, Cambridge, UK: Cambridge University Press, 2011.

Jouannet, Emmanuelle, and Hélène Ruiz-Fabri, *Droit International et Impérialisme en Europe et aux Etats-Unis*, Paris: Société de Législation Comparée, 2007.

Junod, Dominique-Debora, *The Imperiled Red Cross and the Palestine-Eretz-Yisrael Conflict 1945-1952. The Influence of Institutional Concerns on a Humanitarian* Operation, New York: Kegan Paul International, 1996.

Kalmanovitz, Pablo, *The Laws of War in International Thought*, Oxford: Oxford University Press, 2020.

Kalshoven, Frits, *Belligerent Reprisals*, Leiden: Sijthoff, 1971.

Kalshoven, Frits, *Reflections on the Law of War: Collected Essays*, Leiden: Martinus Nijhoff, 2007.

Kalshoven, Frits, "The International Humanitarian Fact-Finding Commission: A Sleeping Beauty?" *Humanitäires Völkerrecht* (2002).

Kalyvas, Stathis, *The Logic of Violence in Civil War*, Cambridge, UK: Cambridge University Press, 2006.

Kedward, Rod, *In Search of the Maquis: Rural Resistance in Southern France, 1942-1944*, Oxford: Oxford University Press, 1993.

Kelly, Tobias, "What We Talk about When We Talk about Torture," *Humanity* 2:2 (2011): 327–343.

Kennedy, David, *Of War and Law*, Princeton, NJ: Princeton University Press, 2006.

Kessler, Birgit, "The Duty to 'Ensure Respect' Under Common Article 1 of the Geneva Conventions: Its Implications on International and Non-International Armed Conflicts," *German Yearbook of International Law* 44 (2001): 498–516.

Kinsella, Helen, and Giovanni Mantilla, "Contestation before Compliance: History, Politics, and Power in International Humanitarian Law," *International Studies Quarterly* 64:3 (2020): 649–656.

Kinsella, Helen, *The Image before the Weapon: A Critical History of the Distinction Between Combatant and Civilian*, Ithaca, NY: Cornell University Press, 2011.

Kinsella, Helen, "Superfluous Injury and Unnecessary Suffering: National Liberation and the Laws of War," *Political Power and Social Theory* 32 (2017): 205–231.

Kinzer, Stephen, *The Brothers: John Foster Dulles, Allen Dulles, and Their Secret World War*, New York: St. Martin's Griffin, 2014.

Kitching, Carolyn, *Britain and the Geneva Disarmament Conference*, New York: Palgrave, 2003.

Kleinfeld, Margot, "The 1934 Monaco Draft: How the Military Medical Services Worked to Strengthen the Laws of War," *International Review of the Armed Forces Medical Services* 88:1 (2015): 91–97.

Klose, Fabian, *Menschenrechte im Schatten kolonialer Gewalt: Die Dekolonisierungskriege in Kenia und Algerien, 1945–1962,*" Munich: R. Oldenbourg, 2009.

Klose, Fabian, "The Colonial Testing Ground: The International Committee of the Red Cross and the Violent End of Empire," *Humanity* 2:1 (2011): 107–126.

Klose, Fabian, and Mirjam Thulin, eds., *Humanity: A History of European Concepts in Practice from the Sixteenth Century to the Present*, Göttingen: Vandenhoeck & Ruprecht, 2016.

Knop, Karen, *Diversity and Self-Determination in International Law*, Cambridge, UK: Cambridge University Press, 2004.

Kolb, Robert, and Richard Hyde, eds., *An Introduction to the International Law of Armed Conflicts*, Oxford: Hart, 2008.

Koskenniemi, Martti, *Gentle Civilizer of Nations: The Rise and Fall of International Law 1870-1960*, Cambridge, UK: Cambridge University Press, 2001.

Koskenniemi, Martti, "International Law as Political Theology: How to Read Nomos der Erde?" *Constellations* (2004): 492–511.

Koskenniemi, Martti, "Histories of International Law: Dealing with Eurocentrism," *Rechtsgeschichte* (2011): 152–177.

Koskenniemi, Martti, Walter Rech, Manual Jiménez Fonseca, eds., *International Law and Empire*, Oxford: Oxford University Press, 2017.

Kovner, Sarah, "A War of Words: Allied Captivity and Swiss Neutrality in the Pacific, 1941–1945," *Diplomatic History* 41:4 (2017): 719–746.

Kovner, Sarah, *Prisoners of the Empire: Inside Japanese POW Camps*, Cambridge, MA: Harvard University Press, 2020.

Kramer, Alan, "The First Wave of International War Crimes Trials: Istanbul and Leipzig," *European Review* 14:4 (2006): 441–455.

Kurz, Nathan, "'Hide a Fact Rather than State It': The Holocaust, the 1940s Human Rights Surge, and the Cosmopolitan Imperative of International Law," *Journal of Genocide Research* 23:1 (2020): 1–21.

Kushner, Barak, *Men to Devils, Devils to Men: Japanese War Crimes and Chinese Justice*, Cambridge, MA: Harvard University Press, 2015.

Lagrou, Pieter, *The Legacy of Nazi Occupation: Patriotic Memory and National Recovery in Western Europe, 1945-1965*, Cambridge, UK: Cambridge University Press, 2003.

La Porte, Pablo, "Humanitarian Assistance during the Rif War (Morocco, 1921-6): The International Committee of the Red Cross and 'an Unfortunate Affair,'" *Historical Research* 89:243 (2016): 114–135.

Laqueur, Walter, "The Origins of Guerrilla Doctrine," *Journal of Contemporary History* 10:3 (1975): 341–382.

Leffler, Melvyn, *A Preponderance of Power: National Security, the Truman Administration, and the Cold War*, Stanford, CA: Stanford University Press, 1992.

Leffler, Melvyn, *The Specter of Communism: The United States and the Origins of the Cold War, 1917-1953*, New York: Hill and Wang, 1994.

Leffler, Melvyn, and David Painter, eds., *The Origins of the Cold War: An International History*, New York: Routledge, 2002.

Leffler, Melvyn, and Odd Arne Westad, eds., *The Cambridge History of the Cold War, Vol. I*, Cambridge, UK: Cambridge University Press, 2010.

350 BIBLIOGRAPHY

Lepick, Olivier, *Les Armes Chimiques*, Paris: Presses Universaitaires de France, 1999.

Levie, Howard, "Prisoners of War and the Protecting Power," *American Journal of International Law* 55:2 (1961): 374–397.

Levie, Howard, "History of the Law of War on Land," *International Review of the Red Cross* 838 (2000): 339–350.

Lemnitzer, Jan, *Power, Law, and the End of Privateering*, New York: Palgrave Macmillan, 2014.

Lewis, Mark, "The World Jewish Congress and the Institute for International Affairs at Nuremberg: Ideas, Strategies, and Political Goals, 1942-1946," *Yad Vashem Studies* 36:1 (2008): 181–210.

Lewis, Mark, *The Birth of the New Justice. The Internationalization of Crime and Punishment*, Oxford: Oxford University Press, 2014.

von Lingen, Kerstin, *"Crimes against Humanity": Zur Ideengeschichte der Zivilisierung von Kriegsgewalt, 1864-1945*, Paderborn: Schoeningh, 2018.

von Lingen, Kerstin, *Transcultural Justice at the Tokyo Tribunal*, Leiden: Brill, 2018.

von Lingen, Kerstin, *War Crimes Trials in the Wake of Decolonization and Cold War in Asia, 1945-1956*, London: Springer, 2018.

Liivoja, Rain, and Tim McCormack, eds., *Routledge Handbook of the Law of Armed Conflicts*, New York: Routledge, 2016.

Linstrum, Erik, "Domesticating Chemical Weapons: Tear Gas and the Militarization of Policing in the British Imperial World, 1919-1981," *Journal of Modern History* 91:3 (2019): 557–585.

Loeffler, James, *Rooted Cosmopolitans: Jews and Human Rights in the Twentieth Century*, New Haven, CT: Yale University Press, 2016.

Lowe, Kimberly, "Humanitarianism and National Sovereignty: Red Cross Intervention on behalf of Political Prisoners in Soviet Russia, 1921-3," *Journal of Contemporary History* 49:4 (2014): 652–674.

Luthi, Lorenz, *Cold Wars: Asia, the Middle East, Europe*, Cambridge, UK: Cambridge University Press, 2020.

Luttikhuis, Bart, and Dirk Moses, eds., *Colonial Counterinsurgency and Mass Violence. The Dutch Empire in Indonesia*, New York: Routledge, 2014.

van der Maar, Rimko, Ruud van Dijk, Samuel Kruizinga, and Vincent Kuitenbrouwer, eds., *Shaping the International Relations of the Netherlands, 1815-2000*, London: Routledge, 2019.

Maier, Charles, "Targeting the City: Debates and Silences about the Aerial Bombing of World War II, *International Review of the Red Cross* 87:859 (2005): 429–444.

Manacordan, Stefano, and Adan Nieto, eds., *Criminal Law Between War and Peace: Justice and Cooperation in Criminal Matters in International Military Interventions*, Cuenca: Ediciones de la Universidad de Castilla-La Mancha, 2009.

Manela, Erez, *The Wilsonian Moment: Self-determination and the International Origins of Anticolonial Nationalism*, Oxford: Oxford University Press, 2007.

Mantilla, Giovanni, Under (Social) Pressure: The Historical Regulation of Internal Armed Conflicts through International Law, Ph.D. Dissertation, University of Minnesota, 2013.

Mantilla, Giovanni, "Conforming Instrumentalists: Why the USA and the United Kingdom Joined the 1949 Geneva Conventions," *European Journal of International Law* 28:2 (2017): 483–511.

Mantilla, Giovanni, "Forum Isolation: Social Opprobrium and the Origins of the International Law of Internal Conflict," *International Organization* 72:2 (2018): 317–349.

Mantilla, Giovanni, "Social Pressure and the Making of Wartime Legal Protection for Civilians," *European Journal of International Relations* 26:2 (2019): 444–468.

Mantilla, Giovanni, "*Lawmaking under Pressure: International Humanitarian Law and Internal Armed Conflict*," Ithaca, NY: Cornell University Press, 2020

Mastny, Vojtech, Sven Holtsmark, and Andreas Wagner, eds., *War Plans and Alliances in the Cold War: Threat Perceptions in the East and West*, New York: Routledge, 2006.

Mayer, Jane, *The Dark Side: The Inside Story of How the War on Terror Turned into a War on American Ideals*, New York: Doubleday, 2008.

Mazower, Mark, "Strange Triumph of Human Rights, 1933-1950," *Historical Journal* 47:2 (2004): 379–398.

Mazower, Mark, *Hitler's Empire: Nazi Rule in Occupied Europe*, London: Allen Lane, 2008.

Mazower, Mark, *No Enchanted Palace*, Princeton, NJ: Princeton University Press, 2009.

McDougall, Carrie, *The Crime of Aggression under the Rome Statute of the International Criminal Court*, Cambridge, UK: Cambridge University Press, 2013.

McMahon, Darrin, and Samuel Moyn, eds., *Rethinking Modern European Intellectual History*, New York: Oxford University Press, 2014.

McMahon, Jeff, *Killing in War*, Oxford: Oxford University Press, 2009.

McQuade, Joseph, *A Genealogy of Terrorism: Colonial Law and the Origins of an Idea*, Cambridge, UK, Cambridge University Press, 2020.

Mégret, Frédéric, and Immi Tallgren, eds., *The Dawn of a Discipline*, Cambridge, UK: Cambridge University Press, 2020.

Melzer, Nils, *Interpretative Guidance on the Notion of Direct Participation in Hostilities under International Humanitarian Law*, Geneva: ICRC, 2009.

Mendelsohn, Ezra, Stefani Hoffman, and Richard Cohen, eds., *Against the Grain: Jewish Intellectuals in Hard Times*, New York and Oxford: Berghahn Books, 2014.

Menon, P.K., *The Law of Recognition in International Law: Basic Principles*, Lewiston, NY: Edwin Mellen Press, 1994.

Merrills, John, *International Dispute Settlement*, Cambridge, UK: Cambridge University Press, 2017.

Meron, Theodor, "The Humanization of Humanitarian Law," *The American Journal of International Law* 94:2 (2000): 239–278.

Meyer, Michael, and Hilaire McCoubrey, eds., *Reflections on Law and Armed Conflicts: The Selected Works on the Laws of War by the Late Professor G.I.A.D. Draper*, The Hague: Kluwer, 1998.

Meyrowitz, Henri, "Les Guerres de Libération et les Conventions de Genève," *Politique Étrangère* 39:6 (1974): 607–627.

Moir, Lindsay, *The Law of Internal Armed Conflict*, Cambridge, UK: Cambridge University Press, 2002.

Moorehead, Caroline, *Dunant's Dream. War, Switzerland, and the History of the Red Cross*, New York: Carroll & Graf Publishers, 1999.

Moreillon, Jacques, *Le Comité international de la Croix-Rouge et la Protection des Détenus Politiques*, Lausanne: L'Age d'Homme, 1973.

Moreillon, Jacques, "The ICRC and the Future," *Revue Internationale de la Croix-Rouge* (1983) 231–245.

Morgan-Owen, David, and Louis Halewood, *Economic Warfare and the Sea: Grand Strategies for Maritime Powers, 1650-1945*, Liverpool: Liverpool University Press, 2020.

Morrow, James, "When Do States Follow the Laws of War?" *American Political Science Review* (2007): 559–572.

Moses, Dirk, and Lasse Heerten, eds., *Postcolonial Conflict and the Question of Genocide: The Nigeria-Biafra War, 1967-1970*, Abingdon: Routledge, 2018.

352 BIBLIOGRAPHY

Moses, Dirk, Marco Duranti, and Roland Burke, eds., *Decolonization, Self-Determination, and the Rise of Global Human Rights Politics*, Cambridge, UK: Cambridge University Press, 2020.

Moses, Dirk, *The Problems of Genocide: Permanent Security and the Language of Transgression*, Cambridge, UK: Cambridge University Press, 2021.

Moyn, Samuel, *The Last Utopia: Human Rights in History*, Cambridge, MA: Harvard University Press, 2012.

Moyn, Samuel, *Humane: How the United States Abandoned Peace and Reinvented War*, New York: Farrar, Straus and Giroux, 2021.

Mulder, Nicholas, *The Economic Weapon: Interwar Internationalism and the Rise of Sanctions, 1914-1945*, forthcoming.

Murphy, Mahon, *Colonial Captivity during the First World War: Internment and the Fall of the German Empire, 1914-1919*, Cambridge, UK: Cambridge University Press, 2017.

Nabulsi, Karma, *Traditions of War: Occupation, Resistance and the Law*, Oxford: Oxford University Press, 1999.

Neep, Daniel, *Occupying Syria under the French Mandate. Insurgency, Space and State Formation*, New York: Cambridge University Press, 2012.

Neff, Stephen, *War and the Law of Nations: A General History*, Cambridge, UK: Cambridge University Press, 2006.

Nelson, Robert, and Christopher Waters, "The Allied Bombing of German Cities during the Second World War from a Canadian Perspective," *Journal of the History of International Law* 14:1 (2012): 87–122.

Nevers, Renée de, "The Geneva Conventions and New Wars," *Political Science Quarterly* 121:3 (2006): 369–395.

Newman, Edward, "The 'New Wars' Debate: A Historical Perspective Is Needed," *Security Dialogue* 35:2 (2004): 173–189.

Normand, Roger, and Chris af Jochnick, "The Legitimation of Violence: A Critical History of the Laws of War," *Harvard International Law Journal* (1994): 49–95.

Nystuen, Gro, Stuart Casey-Maslen, and Annie Golden Bersagel, eds., *Nuclear Weapons under International Law*, Cambridge, UK: Cambridge University Press, 2014.

Oberleitner, Gerd, *Human Rights Institutions, Tribunals and Courts: Legacy and Promise*, Singapore: Springer, 2019.

Ohlin, Jens, *The Assault on International Law*, Oxford: Oxford University Press, 2015.

Ohlin, Jens, *Theoretical Boundaries of Armed Conflict and Human Rights*, Cambridge, UK: Cambridge University Press, 2016.

Ó Longaigh, Seosamh, *Emergency Law in Independent Ireland, 1922–1948*, Bodmin: Four Courts, 2006.

Omissi, David, *Air Power and Colonial Control: The Royal Air Force 1919-1939*, Manchester: Manchester University Press, 1990.

Orford, Anne, *International Law and its Others*, Cambridge, UK: Cambridge University Press, 2009.

Orford, Anne, and Florian Hoffmann, eds., *The Oxford Handbook of the Theory of International Law*, Oxford: Oxford University Press, 2016.

O'Rourke, Catherine, *Women's Rights in Armed Conflict under International Law*, Cambridge, UK: Cambridge University Press, 2020.

Otto, Roland, *Targeted Killings and International Law. With Special Regard to Human Rights and International Humanitarian Law*, Heidelberg: Springer, 2012.

Overmans, Rüdiger, *In der Hand des Feindes. Kriegsgefangenschaft von der Antike bis zum Zweiten Weltkrieg*, Cologne: Böhlau, 1999.

Overy, Richard, *The Bombing War: Europe 1939-1945*, London: Penguin Books, 2014.

Özsu, Umut, *Formalizing Displacement: International Law and Population Transfers*, Oxford: Oxford University Press, 2015.

Pahuja, Sundhya, *Decolonizing International Law: Development, Economic Growth and the Politics of Universality*, Cambridge, UK: Cambridge University Press, 2011.

Palmieri, Daniel, "Une Neutralité Sous Influence?: Le CICR, Franco et les Victimes," *Revue Suisse d'Histoire* 59:3 (2009): 279–297.

Palwankar, Umesh, "Measures Available to States for Fulfilling their Obligation to Ensure Respect for International Humanitarian Law," *International Review of the Red Cross* 298 (1994): 227–240.

Panayi, Panikos, *The Enemy in our Midst. Germans in Britain during the First World War*, New York: Berg, 1991.

Parker, James, *Brother's Keeper: The United States, Race, and Empire in the British Caribbean, 1937-1962*, Oxford: Oxford University Press, 2008.

Paulmann, Johannes, "Conjunctures in the History of International Humanitarian Aid during the Twentieth Century," *Humanity* (2013): 215–238.

Paulmann, Johannes, eds., *Dilemmas of Humanitarian Aid in the Twentieth Century*, Oxford: Oxford University Press, 2016.

Pedersen, Susan, *The Guardians: The League of Nations and the Crisis of Empire*, Oxford: Oxford University Press, 2015.

Penkower, Noam, "The World Jewish Congress Confronts the International Red Cross during the Holocaust," *Jewish Social Studies* 41:3/4 (1979): 229–256.

Penter, Tanja, "Local Collaborators on Trial: Soviet War Crimes Trials under Stalin (1943-1953)," *Cahiers du monde russe* 49:2/3 (2008): 341–364.

Perrigo, Sarah, and Jim Whitmann, eds., *The Geneva Conventions Under Assault*, London: Pluto Press, 2010.

Plokhy, Serhii, *Forgotten Bastards of the Eastern Front: American Airmen behind Soviet Lines and the Collapse of the Grand Alliance*, Oxford: Oxford University Press, 2019.

Pillonel, Jessica, La Grande Guerre 1914-18. Un Nouveau Défi Pour le CICR? L'Agence Internationale des Prisonniers de Guerre et son Action en Faveur des Civils, Geneva: MA Thesis, 2012.

Pitts, Jennifer, "The Critical History of International Law," *Political Theory* 43 (2015): 541–552.

Pralong, Estelle, *La Guerre Chimique: de la Grande Guerre à la Guerre d'Abyssinie. Les Faiblesses du Nouvel Ordre International*, Geneva: MA Thesis, 2002.

Price, Richard, *The Chemical Weapons Taboo*, Ithaca, NY: Cornell University Press, 1997.

Priemel, Kim, and Alexa Stiller, *Reassessing the Nuremberg Military Tribunals: Transitional Justice, Trial Narratives, and Historiography*, New York: Beghahn Books, 2014.

Primoratz, Igor, *Civilian Immunity in War*, Oxford: Oxford University Press, 2010.

Prochason, Christophe, and Anne Rasmussen, *Vrai et Faux dans la Grande Guerre*, Paris: Découverte, 2004.

Ralph, Jason, "The Laws of War and the State of the American Exception," *Review of International Studies* 35:3 (2009): 631–649.

de la Rasilla, Ignacio, and Jorge Viñuales, eds., *Experiments in International Adjudication: Historical Accounts*, Cambridge, UK: Cambridge University Press, 2019.

Rejali, Darius, *Torture and Democracy*, Princeton, NJ: Princeton University Press, 2007.

Rey-Schyrr, Catherine, *De Yalta à Dien Bien Phu. Histoire du Comité international de la Croix- Rouge 1945-1955*, Geneva: Georg-CICR, 2007.

Riesenberger, Dieter, *Für Humanität in Krieg und Frieden. Das Internationale Rote Kreuz, 1863-1977*, Göttingen: Vandenhoeck & Ruprecht, 1992.

354 BIBLIOGRAPHY

Ristaino, Marcia, *The Jacquinot Safe Zone: Wartime Refugees in Shanghai*, Stanford, CA: Stanford University Press, 2008.

Roberts, Adam, and Richard Guelff, *Documents on the Laws of War*, Oxford: Oxford University Press, 2000.

Roberts, Adam, "The Laws of War: Problems of Implementation in Contemporary Conflicts," *Duke Journal of Comparative & International Law* 6 (1995): 11–78.

Roberts, Adam, "Transformative Military Occupation: Applying the Laws of War and Human Rights," *American Journal of International Law* 100:3 (2006): 580–622.

Roden, David, and Henry Shue, *Just and Unjust Warriors: The Moral and Legal Status of Soldiers*, Oxford: Oxford University Press, 2008.

Rosen, David, *Child Soldiers in the Western Imagination: From Patriots to Victims*, New Brunswick, NY: Rutgers University Press, 2015.

Rosenau, James, *International Aspects of Civil Strife*, Princeton, NJ: Princeton University Press, 1964.

Rosenberg, David, "The Origins of Overkill: Nuclear Weapons and American Strategy, 1945-1960," *International Security* 7:4 (1983): 3–71.

Saada, Emmanuelle, *Empire's Children: Race, Filiation, and Citizenship in the French Colonies*, Chicago: University of Chicago Press, 2012.

Sandholtz, Wayne, *Prohibiting Plunder: How Norms Change*, Oxford: Oxford University Press, 2009.

Sandoz, Yves, "Le Demi-siècle des Conventions de Genève," *International Review of the Red Cross* 81:834 (1999): 241–264.

Sandoz, Yves, "The History of the Grave Breaches Regime," *Journal of International Criminal Justice* 7:4 (2009): 657–682.

Sands, Philippe, *East West Street: On the Origins of Genocide and Crimes against Humanity*, London: Weidenfeld & Nicolson, 2017.

Sanger, David, *The Perfect Weapon: War, Sabotage, and Fear in the Cyber Age*, New York: Broadway Books, 2019.

Sarat, Austin, Lawrence Douglas, and Martha Merrill Umphrey, eds., *Law and War*, Stanford, CA: Stanford University Press, 2014.

Sasson, Tehila, "From Empire to Humanity: The Russian Famine and the Imperial Origins of International Humanitarianism," *Journal of British Studies* 55 (2016): 519–537.

Satia, Priya, *Spies in Arabia: The Great War and the Cultural Foundations of Britain's Covert Empire in the Middle East*, Oxford: Oxford University Press, 2008.

Saul, Ben, *Defining Terrorism in International Law*, Oxford: Oxford University Press, 2006.

Savage, Charlie, *Power Wars: Inside Obama's Post-9/11 Presidency*, New York: Little, Brown & Company, 2016.

Scarfi, Juan, *The Hidden History of International Law in the Americas. Empire and Legal Networks*, Oxford: Oxford University Press, 2017.

Schabas, William, *The International Criminal Court: A Commentary on the Rome Statute*, Oxford: Oxford University Press, 2010.

Scheck, Raffael, "The Prisoner of War Question and the Beginnings of Collaboration: The Franco-German Agreement of 16 November 1940," *Journal of Contemporary History* 45:2 (2010): 364–388.

Scheipers, Sibylle, *Prisoners in War*, Oxford: Oxford University Press, 2010.

Scheipers, Sibylle, "'Unlawful Combatants': The West's Treatment of Irregular Fighters in the 'War on Terror,'" *Orbis* 58:4 (2014): 566–583.

Scheipers, Sibylle, *Unlawful Combatants: A Genealogy of the Irregular Fighter*, Oxford: Oxford University Press, 2015.

Schindler, Dietrich, "Human rights and Humanitarian Law: Interrelationship of the Laws," *American University Law Review* 31:935 (1981): 935–937.

Schindler, Dietrich, "International Humanitarian Law: Its Remarkable Development and its Persistent Violation," *Journal of the History of International Law* (2003): 165–188.

Schindler, Dietrich, "Max Huber - His Life," *The European Journal of International Law* 18:1 (2007): 81–95.

Schmitt, Carl, *Politische Theologie: Vier Kapitel zur Lehre von der Souveränität*, Munich: Duncker & Humblot, 1934.

Schmitt, Carl, *Theorie des Partisanen. Zwischenbemerkung zum Begriff des Politischen*, Berlin: Duncker & Humbolt, 1963.

Schmitt, Carl, *The Nomos of the Earth in the International Law of the Jus Publicum Europaeum*, New York: Telos Press, 2003.

Schmitt, Michael, "Military Necessity and Humanity in International Humanitarian Law: Preserving the Delicate Balance," *Virginia Journal of International Law* 50:4 (2010): 795–839.

Schmitt, Michael, *Tallinn Manual on the International Law Applicable to Cyber Warfare*, Cambridge, UK: Cambridge University Press, 2013.

Schwarzenberger, Georg, *International Law. The Law of Armed Conflict, Vol. 2*, London: Stevens, 1968.

Schwarzenberger, Georg, *International Law as Applied by International Courts and Tribunals, Volume II, The Law of Armed Conflict*, London: Stevens, 1968.

Segesser, Daniel, "Dissolve or Punish? The International Debate amongst Jurists and Publicists on the Consequences of the Armenian Genocide for the Ottoman Empire, 1915-1923," *Journal of Genocide Research* 10:1 (2008): 95–110.

Segesser, Daniel, "The Punishment of War Crimes Committed against Prisoners of War, Deportees and Refugees during and after the First World War," *Immigrants & Minorities* 26 (2008): 134–156.

Segesser, Daniel, *Recht statt Rache oder Rache durch Recht? Die Ahndung von Kriegsverbrechen in der internationale wissenschaftlichen Debatte, 1872-1945*, Paderborn: Ferdinand Schöningh, 2010.

Sellars, Kirsten, *"Crimes against Peace" and International Law*, Cambridge, UK: Cambridge University Press, 2013.

Sellars, Kirsten, *Trials for International Crimes in Asia*, Cambridge, UK: Cambridge University Press, 2016.

Shah, Reema, and Sam Kleiner, "Running Out of Options: Expiring Detention Authority and the Viability of Prosecutions in the Military Commissions under Hamdan II," *Yale Law Review* 32:2 (2013): 465–504.

Shealy, Gwendolyn, *A Critical History of the American Red Cross, 1882-1945*, New York: The Edwin Mellen Press, 2003.

Shepherd, Ben, *Terror in the Balkans: German Armies and Partisan Warfare*, Cambridge, MA: Harvard University Press, 2012.

Siegelberg, Mira, *Statelessness: A Modern History*, Cambridge, MA: Harvard University Press, 2020.

Simpson, Brian, *Human Rights and the End of Empire: Britain and the Genesis of the European Convention*, Oxford: Oxford University Press, 2010.

Sinclair, Guy Fiti, *To Reform the World: International Organizations and the Making of Modern States*, New York: Oxford University Press, 2017.

Sivakumaran, Sandesh, *The Law of Non-international Armed Conflict*, Oxford: Oxford University Press, 2014.

356 BIBLIOGRAPHY

Sivakumaran, Sandesh, "Making and Shaping the Law on Armed Conflict," *Current Legal Problems* 71:1 (2018): 119–160.

Sjoberg, Laura, "Gendered Realities of the Immunity Principle: Why Gender Analysis Needs Feminism," *International Studies Quarterly* 50:4 (2006): 889–910.

Skinner, Rob, and Alan Lester, "Humanitarianism and Empire: New Research Agendas," *Journal of Imperial and Commonwealth History* 40:5 (2012): 729–747.

Sluga, Glenda, *Internationalism in the Age of Nationalism*, Philadelphia, PA: Philadelphia University of Pennsylvania Press, 2015.

Sluga, Glenda, and Carolyn James, *Women, Diplomacy and International Politics Since 1500*, New York: Routledge, 2016.

Sluga, Glenda, and Patricia Clavin, eds., *Internationalisms: A Twentieth-Century History*, Cambridge, UK: Cambridge University Press, 2016.

Solf, Waldemar, "Protection of Civilians Against the Effects of Hostilities under Customary International Law and Under Protocol I," *American University International Law Review* 1:1 (1986): 117–135.

Solis, Gary, *The Law of Armed Conflict: International Humanitarian Law in War*, New York: Cambridge University Press, 2010.

Stanton, Jessica, "Rebel Groups, International Humanitarian Law, and Civil War Outcomes in the Post-Cold War Era," *International Organization* 74:3 (2020): 523–559.

Steinacher, Gerald, *Humanitarians at War: The Red Cross in the Shadow of the Holocaust*, Oxford: Oxford University Press, 2017.

Stibbe, Matthew, "The Internment of Civilians by Belligerent States during the First World War and the Response of the International Committee of the Red Cross," *Journal of Contemporary History* 41:1 (2006): 5–19.

Strachan, Hew, "Essay and Reflection: On Total War and Modern War," *The International History Review* 22:2 (2000): 341–370.

Stubbins Bates, Elizabeth, "Towards Effective Military Training in International Humanitarian Law," *International Review of the Red Cross* 96: 895/896 (2014): 795–816

Stubbins Bates, Elizabeth, "The British Army's Training in International Humanitarian Law," *Journal of Conflict & Security Law* 25:2 (2020): 291–315.

Surkis, Judith, Gary Wilder, James W. Cook, Durba Ghosh, Julia Adeney Thomas, and Nathan Perl-Rosenthal, "AHR Forum: Historiographic 'Turns' in Critical Perspective," *American Historical Review* (2012): 698–813.

Suter, Keith, *An International Law of Guerrilla Warfare. The Global Politics of Law-Making*, London: Frances Pinter, 1984.

Suzuki, Michiko, History of Disaster, Recovery, and Humanitarianism: The Japanese Red Cross Society in the Modern World, 1877-1945, Ph.D. Dissertation, SOAS, 2019.

Swinarski, Christophe, *Studies and Essays on International Humanitarian Law and Red Cross Principles in Honour of Jean Pictet*, The Hague: Martinus Nijhoff, 1984.

Tallgren, Immi, and Thomas Skouteris, eds., *The New Histories of International Criminal Law: Retrials*, Oxford: Oxford University Press, 2019.

Tallgren, Immi, *Portraits of Women in International Law: New Names and Forgotten Faces?* Cambridge, UK: Cambridge University Press, forthcoming.

Tanaka, Yuki, and Marilyn Young, eds., *Bombing Civilians: A Twentieth-Century History*, New York: New Press, 2010.

Tanaka, Yuki, Timothy McCormack, and Gerry Simpson, eds., *Beyond Victor's Justice? The Tokyo War Crimes Trial Revisited*, Leiden: Brill, 2011.

Teitel, Ruti, *Humanity's Law*, Oxford: Oxford University Press, 2011.

Thompson, Andrew, "Humanitarian Principles Put to the Test: Challenges to Humanitarian Action during Decolonization," *International Review of the Red Cross* 97:897/898 (2015): 45–76.

Tirman, John, *The Deaths of Others: The Fate of Civilians in America's Wars*, Oxford: Oxford University Press, 2011.

Tolley, Howard, *The International Commission of Jurists: Global Advocates for Human Rights*, Philadelphia: University of Pennsylvania Press, 1994.

Toman, Jiří, *The Protection of Cultural Property in the Event of Armed Conflict*, Aldershot: Dartmouth Publishing, 1996.

Toman, Jiří, 'L'Union Soviètique et le Droit des Conflits Armés, Ph.D. Dissertation, University of Geneva, 1997.

Totani, Yuma, *The Tokyo War Crimes Trial: The Pursuit of Justice in the Wake of World War II*, Cambridge, MA: Harvard University Press, 2008.

Totani, Yuma, and David Cohen, eds., *The Tokyo War Crimes Tribunal: Law, History, and Jurisprudence*, Cambridge, UK: Cambridge University Press, 2018.

Tov, Arieh Ben, *Facing the Holocaust in Budapest. The International Committee of the Red Cross and the Jews in Hungary, 1943-1945*, Geneva: Henry Dunant Institute, 1988.

Tuck, Richard, *Rights of War and Peace: Political Thought and the International Order from Grotius to Kant*, Oxford: Oxford University Press, 1999.

Vagts, Detlev, Theodor Meron, Stephen M. Schwebel, and Charles Keever, eds., *Humanizing the Laws of War. Selected Writings of Richard Baxter*, Oxford: Oxford University Press, 2014.

Valentino, Benjamin, Paul Huth, and Sarah Croco, "Covenants without the Sword: International Law and the Protection of Civilians in Times of War," *World Politics* 58:3 (2006): 339–377.

Venzke, Ingo, and Kevin Jon Heller, eds., *Contingency in International Law: On the Possibility of Different Legal Histories*, Oxford: Oxford University Press, 2021.

Viegnes, Michel, ed., *La Peur et ses Miroirs*, Paris: Editions Imago, 2009.

Vonèche Cardia, Isabelle, *Neutralité Entre le Comité International de la Croix-Rouge (CICR) et le Gouvernement Suisse*, Lausanne: SHSR, 2012.

Vrdoljak, Ana Filipa, *International Law, Museums, and the Return of Cultural Objects*, Cambridge, UK: Cambridge University Press, 2008.

de Waal, Alex, *Mass Starvation: The History and Future of Famine*, Cambridge, UK: Polity, 2018.

Wagner, Kim, "'Calculated to Strike Terror': The Amritsar Massacre and the Spectacle of Colonial Violence," *Past & Present* 233:1 (2016): 185–225.

Waterlow, Jonathan, and Jacques Schuhmacher, eds., *War Crimes Trials and Investigations: A Multi-Disciplinary Introduction*, Basingstoke: Palgrave, 2019.

Webster, Andrew, "Making Disarmament Work: The Implementation of the International Disarmament Provisions in the League of Nations Covenant, 1919-1925," *Diplomacy & Statecraft* 16:3 (2006): 551–569.

Weiss-Wendt, Adam, *The Soviet Union and the Gutting of the UN Genocide Convention*, Madison: University of Wisconsin Press, 2017.

Weitz, Eric, "From the Vienna to the Paris System: International Politics and the Entangled Histories of Human Rights, Forced Deportations, and Civilizing Missions," *American Historical Review* 113:5 (2004): 1313–1343.

Weitz, Eric, *A World Divided: The Global Struggle for Human Rights in the Age of Nation-States*, Princeton, NJ: Princeton University Press, 2019.

BIBLIOGRAPHY

Werner, Wouter, Marieke de Hoon, and Alexis Galán, *The Law of International Lawyers: Reading Martti Koskenniemi*, Cambridge, UK: Cambridge University Press, 2015.

Wertheim, Stephen, *Tomorrow, the World: The Birth of US Global Supremacy in World War II*, Cambridge, MA: Harvard University Press, 2020.

Westad, Odd Arne, *The Global Cold War: Third World Interventions and the Making of Our Times*, Cambridge, UK: Cambridge University Press, 2005.

Westad, Odd Arne, *The Cold War: A World History*, New York: Basic Books, 2017.

Whitman, James, *The Verdict of Battle. The Law of Victory and the Making of Modern War*, Cambridge, MA: Harvard University Press, 2012.

Whyte, Jessica, "The 'Dangerous Concept of the Just War': Decolonization, Wars of National Liberation, and the Additional Protocols to the Geneva Conventions," *Humanity* (2018): 313–341.

Wieviorka, Olivier, *The French Resistance*, Cambridge, MA: Harvard University Press, 2016.

Wildenthal, Lora, *The Language of Human Rights in West Germany*, Philadelphia, PA: University of Pennsylvania Press, 2012.

Wilder, Gary, *Freedom Time: Negritude, Decolonization, and the Future of the World*, Durham, NC: Duke University Press, 2015.

Wilke, Christiane, "How International Law Learned to Love the Bomb: Civilians and the Regulation of Aerial Warfare in the 1920s," *Australian Feminist Law Journal* 44:1 (2018): 29–47.

Winter, Jay, and Antoine Prost, *René Cassin and Human Rights. From the Great War to the Universal Declaration*, Cambridge, UK: Cambridge University Press, 2013.

Witt, John Fabian, *Lincoln's Code: The Laws of War in American History*, New York: Free Press, 2012.

Wylie, Neville, *Barbed Wire Diplomacy: Britain, Germany, and the Politics of Prisoners of War, 1939-1945*, Oxford: Oxford University Press, 2010.

Wylie, Neville, and James Crossland, "The Korean War and the Post-War Prisoners of War Regime, 1945-1956," *War in History* 23:4 (2016): 439–456.

Wylie, Neville, and Lindsey Cameron, "The Impact of World War I on the Law Governing the Treatment of Prisoners of War and the Making of a Humanitarian Subject," *European Journal of International Law* 29:4 (2018): 1327–1351.

Yoo, John, *War By Other Means*, New York: Atlantic Monthly Press, 2006.

Zarakol, Ayşe, "What Made the Modern World Hang Together: Socialisation or Stigmatisation?" *International Theory* 6:2 (2014): 311–332.

Index

Acheson, Dean 32, 43, 46, 189, 241, 243, 245–247, 307
Additional Protocols
    Additional Protocol I 147–148, 174, 183, 194, 323, 325–327
    Additional Protocol II 143–144, 147–148, 325–326
aerial bombardment *see* bombing
Afghanistan 196
Africa 21, 32, 216, 322
African-Americans 119
Afro-Asian states 326–327
aggression 106–107, 207, 213, 297, 319
air bombing *see* bombing
aircraft carrier 222
air-gas warfare *see* bombing; gas
air-nuclear warfare *see* bombing; nuclear
airplanes 208, 326
air policing 213, 225, 250
    see also bombing; empire
air raids *see* bombing
Albania 305
Aldrich, George 199
Algeria 110–111, 312, 322
Allies
    Allied Commission Report of 1919 58, 260
    bombing 30, 38, 197–198, 222–223
    indiscriminate warfare 222
    planning 72, 222
    powers 30–31, 35–37, 55, 113, 162–164, 167, 206–208, 222
alternative paths *see* contingency
Al Qaeda 144, 323, 328
ambassador 13, 45
ambulance personnel 157
    see also hospital
American Civil War (1861–1865) 101–102, 142, 153–154
American Red Cross 32, 103, 226, 230–231, 278
Amnesty International 328

ancient world 22
anti-colonial
    guerrillas 56, 142–143, 147–148, 167, 176, 238, 326–327
    insurgencies 6, 103–6, 110–111, 121–122, 143–144, 195, 208, 210
    politicking 7, 322
anti-communist
    insurgencies 6, 12, 319
    prisoners 6, 104–105
anti-Semitism 119, 265
Arab states 21, 44
arbitrary treatment *see* ill-treatment; torture
archive
    archival materials 14–17, 21–24
    Swiss archives 23
area bombing *see* bombing
Argentina 142, 196
armaments 203
    see also disarmament; weapons
'armed bands' *see* partisan
armed conflict 1, 2, 8, 12, 23–24, 42, 53, 106–107, 116–117, 150, 162, 312, 322–323, 333
    international armed conflict 23, 323
    see also non-international armed conflict; war
armed forces 299
Armenian Genocide 60, 260
Article 5 hearings 185–186, 194
Asakai, Koichiro 45
Asia 1, 5, 7, 34, 37–38, 111–112, 118, 177, 264, 321
atomic weapons 41, 135, 289, 297
    see also bombing; nuclear
atrocity 10, 34, 55, 58, 68, 75, 106, 161, 180, 253, 273, 307–308, 333
Attlee, Clement 84, 131, 176–177, 239, 285
Augunas, Algy 197
Auriti, Giacinto 45, 309
Auschwitz 50, 72, 235, 247

360 INDEX

Australia 129, 132, 138, 187, 196, 240, 247, 291, 293, 311
Austria 312
Austria-Hungary 105, 204–205
Axis
  occupation 8, 12, 34
  powers 3, 37, 45, 67, 88, 167, 219, 222–223, 333
  prisoners of war 32

Badoglio, Pietro 166
balloons 203–206
  balloon declaration 203–204
  see also bombing
Baltic 29
'bandits' *see* partisan; spies
'barbarians' 155–156
  see also 'civilization'
Baruch, Bernard 223–224, 234
  Baruch Plan 224, 234
Bâtiment Électoral 1, 321
battlefield 5, 155, 253, 255, 270, 291, 295, 328
Baxter, Richard 163, 194
Belgium 68, 74, 87, 98, 162, 183–184, 215, 243, 267, 306
Bellan, Pierre 168, 174
belligerency 101–102, 106–109, 113–116, 120, 132, 142
belligerent
  equality 183
  nexus 157, 167
  rights 124, 150–151, 157, 163, 224
  status 114–118, 136–138, 163–167
  territory 64, 75, 93–94, 188–190, 200, 229, 329
Bellot, Hugh 64
Belorussia 305
Benes resolution 212
Berlin blockade (1948) 40, 44, 83, 123, 178, 231–232, 236
Bern agreements (1918) 58–59, 259
Best, Geoffrey 16, 53, 99, 134, 194, 233, 244, 247–248
Betolaud, Robert 47, 189, 243
Betts, Paul 318
Bevin, Ernest 133, 177, 239, 243, 246
Biafra 325–326
bipartisanship 3
bipolar spectrum 15, 21, 46

Blanco, Hector 135, 139
'blind weapons' 224, 229, 240, 251, 324
  see also bombing; nuclear
Blitz *see* bombing
blockade 25, 56, 96, 197–251, 325–326, 332
  hunger blockade 58, 201, 208, 213, 218–219, 224, 227, 251
blueprint 2, 4, 330
Boissier, Pierre 274–275, 280, 282
Bolla, Plinio 47, 132, 247–248
Bolshevism 100, 104–106
bombing 1, 6–8, 11, 22, 25, 30, 32, 48, 50, 63, 65, 135–137, 197–251, 271, 283, 285, 287–289, 296–297, 309, 314, 316–317, 319–320, 324–325, 331–332
  bomber pilots 180, 197–198, 227–228, 232, 238, 240, 276–277, 289, 318
  bombing of French cities 32, 206, 225
  for 'psychological reasons' 6, 204
Bonnet, Marie-Jo 50
Bourdet, Claude 38, 50, 74, 168–170, 179, 310, 320
Bourquin, Maurice 68, 74, 87, 98, 243, 245, 267–268
Brazil 37, 227
Brigadier Page 73
Brussels conference (1874) 156–160, 203
Brussels draft 159
Brussels Pact (1948) 40
Burckhardt, Carl 33, 265
Burma
  delegation 14, 129–130, 132, 135, 138–142, 196, 244
Bush Administration 18, 328

Cahen-Salvador, Georges 3, 14, 33, 47, 54, 71, 81, 87, 93, 122, 129, 134, 183–184, 233, 240–245, 247, 271–272, 277, 292–293, 312, 326
Callen, Jason 329
Canada
  Canadian delegation 83, 86–90, 93, 128, 140, 174, 190, 230–231, 235, 246
capital punishment 77–78, 81
capitalism 31, 41, 203, 239
captor states 32, 37, 167
carpet bombing *see* bombing
Carry, Paul 235
Cassese, Antonio 160

INDEX 361

Cassin, René 71–72
Castberg, Frede 68, 73–74, 81–82, 98, 100–101, 111–115, 129–132, 135, 149, 187, 236
Central Europe 38–39, 162
Central Powers 207, 259–260
Chaco War 107
Chang, Peng Chun 48
chaplain 21
charity 29
Chayet, Claude 165
children
    child soldiers 81
    children's rights 57–59, 63, 78–79, 94–95, 207–208, 324
China
    delegation 44–45, 48–49, 73, 92, 216, 236–237, 321
    Maoist China 21, 46, 305
    Nationalist China 31, 33, 36–37, 214, 217, 236–237, 306, 321
Chinese Civil War 36, 117, 124
chivalry code 22, 153
Chongqing 48
civil war 1, 5–7, 14, 22, 93, 99–145, 299–300, 317, 327
civilian
    civilian air crews 186
    civilian victim categories 60–70
    civil defense 211–213, 220, 224
    internees 37, 58
    population 63, 197–251, 317, 324–325
    protection 1, 9–13, 19, 22–24, 30–33, 35–36, 38, 42, 53–97, 116, 162, 189, 197–251, 258, 307, 312–314, 317, 319, 321, 324
    rights 47, 50, 54–56, 61–97, 331
Civilian Convention 11, 12, 22, 24–25, 30–32, 36–38, 42, 53–97, 116, 124, 133–134, 148–195, 197–251, 294, 303–305, 309, 312–313, 315–316, 318–319, 324–325, 328, 332
    failure of interwar drafts 56, 65–67, 220, 235, 313
civilization 7, 34, 57, 102, 114, 129, 152, 155, 202–203, 208, 239, 287
Clattenburg, Albert 37, 73, 121–122, 168, 173–180, 226–227, 231–233, 240, 272, 276, 278

Clausewitz, Carl von 152
Clay, Lucius 45
Cohn, Georg 93, 174, 183–184
Cold War
    adversary 9, 191–193, 297
    battleground 11, 201, 289, 320
    early Cold War 3, 40, 56, 231, 276, 306–308, 321
    interests 12, 82
    politics 5–9, 15, 20, 25, 37–38, 46–47, 92, 100–101, 176–181, 231, 238–240, 242, 249, 250, 275, 285, 290, 293–294, 296–298, 304, 311, 314–315, 327–328, 330, 333
collective
    collective memory 3, 79, 308, 333
    collective penalties 38, 55–57, 68–70, 74–78, 81, 87–88, 95, 136–137, 162, 253
colonial
    auxiliaries 155
    interests 12
    laws 96
    official 13
    starvation 202, 208
    torture 6
    war 7, 22, 47, 93, 99–145, 188–189, 208, 312, 319
    see also empire
colonialism 21, 46, 312, 323
    see also empire
Combat 50, 166, 170
Comité de Luxembourg 217
Comité International d'Information et d'Action pour la Protection de la Population Civile en temps de Guerre 217
Commentary 4, 15, 99, 123, 134, 147, 200, 299–300, 309
Committee of National Front (CFLN) 166
Common Article 1 10, 299–300
Common Article 2 10, 117–118
Common Article 3 10, 93, 99–145, 185, 191, 250, 305, 307, 310, 312, 316–318, 321–323, 325, 328
    legacies 321–323
Commonwealth 44, 86, 92–93, 130, 187, 190, 192, 242, 246
Communism
    communist parties 40, 195
    communist powers 36, 122, 125, 237, 276

362 INDEX

compensation 257
'competent international body' 272–274,
  278–279
  see also Protecting Power; substitute
competing projects 22
compliance 26, 211, 255, 258, 261, 266,
  269–270, 273, 294–295, 328
concentration camp 1, 47, 74, 263
conciliation procedures 278–301
Confederacy 155
conference
  Brussels conference (1874) 156–160, 203
  diplomatic conference (1929) 62–63,
    162–163, 212, 262–263, 298
  diplomatic conference (1949) 1–2, 4,
    11–12, 19–21, 24, 28, 42–51, 54, 83–
    97, 127–142, 178–192, 235–249, 284–
    295, 315–316, 318–321, 326–327
  Geneva conference (1864) 34, 157, 303
  government experts' conference
    (1947) 21, 34, 36–39, 72–74, 112–115,
    167–170, 226–228, 252, 269–273, 283
  procedures 49, 158, 191, 241–246, 249, 314
  Red Cross conference (1912) 103–104
  Red Cross conference (1921) 59–60,
    106–107, 207–208, 261
  Red Cross conference (1923) 60–61
  Red Cross conference (1925) 211–212
  Red Cross conference (1934) 63–64,
    107–108, 215
  Red Cross experts' conference
    (1937) 108–109, 216
  Red Cross conference (1938) 65, 109–110,
    216
  Red Cross conference (1946) 34, 68–69,
    111–112, 221, 223–224, 266–268
  second government experts'
    conference 41
  Stockholm conference (1948) 41–42,
    77–78, 81–83, 119–121, 150, 173–175,
    196, 201, 228–235, 254, 273–279, 313,
    315
Congo 331
Congress of Paris (1856) 203
conscientious objector 60
Conseil d'État 33, 71
conservatism 13, 30, 33
containment 36, 250
contingency 10–12, 18, 24, 53, 100–101, 330
contraband 202–203

Convention for the Protection of Historic
  Buildings 210
counterinsurgency
  policies 6, 7, 24, 33, 42, 55, 58–61, 67–91,
    95, 122, 136–137, 148–149, 172, 307
Craigie, Robert 46, 48, 87, 90–91, 125–126,
  130–135, 139–141, 181–185, 188–189,
  236–238, 242–243, 245–246, 263, 271,
  288, 291, 294, 298, 305–306, 316
Cramer, Marguerite 14, 29, 58–63, 69,
  161–162, 269
Crawford, Emily 147
crimes against humanity 259–260,
  264–265
critical legal studies 17
cruiser rules 208
customary law 323
cyber
  manuals 332
  warfare 332–333
Cyprus 192
Czarist Russia
  Czarist Russian Red Cross 104–106
  Foreign Ministry 156
  state 156–160, 203–205, 257
  see also Russia
Czechoslovakia
  delegation 39, 48, 190
  government 40–41

Dachau 50
de Alba, Pedro 48
death penalty 8, 11–12, 77–78, 81, 84–86,
  89–91, 177, 304–306, 313–314, 316,
  318–319
debellatio 166
Declaration of the International Rights of
  Man (1929) 64
Declaration of the Rights of the Child
  (1924) 63
decolonization 5, 8, 25, 47, 56, 68, 99–145,
  100–101, 110–111, 148, 296–298, 309,
  321–322
  see also anti-colonial
Denmark 82–83, 93–94, 174, 295
depoliticized origin story 4, 308–309
deportation 42, 59, 70–71, 74, 80–81, 89,
  137, 329
derogations 84–85
deterrence 9, 40

Dillon, Joseph 32, 50, 237
Dinstein, Yoram 149
disarmament 203–205, 207–208, 212–213,
   223, 227–228, 232, 245, 283, 331–332
   disarmament conference
      (1930s) 212–213
   Washington disarmament conference
      (1921–1922) 208
discipline 153
discretionary powers 117, 159, 162, 173,
   221, 236, 325
discrimination
   non-discrimination 72, 112
   racial discrimination 74, 80, 84, 87, 112,
      120, 315
displaced persons 83, 89
   see also civilian; statelessness
dispute settlement 254, 278–301
   see also enforcement
dissemination 254, 256, 266–268, 278,
   298–299, 307, 324
distinction 11, 25, 57–58, 65, 150–151, 167,
   171, 176, 197–251, 332–333
distinctive sign 152, 154, 157, 160, 167, 170
disturbances see emergency
'Divine Origins of Man' 92
Dogger Bank incident (1904) 257
domestic jurisdiction 256–257, 275, 282,
   284, 289, 296
Douhet, Giulio 210
Dove, Arthur 172
Dresden 30, 197–198
drone 329
Duchosal, Jean 77–78, 98
Dufour, Guillaume Henri 44
Duhamel, Georges 165
Dulles, John Foster 307
Dumbarton Oaks (1944) 47
Dunant, Henri 2, 8, 14, 22, 29, 103, 214,
   234, 303
duration clause 96

East-West
   relations 9, 75, 85, 118, 123, 141, 148,
      177, 185, 188, 227–228, 239–240, 242,
      249, 251, 278, 286, 312–313
Eastern Europe 1, 6, 48, 87–88, 140, 143,
   218, 223, 227, 259, 268, 304, 317
economic warfare see blockade
Ede, James 177

'effects of war' 30, 225, 311, 330
emergency 80, 116, 118, 296
empire 7–8, 13, 16, 47, 101–105, 99–145,
   147–195, 207–208, 210, 213, 248, 254,
   315, 319, 322, 326
   see also colonial; colonialism
enemy agents 124, 149–150, 176
   see also partisan; spies
Enemy Airmen's Act (1942) 173, 197
enemy alien see civilian
enemy civilian see civilian
'enemy combatant' see partisan
enforcement 9, 25, 253–300, 314, 319,
   327–328
ensuring respect 254, 299–300
established account 14–15
Eurocentric 19, 21, 46, 166–167, 323
European
   colonial powers 21, 31, 37, 46
   colonial rule 13
   imperial expansion 8, 17
European Convention on Human Rights
   (ECHR) 95–96
ethics 333
Ethiopia 65, 107–108, 244
   Ethiopian-Italian War (1935–1937) 65,
      107–108, 216
ethnic cleansing 137
   see also genocide
Ex Parte Quirin trials (1942) 167
exclusion 16–17, 25, 57, 96, 148, 202, 324,
   327, 329, 331
experiences of war 13
   see also victim
extermination 137, 222, 237–238, 247, 329
   see also civilian; genocide
extradition 270, 282, 284, 296
extrajudicial 74, 148–151, 172, 176–179,
   188, 192–193, 329
   see also security clause

fact-finding 260–301, 327, 331
   see also enforcement; inquiry
fair trial 171, 198, 264, 274, 280
'fall back option' 82–83, 86, 149–150,
   186–192
famine 224, 325
   see also blockade; food; starvation
'farmer-by-day-guerrilla-by-night' see
   partisan; spies

364 INDEX

fascism 45, 129, 267, 309, 318
  fascist practices 7, 311, 326
fear of war 20–21, 319–320
Ferrière, Frédéric 58, 60–64, 95
Ferrière, Suzanne 63, 69, 73, 77
field manuals 161, 254
'fifth columns' 148, 165, 173, 177
  see also partisan; spies
Finland 37, 45, 105, 244
Firestorm 197–198
First Geneva Convention 12, 29, 42, 116,
  120, 202, 212, 216, 228, 256–257,
  262–263, 273–274
First World War 22, 56, 58, 100, 104–105,
  150, 161–162, 206–207, 212, 214,
  254–255, 258–259, 281, 311, 330
food 202, 205, 211, 218, 229, 234, 236
  see also famine; starvation
forced disappearances 187
forced labor 59, 80, 258
foreign nationals 102
Foreign Office *see* Great Britain
fortified towns 202–203
foundation myths 2, 14, 308–310
  see also contingency; popular mythology
Fourth Geneva Convention *see* Civilian
  Convention
France
  Air Force 210, 225
  Army 225
  communist officials 36
  delegation at Geneva 1947 73–75, 226–227,
    270, 273–274
  delegation at Geneva 1949 6, 9–12, 14,
    19–20, 44, 47, 49–50, 87–90, 92–93, 132,
    138–140, 178–192, 235–251, 286–301
  delegation at Stockholm 1948 82–83,
    122–123, 175, 231–233, 277–279
  Foreign Ministry 43, 125, 131–134, 164,
    179, 244
  French military doctors 13, 214–215,
    311, 317
  French-Soviet relations 41, 86, 179, 290
  legal attitudes 6, 8–9, 31–33, 35–36,
    38–39, 59, 61–62, 65, 71–75, 86–87,
    109–110, 113–114, 122–123, 125–126,
    128–135, 138–140, 143, 157, 162, 164–
    166, 178–195, 204, 209, 210, 213, 224–
    251, 286–301, 306–307, 311–313, 316

Ministry for Prisoners, Deportees, and
  Refugees 33, 50, 311
Ministry of Defense 133
Ministry of Interior 131–133
Ministry of Overseas Territories 113,
  131, 164
Ministry of War 156, 164–165
National Council of the Resistance 33
occupation of Germany 9, 61, 96–97,
  165, 168, 311–312
prisoners of war 33, 272
Provisional Government 32, 71, 164
ratification 306–307
reservation 306–307
resistance 13, 33, 50
US-French relations 43, 178–179, 189,
  225, 312
war crimes' tribunals 198, 265, 274
Franco, Francisco 108
Franco-Prussian War (1870–1871) 58,
  156–158, 255–256
francs tireurs *see* partisan; spies
free-corps 154
freedom of religion 65
'freedom fighters' 326–327
  see also partisan; spies
Free French Forces 163–166, 225, 312
free passage 224, 227, 229, 234, 236
Freiburg 206
Frenay, Henry 33, 38, 47, 50, 164–166, 311–312
French Forces of the Interior (FFI) 163,
  166–168
French Red Cross 33, 233
French Revolution 152–153

Gandhi, Indira 48
Garde Nationale Mobile 156
Gardner, William 47, 50, 113–116, 124–125,
  131, 172, 174, 177–178, 181–182, 188,
  237, 242, 287, 291
gas
  chamber 221, 247
  poison gas 203, 208, 215, 268
  tear gas 208
  warfare 63, 207–208, 211, 215, 219, 229,
    240, 247
  weaponry 207, 210, 222, 240, 283
de Gaulle, Charles 31–33, 36, 71, 164–166,
  225

Gautier, Alfred 59
gender 161, 324
genealogy 17–22, 99–100
General Order No. 100 154–155, 202
Geneva
  Conference of 1864 34, 157, 303 *see also* conference
  Convention of 1906 256–257
  Conventions Act (1957) 308
  Conventions of 1929 30, 32–34, 36, 79, 108, 269, 276, 313 *see also* First Geneva Convention; POW Convention
  Protocol (1925) 208, 211, 221, 229, 240, 283 *see also* gas
  University of Geneva 35
'Geneva Law' 25, 54, 199–202, 219–220, 250
genocide 70, 163, 218, 247, 265
  Genocide Convention (1948) 86, 120, 179, 184, 222, 238, 281, 286–289, 295
Germany 6, 20, 38, 40, 45, 73, 76, 87–88, 105, 158, 164, 203–207, 218, 220–221, 225, 235, 260, 263, 276, 277, 282, 309, 312, 315, 329
  aggression 213
  aliens 37
  camps 47
  communists 70
  deportations 96
  German captivity 305
  German-Soviet War 41
  Red Cross 34, 266
  rocket campaign 220–221, 229, 240
Gestapo 168
Gillespie, Alexander 199
global
  Global South 20, 299, 322–323
  history 12, 19
  justice 249
  leadership 31
  politics 269, 331
Goldsmith, Jack 329
good offices 259, 269, 278–301
  see also enforcement
des Gouttes, Paul 63–64, 109, 117
government experts' conference (1947) *see* conference
grave breaches 11, 252–300, 327, 331
  see also enforcement

Graven, Jean 279–283
Great Britain
  Admiralty 236
  atomic weapon's program 241
  Chiefs of Staff 233
  Colonial Office 13, 42, 123, 136, 315
  delegation at Geneva 1947 73–76, 168–170, 226–227, 270
  delegation at Geneva 1949 9, 11–13, 19–20, 44, 46–47, 50, 87–91, 138–139, 179–184, 188–192, 235–251, 285–301, 314–316
  delegation at Stockholm 1948 42, 82–83
  Foreign Office 9, 30, 42, 50, 72, 84, 90, 123, 130–131, 176, 188, 193, 239, 241, 243, 246, 287, 306
  General Staff 172, 187, 287
  Home Office 31, 47, 123, 176
  Home Office Committee 42, 75, 116, 123–124, 173
  legal attitudes 6–9, 12, 30–34, 38, 42, 62, 65–67, 72–76, 79–85, 90–91, 111–116, 123–131, 138–139, 143, 150, 157–158, 164, 176–195, 205–207, 209–210, 213, 216–219, 222–251, 257, 276, 285–301, 305–307, 309, 315–316, 321
  Royal Air Force (RAF) 209, 213, 218, 228, 233–234, 237, 315
  Security Services 9, 123, 187, 315
  War Office 9, 31, 47, 83–84, 90, 164, 172, 188, 285, 287–288, 291, 295, 305, 315
  War Office Committee 42, 115–116, 124–125, 171–172
  War Office Prisoner of War Department 38, 168, 265
Great Powers 4, 10, 13, 19, 30, 33–34, 56, 61–62, 65, 70, 79, 85–86, 93–94, 101, 121, 127, 156–160, 211, 215, 217, 219, 223, 234–235, 248, 254, 268–269, 281, 290–291, 294, 298, 300, 307, 316–317, 321, 327, 330, 333
Greece 29, 36, 113–114, 120, 163, 218, 224
Greek Civil War 113–114, 118, 122, 127
guerrilla *see* partisan
Gutteridge, Joyce 2, 50, 123, 147, 182, 188, 200, 287, 295

Hague Air Rules (1923) 208–210, 214–215, 217, 219

366 INDEX

Hague Conventions
  Hague Convention of 1954 210, 219
  Hague Conventions of 1899 160–162,
    203, 258
  Hague Conventions of 1907 199–200,
    204–205, 209
  Regulations of 1907 57, 64, 67, 157, 163–
    164, 171, 204, 206, 217, 219, 234, 283
  see also 'Hague Law'; Hague Peace
    Conference
'Hague Law' 25, 199–202, 250
  see also Hague Conventions; Hague
    Peace Conference
Hague Peace Conference
  1899 50, 159–160, 203, 256–257
  1907 50, 161–162, 199–200, 204–205,
    257
  see also Hague Conventions; 'Hague Law'
Haksar, Parmeshwar Narayan 48
Halleck, Henry 153
Hamdan vs. Rumsfeld (2006) 144, 328
Harrison, Leland 46, 48, 85, 91, 126, 130,
    135, 182–185, 238, 240, 243–244, 316
Hemery, Pierre 165
hierarchy 17, 96, 331
high international committee 278,
    292–293
  see also enforcement; substitute
high seas 205
Hiroshima 197, 227, 297
'historicizing moment' 16–19
historiographical amnesia 14, 333
Hitler, Adolf 4, 31, 34–35, 38, 43, 66, 81,
    163–164, 169–170, 180, 213, 218–219,
    232
Ho Chi Minh 307
Hodgson, William 247
Holocaust 10, 33, 35, 50, 53, 54, 66, 69, 80,
    87, 117, 183, 190, 237, 247, 263, 304,
    309, 329
hospital
  civilian hospital, 221, 223, 233, 235, 249
  neutralized military hospitals 202–203,
    205, 212, 221, 223, 233, 235, 249
  ships 21
  town 65, 214, 216
  see also Red Cross
hostage 7, 38, 55, 57–59, 61, 64, 67–71, 74–
    76, 81, 87–88, 105, 113, 319

Huber, Max 35, 38, 64, 70, 73, 77–80, 98,
    111, 167, 213, 215, 220, 224, 234, 265,
    280–283, 317
Hull, Isabell 158
human dignity 8, 34, 55, 65, 69, 72
  see also human rights
human rights
  agenda 68
  duties 60, 69
  groups 331
  relationship human rights and
    humanitarian law 10, 12–14, 18, 24,
    35, 42, 54–56, 59–62, 64–95, 104–105,
    111–112, 125, 134–136, 149, 163–166,
    171–175, 178–179, 189, 194, 237,
    254, 266, 282–284, 303, 308, 312, 317,
    321–322
  see also human dignity
Human Rights Watch 328
human shields 205–206, 212, 218–219,
    222, 225–226, 233, 250
human suffering 29, 104, 255, 258, 321,
    326, 329–330
humanitarian
  aid 29
  assistance 228
  organization 29
  principles 10
  'The Great Humanitarian' 320
  see also humanitarianism
humanitarianism 15–16, 254, 266
  'unbridled humanitarianism' 10
  see also humanitarian
'humanizing air war' 214, 221
Hungary 105, 127, 304, 319
hunger blockade see blockade; starvation

ideology 333
'illegal combatants' see partisan; spies
ill-treatment 50, 63–64, 67–74, 80–91, 172,
    190, 237, 258, 276
  see also torture
illiberal 6, 189
imperial rule 5, 10, 25, 99–145, 147–195,
    213
  see also empire
implementation 254, 305
  see also enforcement
incendiary weapons 30, 197, 210–211, 218

see also bombing
inclusive process 4, 6, 329
India 36, 110, 264, 306, 326
   delegation 44, 48–49, 92, 184, 248
   Foreign Service 48
   Ministry of Defense 48, 184
indiscriminate bombing *see* bombing; nuclear
individual criminal responsibility 261, 263,
   280, 282, 285
   see also enforcement; grave breaches
Indochina 6, 101, 110–111, 113–114, 117,
   122, 125, 129, 133–134, 165, 179, 188,
   195, 225, 307, 312
Indonesia 110–114, 124–126
   Republicans 21, 37, 46, 111, 126
inquiry 254, 257–258, 260–301
   commission of inquiry 257
   investigators 256
   see also enforcement; fact-finding
inspector 171, 178–179, 193, 253–300
   see also enforcement
Institut Henry Dunant (IHD) 14
Institute of International Law (IIL) 159,
   204–205
insurgency 84, 101–103, 110, 116, 123–124,
   129–130, 137, 176, 305
intelligence 178–179
   see also interrogation
internal wars 25, 99–145, 174, 191–192
   see also civil war; colonial war
inter-belligerent conferences 161
   see also Bern Agreements
Interdepartmental Prisoners of War
   Committee (POWC) 32, 37, 73,
   76–77, 85–86, 118–119, 126, 167–168,
   173–174, 178, 226, 228, 266, 313–314
   see also United States
Inter-Ministerial Commission 33, 36, 50,
   56, 71–72, 113, 125–126, 164, 224–226
   see also France
'intermittent guerrilla' *see* partisan ; spies
international
   humanitarian law (IHL) 23
   internationalism 15, 254
   lawyer 326
   legal personality 59, 323
   (legal) order 8, 13, 15, 19, 31
   organization 19, 43, 213
   relations 16

International Association for the Protection
   of Civilian Populations and Historic
   Buildings in Wartime 214
International Association of Penal Law
   (IAPL) 269, 280
International Commission to Inquire into
   the Causes and Conduct of the Balkan
   Wars (1913) 258
International Committee of the Red Cross
   (ICRC)
   appeals 35, 217, 251
   Assembly 117
   Committee 1, 3, 5, 8–16, 19–21, 23–25,
     29–38, 42–46, 58–63, 66–67, 72–74,
     99–100, 104–109, 110–111, 122–123,
     141–144, 147–149, 165–168, 175–196,
     199–200, 211–217, 219–251, 253–256,
     258–300, 303–333
   delegation at Geneva 1946 266–267
   delegation at Geneva 1947 169–170
   delegation at Geneva 1949 47, 49, 87–89,
     141–142
   delegation at Stockholm 1948 42, 122–123
   Greek relief campaign 218, 224
   ICRC-French relations 39, 272–273
   ICRC-Soviet relations 190–191, 290,
     318–320
   impartiality 281
   inspections 102–103, 173, 176–179, 193,
     254–300, 319, 324, 327–328
   legal attitudes 56, 60–68, 72–83, 93–94,
     99–100, 105–106, 110–111, 117–118,
     147–148, 163, 170–174, 186–195,
     211–217, 219–251, 255–300
   Legal Division 35, 67–68, 77–78, 109
   neutrality 15, 25, 215, 220–221, 236, 257,
     266, 269, 281, 298, 316
   POW Agency 44, 58, 161, 259
   right of intervention 105, 109, 117,
     136–138, 322
   Secretariat 35
   Special Committee 60–64
International Congress of Military Medicine
   and Pharmacy (ICMMP) 214–216
international criminal law 18, 254, 256–300,
   323
   criminal repression 23, 25, 256–300
   criminal tribunal 261–262, 277, 280–281,
     286–287, 289, 297

368 INDEX

International Criminal Tribunal for the former Yugoslavia (ICTY) 323
international law
  boundaries of international law 12
  discipline of international law 16–17
  lawmaking 10–11, 19
International Law Association (ILA) 62, 64, 216–217
International Union for Child Welfare (IUCW) 78, 81, 94
internment 37, 57–59, 62, 77, 82, 161, 261
  see also civilian
interrogations 76, 84, 172–173, 190, 328–329
  see also torture
interstate non-aggression 31, 213
interwar proposals 3, 13, 22, 56, 66–68, 74, 88, 110, 201, 210, 212, 214, 220, 224, 227, 262, 267, 271
invasion 12, 107, 158, 181, 213, 311–312
invitation policies 19–21
Iraq 328–329
Ireland 105, 321
irregular
  combatants 148
  warfare 9, 152, 162
  see also partisan; spies
Israel 44, 46, 48, 183–184, 244, 248
Istanbul Trials (1919–1920) 260
Italy 29, 50, 166, 205, 306
  fascist Italy 45, 62, 106, 109, 216
  Italian delegation 45, 135–136, 185
Iwao, Ayusawa 45

Jackson, Robert 263, 281
Jacob, Andrée 49–50, 72–73, 81, 165, 174, 196
Jacquinot, Robert 214, 219
Japan 20–21, 34, 37–38, 63, 73, 96, 107, 197–198, 212, 218–221, 235, 237, 262, 276
  delegation 20, 45
  Japanese Red Cross 34, 63, 107
  Japanese soldiers 166
Japanese-Americans 73–74
Jewish
  civilians 10, 218, 221, 247, 262–263, 268
  internationalism 13, 66
  minorities 70, 119
  organizations 35, 69, 129

Jews 10, 35, 66, 70, 78–80, 93–94, 119, 162–163, 247, 309
Jim Crow laws 96
Joint Committee 129, 139–140, 186, 237
journalists 189, 232, 239, 244, 247–249, 280, 307–311, 331
just war
  'just cause' 180, 183–184, 318, 327
  Soviet just war theory 180, 318–319, 327
justice
  ideals of justice 31, 69, 253, 296, 317, 331

Kalshoven, Frits, 300
Kara, Anna 304
Kassem Case (1969) 186
Kellogg-Briand Pact (1928) 106–107
Kenya 307, 322
Kharkov Trials (1943) 280
Khrushchev, Nikita 137
Klose, Fabian 99
'knockout blow' 205–206, 210
  see also bombing
Kobe 197
Kommandobefehl (1942) 163, 167
Korean War (1950–1953) 239, 305, 307, 324
Kouchner, Bernard 325–326
Kristallnacht (1938) 119

Labour
  Cabinet 9, 84–85, 124–125, 131, 135, 176–177, 239, 285, 306
  Ministers 306
  MPs 239
Lamarle, Albert 43, 47, 72–74, 90, 93, 98, 114, 125, 129–130, 133–134, 138–140, 165, 168, 178–179, 181–184, 191, 196, 225, 227, 233, 240, 242–243, 272, 277–278, 286, 295, 313
Latin America(n) 1, 34, 331
  states 20, 37, 44, 132, 135, 139, 244, 314
Lauterpacht, Hersch 101–102, 271, 279–283, 288–289, 331
law of nations 57, 202
League of Nations 63, 105, 207, 211–212, 214, 220, 261
  Council 261
  Covenant 207
  sanctions 207, 212, 214, 220
  see also blockade

INDEX 369

League of Red Cross Societies 105, 231, 292
legitimate target 5, 237
   see also bombing
Leiden University 271
Leipzig Trials (1921) 260, 281, 296
Lemkin, Raphael 70, 184, 264–265
levée en masse 152–155, 157–158, 186
lex specialis 274
liberal
   blueprint 4, 318
   humanitarianism 2
   international jurists
   internationalism 15
   origins 3, 6
   powers 65, 236–237, 267
   safeguards 273–277, 280–281, 288–289
Libya 205
Lieber, Francis 57, 142, 151, 153–159, 202,
   308
Lieux de Genève Association (LGA) 213–
   214, 219–220, 234
Lincoln, Abraham 154–155
Lips-Odinot, Rie 306
Lodygensky, Georges 104–105
Logoz, Paul 280
London 271
   London Charter (1945) 281
   London conference (1938) 65, 216 *see*
      also conference; Red Cross
   London Declaration (1909) 205–206
lower-intensity conflicts 11, 123
   see also civil war
Luban, David 55
Luca, Elisabeta 50, 247
Luns, Joseph 193, 306
Lynching 119

MacArthur, Douglas 45
MacBride, Seán 321–322
Malagasy Uprising 114
Malaya 123, 136–137, 176, 188
Manchuria 63, 107
Mandates 103, 105–106, 172
Mandela, Nelson 322
Maoism 21, 36–37
   see also China
'marauders'*see* partisan; spies
Marshall Plan 39
Martens, Fyodor 156–160, 257

Martens Clause 159–162, 166, 185
martial laws *see* emergency
mass civilian death 207, 235, 324
   see also extermination; genocide
master-narrative of the Conventions 2, 4
Mayer, Jane 308
Mayhew, Christopher 133
mediator 13, 237, 273
   see also enforcement
medical
   expert 58
   facilities 202, 214–215
the Mediterranean 31, 36, 112
mercenaries 327
merchant marine 186, 202, 205
Mexico 48, 92, 248
Meylan, Jean 77
MI-5 84, 172, 176–177
   see also Great Britain
Microsoft 332
the Middle East 1, 34, 38, 111–112, 263,
   267
military
   necessity 3, 6, 55, 57, 65, 89, 202–204,
      288, 317
   objectives 206, 209, 217, 226, 237, 249,
      251
   officer 13, 331
militia 157
   see also partisan
mines 218
minority 10
Mitra, Dhiren 49
mobilizable adult men 161
   see also civilian
Moir, Lindsay 99
Monaco Draft (1934) 64–68, 107, 210,
   214–217, 219, 229, 236, 262, 267,
   292, 311
monument protection in war 203, 209–210,
   215
Moore, John Bassett 209–210
'morale bombing' *see* bombing
Morosov, Platon 14, 47, 141, 191, 240, 288
Mott, William 121
Mouton, Willem 183, 185–186, 193, 263,
   270–271, 277, 279–281, 283–284,
   286–287, 289
Moyn, Samuel 314

370 INDEX

Moynier, Gustave 256–257
munition factories 209
  see also bombing
Mussolini, Benito 45, 62, 216
'mutiny' 102

Nagasaki 197
napalm 197
  see also bombing
Napoleonic Wars (1803–1815) 152
national liberation movement 21, 183, 194, 323
nationalism 13, 332
Nationalist China *see* China
nationality 60, 94, 333
  nationals of a non-party belligerent 76
  see also civilian
naval
  bombardment 202–204
  power 226–227, 233
  see also blockade; bombing
Nazi
  Germany 7–9, 55, 68, 71–72, 84, 109, 117–119, 125, 129, 168, 213, 216, 218, 233, 236, 238, 249, 262–263, 265–266, 268, 272, 281–282, 308
  hunger plan 163, 218
  legalism 129
  occupation 6, 7, 9, 32, 72, 80, 90, 180, 190, 193, 222, 224, 271
  persecution 9, 13, 36, 193, 306
  race laws 80
Nehru, Jawaharlal 48, 306
Nelson, Robert 197
the Netherlands 205, 215, 234, 306
  delegation 49, 90, 122, 128, 157, 185, 209, 270, 286
  Dutch East Indies 103, 111, 271
  Dutch survivors of Nazi persecution 306
neutrality 86, 253–254, 266, 271, 280
  see also ICRC; Switzerland
'neutralized zones' 229–230, 237
  see also safety zones
New Delhi
  New Delhi conference (1957) 322
  New Delhi Rules 251, 325
New York 246
New Zealand 128, 134–135, 175, 181, 285, 309

Nigeria 325
Night and Fog Decree (1941) 187
Nobel Peace Prize 258–259
non-aggression pacts 213, 217, 227
non-combatant
  immunity 202–205, 216–217
  protection 57–58, 109, 202, 332
  see also civilian; bombing
non-international armed conflict 19, 23–24, 42, 99, 116–118, 319, 322–323
  see also armed conflict; civil war
non-renunciation clause 69
  see also civilian; intangible rights
North America 13, 35, 48, 262
North Atlantic Treaty Organization (NATO)
  member states 9, 40, 90–91, 133, 182, 185–192, 195, 236–237, 242–243, 306, 312, 316, 325, 333
  preparations for war 88, 178–179, 236, 272, 307
Northern Ireland 83
Norway
  delegation 68, 115, 132, 138, 236
  Norwegian Communists 310
nuclear
  energy 234, 242
  testing 251
  warfare 9, 21, 56, 197–251, 310, 314, 316, 325
  weapons 12, 330
  see also bombing
Nuremberg
  Hostage Tribunal 163
  Indictment 71
  Nuremberg Laws (1935) 78
  Nuremberg Military Tribunals (NMTs) 7, 163, 249
  Trials 6, 7, 25, 107, 125, 168, 187, 201, 212, 222, 230, 252, 263–264, 266, 269–270, 273, 280, 282–286, 289–290, 296, 316

Obama, Barack 328–329
occupation 6, 10–12, 25, 53–96, 147–195, 305, 312, 315
occupied
  'ex-occupied complex' 38

territory 38, 46, 57, 61, 64–77, 147–195, 229, 236, 259, 329
  see also civilian; victim
O'Connor, Basil 231
Odier, Edouard 256
open towns 206, 218–219
opinio juris 323
Oradour-sur-Glane 71
Ottoman empire 260
Oung, Tun Hla 14, 135, 140–142
outside interference 327

the Pacific 31, 267
  Pacific War 38, 46, 75
pacifist 13, 304, 310
Pal, Radhabinod 264
Palais du Conseil Général 1, 44, 321
Palestine 75, 96, 101, 110, 113–115, 118, 124, 133, 170–172, 183, 192, 229, 315, 331
Palestine Liberation Organization (PLO) 183, 194
Paris Commune (1871) 103
Paris Peace Conference (1919) 105–106, 207, 260
partisan
  warfare 1, 7, 9, 11, 22, 25, 32, 36, 38, 47, 78, 82–86, 111–113, 124–125, 147–195, 282–283, 292, 309, 312, 314–316, 318–319, 321, 326–328
  see also irregular; resistance fighter; spies
passivity 25, 57
  see also civilian; partisan
patriotism 152–153, 166–167
peace
  critique 227–228, 236, 242, 248, 304–305, 310, 317 *see also* pacifist
  treaty 45
  zones 211, 213
Peninsular War (1808–1814) 154
Permanent Court of Arbitration 256
Perrin, Dominique 165
Pesmazoglou, Michael 120–122
Pétain, Philippe 272
Petitpierre, Max 1, 5, 48, 52, 94, 141, 191, 242–243, 245, 248–249, 291, 302–304, 307
Phillimore, Henry 168–171, 173, 252, 270, 279–283

Pictet, Jean 3, 4, 10–12, 14, 23, 35–36, 39, 42, 47, 54, 63–72, 77–81, 86, 98, 109, 111, 117, 120–121, 134, 147, 166–167, 170–173, 196, 198, 217–218, 224, 229–236, 240, 251, 268, 274, 279–280, 299, 310, 317, 323–324, 326, 330, 333
Pictet's drafting team 23, 35, 67–69, 77–82, 117–118, 149, 166, 170–172, 191, 220, 223–224, 228–229, 273–274, 279, 316, 321, 329, 331–332
  see also ICRC
pillage 222, 224, 233, 236, 250, 330
Pilloud, Claude 4, 35, 47, 50, 54, 70, 77–79, 82, 87, 90–92, 121, 129, 133, 169, 173, 184–185, 187, 190–191, 229, 244, 247, 269, 275, 280–281, 283, 290–292, 294, 303, 319
Pitts, Jennifer 16
de la Pradelle, Albert 64, 209–210, 214, 217
de la Pradelle, Paul 3, 194, 236, 292, 295
Poland 29, 166, 262, 291, 297
  Polish delegation 38–39, 44, 170, 221, 223, 227–228, 268
  Polish state 262
political prisoner 56, 63, 68–71, 74–75, 78, 82–83, 86, 93–96, 105, 109–110, 120, 289, 317, 319, 322, 324
political scientists 15
Popper, Hans 94
popular mythology 14, 308–310
  see also contingency; foundation myths
Portugal 142
postcolonial
  delegates 9–10
  legal attitudes 8, 297
  states 321–323
  theory 16–17
POW Convention
  POW Convention 1929 32–33, 35, 37, 42, 47, 58–59, 62–63, 65–67, 76, 79, 113, 116
  121, 124, 147–195, 212, 244, 259, 262–263, 268–269, 272, 277, 326
  POW Convention 1949 11, 25, 65, 144
  see also Third Geneva Convention
POW rights 21, 32, 105, 147–195
  see also prisoners of war
powers of occupiers 55, 151, 162, 221, 313, 315

372 INDEX

Prague 41–42
  Prague Coup (1948) 40–41, 178
Pravda 320
preamble 42, 72, 81, 84–87, 91–95, 134,
  179, 233–234, 238, 240, 249
'precision bombing' *see* bombing
'principal artisan' 14
prisoner of war 1, 13, 30–33, 35–37, 44, 50,
  58–59, 72–73, 147–195, 206, 212, 215,
  217–218, 220, 224, 228, 237, 255, 257–
  259, 263, 265–266, 271, 274, 276–278,
  283, 288, 290, 298, 305, 307, 311, 318,
  320–321, 326
  POW treatment 46, 58–59, 147–195
  see also POW Convention
'private citizen' 57
  see also civilian
propaganda 7, 239, 242, 285, 307, 320
  Allied propaganda 58, 66, 260
property 56, 96, 236, 285, 287–288
proportionality 209
protected person 56, 78, 87, 91–95
  see also civilian
Protecting Power 25, 122, 138, 173, 177,
  187, 193, 253–256, 258–300, 275,
  327
provocateur 13
provost marshal 32
  see also United States
public expectations 7
publicists 202–203
punitive powers 253

Quebec 128
Quentin-Baxter, Robert 285

race
  racial hierarchy 49, 57, 74, 155, 175
  racialized outlook 21, 57
  racial segregation 80, 96
  see also discrimination; empire
Rao, Benegal Mukunda 48, 50
rape 95–96, 283, 330
  see also sexual violence
ratification 12, 210, 211, 288, 307–310, 312,
  316, 326
Ravensbrück 306
Reagan Administration 326
realism 3, 6, 10

rebellion 102–103, 138, 172
  anti-colonial rebellion 38, 110, 264
  see also insurgency
reception
  of the Conventions 308–311
  see also ratification; reservations
reciprocity 78, 86, 155, 255, 257, 272, 317
  clause 111–112, 117–118, 120–122, 126,
  129, 154
Red Cross
  emblem 216, 244, 255–256
  hospitals 23, 205–206, 212, 216, 224,
  226, 228, 233, 235, 249 *see also*
  bombing; hospital
  movement 28, 34, 103–108, 221, 228,
  232, 241, 261, 275, 303, 315, 322 *see*
  also conference; ICRC
  societies 68, 103–106, 207, 221, 292
  refugees 11, 83
  Refugee Convention (1951)
relief 29, 224, 325
  societies 257
repatriation 259
reprisals 21, 25, 42, 56–59, 62, 64, 71, 87–88,
  95–96, 124, 136–138, 161, 206, 212, 228,
  253–255, 258, 266, 269, 298
reservations 91, 96, 134, 142, 304–306, 318
resistance *see* partisan; spies
resistance fighter *see* partisan; spies
resistance movement *see* partisan
retrospective narratives 5
Revolutionary Wars (1792–1802)
  152–153
Revue 212, 310
Rey-Schyrr, Catherine 99, 134, 236
Riegner, Gerhart 69, 72, 119–120
rights
  intangible rights 19, 69–71, 78, 166
  labor rights 21, 161
  rights of complaint 298
  see also human dignity; human rights
riots 123
roads not taken *see* contingency
Robert, Denise 47
Roerich Pact (1935) 210
Romania 50, 247
Roosevelt, Eleanor 52, 77, 82, 92, 116
Ruegger, Paul 53, 133, 170–171, 251, 283
Russia 105–106, 156–160, 204–205, 325

Russian Civil War 105–107
Russo-Japanese War (1904–1905) 161

saboteur 90, 328–329
  see also partisan; spies
safety locality 65, 220, 225–227
safety zones 210, 214–217, 219, 221, 224–
  226, 228–230, 233–234, 236, 249, 251,
  309, 317, 324
Saint-Paul, Georges 214
Saint-Petersburg Declaration (1868) 157, 202
sanctions see blockade; League of Nations
Satow, Harold 38, 265
Scandinavia
  neutrals 207, 217
  states 90, 184, 187
Scapini, Georges 272
Schindler, Dietrich 199
Schmitt, Carl 147–148, 154, 195, 314
Schoenholzer, Jean-Pierre 4
Schuman Plan (1950) 292
scorched earth policies 96
Second Geneva Convention 12
second government experts' conference see
  conference
Second World War 1, 2, 5–8, 20–26, 31–35,
  46, 50, 56, 65, 100, 110, 147, 253–254,
  262, 271, 278, 296, 298, 308, 311, 313,
  318, 330
security clause 8, 11, 135, 139–140,
  178–180, 186–192, 304, 312, 314,
  316, 327, 329
  see also extrajudicial; partisan
Sétif 110–111
sex
  character 95
  difference 94–95
  sexuality 94–95
  see also gender
sexual violence 21, 56, 94–96, 330
  see also rape
Shanghai 212, 214
Shawcross, Hartley 124–125, 131, 285–
  286, 306
shifting legal boundaries 18
Sick and Wounded Convention see First
  Geneva Convention
siege warfare 56, 202, 220, 249
  see also blockade

signature
  ceremony 43, 251, 302–307, 311
  see also reservations
Silesia 105
Sino-Japanese War (1937–1945) 65, 214
Siordet, Frédéric 4
Slavin, Nikolay Vasilyevich 47–48, 50, 138,
  146, 240, 242, 247, 302, 319
Smith, Brad 332
social media 331
Solferino
  Battle of Solferino (1859) 2, 29
Solis, Gary 99, 199
South Africa 44
South African War (1899–1902) 57, 161
sovereignty
  colonial sovereignty 13, 83–84, 99–145,
    290–291
  state sovereignty 5, 8, 24–26, 55–56,
    59–61, 64–69, 82–84, 99–145, 165,
    224, 237, 254–256, 258, 262, 270–271,
    275, 279, 284–286, 290–293, 295,
    297–298, 305, 317, 319, 322–323, 327
Soviet Union
  atomic weapons' program 227, 230, 234,
    240, 251
  Civilian Convention 20, 24–25, 319
  Common Article 3 24–25
  contributions 16, 318
  delegation at Geneva 1949 11, 13, 19–20,
    44, 47, 87–93, 127–128, 132, 138–140,
    146, 179–192, 236–251, 288–301, 314,
    318–320
  expansionism 36, 40
  French-Soviet relations 40–41, 312,
    318–319
  Gulag 297, 319
  ICRC-Soviet relations 34, 179, 271–272,
    278, 316
  legal attitudes 5–9, 14, 30–31, 37–40,
    43–44, 56, 67, 76, 87–92, 127–128,
    135–143, 149, 179–195, 213, 217, 220,
    223–224, 230–251, 262, 267, 288–301,
    304–305, 307–308, 318–321, 327
  military planning 87–88, 180–181, 185,
    227, 297
  political prisoner 319
  postcolonial forum 127–128, 319
  POW code 162–163

374 INDEX

Soviet Union (*cont.*)
  Red Army 47
  satellites 40, 44, 294
  Soviet POWs 10, 31, 162–163
  Sovietization 40
  strategic bombing 222, 227
  US-Soviet relations 179–180
Spaight, James 159
Spain
  Nationalist Spain 43, 108–109, 216
  Republican Spain 108–109, 216
Spallicci, Aldo 45
Spanish Civil War 50, 65, 107–110, 116–117, 124
spies 47, 85, 90, 148–149, 153–155, 159–160, 173, 176–179, 189–190, 314, 316
  see also extrajudicial; partisan; security clause
Sri Lanka 331
Stalin, Jozef 39–40, 87–90, 162–163, 221, 223, 227, 234, 242, 318–319
Stalinism 11
  Stalinist show trials 274
Standing Commission 41
starvation 25, 50, 58, 80, 163, 197–251, 258, 325–326
  see also blockade
state
  authorization 151–153, 156
  belligerent states 6
  destruction of states 69
  formation 151
  nation-state 16
  state power 10–13, 20, 253
  state's own nationals 10, 60, 70, 78–79, 81–83, 120, 237
  terror 106, 120, 198, 206, 209
statelessness 8, 68–69, 75
  stateless persons 11, 32, 60, 64, 70–72, 76–78, 83, 86, 94–95, 312
Steinberg, Arieh 183–184
Stockholm
  conference (1948) *see* conference
  drafts 47, 56, 77, 81, 89, 125–128, 139, 177–184, 233–235, 240–241, 288, 291, 313–314, 318–319
strategic bombing *see* bombing
Strutt, Henry 47
'studied vagueness' 110, 116–117, 131

substitutes 272–300, 327
  see also enforcement; Protecting Power
summary execution 81, 95, 136, 149–151, 156, 162–164, 175, 180, 186, 255, 282, 319
superior orders 263, 267, 281–282, 284, 286, 288
  see also grave breaches
supervision 23, 134, 162, 253–301, 317, 319, 328, 331
  see also ICRC; Protecting Power
surrendered enemy personnel 166
  see also prisoner of war
Sweden 20, 112
  Swedish neutrality 35
  Swedish Red Cross 207
Switzerland 8, 15, 41, 130, 221, 230, 235, 239, 241, 244, 247–249, 263, 280–281, 290, 295, 303, 309–310
  Swiss delegation 47, 91–92, 132, 136, 141, 190, 235, 247–248, 292–293, 317
  Swiss diplomacy 33, 39, 43–44, 45–46, 62, 65, 126–127, 239, 241, 247–248, 259, 307, 309, 332
  Swiss-Soviet relations 43, 239, 272, 309, 317
  ICRC-Swiss relations 62, 135
  Swiss-US relations 46, 247–248
  Swiss neutrality 243, 259, 307
  Swiss ratification 307
  Swiss Federal Government 19–21, 30, 37, 47, 235, 259, 263, 317
Syria 110, 326

Taiping Rebellion (1850–1864) 101
Taliban 328
Tauber, Arnöst 48, 50
Teheran Conference (1968) 54, 93, 321
teleology 4
'terror fliers' 219, 222, 232
terrorism 315
terrorizing bombing raids *see* bombing
Thailand 21, 45
Third Geneva Convention *see* POW Convention
Third World politics 321–323, 326–327
Thirty Years' War (1618–1648) 152
Tokyo 45, 46, 63–64, 107–108, 197, 215
  Tokyo Draft 59, 63–71, 81, 212, 215
  Tokyo Trials 7, 201, 222, 264, 285, 288, 296

torture 6, 11, 42, 50, 56, 58, 68, 72–77, 81, 84, 111–112, 149, 164–165, 168, 176–177, 190, 237, 258, 308, 319, 328, 331
    mental torture 11, 76–77, 84, 176, 190, 193, 283, 315
    see also extrajudicial; interrogation; partisan
total war 51, 53, 205
totalitarianism 192
transnationalism 15, 18, 29, 69
treaties 11–12, 21, 56, 303, 314, 321, 324
trench-warfare 210
Trenchard, Hugh 209–210
trials 253, 284
    see also international criminal law; Nuremberg
triumphalist accounts 16
Truman 245
    Administration 32, 40, 223, 276, 305
    Doctrine 36
Turkey 36

Ukraine 93, 213, 305, 331
undeclared wars 106–107
    see also armed conflict
undefended towns 206, 218–219
    see also bombing; open towns
Union forces 153–155
United Kingdom *see* Great Britain
United Nations (UN) 12, 35, 47, 79, 83, 112, 218, 223, 226, 228, 232, 241–243, 246–247, 249, 326, 328, 274, 281, 295, 299, 331
    Atomic Energy Commission (UNAEC) 223–224, 230, 234, 241–242, 245–247
    Charter (1945) 95, 222
    Commission on Human Rights (UNCHR) 48, 70–71, 77–79, 82, 92, 116, 120–121
    Declaration of 1942 21, 37
    Educational, Scientific and Cultural Organization (UNESCO) 219
    General Assembly 246, 281
    International Court of Justice (ICJ) 268, 295–296
    International Law Commission (ILC) 230, 286, 290
    Relief and Rehabilitation Administration (UNRRA) 72–73

Security Council 120, 267
War Crimes Commission (UNWCC) 263, 268, 271
United States (US)
    Air Force 7, 32, 197–198, 230, 232, 237
    Airmen 197–198
    Army 76, 187, 305
    Congress 40
    delegation at Geneva 1947 73–75, 113–114, 169–170, 226–228, 270–271
    delegation at Geneva 1949 20, 44, 87–90, 132, 138–140, 179–192, 235–251, 284–301, 304, 314–316
    delegation at Stockholm 1948 120–121, 175, 230–231, 233, 276–277, 313
    foreign policy 36, 46, 207
    imperial interventionism 103
    Joint Chiefs of Staff 241
    Justice Department 32, 178, 187
    legal attitudes 5–7, 9–12, 19, 31–32, 36–39, 65–67, 73–75, 81–92, 112–114, 118–119 120–122, 127–129, 135–136, 139–140, 164, 177–195, 204, 209, 211, 216–219, 222–251, 258–259, 266, 270–279, 284–301, 304–309, 313–316, 321, 324
    Navy 32, 121
    military and security interests 31, 73, 224, 267, 305
    military predominance 31
    nuclear warfare 46, 135
    occupation 73, 305
    prisoners of war 73
    racial violence 118
    ratification procedure 307–309
    Senate 307–308
    soldiers 32
    State Department 32, 85, 103–104, 126, 173, 175, 189, 230, 232–233, 240–241, 243, 245–246, 285, 291, 307–308
    Supreme Court 144, 276, 323, 328
    War Department 32
    war planning 40–41, 76–77, 85–86, 89–90, 96–97, 178–180, 185, 222, 226, 235, 241, 276, 297, 313–315, 320
    universal core 12
    jurisdiction 270
'universality' 20, 46, 307–309, 317
Universal Declaration of Human Rights (UDHR) 54, 86, 95, 179, 303

376 INDEX

universal jurisdiction 275–277, 280–284, 287–290
unlawful combatants *see* partisan; spies
'unprivileged belligerent' *see* partisan; spies
Uruguay 132, 135, 139
utopia 254
  utopian schemes for humanized war 10
  utopians 13

Vatican 92, 294
de Vattel, Emer 22, 151–155
Versailles *see* Paris Peace Conference
Vichy France 6, 72, 166, 272, 290, 311
victims
  of occupation 8, 38, 73–74, 81–82, 88, 90–91, 180–181, 236, 247, 254, 312–313, 321, 326
  of war 4, 6, 10–12, 25, 33, 60, 94, 199, 235, 248, 250, 258, 311, 325
victors' justice 264
Viet Minh 46, 113, 119, 122, 165–167, 171, 312
Vietnam
  Democratic Republic of Vietnam (DRV) 114, 225
  Vietnamese insurgents 125
  War 240
violations 211, 216, 253–255, 257, 261, 266, 268, 281–284, 288, 296
de Visscher, Charles 210
volunteer corps 152–154, 157
  see also partisan
Voncken, Jules 215, 217
Vyshinky, Andrei 138

wanton destruction 203–204
  see also bombing
war
  air war 197–251
  cabinet wars 152–153
  conduct of warfare 5–9, 12, 61
  maritime warfare 202–206
  people's wars 152–153
  'private wars' 151–152
  proxy war 8, 297, 322
  sanction wars 212
  submarine warfare 203–205, 207–208, 218
  wars of self-defense 106–107
  war-making states 6
war crimes 5, 222, 259–261, 263–300, 314, 323

war crimes' tribunals 12, 91, 197–198, 260, 266, 297
  see also grave breaches; international criminal law; Nuremberg
war criminals 180, 197–198, 222–223, 263, 265–266, 274, 281
'War on Terror' 18, 144, 323, 328
War Office *see* Great Britain
warfare *see* war
Washington *see* United States
weapons
  'weapons of peace' 207, 209
  see also disarmament; war
Werner, Georges 63
Western
  adversaries 7, 21
  drafters 5, 9, 13, 23–25, 39, 56, 122, 128–129, 135, 140, 143, 169, 179, 232, 237–238, 247, 250, 276, 288–289, 304, 313–314, 332–333
West Point 32
Whitehall *see* Great Britain
White Russian civilians *see* civilian; Czarist Russia
Wilhelm, René-Jean 4, 77, 230, 234–235, 251
'Wilsonian moment' 105–106
Winkler, Pavel 190
women 9, 14, 29–30, 47, 49–50, 57–63, 69, 73, 77–78, 81, 94–95, 123, 147, 161, 188, 200, 207–208, 211, 279, 319, 324, 330
World Jewish Congress (WJC) 69, 80–83, 119–123, 266, 298, 309
Wu Nan-ju 48, 130

Yalta Conference (1945) 89, 288
Yamashita Case (1945) 276
Yemen 326
Yingling, Raymund 46, 77, 126, 135, 149, 173, 183, 200, 241, 243, 284–285, 287, 293, 295, 305
Yokohama 198
Yoo, John 328–329
Yugoslavia 34, 37, 44, 68, 267–268, 305
Yung, Walter 109

zeppelin raids 206
  see also bombing